THE HAND OF CAPTAIN DANJOU

CAMERONE AND THE
FRENCH FOREIGN LEGION
IN MEXICO,
30 APRIL 1863

COLIN RICKARDS

The Crowood Press

First published in 2005 by
The Crowood Press Ltd
Ramsbury, Marlborough
Wiltshire SN8 2HR

www.crowood.com

© Colin Rickards 2005

All rights reserved. No part of this publication may be reproduced or transmitted in any form or by any means, electronic or mechanical, including photocopy, recording, or any information storage and retrieval system, without permission in writing from the publishers.

British Library Cataloguing-in-Publication Data
A catalogue record for this book is available from the British Library.

ISBN 1 86126 587 5

Dedication
For Ida and Damian
With All My Love

Photographs, unless otherwise credited, are courtesy of the Bureau Information et Historique de la Légion Étrangere/Musée de la Légion Étrangère, Aubagne, France.

Typeset by Textype, Cambridge

Printed and bound in Great Britain by The Cromwell Press, Trowbridge

Contents

Preface and Acknowledgements   5

1. 'A Legion of Foreigners . . . for Service Outside France'   21
2. Sidi Brahim – A Cautionary Tale   30
3. The First Foreign War   39
4. Tempering the Steel   51
5. Doldrums in Algeria   63
6. 'Let's go to Mexico!'   75
7. 'I leave, resolved to do my duty'   87
8. Into the *Terres Chaudes*   100
9. 'A good Company ours, the 3rd of the 1st'   111
10. 'We will amuse the enemy'   122
11. '*Jusqu'a la mort!*'   136
12. The Aftermath   150
13. 'A brilliant military page for the Regiment'   160
14. Dupin Gets a Free Hand   170
15. 'Everyone did his Duty'   181
16. 'The past will be the guide for the future'   191
17. An Illusive Enemy   200
18. The Emperor Arrives   209
19. Bazaine Plans a Campaign   219
20. Oaxaca Falls   229
21. The Hand of Captain Danjou   238
22. Disaster at Santa Isabel   251
23. The Last Farewell in Mexico   260
24. Fighting for France   272
25. Claiming the Regiment's Heritage   281
26. The Last Survivor, the First Celebration   295
27. The Ascent of Colonel Paul Rollet   308
28. The Centenary of the Foreign Legion   319
29. Voices from the Past   328

Contents

30. Celebrating Camerone in Strange Places	339
31. Camerone at Dien Bien Phu	353
32. A Bitter Homecoming	368
33. End of an Era	379
34. General Penette Dreams a Dream	387
35. Danjou's Hand Goes Back To Mexico	396
36. A New Beginning	409
37. Camerone and the Foreign Legion Today	418
Appendix	429
Source Notes	432
Bibliography	463
Index	471

Preface and Acknowledgements

'The Third of the First is dead, my Colonel, but it did enough for those who speak of it to say: "It had nothing but good soldiers".' – Letter from Corporal Evariste Berg, prisoner-of-war, to Colonel Pierre Jeanningros, commanding the Regiment Etranger, 1 May 1863.*

On 30 April 1863, the half-strength 3rd Company of the 1st Battalion of the Regiment Etranger gave battle to close to two thousand Mexicans – regular troops and guerillas – at a hamlet called Camaron, southwest of Veracruz, Mexico. Before reaching the ruined inn known as the Hacienda de la Trinidad, where they forted up to make a stand, almost a quarter of the sixty-two Legionnaires were cut off from their comrades and captured, several of them badly wounded. Veteran Captain Jean Danjou led his two junior officers and forty-six Legionnaires into the stone-walled corral behind the derelict inn.

Vastly outnumbered, without water or food, burned by the tropical heat, and half-blinded and stifled by smoke from a fire started by their enemies, the Legionnaires fought for nine hours, during which time two of the officers and almost half of the men were killed, several others mortally wounded and the rest injured to a greater or lesser extent.

When Danjou – who wore an articulated wooden left hand, to replace the one lost a decade earlier in an accident in Algeria – was killed, his place was taken by Sous-Lieutenant Jean Vilain. When he fell, Sous-Lieutenant Clement Maudet, the Regimental Standard-Bearer, took over. Near dusk, isolated in a derelict lean-to outbuilding, reduced to one cartridge each, and with only five of his Legionnaires still standing, Maudet called for their last rounds to be fired, then led his men as they charged with the bayonet. Fusilier Jean-Baptiste Leonard, a Belgian, was seriously wounded before they even stepped into the open. Fusilier Victor Catteau, also a Belgian, threw himself in front of his officer, and fell with nineteen bullets in his body. Maudet also went down, hit twice and mortally wounded. The three remaining Legionnaires – Corporal Philippe Maine, a Frenchman, and Fusiliers Gottfried Wensel and Laurent Constantin, respectively a Prussian and yet another Belgian – both wounded – surrendered, but only on condition that their officer and comrades be given medical attention.

---

*Letter quoted in *El Heraldo* [Mexico City], 16 May 1863.

In all, two Officers and twenty-one Other Ranks died in the courtyard of the hacienda, and two of the sixteen Legionnaires captured early in the fight died the next day at the Mexican camp. Maudet and seven of those who had fought at the ill-starred Hacienda de la Trinidad, as well as one of the sixteen taken prisoner before the last stand, died in hospitals over the next few weeks, a total of thirty-four, or two-thirds of those engaged.

Theirs is a story of courage, commitment, tenacity, devotion to duty and, ultimately, of sacrifice. The words on the stone placed almost thirty years later over the grave of the twenty-three who died in the hacienda said it all:

> *They were here less than 60*
> *Opposed by a whole army*
> *Its mass crushed them*
> *Life rather than courage*
> *Abandoned these soldiers of France*
> *On April 30 1863*

Only Captain Danjou had attended the *Ecole Speciale Militaire* at Saint-Cyr, the equivalent of Sandhurst or West Point. His two junior officers had risen from the ranks, and the Legionnaires they led were just ordinary men. All behaved in an extraordinary manner. They had former occupations like student, weaver, blacksmith, saddle-maker, waiter, etc., and the Sergeant-Major had been an actor and professional comedian. Some were long-serving Legionnaires, who had taken part in the Conquest of Algeria, and been through the Crimean War and the Campaign in Italy. Others were new recruits, who had never been under fire. They were from France – or born in France of non-French fathers – Belgium, Holland, Austria, Switzerland, several of the German States, Denmark, Italy and Spain. The youngest was seventeen, the oldest in his fifties.

Over a period of almost eighty years the anniversary of what came to be known as the Combat of Camerone – as the French call the hamlet where the battle took place – has grown to become the most important annual event in the life of the Foreign Legion. It is an occasion for spit-and-polish pageantry, a parade and the retelling of the story *La Compagnie Danjou*, and of the Combat of Camerone, following which there is eating, drinking and merrymaking on a grand scale.

At the parade, the articulated wooden hand of Captain Danjou is carried in an intricately-carved glass-sided casket, usually by a much-decorated soldier, and takes a leading role in the ceremony. To be its custodian for even so short a time is considered a supreme honour. For the rest of the year it resides in a special place in the Crypt of the Foreign Legion Museum at Aubagne, near Marseille.

'Camerone Day,' also called 'The Feast of Camerone' – *Fete du Camerone* – is celebrated wherever Legionnaires are serving, and in whatever conditions, peace or war – under fire if necessary. During the Second World War, one Camerone Day was observed on board a French ship in a British convoy heading for the German-occupied Norwegian port of Narvik. Another was held in Eritrea in the Horn of Africa, just liberated from Italian occupation. Camerone was even celebrated in Tonkin – which the world would come to know as North Vietnam – as General Vo

Nguyen Giap's Viet-Minh hordes closed in on the doomed garrison at Dien Bien Phu in April 1954.

In this book, as well as telling the story of the battle, I have thought to investigate the extraordinary place which Captain Danjou's articulated hand has come to have as the Foreign Legion's most sacred battle relic, and also the seemingly curious phenomenon which has made the story of *La Compagnie Danjou* and what it did at the Hacienda de la Trinidad so very truly the centrepiece of the psyche of the Foreign Legion.

When Colonel Francisco de Paula Milan, the Mexican commander, described the battle as a 'small clash of arms,' he was seeking to obfuscate his own losses – perhaps fourteen times those of the French. General Elie-Frederic Forey, the Commander-in-Chief of the French Expeditionary Corps – a man, let it be said, with no particular liking for the Foreign Legion – saw the battle differently, and called it 'a clash of giants'.

The first of the Camerone survivors were returned to the French lines in a prisoner exchange after almost three months of unusual captivity, and were promoted or decorated, or both. Others who trickled back in the coming weeks simply went back to soldiering. CAMERONE was approved as a Battle Honour on the Regimental Standard, and on the first anniversary there was a remembrance service in the great cathedral at Puebla and the *Expedition du Mexique* campaign medal was presented. The Foreign Legion left Mexico at the end of what was called the French Intervention in early 1867 and after that there was no official remembrance of Camerone for thirty-nine years.

Then, on the morning of 30 April 1906, at the tiny French military post of Ta Lung in northwest Tonkin, a young officer, Lieutenant Marie Jules Victor Leon Francois, entirely on his own initiative, staged a parade and re-telling of the Combat of Camerone with his one hundred and twenty-five-strong Company of the 1st Regiment Etranger.[1]

There appear to have been occasional similar locally-organized Camerone Day parades in Algeria and Morocco in the years prior to the First World War, and in its wake the regimental memory of Camerone began to take on unexpected importance. For example, many Legionnaires from the 1st Battalion of the 1st Regiment Etranger were used as the nucleus of the newly-created 4th *Regiment Etranger d'Infanterie* – 4th REI. It was raised for service in Morocco on 15 November 1920, and a complicated system of 'affiliations' determined that the 3rd Company of the 1st Battalion of the new regiment should be considered as the lineal descendant of *La Compagnie Danjou*.

Lieutenant-Colonel Paul Rollet, who commanded the *Regiment de Marche de la Legion Etrangere* during the First World War, and the 3rd *Regiment Etranger d'Infanterie* – 3rd REI – in the early 1920s, believed that laying emphasis on Camerone would help to inculcate an *esprit de corps* among the men from many nations who had come to fight under the Tricolour of France. He made 30 April a holiday for his regiment, and celebrated Camerone with a parade and with special food and an abundance of drink. When he became Colonel of the renamed 1st *Regiment Etranger d'Infanterie* – 1st REI – near the end of 1925 he made Camerone Day a holiday for all the foreign regiments.

The Centenary of the Foreign Legion was only a few years in the future and Rollet decided to mark it with celebrations on 30 April 1931 – the sixty-eighth anniversary of the Combat of Cameron – rather than on 9 March, the actual one-hundredth birthday of the Foreign Legion. He wanted a regimental history prepared for the occasion, with special emphasis given to Cameron, and charged Captain Paul Rollin of the 1st REI with writing the text. Pierre Benigni, the Official Artist to the Army was asked and agreed to create some special artwork and historian and militaria collector Jean Brunon agreed to assist with material from his famous *Collection Raoul et Jean Brunon*.

It rapidly became clear that there was relatively little in the Foreign Legion's *Salle d'Honneur* – an embryo regimental museum – which could actually document the story of Cameron, although there is evidence that original documents and a collection of photographs of officers had existed up to a few years earlier. Brunon could not help much and he and Rollin were apparently unaware of several secondary sources which would have materially assisted them. So, in preparing the Cameron material for the manuscript, they fell back on a regimental history published in 1888 and a general article on the Foreign Legion written by a former Colonel of the 1st Etranger eight years later. Their book, *Le Livre d'Or de la Legion Etrangere, 1831–1931*, appeared in time for the Centenary Celebrations.[2]

The fact is that the Foreign Legion has always had problems with the telling of the story of Cameron. The articulated wooden hand of Captain Danjou had gone back to Algeria when the Regiment Etranger quit Mexico, and became an emotive relic of the campaign, lying on a red velvet cushion in a special casket. Legionnaires taken to visit the *Salle d'Honneur* have been shown it, and told the story of Cameron, since at least as far back as 1889. Yet there was next to nothing in the way of official reports, or other contemporary paperwork, to support it all – leaving the Foreign Legion with a relic, a story and a tradition, but little real documentation to back them up.

Then, some three years after the Foreign Legion Centenary, and the publication of the *Livre d'Or*, historian Brunon, conducting research on the Regimental Standards of the Foreign Legion, found some truly seminal Cameron documents in the files of the Directorate of Artillery in Paris, where they had lain unseen for seven decades. They were a letter from Colonel Pierre Jeanningros, the Commanding Officer of the Regiment Etranger, to Marshal Jacques Randon, the Minister of War, written five months after the battle at Cameron.[3] It was important in its own right, but one of two attachments was of truly crucial value: a copy of a report sent by Commandant Eloi Regnault, then Interim Commander of the Regiment Etranger, to General Ernest de Maussion, Commanding the Reserve Brigade, on 17 August 1863. In effect, it was the story of the Combat of Cameron as it emerged from the debriefing of twenty survivors who had been prisoners of the Mexicans.[4] There have been other less exciting and valuable discoveries in French Army Archives over the years, including Jeanningros' report of the battle to General Forey.[5]

The story of what happened at Cameron, in many of its tellings, is sprinkled with errors, and the two most common ones involve Captain Danjou's articulated hand – how he got it and how the Foreign Legion got it.

In 1878, fully fifteen years after the battle, the former Corporal Philippe Maine, who had laid down the surrender terms at Camerone, retired as a Captain of the 3rd *Infanterie de Marine*. He gave an interview to Lucien-Louis Lande (1847–1880), which was published in the prestigious magazine *Revue des Deux Mondes*, and because it was an 'I was there' account, it has been much used – and sometimes misused – by those who have sought to write about Camerone. Unfortunately, in it was the statement that as a result of being 'grievously wounded' during the Crimean War, Captain Danjou was 'one-armed' and wore an artificial hand. This was attributed directly to Maine, who had served in the Crimea, but not with the Foreign Legion. The article also claimed that 'among the debris of the battle' the burial party found 'the articulated hand of the Captain,' though this was not attributed to Maine, and was presumably told to Lande during his research.[6]

Neither statement was true, but they became part of the story of Camerone, repeated in a chapter of Lande's book *Souvenirs d'un Soldat*, published later in the year,[7] then by General Alexis de la Hayrie in the little booklet[8] *Le Combat de Camaron, 30 avril 1863*, which he wrote in 1889, and by Military Chaplain Jean Efrem Lanusse in the more ambitious *Les heros de Camaron: 30 avril 1863* two years later.[9] Maine was a Camerone survivor, de La Hayrie had been a formidable Battalion Commander with the Regiment Etranger in Mexico, and Lanusse had ministered to his military flock throughout the French Intervention, which effectively locked the errors into Foreign Legion 'history.'

Unfortunately, because of their backgrounds, and the great esteem in which they came to be held, Maine, de La Hayrie and Lanusse were felt to be infallible, their mistakes and mis-statements slavishly repeated by others – classic examples of 'derivative errors'. It may even be suspected that they have deliberately not been corrected, as the story of Camerone naturally relies on the dramatic: gallant officer, tragically mutilated in the service of his country, soldiers on, and when he is killed his artificial hand is retrieved from 'the debris' of the battlefield. This is a pity, not merely because they are untrue, but because what happened at Camerone is a story replete with drama, and the facts themselves need no embellishment.

In fact, Danjou lost his hand far more prosaically, when a signalling pistol misfired while he was a member of the *Service Topographique* in Algeria nine years before the Crimean War – and nobody in the burial party found the artificial replacement after the battle.

The early 1930s was a time when much effort was being made to raise the profile of the battle, and Danjou's artificial hand made its first official appearance in the Camerone Day Parade of 30 April 1931, when the elaborate *Monument aux Morts* cenotaph at Sidi-bel-Abbes was dedicated during the Centenary ceremonies. Every year since 1936 it has been carried in the Camerone Day Parade by a decorated Officer or Other Rank. It has its own honoured place in the crypt of the Foreign Legion Museum at Aubagne, the most precious and sacred of all the regiments' relics, more poignant – and emotionally potent – than, say, a captured battle flag. It even went back to Mexico in 1963, the one-hundredth anniversary of the battle, to be present at the dedication of a monument built by the Foreign Legion.

The memoirs of General Charles Zede, who had been a high profile Lieutenant in the Regiment Etranger in Mexico, were posthumously published as a magazine serialization a quarter of a century after his death. In the early Summer of 1934 the instalment which dealt with Camerone saw the light of print,[10] containing the statement that Danjou 'had lost his left arm, amputated below the elbow' during the Crimean War. Zede also gave currency to another of de La Hayrie's errors, in saying that nineteen of the Legionnaire prisoners taken at Camerone had died in Mexican captivity – a figure too large by at least nine, possibly more – another 'derivative error,' and one now frozen in time in the regimental history.

Brunon made public in 1935 the documents he had found[11] and an 'Official Story' was developed for the Camerone Celebrations. Fully fifty years ago, a Captain Oudry, writing in the now defunct Foreign Legion magazine *Vert et Rouge: Traditions et souvenirs militaires*, remarked that there were three 'essential documents' concerning the battle: Colonel Jeanningros' report to General Forey, Commandant Regnault's report to General de Maussion and the 1878 interview with Corporal Maine. To this trio he added a section of the memoirs of Zede, who had discussed the battle with a survivor, Corporal Evariste Berg. These four sources, Oudry said, were used as the basis for 'the official story of the Combat'.[12]

At the time he was writing the Feast of Camerone was still growing, still being shaped and re-shaped. Gradually the mystique of *La Compagnie Danjou* and what it did at the Hacienda de la Trinidad took on the mantle of almost a Greek Tragedy, even perhaps a Norse Saga. Eventually, the 'Official Story' became the formalized *Recit du Combat de Camerone* – the 'Official Version' – which is read aloud at Camerone Day parades wherever Legionnaires are serving.

In it, Captain Danjou, his two junior officers and sixty Legionnaires, defend themselves in the walled corral until they are overcome. There are also a number of inaccuracies in the *Recit*, starting with the numbers. Specifically, Danjou and his officers had only forty-six Legionnaires with them in the siege, as sixteen had been captured by the Mexicans in the confusion of the fighting before the hacienda was reached. Their loss as combatants raised what would have been odds of thirty-to-one to odds of fully forty-to-one. However, this 'Official Version' brooks no contradiction or dissent, although parts of it are contrary to demonstrable facts,[13] and anything at all to do with the hand of Captain Danjou is especially sacrosanct, particularly how it came into the possession of the Regiment Etranger.

The facts are that the dead Legionnaires had been stripped naked by the Mexicans and tumbled into a trench for burial, an activity interrupted by reports of the approach of Jeanningros and a relief force. Captain Danjou's articulated hand had been detached from his arm and taken as a souvenir, along with the uniforms, medals, weapons and equipment of the men of the 3rd of the 1st. It was acquired as a curio by a small rancher far away from Camerone, bought more than two years after the battle by an Austrian officer and sent to Marshal Achille Bazaine, then Commander-in-Chief of the French Expeditionary Corps.[14]

Former Foreign Legion officer Pierre Sergent learned this in the late 1970s, while researching a book on the Regiment Etranger's part in the French Intervention in Mexico. To some serving Legion officers the revelation was deemed to be little less than sacrilege, as it contradicted accepted lore. Adjutant-Chef Tibor

Szecsko, the Curator of the Foreign Legion's Museum and Archives at the time, subsequently told U.S. historian Douglas Porch that there had been quite serious discussions about whether or not the information should actually be suppressed.[15]

So there are problems to be encountered in telling the story of the Combat of Cameron and I have sought to work, as far as is possible, from firsthand sources, fleshed out by secondary sources where necessary and relevant. A growing number of researchers now describe themselves as 'documentary scholars', but often do not see themselves also as 'narrative scholars'. I have attempted to be both, using original contemporary documents as primary sources wherever possible. A major preoccupation was to locate the actual Camerone battle reports of both the French and the Mexicans. I have been fortunate with both, and use them in full here for the first time in the telling of the Combat of Camerone. Up to now, nobody has made a serious attempt to determine which Legionnaire did what, or where, or when, during the battle, and in the aftermath. By diligently cross-referencing my assorted sources, I believe I have been able to largely pinpoint much of this information.

As a journalist I was taught many years ago that quotes from people involved give 'life' to a story. As an historian I believe that quotes from participants give a 'feel' of the events. An older colleague, journalist and war correspondent R.W. Thompson, wrote in his autobiographical *An Echo of Trumpets*: 'It is impossible for any one man to be "there", to know what it was like on that day and in that hour for anyone but himself, and it is always, or nearly always[,] so. A semblance of the "true" story may only be built up through the eyes and ears and varied senses and sensibilities of scores of men, dredged out of a chaos of emotion and experience and fashioned into coherence'.[16] I agree wholeheartedly, and while I do not have 'scores' of accounts by Camerone participants, I have rigorously worked the ones at my disposal, in an effort to find the vivid and the significant. I have tried to allow the voices of as many Legionnaires as possible tell how it was to be a member of the 3rd of the 1st at Camerone and overall of the Regiment Etranger in Mexico.

I first came to know of the Combat of Camerone from reading the account in the second – and updated – edition of the *Livre d'Or*.[17] It seemed an extraordinary story of courage in the face of overwhelming odds, and I wondered why it was not better known. Later, while on a newspaper assignment in Southern Mexico, I became aware that the Foreign Legion was actively supporting General Marcel J. Penette, a former Foreign Legion officer, then retired and living in Mexico City, in an effort to erect a suitable memorial in time for the Centenary of the battle. On returning to England I embarked on an attempt to gather whatever I could on both the Centenary plans and the battle. Lieutenant-Colonel Patrick Turnbull, M.C., convinced me that there was much to be learned. Author of *The Foreign Legion*, then the best of several English-language histories,[18] he had spent time working in the Foreign Legion Archives in Sidi-bel-Abbes. He had found some firsthand material on the Combat, but been frustrated over what he could not find.

I first put pen to paper about the battle in an article almost four decades ago,[19] largely basing my story on some almost contemporary reminiscences I had found in the *Bibliotheque Nationale* in Paris, bolstered by Turnbull's account and that given in the *Livre d'Or*. Turnbull was kind enough to say that it easily eclipsed the chapter in his book, but we both knew it was still only part of the story, and when I look at it now I realize how far short it fell. However, it was a step along the way.

Several supercilious French Army officers in Paris told me that the Combat of Camerone had been little more than a skirmish, the very reason that it was largely undocumented. The Foreign Legion, they assured me, was blowing it out of all proportion to reality purely for propaganda purposes. I did not accept this, and on and off over the years sought out and collected documentary evidence in French, Mexican, Belgian and Austrian archives, museums, libraries and collections, some public, some private, and also conducted additional fruitful research in England, the United States, Canada and Eire.

For example, in 1975, I was seeking the source of Corporal Berg's oft-quoted statement: '*The Third of the First is dead, my Colonel, but it did enough for those who speak of it to say: "It had nothing but good soldiers".*' Tradition claimed that it had been made in a note which Berg, a prisoner of the Mexicans, smuggled out of their camp. Nothing could be further from the truth. Although only a Corporal in the Foreign Legion, Berg, a de-commissioned officer – of the 1st Zouaves – was probably the best educated of the Fusiliers of the decimated 3rd Company. He was given permission by the Mexicans to prepare an account of the battle, and a list of the survivors, which would then be sent to Colonel Jeanningros, and he did a careful job.

As it happens, the Colonel of the Foreign Legion quite probably never received the letter. Certainly it is not in the Archives of the Foreign Legion. Nor has it been found – so far – in the records in the possession of the *Service Historique de l'Armee de Terre* at Vincennes, near Paris. At the time, however, the Regiment Etranger certainly knew of it, for within two weeks of the battle the letter received fairly wide publicity in Mexican newspapers.[20] Of course, the original was handwritten – and how legible was Berg's handwriting? Naturally, it had been translated from French into Spanish – and how good was the translator? Many Legionnaires' names are spelled phonetically, at best.

In the handful of other accounts in which Camerone survivors – Corporal Maine, Fusilier Friedrich Fritz, the drummer, *Tambour* Casimir Lai, and Berg himself – are quoted, their words are not of themselves firsthand, in the sense of not having been actually written down by the participants themselves. They are 'as told to' versions, set down on paper by someone else. So Berg's letter is important as the only genuine set-down-by-a-participant account of the battle at Camerone and its aftermath, and I have drawn on it extensively. It has never been published in English – or French, for that matter.

In the late 1970s I was in correspondence with the venerable Jean Brunon, who had long had a special interest in the Foreign Legion, especially the Combat of Camerone, and in the early 1980s I had the good fortune to get to know General Marcel Penette. Along with a small group of dedicated enthusiasts, both French and Mexican, he had laboured hard from 1948 to 1965, with the Foreign Legion's help and blessing, and with support from public fundraising, to have a proper memorial set up to mark the grave of the men of the 3rd Company of the 1st Battalion at Camerone.

A diplomat as well as a soldier, Penette had co-researched and co-authored the first serious study of the Regiment Etranger in Mexico, doing so with a non-Legion colleague, Captain Jean Castaignt, a meticulous historical sleuth. The result of their fruitful collaboration was titled *La Legion Extranjera en la Intervencion Francesca*,[21] and was published in Mexico – in Spanish, of course – in 1962. Penette was the first person to compile a complete roster of the sixty-two Legionnaires involved in the Combat of Camerone, and Brunon subsequently had the Foreign Legion's spellings of their names specifically verified by Adjutant-Chef Szecsko of the Foreign Legion Archives.[22]

It has to be said that it is extremely difficult to write meaningfully about the Foreign Legion for a number of reasons, a prime one being that the guarantees of anonymity – the *anonymat* – given to Legionnaires when they join must not be violated. Consequently, there are no personnel files to be accessed by the historian, no pension records, nothing of a personal nature. Lieutenant-Colonel Pierre Carles of the *Service Historique de l'Armee de Terre*, who attempted serious documentary research on the Foreign Legion fifty years after the publication of the first edition of the *Livre d'Or*, has commented pertinently on the difficulties to be encountered.

Individual Service Files, and the reports in them, as well as compilations of statistics, 'are all covered by regulations which guarantee the anonymity of Legionnaires,' he remarked in a 1981 article to mark the Foreign Legion's 150th Anniversary. 'There are many problems, essentially those of sources. There is no pioneering example of scholarly writing on the subject, not much is known, and the archives available to researchers are very fragmentary.' The *Journaux de Marche* – regimental day-to-day records – in the various military archives, he added, are essentially the only materials which are 'accessible and useable', and, faced with these 'multiple difficulties', at certain points the researcher meets a brick wall.[23]

Yet by a stroke of great good fortune, Camerone, to a limited degree, is something of an exception. The personnel files of French Army officers can be accessed, and five of the principle participants held Commissions either before or after the battle. Only Captain Danjou had entered the French Army as a Commissioned Officer. Sous-Lieutenants Vilain and Maudet had risen through the ranks and their records as officers give some details of their earlier careers. Corporal Berg had also come up through the ranks, had received a Commission in the 1st Zouaves, been allowed to resign it in order to avoid a scandal, and later became an officer again. Corporal Maine earned a Commission for his role at Camerone and had a long military career. Their records can be scrutinized, and much can be gleaned, though I know of no other writer who has bothered to look at them.

Fortunately, along with assorted documents, reports and letters, there are also several officers' diaries or memoirs with a bearing on Camerone. While none of the officers of the 3rd Company survived, the Captain, Lieutenant and Sous-Lieutenant of the 5th Company – which was very closely involved with the various pre- and post-battle events – all left accounts of aspects of their service in Mexico.

So much for the primary sources or lack of them. The secondary sources – good, bad and indifferent – are another matter.

It might have been hoped that Jeanningros, who rose to the rank of General Officer, would have written an autobiography, or otherwise recorded his distinguished military career, and that these reminiscences would have had something to say about Camerone. The same applies to Captain Gustave Saussier, who led the 1st Battalion's Grenadier Company, and who also became a General Officer. Unfortunately, neither did so, and if collections of their papers do exist, I have been unable to locate them. However, a handful of personal memoirs, mostly articles in now widely scattered and long out-of-print, if not defunct, French publications, provided some snippets. So did three rare books, and a pair of even rarer pamphlets, which throw some fresh light on events surrounding the battle.

I have made far more use than any previous writer of Jean Ephrem Lanusse's *Les heros de Camaron: 30 avril 1863*. He was in Mexico as a Military Chaplain before the Regiment Etranger arrived, and had been in the hamlet of Camaron in early 1863. He subsequently managed to meet a number of the battle's survivors, and twice visited the Hacienda de la Trinidad with some of them. In his book he quoted the 3rd Company's *Tambour* Lai, and worked from the notes of his talks with a very observant survivor, who he did not identify by name.

Armed with General Penette's complete roster of the 3rd Company, and by cross-referencing the men named in various primary sources, it was possible to determine that Lanusse's pertinently-quoted survivor was Fusilier Fritz, a well-educated man from Germany's Black Forest region, who lost an arm in the battle and was made a Chevalier of the Legion of Honour for his part in it.

Another source I found very useful was a rare small book, ponderously entitled *Reminiscences of the Franco-German War, by Captain Kirwan, Late Captain Commanding the Irish Legion During the War of 1870-71*. Written by Martin Waters Kirwan, an Irish officer who commanded the 8th Company of the 5th Battalion of the Regiment Etranger in the Franco-Prussian War, it was first published in 1873. While it is an account of the unit's war service, tucked away in it is the first account of the events surrounding the Combat of Camerone to have been published in English. It takes the form of valuable reminiscences by one of Kirwan's fellow officers, Frank M'Alevey, a former Corporal in the 1st Company of the 1st Battalion of the Regiment Etranger in Mexico.[24]

It must be said that M'Alevey's reminiscences, as reported by Kirwan, have to be used with considerable care, as they were not formally given and set down, being conversations shared one night in 1871, near the end of the war. It is not clear whether notes were taken by Kirwan, but it seems unlikely. At the time of the telling, Camerone rated as no more than an obscure battle, fought eight years earlier, in the first month of the four-year Foreign Legion campaign in Mexico. It had achieved little real fame, except within the Regiment Etranger itself, so there was no vicarious glory for M'Alevey to gain by making himself a player in the pre- and post-battle events. Clearly, he was simply talking about it as an anecdote of his earlier service in the Foreign Legion. It can safely be considered that the overall thrust of his account is accurate. The emotions expressed are undoubtedly so, and I have felt able to draw upon it.

I also found useful firsthand reminiscences with a bearing on Camerone specifically – and the activities of the French Army in Mexico generally – in an interesting little book called *Deux ans au Mexique* by a French-Canadian named Narcisse-Henri-Edouard Faucher de Saint-Maurice, published in 1874. He had spent time in Mexico as an Observer with the French forces, and has never featured in any writings on Cameron, in any language.[25]

Clearly, the importance of the reminiscences of Generals de La Hayrie and Zede cannot be discounted. Nor should they be totally relied upon. The gradual acquisition by the *Salle d'Honneur* of various Cameron-related photographs, documents and artifacts – such as uniforms and medals – kept the memory of the battle alive up to the time of the Second World War.

Historian Carles has pointed to the tendency of writers to either exaggerate and glorify, or to be destructively negative, when writing of the Foreign Legion. 'It is to be hoped that one day, a researcher will perhaps attempt a true history which neither overly praises, nor needlessly maligns,' he wrote in his 1981 article,[26] and this problem was somewhat addressed a decade later, when historian Porch published *The French Foreign Legion: A Complete History of the Legendary Fighting Force*. Afforded access to the Foreign Legion Archives at Aubagne – but constantly reminded of the confidentiality quotient – and working with a mass of archival and secondary source materials, he managed to produce a meticulously documented general study of the Foreign Legion from 1831 to 1962. Porch spent the greater part of five Summers poring over the old records and reports, apparently just in time, as towards the end of his research he was told by Sergeant (later Adjutant) Yann Cuba, Adjutant-Chef Szecsko's successor, that there were plans for the Archives 'to be transferred' to the *Bureau des Anciens* in Marseilles.[27] All records were, indeed, subsequently relocated, those predating 1909 to the *Service Historique de l'Armee de Terre* in Vincennes, and the post–1909 ones to the *Bureau des Anciens*.[28]

For the broad story of the several specific French campaigns during the Intervention I have utilized, where necessary, some of the books of reminiscences by serving officers, and have relied in general on Jack Autrey Dabbs' unsurpassed *The French Army in Mexico 1861–1867: A Study in Military Government*, which is drawn from the personal archives of Marshal Achille Bazaine and other documentary collections in the Latin American Library at the University of Texas.[29]

In the French Army what would be a Second Lieutenant in other armies is a Sous-Lieutenant. To Anglicize it somehow seemed cumbersome, and to translate it as Under-Lieutenant even worse, so I have retained the original. A word or two should be said about non-commissioned ranks in the Foreign Legion, which are different from those of the British and American armies. The general phrase Non-Commissioned Officer – NCO – will not work here, as Corporals are not included. Those above the rank of Corporal-Chef are Sous-Officiers, a very privileged group. At the top is the Adjutant-Chef, followed by the Adjutant, then the Sergeant-Chef and the Sergeant. Unable to use the encompassing NCO, for the above reasons, I have retained Sous-Officier for clarity, and – like Sous-Lieutenant – it perhaps adds to the French 'flavour'. (At different times in the history of the Foreign Legion other designations were in use, such as Sergeant-Major, ranks which no longer exist, but which appear in some of the quoted material in this book.) Below the Sous-Officiers come – today – the Corporal-Chef and the Corporal, then the Legionnaire 1st Class and Legionnaire 2nd Class. In the Foreign Legion Cavalry, both the horsemen of yesterday and the mechanized troops of today, the rank *Marechal de Logis* equates to that of Sergeant and *Brigadier* to Corporal.

Something should also be said here about the illustrations in this book.

Photography, if not exactly in its infancy, was still in its youth at the time of the French Intervention. Certainly, Roger Fenton had been very successful with many of his photographs during the Crimean War almost a decade earlier, and Matthew Brady and his associates pioneered the art of military photography as the American Civil War progressed, but the early part of France's invasion of Mexico was almost camera-less.

Studio portraits, taken under controlled conditions, were usually quite satisfactory, and a number of Foreign Legion officers had themselves photographed – mostly in Puebla or Mexico City – during the Mexican Expedition. Photographs taken outside, unless landscapes or views, were often unsatisfactory. (The earliest campaign picture I have seen is of the 4th Company of the 3rd Battalion of the Regiment Etranger taken in the field in February 1866.) Mexico's climate frequently had a bad effect on the delicate photographic chemicals then used, while its roads were not conducive to the lumbering darkroom-wagons of travelling picture-makers, or to the longevity of wet-plate process glass negatives.

The Army relied on the Minister of War's Official Artist, Jean-Adolphe Beauce. Unofficially, examples of the sketching skills – sometimes very advanced – of various officers found their way into several of the illustrated French magazines of the time, providing a good overall picture of the highlights, as well as of the day-to-day events, of the campaign. Illustrations in some of the early books which happen to mention Camerone vary from the hugely imaginative – and wrong – to the very good. A photograph purporting to show a gateway and part of the outside wall of the corral at the Hacienda de la Trinidad, and another, allegedly of the ruined inn on the north side of the road, have done the rounds over the years. I consider them to be of extremely dubious provenance and have ignored them. Along with three quite famous Camerone paintings, by Beauce (1818–1875), Edouard Detaille (1847–1912) and Pierre Benigni (1878–1956), I have preferred to use photographs of individuals, and of artifacts – like Captain Danjou's articulated wooden hand, and some of the medals won – for my pictorial content.

This has been a fascinating and fun book to write, It has also been a singularly difficult one. Material on the French Intervention in Mexico is voluminous, but material on the Regiment Etranger in the campaign is much harder to find. I deliberately challenged myself, as it was necessary to work from both primary and secondary source materials in French, Spanish and, in one case, German. Understandably, there is next to nothing contemporary in English.

So is this the 'last word' on Camerone? Not necessarily. Brunon fortuitously found some wrongly – or peculiarly – filed documents among the French military archives. Historian Carles located others. Corporal Berg's actual letter to Colonel Jeanningros, and other important documents, may yet be providentially found there, and even elsewhere. For reasons which are not entirely clear, Mexico's military archives are not open for inspection by historians, and, though I have been fortunate in obtaining some key material, there may be more than has been forthcoming so far.

Preface and Acknowledgements   17

Hopefully, by using all that can currently be located regarding Camerone, this book will – for this battle, at least – partly meet Carles' call for 'a true history which neither overly praises, nor needlessly maligns'. It may even change the Foreign Legion's 'Official Version' of the Combat of Camerone.

All I can claim is that this book represents the most complete scholarship on the subject to date, and that it has had the benefit of consideration by, and advice from, some noted military specialists. Notwithstanding this, conclusions drawn by me, and errors which may have crept in, are my responsibility alone.

To my wife, Ida, and our son, Damian, to whom this book is dedicated, I owe the kind of debt that authors always incur with their families, and I am grateful to them for their love, and for their patience with me, and with this story, over the years.

Colin Rickards
Toronto, Canada.
31 October 2004

Acknowledgements

As with any book of this kind, the author runs up all sorts of debts of gratitude for help generously given, leads suggested and guidance provided – sometimes simply for a sympathetic ear. Sadly, when research runs over a period of years, as has been the case with *The Hand of Captain Danjou*, not all of those who helped are still around when the project becomes a finished product and a reality.

My greatest debt is to the late General Marcel J. Penette, who spent three years in the Foreign Legion and many more as a soldier-diplomat. In Mexico, working with Captain Jean Castaignt, a French Army Reserve Officer, he authored the first comprehensive study of the Regiment Etranger during the French Intervention, and gave especial attention to Camerone. He also dreamed a dream: to mark the grave of the officers and men of the 3rd Company of the 1st Battalion, and fired Castaignt and a group of fellow enthusiasts, both French and Mexican, with his zeal. The dream was eventually partially realized in 1963, in time for the Camerone Centenary, and completed two years later, though in some ways it is still a work in progress. General Penette encouraged me to continue my research, and provided copies of his own writings, as well as photographs, documents and many fruitful leads, because, as he expressed it, he felt that I shared his enthusiasm for telling the truth about 'the lofty deeds of Camerone'.

My second major debt is to the late Jean Brunon, who developed the famous *Collection Raoul et Jean Brunon*, which the French Army has preserved as the *Musee de l'Emperi* in Salon-de-Provence. He provided copies of some of his own writings, as well as documents, photographs and prints, and, the year before he died, a photocopy of a letter which Captain Jean Danjou wrote to one of his brothers on board ship on the way to Mexico.

I am also indebted to two fellow historians of the Legion – both of whom have painted on a larger canvas than have I. The late Lieutenant-Colonel Patrick Turnbull, M.C., of Oxfordshire, England, provided encouragement, and some

Camerone material he had discovered during his own research. Like Brunon, he died in 1986. Turnbull had spent some weeks with a Squadron of the 1st *Regiment Etranger de Cavalerie* in Morocco shortly before the Second World, and was the author of a number of non-fiction books, and several novels – some of them with Foreign Legion themes – as well as the then pathbreaking history *The Foreign Legion*, published in 1964.

Professor Douglas Porch of the Naval Postgraduate School in Monterrey, California, author of a number of books on French colonial expansion and military conquest, offered guidance on various points, including providing me with an understanding of assorted military matters pertaining to the Foreign Legion, the French Army and writing about both of them. Camerone, indeed Mexico, occupied, of course, only a small portion of his monumental 728-page opus *The French Foreign Legion* – subtitled 'A Complete History of the Legendary Fighting Force' – published in the United States in 1991. It deservedly received awards from the Society for Military History and the French Colonial History Society, while the French edition, published four years later, won the *Prix du Musee d'Armee*.

There are other thanks to be expressed to people in seven countries who went out of their way to be helpful.

In **France**, I am deeply indebted to Adjutant Emilio Condado Madera, Conservateur of the *Musee de la Legion Etrangere* at Aubagne, for his assistance with photographs, suggestions, and his patience and skill in running down some hard-to-find details which were important to my development of the story of *La Compagnie Danjou*. Valerie Vergniaud, Chief Librarian at the *Ecole Speciale Militaire* of Saint-Cyr, and Pierre-Marie Chagneau, Curator of the School's *Musee du Souvenir*, helped me to 'know' the remarkable Chaplain Jean Ephrem Lanusse and his extraordinary life and work. A succession of officers at the *Service Historique de l'Armee de Terre* at Vincennes, beginning with those serving under General Delmas as *Chef du Service* in the early 1980s, located a variety of relevant documents and pictures for me at various times over a period of years. Jean-Francois Chanal of the *Bibliotheque Nationale de France* in Paris helped in my search for important secondary source materials and genealogist Jean-Paul Pinard assisted me in untangling the convoluted military and personal story of Corporal Evariste Berg's pre-Foreign Legion days.

In **Mexico**, where the military archives are not open for inspection by historians, I was fortunate in being able to access some otherwise unobtainable information through the efforts of a distinguished Mexican officer who wishes – in the tradition of the Foreign Legion – to remain anonymous. I am also grateful for input from Louis Hallard, the first Executive Vice-President of The Camerone Association in Mexico City, and from Xavier Sol la Lande, a Founder Member. I was also fortunate in receiving some very useful material through the efforts of Brigadier-General Juan F. Tapia G. during his tenure as Military and Air Attache at the Embassy of Mexico in Ottawa, Canada. Other help was received from Dr. Jose Luis Martinez, Director-General of the Fonda de Cultura Economica, Colonel Leopoldo Martinez Caraza of the Comission de Investigation Historia at the Secretaria de la Defensa National and Enrique Cervantes Sanchez of the Reference

Centre at the Directorate of Historical Archives, at the National Archives, all in Mexico City.

In **Belgium**, M.J. Lorette, Conservateur at the *Musee Royal de l'Armee et d'Histoire Militaire* in Brussels, provided photocopies of some relatively obscure publications under his care, and guided me regarding the so-called 'Belgian Legion' in Mexico.

In **Austria**, at the Osterreichisches Staatsarchiv (Austrian State Archives) in Vienna, Dr. Rainer Egger, Director of the Kriegsarchiv (War Archives), offered guidance concerning documents held in Record Group Five on the Belgish-osterreiche Freikorps (Belgian-Austrian Volunteer Corps), as did Assistant Director, Dr. Peter Broucek, Curator of Old Campaign Files, while Dr. Robert Rill provided advice on the Archives' picture collection.

In the **United States**, pioneer aviator Moye W. Stephens of La Verne, California, shared with me his memories of attending the Foreign Legion's Centenary Celebrations in Sidi-bel-Abbes in 1931, and I am grateful to Danny J. Crawford, Head, Reference Section, History and Museums Division, Department of the Navy, Washington, D.C., for material on Colonel Frank E. Evans of the U.S. Marine Corps, who spent time with the Foreign Legion in the early 1930s. Professor Jack Autrey Dabbs of the Department of Modern Languages at the A. & M. College of Texas in Austin provided guidance concerning the Archives of Marshal Francois-Achille Bazaine and other manuscript materials in the important Latin American Collection at the University of Texas. The Librarians at the famed Bancroft Library at the University of California, in Berkeley, searched a number of rare and otherwise virtually unobtainable old publications for me, while Patrick Shannon, Head of Interlibrary Lending at the University of California's Berkeley Library, was my 'eyes' regarding old Mexican newspapers in the Microfilm Collection of the Doe Library. The Department of Rare Books and Special Collections of the Library of Princeton University in Princeton, New Jersey, provided me with some valuable photocopies of documents and Harvard University Library entrusted me with two rare books which were unavailable in Canada.

In **England**, Nick Wright, Commissioning Editor at The Crowood Press, was exceptionally patient with an author whose sources unexpectedly increased exponentially, causing serious delays in manuscript completion. Tom Gillmore of the Mary Evans Picture Library drew my attention to a rare – and totally inaccurate – contemporary illustration of a German magazine artist's conception of the Combat of Cameron. Lesley Smurthwaite of the Department of Uniforms, Badges and Medals at the National Army Museum in London clarified a number of points concerning medals. The Curators of the Victoria and Albert Museum provided me with interesting illustrative materials on the uniforms of soldiers of France's Second Empire.

In **Canada**, in research concerning Faucher de Saint-Maurice, who served as an Observer with the French Army in Mexico, I was greatly assisted by Ann M. Morris of the Reference Department of The D.B. Waldon Library at The University of Western Ontario, London, Ontario. Other useful information on Saint-Maurice was provided by Richie Allen of the National Archives of Canada and by Lynn Lafontaine and Patrick Labelle of the National Library of Canada, both in Ottawa. I was generously lent old books by the National Library of Canada, the Quebec Provincial Library in Quebec City, the Provincial Library of British Columbia in Victoria, B.C., the Library of Brock University in St. Catharines, Ontario, St. Mary's University in Halifax, Nova Scotia, and the Royal Military College of Canada in Kingston, Ontario.

Specifically in Toronto, I was grateful for the facilities of the Toronto Reference Library, and for permission to use the Library of the University of Toronto, the Library of York University and the Library of the Royal Canadian Military Institute. As always, I have nothing but praise for those who labour fruitfully in the Interloan Department of the Toronto Public Library System, who offered enthusiasm and help, often above and beyond the call of duty.

I am also especially grateful to Dawn Williams of Toronto, who, in the midst of her own publishing activities, made the time to double check the accuracy of my translations of phrases in some older French documents, and to Flora Knight of Ottawa, a friend of many years standing, and Dr. Andrew Scheftsik-Pedery of Toronto, an overworked General Practitioner, who at various times did the same with my translations of Mexican source materials.

As is customary, I absolve all of these people of any blame for the, hopefully rare, but inevitable, error(s) which may have crept in, which are entirely my responsibility.

1
'A Legion of Foreigners . . . for Service Outside France'

In the sun-baked garrison towns of Algeria all the talk among the soldiers of the Regiment Etranger – the Foreign Legion of France – was of Mexico in the early days of 1862. Officers and Sous-Officiers, even the Corporals and Legionnaires, imagined that they would soon be off across the Atlantic to fight in a new war, where glory and promotions would be easily won. Indeed, why should they think otherwise? After all, a battalion of the 2nd Regiment of Zouaves, with whom they had frequently been brigaded in the past, and with whom they had a friendly rivalry, had been among the more than two thousand troops sent to Mexico with Admiral Jurien de la Graviere the previous November.

Now the year had turned and a second battalion of Zouaves had been included among the four thousand-plus troops who had gone to Mexico with General Charles Ferdinand Latrille, Count of Lorencez, in February. Yet the Foreign Legion, a major reorganization completed, was still in Algeria, and there was more talk of road-building and 'colonization work' than there was of fighting.

In its thirty-one years of existence the soldiers of the Foreign Legion – under one or another of several military designations – had participated in virtually all of the campaigns in the 'pacification' of Algeria. The Battle Honours were many and there was still a handful of men, carried on the regimental strength, but of dwindling usefulness, who could remember fighting against Abd-el-Kader and other Algerian leaders in countless battles and skirmishes more than two decades earlier. There were still active men in the ranks who had taken part in the two bloody attacks on the oasis of Zaatcha in 1849, and many officers and men who had been at Alma and Inkermann in the Crimean War, and lived through the dreadful Winter of 1854–55 in the freezing trenches of the allied armies besieging Sebastopol. There were officers and men wearing decorations and medals awarded for the tough 1857 campaign against the warlike Kabyles of Eastern Algeria, and many others had them from the Italian Campaign of two years later.

Yet neither of the two foreign regiments had been called to take part in the Anglo-French Expeditionary Force sent to China in August 1860. Nor had they received marching orders when France sent troops to Syria at the end of the same year to restore order in the wake of anti-French riots, and where their old foe Abd-el-Kader, living in exile in Damascus, had been credited with saving the lives of twelve thousand Christians and was decorated with the Cross of the Legion of Honour. Instead, they had fought those Algerian tribes which still resented French control and taxes, and built the roads and the blockhouses needed for colonial expansion. Now, though slimmed down from two regiments, restructured, and reconstituted as a single Regiment Etranger of three battalions, they languished in North Africa, while other soldiers of France were on their way to fight yet another war on foreign soil.

In Sidi-bel-Abbes, the town which the Foreign Legion had founded in 1843 and built into an important metropolis, Colonel Mathieu Butet, commanding the Regiment Etranger, had no answers for officers who asked when they would be sent to join what was becoming an important Expeditionary Corps. Nor was there any point in asking Captain Jean Danjou, as Adjutant-Major the senior Staff Officer of the 1st Battalion. All they could say was that war between France and Mexico had not been officially declared. It seemed to beg the question.

The first three decades of the Foreign Legion had been a never-ending story of fighting and building, the musket and the pickaxe. The Romans had been on the coast of North Africa almost eighteen centuries earlier, fighting and building, and many officers liked to speak glowingly of the Foreign Legion's 'Mission of Civilization', though few of the men engaged in back-breaking road-building, marsh-draining, irrigation and 'colonization work' under a burning sun had any great enthusiasm about being the 'successors' of the vaunted IIIrd Augusta Legion.

An outpost of the crumbling Ottoman Empire, though only vaguely under Turkish rule, what became Algeria was an area nearly four times the size of France, with forbidding mountains backing the relatively narrow coastal plain, and the thousands of square kilometres of the Sahara Desert behind them. France's King Charles X, in what turned out to be the dying days of his reign, had dispatched an army to North Africa, in a seeming effort to use new territorial acquisitions to distract public attention from his increasingly unpopular rule. An election in May 1830 showed a majority hostile to the King, who then dissolved the National Assembly, imposed censorship on the Press and attempted to rule through Royal Ordinances. Parisians took to the streets in the 'July Revolution' and the Army refused to fire on them, forcing Charles X to abdicate. He was replaced by a distant cousin, Louis-Philippe, who came to power as 'The Citizen King of the French'. He had a sound understanding of what could happen when rabble turned into mobs, having fought in the Army during the French Revolution and been forced to flee in 1793, the year that he became the Duke of Orleans on the death of his father. Some four years of his twenty-four years of living outside France had been spent in the United States, so he had seen his own country at the start of a revolution and one of the countries of his exile in the wake of one.

The year 1830 was a turbulent one for Europe. Austria put down uprisings in the northern Italian states it controlled, Russia ruthlessly suppressed a national revolt in Poland and in England the government led by the Duke of Wellington was forced to resign. Louis-Philippe feared his own Army, so proceeded to substantially purge it at the senior officer level, disbanding the Swiss regiments in French service and beginning to look askance at the fact that France, particularly Paris, was suddenly brimming over with foreigners, many of them ex-soldiers or self-exiled revolutionaries from other countries.

Most were penniless, and the former soldiers seemed a possible threat to the law and order that the 'Citizen-King' intended to enforce, so he listened with interest to those who suggested that such men – and others less suitable – could be usefully employed in the Conquest of Algeria, as part of the newly-formed *Armee d'Afrique*. On 9 March 1831 Louis-Philippe signed a Decree bringing into existence 'a Legion of Foreigners to be known as the Foreign Legion for service outside France'. Recruitment was open to men between the ages of eighteen and forty, and recruits who could produce documentation about themselves were expected to do so. Those who could not would be enlisted at the discretion of the interviewing officer. A false name and nationality was acceptable, providing anonymity to those who sought it. Frenchmen were permitted to engage with the special permission of the War Ministry, but those who felt themselves unlikely to receive it could also enlist with false names and nationalities. Thus the Foreign Legion – the *Legion Etrangere* – was born,[1] and the anonymity of its rank and file, the *anonymat*, was there from the beginning. The seven battalions were to serve as national groups, the 1st, 2nd and 3rd being Germans and a few Swiss, the 4th Spaniards, the 5th Italians, the 6th Belgians and Dutchmen and the 7th Poles. The French, and soldiers who fitted none of the national groups – for example, the ten Englishmen who joined in 1833 – could be slotted in where needed. They were sent across the Mediterranean to Algiers, one of the handful of coastal cities where the French were in control.

Initially, not much was expected of them and they were used as little more than a labour corps. Discipline was a problem, as were desertions, but things gradually settled down and on 7 April 1832 the Foreign Legion was granted the right to form what were known as *Compagnies d'elite* – Elite Companies – a peculiarly French configuration for infantry regiments. In a Battalion of eight Companies there would be a *Compagnie de Voltigeurs*, selected from especially fit, light men, trained in reconnaissance and skirmishing, a *Compagnie de Grenadiers*, usually heavier men, equipped with the primitive grenades of the day, and six *Compagnies du Centre*, armed with musket and bayonet. In a set piece battle the Grenadiers were on the right, the Voltigeurs on the left and the six other Companies in the centre.

Exactly twenty days after their new configuration came into being the 3rd Battalion, largely Germans and Swiss, accompanied a battalion of the 4th Regiment of the Line and several squadrons of the newly-formed *Chasseurs d'Afrique* in a tax-collecting expedition in the area of Maison Caree, a French-held position near the coast. The Arabs objected to paying and gave fight. The Foreign Legion fought back.

Less than a month later, on 23 May, a small working party of twenty-seven men of the 3rd Battalion was again near Maison Caree, with a twenty-five-strong partial-Squadron of the *Chasseurs d'Afrique* ranging around as a screening party. Suddenly, the horsemen came dashing back, their officer yelling that they were being pursued by fifteen hundred Arabs. As he passed the 3rd Battalion's Swiss-born Lieutenant Cham at the gallop he shouted to him to hold on, as the *Chasseurs* were going for help. Their *Clarion* – Trumpeter – apparently ashamed that his officer seemed to be abandoning the Legionnaires, dismounted and offered Cham his horse. When it was refused, he remounted and raced off after his comrades.

The men of the 3rd Battalion were rapidly engulfed by the enemy, some killed and some, including Cham, taken alive. Prisoners were told that they would be spared if they renounced Christianity and embraced Islam. Only one Legionnaire agreed to desert and convert, and subsequently escaped back to the French lines to tell his story. Cham was the first Foreign Legion officer to die in the field.[2] On 9 June, when a Swiss nobleman named Christophe Stoffel arrived from France to take command, he brought the first Regimental Standard. It was inscribed: 'The King of the French to the Foreign Legion.' There have been many flags since then, and while all regiments honour and revere their flags, the Foreign Legion's relationship with its Regimental Standards has always been almost obsessive.

The Conquest of Algeria was a war of hit-and-run skirmishes and firefights, with relatively few full scale battles. The Arabs of Central and Western Algeria, and the Kabyles – Berbers – of Eastern Algeria, preferred to attack small groups of French troops with hundreds, sometimes thousands, of men, both mounted and on foot. Against this largely nomadic enemy the French arrayed the Foreign Legion, a number of regular Regiments of the Line, the horse soldiers of the *Chasseurs d'Afrique*, the baggy-trousered infantrymen of the Regiment of Zouaves, who at their inception were recruited from among French-supporting Kabyles, and the dashing horsemen of the Spahis. There was also the newly-raised *Infanterie Legere d'Afrique*, African Light Infantry, commonly known as the *Bat d'Af* – or *Les Joyeux* or the *Zephyrs* – made up of young French criminals and incorrigibles. In 1834 the French added the locally-raised *Tirailleurs Algeriens* and indigenous irregulars known as *Goumiers*.

French penetration along the coast during 1833 was gradual, and usually opposed, but a year's grace was achieved when it was agreed that Abd-el-Kader, the most powerful of the Algerian leaders, should be recognized as the indigenous authority in Western Algeria. The French used the time to build roads and blockhouses, apparently not realizing that Abd-el-Kader, often referred to simply as the Emir, was quietly amassing a huge army to drive them into the sea. Near the end of the year Colonel Joseph Bernelle took command of the Foreign Legion.

As was always the case, events and decisions in Paris affected the *Armee d'Afrique*. King Ferdinand VII had ruled Spain, with interruptions – including being deposed by Napoleon Bonaparte – since 1808 and his brother, Don Carlos, was considered to be his heir. However, when the king's fourth wife, Maria-Cristina, presented him with a daughter, Ferdinand revoked the Salic Law, which forbade females from succeeding to the throne. When Ferdinand died in 1833 the crown passed to his infant daughter, Isabella II, with her mother ruling as Regent. Don Carlos disputed the line of succession and raised the standard of rebellion in the northern part of Spain. France, Britain and Portugal supported the accession of Isabella, and King Louis-Philippe's initial response was to order the Spaniards of the Foreign Legion's 4th Battalion to be released from their contracts so that they could return home to join Maria-Cristina's army – the 'Cristinos'.[3] The 'Citizen-King' had other plans up his royal sleeve as well, and on 28 January 1835 secretly agreed to cede the entire Foreign Legion, lock, stock and barrel, to the Queen Regent.

In the meantime, the Poles of the 7th Battalion found their unit re-numbered as the 4th, but service remained much the same, with road building, and consolidating small territorial gains. The fighting involved clashes with the Arab leaders of tribes holding sway over particular areas. Early in 1835 General Camille Trezel decided it was time to take to the field against Abd-el-Kader, and assembled a column comprising the *Chasseurs d'Afrique*, the *Bat d'Af*, the 66th Regiment of the Line, some mountain guns, supply wagons and the 5th (Italian) Battalion of the Foreign Legion, along with three Companies from the 4th (Polish) Battalion.

Trezel's forces met those of Abd-el-Kader near Moulay Ishmael, east of Oran, on 26 June. Arab tactics and their overwhelming numbers caused panic among some of the regular French troops. Only the men of the Foreign Legion, led by Lieutenant-Colonel Joseph Conrad, and the *Bat d'Af*, largely held fast in a disorderly retreat. At Macta, two days later, the Arabs fell on the French forces again and once more it was elements of the Foreign Legion and the *Bat d'Af* who saved the day and enabled the battered command to struggle back to the coastal port of Arzew.

At Moulay Ishmael and Macta a twenty-four-year-old Foreign Legion Sous-Lieutenant named Francois Achille Bazaine received a wound in his right wrist. He had enlisted as a private soldier in the 37th Regiment of the Line in 1831 and risen to the rank of sergeant in little more than a year. African service in the field had more appeal than garrison life in France and he was able to retain his rank when he transferred into the Foreign Legion. In 1833 he was commissioned a Sous-Lieutenant, and after the Moulay Ishmael/Macta affair General Trezel wrote in his record: 'The young Bazaine displayed rare bravery and shows most definite promise through his capacity and his conduct. He is blessed'.[4] A nineteen-year-old soldier serving with the 66th Regiment of the Line received his baptism of fire, and his first wound, at Moulay Ishmael/Macta. His name was Pierre Jeanningros. Both men would leave their marks on the Foreign Legion, particularly in Mexico, three decades later. Bazaine was promoted to Lieutenant within a month and made a Chevalier of the Legion of Honour. Trezel would be recalled, and replaced by the aged but energetic Napoleonic veteran General Thomas Bugeaud, and Jeanningros would transfer into the Regiment of Zouaves the following year.

Less than two weeks after the remnants of the 4th and 5th Battalions returned to base they received formal notification of Louis-Philippe's generosity to the Spanish.[5] The ceding of the Foreign Legion to Spain was not well received by officers and a step in rank was offered as an inducement to those willing to remain with the regiment. Fussing over the single nationalities of the battalions of what was officially known as 'The Auxiliary French Division', Bernelle, now a General, took the sensible step of mixing his men broadly, instituting a practice followed ever since. The Spanish Campaign was four years of battles and privations, an overall disaster, costing the lives of the vast majority of the Legionnaires, and also of several drafts of reinforcements, as many through disease, hunger and neglect as in battle against 'Carlist' forces. After a number of victories, Colonel Conrad resigned because of disagreements with his superior officer. Eventually, Bernelle himself quit over strained relations with the Spanish High Command over pay, rations and uniforms.

Conrad returned. Captain Bazaine was at his side when, riding at the head of his men, his hat perched on top of a cane he held aloft, Conrad was killed at Barbastro on 2 June 1837 – the first Colonel of the Foreign Legion to die at the head of his men. 'The Auxiliary French Division' fought on for another year. Bazaine returned to France, dropping to the rank of Lieutenant when he transferred into the 4th *Chasseurs a Pied* – Light Infantry. Finally, unpaid, in rags and nearly starving, the French force was dissolved by Royal Decree on 8 December 1838. The survivors left Spain with heads held high, marching north across the Pyrenees and back into France. Tagging along with them was a Spanish guerilla named Antonio Martinez, one of their former Carlist enemies, who for obscure reasons of his own wished to leave his country. Of the more than four thousand Legionnaires who had sailed from North Africa four years earlier, only a handful of officers and a mere one hundred and fifty-nine other ranks of what was now being referred to as the 'Old Legion' returned to France.

The *Armee d'Afrique* had immediately missed the fighting prowess of the Foreign Legion which their king had so loftily given away. Only five months after the departure of 'The Auxiliary French Division', recruiting began for a new Foreign Legion in July 1835.[6] Bugeaud succeeded in inflicting severe losses on Abd-el-Kader twelve months later, but was constantly short of men and it took almost two years for the 1st Battalion of the 'New Legion', commanded by Major Alphonse Bedeau, to be brought up to strength and shipped to Algeria. When a second battalion was raised, Bedeau was promoted to Lieutenant-Colonel and command of the regiment given to Lithuania-born Colonel von Hulsen. Once in Algeria the two-battalion regiment quickly proved itself, while its predecessor was bleeding and dying in Spain. In little more than two years of fighting the 'New Legion' built a formidable reputation for itself. On 13 October 1837 it participated in a major French assault on the walled city of Constantine, in Eastern Algeria, and the ambitious young Captain Leroy de Saint-Arnaud – a man with a somewhat murky past, and out to redeem himself or die in Africa – not only distinguished himself, but coined what would become a famous rallying cry: '*A moi la Legion!*' which would echo down the years. Sergeant-Major Doze captured an enemy battle flag and in recognition of their actions the Ministry of War decreed that the 'New Legion' should be allowed to form its own *Compagnies d'Elite*, with Voltigeurs and Grenadiers. Perhaps surprisingly, most of the survivors of the 'Old Legion' who had tottered out of Spain promptly joined the 'New Legion', and Bazaine had himself transferred out of the 4th *Chasseurs a Pied*, returning to the Foreign Legion as a Captain.

Abd-el-Kader had been quietly gathering himself an army to launch a major *Jihad*, or Holy War, against the French. The first to feel the strength of the Arab forces was the 16th Company of the 1st Battalion of the *Bat d'Af*, comprising one hundred and twenty-three soldiers under Captain Lelievre. On 1 February 1840 an Arab force of around eight thousand, led by one of Abd-el-Kader's senior commanders, attacked Fort Mazagran. The flagstaff was broken by bullets on three separate occasions, and was each time repaired and the Tricolour re-hoisted. Lawrence Trent Cave, a British officer visiting Algeria some time later, reported: 'On the fourth day Captain Lelievre told his men they would fight to the last shot, then go into the powder magazine and blow up themselves and the fort.' Fortunately, the Arabs had had enough and withdrew. Cave noted that French losses amounted to 'three or four dead and 16 wounded'.[7]

Clemens Lamping, a former officer in the Army of the North German principality of Oldenburg, serving as a Corporal in the Foreign Legion, met some of the Mazagran survivors the following year and 'heard an account of this whole affair from eye-witnesses.' He said he was 'fully persuaded that the defence was one of the most gallant actions of the whole war,' and reported that all the men involved were pardoned, received a special medal and were absorbed into regular French regiments. Lelievre was promoted to Commandant (Major), received the Cross of the Legion of Honour and was transferred into the 53rd Regiment of the Line.[8]

The Foreign Legion was now four battalions strong and a month after the affair at Mazagran the 1st and 4th Battalions took part in engagements around Medea, which was taken in mid-May 1840. Captain de Saint-Arnaud and Lieutenant Louis Espinasse were commended for their actions at Mouzaia, and Captain Meyer and Espinasse for the successful defence of a column attacked by an overwhelming number of Arabs. Captain de Caprez also received commendations for actions in the field.

The same two battalions took part in the assault and occupation of Miliana in June. A battalion of the 3rd Regiment of the Line, a few Sappers, some light guns and the 4th Battalion of the Foreign Legion, a total of some twelve hundred men, were left behind to occupy the town, which was immediately invested by the Emir's forces. Captain Bazaine held the Staff post of Adjutant-Major of the 4th Battalion. Constant attacks were beaten off, but fever and dysentery decimated the garrison. Food ran short. By the time a relief column arrived in October only two hundred and eight men of the 4th Battalion's complement of seven hundred and fifty were still on their feet. Colonel von Hulsen and two other Foreign Legion battalions had occupied a hill post called Fondouk and withstood a similar siege. They were not relieved until December, by which time two hundred and seven officers and men, including von Hulsen, were dead.

Bazaine's reward for surviving Miliana was to be transferred to the north of France where ten battalions of *Chasseurs a Pied* were under training. The nation's brightest young officers were in command. Francois Certain Canrobert was with the 6th Battalion, Bazaine with the 8th and the aristocratic Patrice MacMahon commanded the 10th. France was getting ready for a major offensive in Algeria and no doubt the ambitious Saint-Arnaud was delighted to hear that his patron, Bugeaud, was to be sent back as Governor-General.

Major Gautrin, commanding the 4th Battalion of the Foreign Legion, ran into serious opposition while on a routine swing through the country in January 1841 and fell at the head of his men. Sous-Lieutenant Edouard Collineau and another subaltern retrieved his body under fire. In April the regiment was split into two, with the 1st, 2nd and 3rd Battalions becoming the 1st Regiment Etranger and the 4th and a new 5th becoming the 2nd Regiment Etranger.[9]

While both saw their share of action, it soon became clear that the 2nd Etranger was to be the hard-hitting strike force, and it was soon possible to identify the rising young officers who, if they lived, would be France's future generals. Bugeaud's policy was one of scorched earth and in what came to be a standard form of warfare, flying columns were sent out, 'dissident' Arab and Kabyle villages attacked, houses burned, crops destroyed, fruit trees cut down and flocks of sheep and camels driven off. The Army established supply bases – known as 'Biscuitvilles' – to feed their fast-moving columns, which appeared out of nowhere, devastated whole areas and withdrew.

Beginning in 1842 General Jacques Randon took an aggressive stance, harrying the Kabyles of eastern Algeria. In May, what the French called a *razzia* – marching through mountain villages and small towns, fighting when necessary, but generally showing the flag and collecting taxes in cash or kind – netted two thousand five hundred sheep and three hundred and fifty head of cattle, but Lieutenant Collineau, who was commended for his efforts, and his mixed force of Legionnaires and Zouaves had some stiff fighting on the way home. Major de Caprez and Captain Vinoy of the 1st Etranger were commended for a particular bitter fight in the mountains in September. Abd-el-Kader was badly routed when Bazaine's 8th Battalion of *Chasseurs a Pied* and a Zouave battalion attacked him from one flank, while MacMahon's 10th *Chasseurs a Pied* and a Regiment of the Line swung in from the other. Soon afterwards MacMahon, promoted to Lieutenant-Colonel, took command of the 2nd Etranger.

The war went on and Collineau was commended for his part in two punitive actions fought in February 1843. Abd-el-Kader had changed his tactics to avoid having a static home base where he could be attacked and had established a nomadic camp called a *Smala*, a journeyman tented capital of upwards of thirty thousand men, women and children. In May of that year the Duc d'Aumale, fourth son of King Louis-Philippe, with five hundred cavalrymen, stumbled across the *Smala*. While vastly outnumbered, they had the element of surprise on their side and swept through the camp. Abd-el-Kader was not there, and only token resistance was offered, enabling d'Aumale to capture great herds of animals, a vast quantity of munitions and the Emir's entire treasury.

During the battle, one of the Duke's junior Staff officers, Charles Dupin, saved the life of Colonel Louis Morris, commanding the 4th *Chasseurs d'Afrique*, an action subsequently recorded for posterity as part of a vast seventy-five foot canvas painted by Horace Vernet, which was hung at Versailles.[10] Dupin, an eccentric and ruthless officer, would be important to the Foreign Legion when it went to Mexico twenty years later.

Elsewhere in May 1843 the 1st Etranger was in action in the mountains. Captain Vinoy was again commended and the following month Major de Caprez led a Grenadier Company in a bayonet charge against an Arab position. Later in the year the regiment began fortifying a 'Biscuitville' which had been established at Sidi-bel-Abbes, about a hundred kilometres (sixty miles) south of Oran, near the tomb of a holy man. It would ultimately become the home of the Foreign Legion. MacMahon, taking command of the 2nd Etranger, had found them a strange lot, including about a hundred Carlists who had fought the 'Old Legion' in Spain. There were also forty hungry Englishmen, who could never make their rations last for the prescribed period, and who had come to the Foreign Legion from among the British troops who had been supporting the Cristinos in Spain.

Abd-el-Kader had withdrawn across the barely-defined border into Morocco and not much was heard of him for some time, although resistance to the French was offered by various local chiefs. MacMahon drove his men relentlessly. Captain Espinasse and other officers were commended for their actions during clashes with the Kabyles in June and Captain Meyer was among the officers and men receiving official praise after an especially difficult *razzia*, which lasted from mid-June to early August. Bazaine was appointed head of the *Bureau Arabe* – Arab Bureau – at Tlemcen, filling a difficult position, which combined the duties of Intelligence Officer for the *Army d'Afrique* with the responsibilities of policeman, tax-collector and judge for the local population. Early in 1844 he was promoted to the rank of Major, nominally of the 58th Regiment of the Line, but remained with the Arab Bureau.

On 15 March 1844 the 2nd Etranger was part of the Duc d'Aumale's forces facing the fortified mountain village of Mechounech, which was occupied by hostile Kabyles and some of Abd-el-Kader's regular troops. The 2nd Regiment of the Line took the village at bayonet point and a defensive fortified position was made untenable by an artillery bombardment directed by the Duc de Montpensier, the fifth son of Louis-Philippe. The Kabyles then established themselves on the top of an enormous, and seemingly impregnable, rock formation, and turned back two French frontal attacks. Although dusk was falling, d'Aumale and de Montpensier seized the initiative and led the French attack, scrambling up the side of the rock under heavy fire. Captain Espinasse, leading his Company of the 2nd Etranger, reached the top after being wounded twice, then had to repulse repeated attacks – in which he sustained two more wounds – by some five hundred Kabyles. Eventually, the French, who had not eaten since before dawn, overcame resistance and the enemy slipped off into the night.[11] Major Louis de Granet Lacroix de Chabriere and Captain Meyer, who was wounded, were conspicuous in the fighting, and such had been the regiment's stamina that the Duc d'Aumale convinced his father, the King, to present them with their own Regimental Standard. Not long afterwards MacMahon was promoted and named as Colonel of the 41st Regiment of the Line. Command of the 2nd Etranger passed to Colonel Senihle.

When the Emir returned to the Algeria-Morocco border country several months later he was at the head of a large army, having convinced the Sultan of Morocco that it was his duty to help in driving the French out of North Africa. Bugeaud, however, was ready, crossed the border into Morocco and destroyed the Emir's army at the Battle of Isly on 14 August. It earned him his Marshal's baton and the title of Duc d'Isly, and was one of the few major engagements which did not involve the Foreign Legion.

2
Sidi Brahim – A Cautionary Tale

Abd-el-Kader was desperate now and struck wherever he could, hoping to recapture the magic his name had once had for the Arabs and Kabyles. He needed a highly visible victory, a crushing defeat of French forces, but he had to wait a year for an opportunity to present itself. The *Chasseurs a Pied* had become the *Chasseurs d'Orleans* and in September 1845 Bazaine's old 8th Battalion was decimated through its Commanding Officer's blatant disobedience to orders. Colonel Montagnac, a former Foreign Legion officer, saw himself as a fire-eater and his actions precipitated a catastrophe for the French and a triumph for the Emir. Although under strict instructions to remain on the defensive at the small outpost at Djemmaa-Ghazaouet, east of the frontier with Morocco, when Montagnac heard that Abd-el-Kader was moving across the border into Algeria he decided to strike.

What happened should have been an object lesson for French officers, a matter for the manuals on war, but it was not learned. The *Bat d'Af* had shown at Mazagran what small numbers of soldiers in a defensive position, in that case a fort, could achieve against vastly superior numbers. The affair involving Montagnac's *Chasseurs d'Orleans* began and ended at the military post at Djemmaa-Ghazaouet, but between his full force leaving the fort and the pitifully few stragglers returning there were two costly engagements in the open, a struggle at a defensive position called Sidi Brahim and a ragged retreat. Echoes of this sorry running engagement would occasionally be enacted later in Foreign Legion history, particularly in Mexico, where aspects of the Combat of Camerone in 1863 closely approximated events at Sidi Brahim, and a sanguinary affair at Santa Isabel in 1866 was precipitated by another officer disobeying orders and letting his men be caught in the open by a numerically superior enemy.

Entrusting the fort at Djemmaa-Ghazaouet to Captain Coffyn and little more than a Corporal's Guard, Montagnac left on 21 September with about a dozen officers, some four hundred infantrymen and sixty cavalrymen, marching west to intercept Abd-el-Kader. At daylight two days later an enemy force, estimated at about eight hundred horsemen, was seen on the hills near the French camp. Compounding his disobedience to orders, Montagnac now committed the cardinal sin of dividing his command and took his cavalry and rather more than two-thirds of his infantry forward, leaving Major Froment Coste and around a hundred men to guard the camp. Montagnac's cavalry attacked the enemy, rode through them, lost half their number and had to retreat. By now the infantry had come up and Montagnac attacked again. Suddenly, thousands of robed figures emerged from a ravine. A cavalryman was sent dashing back to Coste as the battle was joined. Montagnac was killed soon afterwards and command passed to Major Courby de Cognord. A Sergeant was now sent to alert Coste. The command was split yet again as he started at once towards Montagnac's force with about sixty men, leaving Captain Gereaux and the others to guard the camp. The sound of firing by Montagnac's men grew less vigorous and then died out. Coste realized that his own only hope was to rejoin Gereaux, but before he could do so his troops were surrounded and overwhelmed.

Gereaux heard the sound of diminished firing by Coste's party and then silence. Suddenly a cavalryman named Davine swept down on them. 'They are all dead . . . it's over,' he shouted as he raced by, heading in the direction of Djemmaa-Ghazaouet. Gereaux and Lieutenant Chapdelaine retreated with their men, falling back on a small, white-domed building, surrounded by a wall. It was the tomb of Sidi Brahim, a venerated Muslim holy man. They took possession and manned the wall, but there was no room for their pack mules, which were soon captured, and when they began checking their supplies – a few bread rolls, some potatoes and a bottle of absinthe – they found there was very little water.

Then the pursuing enemy attacked, flinging themselves, in the words of one of the defenders, a soldier named Tressy, 'like an unstemmed torrent, like the waves of a raging sea against the crumbling walls . . .'. Abd-el-Kader himself appeared and a surrender demand was sent. 'We will never surrender!' replied Gereaux. 'We are few, but we will fight.' The Emir sent a second demand. He had, he said, eighty-two French prisoners and if Gereaux did not surrender they would be executed. 'They are in the hands of God,' replied Gereaux. 'We have plenty of food and ammunition. We will hold out.' A third note came from Abd-el-Kader, saying he knew they had no food and little ammunition, but that he would not sacrifice perhaps five or six hundred of his men to overcome the fifty or sixty Frenchmen. 'I will starve you out,' he said. Gereaux did not want to reply, but a Corporal took the note and wrote: '*Merde* – Shit – to Abd-el-Kader! The *Chasseurs d'Orleans* die, but they never surrender.' Gereaux read it and approved. 'Send it,' he said.

When a fourth messenger approached, the French fired on him. So Abd-el-Kader sent an officer prisoner, Dutertre, the battalion's adjutant, to negotiate. Instead, he told his comrades to 'fight to the death.' His captors promptly shot him and dragged him dying behind a bush. Almost immediately an Arab appeared with the officer's head on a lance. The French killed him. The attacks resumed, but were too costly for Abd-el-Kader's taste.

After dark a friendly Kabyle crept to the wall and offered to take a note to Djemmaa-Ghazaouet. The following morning Abd-el-Kader sent his prisoners away under guard, left three groups of one hundred and fifty men each to contain the besieged Frenchmen and withdrew with his main force. The Kabyle messenger returned under cover of darkness, reporting that Captain Coffyn at Djemmaa-Ghazaouet had declared Gereaux's note to be a forgery and a trap. The Kabyle had been soundly thrashed and thrown out of the fort. Gereaux paid him for his efforts and discussed plans with his men to make a run for it the following day.

At dawn they slipped silently away, Gereaux, who had been slightly wounded, helped by two soldiers, and they covered almost seventeen kilometres (ten miles) with little more than sniping action by a handful of pursuers. Chapdelaine and several others fell, but the balance of the men arrived on the brink of the valley they must cross to reach Djemmaa-Ghazaouet. Below them were two thousand of the enemy. The handful of Frenchmen fought their way downwards, twice forming squares to break infantry assaults. Eventually, their last cartridges fired, and in sight of the fort, they resorted to stones and clubs and fifteen were submerged by their enemies and captured. Gereaux was finished and the fugitives were down to a mere twenty men when the timid Captain Coffyn fired three cannon shots to frighten the Arabs, but he did not open the gates until the survivors actually reached them.

Of the four hundred-plus men of the *Chasseurs d'Orleans* who had marched out a week before only seventeen returned, two of whom dropped dead as they entered the fort. Several died in hospital in a matter of days. Only Corporal Lavayssiere still retained his firearm.

'As for me, almost every night for fifteen years I dreamed of some scene or other of that terrible fight,' the soldier Tressy wrote in 1892. '[E]ven to-day, after forty-seven years, every detail of it is as clear in my memory as it was at the time.'

The 1st Battalion of the 1st Etranger was put into the field as soon as word of the affair at Sidi-Brahim was received. They found the mutilated bodies there and buried them, but there was no sign of the eighty or more prisoners taken when Colonel Montagnac's command was attacked. Abd-el-Kader had marched them across the border into Morocco, where they were joined in October by the fifteen taken in the penultimate dash to Djemmaa-Ghazaouet – soon to be re-named Nemours – and about a hundred and seventy-five other French soldiers, who had been captured when an ammunition convoy had been attacked near Tlemcen. There were several escape attempts, but only one man was successful.

The same month Colonel MacMahon, now commanding the 41st Regiment of the Line, was at Nemours, where he met Sidi Brahim survivor Corporal Lavayssiere. The year turned and in February, while at the battle site, he made arrangements for the temporary burial of the remains of a number of bodies which had lain out in the open for five months.

On 24 April 1846 Major Courby de Cognord and ten other officer prisoners were sent away from the camp inside the Moroccan border where they were being held. They took four soldiers with them and barely were they out of earshot when the massacre of the other prisoners began. A *Clarion* named Roland managed to escape at the beginning of the bloodbath, and another Frenchman, Delpech, left for dead, escaped as well. Roland reached the post at Lalla Maghrnia three weeks later, but it took Delpech three months to get back to the French lines. In early November Abd-el-Kader tried to interest Marshal Bugeaud in ransoming the captives, but received no response. He then approached the authorities in Spanish Morocco, who paid him thirty-three thousand francs, and on 23 November, after fourteen months of captivity, Courby de Cognord and his companions were returned to French-held territory.[1]

MacMahon had met *Clarion* Roland, who had escaped the massacre of prisoners, and later in the year, accompanied by the celebrated author Alexandre Dumas, had an unusual meeting with other survivors. Dumas had published *The Three Musketeers* in 1844, followed by *The Count of Monte Cristo*, and many official and unofficial doors had been opened for him.

'I was at the port of Nemours at the end of 1846 when a French frigate arrived,' MacMahon would write later. 'It had been placed at the disposal of Alexander Dumas, to enable him to visit the Algerian ports. Passing through Melilla he had heard about the prisoners.'

MacMahon arranged for him to meet some of those who had been held captive by Abd-el-Kader and Dumas was able to talk with Major Courby de Cognord, Lieutenants Larrazet and Morin, Sous-Lieutenant Thomas, Doctor Cabasse, *Marechal des Logis* Barbet, Hussars Testard and Metz and *Chasseurs d'Orleans* Tallet and Michel.

'We received them with enthusiasm . . .,' MacMahon would recall. 'Alexander Dumas told me of his desire to visit Sidi-Brahim. I conducted him there with an escort of two of my Squadrons of cavalry and a small *goum*. He visited the field of battle and Commandant [de] Cognord gave him all the details of the fight'.[2]

The year was a busy one for the 2nd Etranger, with marches and skirmishes. Captain Collineau was especially commended for his exertions in June in an engagement with the 1st Battalion. General Randon mentioned battalion commanders Meyer and de Chabriere, several Lieutenants, including Bertrand, and some Sous-Lieutenants, including Mangin, at the end of the campaign, and there was much more of the same the following year. The Foreign Legion now had some unusual officers, including Martinez, the veteran Spanish Carlist who had crossed the Pyrenees with the remnants of the 'Old Legion' seven years earlier, who was now a Captain. Comte Paul de Castellane, who spent some weeks at a Foreign Legion outpost, found himself in the company of the son of a high court judge, the nephew of a cardinal, the son of a Frankfurt banker and a very political Persian. There was also Lieutenant Thomas Moore, eldest son and namesake of the Irish poet, and godson of Lord Byron, who was quietly coughing out his life with tuberculosis.[3]

At the beginning of 1847 the 1st Etranger was headquartered at Sidi-bel-Abbes, and in April the 1st and 2nd Battalions took part in a particularly arduous march. Facing snow and bitter cold in the mountains, and, conversely, sandstorms in the desert proper, the Legionnaires pressed on. Everywhere there were traces of the past. Near Thiout, an oasis of some five thousand palms, they paused to examine rock paintings of great age depicting elephants and giraffes. Days later, at Moghar, the Grenadier Company under Sous-Lieutenant Delabecque was attacked by a large and hostile group and had to fight their way clear. Elsewhere, attempts were being made to put an end to the depredations of Abd-el-Kader, but the Foreign Legion was not involved in the campaign which led to his surrender in September.

The affair at Sidi Brahim had been almost the Emir's last hurrah. Declared *persona non grata* by the Sultan of Morocco, he surrendered to the French on 23 December 1847, and was sent into exile, first to France, then to Egypt and finally to Syria. The next year, with his influence gone, the Province of Oran was peaceful, but the two foreign regiments took part in many lengthy *razzias*. Major Meyer was commended for his work with five Companies from the 2nd Etranger's 2nd Battalion in the campaign of that year, which ended when Colonel Canrobert arrived to take command of the regiment. Bazaine was promoted to Lieutenant-Colonel attached to the 19th *Chasseurs a Pied*, and later transferred to the 5th

Regiment of the Line, but remained in Tlemcen as head of the Arab Bureau.

Most of the Foreign Legion was in the field the following year when news came from Paris that their founder, King Louis-Philippe, had paid the price for what had become an increasingly autocratic regime. He had been overthrown and sought asylum in England. Prince Louis Napoleon – nephew of Napoleon Bonaparte – had himself been in exile in England and returned to France at once. He had long sought to rule, having staged an unsuccessful revolt in 1836, causing the King to exile him to the United States. He had also lived in Switzerland, whose Army he admired, and briefly in Italy – whose desire for unification he endorsed – then moved to England. In 1840 he had tried to spread the seeds of revolt among French soldiers in Boulogne. Arrested and jailed for life, he escaped back to England five years later. Now he ran for and won a seat in the National Assembly.

The year 1848 was a momentous one for Europe, as the troubles in France caused a wave of revolutionary spirit which swept across the Continent. Sicily rebelled against its king and anti-Austria riots broke out in Northern Italy. There were revolutionary rumblings in some of the German States and Principalities. Russia stepped in to assist Austria when Hungary declared its independence. French troops helped the Pope to overturn a new republican regime in Rome. In Germany, Karl Marx and Friedrich Engels published their *Communist Manifesto*, then fled to England, where the Chartist riots had already caused politicians to be thinking of some social reforms.

The 1st Battalion of the 1st Etranger went to Oran to receive its new Regimental Standard from the hands of General Jean-Jacques Pelissier. In June, as a gesture of goodwill, it was announced that all Poles serving in the Foreign Legion could be released from service and twenty-three members of the 1st Etranger took advantage of this, though seventeen of them would return within two months, and the 2nd Etranger also lost a number of men. Canrobert had taken command of the regiment on 18 January, but left it on 14 June, and on returning to Philippeville after a difficult campaign, the Foreign Legion had to deal with more of the egalitarian and fraternal international disposition of the new regime in Paris, as brotherly instincts were extended to the Piedmontese of Northern Italy and the two regiments were expected to release those who wished to end their contracts. All told, the haemorrhaging of Poles and Italians cost the 2nd Etranger six hundred and eighteen trained men, roughly the equivalent of a full battalion.

Recruiting, however, was not a problem, as a flood of defeated and dispossessed men from all over Europe was increasingly beating down the doors of the Foreign Legion depots. Then, when mid-year the Paris regime instituted a wave of repression, ordering a crackdown on workers, Frenchmen – artisans, journalists and others – fearful for their safety and quality of life, also began turning up at the recruiting depots.

Among them was a young journalist named Clement Maudet, whose opinions, writings and affiliations were likely to make him a target for unwelcome attention from the authorities. On 6 July he chose soldiering as offering better prospects for a future than the probability of becoming a political prisoner. When he engaged for seven years in the 1st Etranger, the keepers of the records noted that he was born 8 July 1829 at St. Mars d'Outille, the son of Julien Maudet and his wife,

Marie, nee Connier. He was two days short of his nineteenth birthday, 1.56 metres (5 feet 3 inches) tall, had brown hair and eyebrows, brown eyes and was clean-shaven.[4] He would make a career in the Foreign Legion, gain a Commission, and die after a gallant stand at an abandoned inn in Mexico, at a place called Camerone.

Maudet arrived at Sidi-bel-Abbes on 27 July[5] and, initially at least, must have wondered if he had made a bad choice, as it was immediately clear that there was to be far more 'colonization work' and road-building than real soldiering. The 1st Etranger was undertaking most of the construction of the massive barracks which were going up, as well as laying out parks and building fountains within the town, but Maudet was better off than he might have been in Paris and elsewhere, as the savage repression of students and workers continued. Louis Napoleon was President of France by the end of the year. Maudet was promoted to Corporal[6] on 21 April 1849, at which time his regiment was engaged in irrigation and agricultural work around Sidi-bel-Abbes, turning near-desert into farmland.

The officer who had replaced Canrobert as Colonel of the 2nd Etranger was gone inside three months and on 31 August command passed into the hands of Colonel Jean-Luc Carbuccia, an exuberant character who spent several months settling in, then had his men almost continually in the field. In the first half of 1849 they fought a series of engagements as they marched and built their way over hundreds of kilometres. The grandly-named young Sous-Lieutenant Paul-Amiable de Brian de Foussieres Fonteneuillet, who had joined the regiment straight from Saint-Cyr, was seeing his first campaigning on a major scale. He would ultimately go to Mexico, and would die at Santa Isabel with his Legionnaires, all of them the victims of his disobedience to orders in the grand manner of Montagnac of the *Chasseurs d'Orleans*.

At the end of June the 4th Company of the 3rd Battalion was engaged in a construction project when attacked by an enemy force fifteen hundred-strong. Lieutenant Robert deployed his men behind the walls they had just erected and they gave a good account of themselves for over three hours, after which the enemy retired with its dead and wounded. A huge *razzia* involving six hundred men of the 2nd Etranger, four hundred soldiers of the *Bat d'Af* and two hundred and fifty cavalry confiscated fourteen hundred camels, five thousand sheep and five hundred tents following an engagement at Seriana.

Thus encouraged, the feisty Carbuccia went south with a French column sent to reduce the thickly-palmed and prosperous oasis of Zaatcha, where a leader named Bouzian had excited the local population and needed, in French eyes, some serious attention before he could become another Abd-el-Kader. Captain Collineau of the 2nd Etranger believed that the political events in Paris the previous year were known to the Kabyles, and that 'while they did not understand the exact significance, they think they can take advantage and that awakens hopes among them which were only dormant'.[7] This was only partly true, as the causes which led to the attack on Zaatcha also involved some mishandling of affairs by the local Arab Bureau officer, as well as active resistance to tax collecting based on an annual levy per oasis palm tree.

Carbuccia's men were in the attack on Zaatcha on 16 July, but quickly found that reducing what was in fact something of miniature fortress, deep in the oasis and protected by a moat, presented unexpected problems. It was one thing to lay waste to mountain villages, but attacking a static base, especially in a place where the populace had a reputation for belligerence, was quite another. After losing a number of men he drew off, waited three days and then decided to abandon the exercise altogether. Total casualties were thirty-one killed and one hundred and seventeen wounded, including four officers of the 2nd Etranger wounded, fourteen men killed and sixty-seven wounded. A number of officers, Lieutenant Mangin among them, were cited for gallantry, as was the wounded Sergeant Hauer.

It was soon reported that two hundred Kabyle horsemen and an undetermined number of men on foot were converging on an oasis south-east of Biskra and a force of one hundred and twenty-five French cavalry, two hundred *goums* and three hundred Legionnaires was sent to deal with or disperse them. Collineau said later that the French were over-confident, and were lucky to emerge victorious. Losses included the Foreign Legion officer who was partly responsible for the general unrest, dating back to his time with the Arab Bureau, and a number of others. The enemy was eventually scattered and Collineau and Sous-Lieutenant Rousseau, as well as two other junior officers, were commended for their courage, as were *Tambour* Vireken, who had exchanged his drum for a musket, and Sergeant Hauer, wounded at Zaatcha, who went into the new battle with his arm in a sling.

Despite the fact that Carbuccia had been strongly criticized for his actions at Zaatcha, it had been decided that Bouzian and his followers must be taught a lesson, if only for the very practical reason that his besting of the French column sent the wrong message to the tribes. Whether they were mountain people or oasis dwellers they recognized weakness. General Emile Herbillon, commanding Constantine Province, and Carbuccia, commanding the Batna Sub-division, assembled a force of four thousand four hundred and ninety-three men, which included eight battalions of infantry, four squadrons of cavalry and a detachment of artillery, as well as about a thousand men of the 1st and 3rd Battalions of the 2nd Etranger. They reached Zaatcha on 7 October.

Herbillon proceeded to show that he, too, was under-estimating the zeal of Bouzian's followers, failing to surround the oasis, which allowed outsiders to reinforce the defenders. The farce of the first day was blamed on the enthusiasm of the *Chasseurs a Pied* and the *Tirailleurs Algeriens*, but on 10 October the enemy routed both the 43rd Regiment of the Line and the 2nd Etranger. Trenches were dug and saps pushed forward and Herbillon was reinforced by a further fifteen hundred and twelve men.

An attack on Zaatcha eight days later failed, despite the efforts of Major Bourbaki and the *Bat d'Af.* A wall collapsed on Captain Padro's hundred-strong Company of Voltigeurs from the 2nd Etranger, killing thirteen and injuring forty. On 25 October, when two hundred men of the 2nd Etranger and a like number from the *Bat d'Af* were sent to start cutting down palm trees, the population's only source of wealth, they were driven off with losses. On 8 November twelve hundred Zouaves commanded by General Canrobert arrived, but cholera came with them, too.

Carbuccia and Herbillon disagreed violently on several matters, and it was also becoming apparent that news of Bouzian's stand against the French was exciting tribes all over eastern Algeria, so most of the 2nd Etranger were sent away on convoy duty. The regiment missed the closing act of the ill-conceived siege, when Canrobert's Zouaves broke into Zaatcha on 26 November, achieving what the other troops had failed to do, put down the revolt, and presented their Commanding Officer with Bouzian's head.

Collineau and five other officers of the 2nd Etranger were cited for their parts in the siege, which cost the regiment eighty-five dead and one hundred and seventy-five wounded. Overall French losses from battle and disease may have reached the fifteen hundred mark.[8]

For the 1st Etranger, the year's manual labour was merely punctuated by two brief expeditions and a cholera outbreak. General Herbillon had been replaced by General de Saint-Arnaud, who was busy planning future campaigns. Corporal Maudet made Sergeant on 6 March,[9] but for the 1st Etranger a tax-collecting expedition was the high spot of 1850, while the restless Carbuccia took the 2nd Etranger's 1st Battalion to Lamboesis to start building a prison.

Most of the men settled down to construction work, but Carbuccia turned a portion of them into archaeologists, excavating among the Roman ruins. On the tombstone of a Roman Legionary he wrote: 'Colonel Carbuccia to his colleague in the IIIrd Roman Legion'[10] and would later boast: 'I could have built a city. I had in my Company architects, engineers, artists. When I had need of an expert, a writer or a painter, I only had to give the order, and, the next day, the Sergeant-Majors would bring me ten names, rather than just one. I could have staffed a university from among my troops. Where were these men from? What had they done in their own countries? What were their real names? These questions were unanswerable'.[11]

More campaigns and more *razzias* were the order of the day, and increased when Randon, now a Marshal of France, returned to Algeria, this time as Governor-General, the following year. Colonel Meyer, who had succeeded Carbuccia, had the 2nd Etranger all over Kabylia during 1851, a successful July campaign earning plaudits for Captain Collineau, Sous-Lieutenants Rousseau and de Brian and several other subalterns, in an Order signed by de Saint-Arnaud.

For the 1st Etranger there had also been a change of Commanding Officer. Bazaine, who had risen to head the Arab Bureau for the whole Province of Oran, had been promoted to Colonel of the 55th Regiment of the Line, but on 4 February 1851 returned to the Foreign Legion as Colonel of the 1st Etranger. However, if the regiment imagined that having a fighting Colonel, especially one who was a former Legionnaire, would guarantee some action, they were to be disappointed. In fact, because of political events in Paris, there was even some talk of disbanding the foreign regiments, which young officers found disquieting. 'They are talking of abolishing the Legion,' wrote Captain Collineau on 8 September. 'In that case, where shall I go?'[12]

The political upheaval was caused by President Louis Napoleon's efforts to prolong his tenure in office, and the National Assembly's opposition to his plan to change the Constitution so that he could serve another term. His response, in the early days of December, was to dissolve the Assembly, use the Army – notably troops under General de Saint-Arnaud – to suppress dissent in the streets and have himself 're-elected' for a ten-year term. Soldiers who backed him were rewarded and de Saint-Arnaud became a Marshal of France.

General Paul Grisot, reviewing the regimental *Journaux de Marche* several decades later, would write of this period of limbo for the Foreign Legion: 'The year 1851 was tranquil and the 1st Regiment continued its construction work in Sidi-bel-Abbes and in the Province of Oran',[13] but in April 1852 there was a welcome change of activity, and the 1st Etranger was ordered into the field, as part of a four thousand five hundred-strong force sent against the Beni-Snassen, but it was a campaign with more marching then fighting. Villages were burned, flocks of camels and sheep seized and granaries destroyed. The regiment returned to Sidi-bel-Abbes in mid-July.

Efforts to subdue the Kabyles in Eastern Algeria had a repetitive quality about them, with small pieces of territory conquered in every campaign, but the overall goal left unattained. Now Minister of War, de Saint-Arnaud ordered another campaign. General Pierre Bosquet commanded the 1st Brigade and General MacMahon the Division into which the 2nd Etranger was put. Collineau, now a Major, commanded the 3rd Battalion and Martinez, the old Spanish Carlist, was now Captain of the Grenadier Company. Captain Bertrand, commanding a half-battalion made up of the Voltigeurs of the 1st Battalion, the 4th Company of the 2nd Battalion and three Companies of the 3rd Battalion, was in the field in mid-June. Collineau, now a Battalion Commander and commanding the outpost at Biskra, heard that a Kabyle *harka* was in the field with more than two thousand horsemen and foot soldiers. Deeming it a cavalry matter – while the Foreign Legion was infantry – he set out with fifty-two troopers of the *Chasseurs d'Afrique*, thirty-two Spahis, eighty partisans and a *goum* and confronted them in battle. The Kabyles fled, leaving their leader and one hundred and fifty dead, and Collineau in possession of three hundred and twenty-four muskets and one hundred and fifty-eight camels.

3
The First Foreign War

On 24 September 1852 a twenty-four-year-old Sous-Lieutenant named Jean Danjou joined the 2nd Regiment of the Foreign Legion. His service record described him as 1.71 metres (just over 5 feet 8 inches) tall, with brown eyes, clean-shaven, brown hair and eyebrows, and his hairline was noted as receding.[1] Little more than a decade later he would become the best-known Legionnaire in the history of France's foreign regiments.

Born on 15 April 1828, he was the fourth of the eight sons of hatmaker Jean Danjou and his wife, Marguerite, née Balusson, of the southern town of Chalabre. Their oldest son, Philippe, was in a seminary in Carcassonne, training for the priesthood, and the second, Jean-Baptiste, was farming family land. The third son was studying engineering and it had been more or less taken for granted that Jean, his father's namesake, would enter the family business. However, when he was fifteen years old an Army officer who was a former employee of Danjou Senior returned to Chalabre on leave. Now a Sous-Lieutenant in a Regiment of the Line, he was invited to the Danjou home for dinner and his tales of Algerian campaigning fired young Jean with military zeal. He subsequently talked of nothing else, and his father, bowing to the inevitable, sent him to a tutor in Carcassonne to prepare him for officers' school.[2] Young Danjou entered Saint-Cyr on 5 December 1847, graduated near the top of his class two years later and, at his own request, joined the 51st Regiment of the Line on 1 October, 1849. He stayed with them for just less than three years, then transferred into the 2nd Etranger, which had seen considerable action in the early part of the year.

Collineau, who had been in the Foreign Legion since 1836, and who had been named an Officer of the Legion of Honour at the end of the previous year's campaign, was again in the field, this time pressing south into the Sahara with two hundred Legionnaires mounted on camels. It was his last full campaign with the Foreign Legion, as he would leave later in the year, when promoted to Lieutenant-Colonel.

Sergeant Maudet of the 1st Etranger had been out with the 2nd Battalion against the Beni-Snassen near the border with Morocco in May. In mid-June, in a difficult campaign, in which the 1st and 2nd Battalions were part of a column of four thousand five hundred French troops, almost two thousand camels and mules and the enemy's entire reserve of grain was captured. The Beni-Snassen, who had put six thousand men into the field, and facing starvation if they lost their herds and grain, fought hard to prevent the French from leaving with their spoils. The 2nd Battalion, especially, was heavily engaged in protecting other troops during the withdrawal and was favourably mentioned in Orders for its 'unprecedented acts of courage'. A month later the soldiers were navvies again, engaged in 'colonization work' around Sidi-bel-Abbes. Near the end of the year came news from France that President Louis Napoleon, having solidified his position after what had amounted to the *coup d'etat* of the previous year, had now declared the creation of the Second Empire, with himself as Emperor Napoleon III.

Part of the problem with campaigning against the Kabyles was the mountainous nature of the country they occupied, deep valleys, narrow tracks, often along precipitous cliff faces, and a foe who new every nook and cranny, while the French had little more than a basic knowledge. Detached to the *Service Topographique*, Sous-Lieutenant Danjou was sent to help map a remote area, back-breaking and hazardous work, with constant danger from wandering mountaineers with their long-barrelled muskets.

Yet when his map-making career came to an end on 21 May 1853, it was not from a Kabyle bullet. While engaged in a topographical survey with the veteran Captain Rousseau, a faulty cartridge exploded prematurely in a signalling pistol Danjou was loading, almost blowing off his left hand.[3] The injury would probably have ended his military career in any part of the French Army other than the Foreign Legion. Quick first aid by Rousseau, followed by skilful medical attention by a military doctor, prevented gangrene and saved Danjou's forearm.

Once the stump had healed he had an articulated wooden hand made, complete with hinged fingers. It was then attached to a deep leather cup, which fitted over the lower part of his forearm. When it was in place, the sleeves of his shirt and jacket concealed the cuff, and he wore a white glove. There is no way of knowing who made this intricately-crafted hand, but considering the skills present in the regiment, it seems entirely possible that it was the work of a Legionnaire, perhaps several, schooled in carving and cabinet-making. The loss of his hand obviously meant that Danjou's fighting abilities would be limited to some extent, though it in no way impeded him in mounting a horse. Nor would it affect his usefulness in a Staff capacity, or prevent his career progress, and he was promoted to Lieutenant before the end of the year.[4]

The 1st Etranger's life that year had been dull, General Grisot noting[5] that there was 'little to report that was singular in 1853.' Maudet took on additional responsibilities when promoted to Quartermaster Sergeant on 26 November,[6] but the job mainly involved paperwork and accounts and, at his own request, he gratefully reverted to the rank of Sergeant on 1 December.[7]

The two Regiments Etranger continued to draw many recruits from the German States and Principalities and during 1853 they included Gottfried Wensel, a Prussian, and Friedrich Fritz from the South German state of Wurttemberg, both of whom would re-engage, making careers for themselves under the French flag. Early the next year Heindrich Pinzinger, a Bavarian, signed engagement papers, as did a Belgian, Luitpold Van Opstal.

The new men rapidly learned to identify the uniforms and badges of rank of their superiors, Leading Sergeants and upwards to Adjutant were Sous-Officiers, and were the real power in the Foreign Legion. Officers, except on campaign, were aloof and lived in a world of their own. On campaign things were very different. They often used the familiar *tu*, rather than *vous*, in conversations with their men, and were prone to refer to them collectively as *mes enfants* – as in '*Allons, mes enfants!*' – which, while translating as 'Let's go, my children!' was equivalent to the British Army's 'Up boys, and at 'em!' or the American Army's 'Let's go, guys!'

They quickly learned that *soupe* was not just soup, and could mean any meal, and that when a Corporal yelled *Garde a vous!* they were required to snap to attention, as an officer or Sous-Officier was approaching. Their basic skills in French rapidly made them aware that *corvee* meant fatigues, which as new men were their especial chore. They were told that once they had completed their training they would be known as Fusiliers, that as vacancies occurred the best of them might be transferred into the Companies of Voltigeurs or Grenadiers, and that a *peleton* was a training course for Corporals or Sergeants. They also discovered that in its twenty-two years of existence the Foreign Legion had developed a definable regimental personality, and almost its own language – an argot, really – which was a mixture of French and German, with a smattering of Arabic words, and others, thrown in. The regimental doctor was the *Toubib*, and officers and men spoke of the *Tell*, meaning the coastal strip south of the Mediterranean, or the *bled*, meaning the desert to the South, the edges of the Sahara. They also discovered that abusing another Legionnaire because of his nationality quickly brought down official wrath, and that laying undue emphasis on one's own nationality was frowned on, which would lead in time to the Foreign Legion adopting the motto *Legio Patria Nostra* – The Legion is Our Country.

By the Spring of 1854 it was obvious that France was about to become involved in a war with Russia. The Tsar's armies had invaded the Turkish Provinces on the Danube the previous year. The Ottoman Empire had declared war on Russia in September 1853 and the Russian navy had then destroyed a Turkish fleet in the Black Sea. Turkey had been able to form an alliance with Britain and France, who similarly declared war on Russia on 28 March 1854. King Victor Emmanuel II of Sardinia was expected to do the same. Marshal de Saint-Arnaud, named as the French Commander-in-Chief, decided against including the Foreign Legion in his Expeditionary Corps, it being felt unwise to strip Algeria of two of the most effective regiments, then he changed his mind. On 10 May a telegram brought instructions for the 1st and 2nd Etrangers to prepare to leave for Turkey.

It may have seemed odd to thinking Legionnaires that France's ally was England – with whom the French had fought on and off for at least two centuries – while the lesser ally was Turkey, regarded as France's enemy in North Africa. They had not really understood why de Saint-Arnaud, as an old Foreign Legion officer, had initially not wanted the regiments as part of his military command, and they did not understand why he had reversed his decision. No matter. It was a war, and to the 1st Etranger it was certainly far better than the interminable road-building and 'colonization work' in Algeria.

Scattered at different posts in the Province of Oran, it took two full weeks to bring all the Companies together. Orders from Paris called for two battalions to be made ready for war, while the third was to be considered a Depot Battalion and would be based at the Turkish port of Gallipoli. Major Nayral led the 3rd Battalion out of Sidi-bel-Abbes on 25 May, with a send-off from General Pelissier ringing in their ears. 'At Sidi-bel-Abbes, you have turned an encampment into a flourishing city, created from desolation a fertile region, an image of France,' he had declared in a Divisional Order. 'To you are due these fine roads, these canals, these bridges, which have changed the entire aspect of the countryside.' He could not resist a comparison with the much earlier works of 'the Legions of Rome'.[8] The 1st Battalion followed five days later and on 11 June, joined by Colonel Bazaine and the Headquarters Staff, they embarked on the *Napoleon* and set sail for Gallipoli. Sergeant Maudet was with the 2nd Battalion which embarked on the *Jean Bart* at Oran four days later and sailed along the coast to Philippeville.

The orders for the 2nd Etranger had called for two battalions to be equipped for Turkey, while the third would be sent to Corsica to form the Regimental Depot.

As always, news of war brought a rush of new recruits.

On 27 May eighteen-year-old Jean Vilain became one of them when he signed a seven-year engagement with the 2nd Etranger,[9] but he had not completed his training by the time the regiment embarked for Gallipoli less than a month later. Consequently, he was transferred to the 1st Etranger,[10] which had many other young soldiers undergoing instruction, and would be sending a draft of reinforcements to join the regiment in due course.

Born on 3 August 1836 to Jean Vilain, an officer in the 4th Lancers, and his wife, Catherine, née Talonnier, the young man had grown up in the town of Poitiers. His father had sent him to a military school to prepare him for entry into Saint-Cyr, but an accident had caused him to miss his examinations and, faced with another year of study, he simply ran away to follow his father's profession of arms as a simple soldier. His engagement papers for the Foreign Legion noted that his full name was Jean Nicolas Napoleon Vilain and that he stood 1.56 metres (5 feet 3 inches) tall, had blue eyes, fair hair and eyebrows and was clean-shaven.[11] He, too, would achieve fame in Mexico.

When the *Jean Bart* reached Philippeville carrying the 2nd Battalion of the 1st Etranger, three officers and two hundred and thirty-eight men of the 2nd Etranger were promptly embarked and the troopship sailed for Gallipoli on 22 June. Lieutenant Danjou and the remainder of the 2nd Etranger, in two battalions eighteen hundred strong, including Colonel de Caprez and his Headquarters Staff, sailed on the *Labrador* and the *Albatros* five days later.

From the deck of the *Napoleon* the town of Gallipoli looked pretty enough to the Legionnaires of the 1st Etranger when they arrived on 21 June, but ashore was another matter. Narrow, dirty streets, with raw sewage running down the middle, turned the toughest stomachs and the 1st Battalion was glad to be marched to a camp called Boulahir, outside the town, while the 3rd Battalion remained behind to build fortifications. The 2nd Battalion arrived on the *Jean Bart* on 29 June and also went into camp at Boulahir. The two battalions of the 2nd Etranger arrived on 7 and 8 July and joined them there, finding their comrades who had travelled with the 1st Etranger waiting for them.

The men of the two regiments of the Foreign Legion were designated as the 2nd Brigade of the 5th Division of the Army of the Orient and learned that they would be commanded by the colourful General Jean-Luc Carbuccia, who had led the 2nd Etranger on so many *razzias*, and at Zaatcha five years earlier. Then cholera struck, carrying him off, along with other Foreign Legion officers and men. The 1st

Etranger lost four officers and one hundred and seventy-five other ranks to the outbreak and looked forward to getting away from Boulahir. In the event, most would be there for a while, as the orders which came from Marshal de Saint-Arnaud were to provide a *Bataillon de Marche* made up of the Grenadiers and Voltigeurs – the Elite Companies – of both regiments. The *Compagnies du Centre* would remain where they were. Commanded by Major Nayral, the four Companies of Grenadiers and four of Voltigeurs, each with its own Captain, Lieutenant and Sous-Lieutenant, in all some nine hundred and fifty strong, along with a handful of Staff Officers, were embarked on the *Mouette* and the *Albatros* and taken across the Black Sea to Varna. Sent into camp behind the Regiments of the Line which made up the 2nd Brigade of the 1st Division, they found themselves under the orders of General Vinoy, who had fought in Algeria as an officer in the Foreign Legion a decade earlier, and the next day were presented to General Canrobert, who recognized a number of the officers who had served under him during his brief period with 2nd Etranger.

On 1 September, leaving one hundred and fifty of their number behind, the *Bataillon de Marche* embarked on the *Montezuma* and *Jupiter* and sailed across the Black Sea with an Anglo-French fleet to begin the invasion of the Crimean Peninsula and the planned reduction and capture of the great Russian naval dockyard at Sebastopol.

The landing at Calamita Bay on 14 September was uncontested and the Allied Army began to march south. Canrobert took personal command of the Foreign Legion's *Bataillon de Marche* three days later. The morning of 20 September found the Allies on the north side of the Alma River, looking across at an escarpment, at the top of which the Russians had emplaced guns and an army said to be 40,000 strong. Sergeant Clement Maudet and Lieutenant Jean Danjou were among those waiting for orders when General Canrobert, passing the *Bataillon de Marche* where it was drawn up, called out: 'At the right moment, set an example for the others, my brave Legionnaires.'

When the word came to advance the French and British troops crossed the river and began the climb under heavy fire. The Zouaves surged forward and the disciplined Legionnaires scrambled up the Heights of Alma in the face of the guns, went in with the bayonet, killed the gunners or sent them running, then held their ground until the rest of the Army reached the top. De Saint-Arnaud, who had a serious heart condition and was now stricken with cholera, saw them do it and rejoiced. The losses of the *Bataillon de Marche* were five officers wounded and fifty-five men killed or wounded.

The Russians withdrew into Sebastopol, near the tip of the peninsula, which the advancing Allies passed by in order to take possession of the land overlooking the city, the British selecting the narrow inlet of Balaclava as their main port and base. The French chose the rather more open bay at Kamiesh. After turning over his command to Canrobert on 26 September the ailing de Saint-Arnaud was taken to Balaclava and carried aboard a French steamer. He died before reaching Gallipoli and on the Crimean plateau the French and British began digging in for the siege of Sebastopol. Between them and their goal were major Russian defensive works, including the formidable Malakoff Redoubt and numerous other strongpoints, like the Great and Little Redans, against which the British and French armies would hurl themselves several times in the coming months.

On 10 October the *Compagnies du Centre* of the Foreign Legion, who had remained near Gallipoli, received orders to embark. The men of the 2nd Etranger arrived at Kamiesh Bay on British ships mid-month. The 1st Etranger's troops arrived from Gallipoli on a French vessel on 17 October. The *Bataillon de Marche* was disbanded by Canrobert, who spoke favourably of 'the vigorous attitude shown by the *Corps d'elite* since its formation'. General Vinoy, the old Foreign Legion officer, bid farewell to the Legionnaires, now no longer under his command, saying that he was losing 'the brightest jewel in my crown'. Bazaine, promoted to General of Brigade, assumed command of the newly-designated *Brigade Etrangere* and Colonel Raphael Vienot replaced him in command of the 1st Etranger.

The Foreign Legion settled down to digging trenches for what would be a long siege. Dysentery and cholera appeared again. From their position overlooking Sebastopol they were not able to witness the ill-fated Charge of the Light Brigade down the North Valley to attack the Russian guns near Balaclava on 25 October, but General Bosquet saw, declared it to be 'magnificent' but a waste, and sent two Squadrons of the 4th *Chasseurs d'Afrique* in a dashing attack to clear the flanking Russian guns and make the British withdrawal somewhat less hazardous.

On 5 November, in drizzle and heavy fog, the grey-coated Russians came boiling out of the ravines and gullies at Inkermann in an attempt to break the siege. Cavalry and artillery were rendered useless by the visibility and terrain and most of the battle was fought bayonet-to-bayonet. The *Brigade Etrangere* was fighting alongside men of the *Infanterie de Marine*, and Captain Marty, with half of the 1st Battalion of the 1st Etranger, repeatedly charged Russian-held positions, as did the other half of the battalion some distance away. The Foreign Legion had three officers and forty-three men killed and nine officers and eighty-five men wounded, but the overall casualty toll at the end of the day ran to twenty thousand Russians, thirteen thousand French and two thousand five hundred British.

Fortunately, the *Brigade Etrangere* soon received reinforcements from Algeria. The five hundred and seven men who arrived for the 2nd Etranger on 12 November received a dose of Crimean weather two days later when a cyclone of winds and driving rain struck suddenly, blowing away tents and flooding trenches. The troops were hardly dry four days later when Canrobert visited their camp to discuss redeployments. He hardly expected a smart turnout under the circumstances, but was furious to find one Legionnaire who had sold his boots for drink and had blackened his feet in the hope that his equipment shortage would not be noticed. Canrobert knew how Legionnaires were, but went away grumbling about disgraced noblemen in the ranks, and wondering why one of the Fusiliers was a former Prefect of the Rome Police. Young Fusilier Jean Vilain was with the draft of five hundred men who arrived for the 1st Etranger a week later.[12]

The *Brigade Etrangere*, designated as part of the 2nd Brigade of the 6th Division, continued its trench-digging and sapping towards the Russian lines. Daylight excavations attracted snipers, causing losses among both officers and men, so much of the work had to be done under cover of darkness. Canrobert recognized both their fighting abilities and dedicated muscle power and ended the year by conferring the Cross of Officer of the Legion of Honour on Captain Marty of the 1st Etranger and Captain of Voltigeurs Bertrand of the 2nd Etranger, decorating a number of other officers and men with the Cross of Chevalier of the Legion of Honour and awarding seven *Medailles Militaire* to each regiment.

While the greater part of the *Brigade Etrangere* was settling into the trenches before Sebastopol, Napoleon III, who had always been impressed by the fighting prowess of the Swiss, had decided to create a second Legion Etrangere, made up of two regiments, each of two battalions, plus a special ten-company battalion of sharpshooters. A decree of 17 January 1855 established the new entity,[13] and automatically transferred all officers and men of the existing 1st and 2nd Etrangers into a new I Legion Etrangere. The new II Legion Etrangere would be commanded by the Emperor's old friend Baron Ochsenbein, who was given general officer rank in March, and would consist entirely of Swiss volunteers, kitted out in a new green uniform. The plan was that it would be sent to Algeria to fill the void left by the departure of the 1st and 2nd Etrangers for the Crimea. Meyer and de Chabriere, respectively the Lieutenant-Colonels of the existing 1st and 2nd foreign regiments, were pulled out of the Crimea, given a step in rank and sent back to France to take command of the two new regiments. A recruiting depot was established at Besancon, near the Swiss border.

Despite the dreadful Crimean Winter there was no let-up of hostilities, and on the night of 19/20 January 1855 the Russians attacked the trenches of the 2nd Battalion of the 2nd Etranger. Notwithstanding the desperate defence of the Grenadiers, Voltigeurs and the 1st and 5th Companies, by the time it was over an officer, a sergeant and five Fusiliers had been captured, a sergeant and three Fusiliers were dead and Lieutenant Saussier and seventeen men were wounded. An Order of the Army three days later commended the behaviour of Captain Rousseau, among others, while Saussier became a Chevalier of the Legion of Honour and five other ranks – including Fusilier Jean Germeys, a former blacksmith from Belgium – received the *Medaille Militaire*.

On 15 March the Russians again attacked the positions held by the 2nd Etranger's 2nd Battalion, but were beaten off with losses. Captain Bertrand of the Voltigeurs was cited for gallantry and a number of officers and men were made Chevaliers of the Legion of Honour. The month of April was little better for the 2nd Etranger, a serious clash with the Russians on 13 April producing the inevitable losses. Captain Robert of the Grenadiers and Sous-Lieutenant Bernard were cited in Orders, along with some men, and there was a further distribution of decorations and medals.

On 1 May the *Brigade Etrangere* was sent to take some strongly defended Russian trenches, initially deploying four companies of Voltigeurs and Grenadiers from the 1st Etranger and two similar ones from the 2nd Etranger.

The attacking force was divided into three echelons, commanded by Captain Franzini, Major Nayral and Lieutenant-Colonel Martenot de Cordoue, and the Russian trenches were taken at bayonet point. Nayral and Captains Auguste Aubry and Louis de Massol were wounded and Captain Koch of the Voltigeurs was bayoneted several times. *Clarion* Wanderput struck down a Russian officer who was about to kill Lieutenant Paul de Choulot of the Voltigeurs, but soon afterwards de Choulot, along with Lieutenant Jean Abrial and four other officers of the same rank, was injured when a Russian cannon was fired point blank, just as they reached a battery. De Choulot,[14] who had been serving since 1842, and de Massol[15] were both minor members of the French aristocracy, and would survive to later write of their days in the Foreign Legion.

Colonel Vienot, arriving on the run at the head of the 1st Etranger, sword in hand, was shot dead almost at once, becoming the second Colonel of the Foreign Legion to die at the head of his men. Although wounded in several places, Corporal Olivera, more than fifty years old and a former Captain of Cavalry in the Spanish Army, carried from the field the body of Captain Motchevski, a Pole. Captains Delebecque and Franzini immediately organized the trenches to receive the expected counter-attacks, and counting heads found that their victory so far had cost the 1st Etranger's Elite Companies three Sous-Officiers and thirty-four men dead, and twelve Sous-Officiers and forty-three men wounded or missing. The elite detachment from the 2nd Etranger, only half the size, had fared better, with seven men killed, and Sous-Lieutenant Bernard and eighteen men wounded. In the aftermath of the battle, the officers who had led the three-pronged attack – Martenot de Cordoue, Nayral and Franzini – were commended for gallantry, along with Captain Delebecque of the 1st Etranger and Captain Robert and Sous-Lieutenant Bernard of the 2nd Etranger.

The Russians struck back the following day, three waves of infantry attacking the trenches held by the 1st Etranger, and Sergeant Maudet was swiftly felled by a bullet in the chest.[16] The two Companies of the 2nd Etranger, commanded by Captain Robert, were also attacked by Russian infantry and his conduct again earned him a citation. Sous-Lieutenant Bernard was wounded, while eleven more men were killed and twenty-nine wounded before the arrival of three regular Army companies drove the Russians back.

The Regiments Etranger had left General Jean-Jacques Pelissier in Algeria as Governor-General. Now he was in the Crimea and at Canrobert's request took command of the French Expeditionary Corps. Canrobert was viewed by many as being overly cautious. By contrast, Pelissier was prone to attack, sometimes at almost any cost.

In late May the two Regiments Etranger were involved in the taking and holding of a critical Russian defensive position known as the *Ouvrages Blancs* – the White Works – which became an equally critical French offensive position. In one sortie against the Russians the two Battalions of the 2nd Etranger had three Captains, three Lieutenants and thirty-two men killed and eight officers and one hundred and seventy-four men wounded. The 1st Etranger's losses were two Lieutenants, four Sous-Officiers and twenty men killed. The daring Captain Franzini was mortally wounded and Delebecque of the Voltigeurs and three other Captains were wounded, along with ten Sous-Officiers and ten men.

Although the 1st and 2nd Etrangers had each received further reinforcements of two hundred men on 11 May, much reorganization was required because of the recent losses. A temporary commander took over the 1st Etranger, replacing the dead Vienot, but four months later Martenot de Cordoue would be promoted to

Colonel. In a sort of military musical chairs, Colonel de Caprez of the 2nd Etranger exchanged positions with Colonel de Chabriere, who had been sent to France four months earlier to take command of the Emperor's new II Legion Etrangere. Casualties inevitably created vacancies at all levels of command. Among the 1st Etranger, convalescing from his wound, and greatly to his distaste, Sergeant Maudet found himself once more saddled with the position of Quartermaster Sergeant, a situation which changed on 1 June, when he was promoted to Sergeant-Major.[17] Fusilier Vilain was promoted to Corporal on 8 June[18] and Lieutenant Danjou of the 2nd Etranger was promoted to Captain the following day.[19]

The *Brigade Etrangere* had not taken part in the French assault on the Russian defensive position known as the Mamelon on 7 June, which was stormed by the Zouaves and held, despite fierce resistance, largely because General Bosquet had sufficient men in reserve to ensure success. The significance of 18 June as the fortieth anniversary of the Battle of Waterloo was not lost on either of the Allies, but the *Brigade Etrangere* was not involved in the abortive attacks of the day, when the French tried and failed to take the Malakoff and the British were thrown back at the Great Redan.[20]

The carnage of the assaults on the Mamelon, which had fallen to the French, and the Malakoff, which had remained in Russian hands, had been enormous. The Malakoff was the key to the capture of Sebastopol and the Russians defended it tenaciously, while for almost three months the French laid elaborate plans for its storming and capture. Concurrently, the British were to assault and take the Great Redan and 8 September was set for the operation. General Bosquet would again be in command of the French assault and General MacMahon's 1st Division was assigned the task of the actual attack, which would be spearheaded by the 1st and 2nd Zouaves.

Evariste Berg, a young man from the French island of Reunion in the Indian Ocean, was serving with the 1st Zouaves, into which he had transferred from the *Artillerie de Marine* at the end of June, after being wounded in action in one of the Baltic Sea actions in the early days of the Crimean War.[21]

The planning called for 'ladder parties' of volunteers from other regiments to accompany the Zouaves, using the ladders first as 'bridges' to cross Russian trenches, and then to help the attackers scale the walls of the bastion.

Among the first to volunteer for this hazardous task was a Quartermaster Sergeant with the 4th Battalion of the *Chasseurs a Pied* named Philippe Maine. He was an ex-Zouave himself, with considerable fighting experience in Algeria, and, after a return to civilian life, had joined the *Chasseurs a Pied* at the beginning of the war and been in the Crimea since January. He had volunteered for the 'ladder party' for the French attack on the Mamelon on 7 June, and was doing so again for the assault on the Malakoff.[22]

The *Brigade Etrangere* learned that it would again be held in reserve, but they also answered the call for 'ladder party' volunteers. As they were both in the 1st Etranger, it is obvious that Corporal Vilain was deferentially acquainted with veteran Sergeant-Major Maudet, who undoubtedly deigned to at least recognize the existence of the younger man. Further than that their relationship cannot have gone at the time, as the yawning gulf of rank separated them. Both men stepped forward when the call came for a one hundred-strong volunteer 'ladder party,' to be led by Sergeant-Major Valliez.

So, on 8 September, these four men, two already Legionnaires, two in other regiments, and all destined for Commissions and to fight together in Mexico, were in various trenches, some a scant twenty metres (twenty-five yards) in front of the Malakoff, awaiting the signal to attack.

When it came they leapt forward, sprinting for the walls, throwing their ladders across trenches for the charging Zouaves and then following them to the walls of the Redoubt. The Russians, taken by surprise, rallied and poured a withering fire into the attackers. *Chasseur a Pied* Maine was slightly wounded in the face, but followed the Zouaves, who were so quickly among the enemy that the Tricolour fluttered from atop the Malakoff ten minutes after the assault began. Repeated Russian attempts to retake it were repulsed under the personal direction of MacMahon.

French assaults on two other positions were less successful. Stopped in their tracks before the Little Redan, the French lost more than a thousand men in a five-hour struggle. The British attack on the Great Redan, which started with a dash by 'ladder parties' and assault troops across a hundred and eighty metres (almost two hundred yards) of open ground, was another costly failure, but the following morning it was discovered that the Russians were setting fire to buildings, blowing up the dockyard and abandoning Sebastopol.

Bazaine, appointed Commandant Superior, led the Foreign Legion into the almost deserted and still smouldering city. Apart from rooting out a few stray Russian soldiers who had been left behind, the Legionnaires spent much of their time eating, drinking and collecting souvenirs. In further reorganization at the command level, Captain Danjou was made Adjutant-Major of the 2nd Etranger on 18 September, an important Headquarters Staff post – roughly equivalent to Adjutant in the British Army – which would make him familiar with the officers and men who would play roles in his future career.[23]

This easy time was short-lived, however, as the *Brigade Etrangere* was soon sent deep into the valleys and hills of the Crimean Peninsula in mopping-up operations. Occasional clashes with roving bands of Cossaks, usually at long range, took a toll of both officers and men. On 4 October, with a new operation imminent, Corporal Jean Vilain was promoted to Sergeant[24] and three days later left with the 1st Etranger as part of an Anglo-French expedition commanded by Bazaine himself to take the forts at Kinburn, east of Odessa. It was a comparatively simple, and wholly successful, expedition, but among the relatively few casualties was Fusilier Gottfried Wensel, who was badly injured by an exploding shell and had to be sent back to France to convalesce. He rejoined the 2nd Etranger in the Crimea several months later.

Even though the war was won, peace had not been declared, and the armies cooled their heels while the diplomats talked. Just after the year turned, on 3 January 1856, Sergeant Vilain was promoted to Quartermaster Sergeant.[25] His career had been quite spectacular, from Fusilier to Quartermaster Sergeant in eighteen months. In February a formal armistice was arranged. It was heralded by a salvo of one hundred and one cannons. The peace treaty was signed at the end of

March.

Captain Danjou went on leave on 16 April,[26] so missed the huge parade staged the following day. For the *Brigade Etrangere* activities began with the dedication of their regimental cemetery at Strelitzka, followed by the parade, at which Pelissier, now a Marshal of France, and the British Commander-in-Chief, General Sir William Codrington, hosted their Russian recent enemies. The officers and men of the *Brigade Etrangere* were told that in recognition of their services French nationality would be conferred on all those who might wish to transfer into a Regiment of the Line. There were relatively few takers, despite the seemingly ominous concurrent announcement that the two Regiments Etranger were soon to be merged into a single regiment, but would maintain their present formations until details were received.

Decorations and medals were awarded at a ceremony on 26 May, and Danjou, who had returned from leave, became a Chevalier of the Legion of Honour.[27] Sergeant-Major Maudet received the *Medaille Militaire*.[28] Bazaine was advanced a grade in the Legion of Honour and the British made him a Knight Commander of the Order of the Bath. All three men, along with a number of others, both officers and other ranks, also received what the French called 'The English Crimean Medal.'

The British had struck it for themselves and their Allies in 1854 and soon added special 'clasps,' which could be attached to the yellow-edged light blue ribbon, commemorating the recipient's participation in particular battles. Overall, it was rather handsome, with the head of Queen Victoria, the words VICTORIA REGINA and the date on the obverse. The reverse featured a Roman warrior holding a sword in his right hand and a circular shield in front of him with his left, while being crowned by a small winged figure of Victory. The word CRIMEA was written vertically on the left side. Much criticized for supposedly looking like the tags on decanters of spirits, the oak leaf-shaped 'clasps' were awarded for participation in the battles of the Alma, Balaklava and Inkermann and the Sebastopol siege and could be attached to the ribbon.

In all 275,000 were struck and each French regiment received an allotment of medals and 'clasps' to distribute appropriately to officers and men.[29] The only French troops who qualified for the Balaklava 'clasp' were the surviving members of the two Squadrons of the 4th *Chasseurs d'Afrique*, who had charged the flanking Russian guns as the remnants of the Light Brigade struggled back to their lines, but some officers and men of the *Brigade Etrangere* qualified for all or some of the other three.

Danjou was among the officer recipients of the Crimean Medal, with Alma, Inkermann and Sebastopol 'clasps', as were Maudet and a number of the other men, including Fusiliers Pinzinger, Wensel, Fritz and Van Opstal.

Among the first to leave the Crimea, departing on 16 June, Danjou was, in fact, also leaving the Foreign Legion, one of fourteen officers being transferred to Regiments of the Line, as the strength of the 1st and 2nd Etrangers was reduced now that hostilities were ended. He joined the 26th Infantry of the Line nine days later.[30] Most of the officers and men of the *Brigade Etrangere* embarked on the *Ulm* and the *Jemmapes* on 17 June and arrived at Algiers on 2 July, after a brief stop in

Malta. They sailed on to Mers-el-Kebir and were back in Sidi-bel-Abbes on 10 July. The handful of members of the two regiments who had remained in the Crimea – Sergeant-Major Maudet among them[31] – embarked on 6 July and reached Sidi-bel-Abbes by month-end. The pointless and costly Crimean War had cost the two Regiments Etranger twelve officers killed and sixty-six wounded and a total of one thousand six hundred and twenty-five other ranks killed and wounded. The fallen Colonel Vienot had joined the Foreign Legion as a Lieutenant in 1831 and his regiment remembered him by giving his name to their barracks in Sidi-bel-Abbes.

Already warned that there would be an amalgamation of the two regiments, the Legionnaires endured a period of anxiety while awaiting details of the merger. Officers who were well informed had some idea of what was planned, and explained it to their comrades. It had soon become clear that Napoleon III's ideas for an all-Swiss II Legion Etrangere had been overly ambitious, as relatively small numbers of volunteers had come forward to sign engagement papers. When the Emperor saw that his pet project was foundering he lost interest in it, as was usually the case when his schemes failed to meet his expectations. The overall lack of recruits may have had something to do with the fact that the British had also been enlisting Swiss, Germans and Italians at the same time. Nevertheless, the II Legion Etrangere had remained in existence, though inactive, and in April 1856 the disappointing recruiting results were reviewed. The 1st Regiment had been formed at Dijon in March 1855, but in thirteen months had been able to attract only twenty officers and four hundred and forty-eight men. The recruiting for the 2nd Regiment and the Battalion of Sharpshooters over the same period had been equally disappointing. The 2nd, formed at Besancon at the same time, and moved to Langres shortly afterwards, had a strength of only twenty-five officers and five hundred and nine men and the Battalion of Sharpshooters, created at Auxonne, had attracted only thirteen officers and two hundred and thirteen men. By an Imperial Decree dated 16 April the II Legion Etrangere was dissolved[32] and no impediment was put in the way of officers or men who wished to leave. Members of the two disbanded regiments and the sharpshooters who wished to remain in the service of France were moved to Sathonay, near Lyon.

On 8 August the details of the two new regiments, as laid out in the April Decree, were announced. A new 1st Regiment Etranger, keeping the green uniforms which had been created for them in their former persona, was being created from the Swiss volunteers at the camp at Sathonay. For the sake of continuity, Colonel Meyer, who had commanded the 1st Regiment of the II Legion Etrangere, would command the new 1st Regiment. Colonel de Chabriere would command the new 2nd Regiment Etranger being created from the veterans of the old 1st and 2nd Regiments who had fought in the Crimea.

There was much grumbling by many who felt that the numbering should have been reversed, and that those who had fought so long and hard in the Crimea should have constituted the new 1st Etranger, while those who had not, and who were seen as untried troops, should have been the new 2nd Etranger. It would create a rivalry which would last for several years.

4
Tempering the Steel

Only eight months after leaving the Foreign Legion, Captain Jean Danjou returned to Sidi-bel-Abbes,[1] arriving on 6 February 1857, having transferred back into the 2nd Etranger. He found many old friends who were happy to see him, and also many changes. The new 1st Etranger, with its green uniforms, and generally referred to as the *Regiment Suisse* because of its make-up, had its headquarters at Philippeville. Various companies were out building roads and doing 'colonization work', but the regiment's officers had cause to visit Sidi-bel-Abbes from time to time.

Among them was an elegant young man named Gabriel de Diesbach de Torny, an impoverished twenty-seven-year-old Swiss nobleman, from a family with a tradition of service in the French Army going back almost three hundred years, to the *Regiment Suisse de Diesbach*. Founded by one of his ancestors in 1689, it had gallantly defended Louis XVI against a Paris mob[2] in 1792, and his own father, Philippe de Diesbach-Torny, had commanded the *Compagnie Francaise Cente-Suisses* at the time of the Restoration of the Monarchy. Young Sous-Lieutenant Diesbach, born in the Swiss city of Friborg in 1830, blamed his step-father for the loss of the family fortune, and had once needed to be physically prevented from killing him. Believing his financial state made it impossible for him to marry, Diesbach, who was something of a dandy, had left home in December 1855 to join the II Legion Etrangere, which was then recruiting, and remained in the service of the French through the embryo regiment's transition to the new 1st Etranger, the *Regiment Suisse*. He maintained a personal campaign diary while with the Foreign Legion.[3]

Numbering only one thousand and twenty-one men when it embarked at Toulon on 6 July 1856 under the orders of Colonel Meyer, the new 1st Etranger was too small to be a viable regiment, though it had some men in its ranks who would make their marks in the Foreign Legion, including Diesbach and Sous-Lieutenant Jean Lebre from Lausanne and Fusiliers Henri-Guido Kauffmann, a talented artist, and Karl Schaffner. The new 2nd Etranger, due to the influx of men from their former sister regiment, was too large, so six hundred of the Crimean veterans, most of them from the former 1st Etranger, were transferred from the new 2nd Etranger to the *Regiment Suisse*, among them newly-promoted Sergeant-Major Jean Vilain,[4] who joined the 2nd Battalion. Just before Christmas it received its Regimental Standard, which was inscribed '*L'Empereur Napoleon III au 1e etranger*' and bore the motto '*Valeur et Discipline*'.

The new 2nd Etranger had been created on 9 August 1856 in Sidi-bel-Abbes and three Companies of the 1st Battalion were immediately sent out to dig irrigation ditches and drain swamps, while the other five Companies were assigned road work. The 2nd and 3rd Battalions, led by Lieutenant-Colonel Martinez, became part of the 2nd Brigade under General Deligny in the latest campaign in Grand Kabylia.

The regiment saw its first action on 25 September when a section of the Voltigeur Company was surrounded by the enemy and had to fight their way clear. Captain Saussier's Company was involved in several clashes the same day. During one of them he plunged into a group of Kabyles who had captured one of his men. Followed by several Legionnaires, Saussier reached the soldier, snatched him from his captors and succeeded in escaping with him. Just five days later Captain Aubry's Company had a Sergeant-Major killed and twelve Legionnaires wounded in another clash.

On 4 October, under the personal direction of General Deligny, the Voltigeur and Grenadier Companies of the two battalions, commanded by Captain Mariotti, and the Companies of the Centre commanded by Lieutenant-Colonel Martinez, fought a major engagement, but the campaign was winding down and ended six days later. Most of the troops returned to Sidi-bel-Abbes, where it was learned that many of the men of the 1st Battalion had come down with fever while working in a swampy area. There were a number of deaths. Almost the entire regiment was back in Sidi-bel-Abbes by year-end.

Captain Danjou learned all this when he re-joined the 2nd Etranger in early 1857, at the beginning of what would turn out to be a very busy year. Marshal Randon had first directed operations against the Kabyles as far back as 1842. Now, as Military Governor of Algeria, he was determined to put an end to the annual campaigns, which had always been so costly in terms of money and lives. He put another army into Grand Kabylia in April. The 1st and 2nd Battalions of the 2nd Etranger were below strength, but Colonel de Chabriere managed to muster fifteen hundred and seventy-six men for the campaign.

Along with the 2nd Regiment of Zouaves and the 54th Regiment of the Line they became part of General Bourbaki's 1st Brigade, itself part of the 2nd Division led by General MacMahon. The Foreign Legion battalions were heavily engaged on 23 May and sustained losses. Captain and Adjutant-Major Delebecque and Fusilier Brandt, who had brought several wounded comrades in under heavy fire, were mentioned in Orders. Guns were briefly exchanged for pickaxes to build a road to the site of the proposed Fort Napoleon, Randon personally laying the foundation stone on 14 June. Then it was back to campaigning.

When the French arrived at the foot of a Kabyle-held mountain fastness called Ischeriden ten days later it was clear that they faced a difficult situation. The village was perched at the top of a steep ridge, protected on one side by a deep ravine. MacMahon ordered Bourbaki's brigade to attack and the Zouaves and the 54th advanced. Suddenly, the Kabyles popped up from well-prepared and dug-in positions at the top of the ridge and poured a steady fire into the advancing troops. The 1st Battalion of the 2nd Etranger was rushed to their aid, but MacMahon believed he saw an opportunity to take the ridge and ordered Major Mangin to take his 2nd Battalion forward.

It was then, to the left of Bourbaki's brigade, that I saw a Legion battalion begin to move up, its officers on horseback at the head of their Companies, its veterans, superbly disciplined, indifferent to the whistling bullets [*wrote Sous-Lieutenant Perret of the 3rd Zouaves, who watched the Foreign Legion move forward*]. A withering fire was directed on them. They advanced unflinching, without replying, and in a few minutes had reached the [Kabyle] trenches, swarmed into them and exterminated the defenders with the bayonet. (⁵)

As the Legion had advanced on the enemy trenches Captain Mariotti had slipped and fallen and the Kabyles had rushed in to finish him. Sergeant Mori, followed by Corporal Van-Leyden and Grenadiers Pietrovitz, and Donven and Voltigeurs Coulman and Sommer, had charged through them with their bayonets, grabbed their officer and dragged him away. Ischeriden had been taken, but Kabyle resistance continued all around. On three occasions the 1st Battalion had to charge with the bayonet to dislodge snipers, and the 4th Company rushed to the assistance of a detachment of Zouaves about to be overrun in a forward defensive post. Sous-Lieutenant Adolphe Gans and another officer, as well as thirteen Legionnaires, were wounded before the Kabyles were beaten off.[6]

Marshal Randon, in congratulating Mariotti, referred to his actions in the previous October's Kabylia campaign, and suggested that he sometimes exposed himself recklessly: 'You should be careful with your life,' Randon told him. 'In 1856, you were cited for heroism. You will get yourself killed some day.' Mariotti smiled and said: 'Oh, *Monsieur le Marechal*, there was not much danger, my Legionnaires were behind me'.[7]

The clashes at and around Ischeriden cost the 2nd Etranger one officer and eight men killed and three officers and eighty-seven men wounded. The Grenadiers had taken the brunt of the casualties, with two killed and twenty wounded, while the Voltigeurs had twenty-five wounded. Some time later Captain Mariotti transferred into the 90th Regiment of the Line.

In the ranks of those who had fought that day was a young German named Gerhardt Rohlfs, who would fall in love with the desert and, after leaving the Foreign Legion, achieve fame as a Saharan explorer. Sergeant Mori, who had helped save Mariotti, would become a well-known figure in the 2nd Etranger. He carried in his pack documents which proved that he was actually Prince Mori-Ubaldini, an ordained priest, from one of the richest noble families in Florence. He was awarded the *Medaille Militaire* and he would earn a commission in Mexico. Corporal Van-Leyden, who was also awarded the *Medaille Militaire*, was later decorated with the Cross of a Chevalier of the Legion of Honour and retired after twenty-five years of service in the Foreign Legion, having taken part in forty-four campaigns.

A month later the regiment returned to an enthusiastic welcome in Sidi-bel-Abbes, but to be greeted with the unhappy news that the 3rd Battalion had been decimated by fever and reduced from six hundred men to only one hundred and twenty effectives. The rest were either dead or in hospital.

The deaths of officers in the Grand Kabylia campaign opened vacancies in the regiment and one of the newcomers was Sous-Lieutenant Charles Zede, an outspoken, somewhat brash twenty-year-old, just out of Saint-Cyr. He was assigned to the 3rd Battalion and would spend ten years in the Foreign Legion, fighting with them in Italy and Mexico, then transfer into the regular French Army, rise to the rank of General and leave a long and detailed account of his military life.

Among the more interesting men who engaged during 1857 was Jean-Baptiste Verjus, a Parisian who had already served eleven years in the French Navy, but young Zede was shocked at what he found. 'The Legion was then permeated with the wreckage of [Europe's] vanquished parties,' he wrote, as though that was anything new, or that it necessarily detracted from such men's efficiency as soldiers. He found Spanish Carlists, but failed to mention that Lieutenant-Colonel Martinez was one. He also found Parisian revolutionaries of 1848, of whom Sergeant-Major Clement Maudet was an example, and other somewhat 'exotic' Legionnaires, including, he reported, 'a Chinese who looked strange with his pigtail hanging from beneath his kepi'.[8]

On 15 August a *Bataillon de Marche*, made up of the Grenadier and Voltigeur Companies of all three battalions of the 2nd Etranger, travelled to Oran to receive a new Regimental Standard. There was disagreement as to whether the Voltigeurs or the Grenadiers should be the first to provide the Colour Guard and Colonel de Chabriere had to step in with a ruling that one Grenadier and one Voltigeur would share the distinction. On the face of the Standard was written: '*L'Empereur Napoleon III au 2e Regiment Etranger*'.

The Battle Honours were shown as: CONSTANTINE (1837), MOSTAGANEM (1839), MOUZAIA (1840), COLEAH (1841), DJGELLY (1842), ZAATCHA (1849), ALMA (1854) and SEBASTOPOL (1855). The Directorate of Artillery was responsible for regimental flags and standards and there was much grumbling, because there were errors in two of the Battle Honours, and two others had been left out. On 10 May 1852 new Regimental Standards had been presented to the 1st and 2nd Etrangers. The Battle Honours shown for the 1st Etranger were CONSTANTINE (1837), MOSTAGANEM (1839), MOUZAI (1840), COLEAH (1841) and TEDJENNA (1845), and it was immediately noted that the campaign involving MOSTAGANEM had taken place in 1833, when the Foreign Legion had been only two years old, and so should have appeared on the flag above CONSTANTINE , which occurred almost four years later. The Battle Honours on the Regimental Standard of the 2nd Etranger were shown as CONSTANTINE (1837), COLEAH (1841), DJGELLY (1842), ZAATCHA (1849) and FEDJ-MENAZEL (1851) and there were complaints that the correct spelling for the 1842 Honour should have been DJIGELLY, not DJGELLY.

Now, five years later, the same errors concerning MOSTAGANEM and DJIGELLY had been repeated by the Directorate of the Artillery[9] and complaints were again lodged, but nothing could be done about it. So the new Regimental Standard went with the regiment to fight the Kabyles, and would subsequently go with them to Italy and eventually to Mexico.

The year 1857 was less active for the 1st Etranger, though, stiffened by the influx of Crimean veterans, regimental instruction had gone well and in May it had provided a *Bataillon de Marche* of two Companies of Grenadiers, two Companies of Voltigeurs and two Companies of the Centre, to take part in the annual campaign against the Kabyles. It had joined a large force, which included Zouaves and Regiments of the Line, and was under Randon's personal direction. While there were no major engagements, the presence of such a large number of troops had the desired effect of suppressing any serious acts of rebellion. A section of the 1st Etranger then began construction work on Fort Napoleon, while others were set to road building. In October the 2nd Battalion took part in a small punitive operation and at the end of the year was based at new headquarters at Setif.

The 2nd Etranger had ended the year with construction work, and when Captain Danjou was once again named Adjutant-Major[10] on 25 February 1858 he suspected that, unless there were to be a serious uprising, almost the entire coming year would be spent in much the same manner, which turned out to be the case. The 1st Battalion worked on road building between Sidi-bel-Abbes and Oran, the 2nd in construction and engineering work in and around Sidi-bel-Abbes and the 3rd on the road between Oran and Tlemcen.

It was the 1st Etranger which had the major share of the fighting that year. Sergeant-Major Vilain was in the field with the 2nd Battalion in early April when word was received that the Company of Voltigeurs, commanded by Captain Rembert, was under seige by a large body of Kabyles at an isolated post. He had sustained almost ten hours of continuous fighting when the approach of the relieving force sent the attackers scurrying back into the hills. The same month Colonel Meyer retired after a long career with the Foreign Legion. There were two short term commanding officers in the next few months, but in December command of the regiment passed into the hands of Colonel de Brayer.

Along with his admiration for the fighting prowess of the Swiss, Napoleon III had always harboured romantic notions about Italian efforts to unite the various small states and kingdoms into a single nation. The modest but gallant part played by the Piedmontese troops in the Crimean War had further endeared the Italians to the Emperor of the French, and he was always supportive of Victor Emmanuel II, King of Sardinia, Piedmont, Genoa and Savoy and Comte of Nice. The Provinces of Venice and Lombardy were part of Austria, spoils of the Napoleonic War, and Austria was also the dominating influence in the Duchies of Parma, Modena and Tuscany. A secret discussion between Piedmontese Prime Minister Count Camillo Benso di Cavour and Napoleon III brought forth an agreement that France would come to the aid of Victor Emmanuel in the event of war with Austria. The price would be Savoy and Nice. In April 1859 Cavour tricked the Austrians into declaring war and France mobilized.

Sous-Lieutenant Zede remembered later how excited Italian-born Sous-Lieutenant Valentin Barera had been as he rushed into the officers' mess to announce: 'A telegram arrived this evening. War has been declared! The Austrians have invaded Piedmont, we are going to turf them out. Italy will be free!' In the evening Colonel de Chabriere lifted his glass at the dinner table and gave a toast: '*Vive l'Empereur!* Down with the Austrians!' The excitement was tempered a few days later when it was learned that Napoleon III intended to personally lead his army in the field.

The *Regiment Suisse*, well under strength, was sent to Corsica on 8 April in the hope that patriotic Italians would rally to its Colours. Some did, including a young man named Casimir Lai, from Cagliari, in the neighbouring island of Sardinia, who engaged as a *Tambour*. Overall, however, the results were disappointing and after little more than a month the regiment embarked for Genoa to join the 2nd Etranger, which had been there for more than two weeks.[11] It had arrived with all its paraphernalia, including rear echelon people like washerwomen, sutlers and *cantinieres*, who operated mobile recreational facilities for troops pulled out of the front line, and *vivandieres*, young women who carried small barrels of brandy and went where the fighting was, bringing relief, and often nursing skills, to troops on the battlefield. Along with the 2nd Regiment of Zouaves, the Foreign Legion became General Armand Castagny's 2nd Brigade, part of the 2nd Division, commanded by former Foreign Legion officer General Espinasse, in General MacMahon's 2nd Corps. The 1st Etranger comprised two battalions, each with seven companies, while the 2nd Etranger had three battalions, each with six companies.

The flower of the French Army was taking to the field with Napoleon III and the Imperial Guard, many of them officers who had served in or commanded the Foreign Legion at one time or another. General Bazaine was a Divisional Commander with the 1st Corps, Marshal Canrobert commanded the 3rd Corps, General Vinoy was a Divisional Commander with the 4th Corps, and there were many others serving as Battalion Commanders and Company Officers.

The Austrians and Piedmontese had fought three battles already and, making their way almost straight north from Genoa, the French guessed that battle would be joined on the Plain of Lombardy. Just as the Austrians had no real idea where the French were to be found, the French did not know with any certainty where the Austrians intended to make a stand. By the first days of June the French were within striking distance of the City of Milan, but Magenta, a prosperous market town lay in the way.

Among the Old Sweats in the ranks of the Foreign Legion were a number who had fought in the Crimea, and many who had taken part in the 1857 campaign against the Kabyles. The 2nd Etranger's German-born *Tambour-major*, Christophe Schaefer, had been in the Foreign Legion since 1845, been wounded at Zaatcha, served throughout the Crimean War with both regiments of the *Brigade Etrangere*, and was wounded again at Sebastopol.[12] Other Crimean veterans humping their packs along the highways were Sergeant Jean Germeys, who had won a *Medaille Militaire* as a Corporal before Sebastopol, and Fusiliers Gottfried Wensel, Luitpold Van Opstal – both of whom had been wounded in the Crimea – and Friedrich Fritz. The former sailor Jean-Baptiste Verjus had just signed a new two-year engagement.

On 3 June, the 2nd Etranger began attempting to determine the whereabouts of the Austrians and, while the engineers were trying to repair a damaged bridge, Captain Jules Dubosq and a few men took a boat and stole stealthily along the Ticino River. When they drew fire from an outlying enemy position they had their answer and returned the way they had come.[13] Captains Delebecque and Danjou, respectively the Adjutants-Major of the 1st and 2nd Etrangers, were scouting on horseback. Cantering across a large hayfield, Danjou's mount stepped into a hole, pitched its rider and went down with a broken leg. It had to be shot, and the two officers, after stripping it of saddle and accoutrements, set off back to their lines. The two regiments of the Foreign Legion, fairly scattered because of the terrain, were still moving forward at dusk and made camp over a large area. They had not eaten since the previous evening and the small group of Legionnaires who discovered the dead horse considered themselves fortunate indeed.

'Captain Danjou's horse was cut up and eaten,' General Grisot reported later. 'The men who were not able to profit from this godsend had to be content with a little coffee which they shared with their officers.' By the following morning the commissariat had caught up with the regiments and the normal four a.m. departure was delayed while rations were given out. Orders to advance were received as the meal was ending and the regiment started moving out before wine was distributed. Grisot noted that it 'was drunk by the men doing fatigues, who then hurried to catch up with their Companies'.[14]

The small walls around fields, and the many mulberry trees, prevented anyone having a clear view of what was ahead and the Austrians and French more or less bumped into each other by accident. The first hint of action came for the 1st Etranger, moving forward beside the 2nd Zouaves, when they saw the detachment of the 7th *Chasseurs a Cheval* riding ahead of them begin to fall back. Then bullets came whistling through the trees, and those near them front saw white-uniformed Austrian infantry advancing.

> The Colonel of the 1st Regiment, with the Company of Voltigeurs commanded by Captain Rembert, moved off to the flank to intercept the Austrians and, deploying his men, opened fire at 100 metres [ninety yards] [*noted the* Journal de Marche *of the 2nd Etranger*]. The enemy was halted for a few moments but, vastly superior in numbers, began to move forward again. At this moment, Colonel de Chabriere, commanding the 2nd Regiment, a brilliant figure in his epauletted tunic, coolly sitting his charger, decided to intervene and gave the order: 'Off with your packs! Forward the Legion!' Levelling their bayonets, the two leading battalions broke into the double; but, because of the rough road, ranks were broken and contact was lost between the advancing companies. In spite of this, shouting '*En Avant!*' they swept down on the Austrians like a tidal wave. Surprised, the enemy began to give way, though still maintaining good order. In vain Colonel Chabriere tried to regroup his regiment. He was carried along by the human current to the accompaniment of shouts of 'Forward! Forward!' till, an easy target on his plunging charger, he was killed outright by a well-aimed bullet.[15]

The third Colonel of the Foreign Legion to fall at the head of his regiment, de Chabriere pitched to the ground and died in the arms of Sergeant-Major Victor Maire, and his men swept on towards the Austrians.

> The charge was spontaneous [*recalled Sous-Lieutenant Zede, who was with the 3rd Battalion*]. The hurrahs, the cries of *En avant!* were shouted, Zouaves and Legionnaires hurried forward. Neither cannon nor the volleys of the Austrians could stop them and this torrent rolled toward Magenta carrying all before it.[16]

The Austrians took cover behind the railway bank and several bayonet charges failed to dislodge them. Those of the 1st Etranger were directed by Colonel Brayer and Lieutenant-Colonel Mathieu Butet. In one of the attacks Sergeant-Major Vilain was hit in the left thigh and put out of action,[17] Sergeant Germeys was also wounded in the fighting. Newly-recruited *Tambour* Lai, with only weeks of service, was struggling to remember the correct drum calls. Corporal Schaffner was noticed by his officers as a soldier to watch, as was the veteran Pinzinger, now also a Corporal.

The 2nd Etranger had been able to do little better than their sister regiment, although Lieutenant-Colonel Martinez, leading the 3rd Battalion, briefly managed to get to the first houses, only to be driven back. The precious Regimental Standard was in danger of being captured by the Austrians at one point, but a quick-thinking *Clarion* sounded '*Au Drapeau!*' which brought Legionnaires and Zouaves dashing to the rescue. Then the French artillery took a hand and at half past seven in the evening General MacMahon watched the Foreign Legion begin edging forward as the Austrians withdrew.

'The Legion is in Magenta!' he exclaimed. 'The affair is in the bag!'

Despite his enthusiasm, there was house-to-house fighting as the Austrians contested every inch of ground. 'From this moment, all was disorder and confusion,' Zede said later. 'Everything dissolved into desperate struggles among small groups'.[18] Martinez, his face covered with blood from a superficial wound, sword in one hand and a captured rifle in the other, urged his men on. General Espinasse, forgetting perhaps that he was no longer an officer of the Foreign Legion, was at the front of things and was killed attacking a barricade. Years later, Zede wrote of the moment when the defenders quit: 'The Austrians hardly resisted but surrendered *en masse*, and we were furious to see the officers ride away with their flags. Only one was captured, and that was by the Zouaves'.[19] This was the flag of the 3rd Battalion of the Graf-Klarnstein Regiment, and it would be claimed – and denied – forty-five years later that Sous-Lieutenant Callet of the 2nd Etranger actually took possession of it, but that when it slipped from his grasp some Zouaves snatched it up and carried it away as a trophy.

Walking through the town, Zede was shocked at the number of casualties.

'One heard nothing but the moans of the wounded,' he remembered. There was little help. 'The railway station, where the hospital had been established, overflowed with unfortunates laid out on the bare earth,' he said. 'During the entire night, the doctors had only their medical bags which they carried with them, no linen for bandages, no chloroform . . . They could do little more than give water to the wounded'.[20]

Polish-born Legionnaire Miccilas Kamienski, his arm shattered by a bullet, lay out all night with three other wounded men. In the morning one of them advised him to go to the railway station. 'As for me,' he said, 'I'm going to die here without bothering'.[21] Among those already dead was Legionnaire Sobieski. A comrade confided the dead man's secret to an officer: Sobieski was the last descendant of King Sobieski of Poland, who had saved Vienna from the Turks in 1683.

The victory had cost the Foreign Legion dearly. The under-strength 1st Etranger had five officers killed, along with fourteen men, and a further thirty Sous-Officiers – including Vilain – and soldiers wounded. The 2nd Etranger's losses were greater, for not only had Colonel de Chabriere been killed, but two Captains, a Lieutenant and forty-one Sous-Officiers and men were dead, while six officers – including Captain Delebecque and Lieutenant Jaudon – had been wounded, along with one hundred and thirteen Sous-Officiers and men. Lieutenant-Colonel Martinez was named as provisional Colonel. A few hours later the 2nd Etranger's officers heard the melancholy news that their old comrade Captain Mariotti, who had transferred into the 90th Regiment of the Line, was also among the dead. Marshal Randon's words of caution to the hero of Ischeriden two years earlier had come true.

Napoleon III had arrived on the scene late in the battle and the following day made MacMahon a Marshal of France, adding the title Duke of Magenta. The Regimental Standard of the 2nd Zouaves, who had captured the Austrian flag, was decorated with the Cross of the Legion of Honour, and the Emperor of the French also pinned the decoration on the bosom of one of their *vivandieres*, Antoinette Tremoneau. The French spent most of the day getting their scattered regiments back into some semblance of order, and on 7 June started down the road towards Milan, only half-believing evidence which indicated that the Austrians had abandoned any thought of contesting the most important city in Lombardy. Yet it was true and the Foreign Legion went into camp on the outskirts of the city. The Piedmontese had missed the Battle of Magenta, but had now caught up with the French and Napoleon III and Victor Emmanuel II rode together through streets thronged with cheering people the following day. Their armies might have finished the campaign if the Austrians had been vigorously pursued, but took a few days break.

'Our camp was invaded by a population drunk with joy,' Zede wrote. 'Our soldiers were showered with food and wine, and taken into the houses where they were feted endlessly'.[22]

It was at Magenta that the Foreign Legion first became acquainted with Jean Ephrem Lanusse, a forty-one-year-old Army Chaplain known as Abbe Lanusse, a military-minded cleric who found his calling on the battlefield, and who would be a good friend to Legionnaires wherever he found them. A parish priest in France when the Crimean War broke out, he had obtained approval to join the Military Chaplain Service, but the permission was mysteriously withdrawn. As soon as war was declared against Austria, Lanusse had again applied to be an Army Chaplain, and this time he was successful. Attached to General Bourbaki's Division he became a familiar figure, hearing Confessions, ministering to his new flock and writing letters home for illiterate soldiers.[23]

The 1st Etranger was now down to only about four hundred men, so it was decided to leave them to garrison Milan, where, hopefully, military success would be an encouragement to recruiting. Decorations and medals were distributed a few days later and Sergeant-Major Vilain was heartened to find that his efforts at Magenta had earned him the Cross of a Chevalier of the Legion of Honour.[24] He also received the prestigious *Medaille d'Or*.

The 2nd Etranger and the Zouaves moved southeast, following the withdrawing Austrians. It was a somewhat leisurely pursuit. On 19 July medals and decorations for the action at Magenta were received and by day's end there were seven new Chevaliers of the Legion of Honour, including Captain Dubosq,[25] and two days later, when promotions were announced, Sergeant-Major Clement Maudet was pleased to find he had been advanced to the rank of Adjutant.[26] Lieutenant-Colonel Martinez was no doubt disappointed when he learned that Colonel Signorino had been named as Colonel of the Regiment, and that he would be reverting to second-in-command.

The following day the 2nd Etranger was at Castiglioni, still without any very clear idea of the whereabouts of the Austrians, and some effort was made to ensure that no ambush was being laid. There was much excitement by the unexpected arrival of balloonist Jules Godard and his equipment. This was the first time that a captive balloon – one allowed to rise from a ground base, attached to a winch so that it could be brought down – would be used for aerial observation in a military campaign. It was late afternoon, but there was still plenty of light and three officers, two from Division Headquarters and one from the 2nd Etranger, were assigned to go aloft with Godard. Extant records do not identify the Foreign Legion officer, but as he possessed superior topographical skills and held the position of Adjutant-Major, it is probable that it was Captain Danjou who was chosen for the task. The four men duly ascended, scanned the land, saw but three Austrian soldiers and were winched down to report that no enemy troops were in that vicinity.[27]

In point of fact, the French had convinced themselves that the Austrians would continue withdrawing all the way to their frontier. They did not know that Emperor Franz Joseph had now personally taken to the field and was ordering his troops to prepare to regain the ground they had lost. The Austrians continued to fall back slowly the next day, with the French in cautious pursuit. The undulating country they were traversing had often been used by the Austrians for military manoeuvres and the weather was unseasonably hot. The French had more than one hundred and seventy thousand men in the field, the Piedmontese fifty-five thousand and the Austrians almost one hundred and fifty thousand, but little serious reconnaissance work had been done by any of them.

MacMahon's 2nd Corps was on the move again in the pre-dawn of 24 June, and in an almost carbon copy of the early hours of the Battle of Magenta, the French and the Austrians blundered into each other, this time near Solferino. Screened again by the 7th *Chasseurs a Cheval*, the 2nd Etranger and the 2nd Zouaves were moving forward when they encountered an Austrian column. The *Chasseurs a Pied*, Zouaves and the Companies of Voltigeurs from the three battalions of the 2nd Etranger were in the van. The Foreign Legion's 3rd Battalion and the Zouaves engaged the enemy and MacMahon gave orders for them to maintain contact while the other Army Corps closed in on Solferino.

Suddenly, the three armies found each other and fighting broke out on a fifteen-kilometre (nine-mile) front, attack and counter-attack. The 2nd Etranger moved against the walled village of Cavriana, but found the Austrian defence fierce. Pinned down by the tough Croatian troops in the San Pietro Cemetery, they took, lost and re-took it, as the battle swayed back and forth. Elsewhere around Solferino, the French, Piedmontese and Austrians were exterminating each other. Bazaine, who had missed the Battle of Magenta, but had sustained a slight head wound in a clash with the Austrians north of the city several days later, was in the thick of things at Solferino. Near two o'clock in the afternoon a freak storm, with high winds, lightning and drenching rain bore down on the battlefield, turning the dusty ground into mud and effectively bringing an end to the fighting.

Soaked to the skin and exhausted, the 2nd Etranger made camp by the cemetery, huddling against its walls. The commissariat had not caught up, and the officers could buy no food for the men in the village. Considering the ferocity of the fighting the 2nd Etranger's losses were relatively small, including two officers wounded, one of whom, Lieutenant Antoine Astolfi, was not a casualty of the actual fighting, as he was sitting behind a wall with Sous-Lieutenant Zede, in the late afternoon, eating a chicken leg when a sniper's bullet hit him in the nose and cheek. There were forty men wounded and six dead, among them a quiet and efficient Legionnaire named Wildermann, in a former life one of seventeen Austrian Generals involved in a revolt against Russia in 1849, and condemned to death in absentia by the Tsar. The regiment's losses were tiny in comparison to the overall battle, which cost the French twelve thousand in dead and wounded, the Piedmontese five thousand and the Austrians thirteen thousand.[28]

Around six in the evening a watery sun came out and the full state of the horror could be seen. Dead and dying men were everywhere, but for a while almost the only figure moving over the sodden ground was Military Chaplain Lanusse, stopping now and again to administer the Last Rites, or to call, usually fruitlessly, for stretcher-bearers. 'Days of glory for France, [but] days of great sacrifice!' he would say sadly later.[29] Night fell, but the dawn of the new day revealed a horrendous picture of destruction and death, havoc created by the guns and the exploding shells, by bullets and sabres and bayonets. 'What a dismal sight is the battlefield covered with dead and wounded,' Bazaine remarked in a private letter a few days later. 'I was lucky enough to get through without losing any bits of myself'.[30] A Swiss businessman named Henry Dunant, who was travelling with Napoleon III, was deeply affected by the carnage and subsequently wrote a vivid book about what he had seen, which set in motion the steps which led to the founding of the International Red Cross.

The Piedmontese wanted to continue the war, and to drive the Austrians out of all of Italy, not merely from Lombardy, but the French and Austrian Emperors had been appalled at the losses and peace was made. Napoleon III approved eleven Chevalier of the Legion of Honour decorations for the 2nd Etranger, ten of them for officers – including Lieutenants Jaudon and Lebre – one for a Sergeant, and twenty-two *Medailles Militaire*.[31] Captain Danjou was named a Chevalier of the Order Militaire de Saint-Maurice et Lazare.[32] An Italian Campaign Medal was issued later to those who had taken part.

Greatly to the disappointment of Sous-Lieutenant Zede the 3rd Battalion was left at Milan, and would soon head back to Algeria, while the 1st and 2nd Battalions were entrained for Paris, but one man who did not go with them was Sergeant Mori, whose engagement was up, and who opted to remain in his native country in the hope of continuing the fight for unification.

In early August, for the very first time, the men of the Foreign Legion, band playing, marched down the Champs-Elysées in Paris in a victory parade. Captain Danjou was among them, a freshly laundered white glove covering his articulated left hand, his medals, old and new, sparkling in the sun. It was a defining moment for many of the officers and men. They spent a few days in the capital, then entrained for Toulon and took ship across the Mediterranean to Algeria.

5
Doldrums in Algeria

Unlike the Crimean War, the Italian Campaign had been short, vigorous and successful. The 1st and 2nd Battalions of the 2nd Etranger returned to Sidi-bel-Abbes on 29 August, refreshed from their trip to Paris. This was just as well, for three days later Lieutenant-Colonel Martinez took them to Western Algeria to campaign once again against the rebellious Beni-Snassen, near the Moroccan border. At Lalla-Mahrina they joined a brigade of two battalions of the 9th Regiment of the Line, and two of the 2nd Zouaves, commanded by General Charles Thoumas. A successful *razzia* netted seven thousand sheep, but then cholera hit the brigade, putting an end to campaigning for the time being. The epidemic had still not run its course by 12 October, when they were unexpectedly joined by Lieutenant-Colonel Mathieu Butet of the 1st Etranger, who brought the news that he had been transferred and promoted to Colonel of the 2nd Etranger, replacing Signorino, who had gone to the 86th Regiment of the Line.

Butet was a popular and well respected officer[1] with more than thirty years of soldiering behind him, having joined the Army in 1828 and served in the ranks for nine years before receiving a commission. As General Thoumas was one of those felled by cholera, Butet was named to replace him as Brigade Commander, with Martinez continuing to command the 2nd Etranger for the remainder of the campaign. The Beni-Snassen, who had been intriguing with the Sultan of Morocco, had assembled more than ten thousand fighting men, and it was considered unwise to face them in a serious confrontation because of the physically weakened state of the brigade. Instead, their villages were threatened, which brought them down from the mountains. Due to the Moroccan connection, the whole campaign was as much political as military and ended with the French offering, and the Beni-Snassen accepting, a hundred francs for each musket surrendered. The 2nd Etranger did not return to Sidi-bel-Abbes until mid-November.

The 1st Etranger, the *Regiment Suisse*, had felt themselves fairly successful in their recruiting drive in Italy in the second half of 1859, adding two hundred and fifty men to the ranks, partly as a result of an Imperial Decree, signed by Empress Eugenie at the end of June, permitting engagements of two-to-five years and re-engagements of one-to-five years – as was the case with the 2nd Etranger. Another Imperial Decree some three months later, signed by the Emperor, abolished the green uniform and set the two Regiments Etranger on exactly the same footing.[2] However, by the time the *Regiment Suisse* left Milan for a second recruiting effort in Corsica many of the Italians who had signed engagement papers had already deserted. Recruiting in Corsica was even less successful than it had been in Italy and on 5 February 1860 the regiment returned to Algeria, setting up headquarters in Philippeville. The three battalions were all under strength and would now have to rely on traditional recruiting.

Near the end of the month Sous-Lieutenant Ernest Milson von Bolt, a member of the Royal Family of Prussia, arrived to begin what would be a seven-year career in the Foreign Legion. Born in Samter, in the Duchy of Poser, he had appeared to have a brilliant career ahead of him in the 4th Regiment of Prussian Hussars, of which he was already Standard-Bearer, when he killed a superior officer in a duel. Needing to quickly find employment outside Prussia he joined the Foreign Legion. Another new face in the officers' mess was that of twenty-eight-year-old Captain Jean Cazes, who transferred in from the 65th Regiment of the Line, which he had joined eight years earlier after leaving Saint-Cyr.

The 2nd Battalion, stationed at Setif, was nearly overwhelmed in a vicious snowstorm on 4 March while marching through the mountains, and might have been completely wiped out had it not been for the leadership of the officers, and Sous-Officiers like Sergeant-Major Vilain and his comrades, the Legionnaires' sense of discipline, and the efforts of local tribesmen travelling with the column. The battalion staggered back into Setif, regrouped and was then sent out on a another march through the mountains to the south, once again facing bitter temperatures in difficult terrain. On 1 December the promotion of Vilain to Sergeant-Major of Voltigeurs was promulgated in Battalion Orders.[3] Later in the month Lieutenant-Colonel Martinez of the 2nd Etranger was transferred, promoted and named Colonel of the 1st and Captain Aubry went with him to be a Battalion Commander. The Swiss artist Henri-Guido Kauffmann had risen through the ranks and received a commission as a Sous-Lieutenant in the final days of the year.

Overall, the year 1860 was a quiet one for the 2nd Etranger, with various Companies of the 2nd and 3rd Battalions garrisoning small military posts in Western Algeria and the majority of the regiment based at Sidi-bel-Abbes. Lieutenant-Colonel Jean-Baptiste Giraud had been transferred in from the *Chasseurs a Pied* to be Butet's second-in-command, and on 28 March, after just less than twelve years of service, Adjutant Clement Maudet received a Commission as a Sous-Lieutenant.[4] In the middle of the following month the regiment lost one of its old warriors, when Captain Delebecque was transferred to the 81st Regiment of the Line to become a Battalion Commander. He had been in the Foreign Legion since 1847, gradually working his way up through the hierarchy, often cited in Orders. Captain Danjou was sorry to see him go, remembering how he had been with Delebecque when unhorsed in Italy the afternoon before the Battle of Magenta. Delebeque's distinguished years of service stood him in good stead and he went on to achieve General Officer rank and ultimately to command the 19th Army Corps, the *Armee d'Afrique*.

In September, Colonel Butet took the 1st Battalion's 2nd and 3rd Companies – the Grenadiers of Captain Gustave Saussier and the Voltigeurs of Captain Philippe Wolkensinger – to Algiers to be part of the military welcome for the visit of the Emperor Napoleon III and Empress Eugenie.[5] They returned to Sidi-bel-Abbes for the annual inspection, conducted by General Deligny, following which the regiment was dispersed to carry out building and repair work on a number of small military posts.

This was much more popular than road-building, where Legionnaires were employed essentially as armed labourers, rather than as soldiers. Men who had joined up to fight failed to share their superiors' enthusiasm for work with the pick and shovel. However, in building, expanding or repairing military posts Legionnaires with skills as masons, bricklayers and carpenters quite enjoyed the construction work and took pride in what they built.

'This existence is much liked by the soldiers who, in their work clothes, are usefully occupied, under only very casual surveillance by Sous-Officiers and Corporals, in relative independence,' General Grisot would write later. He felt that the open air life also kept the men in good physical shape, but remarked: 'The officers use their leisure time for hunting, but other than that distraction their existence is desperately monotonous'.[6]

There was more of the same in 1861.

'The Companies of the regiment were employed in the same public works,' said Grisot. Some of the Legionnaires were allowed to hire themselves out to town administrations as labourers, which was quite popular, as it added a few more coins to their pitifully small pay. At one point in the year a total of sixteen Companies was engaged in labouring jobs. Grisot commented: 'The needs of the colonization had priority over all other considerations'.[7]

In May 1861 the 3rd Battalion of the 1st Etranger, stationed at Constantine, took part in a tough campaign against the Kabyle. Commanded by Major Aubry, they were part of a column which included the 58th Regiment of the Line and a battalion of *Tirailleurs Algeriens*. There were night attacks by the enemy, at one point it was necessary to construct a road and the Legionnaires constantly had responsibility for guarding the rear of the column. Men who could take it no more deserted. Often the Legionnaires marched without their packs, staggered into camp in the small hours of the morning, ate cold rations and then got up and did the same thing all over again the next day. At the end of the campaign the battalion returned to Constantine.[8]

Desertions multiplied. Men sold their kit and were duly punished. It was not a happy regiment. Even so, Sergeant-Major Vilain re-engaged[9] on 27 May 1861. General Ulrich, conducting the 1st Etranger's annual inspection on 6 August, reported unfavourably on a number of aspects. Discipline, he said, was 'severe, often too rigorous', and sometimes enforced by 'coercive means forbidden by the regulations and by the sentiment of humanity'. As an example, he charged that 'Major Aubry ordered a man who was merely suspected of theft tied up and exposed in the sun for nine days.' Some, but certainly not all, of the Sous-Officiers in the three battalions came off better.

> The Sous-Officiers are generally good, [but] several have brought brutality into the service [*Ulrich reported*]. A good number of the Sergeant-Majors are likely to make good officers. Several Sergeants have been severely punished for misconduct... [Overall,] misdemeanors [and] serious infractions are very frequent and denote an advanced state of demoralization. A regiment

which counts 648 deserters, in which one does not dare hand out the munitions which each soldier must carry, in which only one pair of shoes per man can be distributed lest they sell them, is far from being a disciplined regiment . . . It is unworthy of confidence, perhaps even dangerous.

Clearly this was a serious slap in the face for Colonel Martinez, who had commanded the regiment for twenty months, but it is also possible to detect a xenophobic bias in Ulrich's sweeping conclusion that the 1st Etranger was '. . . nothing more than an amalgamation of all the nations of Europe, [and] does not have nor can it have an *esprit de corps*'.[10]

The inspection of the 2nd Etranger was conducted by General Deligny the same day and he found things very different from the depressing picture Ulrich had painted of the sister regiment. Deligny had never served in the Foreign Legion, but the 2nd Etranger had been under his command in some gruelling campaigns and he knew their capabilities.

> The Sous-Officiers and Corporals are very vigorous soldiers [*he wrote*]. Many among them, the foreigners especially, are well educated and their military skills are very good. Sous-Officiers and Corporals are, in general, good instructors; they learn the manoeuvres efficiently . . .

Moreover, Deligny's views on the multi-nation make-up of the force were quite the opposite of those of Ulrich, and he wrote: 'Sous-Officiers and soldiers, though being an assembly of all the nationalities of Europe, are generally disciplined, vigorous and devoted; one finds among them a solidarity which makes for troops with remarkable firmness'.[11]

The average age of the Sous-Officiers in the 1st Etranger that year was thirty. In the 2nd Etranger it was thirty-two. The oldest Sous-Officier had completed ten years of service in Line regiments, followed by nine-and-a-half with the 1st Etranger and eleven-and-a-half with the 2nd Etranger.[12]

From mid-year officers with contacts in Paris, and those who received newspapers from the capital, became aware that possible trouble was brewing in Mexico. Details were sketchy, but it appeared that the Government headed by President Benito Juarez, had angered France, Britain and Spain, all of whom were major creditors, by unilaterally placing a moratorium on the repayment of foreign debts. He had also confiscated the property of the Roman Catholic Church. In October it was learned that, following a tripartite meeting in London, Britain, Spain and France had withdrawn diplomatic recognition of the Juarez Government, and had – with varying degrees of enthusiasm – agreed on armed intervention, so the announcement in November that France was despatching a small Expeditionary Corps to Mexico did not come as much of a surprise.

During the previous eight years France had sent troops to the Crimea, Italy, China and Syria, as well as fighting numerous campaigns in Algeria. It was noted with interest that a battalion of the 2nd Regiment of Zouaves was going to Mexico, but as reports were circulating that the two regiments of the Foreign Legion were poised for a major reorganization, it was clear that there was no immediate possibility of them being considered for overseas service.

For the 2nd Etranger the most exciting event of the year came early in November, when Colonel Butet took the 1st Battalion to Oran to be part of the celebrations welcoming Marshal Pelissier, who was returning to Algeria as Governor-General. The ceremonies over, the battalion hastened back to Sidi-bel-Abbes, so as to be on hand when Pelissier arrived to visit the Foreign Legion at home.[13]

New men were still trickling into the 2nd Etranger, among them a handsome young Irishman named Frank M'Alevey, soon popular, 'the soul of humour', according to Captain M.W. Kirwan, his Commanding Officer almost a decade later. 'In appearance he was every inch a soldier, [with] his tall well-knit figure,' Kirwan said. 'If there was evidence of vanity at all, perhaps it was in the twist of his moustachios, which he as carefully trimmed in the field as in quarters'.[14]

Another new man, who became M'Alevey's friend, was Marie Morziki, the French-born son of a self-exiled Polish officer. 'He had been educated for the Church, but preferring the more active life of a soldier, had joined the Legion to try to win his baton,' M'Alevey would say later of the man he called his *camarade de camarades* – best friend.[15] On 18 November a young man named Hippolyte Kuwasseg also signed a two-year engagement with the 2nd Etranger. Born on 22 July 1843 at Villeneuve-Saint-Georges, he was the son of a well-known Austrian painter and except for a brief period as a civilian, and stints with two regular Regiments of the Line, would serve in the Foreign Legion for more than a quarter of a century. Regimental clerks wrote his name down as Kunassec.

Undoubtedly, General Ulrich's strictures on the state of the 1st Etranger were a factor in the decision-making process when Napoleon III and Marshal Randon, now Minister of War, decided to cut back on the overall number of foreign soldiers in the service of France. By Imperial Decree dated 14 December the 1st Regiment Etranger was simply written out of existence[16] and two days later the Ministry of War suspended indefinitely all engagements in the soon-to-be-formed and newly-named Regiment Etranger.[17] There was obviously no place for Colonel Martinez, and he was not offered a transfer into a French Regiment of the Line when it was decided that Colonel Butet would command the new Regiment Etranger. Doubtless bitter, Martinez simply disappeared from Algeria and from history, though rumours eventually reached Sidi-bel-Abbes that he had found opportunities for his fighting prowess in South America. The now defunct 1st Etranger had had a regimental strength of two thousand six hundred, but this was drastically reduced two weeks later as a result of a Ministerial Note which provided authorization for all foreigners in both the 1st and 2nd Etrangers who had completed one year of their two-year enlistments to return to civilian life if they wished.[18]

The brand new Regiment Etranger of three battalions, with an on-paper strength of two thousand six hundred and thirty-five officers and men, came into being on 1 January 1862, with Colonel Butet making a smooth transition from being Colonel of the old 2nd Etranger. Despite Colonel Martinez' more than two decades of loyal service, during which time he had risen through the ranks from common soldier to command a regiment, there was now no 1st Etranger, and clearly no place was made for him the French Army. He resigned his Commission, left Algeria and simply disappeared, though rumours subsequently drifted back to Sidi-bel-Abbes that he had found another country and another war in South America.

The final disposition of soldiers and officers of the defunct 1st Etranger took place on 29 January and the new Regiment Etranger absorbed four Captains and four Lieutenants from the old regiment, along with seven Sous-Lieutenants, among whom were Diesbach, Kauffman and Milson von Bolt. There were no positions for any of them, as all Battalions and Companies had their full complement of officers, so they became – in the terminology of the French Army – *a-la-suite*, officers on the strength, but unassigned to specific duties.[19]

Once the reorganization was completed, officers had time to take a greater interest in the reports coming out of Mexico, and began badgering Butet with questions about future campaigning. His chain of command ran through Colonel Faidherbe, Commanding Officer of the Sub-Division of Sidi-bel-Abbes, upwards to General Deligny, Commanding Officer of the Division of Oran, but no information was to be had, so those with access to books and newspapers started reading up on Mexico.

These interested readers discovered that even under Spanish Colonial rule in the early part of the century Mexico had not been politically stable, and that things had become worse as ideas about self-determination and Independence took root. In September 1810 Father Miguel Hidalgo y Costilla had proclaimed a revolt against Spain. He was captured by government troops four months later and shot. Leadership of the *Independistas* fell to another priest, Father Jose Maria Morelos. Napoleon Bonaparte's expulsion from Spain in 1814 led to the deposed King Ferdinand VII being restored to the throne, and to further activities in Mexico on the part of the *Independistas*. These were countered by increased Spanish efforts to cling to power. The following year Morelos was captured and shot. King Ferdinand's autocratic rule led to a revolt in Spain in 1820 and the establishment of a constitutional monarchy. In Mexico, the Conservatives, opposed to constitutional government, made common cause with the *Independistas*, now headed by Vincente Guerrero.

Antonio Lopez de Santa Anna, a young Lieutenant in the Spanish Army, deserted to the *Independistas* and was with them when Augustine de Iturbide, also an Army officer, succeeded in deposing the Spanish Viceroy and finally wresting the government from Spain. Iturbide managed to have himself declared Emperor, but his despotic regime lasted less than two years and Santa Anna was involved in the upheaval which ousted him and sent him into exile in the United Sates with his family. A federal republic, the United States of Mexico, was established in 1824 and when Iturbide attempted a return to power he was shot. Guadalupe Victoria served the first Presidential term, which ended in 1829, and was briefly succeeded by Guerrero.

Later in the year Anastasio Bustamante took power. He lasted until 1832, but the ambitious Santa Anna was active in the background and became Head of State for the first time the following year. During his two years in office he sought to put in place the necessary machinery for his continued dominance of Mexican politics even when not actually President.

Doldrums in Algeria

In March of 1836 he took his Army northward in an attempt to bring to heel the breakaway Republic of Texas, sending more than three thousand Mexican soldiers against one hundred and eighty-seven armed settlers and their supporters forted up in a venerable semi-ruined Spanish Mission in San Antonio. With odds in his favour of more than sixteen-to-one, Santa Anna overran the 'rebels,' only to be defeated shortly afterwards by an army under General Sam Houston, which fell on the Mexican position at San Jacinto with cries of 'Remember the Alamo!'

Now, twenty-six years later, his name was featuring in French newspapers again, for, even in exile, he was a behind-the-scenes player in the events which were taking shape. He had failed in a bid for office in 1837, being beaten by Bustamante, who the following year suffered the ignominy of having the French Navy capture the port of Veracruz, on the coast of the Gulf of Mexico, to collect monetary damages for losses suffered by French citizens during civil unrest. Bustamante lost power to Santa Anna in 1839, got it back and remained President until 1841, when Santa Anna again became Head of State. The two men had each held office three times, and Santa Anna became President three more times between 1843 and 1847, but was ousted that year when American troops landed at Veracruz, fought their way inland and captured Mexico City. The hostilities ended with Mexico losing California and much of the land which now makes up the Southwestern United States.

Incredibly, Santa Anna was back in office again for a seventh time in 1853, and raised several million dollars by selling the United States a huge chunk of northern Mexico in a deal which at least established a demarcated – but porous – international border. Assorted Presidential comings and goings during the decade created a situation where parts of the vast, sprawling country that was Mexico became subject to the whims of ambitious local strongmen, while the Far West was plagued by foreign filibustering expeditions, headed by adventurers – some of them French – attracted by dreams of empire and of the legendary wealth of the mines of Sonora.

A filibustering expedition led by Count Charles de Pindray ended in June 1852, when he was found in his tent with a bullet in his head, the victim of either suicide or murder. Another high-born Frenchman, Count Gaston Raousset-Boulbon, leading other filibusters, barely escaped with his life in November, managing to retreat across the U.S. border. In May 1854, an American, William Walker, who had tried to seize Sonora, was very lucky to get back into the United States, while Raousset-Boulbon's second filibustering expedition led to his capture and execution by firing squad in August.[20]

The Liberals finally deposed Santa Anna in 1855, and banished him from Mexico. President Ignacio Comonfort began to reorganize the whole machinery of government. His Minister of Justice, Benito Juarez, drafted laws limiting the power of military courts, separating Church and State and establishing the legal equality of all citizens. He became Minister of the Interior and the nation's Chief Justice in 1857, but Comonfort was overthrown the following year and fled into exile in the United States. In the first thirty-three years of the Republic – counting Acting Presidents – there had been thirty-seven Heads of State. Juarez was the legal successor to Comonfort, but the Conservatives, supported by General Felix

Zuloaga, seized Mexico City. The Liberals, with Juarez as Provisional President, withdrew to Veracruz, and thus began the War of the Reform.

It lasted three years, laid waste to huge areas of southeastern Mexico, and saw the violation of the property rights of foreigners in several major incidents, one in Mexico City, when the Conservatives carried off a considerable amount of British property, including a large quantity of bullion. The war eventually ended with victory for the Liberals and exile for many of the leading Conservatives, but the country's economy was ruined, and it owed huge sums to bankers and business houses in Britain, Spain, France and elsewhere. Trying to drag Mexico up from the economic pit into which it had descended, Juarez nationalized the property of the Roman Catholic Church and on 17 July 1861 signed into law a two-year moratorium on the repayment of all foreign debts.

In the climate of the times it was an invitation to military intervention and reactions were not long in coming. Britain, Spain and France met in London in October, withdrew diplomatic recognition of the Juarez Government, and agreed on armed intervention. Under the terms of the tripartite Convention of London, the French and British Ambassadors left Mexico City and Juarez took steps to strengthen his Army by placing an order with a private contractor for twenty-five thousand rifles.[21]

Initially at least, Britain and Spain were apparently unaware that Napoleon III had more in mind in invading Mexico than simply collecting debts, but about that time they were hearing rumours that there were money scandals concerning what was owed to the French, and that the hands of some people close to the Court were less than clean, they also learned that Napoleon was talking about installing a ruler in Mexico, and an Emperor, no less. Despite the 1859 war over Italy, his relations with Emperor Franz Joseph of the Austro-Hungarian Empire were relatively cordial, and he had begun sounding him out about perhaps placing his younger brother, Archduke Maximilian, on an imperial throne in Mexico. The Austrian Emperor was interested, as Maximilian was very popular with the masses, perhaps embarrassingly so, and vaguely seen as a threat.

The French Expeditionary Corps, commanded by Admiral Jurien de la Graviere, left France on 12 November 1861 for what, under the best conditions, was a voyage of some six weeks, longer if a break was taken in Martinique before heading west across the Caribbean Sea. The Spanish, having both ships and troops in Cuba, were the first to reach Mexico. On 8 December, two warships approached Veracruz and the commanding general sent a boat ashore to demand the surrender of the city and the fortress of San Juan de Ulloa within twenty-four hours. Governor La Llave complied and withdrew his forces. Watching the Spanish land, no doubt with mixed emotions, was the Port Captain, a Frenchman named Laine, long resident in Veracruz, whose son was an officer in the Mexican Army.

In a frantic effort to avert actual fighting, the Mexican Congress hurriedly repealed, by a vote of sixty-three to thirty-four, the moratorium on debt repayment as it applied to the three parties who had met in London. This can only have been an attempt to seize the moral high ground, as Juarez immediately issued a manifesto calling for unified resistance and instructed General Jose Lopez Uraga, commanding the Army in the East, to take all necessary steps against the initial invaders and their expected Allies, when they arrived.[22]

Admiral Jurien de la Graviere, with a force of two thousand four hundred men, reached Veracruz on 7 January 1862, coming ashore to find that the Spanish had already set up a functioning government, and that General Prim, the Conde de Reus, was in supreme command. The British also landed Royal Navy personnel and Marines, and the three Allies had an immediate meeting and issued a public broadside assuring the Mexican people that their intentions were not hostile. It was signed by the three military commanders, General Prim for Spain, Admiral Jurien de la Graviere for France and Sir Charles Wyke for Britain.[23] Juarez, prepared for anything, including duplicity, declared a state of siege in the Department of Veracruz, taking all control out of the hands of the civilian government and placing it under total military control.[24]

Founded by Hernando Cortez in 1519, the city of Veracruz, with a population of thirteen thousand, presented a rundown appearance, Spanish Colonial architecture cheek-by-jowl with squalid dwellings, open unpaved squares, insanitary fruit, vegetable and meat markets, and, everywhere the ugly black *Zopilotes*, scavenger birds, whose usefulness as garbage cleaners could not be denied. Veracruz was the major port on the Gulf Coast and the starting point for both of the main routes inland to Mexico City. It was either the point of entry to southeastern Mexico, or the point of exit. It was also hugely unhealthy from May to October, when yellow fever ran rife, though it was endemic on a year-round basis. Locally known as the *vomito negro*, it was frequently fatal within a matter of hours, and while the local population had built up some immunity, newcomers often rapidly fell victim to the sickness. The local wisdom was that it was contracted from fetid air, swampy areas and bad water, and it would be another twenty years before Dr. Carlos Juan Finlay of Cuba tentatively suggested it as being mosquito-borne, and almost forty years before this was finally confirmed by the Yellow Fever Commission of the U.S. Army.

Up to this point, the overall situation between the Allies and the Mexicans was fairly harmonious, and, taking into account the fact that the *vomito negro* rapidly began to show itself among the foreign troops, it seemed a sound military decision to send the majority of the soldiers to La Tejeria, some eight kilometres (about five miles) from Veracruz, and more than thirty metres (about a hundred feet) above sea level, hopefully a healthier place.

After being ordered by his government to leave Mexico City, France's Ambassador, Dubois de Saligny, had gone only as far as Orizaba, where he had awaited news of the arrival of the French forces. A cunning and devious diplomat, he now joined Jurien de la Graviere's headquarters at Veracruz, where he was instructed to produce a document to form the basis for the Allies' demands on the Juarez Government. However, when the representatives of Britain, Spain and France sat down on 13 January to examine the draft they found it excessively belligerent. After removing all references to reparations, they devoted further time to making the wording milder in tone, if not in intent, and then sent it to Lopez Uraga. He forwarded it to General Manuel Doblado, the Minister of Foreign Affairs.[25]

For the Allies things proceeded at a relatively leisurely pace while they awaited Doblado's response. Admiral Jurien de la Graviere even had time to think of the health considerations for the French forces if they were to be long in Mexico, with men stationed in the unhealthy flatlands known to the Mexicans as *Tierra Caliente* – Hot Land – and to become infamous to the French as the *Terres Chaudes*, and suggested to the Minister for the Navy that Senegalese or French West Indian troops might have a greater immunity to the *vomito negro* than Frenchmen. It seemed a good idea and Napoleon III asked the Khedive of Egypt if he could loan France between twelve hundred and fifteen hundred African soldiers. For the Mexicans it was a busy time, and General Ignacio Zaragoza, who had been named to replace Lopez Uraga, expended considerable effort on defensive works at various points along the two roads which led inland. Doblado, on 9 February, bought Zaragoza some more time by asking for further details of financial claims, and suggesting a full meeting in ten days. Clearly, the Mexican Government's representatives could not be expected to hold talks in occupied Veracruz, so the meeting was scheduled for La Soledad, a very small town thirty-five kilometres (some twenty miles) inland from the coast.

The roads in southern Mexico did not lend themselves to normal wheeled traffic. Rutted from wagon wheels, scoured by rains, and bisected by rivers and streams, sometimes merely dried-up waterways, at other times torrents, the southern road was often impassable for days at a time, and was always difficult. Some of the once handsome stone bridges had been deliberately destroyed during the War of Reform. Journeys were made by *diligences*, mule-drawn conveyances much like the stagecoaches of the American West and Northern Mexico, well-suited to the terrain. The Allied negotiators travelled to La Soledad by *diligences*, heading west from Veracruz along what had once been grandly designated the Royal Highway, then taking the southern fork, known as the Orizaba Road, passing through tiny hamlets, often no more than a few kilometres apart, some of which, in times of peace, were staging posts, where mule teams could be rotated and modest meals purchased.

The conference went reasonably well, especially as the Allies specifically stated that they had no intention of interfering with Mexican sovereignty. There was almost a feeling that these were negotiations between equals, brought together to solve a knotty problem, and no doubt the repealing of the moratorium on British, Spanish and French debt repayments helped to make for a somewhat cordial atmosphere. Concessions were made, including agreement that the Customs revenues from Veracruz – a major generator of funds – would be returned to Mexican control.

There was a mutual recognition that there might be further claims against the Government of Mexico, and that these would take time to prepare by the creditors, and would then have to be examined by the regime. Doblado suggested that the foreign troops should be moved from La Tejeria and Veracruz and sent inland, to get them away from the *vomito negro* of the unhealthy *Terres Chaudes*. The Spanish troops were assigned to Orizaba, the British to Cordoba and the French to Tehuacan, all of them towns located at healthy elevations of more than a thousand metres (three thousand feet) above sea level, well beyond the *Terres Chaudes*. The suggestion was accepted by the Spanish and French, but Sir Charles Wyke declined it, saying that his force of seven hundred Marines could be accommodated on board the ships which had brought them. It was agreed that in the event of the negotiations breaking down the French and Spanish troops would be pulled back to the Chiquihuite River, on the western edge of the *Terres Chaudes*.

The meeting ended in accord, General Prim signing what became known as the Convention of La Soledad almost with alacrity. Admiral Jurien de la Graviere and Sir Charles signed, with some misgivings, the following morning, and the Allied party returned to Veracruz in their convoy of *diligences*, the Spanish and French to prepare for their troops to march inland.[26]

In Paris, Napoleon III met regularly with a number of exiled Conservatives from Mexico and thirsted for news from his Commander-in-Chief. Many things were happening on the Imperial front. The Emperor was enthusiastic, and believed that the American Civil War, which had broken out between the Union and the Confederacy in April 1861, would mean that Washington would be far too preoccupied with its own problems to mount any really serious opposition to a French invasion of its southern neighbour. Empress Eugenie believed that France should support Roman Catholicism south of the border with the Protestant United States. Franz Joseph of Austria looked forward to ridding himself of his too-popular brother. Maximilian's wife, the former Princess Charlotte of Belgium, liked the idea of her husband becoming an Emperor, and her father, King Leopold, approved of the idea of his daughter becoming an Empress. Maximilian himself, somewhat naive and generally well-meaning, was not quite so sure, and wanted assurances that the Mexican people really wanted him to become their Emperor.

In late February, Napoleon III decided to beef up his Army in Mexico, dispatching General Charles Ferdinand Latrille, Count de Lorencez, to Veracruz with a force of four thousand seven hundred and eleven men – including a second battalion of Zouaves – almost twice the number of troops sent out with Jurien de la Graviere three months earlier. Jean-Adolphe Beauce, who had been with the Army in both Italy and Syria, accompanied them as Official Military Artist to the War Ministry to record the campaign.

This troop movement, and General de Lorencez's instructions to take command of all French field forces in Mexico, quickly became known in Algeria. Once again Colonel Butet was besieged with questions about the possible deployment of the Regiment Etranger. He still had no answers, and it may be guessed that during the month he wore out his welcome with Colonel Faidherbe in Sidi-bel-Abbes and General Deligny in Oran, seeking answers to the questions his officers were asking him, and getting no satisfactory responses. A gentle man, much liked by both officers and men, he apparently concluded that he lacked the fire to forcefully press the Regiment Etranger's case.

> Our excellent Colonel, 'Papa' Butet, told us: 'I do not have the stuff that makes for generals, and I am rather surprised that I even made Colonel' [*Zede reported him as saying*]. 'So you see, gentlemen, I think that my personality may even be an obstacle to the realization of your wishes. Therefore, I have decided to leave. I have asked to be transferred to Divisional Headquarters'.[27]

On 8 March the Emperor named Butet as 'Commandant 1st Class in the city of Oran,' a post he assumed six days later.

In the long run, of course, the Regiment Etranger neither knew – nor really cared – what was causing the Mexican Crisis. The politics and machinations of the Emperor they served were of little interest to them. They merely existed – as they had always done – to effect the wishes of France's ruler. They had enlisted to fight, and the fact was that other soldiers were being sent overseas to do so, while they were staying at home. They would have no say in shaping events which were beyond their control – unless, of course, their new Commanding Officer had greater persuasive powers than his predecessor, and Pierre Jeanningros, the incoming Colonel of the Regiment Etranger, was certainly the very opposite of Mathieu Butet.

6
'Let's go to Mexico!'

A forty-six-year-old rough diamond, who had been with the Army since he was fourteen as the *enfant de troupe* – child of the troop – in the 66th Regiment of the Line, Pierre Jeanningros had been a soldier with the regiment at nineteen. His first battle had been the debacle with Abd-el-Kader's forces at Moulay-Ismael in June 1835, where he had also received his first wound. The following year he had transferred into the Regiment of Zouaves, was wounded three times within a few months, commissioned a Sous-Lieutenant in 1840 and received the Cross of a Chevalier of the Legion of Honour from the hands of the Duke d'Aumale himself. Jeanningros had risen through military hierarchy, been distinguished in the Crimean War, and wounded three more times before being appointed Colonel of the 43rd Regiment of the Line in 1859.

When Butet sought a quieter military life, Jeanningros had been offered, and had accepted, command of the Regiment Etranger[1] and assumed his new post on 15 March 1862. Heavy-set and muscular, with a short beard, he had the kind of fighting reputation which appealed to Legionnaires, and which negated the fact that he had never served with them.

> [He was] a fine figure of a man who had all the virile and soldierly qualities needed to command this *troupe d'elite* [*said Zede, a Sous-Lieutenant when Jeanningros joined the regiment*]. Although of modest origin – his father at the time of his birth was a retired Captain – and never having been to any military school, owing his knowledge of the art of war entirely to practical experience on the battlefield, he was well above the average standard. He approached every problem with a startling realism and invariably found the most practical solution.[2]

To his public embarrassment, though possibly to his private pleasure, Jeanningros had been dubbed the 'Bayard of the Zouaves' – a reference to the great French soldier Pierre Terrail, Seigneur de Bayard, of three centuries earlier, known as 'The Knight Without Fear and Beyond Reproach.' A French-Canadian who campaigned under his orders in Mexico in 1864–65 remembered him with respect and a degree of fondness.

> Colonel Jeanningros had risen to the rank he occupied by a combination of energy and valour, coupled with the protection afforded by muscles of iron, a strong wrist and the omen of a Lucky Star . . . [*Faucher de Saint-Maurice wrote in his memoirs*]. To his qualities as a rough soldier and a formidable

swordsman, Colonel Jeanningros added the delicate manners which are the attributes of those of sensibility and good hearts.[3]

The news coming from Mexico was not encouraging. General de Lorencez had made a fast trip from France, landing at Veracruz on 6 March, accompanied by a number of Mexican exiles, including Juan Almonte, a former Mexican Ambassador to France. De Lorencez' instructions called for him to take over all field operations, and for Admiral Jurien de la Graviere to deal with 'political, maritime and commercial matters'. General Doblado, the Mexican Minister of Foreign Affairs, was now pressing for compliance in implementing the clause in the Convention of La Soledad which had agreed that the Customs House in Veracruz be returned to Mexican control.

De Lorencez had found upon landing that the French troops had moved out into the *Terres Chaudes* proper, on their way to Tehuacan. By now the *vomito negro* was raging among them and many who started the journey healthy simply died on the way or reached the uplands so debilitated that they would have been useless in an emergency. Winding their way westward through La Loma, Santa Rita, La Purga and Arroyo de Piedras, they buried men at every little hamlet, or simply by the side of the road, and the *vomito negro* was no respecter of persons or rank. Not long before the column of troops left La Soledad the Abbe de Ribens, Military Chaplain to the Expeditionary Corps, began to show signs of fever. Strong mules, fitted with a saddle which supported a chair or a stretcher, called a *cacolet*, on either side, were provided by the Army's rather primitive ambulance service and one was immediately brought.

'The sickness commenced at La Soledad,' wrote Chaplain Lanusse, who replaced de Ribens months later. 'Everybody else went on with the march and the Abbe de Ribens was placed in a stretcher carried on a mule. Another stretcher provided balance with a Corporal, also burning with fever'.[4]

The column wound its way along the road, passing through El Sordo and Palo Verde. 'The corporal died along the way,' Lanusse reported, but the priest clung to life and the column continued on to a hamlet whose grand-sounding name belied its sorry condition. Formerly known as Temexcal,[5] and now officially designated Villa Tejada o Camaron, it had once boasted a hotel and a large stone building which provided accommodation for the drivers of the *diligences* and for wagon teamsters – known as *arrieros*. Behind it was a large walled yard – a corral – where loaded wagons could be safely parked overnight. Both buildings were now derelict, the doors ripped off and carried away, the windows gaping to the elements and the wagon yard without gates.

'Abbe de Ribens expired a few hours after the column reached Camaron,' Lanusse said,[6] adding that he was buried in a lonely grave outside the southeast corner of the walled corral. Word went back to France for a replacement, and Lanusse was given the appointment.

The troops marched on, past Paso Ancho and Paso del Macho, reached Chiquihuite, which marked the end of the *Terres Chaudes*, then pressed on to Tehuacan and set up camp. General de Lorencez caught up with them there on 26 March.

Doblado was still complaining about the non-compliance with the terms of Convention of La Soledad and Admiral Jurien de la Graviere had come to the conclusion that the Allies had been outsmarted. He felt that Doblado, having bought time for General Zaragoza, was now hoping to provoke a crisis which would enable him to invoke the clause which would force the Spanish and French to move their troops out of the highlands and back down into the unhealthy *Terres Chaudes*.

Among the Mexican nationals who had landed in Veracruz with de Lorencez, under the protection of the Tricolour was Juan N. Almonte, a former Ambassador to France, and several prominent Conservatives who had fled to Europe with prices on their heads at the end of the War of the Reform. Doblado demanded that they be turned over to him. The French refused.[7] Obviously, the usefulness of the Convention of La Soledad was at an end. As it was a political matter, rather than a military one, Jurien de la Graviere gave the order for the French troops to leave Tehuacan and pull back to the Chiquihuite River. Not only was General de Lorencez furious, but the Spanish and British considered this a unilateral action and demanded a meeting of the Allies.

At a stormy conference on 9 April, France's de Lorencez and Spain's Prim quarrelled violently. The British sided with the Spanish, declared that they would not support the French position and announced that they would leave Mexico. They even offered Prim space on their ships for his troops, but, as he was able to call for help from Cuba, he declined.[8] The Spanish and British had seen clearly that the French were going to face problems with the Mexican emigres who had come with de Lorencez and others who would doubtless follow. On 13 March, a week after landing, Almonte, entirely on his own initiative, had issued a Proclamation promising 'firm government'.[9] The *Juaristas* countered by making public some captured documents showing that he was already secretly in touch with known Conservative elements.[10]

Part of France's problem was the fact that it was not officially at war with Mexico. Admiral Jurien de la Graviere and Ambassador de Saligny decided to change that and proclaimed a State of War.[11] Once this was done an excuse had to be found for actual hostilities to commence, and here the *vomito negro* came to the rescue. De Lorencez was required to withdraw his troops to Paso Ancho in the *Terres Chaudes* and had pulled back as far as Cordoba when he received word that sick French troops who had been left in Orizaba were being ill-treated. He turned around and started to march back. Mexican Republicans hung about the fringes of his column and a confrontation was inevitable. It came when Captain Capitan, at the head of a thirty-five-man squadron of *Chasseurs d'Afrique*, charged a Mexican position at Fortin, killed five of the enemy and captured twelve, forcing General Zaragoza to concede that a State of War now definitively existed between the two nations.[12]

Once back in Orizaba, de Lorencez, totally underestimating his foe, decided to attack the City of Puebla, which was not only fortified in its own right, but was protected by several well-constructed and strategically-placed defensive forts, all of them mounting heavy guns. A message from Napoleon III strengthened de Lorencez' hand, as the terms of the Convention of La Soledad had been repudiated in Paris as being 'not in keeping with French dignity'. At the same time, the Emperor stripped Admiral Jurien de la Graviere of even his diplomatic responsibilities, relegating him to the Naval Division, vesting diplomatic matters in the hands of de Saligny and military ones in those of de Lorencez.[13] To beef up his military arm, Napoleon III dispatched General Felix Douay to Mexico at the head of a small force of four hundred and thirty-one men.

Almonte, trying to position himself to the best advantage, issued a second Proclamation on 17 April and on 1 May, Manuel Serrano followed suit with a Proclamation of his own, declaring himself to be Governor of the Department of Veracruz, appointed by the 'Provisional President of the Republic, the honourable General D[on] Juan Almonte'.[14] It also came to the knowledge of the French that their ambitious protégé was preparing yet another Proclamation, intending to declare himself 'Supreme Chief of the Nation'.[15]

Clearly, this put the French were in a difficult position, their enemies determined to resist and their supposed friends ready to undermine them at any time. De Lorencez took his troops back to Orizaba, then on to Puebla. The French High Command completely misunderstood both the strength of the Mexicans' position and their will to win, and with a force far too small to get the job done, de Lorencez attacked Zaragoza's well-entrenched troops. Mainly made up of Zouaves, the French force was resoundingly defeated on 5 May and sent scurrying back to Orizaba. The jubilant Mexicans proclaimed the *Cinco de Mayo* as an historic battle.[16] Mid-month de Lorencez learned that Douay had landed at Veracruz.[17]

In Algeria, the officers of the Regiment Etranger, reading newspaper stories about the deteriorating turn of events, were asking Jeanningros the same kind of questions they had put to Butet and there was much excitement when a new Eagle and staff were received for their Regimental Standard. In 1860 the Minister of War had decided to replace the heavy bronze Eagles and a new design, in gilded aluminium, was approved by Napoleon III the following year. The Eagle, wings spread, stood on a rectangular base with the words 'Regiment Etranger' in raised letters. This topped the blue varnished staff, the foot of which took the form of an eagle's claw in polished brass.[18] The old bronze Eagle had gone through the Crimean and Italian campaigns, and its replacement was felt to be a sure indication that the regiment was again being prepared for foreign service.

The rumour mill moved into even higher gear when it was learned that the Emperor, realizing that he had in Mexico a far more serious problem than he had anticipated, decided that it could only be settled by a full-fledged Expeditionary Corps. General Elie-Frederic Forey was selected as Commander-in-Chief. He had had some experience with Line regiments in Algeria, and was a veteran of the Crimean and Italian Campaigns, a reasonably able officer, but a man who sometimes played favourites, and whose lack of knowledge of people and situations, and reluctance to take advice, could lead him into wrong decisions. The War Minister named General Douay, who was already in Mexico, and General Bazaine, who was still in France, as Forey's two Generals of Division. Forey did not particularly like Bazaine, who was given the 1st Division, and had once lodged an official complaint against him in the Crimea. Douay, who was given the Second Division, was part of Forey's circle, an unfortunate situation, which would require other officers to take sides, supporting either Forey or Bazaine, to the detriment of the service. In Sidi-bel-Abbes, the mess strategists declared that Bazaine, as an old Foreign Legion officer, would certainly want to have the Regiment Etranger with him, and even when the latest batch of French troops left for Mexico in June, and the Regiment Etranger was not among them, it was felt to be only a matter of time.

Individual officers had already taken their own steps to get to Mexico. Captain Paul-Amiable de Brian de Foussieres Fonteneuille, a name mercifully shortened by the Army to simply de Brian, had succeeded in transferring into the 62nd Regiment of the Line, and gone to Mexico with them, though he would rejoin his old regiment in due course. Sous-Lieutenant Zede had tried another method, a direct approach to Marshal Pellisier when he was on one of his periodic visits to Sidi-bel-Abbes. Pellisier, who was in a good mood, had known Zede's father and invited the young man to sit at his table in the mess. Wine and military reminiscences flowed freely and when Zede judged the time was ripe he asked the Marshal to transfer him to one of the Zouave battalions which was getting ready to leave for Mexico.

'You will have to follow your destiny,' Pellisier said not unkindly, though he was not a man who tolerated fools or distributed favours. 'You will go to Mexico when your regiment goes.'

On 2 July Marshal Randon recommended that the Regiment Etranger should be among the troops considered for service in Mexico, but they were not included in a Ministerial Dispatch two days later ordering the formation of a *Regiment de Marche* of six self-contained Companies of the *Tirailleurs Algeriens* for the Mexican Expeditionary Corps. The troopships were leaving Toulon with ever-increasing frequency and Military Chaplain Lanusse, off to his second war, sailed on one on 12 July. In Sidi-bel-Abbes excitement was high, but on 19 July, when the 81st Regiment of the Line, stationed at Oran, received the embarkation orders, there were none for the Regiment Etranger.

For the Foreign Legion this was just too much. It was decided to address a Petition to the Emperor. Colonel Jeanningros was almost certainly aware of the plan, but a Colonel could be replaced for an act of indiscipline. So could a Lieutenant-Colonel or a Major. These were individual officers, upon whom the wrath of officialdom could easily descend. Neither the original Petition to Napoleon III, nor any copy of it, appears to still be in existence,[19] so it is impossible to know exactly who signed it, but as officers serving on the Headquarters Staff would also have been vulnerable, it is unlikely that the Adjutant-Major, Captain Danjou, or any members of Jeanningros' Staff, appended their names. As it would be next to impossible to punish or transfer all of the more junior officers, it was agreed that the Petition would be signed by the Captains, Lieutenants and Sous-Lieutenants of the Regiment. Quite how it was intended to get it to Paris and the Emperor is unclear, but it fell instead into the hands of Colonel Faidherbe, the Commander of the Sub-Division of Sidi-bel-Abbes, and a few days later Jeanningros received a tart communication.

Sous-Lieutenant Edmond Campion, who had joined the Foreign Legion in late 1857, like many officers of his day, kept a personal journal and, perhaps with an eye to incorporating them in a book of memoirs, kept copies of documents he found interesting, including Faidherbe's reaction to the Petition, dated 28 July. It read:

> The subordinate officers of the Regiment Etranger, in by-passing official channels, and collectively addressing a petition to His Majesty the Emperor, seeking to take part in the Mexican campaign, have committed an act which does not conform to good discipline and military spirit. While the sentiment and action are noble and praiseworthy, the manner in which they expressed their desire directly to His Majesty is nevertheless contrary to regulations, and, because of that, is punishable. In consequence, the most senior Captain, Lieutenant and Sous-Lieutenant will be placed under simple arrest until the Colonel Commanding the Sub-Division has received orders from the General Commanding the Division concerning their disposition. This Order is not to be made known to the troops.[20]

This was a mere slap on the wrist from Faidherbe, but also a warning, as French Army punishments always tended to be increased as the paperwork went on up the line. When the file was reviewed by General Deligny, the Officer Commanding the Division of Oran, it produced a rather sterner response. Dated 31 July, and sent to Faidherbe to be forwarded to Jeanningros, it fixed punishment for a larger number of officers and delivered a smart rebuke to the Colonel of the Regiment and his senior officers.

> The three most senior officers of each grade in the Regiment Etranger will submit to four days arrest [*Deligny wrote*]. The officers will not be excused for any reason, and I am obliged to say that the Chief of the Corps, the Lieutenant-Colonel and the other senior officers are even more culpable than the subordinate officers. While not participating directly in these proceedings, it is shown by their abstention that they knew about it; they could not have been ignorant about what was going on in the regiment, so they knew. They are culpable, when they seek to hide behind the responsibilities with which they are charged, and I will not accept this. I desire that you will make known to the senior officers of the Regiment Etranger my disapproval of their conduct in this present matter.[21]

It appears that when the Petition and Deligny's ruling reached Marshal Randon in Paris he decided not to forward it to Napoleon III, and, for the time being, the matter went no further.

There was, however, no holding the enthusiasm of the Regiment Etranger in check, and the Emperor's Birthday Parade seemed an ideal moment for a further expression of patriotic fervour. Given the tight discipline of the Foreign Legion it has to be assumed that at the very least the junior officers knew, and probably even connived at, the 'spontaneous' demonstration, remembered in some detail by Sous-Lieutenant Diesbach, and recorded by him in his personal campaign diary.

> The fifteenth August 1862 – for the Emperor's Birthday – all of Sidi-bel-

> Abbes was in good humour [*he wrote*]. In the barracks, where everything was decked out and decorated with garlands of foliage, the soldiers of the Legion sang and drank while awaiting the arrival of the Colonel who, following tradition, comes, accompanied by his officers, to say a few words and drink a glass of wine to the health of the Emperor. This visit always precedes a very good meal[,] looked forward to by those whose legs can still carry them to the place assigned for the banquet. This day, one could see large placards at the windows, on which were written the numerous military successes of the regiment and all the campaigns, plus other things. The names of all the generals who had come from our ranks were also there. A single blank white placard was prominent. 'What is this, then? What does this big white contrivance mean?' the Colonel demanded. 'It is the place to write the Mexican Campaign,' he was told. And from all parts came the cry: 'Let's go to Mexico!'.[22]

Nothing was initially done about this new act of insubordination, which would certainly have come to the attention of Colonel Faidherbe, and no doubt quickly also reached the ears of General Deligny and then of Marshal Randon, who was known to be opposed to Napoleon III's Mexican adventure. He now decided that he must bring the matter of the Petition to the attention of the Emperor, and communicated the result of their interview directly to Jeanningros on 28 August.

> His Majesty was surprised to receive the Petition which the Officers of your Corps thought to address to him in contravention of all military regulations [*Randon wrote*]. Although His Majesty understands the noble sentiments which animated their action[,] he is not able to sanction such an act of indiscipline. He has done me the honour of having me transmit to you his instruction that the most senior Officers in each grade who are under your command are to be placed under arrest for a period of fifteen days. Nevertheless, His Majesty has also ordered me to look into the eventual possibility of the participation of the Regiment Etranger in the expedition to Mexico. He will make his decision known in due course.[23]

This time the punishment was increased from four days to fifteen. A few days later the first inspection of the newly-constituted Regiment Etranger as a single unit was conducted by General Deligny. There is some evidence that he favoured the regiment being sent to Mexico, and told Jeanningros that in the light of his satisfactory inspection he would send forward a favourable recommendation to Marshal Randon.[24]

Life at Sidi-bel-Abbes went on, and although general recruiting was still suspended, it was possible to sign engagement papers under certain circumstances. Abel Huart, a young Frenchman from Orleans, who had been in petty trouble with the authorities, had jumped at a suggestion that he should join the Foreign Legion rather than be sent to the *Bat d'Af*, and was intrigued with his new companions.

> [This was] a singular regiment, where the diversity of languages reminded one of the Tower of Babel, where all the classes of society, all the races were represented [*he wrote later*]. It had Belgians, Frenchmen, Italians, Americans, Englishmen, Spaniards, Negroes and even inhabitants of the Celestial Empire. Among these descendants of Sem, Cham and Japhet there were counts, princes, men with university degrees, qualified doctors; but one also found unfrocked priests, escaped convicts on the run, Corsicans who had 'done a skin,' as they put it, and preferred life in the regiment in preference to hiding out in the mountains.²⁵

Sergeant Mori, who had fought so gallantly at Ischeriden and in Italy, and had then quit the Foreign Legion to fight for the cause of Italian unity, was back, and he was certainly a real life prince, and a priest, though not unfrocked. There may well have been all the varieties that Huart claimed to have found among the mass of soldiers, perhaps typical of the make-up of the times, a conglomeration of nationalities and races, many anonymous in their names and their pasts, others simple men serving under their own names, their former occupations known.

The movement of troops to Mexico in successive convoys was closely monitored by the officers of the Regiment Etranger. General Bazaine went out in August, Colonel Ernest de Maussion embarked his 7th Regiment of the Line on the *Tilsitt* and the *Turenne*, but, despite regular rumours that the Regiment Etranger was also earmarked to become part of the Expeditionary Corps, nothing happened. Such news from Mexico as reached Paris appeared in the *Echo d'Oran* a few days later and was eagerly scanned and discussed.

General Forey had landed at Veracruz on 27 September with eight hundred and twenty men of the 20th Battalion of *Chasseurs a Pied*, at a time when the *vomito negro* was raging. It became generally known in France that he had lost a number of men to the disease, but few details were made public as the statistics were too shocking. The facts were that by the time he was ready to move inland, on 10 October, more than a third of his men had been sick. Only five hundred and fifteen were fit enough to march inland, and to help them retain their strength arrangements were made for their kit to be carried on mules. It had been decided to make three stops along the thirty-five-kilometre (twenty-mile) route to La Soledad, and then camp there. A further sixty-five men had to be hospitalized when they reached the little town and twenty kilometres (twelve miles) further on it was found necessary to spend two unplanned days at Palo Verde. Forey had fifteen more sick men by the time he reached Chiquihuite, and a further twenty along the road to Cordoba. He arrived at Orizaba, which was one hundred and thirty-six kilometres (eighty miles) from Veracruz, with just one hundred and eighty-two men, sixty-six of them being carried on mules. Only ten were completely well and able to march.²⁶

These were the sort of figures it was thought should be kept from the reading public. In the hope that their constitutions might better withstand exposure to the *vomito negro*, the *Tirailleurs Algeriens*, landing at Veracruz on 29 October, were immediately assigned to the *Terres Chaudes*.

In Sidi-bel-Abbes the hopes of the Regiment Etranger were continually raised and in November, Sous-Lieutenant Diesbach noted in his private journal: 'Big rumour in the air, and all ambitions are focused on promotion and victories!'[27] Once again it was a false alarm.

Officers with friends in Mexico received occasional letters and came to hear of their old colleague Captain de Brian, who was seeing considerable action with the 62nd Regiment of the Line. On 30 November he had been the senior officer with a convoy of eight wagons, guarded by three companies of his regiment, an effective force of one hundred and eighty-four men, when it was attacked close to La Rinconada by eight hundred *Juarista* regulars, both mounted and on foot, under the command of General Diaz Miron. The French troops gave a good account of themselves, killing one hundred and forty Mexicans before the action was broken off. This was the kind of thing about which his former companions in Algeria could only dream.

The rumours, perhaps a case of no smoke without fire, caused the Foreign Legion's recruiting to pick up and nobody looked very hard at twenty-eight-year-old Evariste Berg when he signed a two-year engagement on 27 December. He made no reference to the fact that his uncle was an officer in the regiment, or to having previous military service, though he had almost a decade of soldiering behind him, and six months earlier had been a Sous-Lieutenant in the 1st Regiment of Zouaves.

Born in St. Benoit on the Indian Ocean island of Réunion – also called Isle Bourbon – on 13 February 1834, Berg came from a well-to-do family with a military tradition. His father, Alexandre Louis Berg, was a Naval officer. His mother, the former Marie-Antoinette Rolland, had one brother who had been decorated in the field in Senegal, while the other was Major Charles-Elie Rolland of the Regiment Etranger. After receiving a good education and a matriculation certificate, Berg had decided to follow the family tradition and enlist.

France's *Troupes de Marine* were not Marines in the sense understood elsewhere, having been raised for Colonial Service and for guarding ports and coastal positions in Metropolitan France. Members of the *Infanterie de Marine* were colloquially know as *Marsouins* – Dolphins – and those of the *Artillerie de Marine* as *Bigors* – a contraction of *Bigorneau*, meaning Sea Snail. On 12 November 1852 Berg became a *Bigor*, signing on for seven years with the *Artillerie de Marine*, starting as a 2nd Class Cannoneer. He made Corporal on 21 July 1853, Sergeant on 1 April 1854 and Quartermaster Sergeant two days later. By this time the Crimean War had broken out and less than a week afterwards he went on board the steamship *Darien*, and would be involved in the largely indecisive campaign in the Baltic Sea. By the time an Anglo-French fleet had decided that attacks on the Russian coast were likely to be costly, and had settled instead for an assault on the Bomarsund fort on Russia's Aaland Islands – off the southwestern tip of Finland – Berg was serving on his fourth ship. He went ashore, south of the fort, with three thousand other French troops on 10 August, while an Anglo-French force landed to the north. In less than a week Bomarsund had been besieged, attacked and taken and its garrison, most of whom were Finns, marched away as prisoners-of-war.

Tiring of the *Artillerie de Marine*, Berg, who had been slightly wounded during the action at Bomarsund, was able to transfer into the 1st Zouaves on 27 June

1855 and embarked for the Crimea four days later. It meant starting from the bottom again, and hard fighting to boot, as the 1st Zouaves bore the brunt of the bloody assault on the Malakoff Redoubt on 8 September, the battle which effectively ended the siege of Sebastopol. Berg was promoted to Corporal on 1 April 1856 and Quartermaster Corporal on 6 August, at the time the regiment was leaving the Crimea to return to Africa. Sporting his campaign medal for the engagement at Bomarsund and Queen Victoria's Crimean Medal, he was promoted to Sergeant on 10 March 1857, Quartermaster Sergeant on 16 July, and served with the regiment in Algeria for the next two years.

Granted a Commission on 15 July 1859, when the 1st Zouaves were being sent to take part in the Italian Campaign, Berg fought at both Magenta – where the regiment particularly distinguished itself – and Solferino. The following year he was sent with a battalion of his regiment to Syria. However, his military evaluations in 1860, and again in 1861, were generally unfavourable. Interviewing officers were highly critical of his personal conduct and spoke of his 'bad behaviour' and 'habitual debauchery', characterizing him as 'a very bad officer', who was 'disrespectful to his comrades', and often unduly harsh on his subordinates. They admitted that he possessed certain military skills, but said that in some instances they were at best no more than adequate, and in others much less than what were required. He had also earned a reputation for associating with bad company.

Berg knew he was in trouble by the time he returned to Algeria and, in an effort to avoid a full inquiry into his behaviour, tried unsuccessfully to effect a transfer, but – as was tartly noted in an official document – he 'could not find a Chef de Corps who would consent to receive him.' Berg was relieved of his duties on 7 November 1861 and sent before a Council of Inquiry. Comprising five officers of the 1st Zouaves, it accepted into evidence a letter from Captain Desandre, who had been Berg's commanding officer in Syria. He stated that his former subordinate was 'very educated, very intelligent', and that while he had his faults, he might yet be able to reform. He admitted, however, that Berg was 'hot-headed, arrogant', and had got into the hands of moneylenders. Allegations had been made against him by a Zouave named Lambert, but Berg airily dismissed them as having come from 'a bad soldier.' The Council thought otherwise and by a vote of three-to-two, found him Guilty of 'habitual misconduct', Not Guilty – by a vote of four-to-one – of 'acts against discipline' and Guilty, by another vote of three-to-two, of 'acts against honour'.

The matter went up the line, and, at a hearing in Avignon in France, it was made clear to Berg that he was no longer wanted in the Zouaves. With the stigma of being cashiered staring him in the face, he 'offered to resign so as to be able to return to his family in Reunion'. Probably more to save embarrassment to his military relatives, and to the regiment, than out of consideration for the accused, this course of action was accepted on 30 May 1862. Berg probably did return home for a while, as some six months elapsed between his resignation from the 1st Zouaves and his signing engagement papers with the Regiment Etranger just after Christmas. He was once again starting from the bottom.[28]

The year 1863 was ushered in with the usual parties in the Officers' and Sous-Officiers' messes and with extra food for the men, and now there was a real excitement in the air. It was being apparently reliably reported that the War Ministry was preparing to send even more troops for the Expeditionary Corps in Mexico, and the Foreign Legion suddenly experienced a small flood of men anxious to sign engagement papers. They were a mixed bag, as was always the case, and some of them were very young.

Pharaon Clovis Van den Bulcke, a French youth from Lille, was only just seventeen, while a German, Johann Reus, was but a few months older, both below the official age for acceptance. Jean Timmermans, a Belgian, was eighteen-and-a-half, and Leon Gorski, the son of a Polish officer who had fled his own country after the Polish uprising against the Russians in 1830, and settled in Nimes, in the South of France, was only nineteen.[29] Other men, already serving in regular Regiments of the Line, began trying to effect transfers into the Regiment Etranger, which was difficult, but sometimes possible.

On 10 January a fine soldierly-looking man in his early thirties turned up at the Quartier Vienot in Sidi-bel-Abbes. His name, he told the officer who interviewed him, was Philippe Maine and he not only claimed twelve years of military service in Africa and the Crimea, with three different regiments, but said he had twice risen to be Quartermaster Sergeant and had never been broken to the ranks. It was an impressive – if unusual – record, and Maine was able to provide the necessary military paperwork to back it up.

The Foreign Legion knows Maine as Philippe, as given in his very detailed service record, with no middle name shown. Yet there is evidence that he answered to, or at least used, the first name of Louis, which might have been a middle name, or may simply have been one he liked and had adopted. A scrap of reminiscence by Robert Benoit, a family friend who knew him as Louis, describes Maine as being 'of average build, very small . . . [with] jet black hair' and with eyes 'lively, brilliant like a carbuncle under thin eyebrows'.[30]

Born at Mussidan in the Department of Dadogne in Southwestern France on 4 September 1830, with one short break Maine had followed the flag for a dozen years. His father, Joseph Maine, was a successful bootmaker, while his mother, the former Therese Felix, ran the Grand Hotel du Cheval Blanc. Young Philippe had been apprenticed to a maker of ropes, a profession which had little appeal. On 21 December 1850 he signed an engagement with the Regiment of Zouaves, arriving in Africa in the early days of January and being assigned to the 2nd Battalion. There was some rough soldiering against the Kabyles that year, the final armed clash of the campaign being the Zouaves' three hundred and thirtieth engagement in more than two decades of Algerian warfare. Maine was still a simple Zouave when the three Battalions were reorganized into three individual regiments in March 1852, and saw out his service at Oran with the 2nd Regiment. Seemingly, his engagement, which ended on 14 December of that year, had not provided whatever it was he was seeking. He remained on the strength of the regiment for a week making up his mind whether or not to re-enlist, then decided against it, and returned to France.

The outbreak of the Crimean War settled things for Maine. He would go back to soldiering. On 25 April 1854 he joined the 4th Battalion of the *Chasseurs a Pied*, though if he had hoped he would be shipped at once to fight the Russians he must have been disappointed, for he was promptly sent to Algeria and it was not until 13 January 1855 that the regiment was mobilized for the war. Maine was promoted to Corporal two months later. On 7 June, 1855, when the French launched their successful attack on the Mamelon hill – the Little Redan – in front of Sebastopol, he volunteered for the 'ladder party' to carry scaling ladders across the open ground between the French trenches and the Russian strongpoint. The attack was successful and he was commended for his 'heroism' and promoted to Sergeant eight days later. He became Quartermaster Sergeant on 19 August and less than a month later volunteered for the 'ladder party' needed for the assault on the Malakoff Redoubt, during which he was slightly wounded in the face.

Maine was named a Chevalier of the Legion of Honour on 16 April 1856, received Queen Victoria's Crimean Medal and returned to Africa with his regiment in the middle of the following month. He served until 14 November 1857, leaving the *Chasseurs a Pied* – 'at his demand,' as his military file puts it – as a simple soldier. He probably went home to France, but not for long, as he engaged for a second time in the 2nd Zouaves on 28 March 1858, making Corporal less than two months later. When he heard that the 1st Battalion of the *Infanterie Legere d'Afrique* – the *Bat d'Af* – was in need of experienced soldiers of his rank he transferred into the regiment on 22 December the same year. He was a Sergeant some six months later and a Quartermaster Sergeant after little more than a year's service.

If it was action Maine had wanted, he had played his hand badly. By leaving the 2nd Zouaves in 1858 he missed going to Italy with them the following year. Certainly it was the 1st Regiment – rather than the 2nd – which provided a Battalion for Syria in 1860, but he also missed going to Mexico with the regiment in the early part of 1862. Heeding the now strong rumours that the Foreign Legion would soon be crossing the Atlantic, Maine left the *Bat d'Af* on 8 January 1863 and was interviewed at Sidi-bel-Abbes the following day. It was made clear to him that he could not transfer in with his old rank, though he was doubtless also told that early promotion was almost a certainty, even though he must start as a common Fusilier. He signed his engagement papers the next day. So the man who wore the Cross of a Chevalier of the Legion of Honour on his jacket became, on 10 January, a simple soldier once more. Coincidentally, it was the twelfth anniversary of his arrival in Africa as a young Zouave eager for an introduction to Algerian soldiering.[31]

7
'I leave, resolved to do my duty'

It took just four days for Philippe Maine's papers to be checked and his claims verified. He was then promoted to Corporal,[1] as was the ex-Zouave officer Evariste Berg.[2] The very next day, 15 January, General Deligny in Oran sent Colonel Faidherbe the news everyone had been hoping for.

> The Regiment Etranger is to go to Mexico and will probably embark during the last days of this month [*the Order read*]. It will move without delay to Oran, the point of embarkation. It will be commanded by the Colonel and the Lieutenant-Colonel and will be organized into two battalions, each of seven Companies.
>
> The effective will comprise *La Musique*, the Company *hors-rang* (as regularly constituted) the *cantinieres* and sutlers, and will number as nearly as possible two thousand men.
>
> You will choose the strongest men in terms of good morals and physique. Officers *a la suite* will accompany the battalions. Arrange the necessary transfers and proceed preferably as laid down in regulations. Make the arrangements for running the administration of the Corps, then send me a copy immediately.
>
> The Regiment Etranger will assign mules on the basis of Regulations.
>
> Keep me current with this information.[3]

Faidherbe transmitted Deligny's orders to Colonel Jeanningros four days later and provided additional specifics. The regiment had an allocation of thirty-seven mules, on the basis of four for the Headquarters and two for each of the fourteen Companies. The ambulance and the regiment's *cantinieres*, and the sutlers, who ran the canteens for the soldiers, were allocated four mules, as was the Company *Hors-Rang*, made up of administrative soldiers, like the postmaster and tailors, and one was allocated for the armourer, to carry the tools of his essential trade. Each soldier was to be provided with new kit – clothing and accoutrements – and weapons. On campaign, in addition to his regulation allowance of ammunition, each man would carry a reserve of sixty cartridges. There was to be an issue of certain items deemed sufficient for a year's campaigning: three shirts, three pairs of shoes and three pairs of leggings. Extra *bidons* – water-bottles – bowls, light tents and half-blankets were also to be drawn from stores.[4]

All was activity, the inevitable confusion of a regiment ordered overseas at short notice. Although nominally two thousand six hundred men strong, the Regiment Etranger was under-strength and Jeanningros knew he would be hard put to muster two seven-Company battalions. It was a time for thinning out the three battalions, picking only those Legionnaires who could be reasonably expected to give of their best in an overseas campaign. Some of the fittest men in the 3rd Battalion were transferred into the 1st and 2nd Battalions. Many of the long service Legionnaires, veterans of the Crimea, Algeria and Italy, were devastated at being told they were now considered too old for a foreign war, where much would be demanded of the troops, but there was no appeal.

For a few the Foreign Legion was a family affair. Sergeant-Major Joseph Ceccioni had joined in 1832, and his three sons had followed him into the regiment. Hippolyte had been killed before Sebastopol in 1855, Marius was now serving as a Sergeant and another son, Auguste, was the *enfant de troupe* of the 2nd Regiment Etranger from 1852 to 1863. All went to Mexico, but the strict selection criteria made it impossible for Jeanningros to get even close to Deligny's call for 'as nearly as possible two thousand men'.

The ideal size of a Company was considered to be between one hundred and one hundred and twenty, and there were not enough men for fourteen Companies of that size. In the end, Jeanningros decided to leave the 6th Companies of each Battalion behind. They would be made up of young and as yet untrained men felt unlikely to be able to stand up to the expected rigours of the campaign, the old veterans, men who were nearing the end of their time and did not wish to re-engage and those whose records showed them to be troublemakers or unstable. They would remain in Sidi-bel-Abbes.

A new officer arrived, Captain Auguste Ballue, wearing the Cross of a Chevalier of the Legion of Honour on his tunic. Born on 16 December 1835 in Conti, Ballue had graduated from the *Ecole Imperiale Speciale Militaire* at the age of twenty, fought in the Crimean War and was a Captain when he went to Italy three years later. His progress had been rapid and Zede remembered him as being remarkable for his 'intelligence and also for his deportment and manners'. This was a time, too, for promotions and appointments within the regiment and these were announced on 21 January. Sergeant-Major Jean Vilain was to be Commissioned a Sous-Lieutenant.[5] He asked to be assigned to the 3rd Company of the 1st Battalion. Sous-Lieutenant Adolphe Gans was promoted to Lieutenant, as was Zede. Former Sergeant-Major Clement Maudet, fifteen years in the Foreign Legion, a Sous-Lieutenant since 1860, and now wearing the kind of beard favoured by Napoleon III and referred to as an 'Imperial', was selected for a signal honour. Zede, looking back over the years, would later remark that Maudet was 'one of those old soldiers of the kind they liked then to choose as Regimental Standard-Bearers',[6] meaning 'old' in terms of service, rather than age, for Maudet was only thirty-four years old.

Each man was issued with a short dark blue jacket, known as a 'basquine', with a collar in pale yellow, piped in blue. The front, sides and cuffs of the jackets were piped in red, as were the loops for the heavy fringed epaulettes. These were colour coded: red for Grenadiers, yellow for Voltigeurs and green with red edging for Fusiliers. Buttoned down the front, the jacket also had three brass buttons at the wrists, all stamped 'Regiment Etranger'. The tips of the high collars of the Voltigeurs featured an embroidered *cor de chasse* – hunting horn – while those of the Grenadiers featured the Foreign Legion's seven-flamed grenade insignia. The traditional red trousers of the French infantryman ended just below the knee, so that they could be tucked into leather leggings. The gaiters were made of unbleached or grey canvas. A second pair of trousers, in white or unbleached canvas, was also issued, as was a dark blue cravat. A *ceinture* – a long cloth sash, which wrapped many times around the waist – came in various colours, but was most often red. The uniform conformed to regulations issued on 3 March 1860. The Legionnaires' kepi was blue and red, with a square peak and was issued with a white light canvas cover, with a *couvre-nuque* – neck cloth – which hung down behind to protect the nape of the neck from the sun, in the style of what the British Army in India called a 'Havelock'. Rank was denoted by broad red stripes on the sleeves.

The men received a *bidon*, to be slung over the left shoulder on a black leather strap so that it fell below waist level on the right side, and a *musette* – leather pouch – on a black strap, slung over the right should so that it fell at waist level on the left side. A black leather belt with a brass buckle was worn over the *ceinture* and had a black leather cartridge box attached on the left side at the front. The bayonet, in a black leather scabbard with brass fittings, was carried on the left side. The canvas and leather *sac* – haversack – was the Legionnaire's mobile home, containing compartments for rations, spare ammunition, the pair of trousers not being worn, shirts, underwear and cleaning brushes. It was topped off with the rolled grey *capote* – greatcoat – half of a two-man tent and tent poles and each man carried part of his squad's equipment, either a *marmite* – large cooking pot – or a large *bidon*.

The 1857 muzzle-loading fusil, which had been issued just before the Italian Campaign, would also be the weapon of Fusiliers in the Mexican Campaign. It had a rifled barrel and fired a cylindrical seventeen millimetre bullet and could be fitted with a long steel bayonet. The Grenadiers were also armed with the 1857 fusil, but with a sabre bayonet, while the Voltigeurs had the newer and more effective Mine rifle and bayonet.

Officers were issued with a dark blue frock coat reaching to just below the knee, with their rank indicated on the sleeves in embroidered swirls, known as Hungarian knots. The collar was yellow, with the seven-flamed grenade embroidered on it. The coat, with its nine brass buttons stamped 'Regiment Etranger,' was generally worn open over a dark blue waistcoat, whose top button was usually left open as a matter of style. A black bow tie was worn, with the strings dangling. The blue *ceinture* was worn with a black leather belt over it. The uniform regulations had also been laid down on 3 March 1860 for the *Armee d'Afrique*, and modified on 14 November 1861, but even in Algeria some leeway had been unofficially permitted for individual taste, and this was to be even more the case in Mexico.[7]

Officers' sabres were of various official models – particularly those of 1845, modified in 1855 – usually the one being issued at the time of an officer's Commission, and they were expected to provide their own handguns. Lefaucheux's 1858 model six-shot single-action percussion revolver was popular and fired an eleven millimetre bullet. The Perrin 1859 model looked clumsy, but was also a six-shot percussion revolver of the same calibre, and had the advantage of being double-action.

Decorations – usually grades of the Legion of Honour – were worn by both officers and men, the medals on the left side of the outer garment, over the heart.

In making his dispositions, Colonel Jeanningros naturally kept the Foreign Legion under his direct overall control, and giving command of the 1st Battalion to Commandant (Major) Eloi Regnault. It would be based at the Regimental Headquarters, wherever that was to be. The 2nd Battalion would be under Lieutenant-Colonel Jean-Baptiste Giraud, wherever it was to be based, with Commandant Gustave Munier in day-to-day command.

A number of the regiment's officers were elderly, and would be remaining at Sidi-bel-Abbes, and there was a shortage of senior subalterns. Jeanningros made his appointments with that in mind. The on-paper position of Headquarters Lieutenant could not be filled, so it went to the Swiss artist Sous-Lieutenant Henri-Guido Kauffmann. The position of Pay Officer called for a Captain, but without a suitable one available Jeanningros chose Lieutenant Valentin Barera, with Sous-Lieutenant Philippe Galloni d'Istria to assist him, while also filling the position of Colonel's Secretary. Sous-Lieutenant Maudet, as Regimental Standard-Bearer, would also be one of the Headquarters Officers.

Captain Gustave Saussier commanded the 1st Battalion's Company of Grenadiers, with Sous-Lieutenant Charles Pertusati as one of his junior officers. Captain Charles Cabossel commanded the Company of Voltigeurs, assisted by the experienced Lieutenant Philippe Jaudon. The two key Companies of the Centre were both led by seasoned officers. Captain Jean Cazes commanded the 3rd Company, with newly-promoted Lieutenant Adolphe Gans and newly-commissioned Sous-Lieutenant Jean Vilain as his subordinates. The 5th Company was placed under the command of the recently-arrived Captain Auguste Ballue, with two Sous-Lieutenants, Edmond Campion and Gabriel de Diesbach, as his subordinates. Captain Jules Dubosq commanded the 2nd Battalion's Company of Voltigeurs, with Sous-Lieutenant Pascase Achilli as his subordinate.

The *a-la-suite* – unassigned – officers included Captain Jean Baptiste Munos de Recuerdo, Duke of Montmoro, who was a member of the Spanish Royal Family, Sous-Lieutenant Ernest Milson von Bolt, a member of the Royal Family of Prussia, and Sous-Lieutenant Joseph Rehmann, a Polish-born officer who had fought against the French at Magenta as a member of the Austrian Army.[8]

In all, just over fourteen hundred and fifty men were selected for the campaign and the Companies which mustered for review on 24 January, looked somewhat different from those of five days earlier, when Deligny's orders had been delivered by Colonel Faidherbe.

The Regiment Etranger in Sidi-bel-Abbes would now to be commanded by Major Rolland, and would consist of only the 3rd Battalion, under Battalion Commander Jules Delettre, and the 6th Companies of both the 1st and 2nd Battalions. While it was not exactly a regimental fragment of geriatric officers and over-the-hill soldiers, neophytes, riffraff and misfits, it was certainly one which had been stripped of its best and fittest men. Among the 3rd Battalion's young officers being left behind in Algeria, and fuming about it, was Lieutenant Zede.

On Monday, 26 January, Colonel Jeanningros, preceded by *La Musique*, led the 1st Battalion through the streets of Sidi-bel-Abbes, en route to Oran and the port of Mers-el-Kebir. Sous-Lieutenant Maudet made his first official appearance as Standard-Bearer for the regiment. The new gilded aluminium Eagle, glittering in the sun, was atop the new blue staff. Yet the Standard itself was the one which the 2nd Etranger had received on 15 August 1857, and which had gone with them to Italy two years later.[9] It was the responsibility of the Directorate of Artillery to make new Regimental Standards, but although the Regiment Etranger had existed as an entity for thirteen months none had been made for it, which was especially disappointing, as the mistakes in the names and positioning of the Battle Honours could have been corrected. Moreover, on 20 January 1861, the 2nd Etranger had been awarded the Battle Honours MAGENTA (1859) and SOLFERINO (1859) for the Italian Campaign, but it had been decided that these would not be added to those on the existing Regimental Standard, and would have to wait until a new one was prepared.[10]

Sidi-bel-Abbes was bedecked with flags and bunting and the citizenry turned out to watch as the regiment passed by, stepping out to a stirring new march – as yet unnamed – composed by *Chef de Musique* Monsieur Wilhelm. They arrived at Oran two days later, just as the 2nd Battalion under Lieutenant-Colonel Giraud was marching out of Sidi-bel-Abbes. The two battalions were reunited in camp outside Oran on 30 January, where the final dispositions of personnel were made.

The officers and men had an opportunity to shop for whatever they could afford, and Captain Danjou found a local photographic studio, where he had his picture taken to send to his family in Chalabre. In a typical photographer's set-up of the day, the subject posed between a small table, on which lay a book, and a piece of wooden-pillared furniture, over which a blanket had been draped. In the photograph, Danjou, with his strong face, high forehead and flowing moustache and goatee, looks manfully into the middle distance.[11] He appears formal, rather than heroic, but the photograph captures well what Corporal Maine would later describe as 'his fine intelligent head [and] the energy, tempered with gentleness'.[12] On the breast of his tunic is the Cross of a Chevalier of the Legion of Honour, while his right arm is bent, the fingers gripping the buttons of the tunic. His officer's kepi is under his left arm, which hangs by his side, the articulated wooden hand sheathed in a white glove.

On 7 February the Regiment Etranger was reviewed by General Deligny, who knew he would please the troops if he inserted into his speech at least a passing reference to their Regimental Standard, so he did, unburdening himself of a rolling oration:

> Soldiers!
> I have come to take a last look at your organization and to assure myself that you are completely provided with the equipment and materials necessary for going on this campaign.
>
> You leave in excellent condition, strongly constituted, well commanded. You have worthy leaders and valiant officers. Be disciplined and obedient and I am confident that success will be yours. Although your ranks are filled

with men from many nations, there are no rivalries of nationality, of race, of religion and you live as brothers, formed into a single family, united by the sentiment of devotion and faith in your flag. France has no fears in conferring her honour to you before the enemy. Be proud of this distinction, which is so amply justified. You are the only remaining one of our ancient Foreign Regiments.

Your flag does not have sufficient space to contain all your noble Battle Honours. It has figured with distinction in all the battles and actions where you have assisted in our time.

It is not only a glorious emblem, it also has a particular significance. It is the symbol of sanctuary and of hospitality. It encompasses the generous ideas of France, who has been given the mission of spreading them throughout the world, and you will be the living ambassadors of these ideas in Mexico. Show a firm hand, inspire people with your devotion.

Whenever your war or rallying cry has been heard it has given you many victories, in the mountains of the Atlas, on the plain of the Crimea and in Italy.

Vive l'Empereur![13]

The following day the troopships *Saint-Louis* and *Wagram* hove-to in the roadstead at Mers-el-Kebir and began disembarking the men of the 24th Regiment of the Line, who were to replace the Foreign Legion in Algeria. The *Saint-Louis*, built in 1848, had taken part in both the Baltic and Black Sea campaigns of the Crimean War, been converted to a mixed steam and sailing vessel and was commanded by Captain Duroch. The *Wagram*, an older ship, built in 1833 and originally called the *Bucentaure*, had been converted to a mix of steam and sail in 1852 and was commanded by Captain Huget de Majoureaux.

The officers of the Regiment Etranger were hosted by Colonel de Brayere of the *Chasseurs d'Afrique* of the Oran Garrison, some of whose men would be travelling to Mexico on the *Saint-Louis*. On Monday, 9 February, the Legionnaires marched from their camp to the port to begin embarking. Their send-off left a vivid impression on Corporal Frank M'Alevey, who was going to Mexico as a member of the 2nd Battalion.

> The inhabitants of Oran turned out *en masse* to see the troops embark – not that the sight was in any way novel to the good people of Oran, for it was the third time in less than ten years they had seen the same regiment embarking at the same place for the Crimean and Italian campaigns [*he recalled*]. There were no loud *hurrahs* or vivas, either by the troops or the people, but there was a good deal of fervent hand-shaking, and kissing and sobbing between the young fellows of the regiment and the mesdemoiselles and senoritas . . .[14].

Sergeant-Major Henri Tonel ran a critical eye over the 1st Battalion's 3rd Company, drawn up on the wharf, and was probably not unpleased with what he saw. The Company, like all the others, was slightly under-strength, but it had a good mix of tried veterans, solid soldiers with experience, and young men, some of them very young. Tonel himself, a large man who cut an imposing figure, was a *Lignard*, a slang term meaning that he had not come up through the ranks of the Foreign Legion, having transferred in from a Regiment of the Line, as was the case with Corporal Maine and a number of others.

The three officers had considerable fighting experience: Captain Jean Cazes had graduated from Saint-Cyr in 1852 at the age of twenty and joined the 65th Regiment of the line, transferring into the Foreign Legion in 1860. The heavily-bearded Lieutenant Gans had seen service in the 1857 Kabyle Campaign, in which he had been wounded, and in Italy. Sous-Lieutenant Jean Vilain, the up-from-the-ranks veteran of the Crimea, Algeria and Italy, now also wore an 'Imperial', the mustachios upturned, and sported the Cross of a Chevalier of the Legion of Honour on his chest.

Tonel's own immediate subordinates reflected the mix of veterans and younger men: Sergeant Jean Germeys, a thirty-one-year-old Belgian, decorated in the Crimea and wounded in Italy; Sergeant Karl Schaffner, also thirty-one, a Swiss from Berne who had served in Italy; Sergeant Alfred Palmaert, another Belgian; and Sergeant Marie Morziki, French-born son of a Polish officer father.

The six Corporals likewise reflected the veteran/young man mix: Corporal Heindrich Pinzinger, a Bavarian, had been nine years in the Foreign Legion and had served in the Crimea and Italy; Corporal Adolfi Delcaretto, Algerian-born – a *Pied Noir* – was a twenty-eight-year-old from Oran; Corporal Aime Favas, also twenty-eight, was a French-speaking Swiss; Corporal Karl Magnin was a twenty-year-old Austrian; Corporal Evariste Berg, aged twenty-nine and less than a month in the rank, had been in the Crimea, Italy and Syria with the Zouaves, and had been an officer; Corporal Philippe Maine, thirty-two years old and also newly promoted, had been a Zouave and later a Sous-Officier in the *Chasseurs a Pied* and the *Bat d'Af*.

Among the Fusiliers were the Crimean veterans Friedrich Fritz, a Wurttemberger with more than ten years in the Foreign Legion, and the oldest man in the company, and Gottfried Wensel, a Prussian, wounded after Sebastopol fell, and also with more than ten years of service. There was the former sailor Jean-Baptiste Verjus, a Parisian, and another Frenchman, Claude Billod, from Dijon, who had engaged at the age of nineteen, made Corporal, then Sergeant at twenty and been broken to the ranks after a mere six months. The Belgians included Victor Catteau, Laurent Constantine and Jean-Baptiste Leonard. Hartog De Vries was a Dutchman from Amsterdam, Aloysio Bernardo a Spaniard from Asturias. Standing in front of the 3rd Company as it was drawn up for inspection was *Tambour* Casimir Lai, the Sardinian, a young man, but even so a veteran of the Italian Campaign.

When Colonel Jeanningros inspected the 3rd Company, accompanied by Commandant Regnault and Captain Adjutant-Major Danjou, he cannot have been unimpressed by the number of medals glinting in the morning sun, and by their variety.

As Captain Cazes was embarking on the *Saint-Louis* with the 3rd Company he slipped on the gangplank and fell heavily, badly twisting his back. Dr. Alexandre

Rustegho, the Medicine Aide-Major, or regimental physician, recommended that he should be hospitalized, but Cazes begged to be allowed to go with the regiment, saying that the rest he would get on the voyage would undoubtedly be therapeutic. He was carried aboard on a stretcher and taken to a cabin. The official record shows that Colonel Jeanningros, the Headquarters Staff, *La Musique* and the six Companies of the 1st Battalion embarked with a strength of twenty-one officers, seven hundred and sixty-one Legionnaires and three *cantinieres*.[15] Sous-Lieutenant Campion, who had a penchant for detail, reported thirty-four officers and seven hundred and sixty-three men, plus a detachment of sixty-one *Chasseurs d'Afrique*, two hundred and three Zouaves and a crew of four hundred and thirty-one, a total, by his count, of one thousand four hundred and ninety-two men.[16] Lieutenant-Colonel Giraud and the 2nd Battalion embarked on the *Wagram* with a total of twenty-seven officers, six hundred and seventy-one Legionnaires and five *cantinieres*.[17] The officers' horses and the regiment's mules and equipment were carefully loaded on board the *Finistere*, under the watchful eye of Captain Tardin Esteve, whose vessel had already transported many animals to Mexico.

The next day, as the shores of Algeria slipped from sight at the beginning of what would be a forty-eight day voyage, the men of the Regiment Etranger on the *Saint-Louis* stood on deck and sang *Eugenie*, a haunting ballad dedicated to the Empress.

> Eugenie, with tears in our eyes,
> We have come to say goodbye.
> We leave in the morning,
> Under a cloudless sky.
> We leave for Mexico.
> We go with the wind in the sails.
> Adieu then, pretty Eugenie.
> We will be back in a year.[18]

Cruising past Gibraltar and the 'Pillars of Hercules', with Europe on the starboard side and the tip of Africa on the port, little could they know that more than half of them would be dead within the year, and that very few of this original draft of a little over fourteen hundred men would be alive to return to Algeria at the end of the desperately hard four-year campaign.

The *Saint-Louis* and *Wagram* used steam or sail as the winds dictated as they headed west. The Legionnaires occupied cramped quarters, going barefoot like the sailors, their days punctuated by the morning parade on deck for prayers and the announcement of punishments for malefactors, and the trumpet calls announcing mealtimes.

While the senior Army officers were always responsible for their men on board, the Captains of the troopships were the overall authority, and their rules sometimes caused ill-feeling with prickly soldiers. Army officers were banned from the wardrooms except at mealtimes and on an earlier voyage of the *Wagram* Captain Alexis de La Hayrie, on his way to Mexico with a Zouave battalion, had unthinkingly wandered into one of them, looking for some water, and promptly been placed under arrest by the ship's second-in-command.

'Very well,' de La Hayrie, a hot-headed Breton, had responded icily. 'You are within your rights, and I submit to your authority – but once we are back on land I will again be your equal, and I warn you that I will kill you.'

De La Hayrie, who would leave the Zouaves for the *Tirailleurs Algeriens* and then become an outstanding Battalion Commander with the Regiment Etranger, was known to be a first-class pistol shot and an expert swordsman. In Veracruz, Admiral Jurien de la Graviere heard of the affair and forbade the duel, threatening to have de La Hayrie returned to Algeria on the first available ship if he did not drop the matter.[19]

The Legionnaires' only entertainment came from singing, often to the accompaniment of music from home-made instruments, and they eagerly looked forward to the first landfall, the Portuguese island of Madeira, which was a coaling station for French vessels crossing the Atlantic to Mexico. Corporal M'Alevey spoke years later of having come on deck on the morning of 16 February, when the *Wagram* anchored in the harbour of Funchal, and being struck by the beauty of the island. He was given permission to go ashore at midday, and while he considered that the town had little to offer the tourist, he visited the local Franciscan Convent and marvelled at the beauty of the flowers and shrubs blooming beside the roads.[20] Officers were permitted to disembark, ate meals in the town's little restaurants, drank some of the sticky sweet Madeira wine and returned to their ships when the coaling was completed.

The crossing of the Tropic of Cancer was an occasion for levity on every French vessel heading for Mexico. Plays were put on, with skits and songs. The *Tirailleurs Algeriens* had staged a popular entertainment of the time called 'The Corporal and the Country' on board the *Jura*,[21] en route to Mexico in March 1862 and a Captain Bochet of the 7th Regiment of the Line, on board the *Tilsitt* in September, went through the ritual involving *Pere Tropique* and his acolytes. The junior officers, wearing old clothes and huge hats, sat on a plank over a large tub of water. There was a ritual 'shaving' with a giant wooden razor, which had to be kissed, and then the officer 'on trial' was charged with having tried to win the heart of a sailor's wife. The response of 'I am guilty' resulted in immediately being pushed over backwards into the tub of water. However, the prompt production of five francs to pay the 'fine' saved the victim from a dunking, though it resulted in him being doused with flour or powdered rice.[22] It is likely that the ceremonies were little different for the junior officers of the Regiment Etranger on board the *Saint-Louis* and the *Wagram*. On its previous voyage the *Saint-Louis* had carried the 95th Regiment of the Line, whose men had only one uniform, so were not allowed to engage in any horse-play involving water. The officers, however, had a change of kit and *Pere Tropique*'s acolytes had subjected them to the usual dunking.[23] Although no firsthand account has survived concerning the Regiment Etranger's involvement in this maritime tradition, it is known that Sergeant-Major Tonel of the 3rd Company, a former professional comedian and actor, presented an entertainment of folk songs and dances by Legionnaires from many countries on the *Saint-Louis* for the 'Crossing of the Line' on 22 February.

Once in the tropics, with their steady winds, the sails alone provided sufficient power for the ships and the boilers were shut down. As they neared the chain of islands of the eastern Caribbean flying fish and patches of seaweed provided interest for the Legionnaires. The French at the time tended to give distances in *lieues* – equal to four kilometres, or two-and-a-half miles – and on 4 March, finding a quiet place to write, Captain Danjou began a letter to one of his brothers.

> We left Oran on 10 February; the 16th we were at Madeira and tomorrow[,] 5th March[,] we will reach Martinique, where will spend a short time to give some leisure to the men, horses and mules [*he wrote in his right-sloping, careful handwriting*]. We still have 700 *lieues* to go; there are already 1,300 behind us. We will be separated by a distance of 2000 *lieues* by the time I arrive at the end of my sea voyage. We should arrive at Veracruz about the 28th. At sea all the days resemble each other . . .
>
> Adieu. I leave, resolved to do my duty and more than my duty . . . .[24]

The little convoy sailed into the harbour at Fort-de-France the following day and the Regiment Etranger disembarked from the *Saint-Louis* and the *Wagram*, while their mules and officers' horses came ashore from the *Finistere*. The next six days, camped on the savannah, were a welcome relief from the confined space on board ship, and the break seemed too short. Medical wisdom had decided that the peaked kepi was less than satisfactory for the tropical sun. Apart from having to be present for the issuing of a type of straw hat used by French sailors, considerable freedom was allowed. A statue of Josephine Bonaparte stood in a prominent place in the city and the women of Martinique enjoyed a reputation as the most beautiful in the world. Certainly, many were hospitable. Officers avoided camp living by taking rooms in boarding houses and it was as well for Sous-Lieutenant Diesbach that he made a friend named Andrinetta, for she took care of him when he came down suddenly with fever. The day before the *Saint-Louis* was to sail she took Dr. Romain to her house to examine Diesbach, who was promptly told that he was too sick to continue his journey and was sent off to hospital. The Regiment Etranger left on 11 March without him.[25]

In Mexico, General Forey and his two Divisional Generals, Bazaine and Douay, had been gradually gathering enough troops, eventually twenty-six thousand of them, to stage an attack on Puebla, and by 17 March had succeeded in investing the city and its various protective outlying forts. General Comonfort was known to be in the vicinity with a strong Republican force, and four days later was engaged in a clash with troops under General Leonardo Marquez, a Mexican who had rallied to the French. Then Forey ordered the digging of a series of trenches to ring Puebla, with the intention of keeping General Jesus Gonzalez Ortega from attempting a breakout, while the besiegers began destroying the outposts. All this had stretched supply lines dangerously thin, as relatively little food could be obtained locally and all war supplies had to be brought up from the coast, but it was obviously only a matter of time before the city would be beaten or starved into submission.

The passage of the *Saint-Louis*, *Wagram* and *Finistere* westward across the Caribbean Sea, then north through the Yucatan Passage, with the tip of Cuba on the starboard side and the Yucatan on the port, was dull and uneventful. The ships sailed on and fifteen days after leaving Martinique the coast of Mexico came in view and those on deck could see the snow-capped cone of Mount Orizaba. A little later the convoy passed the sinisterly-named Isla de los Sacrificios, once a religious site for the Indians, but now the place where the French had buried victims of the *vomito negro* and other fevers which had decimated earlier military arrivals. Some wag had named it the 'Garden of Acclimatization'.

The troopships arrived off Veracruz on 26 March and the regiment disembarked the following day, the Legionnaires climbing down rope ladders into small boats to go ashore, where their impressions of the town were anything but favourable.

> In my opinion a more God-forsaken looking place there is not in the world [*Corporal M'Alevey would say later*]. The town was built on an arid plain, and the whole coast as far as the eye can see, presents nothing but barren sand hills to the view, with here and there a patch of grovelling brushwood, that but helps to make the sterility conspicuous . . . The bay and the beach was strewn with the hulls and masts of seventeen large ships, that had been wrecked a year or two previous, during a gale from the north.[26]

The Regiment Etranger marched through Veracruz and set up camp on the edge of town. Colonel Jeanningros and his Headquarters Staff were soon closeted with Colonel de Maussion of the 7th Regiment of the Line, who commanded the Reserve Brigade, of which the Regiment Etranger was to become part. It had been assumed by the officers and men of the Foreign Legion that they would be marched briskly westward through Cordoba and Orizaba and would join the besieging army outside Puebla. Now, however, Jeanningros was told that General Forey had decided that the regiment would have overall responsibility for guarding the road through the *Terres Chaudes* from Veracruz to Chiquihuite, escorting convoys and groups of travellers, and protecting the construction workers pushing westward with a narrow gauge railway, intended to ultimately link the coast with Mexico City, and that he could expect a long stay in the unhealthy lowlands.

'I had to leave the foreigners, in preference to the French, in a position where there was more sickness than glory to acquire,' Forey, who had little liking for the Foreign Legion, was reported to have said.[27]

Jeanningros protested, of course, but the orders were confirmed, and briefings were given on the key components of the regiment's assignment, particularly the road into the interior and the *vomito negro*.

The Royal Highway ran westwards a relatively short distance from Veracruz, then forked. The most direct route to Puebla was often called the Orizaba Road, to differentiate it from the more northerly one, known as the Jalapa Road. The Orizaba Road passed through La Soledad, where the ill-starred tripartite conference with the Mexicans had been held a year earlier, then on to Chiquihuite, Cordoba and Orizaba, and ultimately to Puebla and then Mexico City. It was an old Indian track and had been marked on maps as far back as 1590, but had only been a recognized road for about eighty years. Prior to that travellers to Mexico had gone via the northern road through La Rinconada and Jalapa. American General Winfield Scott had chosen the Jalapa Road during the U.S. invasion less than two decades earlier, and Bazaine had used it for his own move westward the previous year. Both roads had their adherents, and the Jalapa Road had dominated traffic for almost four centuries, until the Orizaba Road had finally been improved, and rivers and ravines bridged where necessary, as a result of the efforts of the Consulado, an association of businessmen involved in the Veracruz–Mexico City trade.

Jeanningros was told that the Orizaba Road ran through swampy ground and scrubland, criss-crossed by deep gullies – called *barrancas* – which were torrents in the rainy season, dust baths in the dry one. This was the occasional hunting ground for the Mexican Republican Army, but mostly for the numerous guerilla bands, some of them loyal to the Liberal regime of President Juarez, others mere *bandidos*, out for loot and blood. The French convoys moving through the *Terres Chaudes* were constant targets, and there was a depressing catalogue of successful or partially-successful attacks on them. The Regiment Etranger would have the most dangerous section of the Orizaba Road, the sixty kilometres (thirty-six miles) across the fever swamps and plains from Veracruz on the coast to Chiquihuite, where the *Terres Chaudes* gave way to the higher, healthier elevation of the *Terres Temperees*. This section of the road was currently being guarded by members of the *Infanterie de Marine*, the Egyptian Battalion – whose soldiers were Sudanese – lent to the French by Egypt's ruler and the *Tirailleurs Algeriens*. Now it was to be the Foreign Legion's turn. De Maussion's 7th of the Line was responsible for the safety of the road through the *Terres Temperees*.

Seeking to sugar the bitter pill of convoy duty that he was inflicting on the Regiment Etranger, de Maussion emphasized that ever since the French had begun the actual investment of Puebla the road had taken on a roll of even more critical importance in the campaign. It was difficult to obtain adequate food for the soldiers up-country, so practically every morsel they ate had to be moved along the road in the convoys of big-wheeled Mexican carts pulled by mules, or on individual pack mules, and siege guns, ammunition and pay for the troops moved inland the same way.

Jeanningros was told that both the *Juaristas* and the French had spies everywhere. Often, those who worked for the French as informants or messengers were the simple Indians, despised by the Mexican grandees, abused by the guerilas. Their knowledge of the *Terres Chaudes* made them invaluable, and their ability to come and go silently – often openly, their presence ignored – made them ideal allies. Informants and hired labour, like everything else, were paid in local currency, which the Expeditionary Corps chose to call piastres. It had an exchange rate of five French francs to one piastre. Jeanningros was warned that Veracruz was staunchly Republican in its sympathies and the ever-watchful townspeople ensured that few movements of troops or supplies remained secret from the guerillas for very long. Conversely, the French often knew ahead of time where irregular horsemen or units of the Mexican Republican Army intended to strike.

There was much talk of the *vomito negro* and the usually fatal effect it had, not only on non-Mexican newcomers but even on Mexicans from outside the *Terres Chaudes*. This was another centuries-old problem. As far back as 1556 an Englishman named Robert Tomson had noted that merchants only lived in

Veracruz between August and April, during the visit of the Spanish fleet, and then went back to their homes in Jalapa. Undoubtedly, Jeanningros was told of General Forey's experiences as he had moved up-country the previous year, and he may also have been shown a report prepared by Colonel Hennique of the *Infanterie de Marine*, who had described his regiment's service as 'the most active and the most labourious', consisting of 'escorting convoys, fatigues loading wagons, work on fortifications'. Concerning the health of his troops he had written: 'Distressing. Diarrhoea, dysentery and anaemia overwhelmed the men'.[28]

8
Into the *Terres Chaudes*

The Regiment Etranger would be taking over the convoy and guard post duties at isolated points along the Orizaba Road between La Tejeria and Chiquihuite from detachments of the 7th Regiment of the Line, the *Infanterie de Marine* and the *Tirailleurs Algeriens*, who had been supported by some part-Squadrons of French cavalry. The regiment would be brigaded with the 7th of the Line, the Egyptian Battalion,[1] and the *Contra-guerilla*, led by Colonel Charles Dupin, a colourful, but publicly-disgraced French officer, who had once enjoyed an excellent reputation.

Based at Medellin, south of Veracruz, the *Contra-guerilla* had been initially formed by a Swiss civil engineer named de Stoecklin in the early days of the French Intervention. Admiral Jurien de la Graviere, who had seen a need for a highly mobile strike force to counter guerilla activity, had felt that a *Contre-guerilla* unit, almost constantly on the move, and living off the land, could be useful in intelligence gathering, identifying those who were pro-French, or at least neutral, and guarding convoys when needed. Unfortunately, de Stoecklin tended to see his unit as autonomous, almost independent of French control, and was prone to ignoring orders. General Forey had shared Jurien de la Graviere's enthusiasm for the idea of the *Contre-guerilla*, but not for its leader, and events were to confirm his concerns.

In mid-January 1863 de Stoecklin was in command of about fifty mounted members of his unit charged with escorting a convoy of wagons of gunpowder travelling from Veracruz to Orizaba. They were accompanied by a sutler named Rousseau and two *cantinieres* serving with the 2nd Regiment of Zouaves. At Arroyo de Piedras, only a relatively short distance from La Tejeria, the convoy had been ambushed by a strong force of guerillas. De Stoecklin and his men had abandoned their charges and bolted from the scene. The guerillas then pillaged the wagons at their leisure, rejecting only what they could not carry away. Several turned their attention to the two *cantinieres*, one of whom was pregnant, repeatedly raping them. They then disembowelled the pregnant woman and threw first the baby, then the mother, onto a huge bonfire which the other guerillas had made with what they did not want from the wagons. The other *cantiniere* was also thrown into the flames, followed by Rousseau.

Forey decided that he wanted a French officer to command the *Contre-guerilla*, and at a reception held by Ambassador de Saligny on 14 February offered the position to Colonel Dupin, who was serving as an aide-de-camp to General Almonte.[2] Dupin had graduated from the *Ecole Polytechnique* in 1834 and joined the 61st Regiment of the Line. He then went back to school, graduating from Saint-Cyr and switching to the Cavalry, being promoted to Lieutenant in 1839 and joining the *Service Topographique*. He was with the troops of the Duc d'Aumale in May 1843, when Abd-el-Kader's *smala* was attacked and dispersed, and attained a kind of immortality by being depicted saving the life of Colonel Louis Morris of the 4th *Chasseurs d'Afrique* in Horace Vernet's vast painting of the engagement, which hung at Versailles.

Dupin had served in the Crimean War, emerging as a Lieutenant-Colonel, and in Italy in 1859. He was a Staff Officer with the French component of the Anglo-French Expeditionary Force to China the following year. During the campaign the Summer Palace in Pekin was looted by the French – and then burned by the British – which caused much international criticism. After returning to France, Dupin, who was in possession of numerous priceless pieces of jewellery and ornaments, took out a newspaper advertisement offering some of them for sale. This unwise move led to an inquiry, and while Dupin asserted that the treasures were not Summer Palace loot, and that he had bought and paid for them, there was some doubt about the legality of their acquisition and the Army retired him on half pay. He had gone to Mexico hoping to redeem himself.[3] He accepted the offer of command of the *Contre-guerilla* and de Stoecklin was demoted to second-in-command, but, to make the pill less bitter, was given the Cross of a Chevalier of the Legion of Honour. Dupin was seconded several young officers to help him turn the ragtag unit into something approximating a military force and one of them, Sous-Lieutenant the Compte Emile de Keratry of the 3rd *Chasseurs d'Afrique*, arriving at Medellin to take up his duties, found some very odd characters among both the officers and other ranks.

> All the nations of the world seemed to have found it to be a rendezvous [*he wrote*]. Frenchmen, Greeks, Spaniards, Mexicans, Americans of the North and of the South, Englishmen, Piedmontese, Neapolitans, Dutchmen and Swiss rubbed elbows . . . Almost all the men had left their own countries to chase after a fortune which was always illusive. One found the sailor disillusioned with the sea; the Black man from Havana ruined by typhus and the survivor of a shipwreck; the merchant seaman, former companion of the filibuster [William] Walker; the buffalo hunter from the Great Lakes; the factory owner from Louisiana, ruined by the Yankees. This band of adventurers had no discipline: officers and soldiers got drunk in the same tent, revolver shots sounded instead of reveille.[4]

Reaching Medellin six days after his appointment, Dupin left nobody in any doubt that change had come to the *Contre-guerilla*.

'I am Colonel Dupin,' he told told the bunch of semi-freebooters he was inheriting. 'You will obey my orders, whatever they are, without question, or you will be dead like that bird!'

Whipping out his revolver, he shot a large toucan as it flew past.[5]

His first job was to get the eighty horsemen and forty-five foot soldiers out of their come-as-you-please garb and into uniforms, similar to the short red jackets of the Spahis, and arm them with regular French weapons, and he began kneading them into some form of shape. The population living south of the Orizaba Road was known to be almost wholly Republican in its sympathies and he rapidly identified three particular villages as worthy of *Contre-guerilla* attention. Tlalixcoyan, sixty kilometres (thirty-seven miles) south of Medellin, was hit in a raid on 21 March and a hundred rifles and several hundred kilograms of powder were seized. Dupin also had his eye on the southern village of Jamapa, and on Cotaxtla, which was further west. Receiving his briefing in Veracruz, Jeanningros was told that apart from the de Stoecklin debacle of mid-January, the year had started badly and that the guerillas had become increasingly bold.

On 28 January a strong force had ambushed a convoy of eleven wagons and forty-two mules just west of La Soledad. Guarded by forty-one *Tirailleurs Algeriens* and twenty-eight men of the 3rd *Chasseurs d'Afrique*, as well as twenty-two Artillerymen and eleven other soldiers from different regiments, the convoy had been attacked at it approached Palo Verde. The defence was effective, the guerillas had been driven off with losses and the convoy had continued on its way. However, showing a rare persistence, the enemy had attacked it again, and, with ammunition running low, word had been sent to La Soledad for reinforcements. The timely arrival of a strong escort of troops coming eastwards from Orizaba accompanying a diplomatic courier caused the guerillas to break off the action.[6]

Then there was the matter of the railway, slowly pushing its way west, part of a dream to link Mexico City to the coast. In 1855, President Santa Anna had granted the Rosso brothers a concession to build a railway from Veracruz to the capital. From them it had passed to financier Don Antonio Escandon. A survey of the full route had been carried out by an American railway engineer named Andrew Talcott in 1858 and rails had been ordered from the United States. A station was established on the outskirts of Veracruz, along with a huge area where supplies could be accumulated. Initially, the rails were laid southwest for some two kilometres (less than a mile-and-a-quarter), to a point where a planned branch line would split off and push as far south as Medellin. The main line was then continued to La Tejeria, eight kilometres (almost five miles) from Veracruz, where the initial railhead and construction yard was established. As with everything else, the railway became the object of regular depredations by guerillas.

There had been an attack in February and another on 12 March, with a man killed each time, and on the last day the month, as Jeanningros and his Staff were being briefed in Veracruz, word was received of a guerilla raid on the construction camp at La Loma, west of La Tejeria. Jeanningros decided to see for himself, and incidentally to take a look at the camp at La Tejeria. He went with Captains Remi Debay and Jean Abrial, marching overland to La Loma with the 3rd and 4th Companies of the 2nd Battalion. They found that there had been perhaps as many as three hundred attackers and the construction camp was a slaughter house. The workers had been killed and their wives raped, then murdered, along with their children. The baker, a Frenchman, making dough when the guerillas hit the camp, had been decapitated with a machete and the raiders had departed with the payroll money for the construction crew. Jeanningros and his men arrived too late to be of any help, but the camp would have to be repopulated, so he left his two Companies there and returned to La Tejeria, wondering about the possible connection between the guerilla raid and the fact that the camp had been visited by

Honorato Dominguez, a well-known guerilla, the night before the attack.[7]

Unimpressed by La Tejeria, but preferring it to Veracruz as being perhaps marginally healthier, Jeanningros decided to make it his base for the few days his troops would spend in the area before moving out into the *Terres Chaudes* proper. He gave orders for his two battalions to be moved out of the port city, leaving only Lieutenant Lebre and a handful of men to establish a small Foreign Legion Depot and keep an eye on the progress of several Legionnaires who had already come down with fevers. There had also already been one desertion, as a Legionnaire had apparently decided that he wanted nothing to do with the coming campaign and had simply slipped away.[8]

Overseeing a two-man work party in town, Corporal M'Alevey chanced upon an Austrian named Louis Docir, who had deserted months earlier in Sidi-bel-Abbes and somehow made his way to Mexico. He gave M'Alevey a fatuous story about having 'bought my discharge before I left Algeria', which was obviously untrue, and was promptly taken into custody. He escaped that same night, but would be seen again later in strange circumstances.[9]

At Puebla the French trenches had enabled heavy guns to be brought to almost point blank range of the defences at San Xavier and reduce the walls to rubble. The Mexicans, seeing no point in losing their own heavy guns, withdrew them, but left infantry at the fort. It was taken by storm by the 2nd Battalion of the 2nd Zouaves and the 1st Battalion of the *Chasseurs a Pied* – both veterans of the *Cinco de Mayo* defeat of the previous year – in hand-to-hand fighting.

The attack on the strong point known as the Penitenciaro on 31 March was led by Bazaine himself. After the shelling had stopped, he stepped from a trench, waved his sword and shouted: 'First echelon of Zouaves and *Chasseurs* – forward! *Vive l'Empereur!*' General Xavier Vernhet de Laumiere of the Artillery, who was next to him, was shot in the forehead and killed and Colonel Isidore Garnier struck in the arm, but the strongpoint was taken and the siege continued.

On 1 April the steamer *Rhone* hove-to in the roadstead at Veracruz. Word was sent ashore that a sick French officer was on board and the ship's captain had Sous-Lieutenant Diesbach landed from his personal launch. In hospital in Martinique the young officer had been diagnosed with diphtheria and Andrinetta and several of her friends visited him every day. Hearing that the *Rhone* was the last Mexico-bound ship in port, Diesbach had insisted on sailing with her and on 17 March was taken from the hospital to the ship on a stretcher. Andrinetta knew the ship's First Officer and had given Diesbach a note for him. The two-week sea voyage had helped recoup his strength somewhat. As he stepped ashore he met Lieutenant-Colonel L.E. Mangin of the 3rd Zouaves and learned from him that the Regiment Etranger had been moved to La Tejeria. Diesbach immediately sought overnight accommodation at the Hotel de la Louisiane, but received an unfriendly reception and would have been turned away had not three Americans guests offered him the fourth cot in their room.

Walking through the town, which he found to be 'depressing and dead, wide streets with grass growing in them and few inhabitants,' Diesbach met his fellow countryman Lieutenant Lebre and at the Hotel des Diligences they encountered de Stoecklin, who Diesbach knew, but had not seen in eleven years. Although no longer commanding the *Contre-guerilla* he appears to have been allowed to continue recruiting for them, and invited his fellow Swiss, Diesbach and Lebre, to join. They refused, of course, but Diesbach introduced him to the three Americans from the hotel who were immediately recruited.[10] The following morning Diesbach took the train to La Tejeria to rejoin his regiment.

Up to that time the protection of traffic along the Orizaba Road had been divided into two distinct divisions, Veracruz and Orizaba. The Veracruz Division had been responsible for maintaining posts at La Tejeria and La Soledad, as well as at Medellin and Alvarado, both of which were south of Veracruz. The Orizaba Division, where Colonel de Maussion had his headquarters with the 7th Regiment of the Line, was responsible for the post there and ones at Fortin, Cordoba, Rio Seco, Chiquihuite and Paso de Macho.

Based on what he was told, and the maps put at his disposal, Jeanningros suggested that Medellin and Alvarado could be adequately controlled and/or defended by Colonel Dupin and his *Contre-guerilla*, and suggested that the Divisions be reorganized. How de Maussion chose to deploy the 7th Regiment of the Line was of no concern to Jeanningros and he mapped out a plan which he believed would enable him to carry out his own responsibilities. La Soledad, although it had been attacked and partially destroyed in a guerilla raid, was geographically situated in a commanding position, approximately midway between Veracruz and Chiquihuite.

He proposed establishing his own Regimental Headquarters at Chiquihuite, and that the 1st Battalion, under Commandant Regnault, should also be based there, where it could provide troops for the small post at Atoyac, just to the west, and at Paso del Macho, just to the east. Lieutenant-Colonel Giraud would command the 2nd Battalion from a base at La Tejeria, where Commandant Munier would be responsible for day-to-day operations. Thus anchoring the regiment with commanding officers at both ends of their area of responsibility, Jeanningros proposed that La Soledad, the approximate midway point, should have a small permanent garrison and be the place where westbound convoys guarded by the 2nd Battalion handed over to 1st Battalion guards for the continuation of their journeys. The reverse would be true for empty eastbound wagons returning to the coast.

Jeanningros' plan was accepted by de Maussion and the Foreign Legion made ready for its foray into the *Terres Chaudes*. There were some final adjustments to the composition of various Companies – Corporal M'Alevey succeeded in transferring out of the 2nd Battalion into the 1st and was assigned to the 1st Company – and then Jeanningros was ready to reveal to his regiment the task they had been given.

At the evening parade on 3 April, emphasizing the importance of the Orizaba Road as the very lifeline of the French Army at Puebla, their only means of receiving siege guns, ammunition, food and pay, Jeanningros laid out in detail how he intended to carry out the regiment's responsibilities. M'Alevey called it 'a brilliant speech',[11] and it was nothing less than the truth, though the harsh and dangerous reality of convoy duty would soon become apparent.

The 3rd Company's Captain Cazes, who had been carried on board the *Saint-*

Louis in Mers-el-Kebir on a stretcher, his back injured by a fall, had managed to disembark at Veracruz under his own steam. He was not, however, considered fit for duty and would for the time being be staying at La Tejeria with Lieutenant-Colonel Giraud's headquarters, along with Sous-Lieutenant Milson, who was still classed as *a la suite* – unattached. It had been decided by Commandant Munier that the 2nd Battalion's Company of Voltigeurs, commanded by Captain Dubosq, would also remain at La Tejeria, replacing two-and-a-half Companies of the *Infanterie de Marine*.

Jeanningros led his men out of La Tejeria on 4 April, leaving behind a force of perhaps one hundred and twenty officers and men to hold the eastern point of the Regiment Etranger's responsibilities. They would be supported by a detachment of Martinique Engineers and a Squadron of the Mexican Auxiliary Cavalry under Colonel Figuerero, known as 'El Negro'. As they moved southwest along the Orizaba Eoad the Regimental Standard, borne by Standard-Bearer Maudet, preceded the troops, whose kit was carried by a string of mules. Wagons and other pack mules brought up the rear.

The column paused at the railhead camp of La Loma, where the 2nd Battalion's 3rd Company, under Captain Debay, and 4th Company, under Captain Abrial, had been since the guerilla attack of five days earlier, and where they were to stay. After passing through La Purga, known for the laxative effect of its waters, the column halted again, this time at Arroyo de Piedras, scene of the ignominious retreat of de Stoecklin and his *Contre-guerillas* in mid-January. The remains, such as they were, of those who had died there were gathered up. Many of the Legionnaires had known Sutler Rousseau, as he had carried on his trade at Sidi-bel-Abbes for several years. His skeletal remains were located, identified by the buttons on his tattered jacket, and Fusiliers from Captain Ballue's 5th Company of the 1st Battalion dug a grave, buried him with the remains of the two Zouave *cantinieres*, and erected a marker before the column moved on.

The road was rising now, the pace of the column slow, as marching was hard on the sandy surface. Much effort had to be expended in constantly manhandling the wagons through the deep ruts that months of traffic had worn into the ground.

The Foreign Legion was moving into and through the *Terres Chaudes* at a time of year when under normal conditions travel along the Orizaba Road, particularly with wagons, was avoided whenever possible. Lieutenant Jean Lafont of the 1st Zouaves, who had made the journey from La Tejeria to Orizaba at the end of January, remembered it vividly.

> The Mexican freight wagons are very heavy [*he wrote in an account of the campaign*]. They are mounted on four huge wheels and carry at least a load of thirty metric fifths. Usually the team consists of twelve or even sixteen mules . . . It was at this time, the worst part of the rainy season, that we were going to set out with this huge convoy of heavily overloaded wagons, drawn by worn out teams and driven by *arrieros* who are taken, you might say, by force and who would take advantage of the first opportunity to escape. The wooded areas which abound along the road that we had to travel were infested with numerous guerrilla bands, who waited in the best ambushes

for a favourable moment to fall on the mired teams and pepper us with shots and then disappear into a terrain so difficult that it was impossible for us to reconnoitre it in advance. They could then continue their attack on another part of our long column, disappearing as if by magic as soon as our men started out in pursuit.[12]

Lafont would remark later that 'during the winter season the roads become quagmires, and all transport of this sort stops from October, the time the rains inundate the *Terres Chaude[s]* until the month of May.' Much of the road was essentially impassable, but the siege at Puebla meant that wagons must move along it regardless, in order to conduct the campaign. Apart from the harassing attacks by guerillas on his column, Lafont could have been describing the westward journey of the Regiment Etranger two months later, except that they had only their few regimental wagons with them, constituted a large body of men, rather than a scattered escort guarding a big wagon train, and that the rain held off until about a week after they had reached their destination. Instead, it was enervating humidity and heat which sapped the strength of the marching men.

'In Africa we were burnt brown, roasted if you will, but it was a dry, healthy heat,' Corporal M'Alevey would say later. 'In *La Terre Chaude*, we were boiled, steamed as it were, in a pestilential vapour'.[13]

After what seemed an eternity of marching, the first houses of La Soledad came into view. About twenty-three kilometres (some fifteen miles) from La Tejeria, it was reached late in the afternoon. The little town stood in the middle of a dry plain of grassland and low scrub and had once been quite a busy place. Now it was almost deserted and the French, British and Spanish Commissioners who had met General Doblado there to sign the subsequently repudiated Convention of La Soledad fourteen months before would hardly have recognized it. The church and the house in which they had met had been badly damaged by fire and other stone buildings, with the exception of the house of the village priest, had been partially raised in the guerilla raid.

The military post was held by four Companies of the *Infanterie de Marine* and a small detachment of the 12th *Chasseurs a Cheval*, who were happy to be leaving. The priest seemed a curious fellow, but Legionnaires who had been stationed in Bone in Algeria quickly identified him. A Corsican, he had served the church there, and the fact that he had a mistress made him the subject of gossip. It was understood that the pair had fled Corsica after the priest had killed his lady friend's father and brother. In due course he had departed from Bone under cover of darkness. The body of the mistress was discovered in a ravine a few days later, but by that time he was long gone. Now he was found in the middle of nowhere in the *Terres Chaudes*, apparently financially well fixed from the fees he charged for marriages, baptisms and funerals, as well as what he earned from providing the French with information about the guerillas, and, it was suspected, vice versa. At the time, the circumstances seemed unimportant and Jeanningros inspected the camp area occupied by the *Infanterie de Marine*, found it suitable and assigned it to the Companies of the 2nd Battalion who were to take up position at La Soledad and shuttle between there and La Tejeria, guarding loaded westbound convoys and empty wagons returning to the coast.

He had no intention of lingering and from now on the 1st Battalion would pay particular attention to its route, for between La Soledad and Chiquihuite was the section of the Orizaba Road which would be their special responsibility. Jeanningros led the battalion out of La Soledad, heading for what he had been told would be a difficult crossing of the Rio Jamapa a short distance to the west. Guards were put out both ahead of the column and in the rear as it approached the deep slash the river had made through the plateau. Now carrying not much more than a trickle of water, it was often a raging torrent, and had formerly been spanned by a handsome bridge, built on solid stone buttresses and running from one side of the plateau to the other. The buttresses were still there, but the bridge itself had been destroyed during the War of the Reform and it was necessary to attach ropes to the wagons and lower them slowly down the steep eastern bank of the Jamapa to the level of a temporary bridge built by French engineers, then to use ropes again to help the draught mules haul the wagons up the river's equally steep western bank.

The road, still rising gently, now ran through different terrain and the vegetation was changing visibly, becoming more tropical, with trees rather than scrub bushes. The column passed through a spot marked on maps as El Sordo and saw much scattered debris, mute evidence of the clash between guerillas the *Tirailleurs Algeriens* at the end of January. As dusk was falling, the column reached the flat grassland plateau known as Palo Verde, where at least one of the two small natural ponds usually retained water all year round. Military Chaplain Lanusse, who had been there more than a year earlier, later recalled the 'clear and excellent water'.[14]

The campsite, however, had its shortcomings, too, and the detachment of the 7th of the Line, in residence under canvas, was constantly on the lookout for snakes, scorpions and other insects. They were very pleased to be relieved by the Regiment Etranger. While there were no solid buildings, a sort of framework arbour had been built by the ponds to provide some shade and Jeanningros, after securing the area, had the *arrieros* water the thirsty animals and his men fill their *bidons*.

On Thursday, 7 April, the Regiment Etranger was on the move again, this time before dawn to profit from the cooler hours of the day. Jeanningros had left no men at Palo Verde, though there would be times in the future months when the place would be garrisoned by small detachments of troops. The landscape was changing again, becoming even more tropical as the column moved west, eating up the twenty kilometres (twelve-and-a-half miles) to the little hamlet of Camaron. Just before reaching it they passed the junction with the road which ran north to La Joya, and then entered the deserted settlement, which was dominated by two semi-ruined stone buildings collectively known as the Hacienda de la Trinidad. Jeanningros halted the column there and, after throwing out a perimeter guard, the men of 1st Battalion had an opportunity to examine their surroundings.

> Like all the villages in the vicinity, this one was completely ruined by the war . . . [*Corporal Maine would say later*]. On the south side of the road was a large square building, measuring a little more than fifty metres [fifty-four yards] on all sides and built in the style of all the *haciendas* or farmhouses of the country. Oriented to the north and fronting on the road, it was of two

storeys, rough-cast and of whitened lime, with a red-tiled roof. The rest was composed of a simple wall, very thick, made of stones and mud, and about three metres [ten feet] high. Two large gates on the west side gave access to the interior courtyard, called a corral; it was there each evening, in normal times, that one could find wagons and mules [sheltering], because of thieves, always very numerous and very enterprising in these localities, as in all of Mexico.[15]

On the north side of the road a two-storey house, formerly an hotel for travellers, stood empty, the rooms echoing, and a few broken sticks of furniture all that remained of its former modest glory. The *hacienda* belonged to the landowning Alarcon family and had once been prosperous, a popular overnight stop for travellers and merchants passing along the Orizaba Road. Now the doors and windows were gone and the wooden veranda overlooking the road sagged from neglect and disrepair. The two-storey building opposite it was similarly without doors and windows. The ground floor had once been a storage place for supplies, and the upper floor a dormitory for the drivers of *diligences* and wagons making overnight stops. An old dam, which had once provided water for the population, was to the north of the road. Partly broken now, it still held enough for the needs of the handful of Indians who had stayed on when the hamlet was abandoned, and lived in primitive huts a few hundred metres to the west. It was also home to freshwater crayfish, known as *camarons*, a local delicacy.

The previous year, Chaplain Lanusse, travelling to Orizaba 'with two Companies, a few officers and fourteen Daughters of Saint-Vincent-and-Saint-Paul', had travelled to La Tejeria by the little train and been 'nearly asphyxiated by the heat in our wagons'. Glad to be making the greater part of their journey in open mule-drawn carts, or walking beside them, they headed west along the Orizaba Road, passing through hamlets with names, but which were rarely anything more than 'a few miserable houses, mostly ruined'.[16] When the party reached Camaron,[17] a place he would later get to know very well, Lanusse went exploring. At a later point he would expend some effort mapping the hamlet, and the two main houses, so his description is the fullest and most complete.

> The [two] large buildings had served as a *hacienda*, or hotel, for *arrieros* of commerce and for *diligences* going from Veracruz to Mexico [City] [*he would write*]. It was a point to stop, in the middle of these vast empty plains, these solitudes where once herds of cattle ran wild. In earlier times, also, the *arrieros* used to hold dances. . .
>
> Now the walls, simply standing there, were merely used as a place for our columns to halt for lunch, or for a few guerillas taking a chance in coming out of the forest to inspect the road. Ah!, if a cloud of dust should appear in the distance, the Indians quickly ran to some high place, from there to ascertain if those approaching were friends or enemies . . .
>
> I saw this building, which was called the Hacienda de Camaron (sic), the only solid building; with its ground floor and its second floor, with its roof of red tiles, like the houses in Orizaba. On the right of the road coming from

Mexico [City], it had a large square courtyard, of about fifty metres [fifty-four yards] on each side. The side which faced the road had several rooms running east to west and facing the north. The courtyard (which the Mexicans call a corral) is enclosed by a wall about three metres [ten feet] high, enclosing several sheds, nearly all in ruins now, in which the *arrieros* shut up their wagons and their mule trains when they stopped at Camaron. It was entered through two gateways, situated on the west side. Among the ruined outbuildings there were two, to the left of the entrance which is furthest away from the road, which would be capable, if needs be, of providing some shelter against an attack. The first was almost intact and made out of boards. The second, situated in the southwest angle of the corral, had no more than a few wooden planks, leaning on a wall of bricks, and a thatched roof. Opposite, in the southeast angle, was the remains of another shed, the brick wall of which had formerly supported some boards... To the right of it was a third outbuilding and a very narrow breach in the wall. A single man could scarcely pass through it.

In front of the living part of the *hacienda*, and on the north side of the road, lay two semi-ruined houses and, here and there, a dozen Indian houses, made out of branches and with thatched roofs.[18]

Lanusse's party had gone on to Chiquihuite, where the *Tirailleurs Algeriens* guarded the road,[19] and then to Cordoba and Orizaba. He would stay there for three months, before joining the troops besieging Puebla.[20]

Lieutenant Lafont of the Zouaves had been struck by the number and variety of the fruit trees, when the convoy he was with, having found the ponds at Palo Verde dry, struggled into Camaron.

We camped in the middle of the village [*he wrote in his account*]. The wagons of the convoy were parked in the centre. We took the time to profit from exploring the nearby gardens. We picked oranges and small citrus fruits which had a superb flavour. The oranges were not completely ripe and tasted bad. All round Camaron were orchards of fruit trees of many kinds... banana... pineapples, guavas, coffee trees, cacao, avocados and other trees originating in the Americas.

Nearby, one saw immense prairies inhabited by herds of wild horses, which dashed off at our approach; closer in were numerous herds of well fed beef cattle which grazed in the middle of abandoned pastures. This country, although insalubrious, has a remarkable fecundity: the vegetation is luxuriant.[21]

The Regiment Etranger left Camaron and marched on westward. Now the heat, and the beginnings of fevers, were beginning to affect some of the men. Jeanningros had lost none yet, but the first cases of sickness appeared at Paso del Muerto, four kilometres (two-and-a-half miles) from Camaron. Several Legionnaires were placed in *cacolets* on the sides of mules to continue the journey. Crossing the deep *barrancas* presented difficulties for the wagons, and it was no easier at Paso Ancho, four-and-a-half kilometres (not quite three miles) further on. Jeanningros called a halt here and the 1st Battalion went into camp. Getting the wagons and pack mules down the steep sides of the *barranca*, across the river bed and up the other side was time-consuming and exhausting. More men were falling sick.

The snow-capped cone of Mount Orizaba was nearer now and the land, rising more steeply, made the marching harder. There were more sick men than *cacolets* and some of the Legionnaires rode on the wagons. The air was becoming less humid and the vegetation ever much more lush and tropical.

Paso del Macho, five kilometres (three miles) further on, was a key defensive post on the Orizaba Road. The tiny village had been abandoned by its inhabitants and some of their livestock, horses and cows, browsed unattended in the fields nearby. Lieutenant Constant, commanding a Company of *Tirailleurs Algeriens*, had billeted his men in the empty houses. A detachment of forty Mexican *Lanceros* from General Leonardo Marquez' cavalry, allies of the French, presented arms as Jeanningros led his battalion into the village. Constant had taken possession of an ancient stone tower, dating back to the early days of Spanish colonization, which provided an ideal location for stores and munitions, and from whose flat roof a good view could be had of the road to the east, as well as of Chiquihuite, nine kilometres (six miles) to the west, at almost six hundred metres (two thousand feet) above sea level, the limit of the *Terres Chaudes* – and theoretically also of the *vomito negro*.

The solid stone bridge which spanned a deep ravine, with the Atoyac River more than thirty metres (a hundred feet) below, was of the same vintage as the tower. This was no mere *barranca* like the ones the battalion and its wagons had earlier crossed with such difficulties. It was a steep-sided gorge and the Mexicans had clearly recognized its strategic importance and built platforms for heavy guns in the early days of the French Intervention. Jeanningros immediately ordered the 4th and 5th Companies to detach themselves from the column and told Captain Ballue to set up such defensive works as would be necessary if the need arose to hold the bridge against a strong enemy force.

It was late in the afternoon of 8 April when Jeanningros led the remaining Companies into Chiquihuite and set up camp. This military base at the foot of the Chiquihuite Mountain would be the headquarters of both the Regiment Etranger and its 1st Battalion for many months, as it controlled the key bridges. Jeanningros' troops relieved two Companies of the 81st Regiment of the Line and Standard-Bearer Maudet placed the Regiment Etranger's flag at the door of Jeanningros' Headquarters tent, while Captain Cabossel's Company of Voltigeurs was setting up a perimeter guard for the night.

9
'A good Company ours, the 3rd of the 1st'

Colonel Dupin, having whipped his *Contre-guerilla* unit into shape, and tried them with their first raid under his direction, was now ready to take them into the field in earnest. When he received word from Colonel Labrousse, the Commanding Officer of Veracruz and the *Terres Chaudes*, that Intelligence sources indicated that Antonio Diaz, the Mayor of Jamapa, a village west of Medellin and south of the Orizaba Road, had been one of the participants in the raid on the railhead camp at La Loma, he went into action.

The *Contre-guerilla* swept into Jamapa in a lightning raid at noon on 8 April. Diaz was not there, and a group of trainee Lancers from the Mexican Republican Army, astonished by the attack, fled at such speed that they left their lances behind. The Mayor's house was searched, some interesting and incriminating letters found and it was then put to the torch.

Soon after dawn on 9 April the 1st Company of the 1st Battalion of the Regiment Etranger left Chiquihuite to take over the little post of Atoyac, the westernmost limit of the regiment's responsibilities. Captain Danjou accompanied them to make a preliminary inspection, while Commandant Regnault and his officers began working out plans for the regular rotation of Companies needed for defensive, guard or convoy duties, and Medicine Aide-Major Rustegho set up his hospital area for those suffering from *vomito negro* and other fevers. The Battalion's position and logistical requirements called for a Company to be based at Headquarters at Chiquihuite, one at Paso del Macho, another to guard the bridge over the Rio Gallego, a third on-post at Atoyac, and two to be available for convoy protection.

The same day, Captain Ballue, commanding the 4th and 5th Companies at Paso del Macho, sent Sous-Lieutenant Diesbach out to hunt meat for the officers' mess. He took his Orderly, a Corporal, a *Clarion* and a Fusilier known to be an excellent marksman. A mule and muleteer went with them to help bring back whatever they might shoot. At the bottom of a ravine they found several cows quietly grazing and Diesbach killed one of them. Then, suddenly, before they could begin butchering it to load on the mule, they were surprised by a number of horsemen. From their dress Diesbach realized they were *Juaristas* and ordered his four men to fix bayonets. The Mexicans made no hostile move and Diesbach slowly started to withdraw, but the mule was stubborn and the muleteer gradually fell behind, and the Mexican horsemen dashed between them and Diesbach's men, separating them. There was nothing to be done and Diesbach began leading his men back to camp. At Paso del Macho, Ballue had been going round the houses of the settlement, checking on his men and looking for anything that might be useful, and had just returned to the fortified tower when Diesbach's muleteer rushed in, gasping out a story that the Sous-Lieutenant and his men had been attacked, and that after killing a number of Mexicans, and firing their last shots, had been overrun and slaughtered. Ballue left at once on horseback with six heavily-armed *Chasseurs de France* and was surprised and happy to meet Diesbach and his men a short distance from the camp. There was no meat that day, and the loss of the precious mule was a blow, but at least the hunting party had returned safely. The following day Diesbach took the same men with him and tried again, this time returning with two cows, which made a welcome addition to the Legionnaires' rations.[1]

Life at Chiquihuite and over at the little post at Atoyac was quiet and the air was clearer. The insects, however, were a continual nuisance, especially after the sun went down, and Corporal M'Alevey would long remember having to cover his hands and resort to tobacco to keep the mosquitoes away.

> The earth is literally teaming with insect life, and night and day there is a continual buzz, and whistling that almost drives you mad [*he would say a few years later*]. Lift the first stone you see on the wayside and you will find beneath it either scorpions, or enormous centipedes, or coral snakes. At night the air swarms with fire-flies and mosquitoes; sleep you cannot, you doze away the night in a broken nightmare, and when the first streak of dawn appears, you are awakened with screaming and yelling, as if ten thousand devils had broken into the camp; snatching your gun you hurry out of your tent, and find the camp surrounded by a cloud of green parrots, that shout and scream the louder, when they see your red cap and breeches.[2]

M'Alevey said that the Legionnaires shot parrots for the pot, and it may be guessed that they probably took some satisfaction in bringing down the noisy pests, though their flesh was tough and stringy and needed much cooking.

Commandant Regnault had organized the Headquarters to his satisfaction. *La Musique* was established in a designated area, and tents had been set up for the regimental administration, with places for Sous-Lieutenant Kauffmann as aide-de-camp to the Colonel, and Lieutenant Barera as Pay Officer. Sous-Lieutenant Galloni d'Istria had charge of the makeshift Orderly Room.

> Soon after our arrival the Colonel was careful to establish an observation post on the first slopes of the mountain [*Corporal Maine recalled*]. It dominated part of the plain, and principally Paso del Macho where we had our advance guard. A telescope at the disposition of the soldiers at the post, permitted them to watch over the country.[3]

The fact that the guerillas had made most of the running in the *Terres Chaudes* in the first three months of the year did not mean that the Mexican Republican Army was inactive. There had, however, been other priorities, as General Jesus Gonzalez Ortega had concentrated his forces at Puebla and its surrounding forts, knowing that he must face a showdown with the French. In February he had named Colonel

Francisco de Paula Milan as both Governor and Military Commander of Veracruz, promising him whatever help might be possible, and charging him with harassing the French line of communications between Chiquihuite and the coast. Milan, who was from Jalapa, was an experienced professional soldier, who had fought the Americans in 1848, been captured and escaped, then served in the War of the Reform and was an ardent supporter of President Juarez.[4]

The fact that the French were assembling a huge convoy for Puebla had become known to the Mexican High Command early in April. Among other things, it was to transport several large siege guns, and ammunition for them, which, if they reached Forey at Puebla, would clearly have a serious impact on the outcome of the coming assault. It was a tempting potential prize and the Mexicans were in need of almost any kind of success, as the news from the besieged city was depressing.

Even so, the French were making slow progress with their siege, in part because of divergent views over tactics. While not ignoring the exterior forts, Forey's strategy was to try to move into the city, taking it public square by public square, if necessary house by house. Bazaine, as Commander of the 1st Division, was wholly opposed to the strategy, condemning it as wasteful of soldiers' lives, pitting them in the open against an enemy they could not see, but who could shoot them down with impunity. Douay, commanding the 2nd Division, although a Forey supporter, found himself sharing Bazaine's views, and the arguments at meetings of the War Council were interminable. Colonel Charles Blanchot, who subsequently authored a very human account of the French Intervention, recalled one such long, and ultimately desultory, meeting.

> The two division commanders, that is, the two executive arms of the High Command, energetically condemned the war of squares and declared themselves against a continuation of this system whereby our soldiers, our officers, showed a wealth of bravery against insurmountable obstacles and against a hidden enemy who killed without showing himself [*he wrote*]. In one month we have taken ten squares out of 200 in the city, not counting the outside forts . . . The division generals favoured taking the exterior forts and letting the garrison surrender or die of hunger. Thus, at least, we would avoid the methodical destruction of a great city and would save our soldiers. These fights are butcheries in which our men are struck down by invisible arms and by a timid enemy who kills from hiding. Attacks on the forts suit our men better because at least there they are fighting in the open and can see their adversaries.

Blanchot said that Forey 'remained cold and indifferent' to arguments about conserving the lives of the troops and appeared bored at the meeting.

'Gentlemen, on my departure from France, I asked for equipment which was refused me,' he said at last. 'So! I decline my responsibility, and you may do the same if you like.'

He rose to leave, remarking to Bazaine, Douay and the other officers present: 'Faith, go on chatting and come to an understanding' – a remark which outraged Blanchot, especially as the War Council soon broke up 'without having decided anything'.[5]

The fact that the Mexicans in Puebla knew that General Comonfort was somewhere behind the French lines trying to raise an army to come to their aid was cheering, but probably more in the sense that it meant they had not been forgotten, than that they seriously expected to be relieved. They did, however, need a victory, almost any victory, to bolster their own and the population's spirits. At the beginning of the previous May they had thrown six thousand Frenchmen back from Puebla on the glorious *Cinco de Mayo*. Now, eleven months later, they faced more than four times that number of enemy troops, and the city seemed as good as lost.

On 12 April, a Republican strategy meeting was held in Jalapa and Colonel Milan was given orders to create a Central Brigade from the 'Independence' battalions, bringing together the National Guard units of Japala, Cordoba and Zamora to be the core of his command.[6] He was given a free hand in deciding at what point on the Orizaba Road he would attack the major Puebla-bound convoy, and settled on the plateau at Palo Verde, where the wagons and mule train would inevitably halt. Working in secret, for the French also had their spies, Milan succeeded in creating a force of cavalry and infantry, and began moving them undetected along the Jalapa Road as far east as Matava, then pushing south to a natural fortress at La Joya, north of Palo Verde.

The same day the drudgery of the 1st Battalion's convoy duty began for the Regiment Etranger, when Captain Cabossel and his Company of Voltigeurs set out for La Soledad with a train of empty wagons returning to the coast from Orizaba. His orders called for him to wait at La Soledad until a convoy came through from Veracruz and then accompany it to Chiquihuite. The following day Sous-Lieutenant Diesbach and a small party of Legionnaires had a chance to see a little more of the country when Jeanningros sent them to Cordoba to buy supplies for the various Companies and for the officers' mess. Perhaps he had it in mind that two days hence would be Captain Danjou's thirty-fifth birthday, which would have to be properly celebrated. Lieutenant-Colonel Giraud had sent Captain Cazes to Medellin as Military Commander, with special responsibility for liaison between the Regiment Etranger and Dupin's *Contre-guerilla*, and had also obtained Jeanningros' permission to move his personal headquarters from La Tejeria to La Soledad.

In the cool of the morning of 14 April, Colonel Jeanningros set off from Chiquihuite with Captain Danjou and Sous-Lieutenant Maudet on an inspection tour, visiting the outposts. The 1st Company had replaced by the 4th at Atoyac, and had returned to Chiquihuite. Captain Ballue's 5th Company was back at Headquarters. The inspecting group paused at the Rio Gallegos bridge, then returned to Headquarters for lunch, before visiting Captain Saussier's Company of Grenadiers which was now manning the post at Paso del Macho.

At almost the same time, way to the southwest, General Comonfort attacked French troops on a foraging expedition, but was routed when General Augustin Brincourt rallied his men and struck back. Comonfort retreated, leaving two hundred men on the field, but Brincourt followed him, caused him to make a stand near Puebla and then inflicted such serious casualties that the Mexican force was obliged to withdraw from the area.

The same day the huge convoy, which had finally been assembled at La Tejeria, began its tortuous journey to Puebla. It was of a size, scope and content such as had never been seen before. Chaplain Lanusse, who saw it when it reached its destination, said that it comprised 'two or three hundred heavy wagons, each pulled by 12 mules, supply wagons, ammunition wagons, five or six hundred mules carrying all sorts of provisions,' as well as badly needed siege guns and a consignment of French gold to the value of three million francs to pay the troops, a long, winding snake of a convoy, extending over some five kilometres (just over three miles).[7]

While Captain Danjou and his fellow officers were celebrating his birthday at Chiquihuite on 15 April the man who would be his nemesis, Colonel Milan, was at Huatusco, where he conferred with a wealthy textiles merchant named Manuel Sousa, whose home was the clandestine headquarters for the local Republican forces. Plans for the attack on the convoy were refined, and when word came that it had left La Tejeria the day before, it was described as being so large and unwieldy that it would be able to make very limited progress each day, and would take at least two weeks to reach Palo Verde. The news indicated that Milan would have plenty of time to gather and position his troops.

At Medellin, spies brought word to Colonel Dupin that guerillas were gathering near the San Juan de Estancia, north of the Orizaba Road, a place often used by General Zenobio, an implacable foe of the French. Dupin had been planning to join the westbound convoy at some point on their route, and accompany it at least as far as La Soledad, which he had begun to see as a more efficient operations base for the *Contre-guerilla*. Reducing possible opposition ahead of time would have demonstrable strategic value, and he set about planning an attack on the guerillas' gathering place.

Dupin led the *Contre-guerilla* out of Medellin on the night of 16 April, striking northwest to cross the Orizaba Road and hit the San Juan Estancia at dawn. Picking their way carefully along barely discernible trails the *Contre-guerilla* entered a heavily wooded area known as La Canada and suddenly heard music. Leaving their horses with the main body of troops, Dupin and several of his officers worked their way forward on foot until they came to the edge of a large clearing. They could hardly believe their eyes, for a full-scale celebration was under way, with lamps hanging in the trees, tables laden with food and a guitar-drum-and-flute band. It was 'like a ballroom', the officer writing up the *Historique* of the *Contre-guerilla* would say. It was also clearly a supply depot, as boxes of stores were to be seen in various places, and perhaps as many as two hundred guerillas were present, as well as singers and dancing girls – 'nearly all of them very pretty', in the opinion of the scribe.

Calling up his horse and the rest of his men, Dupin and his riders surged out of the darkness, shooting right and left. There was total panic, as guerillas, musicians and girls milled around in confusion, then tried to reach the surrounding forest. Surprisingly, most succeeded, but less than half-an-hour later, when the *Contre-guerilla* withdrew, what had been a place of joy and fun was now one of death and smouldering debris. Dawn had broken and at eight o'clock in the morning the *Contrea-guerilla* attacked the San Juan de Estancia itself and put it to the torch.

The one hundred and fifty guerillas who used it as a base had decamped when they had seen the flames from the forest at La Canada. On the way back to Medellin, for good measure Dupin's men attacked and burned a guerilla base at Rancho Espinal, south of the Orizaba Road.[8]

The importance of the huge convoy to the success of the siege at Puebla could not have been greater, as shown in a private letter written on 18 April by Lieutenant-Colonel Napoleon Boyer, a Staff Officer at Forey's headquarters.

> We left France, expecting to have to fight a few strong men and a few miserable Indians quaking in terror at the name of France [*he wrote*]. It can be seen today that we were singularly deluded. We have before us a people who have decided not to be awed by us, and who will fight to the last extremity. We are not assured of an easy victory, but we have great hopes of winning. We came, following many people, believing that there was no chance of a reversal, and we found a city bristling with barricades, and all the houses fortified and menacing, from which death comes incessantly.
>
> They have neglected the most simple precautions, the most elementary ones, to assure our success. Since our arrival at Veracruz the transport which is available is so totally insufficient that it is ridiculous. We do not have sufficient food for three months and the sea biscuits in the administration's stores are damaged or bad. They have given General [Vernhet] de Laumiere (commanding the Artillery), 12 siege guns, with an average of 350 shells each.[9]

At about the same time, at La Tejeria, spies informed Commandant Munier of the 2nd Battalion that another guerilla raid on the railway construction camp at La Loma was being planned by Antonio Diaz, and that he was back at his base at Jamapa with a number of other leaders. Although the Company of Voltigeurs could muster only about fifty fit men, Munier ordered Captain Dubosq and Sous-Lieutenant Achilli to have them ready to march within the hour. Summoning Sous-Lieutenant Milson and the sixty-strong Mexican Auxiliary Cavalry under 'El Negro' Figuerero, Munier took personal command of the column and led it out of La Tejeria. A forced march through the night put them within striking distance of Jamapa soon after dawn, but the guerillas had discovered their presence and fled. Consequently, when Munier's force entered the town at nine o'clock in the morning, it was deserted. After posting guards, he stood his men down for a much-needed rest, though it did not last long. Well before noon bullets began peppering the Legionnaires from positions around the town. Dubosq ordered bayonets to be fixed and his men were ready when Diaz' guerillas rushed them from several points.

Much of the fighting became hand-to-hand and in the swirling mass Munier had his horse knocked from under him. Dubosq, suddenly surrounded by guerillas, was rescued by two of his men, Fusiliers Fuller and Konkewitz – an Englishman and a Pole – who, although wounded themselves, drove into the group with the bayonet and dragged their officer to safety. Elsewhere in the melée Sous-Lieutenant Milson and a group of Fusiliers were closing in on a man apparently giving orders. Positioning himself for a clear shot, Milson killed the man. As they were getting the worst of things, with twelve dead and fifteen wounded, the guerillas gradually withdrew to the outskirts of the village, then disappeared into the trees. The man Milson had killed was quickly identified as Antonio Diaz himself and for an action which had cost the Voltigeurs one dead and two – Fuller and Konkewitz – wounded, Milson became the first officer of the Regiment Etranger to be mentioned in Expeditionary Force Orders. He received the Cross of a Chevalier of the Legion of Honour less than a month later.

The same day, sixty kilometres (about thirty-seven miles) to the west, Captain Cabossel's Voltigeurs returned to Chiquihuite with the convoy from La Soledad, the wagons carrying gunpowder for the siege at Puebla, and pay for the troops. He had been impressed by the changes at La Soledad, many of them directly attributable to the energetic Lieutenant-Colonel Giraud, who had set up a defensive position, using the church and the priest's house as key positions and constructed an entrenched camp on one of the few slight elevations on the plateau. Even before this, the permanent presence of Companies of the Regiment Etranger at the village had given it a new lease of life and various people had arrived to set up small shops and bars. They were the types who always follow an army, and it was clear that this would be no mere flash-in-the-pan boomtown, as plans for the railway called for La Soledad to be a major railhead.

On 23 April, Ballue's 5th Company left Chiquihuite escorting a convoy of empty wagons bound for La Soledad. It began raining as it only rains in the tropics, coming down in sheets, an almost solid wall of water. At least the journey was downhill, but when the convoy went into overnight camp the troops were too exhausted to even erect their two-man tents. No fires could be lit and they made do with chocolate and biscuits. The Company's two mules died and the following morning Ballue ordered the men to put their packs in the wagons. They arrived at La Soledad the next day, had no way of making a hot meal and left the same evening with another Puebla-bound convoy. The rain had not stopped and the Fusiliers had been two days and two nights in their wet clothes. This time the journey was uphill, and when they staggered back into Paso del Macho on 25 April they were in a pitiable state and ten men were showing signs of coming down with fever.

Jeanningros was reluctant to commit the 5th Company again so soon, but needed to send two Companies to La Soledad. There were more empty wagons to be taken there, and the incoming convoy from La Tejeria to be met. However, it was not due at La Soledad until the 29 April and he reasoned that the escorting Companies would get a two-day break while waiting there.

When roll call was taken Ballue found that less than fifty of the one hundred and six other ranks who had disembarked with him in Mexico at the beginning of the month were still fit for duty. Captain Cabossel's Voltigeurs were not much better off, and by the time they left Chiquihuite for La Soledad on 27 April even more were in Dr. Rustegho's hospital and only forty-eight men were fit to march. The rain had still not diminished and Ballue decided to overnight at Paso Ancho before facing the strenuous task of taking the sixty empty wagons and fifty pack mules across the *barranca*. It stopped raining during the night and when the sun came up at dawn the land began to steam. The miserable convoy passed through

Camaron, Ballue riding at the head and Sous-Lieutenant Diesbach following with a squad of only eight men. The second squad was behind the wagons and Cabossel, with thirty Voltigeurs, behind the mules, bringing up the rear.

At ten o'clock in the morning, as they approached Palo Verde, Ballue's *Clarion* touched his arm. A line of Mexican horsemen was sitting motionless across the road some distance away, the sunlight glinting on their lance tips. Ballue quickly ordered Diesbach to take four of his men and make a feint through the brushwood to the left, while he did likewise with the other four, going to the right. Diesbach, a Sergeant and three men disappeared into the bushes, working their way towards where they thought the lancers might be. Coming round a bush Diesbach found himself within arm's length of a richly-dressed mounted man. As he grabbed for the horse's bridle the Mexican fired a pistol at him. Diesbach fired back and believed he had hit the rider in the chest, as he slumped forward, then dug his spurs into his horse's flanks and was gone. Moments later Diesbach and his men found a group of perhaps fifty horsemen behind them and there was a lively exchange of shots, but when the Mexicans saw Diesbach turn to face them they turned away and vanished into the brush. This firefight took place near the two freshwater ponds, which Diesbach then began to circle. A heavy burst of fire sent bullets crashing through the trees, showering his party with twigs and leaves. They returned the fire, but by the time they reached the place where the shots had come from the enemy was gone, but fresh blood spots were found on the ground.

Rejoining the convoy Diesbach was furious to find Ballue and Cabossel calmly eating breakfast. In a bitter outburst he accused his senior officer of abandoning him, but Ballue countered by saying that, while he had heard the gunfire, he had thought Diesbach and his men were probably shooting at waterfowl. He seemed to imply that Diesbach was making up the story of the richly-dressed man and his companions. Cabossel rather supported his fellow Captain, remarking that he had been over this route several times and had never seen any guerillas. The two Captains made light of the whole affair, even when Diesbach called his Sergeant and the three Fusiliers and had them tell what they had seen. Anyway, said Ballue, he had felt unable to leave the convoy of empty wagons and mules unprotected, and Cabossel agreed with him.[10] Diesbach, as a Sous-Lieutenant, was very close to insubordination in this harsh verbal exchange with the two Captains, and must have wondered if he would find himself reported to Colonel Jeanningros. In the event, nothing more was said and the convoy arrived at La Soledad close to dusk. Ballue and Cabossel were told that the big westbound convoy had been delayed and was not now expected to arrive until 30 April, which meant, at the very least, that they would get two days of rest before having to head back to Chiquihuite.[11]

The torrential rains, as well as turning the Orizaba Road into a quagmire, and the *barrancas* into raging torrents, had brought about a new wave of the *vomito negro*. Not only were many of Ballue's and Cabossel's men already in Dr. Rustegho's hospital, but now officers who had not left Chiquihuite since they arrived, and men from other Companies, were coming down with fevers, including a number from the 3rd Company. Lieutenant Barera was showing signs of being in the early stages of *vomito negro*, and Commandant Regnault asked Sous-Lieutenant Vilain to temporarily take his place as Pay Officer, a move which made sense, until

Lieutenant Gans also had to be put under the care of Dr. Rustegho, not for *vomito negro* but for what was described as 'Algerian fever', possibly recurring malaria, leaving the 3rd Company without any officers at all, although it was firmly under the control of Sergeant-Major Tonel.

The morning of 29 April was hot but quiet at Chiquihuite. Colonel Jeanningros was around the camp conducting his business, accompanied by Captain Danjou, who was wearing a new *couvre-nuque* he had collected the previous day from *Caporal-tailleur* Horstein.[12] Corporal Berg was quietly fuming. As an ex-officer, he had expected accelerated promotion and knew that his elevation to the rank of Sergeant was approved. It had not been immediately promulgated,[13] as the 3rd Company already had its complement of Sergeants and Jeanningros had not yet decided whether to transfer him to another Company. Lieutenant Gans was still sick in his tent, and a visit to Dr. Rustegho's hospital showed an ever-increasing number of men of all Companies down with fevers of one kind or another. Many others were desperately in need of rest, teetering on the brink of exhaustion from the physical labour of moving loaded convoys or empty wagons from and to La Soledad.

Late in the afternoon Jeanningros had a visitor.

Much of what is known about the next few hours comes from Captain Ballue, who was not at Chiquihuite at the time, as he was awaiting the westbound convoy at La Soledad, but who subsequently had ample opportunity to talk to those who were present, from Jeanningros downwards. Writing about it twelve years later,[14] he assured his readers that 'these details are strictly factual', and, although he received his information secondhand, there seems little reason to doubt it.

Jeanningros' visitor was a young Indian woman in the pay of the French, who told him that an ambush of the convoy was being planned. She had few details, but spoke of a substantial force of Republican National Guard troops and guerillas being assembled for the attack. Telling Sous-Lieutenant Kauffmann to take the woman to the cook tent for something to eat, Jeanningros sat down to weigh his options. He knew that there was little time to lose, as his information indicated that the convoy should have arrived at La Soledad that very day. Obviously, it would overnight there, and would set off the next morning. He had no way of knowing that it was running a day behind schedule, but his knowledge of the diminished sizes of Ballue's 5th Company and Cabossel's Voltigeurs told him that they would have little chance against a well-directed and numerically superior group of attackers.

He briefed Captain Danjou about his visitor and the news she had brought, saying he intended to have her take a note to Lieutenant-Colonel Giraud instructing him to hold the convoy at La Soledad until a larger escort could be assembled. Danjou listened, and agreed that this was the best course of action, but, playing the devil's advocate, pointed out that were the messenger to be captured on her journey the note would not reach Giraud, who would allow the convoy to continue on its way, which would put it in danger of the ambush.

The 3rd Company was on stand-by duty in the camp, although it had no officers currently active. Captain Cazes was still at Medellin, Lieutenant Gans sick in his tent and Sous-Lieutenant Vilain attached to the Headquarters Staff as Pay

Officer. Since coming to Mexico, Danjou told Jeanningros, he had found 'little occasion to perform his profession as a soldier', and suggested that he should take the 3rd Company eastwards towards La Soledad to scout the road.

'If I leave tonight, I will arrive at Palo Verde near dawn,' Ballue quoted Danjou as saying. 'I will rest my men there for two hours, then push out a reconnaissance along the road to La Soledad. As you know, the movement of a convoy stirs up clouds of dust which can be seen from a long way off. If I see nothing, I will know that the Indian woman arrived as planned, and I will then withdraw rapidly, and will be already long gone when the enemy prepares his ambush. If, on the contrary, I see the convoy coming, I will join it and be able to help with the escort duties, and, of course, this would add a reinforcement of sixty solid men, which would certainly be welcomed.'[15]

The suggestion lifted a weight off Jeanningros' mind, and Danjou's plan was readily accepted. When the Indian girl was brought back to his tent Jeanningros asked her to take a note to Giraud at La Soledad. The Indians often carried messages, either in their shoes or rolled up in their hair, and she agreed to make the journey by a roundabout route. The note was written immediately and the messenger departed, to get as much of her journey as possible done in the few remaining hours of daylight.[16]

Sergeant-Major Tonel was sent for and reported that about forty men of the 3rd Company were in Dr. Rustegho's hospital, leaving sixty effectives available for duty – himself, four Sergeants, six Corporals, a *Tambour* and forty-eight Fusiliers. Over dinner, Danjou discussed his plan with Sous-Lieutenants Vilain and Maudet. Although on detached duty, Vilain pointed out that he was the only *titulaire* of the 3rd Company, and immediately said he would ask Jeanningros' permission to accompany Danjou. Maudet also wanted to go, and accepted Danjou's reminder that while he was the senior of the two Sous-Lieutenants, Vilain in this instance, as a 3rd Company officer, would outrank him. Jeanningros gave permission for both men to join the patrol and Sergeant-Major Tonel was ordered to assemble the men.

The Sergeants, of course, were the first to hear about the assignment. Corporal M'Alevey remembered that he was lying in his tent when his friend Sergeant Morziki entered. 'Just come to say good-bye,' he said. The men shook hands, then Morziki was gone. 'That was the last time I ever saw my friend alive,' M'Alevey would remember sadly.[17] The Corporals were next in line for orders. 'I was on guard duty on the mountain with two Squads of my Company, commanded by a Sergeant,' recalled Corporal Maine, who fifteen years later provided a detailed firsthand account of the next twenty-four hours in the life – and deaths – of the 3rd Company of the 1st Battalion. 'Towards eleven o'clock at night, the order came for us to return at once to our comrades who were encamped lower down'.[18]

Ideally, in a Company of around a hundred men, each of the six Corporals would command a Squad of about sixteen men, with a Sergeant commanding a Section of two Squads. Because of sickness, the Squads of the 3rd Company numbered no more than ten men. Maine said they were ordered to wear what was known as *tenue d'ete* – Summer dress – the short blue *basquine* jacket, white canvas trousers, and the sombreros now being issued by the Army stores.[19] The kepi, with *couvre-nuque*, would be carried, attached to the belt, with *bidons* and *musettes* slung over the shoulders. Packs would not be taken, to make the marching easier, and rations for 36 hours, spare *bidons*, additional ammunition and the *marmites* – cooking pots – would be carried by two mules. The Sergeants checked to see that each man had his sixty cartridges in his *cartouchiere* and coffee was served to the troops. Standing at attention with his companions, Corporal Maine thought well of his comrades.

> A good company ours, the 3rd of the 1st – as they say in the Army – and it was right that it should be considered one of the most solid in the Legion! [*he would remember proudly*]. It had men of many nationalities – as is common in the Corps – Poles, Germans, Belgians, Italians, Spaniards, men of the north and men of the south, but the French were in the majority. Who were these men, so different in origins, in customs, in languages, who found themselves sharing the same perils, so far from the countries where they were born? What had been their pressures, their thirst for adventures, their struggles and disappointments? We could not ask them, but the communal life, the proximity to danger, had moulded in these characters, despite the distances, and their individual needs, elements which were very different, an *entente* and a perfect cohesion. All these gallant men, these soldiers, disciplined, patient, were sincerely devoted to their leaders and their flag.[20]

There were sixty men of the 3rd Company, but sixty-two on parade, one of them a 'mystery man', a Legionnaire, not of the 3rd Company, who seemingly simply attached himself. He would later be identified as Fusilier Holler.[21] Was he a member of Ballue's 5th Company, or of Cabossel's Voltigeurs, who had been left behind sick when his companions set off for La Soledad two days earlier, and who now wished to join them? If so, he was there with Tonel's approval, and presumably that of the officers. Possibly he was a man from the 1st Company who fancied a possible fight, and joined the group surreptitiously, avoiding the watchful eye of the Sergeant-Major, and slipping into line from the shadows as the detachment assembled? Or was he a Legionnaire bent on deserting, who saw a chance to slip away from Headquarters? Who Holler really was, and what his motives were in marching with what would become known as *La Compagnie Danjou*, are as unanswered – and unanswerable – as questions about what happened to him later.

The sixty-second soldier was Danjou's Orderly, Fusilier Ulrich Konrad, a Bavarian, who actually belonged to the 5th Company,[22] but would be marching with his officer. A Mexican muleteer named Jose Dominguez[23] would accompany them to look after the two pack mules.

10
'We will amuse the enemy'

Just after one o'clock in the morning of 30 April, Captain Jean Danjou left Chiquihuite with his patrol. The sixty-five men reached Paso del Macho ninety minutes later, and hearing of their mission, Captain Saussier offered a Section of his Grenadiers. Danjou declined them, but conveyed Jeanningros' order: 'If you hear gunfire, send your Lieutenant with thirty Grenadiers as support'.[1] The officers shook hands and the 3rd Company set out again.

> We marched in two lines in the middle of the road [*Maine would say later*]. It was fully night, and the terrain, very uneven and broken at this point, was covered with bushes and high scrub, which could easily conceal an ambush. At certain points, the two sides of the road had been stripped bare by means of axe or fire to make clearings in the thick woods to assist the passage of the convoys. The road itself, never repaired, was broken up by the torrential rains of Winter and the constant use by carts and ammunition wagons. It was almost invisible, and we followed it with the instinct born of the habit of marching in country where quite suddenly a track or a path could turn into a deep chasm like a precipice.[2]

The column negotiated the steep *barranca* at Paso Ancho in the dark. As expected, they had seen nothing suspicious so far. They marched past the handful of huts of the Indian village at Camaron at half-past five, as dawn was breaking, and approached the Hacienda de la Trinidad.

> On either side of the road there were two or three poor crumbling deserted buildings [*said Maine*]. The house [on the north side] was empty except for bits of furniture, a few old straw mats and scraps of leather left by muleteers. Leaving the village, the Company divided into two sections, one to the right, the other to the left. The Captain, with a Squad of riflemen and the two mules, continued to follow the road. We had already been marching for more than six hours. It was a fine day, and the sun, coming up, promised to be hot.[3]

They passed the road which led north to La Joya and reached Palo Verde at six o'clock, by which time it was full light. The 3rd Company had stopped there while marching west three weeks earlier, and Maine remembered the 'nearby spring which provided excellent water'. Following long Foreign Legion practice, the men poured the water from their *bidons* into the *marmites* in which coffee would be made. The water bottles were then collected, to be refilled from the spring.

> Scouts were put out round the area to prevent any surprises [*said Maine*]. The mules were unloaded, and Corporal Magnin set off for the spring with a Squad. A large bower made of branches, covered with thatch, had been set up under a few trees, as a shade against the sun. While a party of men cut wood, to prepare the coffee, the others stretched out to sleep. Less than an hour passed, water boiled in the *marmites*, and the coffee was being made, when, between us and Camaron, on the same road we had just travelled, two or three of us saw something out of the ordinary.
>
> Dust rose in large clouds. At that distance, and under the blinding rays of the sun, it was not easy to distinguish things clearly. However, we had not met anyone on the road, and if there had been any movement of troops in our rear we would have been alerted. Now all that mattered was that we understood that something was wrong.
>
> The Captain used his field-glasses. 'To Arms!' he cried suddenly. 'The enemy!' With the field-glasses, he had been able to see very clearly.[4]

Danjou noted that the horsemen wore uniforms, meaning that they were Mexican Republican Cavalry, not guerillas. They were not expecting trouble and had folded their leather jackets across the pommels of their saddles, leaving their arms free. It later became known that they were a twenty-strong patrol of Orizaba Lancers, part of a group of two hundred and fifty men brought from Cotaxtla and Cueva-Pentada by Hilario Osario to join Milan's forces.[5]

> At the first cry of alarm we kicked over the *marmites*, and hastily recalled the Squad at the spring, repacked the animals, and in five minutes were ready and under arms [*Maine said*]. During this time, the Mexicans had disappeared. Evidently an ambush was being prepared in our rear ... We left Palo Verde as a column, preceded by a Squad as skirmishers; but then, instead of following the road, at the order of the Captain we moved to the right and into the trees, giving us the double advantage of both hiding our movements and making any attack by cavalry more difficult.[6]

The *bidons* had not been filled, there had been no time to drink the coffee, and now the 3rd Company, using narrow paths, and hacking their way with their bayonets where necessary, pushed northwards through the woods. Danjou had a map and when he felt they were nearing the Rio Jamapa, the banks of which might well be defended, he turned southwest, angling back towards the Orizaba Road. The column emerged into the open three hundred metres (three hundred and twenty-eight yards) east of Camaron. Almost at once a single shot was fired from one of the buildings of the Hacienda de la Trinidad and Fusilier Hans Kurz[7] went down with a bullet in the leg.

> The Company took up the march again [*said Maine*]. At the entrance to the village we split up, to cover both sides simultaneously, and regrouped on the

other side, without having seen anything which would confirm the presence of the enemy. We halted and grounded arms, while a Squad carefully searched the houses.[8]

'Captain Danjou circled the village from the left, Mr. Vilain from the right, but there was no one left in the houses,' Corporal Berg would recall later.[9]

At the same time, as it was very hot, and thirst began to torment us, some men with their *bidons* descended into a little ravine, situated a short distance to the right and where one sometimes found water in rock pools [*said Maine*]. Unfortunately, the hot season had already arrived and we had to suffer with our thirst. The village was carefully searched, but the person who had fired the shot was not found. Doubtless some enemy vedette had fled at our approach.[10]

'After a halt of half an hour the column resumed its march,' said Berg.[11]

We returned to the road to Chiquihuite, moving out again in two sections, one on each flank [*Maine said*]. The Captain was with the mules and a Squad in the middle, and a Squad acted as rearguard a hundred metres behind us.[12]

The column was some distance east of the small group of Indian huts when a number of Mexican horsemen suddenly appeared north of the road.

Up to now we had only a very general idea of where the enemy might be, but suddenly, on a small hill to the right and behind us, the Mexican Cavalry was massing and getting ready to charge [*said Maine*]. They had their leather jackets on, as we could easily see. The sound of the shot from their vedette had alerted them. On seeing this, Captain Danjou rallied the two Sections and the Squad in the rear.[13]

This larger group of Orizaba Lancers was led by Squadron Commander Joaquim Jimenez, and his brother, Lieutenant Anastasio Jimenez. For a moment Danjou thought of launching an attack himself. He ordered *Tambour* Lai to beat the 'Charge,' but then decided against it. His men had not yet fixed bayonets and to attack horsemen poised on a hillside would have been foolhardy.

We formed a square to receive their charge [*said Maine*]. In the middle of it, the mules, remembering the loss of their former freedom, jumped and kicked with such force that we were obliged to open ranks, and they departed at triple gallop into the country. There was no way that they could have been stopped. The enemy had the advantage of us, because the terrain, flat and stripped of vegetation beside the road, favoured the movement of cavalry. They came down the hill, separating into two columns in order to surround us, and when they were within 60 metres (65 yards), charged with loud yells.

The Captain had told us to hold our fire. Fingers on triggers, we let them come. An instant passed, then their mass, like an avalanche, swept down on us. At the command to fire the appalling discharge stunned horses and riders, spread confusion in their ranks and stopped them in their tracks. We continued to fire at will. They drew off.

Losing no time, the Captain jumped over a little ditch with a hedge of thorny cactus which bordered the road on the left and which went almost as far as Camaron. This obstacle would impede the effectiveness of another cavalry charge. For a moment we had hopes of reaching the woods, which we could see 400 or 500 metres (440 or 550 yards) from there, and then use their cover to return to Paso del Macho without difficulty. We were ready to try. Unfortunately, a party of Mexicans had already turned east towards the hacienda. The others were trying to jump over the cactus hedge, but their horses for the most part balked at doing so. For a second time we formed square, and, although the attackers were less numerous, they charged again. We repulsed this assault as resolutely as the previous one. They withdrew again.[14]

The Mexican view of the charge comes from Captain Sebastian I. Campos, who was acting as aide-de-camp to Squadron Commander Jimenez. A twenty-nine-year-old native of Veracruz, Campos was a veteran of the War of the Reform.

'The cavalry formed an unbroken wing to the right of the road and moved forward with their carbines at the ready,' he wrote. 'Despite their reckless bravery the dragoons were driven back by the gunfire'.[15]

The 3rd Company was no longer functioning as a whole. In leaving the road to take advantage of the slightly higher ground south of the cactus hedge it had split into two parts, one grouped around Danjou, Vilain and Maudet and the Sous-Officiers and Corporals, sixteen others a short distance behind and struggling to keep up. Their progress through the cactus had been both painful and slow, made the more so for the little group as it was half-carrying, half-dragging Fusilier Kurz, whose bullet wound was bleeding profusely, and muleteer Dominguez, now also wounded in the leg. With no Sergeant or Corporal on hand to help, the veteran Fusiliers considered it their duty to direct the younger ones and protect those assisting Kurz and Dominguez. Fusilier Van Opstal, who had been through the campaigns in the Crimea and Italy, and Fusilier Verjus, the old sailor who had fought in Algeria and at Magenta and Solferino, did what they could to keep the group together, but watched in alarm as the distance between them and the main body of their comrades increased by the minute. Some of the Mexican horsemen had split away from the Squadron and made individual dashes at the Legionnaires. Others disappeared in the direction of the Hacienda de la Trinidad and some, unable to force their horses through the cactus hedge, spurred round the end of it and backtracked, coming upon the sixteen Fusiliers just as they cleared the obstacle themselves.

Bearing down on them with lances lowered and officers' sabres raised, the Mexicans succeeded in splitting the Legionnaires into little groups, which could be more easily overcome. In the confused melée that ensued Fusilier Bogucki received a serious sabre cut to the head and Fusilier Seffrin fended off a glancing lance thrust, which nevertheless laid open his chest. Another cavalryman sliced open the head of Van Opstal. Fusilier De Vries also suffered a head wound and Fusilier Lemmer took a bullet in the armpit. Fusilier Merlet's head was smashed by a stone[16] and Fusilier Van den Meersche went down with a serious head wound.[17] Then the Mexicans were off their horses, closing in to attack. Professional soldiers, they expected to take prisoners, rather than simply exterminate their enemies as guerillas would have done. The adversaries were too close for effective bayonet work and quickly, through sheer weight of numbers, the horsemen disarmed and captured all sixteen Legionnaires.

The Fusiliers with Danjou probably saw their comrades overwhelmed.

> By now our situation was becoming critical [*said Maine*]. Should we pull back into the woods? It was a pipe dream: the hacienda was a little further away, but with good luck we could get there, take refuge behind the walls and hold on until the probable arrival of help.[18]

Danjou, while seeking to give his little command a fighting chance, had realized that these Mexican troops must be the very ones who had hoped to ambush the Puebla-bound convoy.

'*Mes enfants!* Fall back on the hacienda,' Fusilier Friedrich Fritz heard him call out. 'There we will amuse the enemy. It will thoroughly disrupt their plans, until it is too late. Meanwhile . . . who knows!'[19]

> The group with the Captain was close together [*said Maine*]. On his order, we fixed bayonets, then, heads down, advanced on the groups of cavalrymen in front of us, but they did not wait, and scattered like hares. While the Mexican often shows incontestable courage in the face of bullets, even a little bravado, it seems that any encounter with the bayonet is very little to his taste.[20]

Surging forward with a cry of '*Vive l'Empereur!*' Danjou, Vilain and Maudet led a total of forty-six Fusiliers in a mad dash for the hacienda.

> We covered the distance which separated us from the building and rushed into the corral [*said Maine*]. Everyone began organizing the defence. We did not see much of the enemy. Startled by our French impetuosity, they had gathered on the other side of the wall. The gates had gone a long time before, so we barricaded the two gateways as well as we could with heavy boards, planks and anything else which came to hand.[21]

'Had we remained on the national highway, the cavalry would certainly have cut through us in the blink of an eye,' Corporal Berg said later. 'Captain Danjou made us bar the two large gateways and the two windows which opened onto the courtyard. He positioned a squad at the gateway to the left, and another to the right, and the rest around the interior walls'.[22]

'We will amuse the enemy'

The Mexicans who had broken off from the engagement after their first charge was repulsed by the 3rd Company's square had correctly anticipated Danjou's move on the hacienda and had beaten him to it. The door which faced the street gave access to a number of rooms in the building, and also to the second floor. Only one room, on the ground floor, at the northwest corner, had no access from inside the house and could only be entered from the courtyard. This was immediately occupied by the Legion.

> In the interior of the corral and to the left of the second gateway there were two sheds made of planks and set against the wall [*said Maine*]. The first was completely enclosed and almost intact. The other, the one in the corner, was open, hardly a shelter, the shaky roof supported by two or three beams, the ends of which rested on a little wall made of bricks of a height to support it. To the right of it, at a corresponding angle, a similar shed had previously existed, but the woodwork had disappeared, and the roof rested on a support of bricks, a semi-ruin. In the same place there was an opening in the wall, an old breach, large enough for a man to pass through on a horse.
>
> Under the direction of Captain Danjou, a Squad was placed at each of the two gateways and two others occupied the room ... Another Squad was charged with guarding the breach. We wanted to make loopholes in the wall opposite the gateways, but it was so thick, so well constructed of straw, gravel and stones, that we could only make two, and those with great difficulty. We gave up trying. Finally, Sergeant Morziki, a Pole, was sent up on the roof with several men to observe the movements of the enemy. The rest of the Company was placed in reserve between the two gateways, to keep an eye on the four corners of the courtyard. Danjou inspected everywhere where it appeared that danger was likely to be the most pressing. These dispositions made, we waited patiently for the attack. It was about half past nine o'clock.[23]

The Mexicans made no immediate move. No shots came from the second-floor windows of the house. The Legionnaires were at a disadvantage in that they could not see out of the courtyard, but it was shared by the Mexicans, who could not see in. There was almost complete silence, broken only by the heavy breathing of the men inside the corral and the jingle of military accoutrements and spurs from the horsemen on the other side of the wall.

Captain Campos, reporting that 'the enemy then pulled back slowly, firing occasionally, to a large, rambling and ruined house, where they sought refuge,' said that Jimenez posted 'Captain' Maximo Escobar, the guerilla leader from La Soledad, to watch the building, while he withdrew to 'a safe distance'. Then, calling Campos to his side, he ordered him to take four men and ride to La Joya to alert Colonel Milan.[24]

Inside the courtyard Captain Danjou was taking stock of their situation. He seemed to be everywhere, deploying his men, finding better positions, or suggesting how to strengthen defences. Like them he was thirsty, and he knew the condition of their *bidons*. Fusilier Ulrich Konrad, his Orderly, had prudently included a bottle of wine in his *musette* for the officers' lunch. Danjou now uncorked it, and, accompanied by Konrad, moved from man to man. Maine remembered that he gave 'each one of us a few drops, which we drank from our cupped hands'.[25]

'We suffered from the extreme heat, from hunger and from thirst,' Berg would say. 'Our food had gone with the mules. At Palo Verde we had emptied our *bidons* into the *marmites* to make coffee and at the moment of the first alarm it had been thrown away. There had been no water at Camaron, nobody had eaten or drunk since the evening before'.[26]

When Campos and his detachment pounded into the Mexican camp at La Joya with the news that a French force was forted up at the Hacienda de la Trinidad, Milan moved fast. Within the hour his infantrymen of the Central Brigade – the 'Independence' battalions of the National Guard units of Jalapa, Cordoba and Zamora – were ready to march. Several Companies of the National Guard of Veracruz, who had arrived earlier, were also immediately put under marching orders. At the same time, Milan sent riders in all directions to summon local guerilla leaders to converge on Camaron.

There were many of them, each able to call upon his own adherents and followers: Pascual Rincon of Temexcal (Camaron), who was probably already at Milan's camp, Matias Gonzalez of Cueva Pintada, Honorato Dominguez of San Diego, Marcelino Rosado of Paso del Macho, Zeferino Daquin of Cocuapa, Tomas Algazanas of Cotaxtla, Ignacio Gonzalez of San Jeronimo and Juan Arevalo of Coscomatepec, among others.[27] Milan rode south with two hundred and fifty cavalrymen of the Mexican Republican Army and one hundred and fifty guerillas, and would cover the eight kilometres (five miles) from La Joya to Camaron far more quickly than the infantry's forced march.

A few shots had come from the second-floor windows of the house at the hacienda, but for the most part the Mexicans held their fire. The Legionnaires told themselves that the situation was not too serious, that cavalrymen were not used to fighting infantrymen in defensive positions, and would come off the worse for it. Moreover, there seemed to be every reason to hope that Captain Saussier at Paso del Macho, hearing the sound of gunfire, would alert Colonel Jeanningros, and that they would march to the rescue.

> Up to now there had been firing in one part or another, the exchange of some shots, but the enemy did not seize the occasion to seriously engage us [*Maine would say*]. On the contrary, he seemed to hesitate to commence the attack, and we began to think that he might even leave. We soon found that we were wrong.[28]

'The enemy had neither infantry nor artillery, and in a position like this we could resist for a long time against cavalry, even though there were so many of them,' Berg said later. 'With no bayonets on their short carbines, they did not have the ability to wipe out a Company of the Legion sheltered behind walls'.[29]

The picture changed completely with the arrival of Milan and his horsemen. Morziki and his comrades on the roof of the house reported sombreros as far as the eye could see.

> They were mostly irregulars – guerillas – dressed in the manner of the ordinary Mexican horseman, legs in skin-tight trousers, open at the sides, widening at the foot, and decorated with a triple row of metal buttons, a red cloth waistband, leather jacket and sleeveless vest, ornamented with a profusion of braid and silver embroidery [*said Maine*]. On their heads, worn over a kerchief, the grey wide-brimmed hat, with much braiding in silver or gold, then the enormous spurs, huge stirrups, like square wooden shoes covered with metal, and the heavy saddle with a pommel. All of this was in curious contrast with the size of their horses, a little small for the most part, but with remarkable strength and marvellously trained. Only one Squadron wore military uniform: a tunic of blue cloth, blue trousers and leather leggings, white belts, kepis and couvre-nuques.[30]

After a while Morziki called down to Captain Danjou that a Mexican officer was approaching with a white handkerchief and wanted to talk. This was Captain Ramon Laine, the Mexican-born son of the Frenchman who was Port Captain at Veracruz.[31] He had attended the Mexican military school at Chapultepec and was serving as Orderly Officer for Colonel Milan.

'You are few in number,' he called up to Morziki in perfect French. 'We do not wish a useless massacre. It will be best for you to submit and lay down your arms. We will promise you your lives'.[32]

Morziki slithered down from the roof and delivered the message. Fusilier Fritz was standing nearby.

'I clearly remember the response of Danjou,' he would say later. 'He was calm, and his response was that of a man who fully understood the seriousness of his position. He was determined, without bombast: 'Say that we have cartridges. We will surrender only when they have killed every one of us!''[33]

The die was cast and firing broke out almost at once.

The Republican Army and the area's guerillas had already measured themselves against men of the *Chasseurs d'Afrique*, the *Tirailleurs Algeriens*, the *Infanterie de Marine*, several French Regiments of the Line and the *Contre-guerilla* under both de Stoecklin and Dupin. Apart from Commandant Munier's raid on Jamapa, they had not yet met the Foreign Legion.

Danjou surveyed the corral and its defenders. He had deployed his men with a sure touch. Sergeant-Major Henri Tonel and two Squads – fourteen men, including Fusilier Fritz – were in the northwest ground-floor room of the house. Sergeant Marie Morziki had gone back up onto the roof alone. Corporal Evariste Berg and a Squad guarded the barricaded north gateway and a similar Squad under another Corporal guarded the south gateway. Corporal Philippe Maine was with Sous-Lieutenant Jean Vilain and other men designated by Danjou as reserve troops, hugging the west wall between the gateways. Corporal Karl Magnin and a Squad which included Fusiliers Leon Gorski and Hippolyte Kunassec was holding the breach in the southeast wall.

'Along with his courage, [Danjou] was especially noted for his steadiness and quickness of eye,' Maine would say later. 'He was never found wanting'.[34]

At first Danjou used the ground-floor room of the house as his command post, sharing it with Tonel and his two squads.

> Calm and fearless in the midst of the turmoil, Captain Danjou seemed to be everywhere [*Maine recalled*]. He went from one post to the other, ignoring the bullets as he crossed the courtyard, encouraging the men by his example. He called us by our names, saying to each of us a few stirring words which warmed the heart and rendered the sacrifice of life less painful, even agreeable, in the moment of danger. With such leaders, I felt that nothing was impossible.[35]

'Captain Danjou was splendid in his valour and his coolness,' said Berg. 'He went from one side of the courtyard to the other, and any among us who might have wavered, would have found courage just by watching him'.[36]

> Then the firing broke out everywhere at the same time [*Maine said*]. We were outnumbered ten-to-one, and, if the attack had been vigorously conducted, I do not think it too much to say that we could have been overrun. We were very poorly situated, and several of our men had already fallen, killed or wounded.[37]

In the command post room, surrounding by the swirling, acrid smoke of the gunpowder, deep in the emotion of battle, Danjou may have recognized the true hopelessness of their situation. Facing the Orizaba Lancers in the open they had perhaps been outnumbered two-to-one, but sixteen men, a quarter of his command, had been captured before the hacienda was reached. Now, with the arrival of Milan's cavalry and the guerillas, the Legionnaires were vastly outnumbered about ten-to-one.

Then and there, according to Corporal Berg, Danjou sealed his own fate, and that of the other forty-eight men bottled up within the walls of the corral.

'Raising his hand,' said Berg, 'he swore to fight to the death – *jusqu'a la mort* – and had his men give their word, too'.[38]

In a scene which would be immortalized in a painting entitled '*Le Serment*' – 'The Oath' – by artist Pierre Benigni, Sergeant-Major Tonel and the men in the room promised to die rather than surrender.

Legend-builders and hagiographers would later seek to link Danjou's sharing of his bottle of wine with the swearing of the oath, connecting them, as if the *serment* had been sealed with the wine as some form of sacrament. It has even been preposterously claimed that the Legionnaires individually took the oath while placing their hands on Danjou's gloved articulated one, as if it were a Bible. Clearly, the oath and the wine were not connected, for while Maine, Berg and Fritz all spoke later of swearing to fight *jusqu'a la mort*, only Maine mentioned the wine, which, anyway, was distributed much earlier, in the lull when the initial defences were thrown up and the men deployed.

In the adjacent rooms and the one above them they could hear the Mexicans pounding the wall and ceiling in their attempts to break through and carry the fight to the occupants. Not long afterwards Danjou moved outside, finding a place between the two gateways, where Vilain and the reserves were watching second-floor windows and the roof of the building.

Fritz – who had already sworn to fight to the death – was in the area for the reserves with other Legionnaires when Danjou enjoined them also to fight '*jusqu'a la mort!*' The old Fusilier commented: 'We gave our word'.[39] Corporal Maine remembered: 'A few times before he fell, he had us promise that we would defend ourselves to the last extremity. We swore that we would do so'.[40]

> Towards eleven o'clock, he went to visit the post in the room and quickly recognized the impossibility of holding out there for long [*Maine said*]. When returning to the reserve area, he was struck by a bullet full in the chest. He fell and clutched his heart. A few of us ran to help him, but the wound was mortal. The blood gushed from his chest and ran in rivulets on the ground. Sous-Lieutenant Vilain put a stone under his head. For the next five minutes his wild-looking eyes rolled in their sockets. He gave two or three convulsions, then his body slumped and he died without having regained consciousness.[41]

'We had suffered three or four casualties when Mr. Danjou was wounded by a bullet,' Berg wrote. 'Our poor Captain suffered for an hour and then expired in the arms of Mr. Vilain and Mr. Maudet'.[42] Fusilier Fritz, who said that Danjou was waving his sword at the time he was hit, also spoke of a chest wound[43] – indicating that the bullet had come through the defended north gateway, fired by a marksman outside. To Corporal Berg, defending the gateway, it appeared that the shot came from behind, rather than in front – indicating that it was fired from the house. Other Fusiliers who saw Danjou fall later told Commandant Regnault that the fatal bullet was 'fired from the room occupied by the enemy'.[44] What Maine and Fritz thought was an entry wound over the heart was, in fact, an exit wound, and Corporal Berg was correct when he said that Danjou 'was wounded by a bullet which struck him in the middle of his back and came out below the left nipple'.[45]

Sous-Lieutenant Vilain took command. Although junior to Sous-Lieutenant Maudet in terms of seniority, he belonged to the 3rd Company, so outranked him under the circumstances. He had 'fair curly hair [and] a brave heart, which beat harder in the face of danger', remarked Maine.[46] 'The two remaining officers commanded us calmly and fearlessly, going to all our positions, inspiring us with their voices and often combining their words with actions,' said Berg.[47] The Mexicans hammering at the inside wall of the room where Sergeant-Major Tonel had his squads were making progress, and the position was becoming increasingly perilous. Then a section of the wall between the rooms collapsed and the enemy could fire directly on the Legionnaires.

> The struggle was terrible [*said Maine*]. The Mexicans tried to get in from the outside. At the same time, those who occupied the room next door were trying to break through the wall and the ceiling . . . They were able to force the wall of a room which linked it to others on the ground floor, from which they could fire on our men from all directions at point blank range. This made it necessary for our men to retire, and the room was evacuated, but of the fourteen who were alive at the beginning, there remained no more than five, who were sent to reinforce the various posts in the courtyard.[48]

As Sergeant-Major Tonel stepped from the room into the corral he came under fire. He was a big man, who made a ready target, and was quickly shot down. A Fusilier was killed beside him and two others wounded before they could reach cover.

'Onward, *mes enfants*!' Fritz and the Legionnaires in the area for reserves heard Tonel call out as he died. 'Courage! For France and for the Third! You know the order . . . To the death!'.[49]

> The defence continued [*Maine said*]. The Mexicans were now masters of the entire house, but would not have it all their own way for long. When they tried shooting into the courtyard, we directed a fire so lively, so accurate, against all their efforts that they were forced to quit their positions at the windows of the second floor, then the ground floor. They left marksmen in small numbers, but let a head, an arm, a scrap of uniform appear in a door or a window, then a well aimed bullet from us punished the imprudence.[50]

'The shots of the enemy were almost always fatal for our men,' said Campos. 'The sight of one was immediately greeted by their rifles, so the situation was very dangerous'.[51]

By this time, said Fritz, Corporal Favas had been killed, and Fusiliers Schreiblich, Lernoud, Baas 'and several other comrades' were also dead or mortally wounded.[52]

> Towards midday, we heard from far off the sound of a trumpet [*Maine said*]. We had not lost all hope, and we thought for a moment that the French were coming to our aid. Shaking with joy, we prepared to rush from the corral and run to our rescuers. Suddenly, we recognized the sound of a drum as being one of the little drums of the Mexicans, rolling, raucous and flat in tone, like Basque drums, playing a sort of a skipping march, quite different from our French tunes, and we realized our mistake.[53]

The drum they heard was being beaten by *Tambour* Pablo Ochoa, marching at the head of two Companies of the National Guard of Veracruz, led by Captains Somohano, Migoni and Frias. Others, under the command of Colonel Rafael Estrada, were not far behind. They were followed by the Jalapa Battalion, commanded by Lieutenant-Colonel Ismael Teran, and the Cordoba Battalion, under Major Francisco Talavera.

> It was the arrival of the infantry of Colonel Milan which was being announced [*Maine said*]. Left that morning in the encampment at La Joya, and warned too late be in at the start of the combat being fought at Camaron, it was coming now to add the weight of its arms to the already unequal struggle.[54]

Maine had initially dismissed the Orizaba Lancers and the other cavalrymen as a real factor, saying: 'We had nothing really to fear from these cavalrymen. Forced to fight on foot, encumbered by their large riding trousers, they had little understanding of this kind of fighting'.[55] Now things had changed, and Maine, if not actually during the battle, had plenty of opportunity to observe the National Guardsmen a few hours later, as a prisoner in the Mexican camp.

> The variety of uniforms and of equipment left much to be desired [*he commented*]. However, with all this confusion, beneath all this disorder one could detect a meritorious preoccupation with smartness and drill. All, or almost all, of the men of the Veracruz Battalion wore baggy trousers and a vest of grey linen with blue piping and the big straw hat. Cordoba was different only in the colour of the linen, which was blue. Jalapa, the best dressed of the three, also had the baggy trousers of grey linen and the blue vest, open at the front, but, instead of the Mexican sombrero, the kepi, with the indispensable *couvre-nuque* falling on the shoulders. Most of them wore laced fawn-coloured leather boots. Others had retained their sandals, or sandals with rope soles, rather similar to the Spanish espadrilles. The officers were dressed a little like their men, except for the quality of their uniforms: trousers with blue or red piping and a short campaign tunic with gold buttons. All the senior officers wore boots and carried a revolver at their belt.[56]

The question of the weapons used by the Mexicans – Regulars, National Guardsmen and guerillas – at Camaron has long been contentious. There is no argument about the arms in the hands of the Foreign Legion: the 1857 single shot, muzzle-loading rifle for the Fusiliers, swords and handguns – probably either the six-shot single action Lefaucheux of 1858 or the double action Perrin model of 1859 – for the officers.

The official Mexican position, first raised later by Campos,[57] and subsequently strenuously put forward by Brigadier-General Luis Garfias Magana, the main historian of the battle from the Mexican side, is that the attacking troops, with few exceptions, were amateurs. Garfias Magana has maintained that they were far outclassed in fighting experience, characterizing the National Guardsmen as 'improvised soldiers', who were 'lacking in the most elementary notions of the science of war'.[58] Without doubt, this was at least partly true. Yet many of the officers had attended military schools, been through the Mexican-American War of 1846–48, the later War of Reform and/or the Three Years War, so had a good understanding of 'the science of war', while the guerillas, particularly, essentially made their living by fighting.

Garfias Magana has also maintained that the troops at Colonel Milan's disposal 'were poorly armed with but a few shotguns – any venerable souvenir from the Independence Wars, from our Civil conflicts – and an abundance of machetes and lances'.[59] Yet Maine and other Legionnaires described the weapons they saw in the hands of the Mexicans.

> These troops were well armed with guns made in the United States [*said Maine*]. For the cavalry, the sabre, the revolver and the carbine. A good

number of the guerillas also had lances. The infantry had the rifled carbine and the sabre-bayonet. In truth, the only thing they lacked was artillery!⁶⁰

French collector of militaria Jean Brunon, as curator of items for his museum, accumulated many different types of weapons from the period of French Intervention, and wrote that the range of firearms the Mexicans used against the Foreign Legion at Camerone was so varied that it 'created a problem over ammunition', adding: 'There were Hall flintlocks made in 1819, which had been re-modelled for cartridges in 1842 – a weapon which had been used in the war against the United States in 1846–1847. There were pin-firing model 1855 Springfields [and] Sharps model 1859 breech-loading rifles and carbines.' The revolvers used, Brunon said, were 'of U.S. manufacture: Patterson, Colt, Starr or Remington, of various models made between 1836 and 1858'.⁶¹ A Spencer carbine was pickled up at the scene of the battle the following day by Jeanningros' men. So, while the claim that the Mexican troops were militarily outclassed is true to some degree, the parallel claim that they were also heavily outgunned seems exaggerated.

'The aspect of things changed, for we were now facing regular troops,' Berg said. 'The attack was formidable, but we defended ourselves with the energy of desperation, not believing they would give us any quarter, and wishing to die with our guns in our hands'.⁶²

> Morzicki had rejoined us, and was fighting with us in the courtyard [*said Maine*]. Being supple as a jaguar helped him to use the smallest roughness of the wall to now climb back up to his perilous observation point on the roof. He could see, milling about in front of the house, all these infantrymen.⁶³

Fritz heard him call out: 'They are massed in front of the hacienda!'⁶⁴

Each of the National Guard battalions was between three and four hundred strong, collectively well over a thousand men, and the arrival of groups of hastily-summoned guerillas gave Milan a force of between seventeen hundred and two thousand, outnumbering their enemies in the courtyard of the hacienda by perhaps as much as forty-to-one.

> We looked at each other without saying a word [*Maine remembered*]. In that moment we understood that all of us were lost and that we would be here until we were all dead.⁶⁵

From his perch on the roof Sergeant Morziki could see a small group of Mexican officers, clustered around Colonel Milan. There were two others of his rank, Colonels Mariano Camacho and Angel Luciano Cambas, and three Lieutenant-Colonels: Jose Ayala, Milan's Chief-of-Staff, and Francisco and Manuel Marrero, brothers from Huatusco. Spotting Morziki, Milan at once sent Captain Laine to offer the Legionnaires a second chance to surrender.

> The Sergeant was very hot-headed about the struggle [*said Maine*]. Drunk with gunpowder and anger, he responded as a true soldier, with a word a

little undiplomatic, but which left no doubts about our intentions, then he hastily descended and reported his response.[66]

'You did well,' Sous-Lieutenant Vilain told him. 'We will not surrender'.[67]

It is Foreign Legion lore that the 'undiplomatic' word used by Morziki was: '*Merde!*' – 'Shit!' It may well be so, as it was the word used by General Cambronne, called upon to surrender at Waterloo, almost five decades earlier, and the '*mot de Cambronne*' is a French Army tradition.

After leaving the room in the house where so many had died, Fusilier Fritz had joined the reserve group between the two barricaded gateways. He said later that Sous-Lieutenant Vilain, standing in the open, pointed his sword at the sun and, in an act which sounds just too melodramatic to be true – but probably is – called out to his men.

'Remember that you swore an oath to your Captain!'[68]

At almost the same time, the Legionnaires realized that the wind, which had been blowing from east to west, had shifted and was now blowing from north to south. It was a disastrous discovery. Up till then there had always been the hope that the sound of gunfire might have been heard by Captain Saussier at Paso del Macho, even though it was fourteen kilometres (eight-and-a-half miles) to the west, or even by Captains Ballue and Cabossel at La Soledad, twenty-one kilometres (thirteen miles) to the east.

The change of wind direction now removed even that slim possibility.

Maine, also in the reserve group, was overcome by a strong premonition.

'I had never for a single moment lost my nerve, nor my spirit,' he said later. 'Suddenly I felt sure that I would be killed'.[69]

11
'Jusqu'a la mort!'

It had been decided, said Captain Campos, that the National Guard battalion from Veracruz should spearhead the infantry assault on the Hacienda de la Trinidad. 'The Staff Officers gave the final orders,' he recalled, and some went forward themselves.

'The marksmen,' he said, 'crawling for some distance on the ground, made use of any low cover to avoid the fire of the enemy and to shoot at the gateways on the right of the corral'.[1]

> The first Mexican charge was terrible [*said Maine*]. They rushed from all sides to penetrate the courtyard, shouting, screaming curses and abuse at us in abundance, which to them is proper in such cases, and facilitated by the indisputable richness of the Spanish vocabulary: 'Out with the French dogs!' . . . 'Scoundrels go home!' . . . 'Down with France!' . . . 'Death to Napoleon!' I will not repeat all of them.
>
> For us, calm, silent, each at his post, we sighted our rifles coldly, did not fire until a shot was sure and when we did, knew well that our man went down. Those in front fell. The wave of assailants wavered a little, recovered, re-gathered itself, and was ready to charge again. We hardly had time to load a new cartridge into our guns before they were on us.[2]

'The first of our soldiers to fall was *Tambour* Pablo Ochoa, who, armed with a discarded lance, was attempting to use a heavy wagon loaded with straw as a cover to get to the door of the building,' Campos said. 'He was shot through the heart by a bullet fired from an oblique angle, as was our Chief of Staff [Lieutenant-Colonel Jose Ayala]. His place was taken by Standard-Bearer Rafael Redondo, the Adjutant to Jimenez, who was also killed. A moment later Lieutenant Vicente Guido of the Veracruz Battalion was mortally wounded by a bullet in the stomach, as he attempted to rejoin his companions'.[3]

It was probably Fusilier Fritz who killed Ayala.

'A fine-looking officer appeared, leading his men,' he said. 'I aimed. He fell, stone dead. I think that my bullet hit him in the forehead'.[4]

The attackers fell back, fired a few more shots and then scrambled to get out of range of the Legionnaires at the gateways and the breached wall. 'I must say a word of praise about the courage of the Mexican officers,' Fritz remarked later,[5] and Maine thought they 'were magnificent in their audacity and bravery'.[6] Soon, from inside the house, came more sounds of furious banging, as the Mexicans tried to break through the walls. From outside the east wall of the corral came the sound of hammering and general excavating, as the Mexicans, said Campos, 'between firing, tried to make loopholes'.[7]

> They gathered in force in the main body of the building, which they now fully occupied, opening with picks and crowbars a large breach in the ground floor wall which looked out into the corral [*said Maine*]. At the same time, still others had established themselves behind the part of the walled enclosure which faced the main gateways. From there, they profited from the loopholes which we had ourselves made, but which we could not defend. Piercing more holes level with the ground, which on the outside was a little higher than in the corral, they now directed plunging fire on us.[8]

'They were trying to enlarge the breach and endeavouring to make another in the east wall, facing the main gateway,' Fritz recalled. 'In this way several men were hurt. We saw Fusiliers Langmeier, Wittgens [and] Daglincks fall. Several others were badly wounded and Corporal Delcaretto and Fusilier Hipp were killed. Another man was also killed. I have forgotten his name.'[9]

> Toward half past two in the afternoon, Sous-Lieutenant Vilain was returning from visiting the post by the breach, and crossing the courtyard diagonally in the direction of the big gateways [*said Maine*]. A bullet fired from the building hit him square in the forehead. He fell as if struck by lightning. In that moment, it is fair to say, a feeling of terrible sadness came over us, penetrating to the foundation of the soul.[10]

'Mr. Vilain was hit between the eyes and killed instantly,' Berg said. 'Mr. Maudet was left. We had many dead and wounded, but in spite of that we held on . . . .'.[11]

If Maine was phlegmatic in speaking of Vilain's death fifteen years later, and Berg straightforward in writing of it the following day, Fritz veered on the melodramatic in telling about it only a few months later.

> Our [Sous-]Lieutenant, who I can still see in my mind's eye, his figure so young, was returning from the old breach, which we could see from that angle [*he said*]. He marched forward boldly, in the most natural way. He saluted the dead with his sword, said a word or two to the wounded who lay in the hot sun. Then, brandishing his sword in the air, he cried out to us: '*Vive la France!*' At the same instant a bullet hit him in the forehead. He fell, never to rise again.[12]

Command devolved on Sous-Lieutenant Maudet, who realized that the post between the two gateways was rapidly becoming untenable and immediately redeployed his forces.

'The [Sous-]Lieutenant ordered us to make for the shed which was in the southwest corner,' said Fritz. 'I had time to think that at some point I might take a course in military strategy – after all, I had studied with the best . . . The partly-demolished shed was nothing more than a low wall of bricks, on which rested various pieces of wood, intended to support a thatched roof. Sheltering behind this wall, we fired our bullets at the Mexicans who were trying to open the breach'.[13]

> We changed our position [*Maine said*]. The men of the reserve post between the two gateways, of whom I was one, joined up with the defenders of the south gateway, which had been strongly attacked, and all of us fell back on the open shed in the southwest corner of the courtyard, where we continued to fire.[14]

At almost the same moment a volley of shots brought down Fusiliers Rebers and Brunswick.[15]

'The firing continued to be very lively, quite heavy from some parts,' Berg would say. 'By this time we had about twenty men out of action. The enemy fire came from all sides, the doors of the house as well as the windows'.[16]

Felled in the middle of the corral, two other Fusiliers were too gravely wounded to continue to fight. Seeing *Tambour* Lai, one of them called out: 'Take my rifle. I'm finished. Here are my cartridges.'[17]

> The heat was overpowering [*said Maine*]. The sun, at its zenith, fell directly on our heads, a pitiless sun, devouring us as it can in the tropics. Under its direct rays the walls of the courtyard were a brilliant white, which hurt our eyes. When we opened our mouths to breathe, it was as if we were swallowing fire. The air was heavy as lead, and with the shimmering I had seen on plains and deserts at midday in the Summer. The dust kicked up by the spent bullets hitting the ground in the courtyard rose slowly in heavy spirals. At the same time, overheating because of the sun's rays and the rapidity of our shooting, the barrels of our rifles burned our hands like red hot iron. So intense was the heat that the redoubt was transformed into a furnace. We could see the decomposing bodies of the dead. In the space of an hour, the flesh began to smell and took on a strange palour.[18]

The Mexican plunging fire from the second-floor windows of the house was more frequent now, and harder to prevent.

Major Francisco Talavera of the Cordoba Battalion, a surgeon and doctor in his professional life, began looking for a suitable place to set up a makeshift hospital. He chose a piece of relatively flat land near the old and broken dam, advantageous as it was out of sight of the battle and close to water. Outside and inside the corral of the Hacienda de la Trinidad the Mexican and French troops continued trying to kill each other. The number of wounded grew.

> Jumbled up among the dead, because there was no means of helping them, our wounded lay where fell [*Maine said*]. We could hear the Mexican wounded on the other side of the wall moaning and crying out in their anguish. They invoked the Virgin [Mary] or cursed God and the Saints. Our men, by a supreme effort, despite their suffering, remained silent. They were fearful, the poor fellows, of revealing our losses and giving encouragement to the enemy.[19]

During a lull in the fighting the sixteen Foreign Legion prisoners captured by the Orizaba Lancers in the confusion after the second charge near the cactus hedge were moved eastward to the area behind the old inn on the north side of the road, where Milan had his command post. None of the Legionnaires had been killed in the skirmish, but several, particularly Fusiliers Bogucki and Van den Meerche, were seriously wounded, and five others, along with Kurz and the muleteer, Dominguez, were injured to one degree or another.[20] These wounded men were treated by Dr. Talavera at his field hospital, while the others – Fusiliers Segers, Gaertner, Shifer, Van den Bulcke, Jeannin, Zey, Verjus and the mysterious Fusilier Holler – were started, under guard, northwards along the road to La Joya.[21]

> The thirst dried the throat and we knew again the horrors of our situation [*Maine said*]. A white froth formed in the corners of our mouths and coagulated there. Our lips were dry like leather, our tongues swelled up and every breath was painful. Our chests heaved, our temples pounded as if to burst and our poor heads were spinning. Suffering to this degree was intolerable. Only those who have lived in such a deadly climate, and who know from experience the value of a drop of water, will understand.[22]

A bullet struck down *Tambour* Lai, passing clear through his chest, and he fell near where his comrades were defending the breach. It would not be his only wound that day.

> I saw wounded men dragging themselves on their stomachs, heads thrust forward, and, to appease the fever which consumed them, lick the pools of congealing blood which covered the ground [*said Maine*]. I saw others, mad with pain from their wounds, greedily drink the blood which flowed from their own bodies. Even though it was repugnant, disgusting, the thirst was so acute that we drank our own urine.[23]

There was another lull in the fighting. Parched, wracked by gnawing pains of hunger, light-headed from the heat and the powder smoke, Maine began hallucinating. He thought of rivers, childhood friends, old campaigns and tropical nights.

> I saw again my beautiful and green home of Perigord, and Mussidan, where I had been born, between two rivers, everywhere fragrant with the scent of gardens, and the little friends with whom I played as a child [*he said later*]. I saw myself as a young soldier in the Zouaves, then leaving for the Crimea, wounded in the trenches, taking part in the first assault on the Little Redan, decorated! I saw myself later in Africa, with the *Chasseurs a Pied* and exchanging shots with the Arabs, then giving up my stripes as a Sous-Officier to take part in this new expedition and coming to this country of Mexico where I was going to leave my bones.[24]

The hallucination was vivid and complex, but lasted only a few seconds.

Fritz said later that he thought about his mother.[25]

> Several of the men who had been wounded, and were isolated from their comrades, became delirious and now could not hold back their cries [said Maine]. Their demands for something to drink were heartrending. The hands contracted, the eyes bloodshot and staring, these unfortunates writhed in their agonies and beat their bare heads on the hard, dry ground.[26]

The continual firing of the single-shot rifles gradually clogged the barrels with grains of burned gunpowder, and there was no time to clean them. Fritz wanted to exchange his rifle for one dropped by a comrade. '[It] had been lying for some time in the sun,' he said. 'It was impossible for me to even load, it was so hot'.[27]

> There, right between the four walls, the sun of the tropics bore down on us with all its force [he said]. It burned us, like a rain of sparks and weakened from above those unfortunates lying on the ground, which was like an iron plate burned red in a furnace. Also what fever, the kind which consumes one! I wanted to speak, but I couldn't even think! . . . The mouth was foaming, the tongue swollen by the heat and the thirst, which ignited the throat, and those who were mutilated dragged themselves to lick the pools of blood which had dripped from the wounds of comrades already dead. Eyes on fire, the throat tightened, as if an iron collar was compressing it, the chest burning, we continued to deal out our bullets and death – even using the cartridges of those who, in falling, had left a few behind.[28]

Berg motioned to Fritz to join him.
'You understand?' he said. 'To the end!'[29]
At that moment a bullet ripped into Fritz's left arm.

> It did not take long for us to have an appreciation of the sufferings of our comrades [said Maine]. We had to watch in all directions at once: to the right, to the left, towards the windows of the building, towards the openings in the courtyard walls, because everywhere we could see the sun glistening on rifle barrels, and death was coming from everywhere. The bullets, thick like hail, beat on the shed, ricocheting against the walls, and covering us with showers of stones and rock splinters.
> Occasionally, one of us fell, and then the man beside him bent down to dig in his pockets and get such cartridges as he had left.[30]

'It was magnificent to see Mr. Maudet, alone at the head of a few men, firing his gun like a soldier,' Berg said.[31] Fritz watched Maudet, 'armed with a rifle, doing the job of a simple soldier,' remembering that the officer had volunteered for the mission, and thinking: 'He did not appear to regret it!'[32]

> I think that we got a fresh burst energy and the desire to defend ourselves [he said]. There was nothing like despair. All the weapons which were turned

against us, the rifles, the lances, the sabres – at the breaches, through holes in the walls, and at all the openings – all the bullets which came at us, which ricocheted, ploughed up the ground and showered us with stones, could do nothing to us. We had promised to die, and it would happen, sooner or later, that was all.

Our eyes were burned by the flood of light, by the shimmering, and the heat, which dried us up and penetrated our chests. Yet the fact was that we forced ourselves to keep our eyes open in order to see the enemy and fire the next bullet. Still standing in the hot sun, which weighed us down more and more, it was take aim, and then die. The brave Sous-Lieutenant was not able to go from one post to another. It would have been pointless anyway; the orders were graven on all our souls: fight and die! . . . What strong men, these Legionnaires are! The bullets whistled, like they were the wind of a tempest. They ricocheted and flattened themselves against the wall. They came into our shed. It was a last test of our resistance, a last attempt on us, and also a new suffering, to add to the others. Yet maybe not much against these men who had resolved not to submit, and who had already said the supreme farewell to life?[33]

'I would soon be seriously wounded, but I managed to remain standing,' Fritz added. 'We reloaded our rifles. The shots were fired. There would be more dead.'[34]

Milan tried a new ploy. If he could not destroy the enemy with bullets and manpower, he would use the elements.

The Mexicans now resorted to fire [*Fritz said*]. There was a pile of straw and wood at a shed outside the north-east wall, which they set fire to and which spread to the house. Dreadful, this smoke, which the wind brought to our little corner, and on our poor wounded, and which came down like a veil between us, our enemies and the different positions occupied by our comrades. When the fire had ended, we could see fewer defenders at the gateways and the breach.[35]

'Maudet was always with his gun,' he remarked. 'We crouched down behind the brick wall and fired at them. The Mexicans backed away. To escape our fire they took cover behind the wall of the shed which faced us, and we continued to shoot at each other.'[36]

The Mexicans began to leave, but then, to overcome our resistance, resorted to a new manoeuvre [*Maine said*]. They heaped up piles of straw and wood in the north-east corner and set it on fire. The flames engulfed an exterior shed, outside the wall on the Veracruz side of the courtyard, and rapidly spread to the roof. The wind, blowing from North to South, brought down upon us thick black smoke, which enveloped the courtyard. We were literally blinded and the acrid smoke from the burning straw caught in our throats, making far worse the already terrible thirst which gnawed at our guts. Finally, after about an hour and a half, the fire burned itself out. This incident could have been deadly, as, using the swirling smoke to mask their movements, the Mexicans had been able to come quite close. We fired more accurately.[37]

'The French fought with desperation, making any movement by our people very dangerous,' Campos said. 'Captain [Joaquin] Guido and Adjutant Rojas, arriving at an unfortunate time with the 'Izote' column, were mortally wounded. Those on the road were subjected to a torrent of fire'.[38]

It was probably at this point that 'Captain' Juan Canesco, the most prominent guerilla leader to die that day, fell with the National Guardsmen from the 'Izote' column.[39]

'A new wound flung me to the ground,' said Fritz. 'Weak from the loss of blood, I was not able to dress the wound. I gave away the three or four cartridges which I still had'.[40]

Sous-Lieutenant Maudet's command was now reduced to a mere twelve men. Corporal Berg was alone at the north gateway. Corporals Magnin and Pinzinger and Fusiliers Gorski and Kunassec clung grimly to their positions by the breach in the southeast wall. The others were with their officer in the semi-ruined shed in the southwest corner of the corral. They were Sergeant Morziki, Corporal Maine and Fusiliers Leonard, Catteau, Bertolotto, Wensel and Constantin.

> Not much hope remained, but nobody spoke of surrender [*said Maine*]. Standard-Bearer Maudet . . . a rifle in his hand, fought alongside us in the shed, because the incursions of the enemy did not permit him to move about the courtyard visiting the various positions. In truth, there was not really a need. The order was well known to all: hold out to the end, *jusqu'a la mort.*[41]

The wounded men in the shed did their bit, scrounging for cartridges and helping their comrades as best they could. If still able, they fired at the enemy when they could get a clear shot. Fritz, now with a head wound to add to his smashed left arm, saw Sergeant Germeys, like himself a veteran of the Crimea and Italy, wounded for a third time, and another Fusilier go down.

> Towards five o'clock, we had a moment of respite [*said Maine*]. The attackers withdrew one after the other to obey an order they had received, and we had time to take a breather.[42]

Inside the walls of the corral the Legionnaires waited. It was suddenly quiet outside, a new phase, and they wondered what was next. Then, said Maine, 'in that hot and colourful language which is the foundation of Spanish eloquence, Milan exhorted his men to finish us,' and Fusilier Natale Bertolotto, French-born of Italian descent, understood Spanish and translated for his comrades, 'word for word'.[43]

> What a humiliation, if you do not completely overcome these Frenchmen,

who must certainly be exhausted! [*Milan harangued his men*]. What a disgrace, if the Government of the Republic of Mexico one day has to reproach you for your weakness! Quickly defeat this handful of men, who are already as good as dead. The time has come. Who knows if their comrades are not even now marching to their aid? You can see how few of our enemies are left. Their resistance has given you an idea of the valour of all of them. In the name of the glory, of the honour and of the Independence of our country, launch a last assault – and I promise that you will all be recognized and rewarded. Bring me some of them alive, as visible proof your triumph. Capture these few men. After all you have done, this will be a triumph.[44]

'When he was finished, a huge clamour arose,' said Maine,[45] and Fritz remembered 'applause, many times repeated'.[46] 'We knew that the enemy was preparing for a new effort,' said Maine,[47] and Fritz recognized that 'soon all would perhaps be finished'.[48] 'Nevertheless, before the attack, Milan sent us a third summons to surrender,' said Maine. 'We did not bother to reply.'[49]

The time had, indeed, come.

'At a given signal of drums and bugles reinforcements came streaming from all directions, and the Mexicans bore down on the last twelve defenders of the walls,' said Berg, who was now the sole man at the North gateway. 'They penetrated the courtyard by all the openings, which we were powerless to protect effectively.[50] From all sides they yelled to us to surrender, that they would not harm us – that they were 'soldiers like us, not guerillas'.[51]

Out of ammunition, but having reversed his rifle so as to wield it like a club, Berg was swamped by his attackers, hit on the head, captured and dragged from the corral. Fritz saw the whole thing.

> A single man was by the main gate – in the midst of his comrades who lay on the ground in their last sleep – resting there, like a guard of honour at the door of a military installation or the headquarters of a Marshal of France [*he said*]. Does it matter to him? He has his orders. In effect, a hundred enemies arrived, surrounding him and taking him prisoner, despite his resistance. He envied the fate of his comrades, who lay scattered about on the ground. He also had promised to resist, *jusqu'a la mort*. He expected to die. He was made a prisoner of Milan. All the same, he would have a wound to show. Entry, which until then had been obstructed by a single man, was now possible. The Mexicans were massed to enter. We fired at them. Our bullets, striking the wall, ricocheted on those present, fifteen in a little time. Their bodies formed a new barricade.[52]

Through drifting smoke Fritz thought that it was Corporal Magnin at the gate, but he was at the southeast breach. A Mexican scrambled through it and stabbed him in the hand. Corporal Pinzinger's forearms were badly slashed as he fended off blows from a sword. A Mexican gun-butted Gorski in the face and others fell on Kunassec, bearing him to the ground. The four men were dragged through the breach and flung against the wall outside.[53]

Berg was not the only one who had heard the Mexican soldiers shouting for the Legionnaires to surrender.

> Colonel Milan had told his men not to kill us, because he respected the lives of brave men who were prepared to follow to the last extremity the orders given them: to fight *jusqu'a la mort* [*Fritz said*]. There were some among us who did not seek any such consideration. If they were not killed, they said, it would not be their fault, and they had wounds to prove they had been willing to die.[54]

'At this point the soldier Barrientos, of the Jalapa Battalion, assisted by two or three others, managed to break through the stone wall,' Campos wrote. 'He was killed in the act, but it made the final assault possible. When the attack was launched it gladdened the hearts of the Republicans, until they got into the courtyard and saw the numbers of dead and wounded there. What a waste of lives. French and Mexicans hacked each other with machetes and bayonets. There was no room to use their rifles, as the combatants were so close that they could not shoot without hitting their own men'.[55]

'The assault resumed, more terrible than before,' Maine remembered.[56]

> The enemy came at us from all the openings at the same time [*he said*]. Under the shed, we waited, chests heaving, fingers curled round the triggers of our rifles. Shaking and feverish, we focused all our attention on aiming. Each one of our shots made a hole in their ranks, but for each one killed ten more came at us.
>
> The gateway not long ago defended by Berg, the opening made in the opposite wall, the windows and the door of the hacienda spewed out a flood of assailants, who flung themselves on the ground behind the crumbling little wall of the shed, then from that place advanced into the courtyard. Other adversaries kept coming through the old breach.[57]

Some Lancers, bolder than the rest, spurred their horses through the new break in the East wall. The wounded *Tabour* Lai struggled to his feet and an officer dashed at him, sabre upraised. Lai dodged, put up his hand to fend off the blow and the swinging blade carried away three fingers of his hand.

> The attackers hit us through at all the openings at the same time, turning their efforts towards the shed, our last refuge [*said Fritz*]. They seemed to have little enthusiasm for taking our lives after the harangue by their Colonel. They wanted to take us prisoner, but that was not our intention . . . and we did not consider the mass of troops to be intimidating.[58]

The men in the ruined shed in the southwest corner maintained a steady fire, picking their targets carefully. There were now only eight still standing, some of them already wounded. They were Sous-Lieutenant Maudet, Sergeant Morziki,

Corporal Maine and Fusiliers Bertolotto, Leonard, Wensel, Constantine and Catteau.

> The issue for us was not in any doubt [*said Maine*]. Driven into our corner like wild boars in their lairs, we anticipated the *coup de gras*. Every minute one of us fell, Bertolotto and later Leonard. I found myself between Sergeant Morziki, on my left, and Sous-Lieutenant Maudet, on my right. Suddenly Morziki was hit in the temple by a bullet coming from the corner of the breach. His body sagged and his head fell on my shoulder. I turned and looked him in the face. The mouth and the eyes were wide open.[59]

'Morziki is dead,' he told Maudet.
'Bah!' came the cold reply. 'Another one. It will soon be our turn.'[60]
He continued firing. Morziki's lifeless arm fell against Maine, who pushed his body to the wall and quickly groped in the dead man's pockets for any remaining cartridges.
'He had two,' he said later. 'I took them.'[61]
The wounded Fritz was also searching Morziki's body for cartridges and 'retrieved two from the pockets' and 'a few others from the sergeant's cartridge box'.[62]
The number of whole men was dwindling rapidly. Leonard, though wounded again, was among those still standing, and firing from the back of the shed. Fritz was lying down near the front.

> All the others, dead or wounded [*he said*]. The five comrades were themselves covered with wounds. They knew well that I did not wish to be a prisoner. Only six combatants left! These are their names: Sous-Lieutenant Maudet, Corporal Maine, Fusiliers Catteau, Wensel, Constantine and Leonard.[63]

'Fire all your bullets!' Fritz heard Maudet say. 'Fire – and save the last cartridge.'[64]

> We were no more than five: Sous-Lieutenant Maudet, a Prussian named Wensel, Catteau, Constantine, all three Fusiliers, and me [*he said*]. We always had respect for the enemy, but we continued fighting to the end, when all the cartridges were gone. A few shots more, and then we had just one each. It was about six o'clock, and we had been fighting since the morning.[65]

'Load your weapons,' Maine remembered Maudet saying. 'You will fire on command – then we will charge with the bayonet. You will follow me.'[66]
Fritz recalled Maudet's next to last order in much the same way: 'You will fire on my command, then charge with the bayonet. You will allow me to be the first. *Mes enfants*, I bid you farewell.'[67]

> I was on the ground, not thinking of my wounds, but shaking with rage at not being able to use my rifle, and above all at not being able to be with my comrades, who were going out to die[68] [*Fritz said*]. The silence which reigned within our shed intrigued the Mexicans in the shed in front of us. Little by little they gathered behind the brick wall. They thought that our side was finished, that the Legionnaires had given up all resistance. Finished? . . . Not yet. And the order, where was it? Then they dared to advance into the courtyard.[69]

The final minutes of the Combat of Cameron were recorded by a participant – Corporal Maine – fifteen years later, and by an observer – Fusilier Fritz – only a matter of months later.

'The Mexicans advanced, but were not firing at us,' said Maine. 'The courtyard was filled with them. There was a great silence around us. The moment was solemn: the wounded were quiet. In our little corner we did not stir, we waited.'[70]

> 'Aim! . . . Fire!' was at last ordered by the Standard-Bearer of the Regiment [*said Fritz*]. The five bullets were discharged and he sprang over the wall and charged with the bayonet, followed by his men, who I saw bound forward like lions. All the Mexican guns were turned on them.[71]

'We fired our five shots, and, with him at the head, leapt forward, with bayonets at the ready,' said Maine. 'A formidable volley met us. The air trembled under this explosion of fire and I thought the earth would open. At this moment, Fusilier Catteau flung himself in front of his officer and, as he went to throw his arms around him, to make a shield with his own body, he fell, hit by nineteen bullets. Despite this devotion, the [Sous-]Lieutenant was also struck by two bullets: one in the flank, the other in the right thigh. Wensel was also hit, the bullet hitting him high in the shoulder, but passing through without touching the bone. He got up at once. Then we were three: Wensel, Constantin and myself.'[72]

As Maudet and his men had surged forward, the wounded Fusilier Leonard stood up and tried to follow them, but his legs gave way and he fell back.

Fritz, from his prone position, could see that 'the three of our comrades still standing were disposed to continue the charge, although surrounded by a threatening circle of bayonets.'[73]

'For a moment we looked silently at the [Sous-]Lieutenant, lying on his back, and were about to jump over his body and charge again,' recalled Maine. 'But already the Mexicans had come at us from all directions, the points of their bayonets touching our chests'.[74]

> 'Stop!' a voice shouted [*Fritz recalled*]. He who gave the order, had a strong arm and a great air of authority. He lifted with his sabre the points of the Mexican bayonets.
> 'And you, Gentlemen – do you surrender?'
> I quote, word for word, their response. They were not words of men who felt themselves vanquished:

'We will surrender, if you will assist and take care of our Lieutenant, and all our comrades there who, like him, are wounded, and if you promise to let us retain our equipment and our weapons. Finally, we will surrender if you will agree to attest that, to the last extremity, we have all done our duty.'

All this time, they held their bayonets level, as if to continue the charge. These three soldiers, three soldiers of France, imposed these conditions, one might almost say, on an army! . . .

'One can refuse nothing to men like you!' responded the officer.[75]

Colonel Angel Luciano Cambas had studied in France and spoke the language perfectly. Fritz, used to the gulf in rank between officers and men, was surprised when 'he offered an arm to two of these men, although the blood on them showed that they were wounded'.[76]

'The first words of this exchange had been in Spanish,' Maine said later. ' "Speak to me in French," he said to me. "That would be best, otherwise these men may take you for a Spaniard, and may want to kill you, and perhaps will not wish to obey me . . ." However, the officer spoke to one of his men. He then returned and said to me: "Come with me." He offered me his arm, gave the other to Wensel, and went towards the house. Constantin followed closely behind us.

'As I threw a glance at our officer, he [Cambas] said to me: "I have given an order for care to be given to him. They have gone to look for a stretcher. You can count on me. Nothing bad is going to happen to you."

'It is true to say that I expected to be shot, but I was indifferent about it. I told him this.

' "No! No!" Cambas responded quickly. "I am here for your protection."

'At the same moment, going towards the house, as we came out on the road, still on his arm, an irregular mounted man came at us with pistols in both hands and fired two shots at Wensel and I. Without saying a word, the officer drew his revolver from his belt and coldly pointed it at the head of the wretch, who reeled back in the saddle and veered off. Then we continued along the road with him.

'We came to a small rise in the ground some distance from the hacienda, where Colonel Milan was with his Staff.

' "Is this all?" Milan demanded in Spanish.

'On being told it was, he burst out: "These are not men. They are devils!"

'Then, turning to we three Legionnaires, he spoke in French.

' "You are thirsty, gentlemen, without doubt," he said. "I have already sent for some water. Rest and do not be fearful. We already have several of your comrades who you are soon going to join. We are civilized people, we like to feel, and we know the respect which must be shown to prisoners taken as you have been".'[77]

Back in the corral the Mexicans were moving in to help those Legionnaires who still breathed.

An officer saw me when I raised my head above the wall in front of the shed [*said Fritz*][78]. Because of my wounds, I could not go with the Mexican officer. He had me mounted on a horse.[79]

He looked at his comrades – and knew that he was seeing his own reflection.

> They no longer had their bronzed faces, what with the fatigue, the sweat, the dust, the smoke from the gunpowder [*he said*]. Their clothes were tattered and shredded from the bullets. Moreover, clotted blood was on our clothes and our hands. Immediately we got there we were offered food and water.[80]

'We were given water and *tortillas*, a kind of crepe made of corn which the country people of Mexico make like bread,' said Maine. 'We wolfed it down enthusiastically.'[81]

> The wounded, and [Sous-]Lieutenant Maudet, on a stretcher, were taken to a place called the dam of Camaron [*said Fritz*].[82] We did not have any reason to be ashamed, and were very well treated by the doctors. Milan and his officers did not try to conceal their admiration for the heroes who had been in the fight. Night came – I don't think all the prisoners, but certainly all the walking wounded, and the Mexican troops, took the road to La Joya.[83]

They were accompanied by Squadron Commander Jimenez and his Orizaba Lancers, who had first discovered, then attacked, them almost ten hours earlier.[84] Fusilier Fritz was not among the men making their way to La Joya as Doctor Talavera, after examining his shattered left arm, decided on amputation and removed it just above the elbow. Other Legionnaires, also deemed too badly injured to undertake the eight-kilometre (five-mile) walk to the Mexican camp, were also kept at the dam. Among them were Fusiliers Van den Meersche and Bogucki.

> Accompanied by our captors we took the road towards their encampment at La Joya, [*said Maine*]. It was an emotional journey and helping the wounded slowed us all down. We eventually arrived and there, despite the word of Colonel Cambas, our weapons, which we had not surrendered, were taken from us. We were reunited with our comrades who had been taken prisoner before us. Exhausted by the fatigue and by the suffering, black from the gunpowder, the dust and the sweat, haggard and red-eyed, we did not really resemble human beings. Our clothes and hats were riddled. My own had more than forty bullet holes, but by extraordinary luck, during that long struggle I had not even been touched. How had we managed to come through the day safe and sound? We did not understand it ourselves, and the Mexicans understood it even less. Only the following day I examined my limbs, almost doubting that it had been me and checking to see if I was actually alive![85]

When Milan himself returned to La Joya in the evening, Corporal Berg was taken before him and asked permission to write a letter to Colonel Jeanningros, telling him of the fight at the Hacienda de la Trinidad. The request was approved. In fact, Berg would say later that he was given 'all that I asked for'.[86]

At the scene of the battle a clean-up was in progress and Captain Campos, who had been in at the beginning of the battle, walked through the corral.

> The spectacle in the courtyard was horrifying, yet moving [*he wrote later*]. French and Mexicans lay there, their broken bodies mingled in the eternal sleep of death, the tragic result of their mutual fury. Already they stood before God, purified, nobly having accomplished their duty and made the supreme sacrifice . . .[87]

Milan had ordered that the dead were to be buried and that, as far as possible, all traces of what had taken place be removed, or at least put out of sight. The bodies were sorted out and stripped, while National Guardsmen put down their weapons and took up shovels to dig two trenches outside the southwest wall of the corral, fittingly more or less behind the ruined shed where the last of the men of the Foreign Legion had made their final stand. There was one trench for the Mexican dead, another for the French. By the time the job was completed it was too dark to begin proper burials, so the two piles of bodies were simply pushed into the trenches and left. The trenches could be filled in the morning. In the blackness of the night exhausted National Guardsmen, who had fought since noon, stumbled their way along the road to La Joya.

'The immolation had been complete,' said Fritz. 'Yet we had saved the convoy and the Mexicans in this affair had lost more than three hundred of their men'.[88]

12
The Aftermath

Day One – 1st May

At Chiquihuite, Colonel Jeanningros had not really anticipated any news from *La Compagnie Danjou* to reach him on 30 April, expecting the return of the 3rd Company either very late in the evening or overnight. At dawn on Friday, 1 May, he was no more than mildly surprised when told they had not yet reported in, reasoning that, as Danjou had drawn rations for thirty-six hours, he might well, in reconnoitering east of Palo Verde, have met up with the westbound convoy, in which case he would be accompanying it to Chiquihuite. However, if this were to be the case, he expected some word from Danjou, probably via one of the Indians used as messengers.

By late afternoon, becoming impatient at hearing nothing, Jeanningros began making some tentative plans. In his Official Report, he would explain to Commander-in-Chief Forey that he chose 'my 1st Company, with mules, to go with me to discover if Captain Danjou had been able to meet the convoy, or find out what was the cause of his absence'.[1] The 1st Company drew rations for twenty-four hours[2] and was told to be prepared to move out soon after dark. Then the situation suddenly changed.

'An Indian arrived from [the direction of] Vera Cruz and told me the French had been in a battle with Mexicans,' Jeanningros reported to Forey.[3]

It could be only *La Compagnie Danjou*, or the convoy – or both. After giving the tired messenger food and a chance to rest a little, Jeanningros promised him twenty-five piastres to return to La Soledad by a roundabout route, and wrote a note for Lieutenant-Colonel Giraud of the 2nd Battalion. Then he called his *Clarion*.

> I was half way up the mountain, parrot shooting, and had just sat down to rest myself and enjoy the fine view of the country which the place commanded, when suddenly I heard the clear sharp note of the trumpet sounding the *generale* [*Corporal M'Alevey would say later*]. Starting to my feet, I listened with breathless attention, and in a moment after, the chorus was taken up by a dozen others, so that the entire mountain echoed with the alarming cry. Seizing my gun I ran furiously down the mountain, and found the troops already under arms. I had barely joined my company when the trumpets sounded the regimental march, and off we went, whither I did not yet know. As soon as we were fairly started, I turned to the person next [to] me and asked the cause of the alarm. By him I was informed that the

Company that had set out the night before... had been surrounded at Cameron by guerillas and had been engaged all day. 'God grant', said I, 'that we may not be too late to assist the poor fellows,' and a shudder passed through my body as I thought of my friend Morziki.[4]

Jeanningros planned to add a number of men from Captain Saussier's Company of Grenadiers at Paso del Macho and had instructed Commandant Regnault to send forty Fusiliers from Chiquihuite to replace them as soon as possible. Regnault was also to advise newly-promoted General de Maussion, the Brigade Commander, of the situation and request reinforcements.[5] 'Marching rapidly', Jeanningros reached Paso del Macho, picked up six squads of Grenadiers – bringing his force to just over one hundred and fifty – and two extra mules loaded with ammunition. He continued eastward, feeling, he would tell Forey, 'much anxiety about the 3rd Company'.[6] M'Alevey remembered that they 'marched all night, and at four o'clock in the morning halted and made coffee, and when the sun had well risen, started once more'.[7] The column was still west of Camaron when their attention was drawn to a spectral, near-naked figure, covered with dried blood and dirt, lurking in the bushes on the right-hand side of the road.

> Within a mile of Cameron we came on the first token of the tragedy that had recently taken place [*M'Alevey recalled*]... almost dead from loss of blood and thirst, we found the drummer of the unfortunate Company. A bullet had gone through his chest and out at his back, and three of his fingers had been chopped off by a sabre cut. A little brandy was given to him, the doctor hastily dressed his wounds, and one or two soldiers unpacked their haversacks and gave him the clothing he so badly needed.[8]

'I am the last of the 3rd,' *Tambour* Lai gasped out.[9]

Minutes later, much recovered, and speaking with what Jeanningros considered to be 'great lucidity of spirit', Lai provided an essentially accurate, if understandably slightly garbled, account of the 3rd Company's clash with the enemy at Camaron. Pressed about the number of Mexicans involved, he said that he had 'heard Captain Danjou estimate the enemy forces at 8 or 900 cavalry and 1,500 infantry',[10] but could give no details about the final stages of the battle, as he had lost consciousness after being wounded the second time.

'I remember nothing more till I awoke... and found myself naked lying among the other dead men,' he explained.[11]

> The Mexicans separated their wounded from the others [*said Lai*]. Then they began to separate the bodies. They gathered their compatriots on one side, and the French bodies were placed apart from them. I found myself fainting, and incapable of attempting any movement, and they put me with a number of our dead. Recovering from my light-headedness, doubtless due to the coolness of the night, I found myself in the middle of the bodies. I still had no strength to move. I could hear them digging the trenches... I was thrown in, still alive!... Since I did not cry out they thought I was no

longer alive. Some kind of force seemed to try to move me. I understood that this could be the end. I disengaged myself from the pile of bodies which surrounded me where I had been thrown. I had only one good hand to help me. The other just hung, mutilated, from my arm. I got up and moved away from the bodies of my poor comrades. I dragged myself into the bushes and started to move in the direction from which you came – I don't think I travelled very far. Unable to go any further, I just crouched down, to await death, there where you found me just now. I had commended my soul to God.

Once, a rustling sound woke me up, and then I began to tremble with fear. Coyotes were approaching me. They came to see, no doubt, if they could eat me. Three or four times they came very close. I wanted to shout at them, but my voice froze in my throat. I tried to make a noise with my feet, and to use my good hand to shake the grass and the bushes around me. They fled, but came back, and closer than before. This was perhaps the sight which I found to be the most horrible.[12]

Putting Lai on one of the relief force's mules, Jeanningros led his men down the road towards Camaron, increasingly watchful for Mexicans. They arrived on the outskirts of the hamlet in mid-afternoon and moved cautiously up to the ruined and smoke-begrimed walls of the hacienda, then into the courtyard.

It had been generally cleaned up, bodies removed, along with the more obvious debris of battle, as Milan had ordered. Outside the back wall the Legionnaires found the trench where fifty Mexican bodies had been placed, and another nearby, in which were the naked bodies of the dead of the 3rd of the 1st.[13]

I saw such a sight as I pray God I may never witness again [*M'Alevey would say*] . . . our dead *compagnons d'armes* had been collected by the guerillas and placed in a deep straight trench . . . Shoulder to shoulder in the ranks of death, and divested of every article of clothing, lay the brave fellows – every man of whom I had known personally. A bright warm sun was shining on their ghastly features and cold stiff forms; most of them had their arms extended and their hands tightly clenched in a fighting posture.[14]

Jeanningros, in his Official Report, was less emotional.

I found in a trench, to the right of the house, 16 bodies, all naked, but not having been mutilated [*he wrote*]. I recognized Captain Danjou, Sous-Lieutenant Vilain, the Sergeant-Major [Tonel] and others laid face down against the earth in a deep trench, beyond help. I could find no trace of the wounded or the others.[15]

Dusk was falling, and Jeanningros was faced with a wrenching dilemma. Should he camp that night at Camaron, and bury the dead, or pull back towards Chiquihuite and summon reinforcements? There seemed at least the possibility of a Mexican attack, and properly burying the dead would take several hours at best, if only

The Aftermath 153

because, as M'Alevey would point out, 'we had neither pick nor spade'.[16] A Legionnaire, poking about among some of the debris of the battle, which had been piled out of sight behind the southern wall of the corral, picked up a Spencer carbine.[17] Eventually, Jeanningros made the difficult decision to fall back to Paso Ancho, inform his superiors and make the best of things until first light the following day. Grumbling, said M'Alevey, that they had to retire 'without exchanging a shot with the assassins who had slaughtered our comrades',[18] the Legionnaires retraced their steps to Paso Ancho and went into camp. Every man was engaged with his own thoughts, and they talked in subdued tones.

* * *

Mid-morning on 1 May a courier left the Mexican camp at La Joya heading for Jalapa. He carried Colonel Milan's Official Report of the fight of the previous day, which he had finished writing just after midnight. It was addressed to the Central Brigade's General-in-Chief, Miguel Blanco, at Fort San Lorenzo, near Puebla. Milan knew that the Mexican losses had been huge for what, at the senior military level, would probably be seen as a limited return, and for him to have admitted to some three hundred dead, and perhaps half as many again wounded, would have caused an enormous number of questions. However, the local guerilla bands – which had taken by far and away the heaviest casualties – were always viewed with considerable suspicion by the Mexican Republican Army, as they tended to be indisciplined, to fight beside it when it suited them, and to act as freelance brigands when it did not. Consequently, Milan obfuscated his report, confining his mention of casualties to officers and men of the National Guard units. He apparently also thought it prudent to omit any reference to the munitions and bullion convoy he had originally hoped to capture.

> 30 April 1863
>
> I have the honour to inform you that in accordance with orders from your Government and Headquarters, dated the 12th, I left Jalapa and positioned myself on the road between Veracruz and Orizaba. I had been able to create a Central Brigade, made up of 'Independence' battalions: the National Guard of Jalapa, 'Zamora' and 'Cordoba' are the forces I succeeded in uniting into a body of 650 Infantry and 200 Cavalry. This morning I left with the cavalry, as I often do, to reconnoitre various points along the road.[19] We met a French force going down the road to Chiquihuite, and I at once gave orders to attack them, but having formed a square, they resisted the attack and then withdrew rapidly to the ruined house in Camaron, where they ensconced themselves, opening up embrasures in the walls through which to shoot.[20]
>
> Our cavalry approached the house and came under heavy fire. I had the infantry, who had remained in the encampment, brought up quickly and mounted an attack. However, the enemy was well equipped and we lacked artillery to open a breach in the walls and tools to break through it.

The battle lasted half the day, finishing almost at dusk, and was fought by our opponents with unquestionable valour, in the belief that we were guerillas and that we would never allow them to escape with their lives. At last they succumbed, after two officers had been killed, and the other, being wounded[,] unable to fight for the greater part of the battle.[21] These officers belonged to the 3rd Company of the 1st Battalion of the Foreign Legion, commanded by a Captain, who was acting as a substitute for the Major of the Corps,[22] and who was killed, as was a Sous-Lieutenant. The other Sous-Lieutenant was seriously wounded and was taken prisoner. He was the Standard-Bearer of the regiment. Of the sixty (sic) soldiers, twenty died, and of the others[,] sixteen were seriously wounded, leaving 24 prisoners to fall into our hands, not even one escaping.[23] We cleared the field, picking up all arms, and the wounded prisoners have been given careful attention by the Brigade's medical section. On our part, we have to lament some misfortunes[,] of which I will inform you in detail as soon as I receive the reports of the officers of the units. Lieutenant-Colonel Jose Ayala, my Chief of Staff, was killed at the beginning of the battle, and three lieutenants and three captains were wounded, while our losses in the troop class totalled sixteen dead and eighteen wounded.[24] All the citizens who make up the Central Brigade did their duty. I will send you at the first opportunity the names of those who lost their lives or who shed their blood while in defence of our Independence.[25] In the meantime, I beg you to favour me by informing the President of the Republic of this small clash of arms, which shows that the invaders will not permit themselves to be attacked with impunity in the territory of the State of Veracruz.

Colonel Francisco de P. Milan
Comandante Militar de Veracruz[26]

Corporal Berg, who was probably the best-educated of the men of the 3rd of the 1st, had been hard at work compiling his list of the prisoners to send to Colonel Jeanningros. After collecting the names of those held in the general area for prisoners, Berg, who was unhurt except for a bruised head, visited the wounded men in Dr. Talavera's new makeshift hospital area at La Joya, writing down their names as he encountered them. When he was done he returned to the prisoners' area and began composing his letter, heading it: 'In the Camp, May 1st, 1863.'

'My Colonel,' Berg began. 'In the name of all my comrades I send you this account of the action which took place yesterday, April 30.' He detailed the march from Chiquihuite, the first alarm, the repulsing of the Mexican cavalry at the two defensive squares and the battle at the Hacienda de la Trinidad, praising the conduct of his three officers. Then, buried about two-thirds of the way through the letter, was a phrase which has echoed through the annals of the Foreign Legion for almost a century-and-a-half: 'The 3rd of the 1st is dead, my Colonel, but it did enough to make those who speak of it say: "It had nothing but good soldiers".'

We are now to be found in the camp of Colonel Milan [*the letter continued*]. We are surrounded by consideration and by all the care which can be given to us. The officers are men of heart and honour. They have known misfortune, and the dignity of their behaviour shows that they are true soldiers, who know how to fight and how to honour brave men they have defeated.

Berg explained that he was providing 'the names of all of us who are present in the Mexican camp', and, after noting that Sous-Lieutenant Maudet's 'thigh was shattered by a bullet', went on to identify forty men, including himself, as having emerged alive – though some barely so – from the carnage of the battle. He told Jeanningros that by subtracting the names of the survivors from those of the sixty-five men who had left Chiquihuite some thirty hours earlier, 'you will know the names of the dead', and ended his letter: 'We have, my Colonel, the honour of being your respectful subordinates. For all of us, E. Berg, Corporal.'

He listed, frequently phonetically, nineteen men under the heading 'The Names of the Wounded', and described their injuries:

> Jermet [Germeys], Sergeant, arm broken in three places; they will amputate at the shoulder.
> Delcarreto [Delcaretto], Corporal, a bullet below the left nipple.
> Peninger [Pinzinger], Corporal, both hands mangled.
> Constantin, two wounds, one in the shoulder, and a bullet wound in the arm.
> Baas, a broken arm and a bullet wound in the head.
> Fitz [Fritz], the same.
> Devrisme [De Vries], a head wound (very serious).
> Rebers, a bullet wound in the kidney.
> Leonard, the same in the nape of the neck and another in the arm.
> Kurtz [Kurz], the same, in the foot.
> Lemmer, the same, in the armpit.
> Rohr, his right eye was taken out, and part of the skull to the ear.
> Fimmerman [Timmermans] two bullet wounds in the belly.
> Dael, a bullet wound in the thigh, another in the foot and another in the calf.
> Dalinsky [Daglincks], a bullet wound in the nape of the neck.
> Van-nonsial [Van Opstal], a bayonet wound in the head.
> Bogkiki [Bogucki], a sabre cut on the head.
> Venzel [Wensel], a bad wound in the head and a bullet wound in the neck.
> A man we don't know. I think he is Catteau.

The 'man we don't know' was obviously not Catteau, who had died at the hacienda. A comparison with Berg's lists of wounded and unwounded, and the muster roll for the 3rd of the 1st at midnight on 29 April, shows this man to have been Fusilier Josef Van den Meersche, and his head wound, or wounds, must have been so disfiguring as to have made him unrecognizable. Berg correctly described the serious nature of the wounds of Sergeant Jean Germeys, Corporal Adolfi

Delcaretto and Fusiliers Jean Timmermans, Constant Dael, Ludwig Rohr and Jean Baas. Fusilier Hans Kurz had been the first man to be wounded – by the marksman as *La Compagnie Danjou* approached Camaron from the east – and was probably very weak from loss of blood. Fusiliers Hartog De Vries, Luitpol Van Opstal, Anton Bogucki, the 'man we don't know' – Van den Meersche – and Kurz had been among the sixteen captured before the Hacienda de la Trinidad was reached. As they were infantrymen, attacked by cavalry, it is probable that, like Bogucki, Van Opstal, De Vries – and no doubt Van den Meersche – all the head wounds had been received from sabres, rather than from lances. Apparently, Berg overestimated the seriousness of the injuries of Fusiliers Gottfried Wensel and De Vries, which perhaps looked worse than was actually the case, and perhaps saw Fusilier Fritz before Dr. Talavera amputated his left arm above the elbow.

Berg also mentioned 'Captain Danjou's muleteer [Jose Dominguez], a bullet wound in the leg,' and then went on to list twenty-one men, including himself, under the heading: 'Those not wounded.'

> Palman [Palmaert], Sergeant – bruised shoulder. Schaffner (Sergeant) – wounded by debris in the face. Berg, Corporal – bruised head. Magnin, Corporal – slight hand wound. Maine, Corporal – Segers, Fusilier – Billod, idem – Gautner [Gaertner], idem – Schrublich [Schreiblich] bruised side[,] Verjus – Seffrin, a slight bayonet wound in the chest. Holler – Vandenbruck [Van den Bulcke] – Schiffer [Schifer] – Jeannin – Merlet, hit in the head by a stone – Brunswick – Conrad [Konrad], Mr. Danjou's orderly, from the 5th of the 1st – Gorzki [Gorski], a wound from a blow from a gun butt in the face – Zey – Kunassek [Kunassec].[27]

It was just as well that Berg had drawn up his list, as it was the last time that the survivors of the battle would all be together, either at Dr. Talavera's hospital area or the prisoners' compound, and their numbers even then were fluid.

Puebla was invested by the French, of course, but couriers, moving carefully, and using paths known to the Mexicans but not to their enemies, were still able to come and go, and reaching the surrounding forts was even less difficult. The courier carrying Milan's report to Blanco at Fort San Lorenzo also had Berg's letter to Jeanningros, and would pass through Jalapa.

Shortly after his departure Fusiliers Bogucki and Van den Meersche succumbed to their head wounds, as did a guerilla leader named Donaciano Perez. Milan ordered them buried on the bank of the Rio Chiquito and told the local inhabitants to plant wild white lilies to mark their graves.[28]

Using Berg's method of subtracting the names of the forty-one survivors of the 3rd of the 1st – including Sous-Lieutenant Maudet – and taking into account the fact that *Tambour* Lai had been retrieved by Jeanningros the very day that Berg was writing from La Joya, it can be determined that the dead of Camerone were: Captain Jean Danjou, Sous-Lieutenant Jean Vilain, Sergeant-Major Henri Tonel, Sergeant Marie Morziki and Corporal Aime Favas, along with Fusiliers Aloysio Bernardo, Natale Bertolotto, Nikolas Burgiser, George Catenhusen, Victor Catteau, Peter Conrad, Peter Dicken, Charles Dubois, Friedrich Friedrich, Georg

Fursbaz, Louis Groux, Emile Hipp, Felix Langmeier, Louis Lernoud, Johann Reus, Daniel Seiler, Henri Vandesavel and Karl Wittgens – a total of twenty-three men.[29]

* * *

The convoy, inching its way westward from La Purga, had arrived at La Soledad on the afternoon of 30 April, at a time when the battle at Camaron was at its height. A British courier – a Queen's Messenger, carrying dispatches for the British Embassy in Mexico City – had been at La Soledad for two days, waiting for a military escort to Chiquihuite, and was glad to see the convoy arrive.

It had been accompanied by Colonel Dupin and his *Contre-guerilla*, not merely because they were doing escort duty, but also because he was moving his unit's headquarters to La Soledad,[30] and he arrived with Major Rodriguez and twenty-five men of Colonel Figurero's Mexican Auxiliary Cavalry. Clearly, the convoy would not only overnight at La Soledad, but would need to spend the next day there, too, preparing for the long and difficult haul to Chiquihuite.

Day Two – 2nd May

At Paso Ancho, early in the morning of Saturday, 2 May, Jeanningros called his secretary, Sous-Lieutenant Philippe Galloni d'Istria, and dictated a brief note to General de Maussion at Orizaba.

> My Regiment is scattered . . . [he said]. I am not able to deploy even 250 men at the moment to do everything, without leaving unprotected the posts guarding the sick. It is vital that you send me reinforcements, at least until regular troops are based permanently at Palo Verde.[31]

The message was sent off to Chiquihuite, and a rider would take it on through Cordoba to de Maussion at Orizaba. Alerted by Commandant Regnault the previous day that a crisis might be in the offing, the Commander of the Reserve Brigade had already moved quickly, sending men of the *Infanterie de Marine* to take over the duties of the Regiment Etranger at Chiquihuite and Paso del Macho.

As soon as the first of them arrived on the morning of 2 May, Regnault, having assembled all available men of the Regiment Etranger, marched out of the camp, taking with him a Company of the *Infanterie de Marine*. At Paso del Macho they relieved Captain Saussier's Company of Grenadiers and the forty Legionnaires sent to him the previous day. His force thus well augmented, Regnault marched briskly east to Paso Ancho, where Jeanningros waited impatiently, but did not arrive until late afternoon, necessitating a second night being spent there.

* * *

At La Joya, Colonel Milan's spies had alerted him to the movements of Jeanningros and his column on the previous day, and he knew that they had only retraced their steps as far as Paso Ancho, where they would obviously wait for reinforcements. He was also aware of the arrival of the convoy at La Soledad. Nevertheless, he remained at La Joya, giving Dr. Talavera every opportunity to treat all the wounded, friend and foe alike. Legionnaires subsequently told Commandant Regnault: 'Among the enemy troops, the Jalapa Battalion, officers and soldiers, remarked about the attention and care given to our prisoners'.[32]

Overall, it was a quiet day at La Joya, but in Jalapa there was a sensation. Details of the battle became known to the Editor of the Jalapa *Independiente* from the courier taking Milan's report to General Blanco. He was able to chronicle the death of Chief of Staff, Lieutenant-Colonel Jose Ayala, and the wounding of other officers, but instead of reporting the sixteen National Guardsmen killed and eighteen wounded, simply noted a total of eighteen unspecified casualties. Foreign Legion losses were given, as they had been by Milan, as twenty dead, sixteen wounded and twenty-four taken prisoner.[33]

* * *

At La Soledad, the convoy's day of rest allowed Lieutenant-Colonel Giraud to do some planning. It had been on the road since 14 April and had already faced enormous logistical difficulties in its slow and ponderous progress from La Tejeria. Giraud believed that it was unwieldy and decided to split it into two parts for the remainder of the journey to Chiquihuite.

The first section would be led off by two carriages, one carrying a French Inspector of Mines named Laure, a Mexican architect and a married couple, the other occupied by the Queen's Messenger and the three million in gold francs for the troops at Puebla. The wagons carrying the badly needed ammunition would likewise be part of the first section, while the second section would comprise the heavy siege guns, along with the mule train carrying material destined for the Quartermaster General, largely supplies for the Army canteens, and the wagons loaded with stores for the merchants in Cordoba and Orizaba.[34]

Giraud decided that the first section would be guarded by the 1st Battalion's Voltigeur Company under Captain Cabossel, assisted by the 5th Company's Sous-Lieutenant Campion, and with Major Rodriguez's twenty-five Mexican Auxiliary Cavalry riding ahead as scouts. The section left La Soledad before dawn on 2 May, reaching Palo Verde near seven o'clock in the morning. In activities which paralleled those of *La Compagnie Danjou* two days earlier, fires were kindled, the *marmites* put on to boil water for coffee and guards thrown out.

A few minutes later, one of Rodriguez' men signalled that a lone figure was approaching, and Cabossel, using his telescope, identified it as an Indian. The man turned out to be Jeanningros' messenger, on his way to alert Giraud at La Soledad that a fight had taken place at Camaron. Campion's unpublished manuscript memoir tells how the Indian identified himself as being on a mission for Jeanningros, and refused to deliver his message to anyone other than Giraud. Losing patience, Cabossel threatened to have him beaten and the note was then produced.

Campion and Cabossel read it: 'The 3rd Company completely destroyed ... all dead in battle ... enemy numerous ... convoy impossible ... provide an escort for the courier from men of the three companies'.[35]

The Aftermath

Cabossel immediately sent the Indian on his way, telling him to hurry to La Soledad and deliver his message to Giraud. Then, mindful of his responsibility for the French gold, and for the safety of the Queen's Messenger, he took the decision to turn back, swung the convoy around, assigned Campion to command the rear guard, and set off back to La Soledad.

When Jeanningros' messenger delivered his note to Giraud, Colonel Dupin learned of the fight at Camaron. Giraud apparently believed that the number of men guarding the two sections of the convoy was sufficient, but Dupin promptly rode out with men of the *Contre-guerilla* in an effort to catch up with the slow moving sections.[36] The returning Cabossel, Campion and the first section were not quite a kilometre (about half a mile) from La Soledad when they met the head of the second section, guarded by the 5th Company, under the command of Ballue and Diesbach, who had been joined by Dupin and his men.

Diesbach, who often spoke before ascertaining the facts, began to upbraid Campion for having turned back, but was quickly told by Cabossel about the fight at Camaron. When the first section arrived back at La Soledad, Cabossel's actions were approved by Giraud, once he got over his surprise at seeing the convoy returning,[37] and the decision was later endorsed by Colonel Labrousse, the Commanding Officer of Veracruz and the *Terres Chaudes*.[38]

13
'A brilliant military page for the Regiment'

At the head of the 1st Company, Saussier's Grenadiers, and such odds and ends as Commandant Regnault had been able to gather up from the Headquarters Company and those who had recovered from various forms of sickness, Colonel Jeanningros left Paso Ancho early in the morning of 3 May and marched eastward. His intention, he told General Forey later, was to 'continue my investigations and bury the dead.'[1]

In point of fact, he had already made what he knew would be an unpopular and heart-rending decision. The dead at Camaron were just that – dead. The convoy, however, had not been heard from and, for all Jeanningros knew, might have been ambushed, its escort slaughtered and the guns, ammunition and money dispersed to the many small towns and villages in the *Terres Chaudes*. He took the proper decision and marched straight through Camaron and on towards Palo Verde.[2]

Nearing their goal, the column was suddenly thrown on guard by the sight of a huge cloud of dust, in which horsemen were visible, many of them wearing sombreros. They were taken for Mexican Republican Army troops or guerillas and Jeanningros, fearing the worst, immediately formed square and sent out scouts to determine the identity and size of the approaching force. What he was seeing, in fact, was the convoy. The sombrero-wearing riders were members of Dupin's *Contre-guerilla*, and the sight of Jeanningros' troops had likewise thrown them into some confusion and caused them to go on the defensive.

> On arriving within a short distance of Palo Verde, a military force of some considerable size was seen, but, for the moment, it was impossible to distinguish the uniforms [*explained the* Historique *of the* Contre-guerilla, *in recording the day's events*]. [Colonel Dupin] advanced towards them, with only a few riders, and it was soon realized that it was a battalion of the Regiment Etranger, commanded by Colonel Jeanningros in person. They had formed square, thinking that we were a troop of guerillas planning to attack. Soon the two columns were united.[3]

The convoy, once again a single entity, was being escorted by Dupin, Captain Cabossel and his Company of Voltigeurs and Captain Ballue and the 5th Company, and now Jeanningros quickly briefed them about the action at Camaron.[4] Cabossel explained that after starting out the previous day he had met Jeanningros' Indian messenger, read the note to Giraud, and taken the decision to turn back to La Soledad.

'Thank you, Captain,' enthused Regnault, embracing Cabossel. 'You have saved me a Company'.[5]

'A brilliant military page for the Regiment'

Cabossel, Campion and Diesbach told Jeanningros that Giraud, reversing his earlier decision to send the convoy in two sections, had sent it forward that morning, believing there was now a sufficient number of men for the escort. Adding his own command to those of Dupin, Rodriguez, Cabossel and Ballue, Jeaninngros now had a force of some eight hundred men, and the convoy could certainly proceed without fears of an attack.

They arrived at Camaron not long after noon and Jeanningros sent scouting parties out to scour the country north of the Orizaba Road, while making arrangements for the interment of the men of the 3rd Company. Corporal M'Alevey – almost certainly at his own request – drew burial detail.

> The sight which met my view filled me with horror [*he recalled*]. Owing to the great heat, decomposition had set in, and their bodies were swollen to an enormous size. Already those horrid birds, the *zopilotes*, [had] commenced to prey on their naked bodies.[6]

Only a few of the corpses were still recognizable, as the ravages of coyotes had added to the grisly work begun by the *zopilotes*. 'One could not recognize [most of] the poor unfortunates who after such brave conduct were left for two days to these ignoble animals,' Diesbach noted in his campaign diary.[7] Danjou was recognizable, his famous articulated hand missing from his left forearm. Vilain, too, was identified, as was the large form of Sergeant-Major Tonel, and helping with the burial detail, M'Alevey found the body of his friend Morziki.

> The recollection of his bloated, distorted features, clenched hands, vividly distended eyes, with the flesh torn from the bones by the *zopilotes*, has left upon my mind a picture I cannot contemplate without a shudder [*he told friends years later*].[8]

The trench dug by the Mexicans, outside the southwest corner of the wall of the courtyard, was filled in and the dead of Camaron were buried with as much reverence as possible.

In the mass grave were the bodies of two Officers, two Sous-Officiers, a Corporal and eighteen Fusiliers: Captain Jean Danjou, Sous-Lieutenant Jean Vilain, Sergeant-Major Henri Tonel, Sergeant Marie Morziki, Corporal Aime Favas and Fusliers Aloysio Bernardo, Natale Bertolotto, Nikolas Burgiser, Georg Catenhusen, Victor Catteau, Peter Conrad, Peter Dicken, Charles Dubois, Friedrich Friedrich, George Fursbaz, Louis Groux, Emile Hipp, Felix Langmeier, Louis Lernoud, Johann Reus, Daniel Seiler, Henri Vandesavel and Karl Wittgens.

'Honour to the brave!' intoned Jeanningros, in a strong voice. 'We shall try to be worthy to follow on the road you have laid out for us!'[9]

A rough cross was erected and a board attached to it. On it was written:

> To the memory of Danjou, Vilain and Maudet
> and of the 3rd Company of the 1st Battalion
> of the Legion Etrangere

who succumbed on 30 April 1863
after a ten hour battle with 2000 Mexicans.[10]

A Legionnaire found a bit of broken branch from a Nacaste, a shade tree which bears a multitude of small white flowers. It was known locally as a Camaron, which seemed fitting, and he stuck it in the ground beside the mound with marked the grave.[11]

The various patrols, returning from scouting the road to La Joya and Huatusco, reporting finding many traces of the battle, about ninety bodies, equipment and several dead horses.[12] Cabossel was deeply moved by the events of the day.

'Colonel, would we have compromised our mission if we had come to Camaron yesterday?' he asked Jeanningros.

'Without any doubt,' he was told. 'It seems absolutely certain that the enemy would have attacked you. As they have removed almost all the traces of the battle, it was clearly in the hope of surprising you.'

'I'm certainly convinced,' said Regnault. 'If the 3rd Company had not fought all day, and resisted to the end, I am quite sure that you would have been attacked by the Mexicans, and would have lost the courier and the bullion'.[13]

In truth, the French really had no idea where Milan and his forces were located, or what they might now be planning, and it seemed foolish to linger at Camaron, and possibly expose the convoy to unnecessary risk. So they pulled out, reaching Paso Ancho before dark and making camp for the night. It was probably over dinner that Ballue and others heard from Jeanningros how Captain Danjou had suggested leading what had seemed to be a fairly routine reconnaissance patrol – but which led to the annihilation of the 3rd of the 1st.

North of Camaron, at La Joya, Colonel Milan had broken camp at dawn and begun a sixty-four kilometre (forty mile) withdrawal towards Huatusco. '[He] was concerned about remaining at La Joya,' said Fusilier Fritz. 'The approach of Jeanningros caused him to break camp'.[14] The men of the National Guard of Veracruz headed for home, and guerilla leaders simply buried their dead, patched up their wounded and returned to their villages, taking with them, it appears, some of the less badly wounded Fusilier prisoners. The National Guard battalions from Jalapa and Cordoba headed the westbound column, guided by guerillas whose homes lay in that direction. They used pathways along the north bank of the Rio Jamapa unknown to the French, although they need not have worried about pursuit, as their enemies were too busily engaged in affairs involving Camaron, and in safeguarding the convoy, to begin any pursuit just yet. It was a dreadful march for the wounded, some of whom were taken on stretchers, others in wagons, though there was not much to be said in favour of one over the other.

Colonel Francisco Marrero had taken personal charge of the cart carrying Sous-Lieutenant Maudet, and Corporal Maine walked beside it. In the opinion of Dr. Talavera, if the officer or many of the eight critically wounded Legionnaires survived the journey it would be little short of a miracle. Colonel Cambas and Captain Laine were especially solicitous and were constantly moving among the prisoners.

A halt was made at noon, but Milan was anxious to move on, so as to be at a place he could defend, if needs be, by nightfall. The obvious midway point between La Joya and Huatusco was the village of San Jeronimo, which was reached early in the evening. The only stone building was the church, which quickly became an overnight prison for the men of the 3rd Company.

The Puebla-bound convoy completed its journey to Chiquihuite by mid-afternoon on 4 May and, as soon as responsibility for it had been handed on to officers and men of the 7th of the Line, Colonel Jeanningros sat down to compose an Official Report for the Commander-in-Chief. Writing at his dictation, Sous-Lieutenant Galloni d'Istria, who had apparently never seen the name Camaron written – although it appeared on French maps – made a reasonable French phonetic translation from the Spanish, setting it down as 'Cameronne,' which, with only one n, would become the name of the battle in Foreign Legion annals from that day forth.[15]

Chiquihuite, 4 May 1863

My General,

I have the honour to advise you that I was informed that a convoy which was coming from Vera-Cruz would arrive at La Soledad, where already two of my Companies, the 5th and the Voltigeurs, which had been assigned to escort it[,] had been waiting for three days. Various rumours were circulating that several parties of guerillas were in the area of Palo Verde. To protect this convoy and also the [British] courier, I organized the 3rd Company of the 1st Battalion[,] all the men in good health and the best marchers[,] to reconnoitre the route and be ready to take a strong hand should it be necessary. This Company, which at the time had no Captain, was assigned to Captain Adjutant-Major Danjou. I designated Sous-Lieutenant Standard-Bearer Maudet to complete the 3 officers, and 62 men in all[,] without haversacks and with their complement of cartridges. This detachment left the encampment at Chiquihuite on the 30th of last month, half an hour past midnight. It arrived at Paso d'El Macho at 2 o'clock in the morning. After a rest of half an hour, it continued its march without undue haste, and after giving an order to the Captain of Grenadiers, commanding at Paso d'El Macho, that if he heard gunfire, of which there seemed some probability, to send his Lieutenant with 30 Grenadiers as support. No word had been received and the Company[,] which should have returned during the night of 1st May, after having rested during the day, had not appeared, so I gathered my 1st Company[,] with mules[,] to go myself and find out if Captain Danjou had encountered the convoy, or else to find the cause of his absence. At the same time an Indian, who had come from [the direction of] Vera-Cruz, told me that French soldiers had been in a battle with Mexicans close to Cameronne. At this news, I marched rapidly and took up, when passing Paso d'El Macho[,] the six best squads of Grenadiers, and, as a reserve, two mules loaded with cartridges. At the same time, Commandant Regnault, who I had left in command at Chiquihuite, sent 40 men of the 1st

Company, to replace the Grenadiers I had taken from Paso d'El Macho. I continued my march with increasing concern about the situation of the 3rd Company.

After having left Paso d'El Macho, I found, in bushes on the right hand side of the road, a *Tambour* wearing nothing but a shirt[,] wounded by a sabre cut to the hand and a bullet in the chest, dying of thirst, who[,] after having a drink[,] told us, with great lucidity of spirit, that the Company, arriving at Cameronne towards 6 o'clock in the morning, while stopping to make coffee before returning to Paso d'El Macho, had seen a group of mounted men with lances, coming from the woods, and that the Captain had immediately engaged them with a fusillade, when suddenly numerous cavalry and infantry in very large numbers advanced on the little detachment[,] who stood firm. The *Tambour*, at the orders of the Captain[,] beat the charge to repulse the enemy with the bayonet, but when the infantry was engaged, it was necessary to fall back in good order, and several times to form square. They arrived again close to the first house on the right, where the Captain took position, loopholes were made and all day they fought, repulsing several assaults, but the cartridges began to run out and the enemy was on the roof of the house and had made several gaps in the walls. It was repulsed again, turned back by a charge and in that moment Captain Danjou was killed. The resistance continued unabated, but having many dead and wounded and no more cartridges, the Company was vanquished; the *Tambour* said he had heard Captain Danjou estimate the enemy forces as 8 or 900 cavalrymen and 1,500 infantrymen. When I arrived there with about 150 men, I found in trenches, on the right of the house, 16 bodies, all naked, but not mutilated, and I recognized Captain Danjou, Sous-Lieutenant Vilain, the Sergeant-Major [Tonel] and some of the others face down in a deep trench, past the point of return. However, of the wounded and the others, I could discover nothing at this time. Night fell, I left to return in 24 hours with some reinforcements to collect the courier, continue my investigations and bury the dead. Having formed a small fighting column, I returned today, the 4th, to escort the courier. The encounter with the enemy, and the attack by their infantry had involved very close combat by my Company, because we counted close to 90 Mexican bodies on the road to Hautusco (sic), close to Cameronne, where the battle had started, and which we have estimated at more than 260 of theirs; among them were uniforms with silver or gold insignia, and a man in a long coat who we took to be a priest, and several horses; we think that if we had gone further along the road which goes to Hautusco (sic), we would have found more remains; as for our bodies, we counted 37 or 38, but this may not be correct, as this mass of bodies was heaped together in a pile and it was not possible to move them. The supposition is that this Company, which had fought from 7 in the morning till 7 in the evening, and did not give up until it had no more ammunition, will have been made prisoners; I am waiting for news in two or three days, which I will have the honour of sending to you. I do not doubt, General, that you will appreciate the great valour of the heroic defence by this admirable Company, which adds a brilliant military page for the Regiment, with remarkable feats, like tenacity in an overwhelming combat. It is certain that the devotion of this troop saved the courier who, accompanied by a single Company, would undoubtedly have been captured, with the sacrifice of all the men in the escort. It is, I think, necessary that I receive some reinforcements, if that is possible. My effectives are very restricted, due to the large number of sick, who occupy a great deal of space, and it is not possible to provide escorts for the courier and the convoys from my scattered and isolated companies. I also have the honour to send you a small memoir asking for the Legion of Honour for the wounded *Tambour* . . .

Colonel Commanding the Regiment Etranger
JEANNINGROS.[16]

Some of the details Jeanningros provided about the battle, coming as they did from *Tambour* Lai, were a little garbled – such as the cavalry and infantry both being in position before the Hacienda de la Trinidad was even reached. Overall, however, it was a fairly accurate account, though Jeanningros' counting of '37 or 38' dead Legionnaires among the mass of piled up bodies in the trench – which he admitted might be inaccurate – was a major error. The actual number would have been twenty-three. As well as asking for *Tambour* Lai to be made a Chevalier of the Legion of Honour, Jeanningros requested a *Medaille Militaire* for a *Brigadier* – Corporal – of the *Chasseurs d'Afrique*, who had behaved with uncommon bravery in a wild ride to deliver a message to the Commander-in-Chief.[17]

Word of the affair at Camaron naturally spread though the Foreign Legion like wildfire. All able-bodied soldiers of the 1st Battalion had been with Jeanningros and Regnault on 4 May, so were in a good position to know the facts, but the men of the 2nd Battalion had to pick the story up secondhand, often with embellishments.

Corporal Abel Huart was given a colourful – and wholly apocryphal – tale to the effect that after the Mexican commander's harangue to his troops, and before their final assault, they sang their National Anthem – and that the men of the 3rd of the 1st 'responded with the *Marseillaise*.[18]

Colonel Milan's column had left San Jeronimo at dawn on 4 May and dragged itself into Huatusco before nightfall. It had been a terrible journey for the wounded, both French and Mexican. The most seriously wounded were taken straight to the hospital, which was run by the Daughters of Saint-Vincent-de-Paul. They were received by its director, Dona Juana Marrero de Gomez, the widow of a wealthy merchant, and sister of the Lieutenant-Colonels Francisco and Manuel Marrero. They prevailed upon her to have Sous-Lieutenant Maudet taken to her own home near the centre of town. The hospital was tiny and Dr. Talavera suggested that less seriously wounded men needing hospital treatment should accompany Colonel Milan to Jalapa the next day.

In besieged Puebla an air of gloom was descending. On 5 May the previous year Mexican forces had decisively defeated the predominantly Zouave battalions and thrown back the French. Exactly a year later Puebla was under siege, and some of the same Zouave battalions were with the vastly increased forces which ringed the city. Once the precious convoy from La Tejeria reached the French lines, the siege took on an even more hopeful aspect for the French – and a more despairing one for the Mexicans – as the heavy guns were emplaced and provided with ammunition, the stores, both military and civilian, distributed and the troops paid.

As General Gonzalez Ortega and the besieged garrison in Puebla were celebrating, albeit in a subdued way, the *Cinquo de Mayo*, Colonel Dupin was preparing for what he hoped would be a strike 'to avenge Camaron'. His spies had told him that some of the guerillas who had fought the 3rd of the 1st were to be found at the tiny hamlet of La Mendoza, not far from La Soledad. Lieutenant-Colonel Giraud lent him eighty men of the 2nd Battalion, but before the heavily-armed group could set out an Indian spy arrived to say that the enemy had got wind of their coming and had left hurriedly.

Milan reached Jalapa on 6 May and saw the wounded men admitted to the hospital. There were a number of them, including Fusiliers Fritz, Daglincks and Baas. He then sat down to address a congratulatory despatch to Major Ismael Teran, who had led the city's battalion at Camaron. 'The *Jalapenos* have shed their blood,' Milan wrote, and he asked Teran to convey his thanks to the troops of the National Guard, and tell them that their conduct in the battle inspired 'hope for major glories in the future'.[19]

The life of Sous-Lieutenant Clement Maudet was quietly slipping away at the home of Dona Juana in Huatusco, and several of the Fusiliers in the hospital of Saint Vincent were in little better condition. Despite the best care that could be given, Maudet had lost a great deal of blood on the journey from La Joya and his wounds were not healing, but at least he was in caring hands. Feeling that he was dying, he asked for a pen and paper and wrote: 'I left a mother in France, I have found another in Mexico.'[20]

In the midst of all that he had to contend with, General Miguel Blanco found the time to give some administrative attention to what had taken place at the Hacienda de la Trinidad. Colonel Milan's Official Report of 30 April had reached him safely at Fort San Lorenzo and on 7 May, expressing his 'most cordial congratulations for the victory,' he sent it on to Minister of War and Marine Ignacio Comonfort,[21] who was at Pensa Cola with an army of four thousand men, waiting for an opportunity to join up with another army of three thousand, under General La Garza, at Ocatlan. Another five thousand men were being held in reserve near Tlaxcala, and all were intended to be the relieving force for those besieged in Puebla.

General Bazaine had received word of these gatherings of troops, but could get no real details. Indians were sent out to try to confirm or refute the stories, but when they returned they were questioned by Forey in a hectoring tone, and told him that the enemy had withdrawn. Bazaine, who had frequently dealt with informants in his days with the Arab Bureau in Algeria, and also spoke Spanish, did not believe what Forey had been told and decided to question the Indians himself.

Colonel Charles Blanchot said later that the Indians were 'terrified by the heavy voice of General Forey', but that Bazaine was able to learn from them 'that they had not dared approach the enemy, and that, having seen nothing, they said there was nothing'.[22]

Bazaine and Forey studied the terrain from a hilltop. Forey, using high-powered Artillery binoculars, could not see anything. Bazaine, using ordinary ones, could see a cloud of dust, and decided that it must be a massing of troops. He remarked that there would not be so much if the enemy was merely withdrawing.

'Well, go on, my dear Bazaine,' said Forey. 'If you find nothing, at least you will have had a good walk, and in the meantime, let's have dinner.'[23]

Leaving fires burning, horses picketed and tents pitched, to confuse any Mexican spies, Bazaine took his men quietly out of the camp under cover of darkness, made a forced night march and fell on Comonfort's army in a dawn attack on 8 May, completely routing them, and putting an end to the one serious attempt to relieve Gonzalez Ortega's besieged garrison.[24]

The same day, General Blanco had Milan's letter to Jalapa's Major Teran published in *El Siglo* in Mexico City,[25] and in Huatusco, at the Marrero family home, Sous-Lieutenant Maudet died in his sleep. The family ensured that he was given a proper burial in the hallowed grounds of the small town's church. Maudet was placed in his coffin in uniform, with his sword, wearing his two medals, and with a broad ribbon in the blue-white-and-red of the Tricolour across his chest. Written on it, in gold letters, was: '*Gloria a las Armas Francia.*' Dona Juana placed a small black crucifix in his crossed hands, along with a little glass bottle which contained a piece of paper with his name and date of death. The coffin was lowered into a stone-lined vault close to the wall of the church.[26] The following day Major Jose Maria Camacho sent word from Huatusco to General de Maussion at Orizaba that Maudet had died, and had been buried with military honours.[27]

General Forey had received Jeanningros' 4 May letter from Chiquihuite and recognized an outstanding feat of arms when he saw one. He waited until 10 May, then issued a General Order of the Army, commending the officers and men of the 3rd of the 1st in their battle against overwhelming odds at Camaron.

> Honour to this brave Company [*he wrote*]. Honour to these warriors, whose conduct during the battle has assured them fame and glory everywhere that people understand the sublime principle of soldiers doing their duty even unto death.[28]

Even as the siege tightened around Puebla, Minister of War Comonfort, in a temporary camp, his command scattered by Bazaine's attack of four days earlier, found time to respond to Blanco on 12 May, saying that the action at Camaron had been 'very satisfactory' to President Juarez.[29] Despairing of receiving any help, Gonzalez Ortega made an attempt to break out of Puebla the same day, but was turned back by the French at Totimehuacan, only the cavalry under General Tomas O'Horan managing to get away.[30]

Jeanningros, who had carefully explained his manpower problems to both de Maussion and Forey, cannot have welcomed the news that day that his second-in-command, Lieutenant-Colonel Giraud, had been promoted and was being transferred out of the Regiment Etranger to take command of the 7th of the Line.

De Maussion would remain as Commanding Officer of the Reserve Brigade.[31] There was other news, too, as the critically wounded men of *La Compagnie Danjou* were gradually dying in the hospital in Huatusco: Sergeant Jean Germeys on 11 May, Corporal Adolfi Delcaretto on 13 May and Fusilier Jean Timmermans two days later.[32]

By this time, the events at Camaron were known all over southern Mexico, as the Republican newspapers, with Puebla seemingly about to fall, badly needed a victory to report.

Corporal Berg's 1 May letter to Jeanningros had got into the hands of the Editor of the *Independiente* of Jalapa, who had been happy to publish it. He may also have kept it, as it does not seem to have reached the hands of the Colonel of the Regiment Etranger.[33] In the manner of the 'exchange' agreements existing between newspapers of the time, the letter was reprinted in *El Heraldo* in Mexico City on 16 May, starting on page two and taking up much of page three, under the headline: SUCCESS AT CAMARON. A small news item from Jalapa, dated 2 May, also appeared. Clearly drawn from Milan's Official Report, it claimed that only two hundred cavalry had been involved in the battle, told of the death of Chief of Staff Ayala, and gave the Foreign Legion casualties as twenty dead, sixteen wounded and twenty-four prisoners.[34] The rival newspaper *El Siglo* only had the news report from Jalapa.[35] Badly scooped, they rushed to print Berg's letter next day, under the headline THE ACTION AT CAMARON,[36] and it received fairly wide play in other newspapers, also appearing in *El Monitor Republicano* and elsewhere, sometimes in slightly different versions.[37]

While *El Heraldo* readers in Mexico City were discussing Berg's letter, General Mendoza, Chief of Staff to Gonzalez Ortega, was visiting Forey, proposing that the besieged garrison be permitted to leave Puebla with honour, taking its arms, baggage and part of its artillery, and withdrawing to Mexico City. Forey, of course, rejected the idea, offering a counter-proposal that the honours of war would be observed, but that the garrison must surrender its arms and submit to becoming prisoners-of-war. The following day Gonzalez Ortega gave orders to spike all the guns, blew up the powder magazines and disbanded his army, notifying Forey that he was surrendering the city and placing himself and his officers at the disposal of the French.

The Combat of Camerone does not seem to have been reported by any French newspapers, perhaps because it was seen by them as a defeat, rather than a victory. Additionally, in the early days of the Expeditionary Corps, the *Terres Chaudes* had gained an evil reputation in France, as a place where large number of Frenchmen had died of the *vomito negro*. Indeed, even prior to the Regiment Etranger arriving in Mexico, a Deputy had commented in the National Assembly: 'Families can ease their minds. It is only the *Infanterie de Marine* which occupies the *Terres Chaudes*.'[38] Later, the *Moniteur officiel* in Paris published a news squib to the effect that because the *Terres Chaudes* were injurious to the health of French soldiers the region had been assigned to the Regiment Etranger and the *Contre-guerilla*.[39] Nor did any of the numerous officer-artists who sent their work to the French illustrated magazines bother to depict the events at Camerone.[40] However, a German journal, *Leipzig Illustrirte Zeitung*, heard about the battle, got the regiment and location wrong and published an interesting – but wholly inaccurate – engraving captioned 'The War in Mexico: Resistance of a French Zouave company to an attack by Mexican guerillas at Gemronne'.[41]

After Bazaine had visited Puebla, and judged Gonzalez Ortega's surrender to be genuine, Forey made a triumphal entry into the city on 19 May. The Tricolour of France was flown from one of the twin towers of the cathedral, the flag of Mexico from the other. After the obligatory cries of *'Vive l'Empereur!'* many officers, perhaps with more sycophancy than sincerity, called out: *'Vive General Forey!'* Many soldiers, aware of what the cost in blood would have been if the Commander-in-Chief's strategy for taking the city had been followed, cried out: *'Vive General Bazaine!'* The French then began dealing with huge problems involving prisoners: twenty-six Generals – including Jesus Gonzales Ortega, Porfirio Diaz, Mariano Escobedo and Miguel Negrete – and three hundred and three Field Grade Officers, one thousand one hundred and seventy-nine Company Officers and more than eleven thousand Other Ranks. A prisoner-of-war processing camp was established, but while being taken to it a number of officers, including Gonzalez Ortega, escaped. Few had volunteered to change sides, or were willing to obtain their freedom by giving their word of honour not to take up arms against the French again.

Diplomat de Saligny proposed that they be sent to the penal settlements in French Guiana, which Forey, to his credit, rejected out of hand, saying: 'I will never permit these brave men to be treated as criminals.' When Mexican Conservative elements demanded that the senior generals be shot, Forey, said Colonel Blanchot, 'did not even honour such proposals with an answer'.[42] Eventually, Forey ruled that thirteen of the generals should be sent to Martinique, or even France, as prisoners-of-war, and despatched them under guard for the coast, along with a number of officers of lower grades. They left Puebla, but by the time they arrived at Chiquihuite nine of the generals had escaped, including Diaz, Escobedo and Negrete. All would fight against France during the next three years.

The eleven thousand-plus soldiers – many of whom had been forcibly pressed into the service of the *Juaristas* – were not necessarily wedded to the Republican cause and more than half were taken into the service of the French, while others were formed into work gangs to help build the railway through the *Terres Chaudes*. In Mexico City, as Bazaine was preparing to move his 1st Division to the capital, President Benito Juarez was making plans to give up the city without a fight and move north towards the border with the United States.

14
Dupin Gets a Free Hand

The Mexican losses at Camerone, and the fall of Puebla had, temporarily at least, made even the guerillas wary of provoking further confrontations with the French in the *Terres Chaudes*. Sous-Lieutenant de Keratry of the *Contre-guerilla* reported accompanying another huge convoy – eighty-four wagons and almost two thousand mules – from La Soledad to Chiquihuite on 8 May. There had been rumours that guerillas from Huatusco and Tehuacan were planning to attack it, and Dupin had his men out in force, strengthened by additional infantry companies – presumably from the Regiment Etranger, the Egyptian Battalion and the *Tirailleurs Algeriens*. The convoy made the two-day journey from La Soledad to Chiquihuite without the reported guerilla force 'showing any sign of life'.[1]

Concerns that attempts would be made to free the prisoners-of-war as they were taken to the coast were also to prove groundless. Troops from the 7th of the Line moved them from the holding camp to Chiquihuite, where Regnault's 1st Battalion took over responsibility for the stretch of the Orizaba Road from there to the railhead. Jeanningros assigned the escort duty to Ballue's 5th Company. At La Soledad the prisoners were handed over to the 3rd Company of the Egyptian Battalion, which had been moved from La Tejeria[2] to handle the eastbound escort duties in conjunction with the *Contre-guerilla*.

The senior Mexican officers travelled by wagon, while the French escorts' officers were on foot with their men.

'You must suffer greatly marching in the sun,' General Mendoza said to Sous-Lieutenant Diesbach as the prisoner-of-war group he was escorting sweated along the dusty road.

'No,' replied Diesbach. 'The French soldier marches all the time. It is our habit.'[3]

On a later trip, while escorting a larger party of Field Grade officers, Ballue began feeling unwell when they stopped along the route. Diesbach took off his jacket, placed it under his comrade's head, and was giving him some tea laced with brandy when several Mexican officers approached and imperiously demanded some. Diesbach gave it to them, then fixed them with a steely glance.

'You have been served by a French officer,' he said. 'It is an honour without price.'

The Mexicans had not realized that Diesbach was an officer because he had removed his jacket. There were many apologies and each of them offered him a cigar. The group included Colonel Cazarini, an aide-de-camp to Mendoza, and Colonel Francisco Fernandez, who had been found on the field of battle, unconscious among a number of his dead soldiers.[4] Once they reached La Tejeria the prisoners were put into a camp guarded by the 4th Company of the Egyptian Battalion until they could be taken to Veracruz to be embarked for Martinique.[5] Many of the Mexican officers were accompanied by their wives or sweethearts, who insisted on making the journey to the coast to say goodbye.

In the little hospital of San Vicente in Huatusco the remaining wounded Camerone survivors were losing their individual battles with life. Fusilier Constant Dael died on 23 May and Ludwig Rohr two days later. When Hans Kurz, the first man to be wounded at Camerone, died on 28 May it left only Claude Billod, for whom not much hope was entertained.[6] The men in hospital in Jalapa were still holding their own, and some had actually been released, but concern was being expressed about Fusiliers Baas and Daglincks.

The Mexicans, having no place to confine prisoners-of-war, took the ex-patients with them in their wanderings in the *Terres Chaudes*, and the extraordinary activity of Dupin's *Contre-guerilla* kept them continually on the move. Fusilier Fritz, whose left arm Dr. Talavera had removed above the elbow within hours of the end of the Combat of Camerone, had initially been taken to the hospital at Jalapa. Considering the seriousness of his injury, and the fact that he was the oldest man in the Company, his recovery was nothing short of remarkable and he was soon released and sent back to Colonel Milan's command, where he found Corporal Maine and four other comrades.

> While my wounded companions were being taken care of in the hospitals at Huatusco and Jalapa, we were six whose wounds were judged to be less severe [*he would say later*]. So we duly followed the Mexican [Republican] Army in its peregrinations. In marches and counter-marches, the enemy was harried by our different columns. If anyone came to know the *Terres Chaudes*, it was certainly us. We had more than enough of these unwanted trials and adventures, and quite often their cause was the efforts of the *Contre-guerilla* to come to grips with the Mexicans. Milan and Colonel Cambas did their best to ensure that our wounds were not worsened by all this activity. We – and I say this to the honour and chivalrous spirit of the Mexican people – we were always the object of their concern. Everyone spoke of our glorious defence.[7]

The observant Maine, who had seen what the guerillas were capable of, viewed the Mexican Republican Army quite differently, and thrown together with Cambas and Captain Laine, had plenty of time to observe them and their actions. Despite the difference in rank, he got on well with Laine, saying later: 'Like all my comrades, I will always commend his kindness and his humanity',[8] and remembering the 'imposing and distinguished' Cambas as 'a soldier by choice'.

'Like many of those who we fought, his love of liberty caused him to take up arms against us,' Maine remarked. 'He was, as was Milan, of the class which is among the best educated and most influential in the country. Excellent people, the one and the other, exhibiting honour in the same manner as any other army, because they are soldiers. I do not believe the many slanders which maintain that three-quarters of them are no better than bandits.'[9]

With Puebla in French hands, the way had been opened to Mexico City and President Juarez had fled North with his government. When Bazaine entered the capital on 7 June he was surprised and annoyed to find that, contrary to the usages of war, no effort had been made to leave behind any form of police or military group to maintain order. An old Conservative, General Mariano Salas, had taken the initiative, with the help of the members of the Diplomatic Corps. General Forey formally entered Mexico City three days later and at once set about organizing a civilian government to work with the French Army.

In the *Terres Chaudes* things went on as usual and Fusilier Billod, the last of the Camerone survivors to have been hospitalized in Huatusco, died on 11 June.[10] Dupin and his ever-active *Contre-guerilla* were still hunting Mexicans wherever they could be found, especially if it was thought they had participated in the clash at Camerone. He learned from an Indian spy that men from the village of Cueva-Pentada had been among the two hundred and fifty-strong cavalry unit under Hilario Osario which had fought there, and that eight of them had been killed in the day-long battle.

Dupin left La Soledad on June 13 with a hundred cavalry and one hundred and thirty infantry, marched rapidly and descended on the village, surprising about fifty horsemen, who fled rather than give fight. In the village they found a quantity of Regiment Etranger clothing, badges and weapons, clearly taken from the stripped bodies of the Camerone dead. Dupin burned the village and took several prisoners during this lightning raid.[11]

Colonel Labrousse, the Commanding Officer of Veracruz and the *Terres Chaudes*, had died of the *vomito negro* on 30 May and been temporarily replaced by the Regiment Etranger's Commandant Munier. Forey, however, wanted a more senior officer in the post and on 14 June named Colonel Jeanningros to replace Labrousse.[12] He moved from Chiquihuite to the coast, taking Sous-Lieutenant Achilli with him as aide-de-camp and assuming enormous responsibilities for the smooth running of the port and the despatch of supplies to the interior. He also retained overall command of the Foreign Legion, while Commandant Regnault assumed responsibility for the 1st Battalion's day-to-day operations, and Munier was moved to La Soledad to oversee those of the 2nd. Lieutenant Jean Lebre still commanded the Foreign Legion Depot in the port city.

Although the convoys now moved from La Tejeria to Chiquihuite with less fear of being attacked, the physical work was no less hard.

> These [escorts] are terribly tiring, privations of food, of clothes [*Diesbach wrote in his campaign diary*]. We sleep for five or six days at the foot of trees in the water. Almost always torrential rain, and no change of clothes, no way to get dry. Impossible to light a fire . . . always sleeping in wet clothes. The next day, the march resumes in the same clothes. It is an ordeal few people realize.[13]

It was the torrential rain which Captain Ballue remembered, too.

> The heat is never less than overwhelming [*he wrote twelve years later*]. The

sky is always an implacable blue, or touched with the reddish of copper. Then, a long way off, on the horizon, the light values change rapidly on the bare flank of the Sierra Madre; isolated clouds come together, thickening, darkening the horizon and obscuring the light of day. In the suffocating atmosphere, all of a sudden would come a violent gust of wind, rippling through the high grass of the savannah. At last, with a glimmering, dazzling, a ripping of the clouds, as in the words of the Scriptures, the cataracts of the sky would open.[14]

Dupin was still hitting villages within striking distance of La Soledad and a nocturnal *Contre-guerilla* raid on the hamlet of Tomatlan on the night of 25–26 June had a wholly unexpected result. The population had fled, leaving behind Fusilier Hartog De Vries of the 3rd of the 1st, last heard of in Mexican captivity at La Joya. The Dutchman had been among the sixteen men captured before Captain Danjou reached the Hacienda de la Trinidad, and had suffered what Corporal Berg had described as 'a head wound (very serious).' It must have looked worse than it was, for he had been taken from Milan's camp by departing guerillas and held by them as a captive. Freed by Dupin's men, he became the second Camerone survivor to be returned to the French lines.[15]

Just two days later Dupin's spies told him that Mexican Republican Army troops from Jalapa and Perote, perhaps sixteen hundred to two thousand strong, were marching toward Huatusco. The advance guard was said to have stopped at Elotepec and Dupin decided to strike at once. After a hard march the *Contre-guerilla* more or less bumped into the Mexican outposts an hour before midnight and overwhelmed them, but the element of surprise was lost. Riders fled to warn the main body of troops in the village of San Martin. It was situated on a plateau, which could only be reached by climbing a steep escarpment, so Dupin's cavalry set off to find a track they could negotiate, while the infantry began their ascent at a point where no horse could go.

> The enemy fired very regular volleys, but the bullets went over the heads of our infantrymen on the slope of the mountain, and they continued their climb without returning fire [*reported the* Historique *of the* Contre-guerilla]. They still did not fire and the enemy decamped after a final discharge of shots. Lieutenant Perret gathered his men, who were a little dispersed after the difficulties of the climb[,] and sent them, heads down, in a bayonet charge, accompanied by repeated shouts of '*Vive l'Empereur!*' In a moment, our cavalry appeared behind the enemy, brandishing their sabres and shouting their war cry. The rout was complete. The Mexicans, fleeing from our bayonets, fell under the sabres of our cavalry. A large group trying to avoid being struck down ran in a mass for a ravine known as the 'Barranca Espinosa del Diablo'. Several were killed or mortally wounded in falling from rock to rock. Searching around, we found eleven bodies. We learned later that the enemy lost 35 men killed and 45 wounded. The confusion was so great among them because our soldiers continued to shoot at them for a long time.[16]

In Medellin, the health of Captain Jean Cazes had greatly improved. He was officially still the Captain *titulaire* of the 3rd of the 1st, but was considered as being on special duty and on 6 July took command of a strong detachment of troops in a reconnaissance to Tlalixcoyan, a small town some distance to the South. The column comprised eighty Sudanese riflemen of the Egyptian Battalion, supported by a troop of Mexican Imperial Cavalry and the mission was accomplished without incident. When Cazes returned to Medellin he learned that Lieutenant Lebre, who commanded the Foreign Legion Depot in Veracruz, had died of *vomito negro* and had been replaced by Sous-Lieutenant Jean-Baptiste Borgella-Houra. Almost at once word was received that a guerilla band had moved into Tlalixcoyan and at the end of the month Cazes marched south again with the same troops as the first time, but now reinforced by the 3rd Company of the Regiment Etranger's 2nd Battalion, the 2nd Company of the Egyptian Battalion and twenty cavalrymen. The town was occupied without resistance.[17]

Forey had authorized Dupin to endeavour to arrange a prisoner exchange and the Mexicans were particularly anxious to obtain the release of Colonel Manuel Alba, who had been captured by General Alexis Bertier's troops in November 1862. The *Historique* of the *Contre-guerilla* subsequently reported that newly-promoted Lieutenant-Colonel Jose Maria Camacho, the Republican commander at Huatusco, 'made it known to us that, in accord with an agreement made with the Military Headquarters, he was charged with returning to us the 20 men made prisoner at Camaron, sole survivors of the heroic company which, by its gallant resistance, immortalized a place which was unknown until then'.[18]

The exchange was set for 14 July, apparently chosen by Colonel Milan because of its symbolism as France's National Day. Under the circumstances, the prisoners' journey to Coscomatepec, the place agreed for the exchange, was a curious one.

'When we were being returned, it was a veritable triumph along our route,' Fusilier Fritz would recall. 'Everyone came to see the heroes of Camaron',[19] and Maine would tell journalist Lucien-Louis Lande that the Indians, especially, rushed to see them, and 'cried out and clapped their hands, exclaiming: "Jesus-Maria, they are here!"'[20]

The exchange was duly made and the *Historique* noted that 'our officers, Sous-Officiers and soldiers shared in the cordial reception given by the brave people,' and the next day 'the prisoners departed for Orizaba on the mules of soldiers of the *Contre-guerilla*'.[21] Colonel Jeanningros travelled from Veracruz to Chiquihuite, picked up some members of his regiment and went on to Orizaba to be on hand to welcome the Camerone survivors.

As with so much connected with the 3rd of the 1st, and with Camerone, there are unanswered questions about the prisoner exchange. The *Historique* of the *Contre-guerilla*, which was probably written up later, perhaps by an officer who was not present, is certainly wrong in saying that twenty Camerone survivors were exchanged, although twenty French prisoners-of-war may have been. Chaplain Lanusse, who was in Puebla at the time, heard that the exchange involved 'eight of ours' – meaning Camerone survivors – and that 'other wounded were returned later'.[22] Other accounts suggest that twelve French prisoners were exchanged, or even sixteen.[23] However, Corporal Maine told a friend later that he was one of eight men of the 3rd of the 1st who were exchanged that day.[24] With him were Fusiliers Friedrich Fritz, Gottfried Wensel, Josef Schreiblich, Leon Gorski, Joseph Rebers, Hippolyte Kunassec and Felix Brunswick. On the outskirts of the town the prisoners were greeted by Jeanningros and the officers and men of their regiment, as well as from other regiments.

> Hands were tightly clenched, eyes wet with tears [*the Editor-in-Chief of the* Memorial de la Loire, *who was present, recalled more than fifteen years later*]. After the first moments of awe, the Regiment formed up in a square. The returning prisoners took places in front of the flag, everyone presented arms, and the Colonel, in a strong voice, often choked with emotion, gave the troops a speech which recalled the glorious fight at Camaron, the heroic conduct of the 3rd Company of the 1st Battalion, [and] the part played by each of those who died and those who had returned ... The Regiment passed in review before the prisoners, who were then ceremoniously conducted to the barracks ... The following day, a funeral service was celebrated for the souls of the dead. The remnants of the 3rd of the 1st formed the guard of honour at the church.[25]

Official recognition came four days later in the form of promotions, with Maine being made up to Sergeant, there being obvious vacancies because of the deaths of Morziki during the Combat of Camerone and Germeys after it. The seven returned Fusiliers were upgraded and transferred to the 1st Battalion's Elite Companies, Fritz, Brunswick, Kunassec and Rebers being named as Voltigeurs, and Wensel, Schreiblich and Gorski as Grenadiers.[26] Their return meant that ten of the Camerone survivors – counting *Tambour* Lai and Fusilier De Fries – were now back with the French. A few days later the survivors and their comrades returned to Chiquihuite, where, not long afterwards, a letter was received from the Danjou family in Chalabre asking that the fallen officer's articulated wooden hand be sent to them. As it had not been found there was nothing that could be done.

The 1st and 5th Companies were still involved in convoy duties in the *Terres Chaudes*, and the *vomito negro* continued to decimate the troops. Sous-Lieutenant Diesbach would note in his campaign diary that his company of one hundred and twenty-four men dwindled to a mere twenty-five fit for duty.[27] The work was only marginally less hard when escorting empty wagons and disagreeable pack mules from Chiquihuite to La Soledad, and it was the sheer drudgery of the deadly monotonous work which left vivid memories with Corporal M'Alevey of the 1st Company.

> Now of all the fatiguing and disagreeable duties which a soldier has to perform in campaign[ing], that of escorting convoys of war material and provisions is by far the most disagreeable and fatiguing [*he said*]. If the roads are good and dry, you are smothered with dust, and the pace is killing; if they are bad and wet, you are bespattered with mud and filth, and owing to the slow pace, will perhaps be marching half the night. To this hour I shudder, when I think of the misery and hardships I suffered in *La Terre Chaude*.[28]

On one of the many trips during July, while passing through Camaron, heading east, the men of the 5th Company were angry when they visited the grave of the men of the 3rd of the 1st.

> In passing by Camerone, we did not see the cross which we had put over the bodies of our poor companions [*Diesbach noted*]. Who had thrown it away? We will locate it on our return, I hope. In any case, we will bring another one for it.[29]

Meanwhile, all was not well in Mexico City, where General Forey was engaged in a series of actions which favoured Conservative elements among the Mexican politicians, and also the Clergy. He had arrived in the capital with Ambassador de Saligny, and it was soon clear that he was very much under the diplomat's influence. Among Forey's first acts was to set up a thirty-five member Assembly of Notables as a *Junta Superior*, who were to elect three of their number and two alternates to exercise executive power. De Saligny arranged the election of Generals Almonte and Salas and Archbishop Antonio de Labastida, who was still in Europe. For the time being he was represented by an alternate, Juan B. de Ormeachea, the Bishop of Tulancingo. The other alternate was Supreme Court Judge Ignacio Pavon.

The more observant Army officers in Mexico City watched and understood the political overtones and undertones of what was going on, and wrote home to France about them. Major Adrien de Tuce of the 3rd *Chasseurs d'Afrique*, a sharp and observant officer, regretted the fact that an olive branch had not been extended to senior Mexican officers, particularly General Gonzalez Ortega, after the fall of Puebla. At de Saligny's insistence, he had simply been declared to be just another prisoner-of-war, and had escaped and disappeared on the way to the holding area.

> If General Forey had been free to organize his government to suit himself, he might willingly have included his old adversary [Gonzalez] Ortega, whose brave resistance he admired [*said de Tuce*]. This generosity would have been useful, for there is no enduring peace that is not based on conciliation . . . But Dubois de Saligny was still the diplomatic representative of His Majesty, and he had influence enough to cause the general to sign a series of decrees destined to give complete satisfaction to the most violent clericals and which will end by alienating from us all moderate minds of the national party.[30]

Officers watched Forey taking steps – or delaying taking them – which would inevitably make the coming conquest of Mexico more costly in terms of French lives and money. Reading the despatches which reached him from Mexico City, and the briefs provided by Marshal Randon, Napoleon III came to much the same conclusion. He had not been happy over the length of the siege of Puebla, or the heavy cost in lives, and was even more disturbed about the direction which the Commander-in-Chief was taking with the Conservative and Church elements. When he decided on 16 July that he needed a change of command, he wrote to

Forey, naming him a Marshal of France, and simultaneously recalling him to Paris. De Saligny was recalled at the same time. Even though the letters – and one to Bazaine, appointing him as the new Commander-in-Chief of the French Expeditionary Corps – would take several weeks to reach Mexico City, rumours were rife.

> They will have to send us reinforcements [*Major de Tuce wrote home*]. You cannot expect to keep peace in a country as big as Europe with twenty thousand men. But no one realizes it. They say that we do not want to back any party, though the appointment of the Provisional Government proves the contrary. Arrests which often serve personal ends also prove it. . .
>
> Civil Affairs have been turned over to the priests, in a series of moves attributed to Saligny. It is supposed that he has been recalled. I hope so, for I believe he has done a great deal of harm. From what they say I consider him a rascal, but a very fine and accomplished one, who only toys with General Forey. The latter is more a famous general than a bad diplomat.[31]

Gradually, other Camerone survivors were returned to the French lines. A second exchange gave freedom to Sergeants Alfred Palmaert and Karl Schaffner and Corporals Heindrich Pinzinger and Karl Magnin. Their names, along with those of Maine and the seven men released with him, were sent to Mexico City with recommendations for medals and decorations.

Interestingly, all twelve of the men recommended for recognition were Sergeants, Corporals or Fusiliers who had been promoted into the Elite Companies. Some days later, Corporal Evariste Berg and Fusiliers Laurent Constantine, Jean-Baptiste Leonard and Luitpol Van Opstal were exchanged, making a total of sixteen men all told. Neither Constantine nor Leonard was promoted into the Elite Companies, so only Berg's name was sent to Mexico City for official consideration.

Soldiers in every army in the world, in every war, have known of men who have deserved medals, but missed out. Nevertheless, there must have been some surprise when it was realized that there was no promotion for Constantine and Leonard, as there had been for the first group of Fusiliers exchanged. After all, Constantine had charged at Camerone with Maudet, Maine, Wensel and Catteau, and Leonard would have done so had he not been wounded as he moved forward. Van Opstal, of course, had been one of the sixteen men captured before the Hacienda de la Trinidad was reached, as were Fusiliers Jean-Baptiste Verjus and Pharon Van den Bulcke, who also got back to the French lines.[32]

Their return brought the number of returned Camerone survivors to twenty, and Commandant Regnault, as Interim Commander of the Regiment Etranger, began painstakingly debriefing all of them about the affair at the Hacienda de la Trinidad. He was quite well advanced with the compilation of a full report for Brigade Commander de Maussion when orders came from him to begin preparing for a campaign.

De Maussion was determined to strike Huatusco, which continued to be an important base for the Mexican Republican Army, and a thorn in the side of the

French. In an attempt to ensure surprise, an elaborate plan was developed, aimed at misleading the Mexicans, or at the very least at confusing their spies.

On 27 July the 1st Battalion of the Regiment Etranger assembled a *Bataillon de Marche* – a strike force – largely made up of men of the 1st and 5th Companies. It included some men from the Company of Voltigeurs, commanded by Lieutenant Philippe Jaudon, rather than Captain Cabossel, who had been intermittently on the sick list since mid-June. Captain Saussier had picked men from his Company of Grenadiers who would be able to withstand the long march which would be required. Lieutenant Gans, now recovered from the fever which had prevented him from being with his men at Camerone, commanded the healthy Fusiliers of the 3rd Company, possibly including a few of the survivors of the battle.

Regnault led his men out of Chiquihuite, marching east to La Soledad. A rumour had deliberately been spread that the column was going to meet a convoy. They arrived on 29 July and joined up with a *Bataillon de Marche* assembled by Commandant Munier and made up of the 2nd Battalion's Grenadier Company, under Captain Dubosq, and Voltigeur Company, under Captain Abrial. The column left under cover of darkness two nights later, moving west along the south bank of the Rio Jamapa, guided by a few horsemen from General Galvez' Mexican Auxiliaries, who knew the country.

By this time, three Companies of the 7th of the Line, which had left Cordoba on 30 July under the direct orders of General de Maussion, also on the announced pretext of going to meet a convoy, were well on their way to Huatusco, planning to bypass Coscomatepec, cross the Rio Jamapa and hit the town from the south. The distance they would have to travel was less than half that to be covered by the Regiment Etranger, and it was almost inevitable that, barring the unforeseen, the 7th would be the first to reach their destination.

Regnault crossed the Jamapa mid-morning on 1 August and was almost immediately spotted by a dozen mounted guerillas, who, having assessed the size of the French column, left for Huatusco as fast as they could. The element of surprise was lost, but Regnault picked up the pace in country which made for easy marching, though the heat from the sun took its toll. Almost twelve hours later, as they approached the village of San Jeronimo, Sergeant Copain collapsed of heatstroke and died. The column moved into the village, from which all the adult men had fled, and went into camp. Sous-Lieutenant Diesbach and elements of the 5th Company slept in the church which had served as an overnight prison for the men of the 3rd of the 1st two months earlier.

The following morning the column was on the move again. It crossed the Rio Bravo with difficulty, and when it marched into Huatusco found, as expected, that the Mexican Republican Army was long gone and that the 7th of the Line was there already. Diesbach wrote in his campaign diary that he had been told: 'The people of Huatusco were initially prepared to resist our attack, but when they heard that we were the comrades of those who had fought on 30 April at Camaron, they wavered, then a shout went up: "Save yourselves! We don't want to face them! They fight too hard!" and that all the able-bodied men had rapidly left town.'[33] Regnault heard much the same story, and that Milan, Camacho, Cambas, the Marrero brothers and Laine, with no soldiers to command, had followed suit and headed for Jalapa. He met Dona Juana Marrero de Gomez, heard from her own lips about the last days of Sous-Lieutenant Maudet and visited his grave. He also received details of the successive deaths of Sergeant Germeys, Corporal Delcaretto and Fusiliers Timmermans, Dael, Rohr, Kurz and Billod.

There was some welcome news when General de Maussion told Regnault that the 7th of the Line was to return to Cordoba and then move their headquarters to Orizaba, and that the Regiment Etranger was to move from Chiquhuite to Cordoba. Dubosq and Abrial left with the 2nd Battalion's men and went straight back to La Soledad, while the Regnault column passed through Coscomatepec on the way to Chiquihuite.

Jeanningros felt that it was now time for Captain Cazes to rejoin his regiment, so transferred him from his post at Medellin and sent him to Cordoba. He did not resume command of the 3rd of the 1st, his recent experience as an administrator, as well as a fighting officer, making him well suited to take over Captain Danjou's former position as Adjutant-Major of the 1st Battalion. In the military housekeeping necessary for the move there were some promotions. Sous-Lieutenant Lucien Bosler was named as Maudet's replacement as Regimental Standard-Bearer on 2 August[34] and Voltigeur Kunassec found himself made up to Corporal four days later.

The regimental equipment was packed and the sick in Dr. Rustegho's hospital made ready for the move. Heading for Cordoba with few regrets, Regnault left a Company at Chiquihuite, and another at Atoyac, and, even though they would still be involved in convoy escort duties, the officers and men rejoiced at leaving the hated *Terres Chaudes* for duty in the more salubrious *Terres Temperees*, the Temperate Zone. They reached Cordoba on 10 August, and not a moment too soon, for Regnault himself was now coming down with fever.[35]

Convoys carrying food, ammunition and military payrolls continued to be moved up from the coast and on 11 August a particularly large one left La Tejeria under heavy guard. Commanded by Sous-Lieutenant Grincourt of the 2nd Zouaves, it carried twelve million francs to pay the troops and the escort was made up of the 4th Company of the Egyptian Battalion and both infantry and cavalry from the *Contre-guerilla*.[36] At La Soledad they handed the convoy over to the 1st Company of the Regiment Etranger's 2nd Battalion for the journey to Chiquihuite.

In Cordoba, although sick, Commandant Regnault began designating various officers to make arrangements for the Emperor's Birthday celebrations on 15 August. Much water had flowed under the bridge – and much blood spilled on battlefields – since the event the previous year, when the buildings at Sidi-bel-Abbes had been festooned with signs celebrating earlier Foreign Legion victories, with one left blank, and the Legionnaires had called out to Colonel Jeanningros: 'Let's go to Mexico!'

All of Cordoba was decorated with French and Mexican flags, and bunting in the national colours, and the day went off well, with a parade, the traditional eating and drinking and, for the officers, parties to which leading citizens were invited. Diesbach ended the day issuing a challenge to a fellow Sous-Lieutenant over a heavy-footed older lady who had been foisted off on him at a dance, but as there were neither épées nor sabres available, and pistols seemed to offer too permanent a solution, the matter was dropped. The following day the Mexicans put on a bullfight, something which few of the Legionnaires had seen before.[37] The only gloomy news was a telegraph message from Veracruz reporting that the *vomito negro* had claimed the life of Sous-Lieutenant Borgella-Houra. Lieutenant Auguste Aubin was named as the new commander of the Foreign Legion Depot.

15
'Everyone did his Duty'

Although clearly sickening with something, Commandant Regnault returned to his debriefing of the Camerone survivors, which had been interrupted by the expedition to Huatusco, the move to Cordoba and the celebration of the Emperor's Birthday. From the twenty men he was able to get a fairly clear picture of what had happened at the Hacienda de la Trinidad and afterwards, as well as to learn that two other survivors, Fusiliers Jean Baas and Therese-Francois Daglincks, were still in hospital in Jalapa.

Whether Regnault worked from written or verbal accounts of the battle is unclear. If written depositions were taken, they have not been found in any archives, but his masterly reduction of the information he received formed the basis of a seven-and-a-half page letter headed 'Report on the Affair at Camarone,' which he sent from his headquarters to General de Maussion in Orizaba, on 17 August, setting out their story in narrative form.

Considering the diverse nature of his sources – few of the Legionnaires had seen more of the battle than what was happening in their immediate sectors, and they had only briefly all been together as prisoners – Regnault's report was astonishingly free of errors. He said that Milan had '500 regular cavalry and 350 guerillas' under his command, along with the three National Guard battalions, each with '3 or 400 men in its ranks'. Maudet, he had been told, had 'tears in his eyes' as he called on the last men standing to fire their final cartridges and then 'go out and die fighting in a bayonet charge', after which 'the enemy rushed in and took prisoner all who still breathed.' He estimated Mexican losses at '3 to 400 *hors de combat*', meaning put out of action, killed or wounded, and added: 'With them, as with us, the number of dead was greater than the number who were wounded.' He also paid tribute to Colonel Cambas and Captain Laine, and especially Dr. Talavera.[1]

Regnault mistakenly understood that Fusilier Peter Dicken[2] – who was actually killed in the Hacienda – had been among those who had died later of his wounds, yet, surprisingly, completely missed Fusilier Claude Billod, although having been personally told by Dona Juana Marrero de Gomez that he had died in the hospital at Huatusco. Regnault also wrongly believed that Fusiliers Anton Bogucki and Josef Van den Meersche had survived – not knowing they had died on 1 May in Dr. Talavera's field hospital at La Joya. Additionally, at the time of writing, he did not know that the information that Fusilier Jean Baas was still in hospital in Jalapa, 'gravely wounded', too sick to be moved, had been overtaken by events, for he had died on 8 August.[3]

Regnault's most serious error, however, one which caused much confusion later, involved Fusilier Jean-Baptiste Leonard. While correctly placing him with the other five men just before the final charge, Regnault did not realize that Leonard was severely wounded and had been unable to follow Maudet, Maine, Catteau, Constantine and Wensel out of the ruined shed. He implied that Leonard had been actively involved in the final charge, causing various later accounts to speak of Maudet, Maine and four Fusiliers, rather than three.

Including the officers, Regnault was able to account by name for forty-six members of *La Compagnie Danjou* who had been killed or wounded. For reasons which are not clear he did not name eight of the men who had returned to the French lines – Maine, Berg, Magnin, Gorski, Kunassec, Brunswick, Verjus and Van den Bulcke – which would have taken his total to fifty-two. He had no information about Fusilier Ulrich Konrad, the Orderly of Captain Danjou, who belonged to the 5th Company, or on eleven of the men who had been among the sixteen captured before the Hacienda de la Trinidad was reached. The battle, he correctly said, ended at six o'clock.

> The fatal hour had come [*Regnault told de Maussion*]. The 3rd Company of the 1st Battalion was finished. In this glorious battle, everyone did his duty. There are few men who would not have been happy enough to distinguish themselves as did their comrades . . . I am happy, General, to have been able to give you a good account of the conduct of the 3rd Company of the 1st Battalion. I dare to hope that you will appreciate their bravery and their energy that was so meritorious. Please, I beg you, put before the eyes of His Excellency, Marshal Forey, the names of all the brave men who have been distinguished in this battle, and commend them to him when the occasion presents itself. His Excellency will find in all the Companies of the Regiment Etranger the same resolution as in the campaign at Camarone.[4]

The report became slightly out of date almost at once. For, just three days after Regnault had forwarded it to de Maussion in Orizaba, Camerone survivor Sergeant Alfred Palmaert, his system doubtless weakened by months of captivity, died of dysentery in Cordoba on 20 August.[5]

Diesbach grumbled in his campaign diary that *Juarista* propaganda about France and her Army – which he considered was 'admirably done' and effective – 'perfidiously portrays us as nothing less than liars, puppets and usurpers', and he concluded: 'France has taken Mexico contrary to her own interests'.[6]

Dr. Rustegho and his assistants were more than busy during the month, as an assortment of fevers began plaguing the troops and an outbreak of *vomito negro* was wreaking havoc with both soldiers and townspeople. Captain Ballue, who has shown signs of sickness while escorting Mexican officer prisoners to La Soledad in late May, now came down with a serious case of *vomito negro*. Then Captain Saussier fell sick, along with Sous-Lieutenant Charles Pertusati of the Grenadier Company and Lieutenant Joseph Rehmann, the Polish-born officer who had joined the Regiment Etranger after the Italian Campaign. Captain Cabossel was only marginally better than he had been in June. Lieutenant Barera, whose job as Pay Officer had been taken over by Sous-Lieutenant Vilain, was considered unlikely to make a recovery. Ignorance of the source of *vomito negro* caused it to be believed that it had been brought to Cordoba by a convoy, and Regnault ordered all incoming wagons to be quarantined on the savannah outside town.

In Mexico City the news of General Forey's promotion to Marshal of France was ten days old when Regnault's report, forwarded on by de Maussion, arrived at Army Headquarters. The newly-elevated Commander-in-Chief described the account as 'moving', and wasted no time in dealing with it. The very day he received it, 30 August, Forey issued Order of the Day #195, noting the Herculean efforts of the 3rd of the 1st, which he had originally commended while General-in-Chief on 10 May. Now he praised the men for having 'sustained a battle destined to rank in our military annals beside the greatest feats of arms,' in facing 'an enemy outnumbering them 30-to-1.' Using Regnault's figures, Forey put the Mexican forces at seventeen hundred, and spoke of three officers and twenty-seven men having been killed, sixteen wounded – a total of forty-six of all ranks – and the rest taken prisoner.[7]

Regnault had urged de Maussion to commend his report to Forey, in the hope that the Commander-in-Chief would make some kind of formal recognition of Camerone. Undoubtedly, he got far more than he could reasonably have expected, as Forey took the unusual step of making the report part of Order of the Day #195, which meant that it would be read out at parades wherever French troops were serving in Mexico, and wrote: 'The Marshal Commander-in-Chief wishes that the personnel of the Expeditionary Corps should not ignore even the smallest detail of this clash of giants.'

He then remarked that 'exceptional conduct merits exceptional rewards', and proceeded to distribute decorations and medals. As Maine was already a Chevalier of the Legion of Honour, it seemed fitting to Forey to recommend him for a Commission, and it was ordered that he be promoted to Sous-Lieutenant 'at the first vacancy in the Corps'. Sergeant Schaffner, Corporal Pinzinger, Voltigeurs Fritz and Brunswick and Grenadier Wensel were made Chevaliers of the Legion of Honour, while the late Sergeant Palmaert, Corporal Magnin, Voltigeurs Kunassec and Rebers and Grenadiers Schreiblich and Gorski were awarded the *Medaille Militaire*.[8] The men received their medals and decorations, and more than a year later, official recognition came through publication in the *Moniteur universel*.[9]

Berg did not get a medal, but, like Maine, was promoted to Sergeant and soon received a Commission. Unfortunately, his *Abstract of Services* is silent on the matter,[10] but Lieutenant Zede, who met him in the *Terres Chaudes* in mid-1864, was told by Berg that he received a Commission as a Sous-Lieutenant 'a few days' after being returned.[11] Unlike Corporal Maine's military documents, which specifically mention his participation in the Combat of Camerone, and give the dates when he was a prisoner of the Mexicans,[12] Berg's *Abstract* merely contains a note of his having gained the rank of Sergeant in 1863, no day or month specified, and says nothing about a Commission. However, it is a fact that he did receive one, but in the Zouaves rather than in the Regiment Etranger.[13]

It may have been thought in the regiment that Constantine, wounded in the shoulder and the arm, and Leonard, wounded in the nape of the neck and the arm, had done more than Sergeants Schaffner and Palmaert, but soldiers always know of men whose deeds receive recognition, though are perhaps less deserving than others, and in this case only the names of Sergeants, Corporals and soldiers of the Elite Companies had been sent forward. Quite possibly the Commander-in-Chief felt that Berg's Commission into the Zouaves, the promise of a Commission for Maine, the creation of five Chevaliers of the Legion of Honour – counting that of *Tambour* Lai – and the awarding of five *Medailles Militaire* was sufficient 'reward' for a single action by what was essentially a half-Company of soldiers. Leonard and Constantine do indeed seem to have been glaringly overlooked, but certainly no great case could have been made for decorations or medals for Fusiliers De Vries, Van Opstal, Verjus or Van den Bulcke who, captured on the way to Hacienda de la Trinidad, had not, of course, taken part in the actual combat.

Even after Maine was made up to Sergeant there was still a vacancy in the 3rd of the 1st, because two Sergeants – Morziki and Germeys – had died. Yet neither Magnin nor Pinzinger was promoted at this time, and neither Palmaert nor Schaffner moved up to Sergeant-Major Tonel's position.

In addition to the promotions, decorations and medals, as Chaplain Lanusse noted, Marshal Forey, in a General Order of the Army, 'ordered that any column passing the grave, already considered sacred, should halt, face it and present arms, and the *Tambours* beat *Aux Champs*'.[14]

How many of the men who had fought at Camerone survived?

Writing to Jeanningros on 1 May, Corporal Berg had been able to identify the forty-one men, himself included, who had been taken alive from the Hacienda de la Trinidad. Writing to de Maussion on 17 August, Commandant Regnault had been able to account for forty-six men – living and dead – of the 3rd of the 1st, and failed to mention eight of those who had been among his informants. The fact that Forey promoted Maine and decorated eleven others at the end of August led to a fairly widespread belief among French officers that, counting *Tambour* Lai and Corporal Berg, there had been only fourteen Camerone survivors. The Foreign Legion, in its *Livre d'Or* – the Regimental History, which has to be seen as the official count – perpetuates General de La Hayrie's statement that '19 sous-officiers and soldiers, wounded and taken prisoner, died during their captivity,' which was copied by General Zede – another 'derivative error' – and the figure is certainly at least ten more than was actually the case.[15]

In fact, there were certainly twenty survivors, perhaps even twenty-two. Apart from Lai, Maine and the eleven men decorated by Marshal Forey on August 30, there were Berg, Constantine and Leonard – a total of sixteen.

The matter of the men captured before the Hacienda de la Trinidad was reached is less straight-forward. Of these sixteen, Van den Meersche and Bogucki died early in the morning of 1 May and were buried on the bank of the Rio Chiquito . . . Kurz – the first man wounded in the engagement – died in hospital at Huatusco on 28 May . . . De Vries was rescued by Dupin's *Contre-guerilla* unit on the night of 25–26 June . . . Van Opstal was in the third prisoner exchange, before Regnault wrote his report . . . By some unrecorded means Verjus, the old sailor, returned, as did Van den Bulcke, who was nineteen years old at the time of Camerone and subsequently left the Foreign Legion, was granted a Commission and served in the 20th Regiment of the Line.[16] This accounts for seven of them, four of whom survived, bringing the total number of living Camerone veterans to twenty.

The Mexican Republican Army commander at Huatusco, Lieutenant-Colonel Jose Maria Camacho, had been quite punctilious in reporting the deaths of the Camerone prisoners, so there seems no real reason to believe that Fusilier Daglincks necessarily followed his comrade Baas to the grave from the Jalapa hospital. The Regiment Etranger would almost certainly have been notified if he had died, as had been the case with Baas. Fusilier Konrad would not have been shown on the roll of the 3rd Company, as he belonged to the 5th, to whom he may have returned.

This leaves unaccounted for nine of the sixteen men captured early in the battle, and, with the exception of Lemmer and Seffrin, they had received only superficial wounds, or none at all. Yet these nine men – Gaertner, Holler, Jeannin, Lemmer, Merlet, Schifer, Seffrin, Segers and Zey – just disappeared. Whether they were randomly killed by their guerilla captors, or simply deserted, is not known.

Napoleon III was beginning to be concerned about the cost of the French Expeditionary Corps and was looking for ways to shed some expenditure. Thinking of the terms of the Convention of Miramar, he wrote to Bazaine to suggest that there could be financial savings if the Foreign Legion was transferred to Mexican Service for a period of ten years and its ranks expanded by the recruitment of Indians.[17] Bazaine did not pursue the first suggestion, but gave instructions to Jeanningros to engage Indian volunteers in both Battalions of the Foreign Legion wherever possible.

Sergeant Philippe Maine received his Commission as a Sous-Lieutenant[18] on 14 September, and Marshal Forey was still holding the post of Commander-in-Chief almost a month after being recalled. Despite having been named to succeed him, Bazaine could not exercise that function while Forey remained in Mexico, and it was a frustrating time for the Army, which wished to get on with the campaign of conquest.

Cotaxtla had long been a Republican stronghold and Commandant Regnault began receiving reports that guerillas from the town were pillaging and terrorizing the villages which were well disposed to the French. He decided to send troops into the area, to see if he could flush out the guerillas and put an end to their campaign of intimidation. It seemed to be a job for the Elite Companies. Saussier and his Grenadiers were on post at Paso del Macho and Regnault summoned them to Cordoba to outline his plans. The Grenadiers were short two officers, so were joined by Lieutenant Auguste Legout and Sous-Lieutenant Rehmann, who had been sick earlier in the month, but insisted that he was well enough to accompany them. They left Cordoba by one of the two routes to Cotaxtla on 12 September. Lieutenant Jaudon commanded the Company of Voltigeurs, as Cabossel was still down with fever, so Sous-Lieutenant Diesbach went with them when they left Cordoba the following day, heading for Cotaxtla by the other route. The two Companies rendezvoused at an agreed point and moved on. At Cotaxtla they found only a storekeeper in town, a sure sign that the men were off on guerilla business. The man was very obsequious and Saussier became suspicious, concluding that a trap was to be laid for the column as it returned to Cordoba.

Rehmann began showing signs of illness on 16 September and died the following day. He was buried at Cotaxtla and Saussier and Jaudon began working out a plan to avoid the ambush they believed was being prepared for them. Making sure that the storekeeper understood them to be heading for La Soledad, information they felt he would certainly pass to the guerillas, the two officers set out for Cordoba using Saussier's original route.

Regnault, in the meantime, had heard nothing from his columns, but had been told by Indian spies that large numbers of guerillas were on the move. He promptly sent a small column of Legionnaires along the road which Saussier had taken when leaving Cordoba, and at the same time sent a message to Commandant Munier at La Soledad, asking that a strong column from the 2nd Battalion be sent to Cotaxtla. Many Fusiliers were on the sick list, but Captain Jean-Baptiste Marion managed to put together a mixed infantry force of eighty, which included a number of men from the Egyptian Battalion, and a like number of Mexican Auxiliary Cavalry, and set off. Saussier and Jaudon met up with Regnault's relief force at San Juan de la Punta and they returned to Cordoba together on 20 September, Saussier going on from there to Paso del Macho. Marion's force from La Soledad, which was too large for the guerillas to seriously consider attacking, fruitlessly went all the way to Cotaxtla and back in five days of unremitting rain.[19]

Not long afterwards Jeanningros lost his two most senior officers. Regnault had not really recovered from his bout with fever in July and August and went back to France on sick leave. It was expected that he would be promoted to Lieutenant-Colonel and would return to take the place of the departed Giraud. In the meantime, Battalion Commander Baron Francis de Briche was seconded from the *Tirailleurs Algeriens* on a temporary basis. Then, in the kind of musical chairs and ripple effect which one senior promotion or secondment tended to create, Munier was made up to Lieutenant-Colonel and went to the *Tirailleurs Algeriens*. Commandant Jean-Jules Ligier, an older officer, who had started out in the ranks, gone to Saint-Cyr as far back as 1844, and had served for almost seventeen years with the 39th of the Line, was transferred into the Regiment Etranger to replace Munier.

The ubiquitous Chaplain Lanusse had been with the besieging forces at Puebla when he first heard of the destruction of *La Compagnie Danjou* at Camerone. He was present when the convoy of siege guns, ammunition, food supplies and pay for the troops finally creaked its way into Forey's camp. He was in Mexico City in mid-July, when news came that the first Camerone survivors had been exchanged for Mexican prisoners-of-war, and still there on 30 August, when the Commander-in-Chief issued his Order #195, making public Regnault's account of the battle and decorating survivors.

'Our hearts bounded in our chests,' Lanusse would say later, and admit: 'I had never had a stronger desire: to some day see one of the heroes of Camaron'.[20]

He got his chance when he spent a month with Captain Saussier and his Company of Grenadiers, who were still manning the post at Paso del Macho, and met many of the men of the Foreign Legion – 'soldiers of every country, of all conditions', he called them[21] – who were either based there or shuttling from and to La Soledad on the interminable convoy escorting duties.

> I often saw one of those who had been at Camaron [*Lanusse would write later*]. Gifted with fine intelligence, having received a very well rounded

education, he had a way of telling a story which was very thrilling. From his first words, you were there with him. Wounded in the last moments of the affair, he had been through all the vicissitudes. He had been cared for in the hospital at Jalapa and had not returned to the regiment until a long time afterwards, with several other comrades.[22]

Strangely, Lanusse does not identify this soldier by name, but, by a process of elimination, it can be determined that he was the now one-armed Voltigeur Friedrich Fritz, veteran of the Crimean and Italian Campaigns, and holder of the Cross of a Chevalier of the Legion of Honour. From Wurttemberg, near the Swiss border, he is the only one of the Camerone survivors to fit the description given by Lanusse: 'Wounded in the last moments of the affair' – Fritz, his left arm already shattered, was hit in the head not long before Sergeant Morziki was killed – 'in the hospital at Jalapa' and returned to the regiment 'a long time afterwards' – in the mid-July prisoner exchange.[23]

> One day, we decided on a project to return to Camaron [*Lanusse would write*]. Several of us left on horseback and headed directly there. As we approached, I saw all sorts of emotions appear in succession on the face of the man who would be our narrator and our guide on the field of battle, small and unheralded then, but which would much later come to be very well known.[24]

Arriving at Camaron, the little group left their horses in the corral, and Fritz said excitedly: 'We come to salute our old comrades. For them, this is our first visit.'[25] The grave was outside the walls of the corral, at the southwest corner.

'We gathered at the mound which marked the place where our heroes slept,' Lanusse reported. 'There was a simple wooden cross on which was written:

> To the Memory of Danjou, Vilain and Maudet,
> and the 3rd Company of the 1st Battalion
> of the Legion Etrangere,
> which succumbed on the 30 April,
> after ten hours of battle, with 2000 Mexicans.'[26]

'For a moment, we remained silent,' said Lanusse. 'We knelt, I prayed. My companions prayed with me, their eyes fixed on this ground so precious and sacred. Each wiped the tears from their eyes. It is good to be heroes, it is also pain and grief, and full of emotions which bring tears to all men. The tears flowed from this man[,] bronzed by the suns of Africa and of Mexico. There were tears flowing in the heart, in this chest which had braved so many bullets...After this moment of religious silence, our trusty guide stood up pronounced these words, his eyes fixed on the grave:[27]

> With you, dear friends, to your generous blood, I have added a few drops of my own, but wherever I rest is not important [*said Fritz*]. It doesn't matter

where I am, I speak of you, because you have given to the world the most powerful example of what soldiers can do. You have shown to the utmost degree how far you would go in devotion to duty, discipline and obedience to orders received. It is unusual to see anger on the battlefield, which is itself the expression of the most terrible rage. Those who are fighting do not realize this. They do not have personal hatreds. In the act of killing one another, they do not obey the laws set by the people, sanctioned by the nations. They represent, uphold and live for greater interests, ones superior to the rotten ones when one or the other party thinks it has the most legitimate reasons to fight and destroy. Soldiers obey, and the more they obey, the more they think of duty, the most sacred and the most serious. They are resolved after the battle to conserve their humanity and their rights. Friends, you have fought the most valiant of battles. Since your deaths I have not wished that my ashes were mingled with your ashes, as I have not given up, even after my wounds, the wish to struggle again for the glory and grandeur of France. Friends, I give you my word that I will be worthy of you. We are going to leave this fortress. We leave your sacred rest to a generous enemy and to the friends of tomorrow. We have hope again. It is for the last time that I approach you. Goodbye, then! . . . and *au revoir* in the country of martyrs, of all those whose deaths are justified before God by having obeyed the great principles of duty, and the exigencies of honour.[28]

'A statement, yes, but also almost a prayer,' remarked Lanusse.

They were outside the walls of the courtyard and Fritz began to talk about how the battle had begun, pointing in the direction of the Orizaba Road.

'It was there, in that open area, that sixty men stood fast against an avalanche of seven or eight hundred horses,' he said. 'Several times they were crushed. What a state of mind, not to fear death! In our contempt for death, what strength: outnumbered fifteen-to-one and they wished to kill us – and we resisted them!'[29]

The party went inside the corral.

'There we heard the story of a battle which [had] lasted for close to ten hours,' said Lanusse.[30]

Fritz started by telling his little audience that he had been standing beside Captain Danjou when he told Morziki to reject Milan's first surrender demand.

'This is where I fought,' he said, pointing. 'I was there, very close, at the foot of that wall, with the Captain.'[31]

He pointed across the courtyard to the original breach, which had been defended so staunchly, and where, finally, Corporals Magnin and Pinzinger and Fusiliers Gorski and Kunassec had been eventually overwhelmed.

> That breach, over there, was defended by four or five of ours [*Fritz said*]. The enemy made extraordinary efforts to mass their troops and force an entry. Taken from behind by those who invaded the courtyard, they made use of the bayonet. They were intelligent, and fought back in every way; but finally, after the most heroic defence, overwhelmed by numbers, they were reduced to fighting with their feet and bare hands against their numerous opponents.[32]

Somewhat to Lanusse's surprise, the old soldier also turned out to be something of a philosopher.

> I have thought about this many times since [*Fritz said*]. All children hear stories of the steadfastness of martyrs, of their attitude, so calm in the presence of the most frightful torments. I used not to understand this firm resolve, this contempt of death. I understand it today.[33] Contempt is a weapon. It does not kill, but it is truly terrible! It will encourage a furious attack against the object of its wrath . . . I have often thought that it is contempt for death, above all, which is learned by soldiers.[34]

There was a long silence, each man present caught up with his own thoughts.

'I do not have anything else to add, to end this moving episode,' Fritz said at last.[35] 'It is pure chance that even one of us survived that valiant fight and can tell of the struggles of that day.'[36]

> What kind of men were these? [*marvelled Lanusse*]. The sun, in the brightest of all its splendours, stands in the sky the last hour of the day, and shines on all men: but are they all alike? No![37]

Towards the end of the month, General de Maussion travelled from Orizaba to Cordoba to conduct the annual inspection of the Regiment Etranger. In his report, dated 25 September, he commented: 'The corps of Sous-Officiers is remarkable for its smartness of dress, its discipline, its *esprit de corps* and its energy.' He noted that desertions – largely men from the 2nd Battalion, whose opportunities for undetected flight had been greater – had 'unfortunately been too numerous', though found little cause for serious concern, as, in his view, those who had decamped were 'wretched, worthless.' Overall, de Maussion considered that morale was high, and was generally pleased with what he saw.

> . . . the 3rd Company of the 1st Battalion immortalized the flag and its Regiment in sustaining at Camaron a heroic struggle of 62 against 1,800[,] and did not cease to fight until after having used all its cartridges, [and] losing their officers [and] the senior Sous-Officier [*he wrote*]. As the Regiment Etranger did not have a chance to measure itself against the enemy at Puebla, it has to console itself with the thought that the Combat of Camaron will forever remain one of the most glorious episodes of the campaign in Mexico. In the face of such an example, of what is such a Regiment not capable?[38]

The same day, in Mexico City, Bazaine was endeavouring to give substance to the plan to recruit Indians for the Foreign Legion. Perhaps it was his Arab Bureau experience in Algeria which made him hopeful of success.

> It is quite evident that the Indian race is inferior at present, but it is because since the Conquest no regime has done anything for it . . . [*he told Napoleon*

III in a letter]. This means that this race, which is so worthy of interest[,] has always been treated as an inferior race . . . and as such it remains completely indifferent to what goes on in the country since they have no part in it.[39]

Bazaine told Jeanningros that if he needed further officers he could seek them among the French regiments, but that they must be volunteers, in order to ensure their active enthusiasm for this recruiting experiment.

At last, on 30 September, almost six weeks after being ordered to return to France, Marshal Forey issued his final Proclamation in Mexico City and demitted office, enabling Bazaine to formally take over as Commander-in-Chief of the French Expeditionary Corps the following day.

16
'The past will be the guide for the future'

Sitting in his seaside office, Colonel Pierre Jeanningros, Commanding Officer of Veracruz and the *Terres Chaudes*, was thinking about the *Expedition du Mexique* campaign medal which he knew was being designed in Paris. Napoleon III had made the announcement about the medal on 20 August, and Jeanningros, believing he saw an opportunity to perhaps have the Combat of Camerone immortalized on it, wrote to Minister of War Randon.

Vera-Cruz, 1st October 1863

Expeditionary Corps
of
Supreme Commander
of Vera-Cruz
 [Letter #454]

A S.E.M. Marshal of France
Minister of War

Monsieur le Marechal

I make so bold as to address to you a request which I beg you to submit to His Majesty the Emperor. The battle fought on 30 April last at Camerone by a company of the Regiment Etranger is known today in all its details.

In his General Order of 30 August, No.195, His Excellency the Marshal Commander-in-Chief called it: 'A battle of giants, a battle which deserves to rank in our military annals, beside the greatest feats of arms.' Kindly urge His Majesty to agree to perpetuate the memory of this heroic struggle; and to decree that the name Camerone be added to the legend on the Mexican medal and inscribed on the Standard of the Regiment.

The officers and soldiers of the Regiment Etranger would be proud of such a glorious distinction. They would applaud the benevolence of the Sovereign if he would consent to immortalize the heroism of their comrades at Camerone and they would imitate that heroism when they have to act for France and the Emperor. The past will be the guide for the future.

Colonel Supreme Commander
of Vera-Cruz and the *Terres Chaudes*.
JEANNINGROS[1]

In case Randon had not seen Forey's General Order, Jeanningros included a copy,[2] and also a copy of Commandant Regnault's August 17 battle report to General de Maussion.[3]

It was perhaps eerily coincidental that the Colonel of the Regiment Etranger should be extolling to the Minister of War the military virtues of the men of the 3rd of the 1st on that very day, as not only was General Bazaine, a former Sergeant in the Foreign Legion, taking over as Commander-in-Chief, but, even as Jeanningros was composing his letter in Veracruz, Voltigeur Joseph Rebers, who had won the *Medaille Militaire* for his part in the Combat of Camerone, was dying of dysentery in Dr. Rustegho's hospital in Cordoba.[4]

The actions of Colonel Dupin and his *Contre-guerilla* were directly responsible for the next death in battle of a Foreign Legion officer in the *Terres Chaudes*. In the course of a sweep through the country Dupin had visited the home of a ranchero named Molina, who had been responsible for several attacks on convoys in the area of Paso del Muerto on the Orizaba Road. He found Molina at home with his sons. As Dupin's methods tended to favour executions – with or without the formalities of courts martial – he judged them guilty and, ignoring the pleading of Molina's wife, had them shot. The *Contre-guerilla* rode away with the woman's fury and grief ringing in their ears.

'In a short time, Colonel, you will die!' she screamed.

The widow Molina was a determined woman, and had the resources to exact revenge. Dupin knew this and was cautious, but his business took him to Veracruz, so he was not on the road with his men for some days. However, the port city was full of Republican spies and they sought to learn when he would be returning to La Soledad. The obvious expectation was that he would take the train from Veracruz to La Tejeria and then onwards, but Dupin had decided to travel by horseback, via a circuitous route.

On the morning of 2 October the little train puffed out of the railway station at Veracruz. A seven-man detachment from the Egyptian Battalion, five armed Caribbean sailors and two Sappers from the Martinique Engineers provided the escort. The military passengers included Commandant Jean Ligier of the 2nd Battalion of the Regiment Etranger, returning to La Soledad, Lieutenant Scherer of the Guadeloupe Engineers and Sous-Lieutenant Bontenaille of the *Contre-guerilla*. The civilians included Every Lyons, the British-born Chief Engineer for the railway, and some company employees, Father Savelli, the priest from La Soledad, and several women and children.

The line ran through a cutting almost midway between Veracruz and La Tejeria, an ideal place for an ambush. Fishplates had been loosened, causing the engine and first carriage to jump the track. As Ligier and some of the men of the Egyptian Battalion alighted to see what had happened they were greeted by gunfire from the lip of the cutting on both sides and horsemen closed in the ends to prevent escape. Ligier went down at once, mortally wounded, and Private Bilan Muhammad was killed trying to drag the dying officer back onto the train. Lieutenant Scherer, estimating the attackers as numbering a hundred mounted men and fifty on foot, took command at once.

At the height of the battle the voice of the widow Molina was heard shouting: 'Where is that miserable Dupin?'

The strong defensive position of the train, and the sustained and accurate fire of the defenders, eventually caused the guerillas to break off the attack and retire, with an unknown number of casualties. The cost to the French was three dead and fourteen wounded, including Lyons, Scherer and a woman passenger. A few days later, Sous-Lieutenant Louis Rajaud of the Foreign Legion detachment at La Tejeria, captured and executed six of the guerillas who had taken part.[5]

The departing Marshal Forey passed through Puebla on 4 October, on his way to embark at Veracruz. It was a month which turned out to be a bad one for the Regiment Etranger, as the *vomito negro* struck once again among the men, and with a vengeance. Sous-Lieutenant Diesbach noted in his campaign diary that one hundred and nine members of the 1st Battalion died in eleven days, while another one hundred and sixty were sick.[6] The regimental *Historique* noted on 31 October that Jeanningros had landed at Veracruz at the end of March with just over fourteen hundred men, and that losses in seven months had reduced his force to less than half, with the deaths of eleven officers and some eight hundred men, most to diseases rather than to battle.[7]

On the orders of Bazaine an experimental *Compagnie franche a pied* – quaintly designated the Company of Partisans – was formed from a hundred Foreign Legion volunteers, all classed as exceptional marchers. It was officered by Captain Boechat, Lieutenant von Smolinsky and Sous-Lieutenant Dugenne, and General du Maussion, who liked the idea, had a similar one created for the 7th of the Line.[8]

The 1st Battalion still provided men for convoy duties, the only difference being that now they had exchanged the mud and torrents of the rainy season for the dust of the dry one.

> We were right in the middle of the immense savannah which extends as far as the eye can see, between the Gulf of Mexico and the beginning of the hills which lead to the vast plateau of Anahuac [*wrote Captain Ballue*]. The sun, reaching his zenith, beat down on a land burned by six long months of absolute drought. The silence of the dead was everywhere; not the rustle of an insect, not a chirp of a bird, not a breath of air. The Mexican took a siesta, the bird crouched down in dense foliage, the snake retired to the deepest hole he could find, even the alligator plunged to the very depths of his slime. In truth, nothing moved, unless by an imperious necessity . . . under the burning rays of the sun of the tropics.[9]

While waiting with growing impatience to take over as Commander-in-Chief, Bazaine had been gathering Intelligence about Republican forces and planning his coming campaign with care. The French stance was that the Government of Benito Juarez had ceased to exist when he abandoned Mexico City in June. However, they had to recognize the fact that he was still operating a peripatetic administration in the central part of the country, always a jump ahead of the advancing French forces. In this shadowy government General Ignacio Comonfort held the post of Commander-in-Chief and Minister of War and Marine, with General Jose Lopez Uraga as his second-in-command and General Manuel Doblado as Minister of Foreign Affairs. It was known that *Juarista* General Miguel Negrete had about seven thousand men near Pachuca, while Lopez Uraga was at Morelia with four thousand and Doblado at Queretaro with three thousand. General Juan Alvarez was reported to have gathered an army of four thousand in the State of Guerrero.

Not the least of Bazaine's problems was the arrival from Europe of Archbishop Labastida, who would immediately take his seat – held for him by Bishop Ormeachea – on the three-man Regency. It was immediately clear that his ideas concerning the return of church lands seized by the Juarez regime – and often later sold – would quickly bring him into conflict with Bazaine and French policy. Bazaine watched and waited as the Regency began issuing decrees which flew in the face of declared French objectives, and which he insisted be withdrawn. Labastida took his seat as a member of the Regency on 19 October, taking unto himself the posts of Minister of Justice and Minister of the Interior. The following day Bazaine, in full dress uniform, and backed by two hundred Zouaves, paid the governing body an unexpected visit and laid down the law.

Organizing the Mexican Imperial Army into a fighting force was another problem, and Bazaine was forced to put more faith than he might have wished in the Divisions led by Generals Leonardo Marquez and Tomas Mejia. There were other Mexican generals, but they were lesser lights, with smaller followings, which was partly why Bazaine was anxious to bring the key Republican generals into the French fold. He had been maintaining sporadic communication with Comonfort and Doblado through intermediaries, in the hope of bringing them over to the Empire, and was trying to start similar third party communications with Lopez Uraga.

To all intents and purposes Bazaine was ready to move into the field by late October, but, as he had to remain in Mexico City awaiting despatches from France, he occupied his time with administrative matters.

In Paris, Minister of War Randon was likewise engaged. He received and read Colonel Jeanningros' month-old letter about the possibility of Camerone being commemorated on the *Expedition du Mexique* medal, and as a Battle Honour, and pencilled a notation at the top left-hand corner: 'Impossible on the medal; on the flag, yes'.[10] On 4 November he replied, dashing Jeanningros' hopes about the medal by saying: 'The first of your requests cannot be acceded to, considering that the institution of the medal is to mark and preserve, in a general manner, the memory of the Expedition and not any particular feat of arms by any single corps.' However, he was amenable to the Battle Honour, writing: 'I authorize you, consequently, to give substance to your second request and to take the necessary measures for the name of Camerone to be inscribed on the Standard of the Regiment Etranger in regulation letters'.[11]

He wrote to Bazaine in Mexico City the same day, noting: 'This authorization is given as an exception, because it bends a rule which confers on the Artillery Service the job of making the inscriptions on the flags'.[12] Then, because he was a man who liked order, he notified the 3rd Directorate of Artillery of his decision, assuring them: 'This authorization is given as an exception and under the condition that the inscription will be done in regulation lettering'.[13]

The Regimental Standard of the Regiment Etranger was kept at Headquarters, currently at Cordoba. Whether Commandant Regnault had the 'regulation lettering' done by a professional Mexican tailor or seamstress is unknown, but it is more probable that it fell to the nimble fingers of *Caporal-tailleur* Horstein. Unfortunately, it will never be known exactly what it looked like, as it was destroyed on orders from Paris[14] in July 1871.

The same day that Randon was writing his series of letters in Paris, Battalion Commander de Briche received an order from Bazaine to provide a Sous-Lieutenant, Sous-Officier, two Corporals and two *Tambours* for the Disciplinary Section which had been established at Fort San Juan d'Ulloa at Veracruz. Mindful of the *vomito negro*, which had claimed the lives of Jeanningros' predecessor as Commanding Officer in the city, and of several other officers, including the first two commanders of the small Foreign Legion Depot, de Briche gave thought as to the best way to comply with the order. Eventually, he decided to send the most senior Sous-Lieutenant, working on the basis that he would relatively soon be promoted to Lieutenant, when he could be withdrawn and replaced by the next Sous-Lieutenant in line.

As the senior officer in his rank Sous-Lieutenant Campion duly packed his bags at Cordoba and departed with his small detachment on 6 November. They arrived in Veracruz six days later and after settling his men Campion sought accommodation for himself. He was able to obtain not a room but simply a bed in a room at the Hotel des Diligences and went to report himself to Lieutenant Aubin, commanding the Foreign Legion Depot. Aubin suggested that Campion leave the hotel and move into the house where he had himself been billeted since taking command. Some days later, bored with the very limited facilities of the town, the two young officers went duck hunting in nearby marshes and within hours Aubin came down with a case of *vomito negro*.[15]

Bazaine sent most of his forces, both French and Mexican, northwards from Mexico City at the end of the first week of November. Quite unexpectedly, any hopes he may have seriously entertained of bringing Comonfort over to the French side were dashed on 13 November, when the Minister of War died at the hands of brigands. His escort fled when an ambush was sprung and Comonfort and the small group of Staff Officers with him were all killed. The following day Archbishop Labastida wrote a letter saying that he would not attend any more meetings of the Regency until they revoked their withdrawal of the decrees of early October.

Bazaine kept his Chief of Staff, Lieutenant-Colonel Napoleon Boyer, busy with paperwork and instructions, including the drafting of regulations and edicts which might be required during his absence in the field. Just before leaving Mexico City to go on campaign Bazaine found the time to advise Napoleon III about the apparent success of the plan to enlarge the Foreign Legion by recruiting Indians, telling the Emperor that one hundred and seventy five had engaged, seemed satisfied to serve under French officers and had been organized into two Companies, and adding that he had given orders that they were to receive the same training and equipment as other Legionnaires and be permitted to rise through the lower ranks in the regular manner.[16]

Almonte and Salas issued a public statement on 17 November, declaring that Labastida was no longer a member of the Regency and Bazaine left Mexico City the same day with a political battle won, though certainly not the political war, as he was under no illusions about the loyalty of many of the people with whom he must deal, particularly the Archbishop. Official War Artist Jean-Adolphe Beauce accompanied Bazaine and would be welcomed by both officers and men, living as one of them and seeking no special privileges. The security of the capital was left in the able hands of General Charles Neigre and three thousand five hundred troops.

Commandant de Briche was in Cordoba on 22 November when he received a telegram announcing that Lieutenant Aubin had succumbed to the *vomito negro*, the third death in four months of officers commanding the Foreign Legion Depot. Instead of replacing him, de Briche asked Campion to take over the Depot, in addition to his duties with the Disciplinary Company. Campion agreed, but three days after Aubin's death felt himself coming down with fever. Sous-Lieutenant Rajaud happened to be in town from La Tejeria and immediately summoned a doctor. Quick treatment saved Campion's life, and when he was stronger he assumed command of the Depot and later took on other administrative duties.[17]

General Felix Douay, commanding the French Second Division, with General Marquez' Division protecting his left flank, had moved northward towards Queretaro and entered it on 17 November. General Armand Castaguy, commanding the French First Division, with General Mejia's Division on his right flank, took Acambaro on 24 November and six days later General Bertier, in support of Marquez' Division, entered Morelia without firing a shot. Marquez remained there, but then Bazaine heard that Lopez Uraga and some of Doblado's troops intended to attack him. When the First Division reached Morelia he found that Lopez Uraga, who had swept down on the city with twelve thousand men and thirty-six field guns, had been driven off by Marquez' Division with heavy losses.

The campaign seemed to be going well, as Mejia defeated General Negrete at San Luis Potosi and forced Juarez to move the seat of his government further North. Douay took Guanajuato on 8 December and Bazaine was with Castaguy six days later when they entered Leon, then moved on to Lagos and to Aguacalientes two days before Christmas.

The Foreign Legion was not involved in Bazaine's campaign, being still confined to the *Terres Chaudes*, but there were rumours that their days were numbered there, and that they would soon be taken out of the Reserve Brigade and assigned to active, rather than convoy, service. In the light of this, Chaplain Lanusse made another visit to Camaron, apparently accompanied by one or two other survivors of the battle.[18] Captain Saussier and his Company of Grenadiers were at Atoyac and the survivors may have been the former Fusiliers Leon Gorski and Josef Schreiblich, both of whom had been made Grenadiers after the Combat of Camerone and later awarded the *Medaille Militaire*. This time, Lanusse's little party passed straight through Camaron and rode on to Palo Verde, as he wanted to return by following the route of *La Compagnie Danjou* from there to the Hacienda de la Trinidad.

A Company of the 2nd Battalion of the Regiment Etranger was now based at Palo Verde and the officers greeted Lanusse warmly. He was again taking notes, and this time preparing a map of Camaron, causing a good deal of jocular comment about him being 'a tourist' and a 'topographer.' He and his group spent three hours at Palo Verde, discussing among other things the relative epicurean merits of game birds and waterfowl – as opposed to parrots, which were the best the soldiers could get as a supplement to the standard fare of biscuits – and eating a late breakfast.[19]

Lanusse found the two officers quite sanguine about what had happened to *La Compagnie Danjou*.

'Unhappily, we have not had another Camaron,' said the Captain. The Lieutenant remarked: 'I have always envied the fate of Danjou.'[20]

The Chaplain's party then followed the route of the 3rd Company from Palo Verde to Camaron.

'We took a tour of the corral,' said Lanusse. 'We then left the ruined hacienda and paid a last visit to our dead.'

They found the mound covering the grave had been more fittingly marked.

'On that eminence, there was a bronze column entwined with the branches of a laurel [but] without any inscription,' Lanusse said. 'It would suffice for the coming centuries.'[21]

Prayers were said, and Lanusse had just one more thing to do.

'Gentlemen, we have prayed at the remains of our dear comrades, young heroes whose names have passed into posterity,' he said. 'Permit me to say that there is another grave in this locality which is dear to me: the grave of an obscure hero, it is true, but who succumbed as a victim of his devotion and his charity. It was here, gentlemen, that one of my comrades of the cloth, the Abbe de Ribens, died. He came to Mexico, after [serving in] the Crimea, with the first expedition. His grave is on the other side of the hacienda, the side facing Veracruz. I suggest that we go and pay it a visit.'

The little party adjourned to the old priest's lonely grave outside the southeast corner of the corral's wall, and, said Lanusse, 'after having paid tribute and homage of the memory of Abbe de Ribens we returned to Paso del Macho'.[22]

Bazaine's method of command in the field was unusual, for while he was in constant touch with his Divisional Generals, and spent much time with Castaguy, he also roamed freely with a brigade of his own, commanded by General Francois du Barail, of which the 3rd *Chasseurs d'Afrique* was the most important component. Hearing that Doblado was at Salamanca, Bazaine went after him, but the Republican general had left by the time the French arrived. Bazaine missed him again at Aguacalientes, then, when Doblado sent word that he was willing to talk, Bazaine, deciding that it was probably merely an exercise to buy time, refused to meet him. Near the end of the year Doblado retired into the mountains around Nochistlan amid rumours that he had taken with him a chest containing a million pesos, the remaining treasury of the State of Guanajuato. Lopez Uraga, harried by Douay, tried and failed to join Doblado and then, with the remains of his army, numbering little more than two thousand, finally escaped into rugged country near Colima.

Late in November an order from Minister of War Randon reached Sidi-bel-Abbes instructing Major Charles Rolland, who had been the Commanding Officer of the Regiment Etranger in Algeria, to prepare the 3rd Battalion for service in Mexico and in the last days of December three contingents of Legionnaires were moved to Mers-el-Kebir.

Rolland himself commanded the first, made up of the Depot Company and the 3rd Battalion, minus its 5th and 6th Companies. The second contingent comprised the 6th Companies of both the 1st and 2nd Battalions, who had been left behind when Jeanningros took the Regiment Etranger to Mexico the previous year, along with the men of the 5th Company of the 3rd Battalion.[23] The third contingent, under the command of Lieutenant Zede, was made up of the 6th Company of the 3rd Battalion and a large number of what were referred to as 'isoles', meaning unattached men, some of them returning to Mexico after sick leave, others unassigned specialists. It did not often come to a mere Lieutenant to command five hundred men and Zede had been provided with a few Sergeants, but no Corporals. Innovation seemed the only way to deal with the problem, and he improvised by interviewing men who had served in the armies of their own countries, selecting suitable ones, and, in the time-honoured fashion of the military, making them up to the non-rank of Acting Corporal (Unpaid).[24]

As the year turned Bazaine was personally leading the French forces towards Guadalajara, which had been rapidly evacuated by the Republicans, but in Mexico City political games were being played. General Neigre had the city under military control, but Archbishop Labastida was busily at work behind the scenes. Since his ousting from the Regency he had been meeting with various clerics and with judges of the Supreme Tribunal, and persuaded some of them to sign a protest on 31 December to the effect that they could not in good conscience accept the authority of the two-man Regency. Bazaine had anticipated just such a move and Chief of Staff Boyer called upon Almonte and presented him with the draft of a decree the Commander-in-Chief had prepared before leaving on campaign. It dissolved the Supreme Tribunal – removing Labastida's support – and specified that those who had signed the protest should not be re-employed. Almonte and Salas signed the document and Labastida immediately issued a formal ex-Communication of all those perceived as having taken part or co-operated in 'despoiling' the Church, a sweeping act, which also encompassed the entire French Expeditionary Corps.

In an attempt to show his power the Archbishop declared that he would no longer permit Mass to be held for the French Army in the cathedral, and that its doors would remain closed. His announcement was made on a Saturday, and Neigre acted at once, sending his aide-de-camp to call on Labastida and inform him that if on the following day the doors of the cathedral were found to be closed when soldiers arrived for Mass they would be opened with cannon balls. At seven o'clock the following morning a section of artillery trundled into the plaza and set up their guns, facing the cathedral. A few minutes later the doors were opened and the soldiery entered and heard Mass.

A consistent story in the Foreign Legion concerns a particular Mass while campaigning in Mexico. The place is never identified, and the story – which has been told for well over a hundred years – has been both claimed as true and asserted to be apocryphal. Frederic Martyn, an Englishman serving in the Foreign Legion in the 1890s, heard it as fact only twenty-five years after it allegedly occurred.

As he retold it in his generally reliable book on life in the Foreign Legion, a

'French force in Mexico had taken a small town, and the general in command, wishing to show the shy inhabitants that the French were Christians like themselves, and not savages as they were represented to be, decided to have a parade celebration of High Mass.' The church was decorated with palms and flowers, 'the drummers and buglers were placed so that they could beat and sound the salute at the elevation of the Host' and officers and men of the Regiment Etranger were in their full dress uniforms.

> When all was ready no priest could be found – the cure of the parish had run away, and the monks of a neighbouring monastery refused to open their gate or to hold any communication with the conqueror [*Martyn was told*]. The general was on the point of renouncing the service and ordering the men to be marched away when the sentry on the church door presented arms as the general passed, and asked permission to speak to him.
> 'What do you want?' asked the colonel.
> 'I was thinking, *mon general*, that if you cannot find a priest to perform the functions of the Mass I could do it just as well.'
> 'You! What do you mean?'
> 'I mean,' replied the legionary, 'that before I became a soldier I was a bishop, and that, never having been unfrocked, I am a priest still.'
> After questioning the legionary further the general consented to his performing the service. Putting on the sacred vestments that were found in the vestry, and with the assistance of a Lieutenant as an acolyte, the legionary performed the service of Mass with perfect dignity, and the inhabitants were reassured as the general had hoped they would be.

Martyn thought the story 'a regimental legend,' but said that after leaving the Foreign Legion he saw it reported as fact in a French newspaper, which added the interesting tidbit that 'this ex-bishop was said to have been such a good fighter that he was decorated for exceptional bravery during the campaign'.[25] At the time of Labastida's attempt to deny Mass to French troops in Mexico City, the Foreign Legion was based at Cordoba, which would seem the most likely place that a zealous priest might have decided to absent himself to give local substance to his Archbishop's wish to prevent French troops from participating in ecclesiastical activities. When Martyn heard the story a number of men who had served in Mexico were still in the ranks, and would have been in a position to contradict it were it untrue – just as they would have been in a position to embroider an actual incident.

Chief of Staff Boyer informed the Commander-in-Chief of the extraordinary confrontation in Mexico City in a letter dated 5 January 1864, the very day that its recipient was entering Guadalajara. He explained that Almonte and Salas were anxious, and suggested that Bazaine might think it wise to return to the capital. Turning the conduct of the campaign over to General Douay, Bazaine began to make his way back to the capital, but, having confidence in Neigre, travelled in a leisurely manner, stopping at various towns on the way to check on local civil and political officials. When he reached Mexico City he found it outwardly calm and Neigre well in control, so immediately immersed himself in administrative work.

17
An Illusive Enemy

On New Year's Day 1864, Major Elie Rolland left Mers-el-Kebir with twenty-four officers and nine hundred and sixty men of the 3rd Battalion. For reasons which are unclear, two of the Companies which sailed with him were temporarily left in Martinique.

In theory, at least, the Foreign Legion was not accepting new men, adhering to the ruling made two years earlier. In practice, engagements, and sometimes transfers, had never really ceased. Whatever might be decided in Paris, men were killed in the service, engagements expired and were not renewed and regimental needs had to be met.

Swiss-born Legionnaire Henri Spinner, signing his engagement papers in Strasbourg on 2 January, found his companions to be a very mixed bag.

> My comrades were German deserters, others my compatriots, not counting a man from Vienna, the most terrible of the lot [*Spinner wrote*]. We showed our identification papers, a formality which was dispensed with in the case of the deserters. We were of sufficient quality to have the doors of the regiment opened to us. I remember that two of the deserters did not speak Polish, being originally Prussian Poles. They had deserted from the garrison in Luxembourg. It was amusing to watch their animated gestures as they tried to make themselves understood ... The Bavarians, Austrians and Wurttembergers could not stand the Prussians. The men from Alsace did not like each other. The Swiss got on quite well with everybody, because, although they love their country, the Swiss are not nationalistic.[1]

Most of Spinner's intake had joined the Foreign Legion as much for three meals a day as for any love of soldiering, and talked incessantly about the food. They were sent onwards from Strasbourg to Algeria to begin their training.

In both Paris and in Mexico City the future of the Regiment Etranger was being given much thought in terms of size, activity – even name – and the first four months of the year saw a flurry of activity.

The second Mexico-bound contingent, a mixed bag of men from the 1st, 2nd and 3rd Battalions, finally left Mers-el-Kebir on 31 January,[2] but there was no room for Zede and his men, who remained in Mers-el-Kebir to await another ship. In due course they were joined by other Legionnaires, including Spinner and his comrades.

In Paris, while the first and second contingents were still at sea, and Zede was still waiting impatiently at Mers-el-Kebir, Minister of War Randon decided on 15

February that the Regiment Etranger should be doubled in size from three battalions to six, and that it would revert to its old name of *Legion Etrangere*, a decision which, of course, would not be known in Mexico for more than a month.[3] The Regiment Etranger was officially permitted to accept new men as of 22 March,[4] but now the term of service was increased from two years to five, where it has remained ever since.

Sous-Lieutenant Bosler relinquished the position of Standard-Bearer of the Regiment Etranger to newly-commissioned Sous-Lieutenant Antoine Lafont early in the year. The 2nd Battalion still provided convoy escorts between La Soledad and Chiquihuite, while the 1st Battalion, in addition to escort duties between Chiquihuite and Orizaba, in the *Terres Temperees*, found itself involved in taking the war to the small villages and towns in the area. It was hard work, involving much marching, but usually little fighting, and often seemed a waste of time, as there were seldom enough men to leave to garrison the places which the French, if only for a matter of days, controlled.

> We march, march without stopping [*Sous-Lieutenant Diesbach grumbled in his campaign diary*]. We enter the villages without firing a shot, [but] we do not have the men to hold what we take ... All the troops which retreat before our army re-form in the tropical lowlands in guerilla bands strong enough to give us serious worries. We are too weak to pursue [and] are like prisoners in the posts which we occupy, just happy enough to hold on. Now that they know our weakness, they come [and] shoot at us in broad daylight, something they would not have done before ... Even though we are victorious, we cannot travel without fighting, every day assassinations and stagecoaches stopped ... Send forty men alone, they will be massacred by the small bands of four to five hundred men who come out of nowhere and who are elusive, protected by the inhabitants of the towns and the countryside who keep them abreast of what we do.[5]

Not that the officers and men of the Foreign Legion had any great concern about the shooting ability of the Mexican guerillas in these brief clashes. Diesbach considered them cowardly and 'cruel,' saying: 'Their method is to flee as soon as they fire. They come back later to see what damage they have done and to strip the dead and finish off the wounded by mutilating them horribly'.[6]

The *Contre-guerilla* had been sent up the coast to Tampico in January, though without Colonel Dupin, who was sick, which was a rare occurrence. Zede, who came to have a soft spot for him, thought him 'a valorous soldier and wise leader', and remarked that 'he was blessed with an unbelievable constitution and was marvellously coordinated in physical exercises',[7] but even this iron constitution broke down once in a while. Certainly, the job he was doing had taken its toll. Zede recalled him as a 'small, bald old man, with a long white beard, a hook nose and lively eyes',[8] but he was prematurely old. As he remarked in a letter to his niece in February,[9] just before going to join his men: 'If you knew how much I have aged since I came to this awful country. Everyone thinks I'm 60 when I'm hardly 49.'

An expansion of the *Contre-guerilla* had been authorized. De Stoecklin's place as second-in-command had been taken by Captain du Vallon of the 3rd *Chasseurs d'Afrique* and a second Squadron of Cavalry, with blue jackets, had been raised and was commanded by Sous-Lieutenant Chappell of the 1st *Chasseurs d'Afrique*. The Infantry Company was commanded by Sous-Lieutenant Vallez of the 1st Zouaves.[10]

Encouraging reports of Douay's campaign in the north reached Bazaine in Mexico City. Apart from a worrying period in February, when Lopez Uraga gathered his army and seemed about to threaten Guadalajara, then thought better of it and withdrew once more to Colima, the French were making good progress. Republican General Manuel Lozada declared for the Empire with several thousand men in March, and several lesser generals also changed sides. After taking Real Catorce very easily General Mejia's Division successfully moved against Matehuala, but a serious outbreak of typhus forced them to remain there for a number of weeks. From some captured letters Bazaine learned that Doblado, with an army of six thousand men, planned to attack Mejia's weakened Division. Not wishing to tip his hand Bazaine said nothing, but ordered Colonel Alphonse Aymard to march North from San Luis Potosi, timing his arrival at Matehuala to coincide with that of Doblado. The plan worked, and Doblado, having forced Mejia's troops into the central plaza of the city, was scenting victory when Aymard's 62nd Regiment of the Line fell on him from flank and rear and almost annihilated his men. Doblado himself escaped, but soon resigned his command and sought sanctuary in the United States.[11]

Among Bazaine's more immediate administrative problems in Mexico City was the many times President Antonio Lopez de Santa Anna. From his exile in St. Thomas in the Danish Virgin Islands he had seen the French Intervention as a possible opportunity for himself, and obtained permission from both Bazaine and Almonte to visit Mexico, ostensibly to attend to some personal business in the neighbourhood of Jalapa. When he arrived at Veracruz on an English mailboat, he was visited by a French officer, who required him to sign a document promising not to issue any Proclamations or Manifestos. He signed it, them promptly issued a statement concerning the purposes of his return to the land of his birth.

It was generally friendly towards the Intervention and was published in both Orizaba and Mexico City on 3 March, but as it was dated the day after he had signed his promise, Bazaine issued immediate orders to the French Navy to put a vessel at his disposal and see that he left Mexico on it. The old politico at once claimed that, while he had indeed signed the promise, he had not understood it, as he was unable to read French. He sought leniency, but Bazaine was adamant and Santa Anna sailed away, threatening to take the matter up with Napoleon III.[12]

The Emperor of the French, however, had far more pressing matters at hand than the machinations of Santa Anna. He was following the course of the American Civil War with interest, and also watching the political situation in Europe, especially the flexing of Prussian and Austrian muscle over the duchies of Schleswig and Holstein at the base of the Jutland Peninsula. In 1861 William I had become the Constitutional Monarch of Prussia and the following year named Otto von Bismarck as Minister-President and Foreign Minister. Napoleon III had made no move when Prussia allied itself with Austria in January 1864 to seize Schleswig and Holstein from Denmark, not seeing in this small war the beginnings of the Prussian aggression which would engulf France itself six years later.

Austrian Archduke Maximilian had indicated that he was ready to accept the throne of Mexico, and was engaged in his regal farewells. He and Archduchess Charlotte, now calling herself Carlota, visited England and were received by Queen Victoria at Windsor Castle. Carlota's father, Leopold, King of the Belgians, was with them, as was French Admiral Jurien de la Graviere, whose own experience in Mexico had been so unfortunate. The British politely declined a request to provide a Royal Navy frigate as an escort for Maximilian and Carlota when they were ready to travel from Austria to Mexico, and the Spanish followed suit. The couple also spent time in Brussels, while Napoleon III's military strategists were hard at work in Paris devising a document which would be called the Convention of Miramar, in which the Emperor of the French would promise to provide the Emperor of Mexico with adequate military forces, and agree that when they were repatriated the Foreign Legion would remain to be part of the Mexican Imperial Army.

General Gonzalez Ortega, who had escaped from custody after surrendering Puebla, began actively encouraging the desertion of French troops, issuing handbills, one of which read: 'Soldiers, you should know that you have overthrown a government, who you betrayed. You have come to assassinate a people. You have come to destroy a political party and your conduct will mean the slaughter of eight million men. Your leaders have said that you will annihilate Juarez, but it is Juarez who is right.' It went on to promise that those who deserted to the Republicans would be well treated.[13] Diesbach began shooting Mexicans he caught encouraging men of the 5th Company to desert.[14] Major Rolland's command landed at Veracruz on 21 February and went into camp to await the arrival of their comrades on the *Darien*, and in Mexico City, where General Bazaine was planning redeployment, the decision was made three days later to move the Regiment Etranger from Cordoba to Puebla. The sickly and depleted 2nd Battalion was sent there at once, while the 1st remained where it was, soon to be joined by Colonel Jeanningros, now taking command of his regiment again, after his stint in Veracruz. On 1 March came the happy news that the Regiment Etranger was to be taken out of the Reserve Brigade and positioned for active service. Moving from Cordoba was a major undertaking, and most of the month was occupied with packing, so as to be ready to move out when Rolland and his Legionnaires arrived from the coast. Some of the sick would never reach Puebla, as Dr. Rustegho's little hospital continued to treat men for *vomito negro*, dysentery, other assorted fevers and maladies, and worse. Camerone survivor Fusilier Luitpol Van Opstal died there of cancer[15] on 23 March.

The mail boat having made better time from France than the troopship from Algeria, Randon's instructions regarding expanding the Regiment Etranger and changing its name reached Mexico six days before the *Darien*, which had picked up the two Companies which had been left in Martinique, hove-to off Veracruz on 29 March. The Headquarters Staff wrestled with the logistics of finding a suitable number of Sous-Officiers and Corporals for six battalions of the re-named regiment, but by 1 April the expansion and reorganization was complete, at least on paper, with the Sous-Officiers selected for the new battalions placed *a la suite* – unattached, with unspecified duties – with the three existing battalions.

The same day, united once more under Major Rolland, the 3rd Battalion and the two newly-arrived Companies from the 1st and 2nd Battalions entrained at La Tejeria, heading West to the railhead. There had been an unfortunate shedding of men in Veracruz, as a number of Legionnaires had simply slipped away, and others disappeared at La Tejeria and finally at the railhead, where the battalion began a thirteen-day march to Cordoba – to join up with the 1st Battalion – and ultimately to Puebla.[16] When Bazaine heard about the desertions from the 3rd Battalion, and of others from Cordoba itself, he told War Minister Randon in a letter that he would take stern measures: 'I shall have some of them shot. It is quite clear that a good many of them engaged to get a free trip, but it will cost them dearly if they are caught'.[17]

Also on 1 April, Lieutenant Zede and his contingent at Mers-el-Kebir were finally able to embark for Mexico. They boarded the *Dryade*, and Zede, visiting Captain de Pena to introduce himself and learn the shipboard routine to be followed, was surprised to be received 'politely but coldly'.

> Commander de Pena was displeased at having had to embark such men as the Legionnaires [*Zede would write later*]. I was going to leave with a bad impression, when he asked me my name . . . I spoke of my brother, who was then also a Captain of Frigate and an aide-de-camp to the Minister of the Marine. Then he spoke frankly, and confessed his concerns at having on board for a long voyage, such bandits as the Legionnaires, and [said] he was surprised to see me in such company. I replied that the Legion was perhaps the most rigorously disciplined in all of the Army; that they had covered themselves in glory in Mexico by the Combat of Camerone, and had done the same in the Crimea and in Italy; that Marshal Bazaine, who was now Commander-in-Chief in Mexico, had spent all his career [in the Legion], and was our former Colonel; that I was proud to be part of it, and I would answer for my men; and he would have to leave me to ensure that they understood that on board ship they would recognize him as the authority, compatible with maritime regulations. My protestations reassured him a little. I told him that among my men, I had former sailors, mechanics, workers in iron and in wood and that, if he should judge it appropriate, I would put them at his disposition to build the installations necessary for transporting the horses and for the stowing of stores. The Commander accepted my offer in principle. For the time being, all went well.[18]

Zede may have been outraged by Captain Pena's concerns, but the truth was that his Legionnaires were a varied enough group to excite apprehension on the part of outsiders. Spinner said that one of his comrades was a Chinese – perhaps the very man Zede had seen when he arrived at Sidi-bel-Abbes in 1857, and Legionnaire Huart had noted five years later – who held the rank of Corporal, and that one of the *Tambours* was an African. He subsequently came to know an Armenian in a Company of Grenadiers 'who spoke several languages, besides French and

German'.[19] To Zede, with more than six years service as a Foreign Legion officer, this human agglomeration may have seemed quite normal. To Captain Pena it apparently presented a perceived threat.

In Mexico the conquest was going well in the central part of the country and Bazaine began making plans to deal with the southern portion of the State of Puebla, and ultimately with Oaxaca, further South, where General Porfirio Diaz, who had escaped from French custody after the fall of Puebla, was firmly in control. With an army estimated at more than three thousand men, and able to call on the allegiance of many guerilla bands in the region, he could menace both the Orizaba Road and the railway in the *Terres Chaudes* and be a real threat to the forces of General Augustin Brincourt, who commanded in Puebla and had responsibility for all military operations in the State. The majority of the Companies of the 1st and 3rd Battalions were at the southern post of Acatlan, respectively under Battalion Commanders Gaston Guyot de Leuchey and Paul-Amiable de Brian.

Detachments of the regiment were scattered at various posts, the most northerly ones, at San Juan de los Llanos, Zacatlan and Tlaxcala, charged with controlling *Juarista* activities and keeping open that portion of the road to Mexico City. The most westerly post was at Punte de Texmelucan, but it was Acatlan and Tepeji – nearest to the *Juarista*-controlled State of Oaxaca – which were the most dangerous, and subject to hit-and-run tactics from both Mexican Republican Army units and guerillas.

Captain Cabossel was still not fit for field duty and Lieutenant Gans, re-assigned from the 3rd of the 1st to the Voltigeurs, took the Company – which now included Camerone survivors Fritz, Brunswick, Kunassec and Rebers – to Tepeji. At the end of the first week in April the post was attacked in force by *Juaristas* under the command of Felix 'Chato' Diaz, brother of Porfirio, who was also pillaging and destroying supposedly pro-French villages in the area, and vaguely menacing Acatlan. Word of Gans' predicament was sent to Puebla and Brincourt ordered Colonel Jeanningros to march to his relief, and then to make a general demonstration of sufficient force to convince the Diaz brothers to leave the posts alone.

On 15 April, Saussier, now commanding the 2nd Battalion, was ordered to get ready to go into the field, taking with him all the members of the 1st Battalion still at Puebla. Jeanningros despatched two Companies to make a forced march to Tepeaca, where they were to wait for the main body of troops he was organizing as a mobile relief column. However, if they were to hear gunfire from Tepeji or Acatlan, were to hasten to the rescue. Saussier left Puebla the following day, but when he arrived at Tepeaca on 17 April he found the original two Companies gone. They had heard gunfire and marched south as quickly as they could. He waited for Jeanningros and the rest of the column, which was delayed by the slow pace of the wagons, and the difficulties they faced on the road, and did not arrive until the following day. They stayed at Tepeaca overnight and pushed south the next day, two Companies going ahead to Acatlan. The Mexicans had ceased their attacks when their scouts reported troop reinforcements on the way, and by the time that Jeanningros and the main column arrived they found that de Brian had the 3rd Battalion ready to go in pursuit of the erstwhile attackers. He was annoyed when Jeanningros refused to give permission, reminding him of Bazaine's orders, which had been reiterated by Brincourt, that no pursuits of Diaz's troops or of guerillas were to go beyond Acatlan. Slowly, the Jeanningros column returned to Puebla, arriving on 28 April, completely worn out.[20]

The troopship *Dryade* reached Martinique near the end of April. It had been a quiet voyage and Legionnaire Spinner and his comrades had generally enjoyed it. Once again food was the centre of their focus, and he remembered it as having been 'excellent', with 'soup, meats, pork and seafood, beans, rice, coffee, and brandy of excellent quality', and being issued with 'very good tobacco'.[21]

Once docked, an order from the Governor was handed to Zede. His Legionnaires were to be marched from the ship to Fort Desaix and kept under guard there by soldiers of the *Artillerie de Marine*, a measure made necessary, he was told, because Zouaves from an earlier Mexico-bound vessel had caused serious disturbances in Fort-de-France.

> I could not contain my indignation [*Zede said later*]. How could they treat like convicts the brave soldiers going on campaign and risking their lives for France! I wrote the Governor a respectful letter, but gave free rein to my indignation, and I asked to be permitted to camp on the Savannah, a vast area situated in the centre of the city, which was at the same time close to the sea. I added that I would be unloading two cases of weapons in order to arm my Police Guard, by which means I would be ready for anything. I concluded by saying that if the Governor refused to accept my request, I would comply, but would ask him to relieve me of my command and have me replaced by a firm officer, as the situation would be grave.[22]

Zede's request to camp on the savannah was approved and he marched his men there as soon as they disembarked.

> In an instant the camp was set up, and roped all the way round [*he would recall*]. I placed my sentinels outside the roped-off area, had my tent pitched in the middle of the camp and always assisted in the distribution of food. I anticipated that I would be asked for many permissions [to leave camp], and warned that anyone who got drunk, caused a scandal in town, or was missing at one of the three roll calls each day, would be taken back on board the ship and put in irons until our departure. At the evening roll call, there were five missing drunks. On their return, I had them seized by my Police Guard, tied up and taken on board the ship, where they were put in irons. Seeing this done, nobody else broke the rules.[23]

In Puebla, on 30 April, the first anniversary of Camerone was marked with a service of remembrance at the great cathedral, attended by Jeanningros, just back from the South, and all the officers and men of the Regiment Etranger. At the Tuileries in Paris – and the date was merely coincidental – Napoleon III was signing an Imperial Decree calling for the raising of a 4th Battalion for the

Regiment Etranger.[24] The Emperor's striking *Medaille du Mexique* campaign medal was ready for distribution and Jeanningros presented it to his Legionnaires at a parade the following day.

The ribbon was of white watered silk, with a black Eagle grasping a green Serpent in its talons and beak – from the coat of arms of Mexico – superimposed on a vertical St. Andrew's Cross, with one red stripe and one green. Suspended from the ribbon by a ring was the heavy medal itself, the obverse taking the form of the pseudo-Roman bust of Napoleon III – wearing a crown of laurel leaves – used on French coinage, encircled by a wreath of the same leaves.

The reverse, also bordered with a laurel wreath, bore the legend *Expedition du Mexique* at the top and *1862–1863* at the bottom of an outer circle. As Marshal Randon had told Jeanningros the previous November, the medal was intended to 'preserve, in a general manner, the memory of the expedition and not the feats of arms of any particular regiment',[25] so the words in the centre commemorated five milestones in the campaign: *Cumbres, Cerro-Borrego, San Lorenzo, Puebla* and *Mexico*, not all of which had been battles. *Cumbres* recalled the difficult – though largely unopposed – assent of the Cumbres Mountains in 1862, while *Cerro-Borrego* was for General the Count of Lorencez's victory earlier the same year. *San Lorenzo* was for the taking of the fort of the same name, *Puebla* for the siege and capture of the city and *Mexico* for the occupation of the capital, all in 1863.

The same day, in Paris, Marshal Randon announced a reversal of his mid-February decision to rename the Regiment Etranger and raise its strength to six battalions. Bazaine, who had worked hard to create a framework for a six battalion *Legion Etrangere*, cannot have been pleased to learn six weeks later that what was now needed was a four-battalion Regiment Etranger, with everything to be in place by 1 July. In the meantime, in an effort to give greater mobility for strike efforts, and greater efficiency in scouting, men of the 1st Battalion who could ride were invited to volunteer for what would officially be known as the *Compagnie franche montee* – Company of Mounted Partisans – two men to a horse or mule, taking turns at riding or marching, and informally referred to as the Mounted Company.[26] Command of this new arm was given to Captain Gabriel Menard de Chauglonne, with Lieutenant Jean-Luc Grimaldi and Sous-Lieutenants Henri Graff and Gabriel Collinet de Lasselle as his subordinate officers and it soon achieved a prodigious marching and fighting reputation.

Lieutenant Zede and his five hundred men reached Veracruz on the *Dryade* in mid-May. They found the view from the ship to be sinister rather than romantic: 'On our right, a small island on which sat the dilapidated fortress of San Juan d'Ulloa,' said Zede. 'On the left, the Isla de los Sacrificios, absolutely arid, but covered by a multitude of crosses indicating the graves of our sailors, victims of the insalubrious climate.' They were disembarked, and gladly marched straight to the station to board the train to La Tejeria. Zede noted the gruesome *zopilotes* – '. . . these disgusting animals seem to stalk you like prey'.[27] They stopped at La Soledad, went on to the railhead at Loma Alta, just east of Cameron, and then began the march to Puebla.

As they passed through Camaron, Zede had a chance meeting with Sous-Lieutenant Evariste Berg, now once again an officer of the Zouaves, and they visited the Hacienda de la Trinidad together. Zede already knew the essentials of the Combat of Camerone, but jumped at the chance of a guided tour by an actual participant and survivor. They walked through the corral, Berg giving a running commentary of the battle and pointing out various places where specific things had happened.

'It is worth noting one thing,' he remarked to Zede. 'Contrary to what is ordinarily the case in the defence of such places, we could not see outside. It did not have terraces on which one could place men, nor windows, and we did not have tools to make loopholes. We had to prevent their access to the various openings and be prepared to repel any efforts at scaling the walls.'[28]

Even though they had covered half of the journey through the *Terres Chaudes* by train, as Zede and his column marched on the *vomito negro* began to make itself felt, with men complaining of headaches and cramps in the neck, which soon spread through the entire body. This was followed by the vomiting of dark blood, which Zede thought looked 'like coffee with the grounds suspended in it'. The primitive, and rarely effective, treatment called for victims to be fed olive oil, while 'poultices made from the disgusting mud of Veracruz were applied to the legs'.[29] Most died within six to twelve hours. Once out of the *Terres Chaudes* things were better, though the marching was all uphill, and Zede's column passed through Corboba and Orizaba and eventually reached Puebla, where they found preparations under way for the arrival of Emperor Maximilian and Empress Carlota, who were expected in a matter of days. Arrangements had to be put in place for their protection on the Orizaba Road from Veracruz, onwards to Puebla, their reception in the city and their continued safety in travelling from there to Mexico City.

18
The Emperor Arrives

Archduke Maximilian had signed the Convention of Miramar on 10 April, ensuring himself of the presence of French bayonets for the foreseeable future, and the services of the Foreign Legion for even longer. The same day he accepted the offer of the Crown of Mexico from a visiting delegation of Mexican exiles. The newly-Imperial couple and their party sailed out into the Adriatic aboard the Austrian frigate *Novara* four days later and, accompanied by the French frigate *Themis*, headed for Italy and an audience with the Pope. Then there were four days at Gibraltar, with an Imperial gun salute from the British garrison, and they received the same from the Spanish at Cadiz and the Portuguese at Lisbon.

The ship put into Funchal – where Maximilian and Carlota had spent part of the Winter of 1859–60, after the Franco-Piedmontese defeat of Austria at Magenta and Solferino – and then set out across the Atlantic to Martinique. The soon-to-be-Emperor was determined to create in Mexico a Court as glittering as that of Austria. A month before even formally accepting the throne he had begun putting in place the trappings of an Imperial Court, including the creation of a special *Medaille du Merite Militaire* for those exhibiting conspicuous bravery, and an elegant decoration called the Order of Guadaloupe. On the voyage to Mexico he spent much time in his cabin, creating a handbook of Court Etiquette, complete with the complicated orders of precedence to be observed on every occasion. The *Novara* ran out of coal before Martinique was even in sight and had to be taken in tow by the *Themis*, becoming the butt of many bad jokes about the Emperor of Mexico having to be dragged to his throne by the French. In Jamaica, where Maximilian and Carlota spent two days, Governor Edward John Eyre was lavish with his hospitality.

On 22 May the Regiment Etranger received orders to proceed to Palmar, midway between Puebla and Orizaba, to secure the road, a journey which required three full days for men on foot. They had just arrived when Almonte, now styled Lieutenant-General of the Realm, passed through with a convoy of carriages carrying his wife and an assortment of high-born Mexican women chosen to be ladies-in-waiting to the Empress. They were to wait at Orizaba, as the Imperial party was not expected to arrive for at least another twelve days.

Standard-Bearer Lafont had died and Colonel Jeanningros had just presided over the installation of Sous-Lieutenant Elie Duroux as his replacement, the fourth Standard-Bearer for the regiment in less than eighteen months, but one who would see out the campaign. After deploying his men at Palmar and other permanent and temporary posts in the vicinity, Jeanningros had plenty of time to write a generally optimistic letter home.

The news which comes in from all directions indicates that the enemy is not on the move, and is a great distance from the road, so to the right and to the left, the country is peaceful... [*he informed his 'Louise cherie'*]. The solution of the problems is going to come with the arrival of Maximilian, expected 5 or 6 June. Many French officials expect to return home. While there are some individuals who wish to stay in Mexico, I think that the great majority are against doing so. There is nothing in this country not available in France. The manners, the conveniences, the joy of life are all lacking in Mexico. Society does not exist, the habits are far from being in sympathy with ours, and, finally, there is no attachment. I might add that to this day, no officer is married to a Mexican, though suitors, in general, are always plentiful in the Army. None desire to contract any alliance with a people who know little of our culture and our customs . . .

What a world, my good angel – and may I add that if the Army stays here for a long time in this horrible business, discipline will be lost and events will eventually tarnish the reputations of everyone . . .

The arrival of Maximilian will reduce all the resistance. A large number of the insurgents now adhere to the Empire. All can hope, if this continues, for peace in the land. I ardently desire this, because we can then return to our own country.[1]

At midday on 28 May, well ahead of her expected date of arrival, the *Novara* hove-to off Veracruz. The *Themis* had preceded her, and Maximilian, not wishing to have his ship in the midst of the French fleet, directed his Captain to anchor some distance away. A less than friendly visit from the French Admiral brought what was virtually a reprimand to the effect that the place chosen was notorious for the *vomito negro*.

Just two weeks earlier, Lieutenant Zede – who had come to Mexico to fight – standing on the deck of the *Dryade*, prior to disembarking his Legionnaires, had seen 'a muddy coast devoid of vegetation, signposted with the carcasses of wrecked ships'.[2] Carlota – who had come to Mexico to rule – standing on the deck of the *Novara*, thought the view was 'infinitely pleasing, a more oriental version of Cadiz', at least, that was what she said in a letter to Empress Eugenie.[3] Obviously, there was no welcoming party, as Almonte had not expected the Imperial Couple for some days, and, rather than risk too long an exposure to the possibility of contracting *vomito negro*, had chosen to stay at Orizaba until the last minute. Summoned by the telegraph, he arrived in the evening, full of apologies.

The French ships were hung with lanterns and on landing the following morning the Emperor and Empress were formally welcomed by a gun salute from Fort San Juan d'Ulloa, but not by the citizens of Veracruz, who remained unalterably Republican in their sympathies. Countess Paola Kollonitz, who was accompanying the Empress as a lady-in-waiting, considered that 'the reception was excessively chilling',[4] and was glad that they went quickly to the railway station to take the train. By this time the rails had been pushed west from La Soledad to a new terminus at Loma Alta, where the Imperial party would find *diligences*, and wagons for their luggage, waiting for them. Many of the details of their journey through the *Terres Chaudes* and the *Terres Temperees* were subsequently recalled by Countess Paola in a book which was astonishingly frank for a courtier, and in the Empress-to-Empress letter from Carlota to Eugenie.

The Imperial entourage numbered eighty-five people, with more than five hundred pieces of luggage. As there was insufficient accommodation at either Cordoba or Orizaba for a group of that size it had been agreed that the party would be split into two parts, the first to push on and overnight in Orizaba, while Maximilian and Carlota would only go as far as Cordoba. The plan called for the whole of the Imperial Party to be reunited in Puebla, but Mexico's roads were always full of surprises, especially in the rainy season.

At La Soledad there was a band and a reception, then the party entrained again for Loma Alta, the railhead. The Emperor and Empress were to make the journey to Puebla in the elegant English-built travelling carriage they had brought with them, the others in a veritable fleet of *diligences*. The first contingent, which included Countess Paola, set off, and she was impressed with the skill and courtesy of the drivers, handling their mule teams. Carlota would declare: 'The road across ill-cultivated plains to the Chiquihuite Mountains is abominable. The only civilized spots are the French guard-houses, with the canteens beside them.'[5] Neither she nor Countess Paola made mention of Camaron – where there was just such a French guardhouse and 'canteen' – which they rattled through in their respective conveyances.

Even before they reached Chiquihuite any hopes of the advance party reaching Orizaba that night were long gone, and they creaked into Cordoba two hours before midnight. A wheel on Maximilian and Carlota's travelling-carriage succumbed to the road, and the Imperial Couple transferred to a stagecoach, which ironically still had the words *Diligencia de la Republica* painted on the side. The one travelling ahead of them nearly went over a cliff in the dark, but they arrived in Cordoba two hours after midnight and went straight to a reception, banquet and endless speeches, lasting until five o'clock in the morning. Trying to make up time, the advance party left for Orizaba an hour and a half later, soon to be followed by Maximilian and Carlota.

The Empress thought Orizaba 'as pretty a place as you can find', reminding her, she told Empress Eugenie, of 'Italy and the South Tyrol', and the air was 'delicious and extremely light'.[6] She and Maximilian spent two days there, meeting their new Mexican courtiers and attending services in the cathedral. Then it was back on the road, destination Puebla. Countess Paola would remember that 'large stables, connected with taprooms, appeared at regular intervals in what at times appeared to be inaccessible places'.[7] Many of them were mini-garrisons manned by men of the Foreign Legion, some of whose comrades had been rushed south to investigate a report that Porfirio Diaz had more than a thousand men under arms and planned to seize the Emperor and Empress along the road. It had turned out to be an unfounded rumour and the Regiment Étranger returned to its static posts. At Palmar the Imperial party was met by several thousand Indians and entertained with traditional dances, and Jeanningros and his officers were personally presented to Maximilian. Carlota appeared in riding habit, with sombrero, for the ascent of the Cumbres Mountains, and, hours later, arrived at the country home of the Bishop of Puebla, drenched by a downpour.

The Empress celebrated her twenty-fourth birthday in the city, guest of honour at a ball thrown by the French garrison, and there were fireworks.

The plain of Puebla reminded her of Lombardy and on 8 June the Imperial Party continued its journey towards Mexico City. The road was still guarded by the Foreign Legion, whose responsibilities extended as far as the post at Puente de Texmelucan, where a large bridge spanned the river of the same name. It was commanded by newly-promoted Lieutenant Diesbach, who had arrived several weeks earlier with twenty-five men and, in signing the necessary papers for the change of command, wrote with a flourish: *G. comte de Diesbach, Supreme Military Commander of Puente Texmelucan and the Surrounding Area.* Unfortunately, his first few days at the post had been made miserable by a severe outbreak of boils.

Maximilian and Carlota and their entourage passed through on 11 June, spending an hour-and-a-half there. As the Emperor chatted with Diesbach, a retainer excitedly stood by, and eventually could contain himself no longer. 'Monsieur le comte, I was a cadet in your father's Regiment of Swiss Guards for ten years,' he blurted out. 'He treated me like his son. I carry his memory in my heart. Permit me to present myself and shake your hand. I am the Comte de Bombelles, First Chamberlain to His Majesty.'

A boyhood friend of Maximilian, Charles de Bombelles was actually one of his two gentlemen-in-waiting, and Diesbach was left to wonder at the Fate which had brought a son and his father's protege together at what was little more than a wide spot in the road on the way to Mexico City – and also how he might possibly be able to turn the existence of this unexpected friend at court to his own advantage.[8] He had already confided to his campaign diary that he was fed up, writing: 'This damned war . . . This damned country'.[9] Diesbach escorted the Imperial party to the Rio Frio and saw them safely into other French military hands, before returning to Puente de Texmelucan.

Jeanningros was not the only French officer who expected that 'the solution of the problems is going to come with the arrival of Maximilian', as he had told his wife. Captain Henri Loizillon, an officer on the staff of General Bertier, was always well informed and knew of Napoleon III's plans for the Foreign Legion. He optimistically saw the installation of the Emperor as likely to considerably shorten the French occupation of Mexico.

'Supposing that he can, as is being tried, take over six thousand men of our Foreign Legion, then we would only have to leave a brigade as an occupation force, and the rest of the Army could be returned at the end of the year,' he wrote home to a friend.[10]

In Puebla, Camerone survivor Evariste Berg, now a Sous-Lieutenant in the Zouaves, clashed with a fellow officer of the same rank named Tochon and came off second best in a duel. The details are unfortunately now lost, but while Diesbach was exchanging pleasantries with Maximilian and de Bombelles at Texmelucan, Berg was dying in Puebla's Military Hospital.[11]

On 12 June, exactly a year after Forey had published his first Proclamation to the Mexican people after entering their capital, the Emperor and Empress were greeted there with suitable pomp and ceremony by General Bazaine and high-ranking Mexicans and took up residence in the Castle of Chapultepec.

The arrival of the Emperor, and his safe installation, brought about a surge of confidence in the business world, both nationally and internationally. In London a group of investors registered *La Compania Limitada del Ferrocarril Imperial Mexicana* – The Imperial Mexican Railway Company Limited – to acquire from Don Agostino Escandon's firm the concession to build and operate the railway between Veracruz and Mexico City. The new company was capitalized at thirty million United States dollars and promptly set about ordering new rolling stock. The construction contract was awarded to Smith, Knight and Company, a firm with considerable experience in building railways in Latin America, and they retained the services of Chief Construction Engineer Lyons, who was already questioning the original survey from Paso del Macho to Puebla made by the American engineer Andrew Talcott six years earlier, and suggesting a partial re-survey. Experienced railway planners Dechert and Wilson began looking at the Talcott Survey, and going over the terrain, but the rails continued westward towards Camaron.[12]

Bazaine, looking past the obvious object of conquest, began thinking of the things which a peaceful nation would need, and laid the groundwork for what would in due course become a full-scale and quite sophisticated Scientific Commission. 'I had the idea of collecting a scientific, artistic, and literary commission, including a certain number of Mexican officers, some French officers, and some foreigners, whose work, studies, and private inclinations make them apt to furnish papers and interesting reports that would be of use to Mexico,' he would explain in a letter. Colonel Louis Doutrelaine, the Staff Engineer, was charged with undertaking the organization of the Commission, which Bazaine suggested should include naturalists, geologists, mineralogists, astronomers, geographers, doctors of medicine, agronomists, technicians, financiers, statisticians, historians and archaeologists.[13]

Chief of Staff Boyer was put in charge of organizing the Entomological Section, and recruited Lieutenant Campion, transferred from the 1st Battalion to the 3rd and based at Puebla, as a collector. He soon found kindred spirits among his Mexican and foreign friends and his efforts eventually resulted in the creation of the first scientific collection of Mexican butterflies.[14]

When Jeanningros rejoined the Regiment Etranger he had been replaced as Commanding Officer of Veracruz and the *Terres Chaudes* by J.M. Marechal of the *Artillerie de Marine*. The Egyptian Battalion had its headquarters at Veracruz and Marechal quickly recognized them as a well-disciplined and enthusiastic group of men. As he was an officer who inspired loyalty in his men he and the Sudanese soldiers got on well, despite their language problems. The Foreign Legion was still being required to detach officers to other units, and Sous-Lieutenant Louis Waldejo, who had been commissioned the same day as the late Sous-Lieutenant Vilain, became Marechal's aide-de-camp. They were aware that the Mexican Republican Army had established a strong entrenched camp on a hill overlooking the navigable Rio Papaloapan, some hundred kilometres (sixty miles) south of Medellin, and had also emplaced artillery, which commanded the approach to the small town of Tlacotalpan. Marechal made plans to deal with the situation, but it took him some time to assemble a mixed force of six hundred, which included men from the Egyptian Battalion and the Martinique Engineers, as well as a Squadron of Colonel Figuerero's former Auxiliaries, now part of the Mexican Imperial Cavalry. They were taken down the coast by a French warship on 8 July, and then upriver by two French gunboats and a steam launch to their destination.

The road leading to the entrenched camp, though stiffly defended, was taken after a hundred Mexican regulars had been killed and sixty-five made prisoner, including five officers. The gunboats shelled the hilltop camp into submission and five guns were captured. Marechal then occupied Tlacotalpan, left a small garrison there and returned to Veracruz on 13 July, formally commending his men, including Waldejo, who he said had 'crossed impossibly exposed positions in a hail of lead to carry out my orders'. However, even as Marechal was writing his report, the Mexican Republican Army was attacking the men he had left at Tlacotalpan. While they were beaten off with difficulty, it became clear that it was an indefensible position and the troops were withdrawn, further proof of the very thing Diesbach had complained of in February: the French could take towns, but, having too few men, could rarely hold them.[15]

For the men garrisoning Puebla life was relatively easy, but Legionnaires have always got into more trouble in garrison than in the field. The Disciplinary Section, with its fatigues, was always a threat, as was the possibility of sterner measures. The Regiment Etranger's Disciplinary Section at Veracruz had been closed down when they moved out of the *Terres Chaudes*, but could not be dispensed with altogether, and a new one at Puebla maintained facilities for the 1st Battalion at Fort Loreto and similar ones at Fort Guadalupe for the 2nd Battalion.

The silo was an old-established form of punishment which the Regiment Etranger had brought with it from Algeria, where it was also used by the *Tirailleurs Algeriens* and the Zouaves. Originating as a field punishment, when troublemakers were confined in the underground rooms where Arabs stored their grain, the silo became a feature at every permanent Foreign Legion post. A hole was dug, deeper than a man was tall, tapering inwards and narrow at the bottom, so that it was impossible to lie down. Those sentenced to a stretch in the silo received their regulation ration of bread every day, and water, and *soupe* every second day. Normally, this fare, and the cramped quarters, were enough to give men food for thought.

Camerone survivor Laurent Constantine had been transferred from the 1st Battalion to the 2nd and became a candidate for the silo at Fort Guadalupe for consistently selling his clothing and equipment to buy drink. Foreign Legion records show that he was considered 'headstrong, but good in the field,'[16] and the 'headstrong' part obviously referred to his behaviour when in garrison. He was initially leniently treated by his officers because of his record, and it was perhaps even thought that the drinking might be the result of his experiences at Camerone, and of being passed over for a medal.

Finally he drew a term in the silo. His Company Commander, thinking perhaps to remit part of the sentence, demanded to know if he had learned his lesson, but found Constantine unrepentant.

'Oh no! Captain,' he said. 'I very much like being here because I can sleep, and I do not have to carry out my duties.'

Each time he was released, he immediately sold a piece of his equipment or clothing, drank the proceeds and was sent back to the silo, doing several stretches before the battalion took to the field again.[17]

Captain Louis Rembert led five Companies of the 3rd Battalion out of Puebla on 13 July, heading south to Acatlan. Legionnaire Spinner, who was with the column, said that as they approached the little town five days later they were greeted by the sound of shots, then the smell of burning houses, and realized that it was being attacked and ravaged by guerillas. They fled at the approach of the French column, who could not even give chase, for, as Spinner put it: 'These centaurs, a hundred times faster on their horses than we infantrymen on our legs, had disappeared.'

> We found, lying on the ground, a long row of bodies, mutilated in a frightful manner, to the point of being absolutely unrecognizable [*he recalled years later*]. Faces [were] convulsed with terror, heads split open, eyes gouged out, noses cut off, hair burned or torn out, hands clenched in a convulsive manner.[18]

The Legionnaires pitched in to put out fires, and helped bury the dead, while waiting for the rest of the regiment to join them in a few days. After all the horror, Campion spent his off-duty time chasing butterflies and catching bugs, sometimes accompanied by Diesbach and their friend Sous-Lieutenant Francois Blank.[19]

It had become known that Commandant Regnault, now promoted to Lieutenant-Colonel, would need more time to convalesce in France and Battalion Commander de Briche's secondment to the Regiment Etranger was causing problems for his own regiment, the *Tirailleurs Algeriens*. It was decided to replace him with a more senior officer, who would be Jeanningros' second-in-command until Regnault's return. So Lieutenant-Colonel Simon Carteret-Trecourt joined the Regiment Etranger at a time of much reorganization, as the newly-raised and trained 4th Battalion was ready to take to the field in July. Guyot de Leuchey now commanded the 1st Battalion, Saussier the 2nd, de Brian the 3rd and Paulin Lavollee the 4th.

The road to Oaxaca ran straight South from Acatlan, which could be reached from either Puebla or La Soledad, and Bazaine authorized a reconnaissance of both roads. Brincourt left Puebla on 24 July with thirteen Companies of the Regiment Etranger, drawn from all four battalions, under the personal command of Colonel Jeanningros. At the same time, Colonel Giraud, late of the Foreign Legion and now commanding the 7th Regiment of the Line, left La Soledad, taking with him several Companies of the *Bat d'Af.* The two columns met up at Acatlan, then moved to Huajuapan on 3 August, and stayed there for nine days planning the next move.

> I do not actually know what we are supposed to be doing [*Jeanningros confessed to his wife in a letter*]. We will be here for a rest period of several days, because our men are a little fatigued by the tremendous heat and the rain. The roads are frightful, the assents and descents interminable, the rocks are endless and everywhere.[20]

Bazaine refused Brincourt permission for an assault on Oaxaca for the time being, as it would have severely extended lines of supply and communication, and would also have left the assault force without reserves, should it get into difficulties. The Commander-in-Chief did, however, permit an advance as far as Yanhuitlan and Lieutenant-Colonel Carteret-Trecourt was ordered to establish himself there with the 1st and 2nd Battalions, leaving de Brian as Commanding Officer at Huajuapan with ten Companies of the 3rd and 4th Battalions. Saussier was to remain at Huajuapan, heading a strike force made up of the Voltigeur Companies from all four Battalions.[21] On their return journey to Puebla, Brincourt and Jeanningros were accompanied by six Companies of the Regiment Etranger, but left Lieutenant Auguste Legout and his men at Tepeji and Captain Augustin Romany and Lieutenant Eugene Sevestre with their Companies at Acatlan, arriving back in Puebla with three of the regiment's Grenadier Companies.

In the *Terres Chaudes* the guerillas, on a regular basis, and sometimes even the Mexican Republican Army, were still active along the Orizaba Road, as well as both north and south of it, and the *Contre-guerilla*, which had returned from Tampico some months earlier, roamed at large in an attempt to keep them at bay. Colonel Milan was known to be north of Puebla with Republican Cavalry and the little towns of Cotaxtla and Tlalixcoyan were still seething with guerillas. Colonel Dupin had replaced Commandant Marechal as Commanding Officer of Veracruz and the *Terres Chaudes* and successfully deployed his own troops, the *Tirailleurs Algeriens*, the Egyptian Battalion and sometimes men from Regiments of the Line in convoy protection.

On 15 July, an important convoy carrying twelve million francs for the Army, accompanied by two detachments of Artillerymen and their guns, moved westward towards Cordoba, protected by the *Contre-guerilla* and two Companies of the 7th of the Line. The guerilla leader Honorato Dominguez had mustered six hundred horsemen, with the intention of seizing this prize near Camaron, and then escaping north to La Joya and disappearing into areas where the French seldom ventured. However, when he saw the size and firepower of the protecting force mustered by Dupin, he thought better of the idea, and the convoy continued on his way.[22]

The planners for the Mexican Imperial Railway had come to a conclusion about the route to Cordoba, choosing the survey made by Dechert and Wilson, rather than the earlier one by Talcott, and had begun building west of Loma Alto, with Camaron as the next stop. The railbed was graded south of the Orizaba Road, passing close to Palo Verde,[23] and reached Cameron in August. The Hacienda de la Trinidad lay precisely where the rails were to be laid, so the house and the walls of the corral where the 3rd of the 1st had made their stand were swiftly demolished, as was the old inn on the north side of the road.

A month later, on 19 September, Dupin relinquished his position as Commanding Officer of Veracruz and the *Terres Chaudes*, in order to move the headquarters of the *Contre-guerilla* from La Soledad and re-establish it at Camaron in order to 'protect the new [railhead] work yard'. Camaron was already becoming a bustling little place. Sous-Lieutenant de Keratry, arriving there with the *Contre-guerilla*, noted that the track ran directly to the area of the old corral, that the new station was being built there, and that 'a few yards from it was the cross which had been erected over the grave of the soldiers of the Legion Etrangere.'[24] Most of the stones from the hacienda building and the walls of the corral had been used in the foundations for the railway track, but there were still enough for the *Contre-guerilla* to claim to build their headquarters.

> The parapets in earth and in stone were constructed to protect the defenders in case of a surprise attack [*de Keratry wrote*]. The main entrance was behind an embankment, strengthened by barrels filled with earth. Trees were felled over an area of several hectares, both to clear a field of fire and to provide fuel for the bivouac fires on humid nights. Pleasant wooden huts were built to house the men of the *Contre-guerilla* . . . Camaron was changed into a lively village. In the wink of an eye the canteen-keepers, the proprietors of coffee houses, almost all of them of American origins, moved in, and the local Indians came with their merchandise, their liquors and their fruits . . . Each little trader knew that the next station on the railway after crossing the bridge at La Soledad was at Camaron, and that the travellers were very happy to find a little bread and a thatched roof during their halt.[25]

Within a few days of settling in the *Contre-guerilla* was involved in a serious clash with guerillas, when Honorato Dominguez, having had to abandon his plans to attack the bullion convoy in mid-July, fell upon a much more modest prize.

> A convoy travelling from La Soledad for the new military post to deliver three wagonloads of provisions and materials for the engineers and the railway workers was escorted by five [*Tirailleurs Algeriens*] riflemen and twenty-six horsemen [*de Keratry reported*]. At two lieues from La Soledad, this handful of men, advised by Intelligence from Indians and thinking the route to be secure, was engaged in a wooded area close to Loma Alta. Suddenly, the guerila band of Honorato Dominguez, accompanied by a Squadron of Regulars from Jalapa, surrounded the unfortunate men and inflicted a number of injuries. A desperate struggle ensued, and the chief of the detachment was killed in the first fire of this struggle between three hundred of the enemy and the twenty-six *Contra-guerillas*. The five riflemen formed a little square, back-to-back. One of them, Sergent Soliman, a veteran Algerian, with Herculean strength and bravery, cleared a wide area around them with his musket reversed. Despite all, he fell, and the men with him fell, too, but their bodies were surrounded by many enemy corpses. The horsemen were blinded by blood from wounds inflicted by the lances. One of the riders named Abila, from Martinique, made his way through the brushwood all the way to La Soledad, where he arrived with his head laid open by a sabre cut and his right shoulder broken.[26]

When the *Contre-guerilla* was in the field they lived off the land as much as possible, confiscating cows and pigs and chickens, corn and vegetables for their cooking pots. Those remaining at Headquarters had to largely look after themselves.

There were few amenities at Camerone [*de Keratry would write*]. The military administration had not yet installed shops where the *Contre-guerilla* could draw rations against reimbursement chits. Each day, our men, obliged to make do for themselves, mounted up and instead of chasing after bandits, rounded up a few wild cattle. When the chase was too perilous, because the guerillas were always around, they threw the animals to the ground, killed them in the brushwood, and each horseman returned with a bloody quarter of beef in front of their saddles.[27]

The Gulf Coast was now securely in French hands as far North as Tampico, the main port midway between Veracruz and the border with the United States. An important source of Customs revenue, but very unhealthy because of endemic *vomito negro*, the port had initially been seized by the French 81st Regiment of the Line in December 1862, but the troops were needed elsewhere and it had been abandoned the following month. Bazaine had sent troops to reoccupy it in August, and before returning to Mexico City from his campaign had sent soldiers of the Mexican Imperial Army overland from San Luis Potosi to open up the trade route into the central part of the country.

Reports from the continuing campaign led Bazaine to feel that this phase of the conquest continued to go well. General Edmond L'Heriller entered Durango on 4 July, General Castagny took Venegas and on 20 August entered Saltillo, where he split his forces, sending Colonel Aymard to Parras and himself moving on to Monterrey, which he entered six days later. Some Republican generals gave up the struggle and retired or changed sides, and now that Emperor Maximilian was ensconced in Mexico City it seemed to General Lopez Uraga that it was time to also declare for the Empire. He brought two thousand soldiers with him and accepted a seat on the Council of State.

Napoleon III had sweetened Forey's recall from Mexico by saying: 'The Marshal of France is too great a person to have to bother himself with the details of government.' Of course, this had been diplomatic language to save hurt feelings. General Bazaine was named a Marshal of France on 5 September and the Emperor now felt he was dealing with a fighting soldier, in whom he could place his trust.

19
Bazaine Plans a Campaign

On a typically humid September morning a young French-Canadian who called himself Faucher de Saint-Maurice stepped off a ship in Veracruz. He went straight to the Hotel del Commercio, deposited his luggage, asked the way to the Military Headquarters and set out with a spring in his step. He told the sentry that he had business with the senior military officer and was directed to the office of Commandant J.M. Marechal, once again Commanding Officer of Veracruz and the *Terres Chaudes*.

Saint-Maurice was an unusual young man. Born Narcisse-Henri-Edouard Faucher in Quebec City on 18 April 1844, the son of a lawyer, he had dropped his three first names, adopted Faucher as his given name and tacked on de Saint-Maurice – it came from an ancestor – because he felt that it had a more 'aristocratic' ring. A prodigy at school, but indisciplined, he had authored a well-received pamphlet called *Organisation militaire des Canadas: L'ennemi! L'ennemi! – Military Organization of the Canadas: The Enemy! The Enemy!* – at the age of eighteen, and another called *Cours de tactique – Treatise on Tactics* – the following year. Now having – at least to his own satisfaction – mastered the theory of war at the age of twenty, he had decided to see the reality, and was seeking a post as an Observer with the French forces.[1] Along with the letter of introduction he presented to Marechal, Saint-Maurice carried three despatches for Jules Doazan, a French consular officer in Veracruz.

Marechal listened carefully to his visitor, hurriedly wrote him a note of introduction to Jeanningros, who he believed to be in Orizaba, warned Saint-Maurice that the *vomito negro* was virulently abroad in the land and advised him to deliver his despatches to Doazan as quickly as possible 'and to leave Veracruz that very evening'. Thus began a ten-month adventure, during which Saint-Maurice would be attached to the Foreign Legion, the 3rd Zouaves, the *Bat d'Af*, and several other French regiments, experience war firsthand in both southern and northern Mexico, be wounded, captured, threatened with a firing squad, then be exchanged for *Juarista* prisoners-of-war. He would then return to his native Quebec, and later write an entertaining account of his sojourn.[2]

The young man wasted no time in calling on Doazan, who 'strongly encouraged' him to follow Marechal's advice, and by four o'clock the same afternoon Saint-Maurice was on the train out of La Tejeria, puffing its way west to La Soledad. He learned there that two officers of the Martinique Engineers, who had arrived in Mexico more or less when he had, were already down with the *vomito negro*, or some other form of fever, so wasted no time in boarding a *diligence* which was leaving for Camaron, where it would stop for the night. The passengers were expected to sleep on board, in anticipation of an early start the next morning. Saint-Maurice decided to go for a walk, and soon found a small open-sided canteen – 'a little tap-room made from bamboo, with the counter open to the wind' – where he sampled a *tepache*, a refreshing local drink made from guava and pineapple juice and cane sugar.

> Two soldiers of France were standing in the angle of a wall, and these two *piou-pious* happily accepted a beer [*he would write*]. They belonged to the Legion Etrangere, both smartly turned out, and well spoken, and took the time to tell me of the glorious tragedy which had been played out so bravely a few months earlier, in this place which was so tranquil and so peaceful this night.[3]

Saint-Maurice heard the story of Camerone in considerable detail, and with few errors, although, as he remembered it, Maudet had seven men with him at the end. The Mexican forces were said to have numbered two thousand five hundred, and their losses two hundred and forty dead and one hundred and sixty wounded. He also understood, incorrectly, that only the *Tambour*, who he did not name, survived.

> The mortal remains of this handful of warriors were buried not ten paces from there, and the Captain, like the last of his soldiers, slept in the line of battle [*he would write*]. I listened, bare-headed, to this marvellous story. There was nothing to indicate the scene of the last stop on their journey, except for the grave marked with a big wooden cross, painted black and surmounted with a small Tricolour.
>
> A board carried the following inscription:
>
> HERE LIE THE BRAVE MEN OF THE THIRD COMPANY
> OF THE FIRST BATTALION OF THE LEGION ETRANGERE,
> WHO DIED GLORIOUSLY IN THE COMBAT OF CAMERONE,
> THE 30 APRIL 1863. M. DANJOU, CAPTAIN;
> M. MAUDET, LIEUTENANT; M. VILAIN, SOUS-LIEUTENANT.
>
> This cross indicated to the regiments of France and her allies in Mexico, the fate which might one day be their reward for devotion and self-sacrifice in this this far-off land. Heads bowed, they answer the command: 'Order arms!' to the rolling sound of drums beating *Aux Champs* in front of this modest mausoleum where lie the glorious dead . . . A second beer paid the soldier for the lesson in contemporary history which he had given me.[4]

Saint-Maurice did not see much more of the busy little railhead town, as he left in the *diligence* very early the following morning, but he did not forget about Camerone, and would in due course be present when Jean-Adolphe Beauce, the Official Military Artist, was immortalizing the battle in a painting. Saint-Maurice reached Chiquihuite safely, and found it occupied by a battalion of the *Bat d'Af* under Commandant Emile Colonna d'Ornano.[5] The road from there to Cordoba and Orizaba was almost impassable because of the rains and in Orizaba he began feeling ill. Army doctors advised him to stay for a few days, and when he felt better he explored the pretty little city. He met Battalion Commander Baron de Briche, now back with his *Tirailleurs Algeriens*, who gave him several letters of introduction to senior officers of the Regiment Etranger at Puebla.[6] Saint-Maurice did not leave Orizaba until 30 September, and had no chance to present his letters of introduction in the short time that the Mexico City-bound *diligence* stopped at Puebla. The road was better, his keen eye noticed the many little shrines they rattled past.

> If there was one thing which struck a stranger, it was the multitude of crosses on either side of the road [*he would recall*]. The custom of the country was to erect one wherever someone had been executed or murdered. Passers-by performed an act of pious devotion if they placed a rock and mumbled a *De profundis*.[7]

The *diligence* passed through Texmelucan, where Lieutenant Zede had just replaced Lieutenant Diesbach as Commanding Officer, and stopped at the bridge over the River Frio. Saint-Maurice and the six English mining men who were his fellow passengers 'dined at an excellent inn'. He remembered it later as a 'celebrated' establishment, 'on a road celebrated for brigands and crimes which were committed every day'.[8] The main bands of highwaymen in the area were led by Jose Maria Romero and Luis Cabrera and Zede – just as Diesbach had done – was constantly mounting punitive expeditions against them and their followers. He gradually came to suspect that the inn, which was operated by a 'Mademoiselle G.', was more than a simple roadhouse stop for travellers, having a bar and working girls and rooms rented by the hour. He realized that it was also an important rallying point for the local bandits, and by some skilled detective work, coupled with clandestine night movements with his Legionnaires of the 3rd Battalion, was able to capture eight of them, including both Romero and Cabrera.[9]

Saint-Maurice reached Mexico City safely and was astonished at the number of place-seekers – like himself – and assorted hangers-on and hopeful opportunists to be found there, writing:

> The pavement was literally crowded with German noblemen, English traders, down-and-outs from Paris, Polish and Hungarian refugees of all types, heroes in search of a romance, an adventure, a social position, a military rank, a rich marriage, a humble place as a courtesan, and who knows what else? – in short, a crumb of bread falling from the Imperial table of Maximilian.[10]

He began to manoeuvre for an opportunity to present his letters of introduction to Marshal Bazaine, and was able to do so at a reception hosted by the Marquis de Montholon, who had replaced Dubois de Saligny as French Ambassador. While waiting for a response, he met many interesting people, and was befriended by editors de Barres and Masseras, respectively of the *L'Estafette des deux mondes* – *The Messenger of Two Worlds* – and the *Era Nouvelle* – *New Era* – the two French-language newspapers in Mexico City. Charles de Barres had been born in Virginia in the United States, and had gone to Mexico, where he started *L'Estafette* in 1858. While expressing small L liberal sympathies, it was nearly always supportive of the French.[11]

From these journalist friends Saint-Maurice learned that Bazaine had brought much of Mexico under French control or domination, occupying three-quarters of the country, with the exception of the States of Chiapas, Guerrero and southern Michoacan, but including at least the main cities in Sonora and Chihuahua. He was now planning a major campaign to wrest the State of Oaxaca from the control of the *Juaristas*, which would settle the control of the South and free up men for further penetration of the North during 1865, with the intention of forcing the surrender of the ever-on-the-move Juarez Government or of driving it across the border into the United States.

It was Bazaine's intention that the Regiment Etranger would be in the forefront of the fighting in the Southern Campaign, and he was well aware that the last four hundred Algeria-trained Legionnaires had embarked at Mers-el-Kebir on 1 August.[12] Others would be coming, although recruits for the Foreign Legion would henceforth be trained at 7th Regiment of the Line's facilities at Aix-en-Provence, rather than in Algeria.

Yanhuitlan soon became the Campaign Headquarters for the Foreign Legion. De Brian assigned detachments to the posts at Tepeji and Acatlan, and kept a substantial contingent at Huajuapan, but moved the rest of the Companies of the 3rd and 4th Battalions to Yanhuitlan. The Foreign Legion had always been great builders as well as fighters and the sleepy Mexican town soon took on a completely new face, as the troops established an outer perimeter of defensive positions, repaired the streets, cleared cisterns and wells, and did as much civic beautification as was possible. The largely Indian populace was pro-French and co-operated fully.

General Brincourt arrived from Puebla on 13 September for a two-day visit and immediately complimented Captain Rembert, Adjutant-Major of the 3rd Battalion and de Brian's second-in-command, on the changes he had made. Brincourt had come to Yanhuitlan for several reasons, one of which was to conduct the annual Regimental Inspection. Overall, his report showed a regiment which was well-officered, had good Non-Commissioned Officers and generally motivated Other Ranks. Desertions since de Maussion's Regimental Inspection of the previous year had totalled four hundred and four, out of the regiment's three thousand four hundred and seventy-one men on strength.[13] Nearly all of them had been relatively new arrivals, and the Foreign Legion came to believe that simple men, with little knowledge of geography, had thought it would be easy to 'escape' to a new life in the United States, having no idea of the distances involved in getting to the border, or the nature of the country through which they would have to travel. Some had also no doubt fallen victim to the blandishments of Republican handbills and agents and had changed sides, but men from French Regiments of the Line, the Zouaves and the *Bat d'Af* also went over to the enemy, or simply vanished from their posts.

Brincourt had also come to say goodbye, as he was being assigned other duties, and to announce that Colonel Jeanningros would be the new Commanding Officer at Puebla, with Lieutenant-Colonel Carteret-Trecourt assuming full day-to-day responsibility for the Regiment Etranger. The regiment, Brincourt told them, could look forward to Marshal Bazaine – perhaps in person – launching a campaign against Porfirio Diaz in Oaxaca in the new year, and the build-up of men and munitions would take place during the next three months.

All the Camerone survivors still serving would be involved in the coming Southern Campaign, but their numbers were dwindling, and not merely from disease and death. For some, the lure of Mexico, or of the Foreign Legion, had worn off and, at the end of their engagements, the call of home and family was strong. Grenadier Leon Gorski, for example, declined to re-engage, instead sailing for France, receiving his discharge and returning to his family in Paris, a young man not yet twenty-one, proudly wearing the *Medaille Militaire* and the *Expedition du Mexique* medals on the breast of his civilian suit.[14]

Much of what passed as a roadway between Puebla and Oaxaca seldom saw wheeled traffic of any kind. Most people either walked or rode, and only rarely was the journey made by any of the big-wheeled mule-drawn Mexican wagons. The road, therefore, was totally unsuited for the movement of heavy guns, and serious attention had to be given to making it at the very least passable. So, for the first time in Mexico, the Regiment Etranger got ready to swap rifles for pickaxes, as they had done so often in Algeria.

Work gangs were recruited in Tepeji, Acatlan, Huajuapan and Yanhuitlan and functioned under the direction of Foreign Legion officers. The regiment's Sappers and specialists tacked the jobs which involved bridge building, or actual engineering work, as opposed to merely moving piles of rocks and stones from one place to another. They worked with weapons always in reach to fight off sudden attacks by guerillas, as all the military activity had naturally alerted Porfirio and 'Chato' Diaz to the fact that the French were clearly contemplating an attack on Oaxaca.

Some of the new roadworks were destroyed by a serious earthquake which hit the region two hours after midnight of 2/3 October, and new problems were created by rock slides. Many houses and buildings in Tepeji, Actalan, Huajuapan and Yanhuitlan were damaged, but there was relatively little loss of life. Lieutenant Zede was manning the post at Rio Frio and had three men hurt. Legionnaire Spinner, who was in Puebla, remembered 'a terrible shock, impossible to describe', which woke the city from its slumber, followed by several smaller shocks,[15] and daylight revealed considerable structural damage to buildings, twenty people dead and many injured. Previous experience told the local people that there could be a major after-shock within twenty-four hours and soldiers and citizens stayed in the open, but it never came and life gradually returned to normal. The quake was felt as far afield as Orizaba, Cordoba and Veracruz, all of which suffered some damage.

As a strike force, Saussier's four Companies of Voltigeurs were not subject to the manual labour and elements of his command were often on patrol, trying to determine where guerillas might strike next. Sometimes they took the war to the enemy, as at Sicahyapan, where they destroyed a band four hundred strong.[16]

The Commanding Officer of the post at San Juan de los Llanos had based a Company at the village of Puchingo as a sort of advance base to observe the movements of any guerilla or Mexican Republican Army troops, but local Intelligence was weak and many villagers were ardent *Juaristas*. An attack on the village at three o'clock in the morning was timed to catch the Legionnaires asleep. The Republican force numbered eight hundred mixed cavalry and infantry, and a small cannon, but in almost four hours of continuous fighting the Legionnaires, without losing any of their own, managed to kill thirty-seven of their attackers, who fled when their scouts warned them of the approach of the garrison from San Juan de los Llanos.[17]

The Mexicans had learned from Camerone, the April attack on Gans at Tepeji, and the subsequent one on a detachment at Puchingo, something which the Arabs and Kabyles of Algeria had long known: that the Foreign Legion could give a good account of itself from a defendable position, but that it was vulnerable if attacked in open country by a force hugely superior in numbers. Both methods of attack would punctuate the period of the French Intervention. Meanwhile, brigands loyal only to themselves continued to harass the *diligences* when they could find them travelling without escorts.

Maximilian, in making demands he believed befitted an Emperor, had been insisting that he be provided with Austrian troops and his brother, Emperor Franz Josef, finally authorized recruiting for an all-volunteer force which would be known as the *Osterreichische Freicorps* – Austrian Volunteer Corps.

King Leopold of Belgium then felt that he could not leave his daughter, Carlota, without troops of her own and a Belgian Volunteer Legion of almost sixteen hundred men was raised. In order not to violate Belgium's traditional neutrality, the recruiting had to be done in the name of the Imperial Mexican Government and became a political issue in Brussels.[18] They were commanded by Colonel Baron Alfredo van der Smissen, who had campaigned as an Observer with the Foreign Legion in Algeria some years earlier and probably knew many of the older officers of the Regiment Etranger. The Belgians arrived in Mexico before the Austrians, landing at Veracruz on 13 October. In just the five days they were there they lost several men to the *vomito negro* and had to leave others in hospital when they set off from La Tejeria by train on the morning of the 18 October.

> The worst of the journey was that we felt a sort of malaise brought on by the difficulty in breathing the humid air [*wrote Captain Claude J. Des Loiseau of the* Carabiniers]. We felt that we were passing through a country frequently visited by death . . . In the distance, we saw the little posts manned by the Egyptians, their faces shining, breathing easily, healthy and full of energy.

Mid-morning they stopped briefly at La Soledad and Loma Alta.

'Our passage was not rapid, because the train only burned wood, coal being unknown in Mexico,' Des Loiseau recalled. 'Finally, towards one o'clock, we arrived at Camaron. The name had sad associations'.[19]

The little post was commanded by a Sous-Lieutenant of the Foreign Legion with thirty Egyptian soldiers[20] and Des Loiseau and his companions were shown the 'grave marking the heroic death of a Company of the Legion Etrangere'. Des Loiseau was told that 'only five soldiers' had lived to tell the tale.[21]

Another Belgian officer, Lieutenant Emile Walton of the 2nd Regiment of *Chasseurs a Pied*, also heard the story of the Combat of Camerone – he was told that there had been seventy-six Legionnaires and fifteen survivors – and visited the grave.

> In passing the modest tomb which the Army of France had made for these heroes, I saw the touching inscription which marked this glorious resting place:
>
> HERE LIES
> THE 3RD COMPANY OF THE 1ST BATTALION
> OF THE FOREIGN LEGION

'We laid flowers on the grave,' Walton added.[22]

The Belgians began their march to Mexico City, and for several hours their route paralleled the roadbed of the Mexican Imperial Railway, which was heading for Paso del Macho. A stone bridge had been built over the *barranca* at Paso Ancho, and work was in progress on one at Paso del Macho, but the British investors, well-attuned to the situation in Mexico, were already wondering whether to continue past there, or adopt a wait and see policy. Gustavo Baz and E.L. Gallo, who would write a history of the railway when it finally reached Mexico City, noted that the difficulties encountered in building the seventy-six kilometres (forty-seven miles) from La Tejeria to Paso del Macho had been 'very few',[23] as the elevation was only four hundred and seventy-six metres (some fifteen hundred and sixty feet). Ahead was the daunting task of crossing the Cumbres Mountains, so once the rails reached Paso del Macho they proceeded no further, and by April 1865 it was both the railhead, and, for the time being, the terminus.

Saint-Maurice was still in Mexico City, waiting for a response to his request for an attachment to the French Army, when the Belgian Volunteers arrived. Bazaine was dealing with an unexpected problem, in that Emperor Maximilian, as an economy measure, had announced the reduction of the Imperial Mexican Army to a mere two regiments, and discharged several thousand officers and men. Fortunately, the Marshal's plan for the Southern Campaign called for the involvement of many French troops, but few Mexican ones. He planned that three specific columns would converge on Yanhuitplan, and move south from there. The first left Mexico City under the command of General the Vicomte Charles Courtois Roussel d'Hurbal on 20 November, taking siege artillery with it, and six days later Colonel Osmont of Bazaine's Staff asked Saint-Maurice to appear before a military board to be considered for service. The interview went well and the following day he received a Commission as a Captain and instructions to join the 4th *Tirailleurs Mexicaine*.[24] Unfortunately, they were with d'Hurbal's division, so Saint-Maurice was told to purchase the necessary kit for a campaign and go at once to Puebla, where he might yet be able to join up with the column.

Finding it gone, he reported himself to Colonel Jeanningros, who he found gruff but likeable, and was told that he would have to wait in Puebla for some days, as it would be necessary for him to travel with an escort. Lieutenant Achilli, serving as Orderly Officer for the 1st Battalion, was told to take Saint-Maurice under his wing.

> The officers of the garrison had formed themselves into a club, under the Presidency of *Chef de Bataillon* Rolland [*Saint-Maurice would recall*]. Evenings and mornings they would gather to read the Mexican and French newspapers, take their glass of absinthe and play a game of whist or of lansquenet.[25]

Achilli introduced him into this club and he met many of the officers of the Regiment Etranger, spending much time in the company of Sous-Lieutenant the Vicomte Paul de Montessuit, who had fought as a volunteer in the war between Poland and Russia, been sentenced to death, and only escaped execution through the influence of his family and his diplomat father.[26] The club also served as the unofficial local headquarters of the Scientific Commission and there were many discussions about Mexican antiquities, Lieutenant Campion's butterfly hunting, and the unusual flora and fauna of the region. Migrating birds began arriving from the north and Saint-Maurice knew that some of them had come from as far away as his native Canada.

It was an idyllic period before the coming battle and Saint-Maurice made the most of it. Sometimes the Foreign Legion officers would go to a cantina in town run by one of the regiment's *vivandieres*, a striking blonde affectionately known as 'Aunt Rose'. Saint-Maurice, who thought she looked 'like an Englishwoman', saw her both in her cantina and in her uniform, a black knee-length flared coat, buttoned at the neck, with red cuffs and two broad red bands round the hem. It was worn over black trousers with a red stripe down the side. White gloves were worn, while the flat hat, topped with feathers, was tied below the chin with a wide red ribbon. A lace-edged apron, the traditional short sword and the barrel of brandy, slung across the shoulder completed her outfit. Saint-Maurice was told that Aunt Rose had always been with the Regiment Etranger, braving the bullets of the Kabyles in Algeria to 'take a drink to a soldier dying of thirst', seen scrambling up the Heights of Alma, 'her little cask of brandy on her shoulder', and further distinguishing herself at Solferino.

> My Aunt Rose was the most chic soldier in the entire French Army [*Saint-Maurice reported*]. When walking boldly along the streets of Puebla, in her snappy *vivandiere* uniform, her four decorations proudly displayed, and carrying her hat in her little hand, the sentries honoured her by presenting arms.[27]

The conversation was always entertaining and animated, and if it became overly boisterous Aunt Rose 'always arrived in time to restore peace'.[28] Officers and men wore their *Expedition du Mexique* medal and affected to believe that the Eagle on the ribbon looked more like a Vulture, so had christened it the 'Decoration of the

Zopiloté.[29] Saint-Maurice quickly observed that the Legionnaires had a respect bordering on devotion for Jeanningros, but the wise ones – watching the foolish – knew how far they could push the rules.

There was time to give additional training to newly-arrived Legionnaires, who were now coming via the 7th of the Line's home base at Aix-en-Provence. Eugene Amiable, a twenty-six-year-old Belgian, who was one of the early recruits to pass through the facilities at Aix, found himself totally unprepared for the first three-day march which confronted him on arriving in Mexico. 'I was so exhausted that I could hardly feel my legs,' he would write. At Aix he had also felt the marksmanship instruction to have been insufficient, but once he reach Mexico found that 'three-quarters of the men did not need it, many being officers of different nations'.[30]

It also appears that after considerable initial success at recruiting suitable men, and training them at Aix-en-Provence, the Foreign Legion began to attract too many who had matters other than soldiering on their minds. Unaccustomed discipline, the second thoughts which came early to almost every man who joined the Foreign Legion – and which most got over – and the fact that it was easier to get away in France than it had ever been in Algeria, led to many desertions before even boarding the Mexico-bound ships. There were more desertions soon after arrival in Mexico, doubtless many of them by men unwilling to work as navvies in tropical conditions. There were, of course, Legionnaires who never got used to discipline, and it was a regimental expectation that certain men would always get into far more trouble in garrisons than in the field.

A lifetime of soldiering had taught Jeanningros that there were times for officers to wink the eye at infractions of the rules, times to try the velvet glove, and times when, if all else had failed, other measures were necessary.

> He had the very best record of service in an army where there was no shortage of talent and his twenty-three wounds had earned him the nickname of *Le Pere Balafre* – Papa Scar – among the soldiers [*Saint-Maurice wrote*]. This was the humourous little name, but it was known, too, that he could often be hard as nails. If by chance the cells or the silos did not straighten out a recalcitrant, he took sterner measures and became Colonel *Carrement* – Colonel Stern. By this other nickname, the soldier knew he had brought upon himself the severe discipline of *Le Pere Balafre*...[31]

Saint-Maurice was particularly intrigued by an elderly and dour Lieutenant from Alsace who 'rarely engaged in conversation, passing his time reading an edition of Goethe in German, sometimes quoting a first line, but never smiling.' There were several stories about him and Saint-Maurice remembered being 'under the impression that beneath his austere exterior there was the soul of a poet.' He considered his musing confirmed to some extent a few months later when the officer was killed in a skirmish, and 'the soldier who prepared him for burial found the crumbling dust of a few dried flowers' among his effects.[32]

Word reached Puebla on 13 December that General d'Hurbal had arrived at Yanhuitlan the previous day and would be adding the Regiment Etranger's 1st

Battalion and most of the 2nd to his column as he moved on towards Oaxaca. Saussier and the four Grenadier Companies and two Companies of the 2nd were to return to Puelba. Saint-Maurice was told to hold himself in readiness to be attached to a detachment of Mexican Imperial Cavalry under Squadron Commander Jose de Jesus de Ximenes, which was expected to soon leave Mexico City for Puebla.

In Paris, on 14 December, Camerone survivor Leon Gorski, ex-Grenadier of the 3rd of the 1st, still short of his twenty-first birthday, died in the bosom of his family. They would treasure the medals he had won in Mexico, passing them from generation to generation, until, almost seventy years later, they gave them to the Museum of the Foreign Legion.[33]

20
Oaxaca Falls

As part of Bazaine's plan of attack for the Oaxaca Campaign, his second column, the 3rd Zouaves, commanded by the newly-promoted General Louis Mangin, and third, the 2nd Battalion of the *Bat d'Af,* under Commandant Colonna d'Ornano, were sent to Yanhuitlan. General d'Hurbal, taking with him the 1st and 2nd Battalions of the Regiment Etranger, left with his column on 14 December for Etla, a four-day march away, and only fifteen kilometres (a little more than nine miles) from the City of Oaxaca. The 3rd Battalion was to accompany the siege guns, which each needed four or five pairs of oxen and fifty men to assist it over difficult passages. At the Barranca de las Minas it was necessary to unload the wagons carrying ammunition and stores, and transfer their contents to pack mules. The convoy spent Christmas on the road and the 3rd Battalion did not arrive at Etla until 28 December, the day after the 1st and 2nd had completed a detailed reconnaissance of the fortified city.

Just before the year turned news came that the first members of the *Osterreichische Freicorps* had landed at Veracruz, under the command of General le Comte Francis de Thun, the brother of Austria's Ambassador to Mexico. Bazaine, poised for his Southern Campaign, saw no reason to involve the Austrians in his plans, so simply issued orders that a Company should be left at Veracruz, where they would come under Commandant Marechal, and that the rest should proceed to Mexico City. General de Thun left two half-Companies in Veracruz, each commanded by a Lieutenant, and advised Bazaine that the final group of Austrian Volunteers was still under training, and would not arrive for several months. This suited the Marshal, as in his mind both the Austrians and the Belgians were untried troops, probably destined to become part of the Mexican Imperial Army, and could be left to their own devices for the time being.

Saint-Maurice had spent Christmas in Puebla with his Foreign Legion friends, still without word of the whereabouts of Squadron Commander de Ximenes and the Mexican Imperial Cavalry. Eventually, Jeanningros attached the young French-Canadian to an Oaxaca-bound convoy[1] commanded by Colonel Doutrelaine. Saint-Maurice had bought a notebook and began keeping a campaign diary. The column left the city on New Year's Day 1865, heading southwards with siege guns and heavily loaded wagons of engineering supplies. At Tepeaca a message came from Bazaine, advising them to go by way of Tepeji, as the road was likely to be better.

Doutrelaine sent Saint-Maurice to Tehuacan to join a column of the 3rd Zouaves with two mountain guns, but when he arrived he found that they had left to relieve troops at a post threatened by guerillas. Several days later he and the

Zouaves joined Doutrelaine's column, arriving at Etla on 11 January, four days after Jeanningros had left Puebla with a convoy of siege artillery and almost two hundred wagons. The column was escorted by Saussier and the four Companies of Grenadiers, the two Companies of the 2nd Battalion who had gone with him from Yanhuitlan to Puebla, the *Compagnie franche a pied* – the so-called 'Company of Partisans' – and the *Compagnie franche montee*, the 'Company of Mounted Partisans'. The road was poor and the column moved slowly because of the difficulties with the heavy artillery.

Leaving General Edmond L'Heriller in command in Mexico City, Bazaine rode out on 3 January to personally direct the Oaxaca Campaign. He caught up with Jeanningros' column as it laboured southwards, but rode on ahead of them, reaching Etla on 14 January, a journey of five hundred kilometres (three hundred and ten miles), which he had covered in twelve days. He then went on to the Hacienda Blanca, which would be his Headquarters and Command Post. D'Hurbal was already established there, as was Saint-Maurice, who had found the camp bristling with officers from every regiment and arm taking part in the campaign, among them the Prussian Sous-Lieutenant Milson von Bolt of the Regiment Etranger.[2]

Oaxaca had a population of twenty-five thousand and Porfirio Diaz had brought together an army of seven thousand. There were six battalions from Sinaloa, which had been formed into two regiments, a further six battalions of Indians from the region and sixty cannon. The city had been well prepared for the expected siege, with earthworks built to defend gun positions and several small hills well fortified, and made accessible to each other by combining existing *barrancas* with a system of trenches. 'Chato' Diaz and eight hundred horsemen had left before the arrival of the French, being told to make life as difficult a possible for the attackers.

Bazaine immediately made it clear that the Siege of Oaxaca would be conducted very differently from the Siege of Puebla. There would be no attempt to take the city street by street, with the enormous loss of life which that had entailed. The day after his arrival at Hacienda Blanca he commenced operations, which were aimed at completely isolating Oaxaca and cutting it off from any possibility of help. When all his forces arrived he would have a total of six thousand men and thirty-eight cannon. All roads into and out of the city were constantly patrolled and all ravines and *barrancas* which might have sheltered anyone arriving or departing were guarded. Bazaine then cut the aqueduct which supplied the city with water.[3]

Saint-Maurice, who had been trying to make himself useful wherever he could, but was attached to nobody, had certainly proved himself if only by his enthusiasm and was much excited when summoned by Colonel Osmont and told that French Ambassador de Montholon had recommended that he be appointed an *Officier Stagiaire* – Official Observer – with the 2nd Battalion of the *Bat d'Af.* The appointment was unusual, in that such Observer positions were customarily assigned to officers appointed by friendly governments. Van der Smissen, for example, had been the Belgian Army's Official Observer in French campaigns in Algeria, where he had won the Cross of the Legion of Honour, but Saint-Maurice had no such national status. The Dominion of Canada, as such, did not yet exist, and it would certainly have been news to the British that a twenty-year-old

Quebecois, irregularly-appointed as a Captain in the Mexican Imperial Army, had been named as an Official Observer with the French in Mexico. Untroubled by his unique status, Saint-Maurice hurried off to the village of San Felipe del Agua, the headquarters of the *Bat d'Af*, to present himself and his orders to Commandant Colonna d'Ornano. They had met briefly the previous September, while Saint-Maurice had been on his way to Mexico City, and he would now serve the Commandant as Ordnance Officer.[4]

The ability of Diaz to threaten both the road from Puebla to Mexico City and the Orizaba Road and the Imperial Mexican Railway in the *Terres Chaudes* had been the reason that Bazaine had moved against him. While the distances to be travelled were horrendous for those moving wagons and heavy guns, they were not especially daunting for men on horseback, especially if they knew back trails, short cuts and ways through difficult mountain passes. To deny Diaz just this sort of outside help, Bazaine had ordered his nine Squadrons of Cavalry, the majority of whom were from the Mexican Imperial Army, to be deployed to the north of the city as a mobile screen, principally to protect the infantry, but also to intercept any troops coming to Oaxaca's aid and to prevent any attempt by 'Chato' Diaz to return.

In Veracruz it came to the attention of Commandant Marechal that there was considerable activity by troops of the Mexican Republican Army under Colonel Antonio Garcia, an able regular officer, and by guerillas in the area of the Rio Blanco, south of Medellin, and he decided to keep them busy while his Commander-in-Chief was occupied at Oaxaca.

The Foreign Legion's Lieutenant Charles Chesneau was Commanding Officer at Medellin and Marechal ordered him to take a force south and occupy Cocuite, a known Republican stronghold. He left Medellin on the evening of 21 January with seventy men of the Egyptian Battalion, under Sous-Lieutenant Gabriel Baron of the Foreign Legion, and forty members of the Mexican Imperial *Gendarmerie*. By forced marches they reached Paso del Limon mid-afternoon the following day and forded the Rio Blanco, the foot soldiers clinging to the stirrups of the mounted men. A Mexican force contested their arrival on the south bank, but Chesneau fought hard and the enemy withdrew. The intention had been to press on rapidly to Cocuite, but the troops had already marched sixty-eight kilometres (forty-two miles) and fought an engagement, so a delay seemed wise. They arrived within striking distance of the town before midnight and set up bivouacs.

At dawn the following morning Chesneau swept through Cocuite, killing twenty-two Mexicans in a battle during which he had his horse shot from under him and the Sudanese and *Gendarmerie* each lost two men. In town they learned that they had been fighting a force of some three hundred guerillas, and that Colonel Garcia was camped within striking distance with three hundred and fifty regular troops. Chesneau immediately set off to attack them, passing through villages where there were no men, and learned that the Mexicans planned to ambush him at the gorge of El Palmar. The two sides met not long after dawn on 24 January and the Sudanese sharpshooters soon drove the Mexicans from the heights. They withdrew into a palm grove and a long-range contest between marksmen began. Baron had his horse shot from under him and two Sudanese were killed and three wounded, but their accurate fire accounted for sixty-two enemy dead, among them three uniformed officers of the Mexican Republican Army, before they withdrew with their wounded. The following day Chesneau arrived back at Medellin.[5]

On many occasions while moving south from Puebla, the Jeanningros column took up the pickaxe and shovel to make a road for the guns and wagons. There was a full moon and they travelled day and night, stopping for food and sleep only when the road became too rough. Finally, on 30 January, having covered three hundred and sixty kilometres (two hundred and twenty-three miles) in twenty-two gruelling days, they reached the Hacienda Blanca.

Now Bazaine was able to deploy his forces according to his plan, which involved giving the encircling ring of troops responsibilities for five different sectors. On 1 February he made his dispositions. The northwest sector, which included a fairly large and well-defended hill designated Dominante and a smaller one designated Dominante 2, was assigned to Lieutenant-Colonel Carteret-Trecourt and the 1st and 2nd Battalions of the Regiment Etranger under Commandants Guyot de Leuchey and Saussier. They were supported by Artillery Captain d'Huart's two batteries of guns. The northern sector became the responsibility of the 2nd Battalion of the *Bat d'Af* under Commandant Colonna d'Ornano, supported by a section of mountain guns. The east and southeast sectors were assigned to General Mangin's two battalions of the 3rd Zouaves, supported by mountain guns, while the fifth sector became the responsibility of the 3rd Battalion of the Regiment Etranger under Commandant de Brian, supported by a section of mountain guns. There were daily exchanges of fire in the various sectors, often causing considerable casualties on both sides, as Diaz' gunners served their guns well, duelling with those under d'Hurart, an old and experienced Artillery officer.

The French soon became aware that they would face some of their own former comrades when battle was finally joined, as it had been learned that Diaz had been able to attract a number of deserters, some from French Regiments of the Line, others from the Foreign Legion, and was reported to have put them into a single unit.[6] Corporal M'Alevey would later tell a story about the deserter Louis Docir, who he had arrested in Veracruz soon after the Regiment Etranger had landed, and who had escaped within a matter of hours.

> One day, to the astonishment of everybody, Docir rode boldly into camp mounted on a fine white charger [*M'Alevey said*]. He rode straight to the Colonel's quarters, in order, as he said, to account for his disappearance from the regiment. The Colonel received him with cool suspicion. Docir appeared to be penitent and told a story full of remorse.[7]

Obviously, it was a self-serving tale – and the details of Docir's alleged wanderings were poorly remembered by Captain Kirwan, reporting M'Alevey's words six years later – but it ended with a flourish.

> '[As a deserter] I knew that a dishonourable death awaited me if I did not escape,' [*M'Alevey quoted Docir as telling Jeanningros*]. 'But it was not that I

feared death, for I am here now to court it; but I wanted to die honourably, and I escaped in order that before my light was extinguished I might do something to prove that I was not unworthy of wearing the uniform I did. In order to prove this, I risked my life by entering the town of Oaxaca, and here, *mon Colonel*, is a map of the fortifications and mines of the place,' and he drew from his pocket a beautiful map, drawn by himself.[8]

Jeanningros had Docir placed under arrest to await a court martial. M'Alevey considered him 'a consummate villain', but he had winning ways and was 'a superior man' and 'brilliantly educated'. He ingratiated himself with the officers and was given considerable freedom to be around the siege works, where his maps and local knowledge were considered very useful.[9]

Bazaine made daily visits to the various sectors and on one of them suggested to Lieutenant-Colonel Carteret-Trecourt that a surreptitious investigation of part of his sector should be made. Zede was standing nearby and was immediately volunteered for the job.

That night, accompanied by four Sergeants of Voltigeurs, he led a patrol deep into Mexican-held territory. After an hour they heard voices speaking Spanish and jumping a bank found themselves in an enemy dugout on one side of a road. Leaping out, they jumped another bank and found the situation repeated. Back on the road, they dashed into some bushes as shots rang out. Then an officer on a horse charged them. Sergeant Ritt shot him out of the saddle and the other Sergeants killed three of the horsemen following him. Zede and his four men then rushed off into the darkness, heading east towards the sector assigned to the 3rd Zouaves, where Lieutenant Vadon, having heard the gunfire, was watching for hostile rather than friendly troops to emerge from the inky blackness of the night. Zede's party was lucky not to draw fire, but his nocturnal reconnaissance earned him his first mention in an Order of the Day.[10]

Other less deep penetrations of the Mexican defences revealed a complicated network of ropes and leather thongs strung across tracks and pathways to impede the movement of attacking troops. Lanterns had been hung in some defensive positions, ready to be used to signal attacks. Over the next several days the amount of French activity in the eastern sector led Diaz to believe that the main assault would come from there, but reinforcing his troops in the sector meant pulling them out of others.

Bazaine, while visiting the Regiment Etranger on the morning of 5 February, invited the opinions of Commandants Guyot de Leuchey, Saussier and de Brian. Saussier advanced his belief that the Dominante defensive position had been abandoned, and was given permission to make a dead of night sortie to confirm this. After dark he slipped out of the camp with a picked group of Sous-Officiers and men, volunteers all, and worked his way towards the hill. Stones rattled down into valleys and ravines as they climbed slippery slopes in the dark, but they drew no fire.

At last, Saussier and several of his men jumped into the redoubt at the top of Dominante, expecting to find at least a Corporal's Guard. It was deserted. Saussier drew his sword and cut the strap which held the lantern, which one of his men caught as it dropped. Taking it with them, they returned, unchallenged, to the regiment's lines. Saussier was named an Officer of the Legion of Honour for his exploit, and his men were all decorated.[11] The same night the Sappers of the 2nd Battalion pushed their trenches closer to Dominante and built a platform for two light mortars and two mountain guns.

For the next two days the Mexicans bombarded the northwest sector, forcing the men of the Regiment Etranger to keep their heads down and causing a number of casualties, including, on the night of 7 February, Sous-Lieutenant Dugenne of the *Compagnie franche a Pied*. Bazaine, after a final tour of his positions, issued orders the next day for his men to be ready for a pre-dawn assault on the city on 9 February.

Such news was difficult to keep secret, as Commanding Officers and their subordinates would be involved in the movement of Companies and Sections. As Corporal M'Alevey remembered it, this was the moment that the deserter Docir was found to be missing. M'Alevey thought that 'all orders were countermanded' and plans changed, which may or may not be the case.[12] At any rate, when Jeanningros called his officers together in the afternoon of 8 February, very specific details were presented.

The Regiment Etranger's attacking force would be commanded by de Guyot Leuchey and be spearheaded by fourteen volunteers, led by Sous-Lieutenant Blank, standing in for the wounded Dugenne. They would by followed by the Company of Partisans, then by the Grenadiers of the 1st and 2nd Battalions, who would attack the salient, as the Voltigeurs of the 1st, led by Lieutenant Ange Giovaninelli, attacked the defensive works on the left and the Voltigeurs of the 2nd the works on the right. A second column, made up of the Grenadiers and Voltigeurs of the 3rd and 4th Battalions, under Saussier, would follow the first column, with the Fusiliers of all the Battalions, under de Brian, forming the reserve, behind d'Huart's main battery of guns.

Later that evening the hour of the attack was announced – six o'clock the next morning. Led by Corporal Achille Dufresne, the fourteen volunteers who were to lead off the attack were issued with machetes to cut the cords and leather thongs strung across pathways. Jeanningros would be at Bazaine's headquarters at the Hacienda Blanca and Carteret-Tricourt, with Zede as his Orderly Officer, at the northwest sector's Command Post.

At eight o'clock that evening all the French batteries opened up on chosen targets, pounding Diaz' troops and artillery. Not long after midnight on 9 February, Bazaine's men began taking their positions for the dawn assault.

> I remember we all paraded about 3 a.m., rolls were called, and the men spoke with bated breath [*Corporal M'Alevey said*]. The troops were all ready, and the desperate anxiety which men experience before a battle, took possession of us all. Every moment we expected to hear the bugles sound the advance. Each one felt that once more every minute might be his last. It would be better to move, we all thought, than to stand there.[13]

Then, said M'Alevey, with only fifteen minutes to go, the astonished Legionnaires saw a white flag being raised on Dominante. Along with everyone else, Legionnaire Spinner was amazed.

> The officers in front pointed in the direction of the forts, calling out: 'Look up there!' and we looked where they were pointing and saw a strange manoeuvre... the besieged were hoisting the white flag beside the [Mexican] national flag [*he recalled*]. It was the sign of the surrender of the two forts. We held back, thinking perhaps it is a trick... Stupefaction ran through our ranks; statements like: 'What jokers these Liberals. Ah! this is how they will finish this thing... hum, hum!' Then shouts: 'Hurrah, the forts are taken. The Mexicans have surrendered!'[14]

Carteret-Tricourt ordered Zede to take a Sous-Officier and a *Clarion* with him and go forward with a white flag. He borrowed a serviette from a *vivandiere*, handed it to a Sous-Officier and set out to climb the hill, wondering if it was some kind of trap. The three men advanced gingerly, picking their way among the rocks as they climbed. As they stepped into the redoubt at the top a Mexican officer presented himself.

'Colonel Correia of the 1st Regiment of Sinaloa,' he said. 'This place is at the disposition of the French Army.'

Zede sent the Sous-Officier back down the hill to tell Carteret-Tricourt that the surrender appeared to be genuine, and reached him just as a Staff Officer from Bazaine's headquarters arrived. Unbeknown to those ready to launch the attack, negotiations had been going on between Bazaine and Diaz since the previous evening. Both men had been through the siege of Puebla and Diaz had initially hopefully suggested a conditional surrender. Bazaine had been uninterested. Then, when Diaz offered an unconditional surrender, he was told to come to Bazaine's camp at the Hacienda Blanca and arrived with two of his Colonels. Once terms had been agreed, Bazaine sent Staff officers to all units countermanding the order to attack. The 'Cease Fire' was sounded and the Legionnaires set up a cry of '*Vive l'Empereur!*'

Carteret-Trecourt, taking some of his elite soldiers with him, climbed the hill to join Zede, noticing as he approached, that there was blood on the junior officer's hand. Zede had been bitten by a snake as he worked his way from the French lines to the Mexican strongpoint. A hurriedly summoned doctor made an incision to squeeze out the poison, then seared the wound with the tip of a bayonet heated in a camp fire.[15]

Saint-Maurice, who had gone through an adventurous time with the *Bat d'Af*, being involved in a substantial action on 22 January, and having his left foot slightly injured during a cannonade on 4 February, was with Commandant Colonna d'Ornano, waiting to advance on the fortified church of Xochimilico, when cries of '*Vive l'Empereur!*' were heard coming from the troops on their right and the 'Cease Fire' was sounded.[16]

The capture of Oaxaca yielded two hundred and thirty-five officer prisoners, along with seven thousand eight hundred and forty other ranks, and among them was a man the Foreign Legion particularly wished to meet again.

Docir was captured, and this time made no attempt to disguise his villainy [*M'Alevey said*]. He was as stubborn as a mule. Had Oaxaca been attacked at the points indicated by the ruffian, we would all have been blown into the air. The ground was mined, and Docir, we found, was the concocter of the treacherous deed. He was a Colonel in the Mexican Army.[17]

In the days that followed Bazaine made his dispositions, and Jeanningros deployed his men. A consequence of the victory at Oaxaca was that the Regiment Etranger fell heir to many horses and mules, which had been in short supply until then. Jeanningros was able to expand the Mounted Company, making it far more efficient than had been possible ten months earlier when it had initially been created.[18] Many of the men who volunteered for it were, according to Zede, German ex-cavalrymen,[19] but some others were simply tired of being foot soldiers.

Legionnaire Amiable, announced that he could ride and volunteered, because, as he said, he was tired of foot slogging and humping his *sac*.[20] He quickly found that it took experience to ride a horse, falling off five times on his first patrol,[21] but soon got the hang of it, and the expanded *Compagnie franche Montee* was attached to Commandant de Brian's 3rd Battalion.

The prisoners-of-war started for Puebla on 11 February, guarded by the 3rd Zouaves. Diaz and his senior officers travelled on horseback, while other captured officers joined their captors in making the journey on foot. Saussier left on 14 February, conducting the artillery to Puebla, and would take some of it onwards to Mexico City. The same night de Brian gave a farewell dinner for the officers of the 1st and 2nd Battalions of the Foreign Legion, who were returning to Puebla the following day, and Saint-Maurice counted himself fortunate to have been included on the guest list.[22] General Mangin was remaining at Oaxaca as Commanding Officer, supported by the 3rd and 4th Battalions of the Regiment Etranger and Colonna d'Ornano's 2nd Battalion of the *Bat d'Af.*

Bazaine travelled as far as Puebla with Jeanningros and the 1st and 2nd Battalions, then went on to Mexico City and a hero's welcome. Saint-Maurice said goodbye to his Foreign Legion friends, as he was going to the capital with the Marshal's column. Jeanningros, as Commanding Officer at Puebla, settled back into garrison routine. The traitor Docir had been taken to Puebla and escaped again. This fugitive extraordinaire, now with a reward on his head, was soon captured by Dupin's *Contre-guerilla*. Tried, convicted and sentenced to be shot, he escaped yet again, but was recaptured a week later and executed by a Foreign Legion firing squad commanded by Major Rolland, which included M'Alevey.[23]

On his return to the capital the Marshal had been somewhat surprised to find that the Belgian Volunteers apparently saw themselves specifically as an Imperial Guard for Empress Carlota, rather than as fighting soldiers, as he had believed they would be. The first detachment of the *Osterreichische Freicorps*, which had arrived in Mexico City while the Marshal was away in Oaxaca, had also seemingly been given to believe that it would essentially be an Imperial Guard for the Emperor.[24] It would ultimately number some six thousand men, and these first arrivals were being feted in grand style by the Maximilian, and Bazaine bided his time as he watched their officers swaggering around the city in their dress uniforms, with feathers in their hats. He left them to enjoy the social life of the Court and the city, but wondered how it was – without having seen any action at all – they were being showered with honours and decorations.

Lieutenant Karl Gruber of the *Chasseurs*, for example, had been named as a Chevalier of the Order of Guadaloupe within a month of his arrival in Mexico.[25] A gifted young officer with many talents, he was regarded as one of the rising stars among the Austrian Volunteers. Born in Neusatz, Hungary, in 1834, he had spent six years as a Sous-Lieutenant in the Hungarian Army before transferring into that of Austria as a Lieutenant. Noted as an outstanding artist with the pencil, and a musician of considerable ability – the flute was his instrument of choice – Gruber spoke five languages fluently and enjoyed a reputation as a crack shot with a pistol.

Bazaine's immediate priority was to plan a new campaign and he now intended to push northwards, beyond the cities and towns of central Mexico, going right to the border with the United States if needs be, trying to drive President Juarez across the international line, hoping to make him irrelevant. He planned to do this with French troops, and to a lesser extent, men of the Mexican Imperial Army, and decided that he could use the *Osterreichische Freicorps* to garrison Puebla, freeing up the 3rd Battalion of the Regiment Etranger and the 2nd *Bat d'Af* for the Northern Campaign.

In Oaxaca life was returning to normal, especially social life, and when not out hunting guerillas the officers of the Regiment Etranger had an easy time. Lieutenant Zede, as aide-de-camp to Lieutenant-Colonel Carteret-Trecourt, exercised considerable power within the military administration, with far more authority than was usually given to an officer of his rank. He was fair, but insistent, sometimes to the point of pedantry, about enforcing and not bending the rules. When this caused a falling out with Commandant Colonna d'Ornano of the *Bat d'Af*, Zede won, but felt that he had made an enemy.

Carteret-Trecourt and Zede began making inroads into the social life of Oaxaca, but while they were personally well received, the experience convinced Zede that Emperor Maximilian's position was weak, and France's long-term prospects of real influence poor among all classes of Mexicans.

'They were inspired by an exalted patriotism like that of the Spaniards who have a hatred of all that is foreign', he said. 'From that moment, I had doubts about the success of our Intervention.'[26]

He also spent much time exploring the area and visiting many sites of archaeological interest. Colonel Douletrain made him a member of the Mexican Society of Geography and Statistics, and some of the artefacts he discovered were eventually displayed at the Louvre in Paris.

21

The Hand of Captain Danjou

In Vera Cruz, Commandant Marechal learned that the Republicans had erected defensive works in the vicinity of Thalixcoyan, north of the Rio Blanco, and that the enemy had returned to Cocuite, south of the river. Obviously, they must be dislodged. Perhaps because he planned to involve the two untried half-Companies of Austrian Volunteers who had been put under his command, Marechal decided to lead the expedition himself, which would give him an opportunity to see how these new troops behaved under combat conditions. On 26 February, accompanied by the Foreign Legion's Lieutenant Chesneau, his second-in-command, and with Sous-Lieutenants Baron and Waldejo as his aides-de-camp, Marechal took the train south to Medellin. They had with them a hundred men from the Egyptian Battalion and ninety-six Austrian Volunteers, and at Medellin picked up a ten-man detachment of Martinique Engineers with a howitzer and forty members of the Mexican Imperial Cavalry.

It took them a day-and-a-half to reach Tlalixcoyan, crossing the river of the same name, where they learned that the enemy was waiting for them at two defensive works at Paso de Vaqueros, on the south bank of the Rio Blanco. Shots greeted their arrival at the ford, but they crossed the river and Marechal, being an officer of the *Artillerie de Marine*, personally sighted the howitzer and blew off the corner of one of the earthworks. The enemy promptly retreated and the French went into the mini-forts, destroyed them, along with stores of weapons and ammunition, and burned the buildings which had housed the troops. From there they marched to Cocuite, reaching it on 2 March and destroying the quarters of the infantry and cavalry there, before returning to Tlalixcoyan.

Up to that point the expedition had been a great success, with losses amounting to one dead Austrian and three wounded Sudanese, but things now began to go seriously wrong. Marechal reformed his column for the march back to Medellin by the most direct route, which would take them through a gorge called Callejon de La Laja. An advance guard of twenty Sudanese led the way, followed by ninety-five Austrians, eighty Sudanese, the howitzer and its crew of Martinique Engineers and the staff and baggage, with the forty cavalrymen bringing up the rear.

Marechal was later faulted for not having sent scouts ahead, who might have found that the enemy had prepared an ambush in the gorge. The versions offered by the Austrians, the *Historique* of the Egyptian Battalion and the reminiscences of one of the Sudanese soldiers vary somewhat, but the result is not in dispute. The enemy waited until the French column was well into the gorge before springing their trap. Marechal was among the first to fall, along with the entire Martiniquan gun crew. After the initial shock, the Sudanese at the rear of the straggling column decided that they must bring out the body of their commander, and, if possible, the howitzer. They succeeded in doing both and Lieutenant Chesneau now took charge, rallied the survivors, led the column in a westerly direction to avoid another attack and returned to Medellin.

It was a trying journey and some of the Austrians fell behind and would die of exhaustion. The expedition's losses were serious, apart from its commander and the entire detachment of Martinique Engineers. The untried Austrians had nine killed in the ambush, while six others, seriously wounded, were abandoned there, three unwounded men were taken prisoner and seven men died of exhaustion on the way back to Medellin. The Sudanese had five killed and five wounded.[1]

Bazaine, in his report to Paris, made scant reference to the lack of sound military planning which had led to the disaster at the Callejon de La Laja.[2] Empress Carlota sent money to Marechal's widow in France and Napoleon III, shocked at the disaster, consulted his maps and ordered that the village of Cameron be renamed Villa Marechal, in honour of the dead commander.[3] The Legionnaire still within Bazaine, knowing well what Camaron/Camerone had come to mean to his old regiment, quietly ignored his Emperor's instruction.

Without consulting Bazaine, Maximilian dissolved the Military Commission – of which the Marshal was President – which devised policy recommendations for the Emperor. It was left to the newly organized Ministry of War to continue the policy work, and, while Bazaine remained as Commander-in-Chief of both the French Expeditionary Corps and the Mexican Imperial Army, he began to find himself deliberately marginalized when the new Minister of War started issuing orders directly to Imperial troops, without going through the Marshal's office.

Although this to some extent deprived Bazaine of the ability to maintain a totally clear picture of the overall military situation, the two-regiment Mexican Imperial army was small enough for him to always know where they were and what they were doing. He watched from the sidelines as confusion set in, and as March drew to a close sent Colonel Van der Smissen and his Belgians to occupy Morelia.

A decision taken in Paris on 5 April called for the creation of a 5th Battalion of the Regiment Etranger.[4] The 1st and 2nd Battalions were already in Mexico City and were slimmed down in size so as to be able to transfer men into the four *Compagnies du Centre* of the new 5th, command of which was given to Captain Christophe Koch. Recruits training in France would soon be sent out to add strength to all the battalions, but news came that Regnault would not be returning to Mexico. He never recovered from the pernicious fever which had forced him to go to France on sick leave, and died in Val-de-Grace Hospital in Paris on 8 April.[5] Colonel Dupin was also in Paris, as Bazaine, concerned about many of the extra-legal activities of the *Contre-guerilla*, had sent him home. He was not expected back and his place had been taken by Captain Michel Ney, Duke of Elchingen, the grandson of the first Napoleon's legendary Marshal Ney.

Dupin, in his eccentric self-designed uniform, complete with a large gold-embroidered sombrero, cut an extravagant figure on the boulevards of Paris – until he was placed under house arrest and ordered to appear in public in more orthodox attire. General du Barail felt he was 'like a soldier of fortune of the 16th century, a captain of adventurers' and was 'superb at the head of his 'Lost Souls,' themselves veritable types of brigands'.[6] Also a man of some charm, Dupin met with Napoleon III in Biarritz and convinced the Emperor that he was indispensable to the French cause in Mexico and should be allowed to return.

The tracks for the Imperial Mexican Railway finally reached Paso del Macho during April and it became both the railhead and the terminus, as a decision had been made to suspend construction for the foreseeable future because of the huge geographical obstacles ahead. The small town quickly took on the appearance of a bustling little metropolis, as those businesses, and the roustabouts who ran or patronized them, which had followed the tracks to La Soledad, then to Loma Alto, then Camaron, now established themselves at Paso del Macho in a more permanent way.

In Oaxaca, General Mangin had fallen sick and the Regiment Etranger's Lieutenant-Colonel Carteret-Tricourt had replaced him, with Lieutenant Zede as his aide-de-camp. Now Bazaine ordered Jeanningros to leave Captain Louis Vigneaud's 4th Battalion at Oaxaca for the time being, and to have de Brian's 3rd Battalion wind up their anti-guerilla activities and move to Puebla, which he was planning to place under the command of General de Thun. The final group of men of the *Osterreichische Freicorps* was known to be going to disembark at Veracruz on 5 May, and when they came ashore received orders to march inland to Puebla to join their comrades. General de Thun was named as Commanding Officer of the newly-created Sub-Division of Puebla, and tasked with subduing such pockets of *Juarista* resistance as still remained in the area. A detachment of Austrians was also sent to Oaxaca.

De Brian and the 3rd Battalion moved from Puebla to Mexico City, but had little time for relaxation, as Bazaine had work for them. The main enemies of the French were Generals Miguel Negrette and Mariano Escobedo, both of whom had escaped from French custody after the fall of Puebla, and, closer to the U.S. border, General Juan N. Cortina, alternately, when it suited him, either a patriot or a bandit.

Colonel Brincourt, who had been campaigning in the State of Chihuahua, was recalled and told to march towards Saltillo. De Brian was ordered to take the 3rd Battalion to Veracruz and go by sea up the coast to the port of Bagdad, on the Mexican side of the Rio Bravo. He picked up a detachment of newly-arrived Legionnaires, which brought his Battalion up to a strength of five hundred, and on 30 April – the second anniversary of Camerone – embarked on the warship *Var*. From Bagdad, de Brian marched on Matamoras, which was under siege from forces under Negrete, but by the time he was within striking distance the Mexicans had withdrawn, and it was soon learned that they had gone in the direction of Saltillo.

Saint-Maurice, who had travelled from Oaxaca to Mexico City with Bazaine, had unexpectedly found that the rarefied air of the capital affected his breathing. A possible heart condition was diagnosed and he at once sent in a request for temporary leave to return to Quebec for treatment.[7] He had heard nothing by 10 May, when he received orders to join Jeanningros, who was being sent into the North.[8] The main strength of the column was the 1st and 2nd Battalions of the Regiment Etranger. Commandant Alexis de La Hayrie, who had arrived in Mexico

Captain Jean Danjou, photographed in Oran, on his way to Mexico (Jean Brunon).

Colonel Francisco de Paula Milan, Commander of the Mexican forces at Camerone.

Painting of Sous-Lieutenant Clement Maudet, Regimental Standard-Bearer.

Sous-Lieutenant Jean Vilain of the 3rd Company of the 1st Battalion.

Corporal Philippe Maine of Camerone: as a Sous-Lieutenant in the Regiment Etranger in 1865 . . . as a Captain of Francs-Tireurs in the Franco-Prussian War in 1870 . . . and as a Captain in the 3rd Infanterie de Marine in 1871 (Jean Brunon).

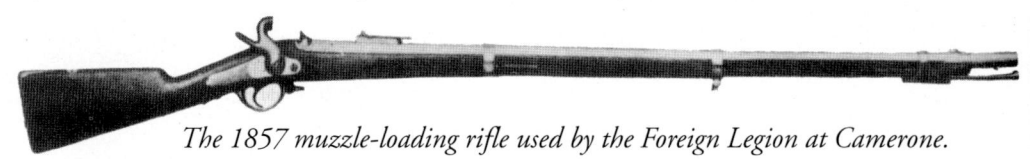

The 1857 muzzle-loading rifle used by the Foreign Legion at Camerone.

Danjou vows to fight to the death in Pierre Benigni's painting 'The Oath'.

Colonel Pierre Jeanningros, Commanding Officer of the Regiment Etranger.

Captain Gustave Saussier (La Legion Etrangere by Roger de Beauvoir, 1892).

Fusilier Hippolyte Kunassec, last known Camerone survivor (Le Petit Journal, 1902).

Corporal Evariste Berg, in the uniform of a Sous-Lieutenant of Zouaves.

Fusilier Pharon Van den Bulcke survived Camerone. Later an officer in 20th Regiment.

Lieutenant Charles Zede.

Captain Charles Cabossel, in the uniform of a Lieutenant-Colonel of the 109th Regiment.

Captain Auguste Ballue, as a Member of the Chamber of Deputies.

Lieutenant Adolphe Gans.

Captain Charles Blin.

Lieutenant Gabriel Diesbach.

'The end of the battle' by Jean-Adolphe Beauce.

Unknown Legionnaire, photographed in Mexico.

Rescued from a curio shop: the Eagle from the staff of the Regimental Standard.

The uniform of the 3rd of the 1st (Musee de l'Emperi, Salon-de-Provence).

General Jules Francois, who organized the first Camerone remembrance in 1906.

Military Chaplain Jean Ephrem Lanusse (Musee de Souvenir, Saint-Cyr).

General Paul Rollet 'Premier Legionnaire of France'.

LEFT: *Inspector-General of the Foreign Legion General Lefort.*

RIGHT: *Pierre Messmer, former Foreign Legion officer, later Minister of Defence.*

BELOW: *'The last survivors of the Hacienda of Camerone' by Edouard Detaille (L'Armee Francaise, 1885).*

...tificial hand of Captain Jean Danjou, the Foreign Legion's most precious relic.

...ase with Captain Danjou's ...edals.

Tambour *Casimir Lai's* Cross of a Chevalier of the Legion of Honour.

Fusilier *Leon Gorski's* Medaille militaire *and* Expedition du Mexique *medals (Jean Brunon).*

ABOVE: General Marcel J. Penette and Captain Jean Castaignt taking measurements in the 1892 grave of the men of the 3rd of the 1st.

The Camerone Monument in 1965 (General Marcel J. Penette).

The grave was protected by a wrought iron fence.

The original gravestone.

as an officer of the Zouaves, then moved to the *Tirailleurs Algeriens*, and now effected an exchange into the Regiment Etranger. He replaced Guyot de Leuchey and assumed command of the 2nd Battalion. The column was accompanied by a Squadron of the 1st *Chasseurs d'Afrique*, several heavy guns and two Squadrons of Cavalry, two Companies of Infantry and two howitzers of the *Contre-guerilla* under Captain Ney.

Campaigning in the South had been done in sub-tropical conditions. Now, in the North, the French were in dry and even semi-desert areas. Passing through Queretaro, Guanajuata – where the 1st Battalion was temporarily left – Matehuala and on to San Luis Potosi, they covered nine hundred and four kilometres (five hundred and sixty-one miles) in twenty-six days, suffering badly from thirst and dust. At San Luis Potosi a fighting column was formed and Bazaine strengthened it by sending Saussier and the Regiment Etranger's four Grenadier Companies.

Jeanningros soon heard that Negrete had occupied a natural fortress at Angostura, not far from Saltillo, with four thousand infantry, fifteen hundred cavalry and twenty guns, well sited in a classic defensive position. Calling for the 1st Battalion to march rapidly from Guanajuato, Jeanningros went into the field on 1 June. In a show of force after taking up a position in front of Negrete, he reconnoitered the Republican position with four Companies of his regiment, three Squadrons of Cavalry and two pieces of artillery.[9]

Saint-Maurice, watching Jeanningros in action, was impressed with 'his eloquence and with his rhetoric', and later recalled that the Colonel of the Foreign Legion had a particular phrase which he 'invariably used to the Regiment during the difficult days' when the chips were down: '*Mes enfants*,' he would say. 'The enemy is in front of us, but they are amateurs and we will drive straight through them! Ready! Char-r-r-ge!'[10]

A message came from Matamoras that Mejia was on his way with three thousand men of the Mexican Imperial Army and Commandant de Brian with the Regiment Etranger's 3rd Battalion, then another that Brincourt was coming from the west with three Battalions of Infantry, two Squadrons of Cavalry and eight guns. Jeanningros decided to await the arrival of the reinforcements, and, in the meantime, make it impossible for Negrete to get away.

The same night, Saint-Maurice, taking sixty mounted men, was sent to seal off a *barranca* which Jeanningros believed might be used as an escape route. It was a pitch black night and Saint-Maurice divided his troops into six units of ten and sent them to take up positions. He was with the last detachment when they ran head on into a large body of Republican troops. Unable to see the enemy, they fired at muzzle flashes, which gave away their own positions. Saint-Maurice took a bullet, which went through his right leg and into his horse. The animal, mad with pain, bolted into a group of Republicans and he was captured, as were his men, all of them wounded.

Taken to Negrete's headquarters, Saint-Maurice asked for food for his men, and for their wounds be dressed, but was told that nobody would get anything until he had been personally interviewed by Negrete. In fact, the meeting never took place. He refused to give a Republican officer any information about Jeanningros' force or his plans, was eventually given some beans and maize cakes, and then told that negotiations were under way for him and his wounded men to be exchanged for twelve Republican officers who had been captured earlier and sentenced to death.

When the exchange took place there was a hitch, as the French had extracted a promise from their Republican prisoners that they would not take up arms again for a year and a day. Learning this, the officer in charge of the exchange wanted the same promise from the French prisoners. The negotiations almost broke down, which would have led to the French prisoners being taken away and probably shot, and eventually Jeanningros sent a note giving Saint-Maurice and his men permission to give their word to be non-combatants.[11]

Jeanningros debriefed Saint-Maurice that night and put wagons at his disposal for himself and his wounded, as well as some other casualties, to be evacuated to Mexico City. Not long after they left Negrete succeeding in getting away from Angostura and, learning that Brincourt was coming at him from the west and Mejia and de Brian from the east, abandoned Saltillo. Jeanningros entered the city without opposition.

When Saint-Maurice reached San Luis Potosi, Marshal Bazaine, hearing of his wound, near brush with death, and that he had been forced to give his word not to fight again for a year and a day, issued immediate approval to the young officer's earlier request for leave to return to Canada for medical treatment. Permission was given for him to depart on the French warship the *Allier*, which would be sailing from Veracruz at the beginning of July and would take on coal at New York, prior to crossing the Atlantic to Brest. Saint-Maurice said his goodbyes on 14 June and left San Luis de Potosi for Mexico City by *diligence*. Soon after his arrival he found to his pleasure that he had been elected as a Corresponding Member of the Mexican Society for Geography and Statistics.[12]

He took lodgings near the dilapidated Convent of Santa Clara and looked up his friend Charles de Barres, editor of *L'Estafette*. De Barres, who knew everybody and everything, suggested a visit to the studio of Official War Artist Jean-Adolphe Beauce in the Convent's former chapel, and told Saint-Maurice that the artist was working on a painting with the tentative title of 'The Last Hour of Camerone', a visual representation – and Beauce had seen the Hacienda de la Trinidad – of the story Saint-Maurice had heard from the two Legionnaires at Camerone on his first night in Mexico.

' "The Last Hour of Camerone" recalls and is dedicated to the most heroic episode of the campaign,' de Barres remarked. 'Everyone knows the story, and I'll not repeat it here. Four [sic] men of this company of the Legion, who had fought all day against 2000 guerillas, held out to the last in a dilapidated farmhouse at Camerone. Then, having no more cartridges, they resolved to die in a final charge with the bayonet. It is the last act of this supreme effort of devotion which Monsieur Beauce has represented in a striking painting, which is especially remarkable for the contrasting expressions of the attackers and the besieged.'[13]

They found Beauce simultaneously at work on three paintings, one of which was 'The Last Hour',[14] and another may have been a vast and allegorical painting, in the grand manner of the military artist, called 'Marshal Forey's entry into Mexico City'.[15] Nor was Beauce above sycophancy, for the previous year he had created a wholly fictitious work showing Napoleon III in the field with his troops in Mexico. Bazaine had sent it to France in care of his aide-de-camp, Captain Henri Willette, who was returning home on sick leave, remarking to Marshal Jean-Baptiste Vaillant in a covering letter: 'The subject, hypothetical though it may be, will prove to His Majesty that His army in Mexico thinks of Him.'[16] The Camerone painting would not be finished by the time Beauce and the French left Mexico, but would in due course become the most famous and evocative of the artistic depictions of the Combat.

Lieutenant-Colonel Carteret-Tricourt, promoted and slated to take command of the 95th Regiment of the Line, was to be replaced by Commandant Emile Colonna d'Ornano, moving from the *Bat d'Af* to become the fourth second-in-command of the Regiment Etranger in two years. Carteret-Tricourt and Zede arrived in Mexico City on 18 June, where Zede was delighted to find that he was being transferred to the 3rd Battalion's Company of Grenadiers. In the few days he had in the capital he looked up his friend Captain Pierron, who was serving as *Chef de Cabinet* to Emperor Maximilian. While visiting his friend at the palace one morning Pierron made an opportunity to introduce Zede to the Emperor, who questioned him closely about the siege and taking of Oaxaca.

Newly-promoted Colonna d'Ornano had come up through the ranks and was known as a no-nonsense officer. Finding no suitable aide-de-camp among the officers of the regiment's new 5th Battalion, he thought of Zede, who had served his predecessor so well, but word reached him that the young officer still had memories of their clash of wills at Oaxaca, and had let it be known that he did not wish to serve the new Lieutenant-Colonel. Colonna d'Ornano sent for Zede at once and laid his cards on the table, assuring him that there was no rancour on his part. Zede, aware that, like it or not, he could be taken as aide-de-camp, and having received what he considered to be an olive branch from his superior, prudently decided to accept the post.

The Orizaba Road and the railway through the *Terres Chaudes* were still subject to raids by guerillas, and the officers commanding the posts at Paso del Macho and La Soledad were encouraged to take action against them whenever they could. As has long been the case, the small town of Cotaxtla on the Rio Atoyac and the village of Cocuite on the Rio Blanco were the major centres of guerilla activity.

Lieutenant Berge, the Commanding Officer at Paso del Macho, decided to garrison Cotaxtla and left his base with forty Sudanese, thirty Guadaloupe Engineers with a howitzer, twenty Mexican Imperial *Exploradores* – light infantry – and a detachment of cavalry on 23 June. Arriving at Cotaxtla at dawn the following day, they found that the guerillas, warned of their coming, had fled. Berge left Sous-Lieutenant Isadore Gonzalez of the Foreign Legion and thirty Sudanese to garrison the town and returned to Paso del Macho.[17]

The Court and the military brass in Mexico City were *en fete* on the morning of 26 June. Marshal Bazaine, a widower, was getting married. His bride was Maria Josefa – known as Pepita – de la Pena y Barragan y Azcarate, a well-connected young woman whose grandfather, Manuel de la Pena y Pena, had been President of Mexico in 1847–48. The marriage – approved of by both the Emperor and Empress of the French and the Emperor and Empress of Mexico – was celebrated in the great cathedral by Archbishop Labastida himself.

It was a glittering occasion, but of little immediate interest to those not invited. Saint-Maurice, who was one of them, left Mexico City that same morning in a special coach with four other officers, bound for Cordoba. In Puebla he tarried only long enough to visit the grave of his friend Lieutenant Joseph Cordier of the Foreign Legion and at the end of his journey met up with the troops who were to be repatriated to France on board the *Allier*. They reached the railhead at Paso del Macho four days later and Saint-Maurice sailed from Veracruz on 1 July. He arrived in New York two weeks later and was back with his family in Montreal by the end of the month.[18]

In Paris, an 8 July decision by the War Ministry called for the creation of a 6th Battalion of the Regiment Etranger,[19] but this one would be raised from recruits, rather from the further cannibalization of the existing battalions in Mexico.[20]

The *Osterreichische Freicorps* had been having a comparatively easy time at Puebla, one of their responsibilities being custody of the prisoners from Oaxaca, of whom Porfirio Diaz was by the far the most important. Consequently, Bazaine was livid when he heard that the General had escaped from his Austrian guards – just as he had escaped from French ones after the fall of Puebla. Diaz was not a man likely to give up, or to declare for the Emperor.

Seeking popularity, and very much against the wishes of the French, Emperor Maximilian ordered the release and pardoning of a number of prisoners-of-war. Then the childless monarch looked back in Mexican history and discovered that the late Emperor Iturbide, who had been executed almost forty years earlier, had two grandsons living in the United States. Augustin, the son of Iturbide's second son and his American wife, Alicia, was two years old. Salvator, the son of Iturbide's third son, was fourteen. Maximilian raised both boys to Royal rank, along with their unmarried aunt, Josefe. He then negotiated a generous financial arrangement with the Iturbide family to renounce any rights they might perceive they had in Mexico, arranged for Salvator to attend school in Paris and moved Augustin – who he apparently saw as an heir to his Imperial dynasty – and Princess Josefe into the palace in Mexico City.

The Regiment Etranger's 4th Battalion was now pulled out of Oaxaca, ordered to move to Mexico City, then sent to San Luis Potosi, which they reached on 15 July, and were assigned to convoy duty between there and Saltillo. In violation of Bazaine's orders, General Mejia had kept de Brian and the 3rd Battalion at Matamoras, where he used them as labourers on defensive works. Eventually, he sent them to Tampico, where almost half died of *vomito negro*, for which the seaport was notorious. Finally, a French warship, the *Tarn*, was sent to pick them up. In less than six months, the more than five hundred healthy men who had boarded the *Var* and sailed up the coast had been reduced to the two hundred fit men who disembarked at Veracruz. By the time de Brian got them to Mexico City there were only one hundred and sixty, and most of them were sick.

Bazaine had never expected very much from General de Thun and his Austrian Volunteer Corps, and Diaz' escape seemed to bear out his feelings. Consequently, he was quite pleased when reports from Puebla indicated that they had begun pushing patrols out into the interior of the State of Puebla, especially around Jalapa and Perote, which remained strongly Republican in their sympathies.

Lieutenant Gruber of the *Chasseurs* had already been awarded the *Medaille du Merite Militaire*, in bronze,[21] and was one of the more diligent and effective of de Thun's officers, raiding deep into *Juarista* territory in search of either the Mexican Republican Army or their guerilla sympathizers. On 17 July, near Cuahutoxa, about a hundred kilometres (sixty miles) north of the Orizaba Road, his mobile column surprised and destroyed an enemy unit, captured General Ramires and took twelve other prisoners and eighteen rifles. From there they moved on to Tesuitlan, where they stopped at the home of a rancher named l'Anglais, before returning to base.

Just nine days later Chief of Staff Boyer laid on Bazaine's desk in Mexico City two letters from General de Thun. The first, detailing Gruber's clash with the *Juaristas*, was a useful update on current Austrian activities in the field, but the second utterly astonished the Commander-in-Chief.

Zacapoaxtla, le 22 juillet 1865

Monsieur le Marechal,

I have true pleasure in announcing to Your Excellency the following: During the expedition of Lieutenant Gruber, this officer learned that the owner of a ranch near Tesuitlan, M. l'Anglais, of French origin, was in possession of the artificial hand of Captain Danjou who died gloriously at Camaron.

Knowing that the family of Captain Danjou had already sought to obtain this precious souvenir, Lieutenant Gruber asked M. l'Anglais if he would be willing to give it up for fifty piastres.

Having received this precious object which I will have the honour to send to you, with a [receipt] issued by Lieutenant Gruber, I request, Monsieur le Marshal, that you let me know if it will be convenient to reimburse the fifty piastres to M. l'Anglais.

Receive, Monsieur le Marechal, etc.

LE GENERAL COMTE DE THUN (22)

Marshal Bazaine replied to the letter the same day.

Mexico [City], 28 julliet 1865

Corps Expeditionnaire
du Mexique
Cabinet de Marechal Commandant
en chef
No. 344

My dear General,

I have the honour to acknowledge receipt of your letter of 22 July, from Zacapoaxtla, in which you informed me that Lieutenant Gruber had the good thought to buy the artificial hand of the brave Captain Danjou who died gloriously at Camaron.

I would ask you to warmly thank Lieutenant Gruber in my name for what he has done on this occasion, and to send the precious souvenir to my headquarters[,] then I will send the purchase price by a warrant for fifty piastres payable to the order of the Commanding Officer at Puebla.

Receive, my dear General, the assurance of my very real consideration.

Le Marechal de France.
BAZAINE[23]

The articulated hand was sent to Bazaine. The tip of the middle finger was missing, presumably damaged in the fight at the Hacienda de la Trinidad, but otherwise it was in good shape. Bazaine was delighted and gave orders for the warrant for fifty piastres to be sent to de Thun. Then bureaucracy kicked in, and, for whatever reason, the money was not sent. Embarrassingly, the matter of the fifty piastres was raised several times in letters from the Austrian Commander-in-Chief over the next four months, but remained unpaid. Bazaine was in the field at various times and the matter clearly received no attention. Eventually, in November, two officers from Bazaine's headquarters sent one hundred piastres to General de Thun, and presumably the rancher was paid.[24]

The American Civil War had ended in April, with the surrender of General Robert E. Lee at Appomattox Courthouse, and many Confederates, having lost everything, began eyeing Mexico. A number were very senior officers, others men of the rank-and-file, and they were soon streaming across the border in large numbers, some offering to serve Juarez, some hoping to serve Maximilian and some simply intending to serve themselves. Bazaine saw them as a possible source of recruits for the Foreign Legion and Maximilian approved the idea.[25]

On 4 August, hearing that General Escobedo had gathered an army of a thousand men, Jeanningros sent de La Hayrie's 2nd Battalion into the field to show the flag, gather Intelligence and make a swing through the countryside to scatter any Republican troops they might find. De La Hayrie took his men on a march of mammoth proportions, covering four hundred and forty kilometres (two hundred and seventy-three miles) in eleven days, at the hottest season of the year, and returned to Monterrey with his command intact. It was the first of the long marches which would come to characterize the Foreign Legion's campaigning until the French left Mexico.[26]

An Imperial Decree signed early in July authorized the raising of a 6th Battalion of the Foreign Legion,[27] and Marshal Bazaine was quite hopeful that Confederates would be persuaded to join. So was Jeanningros, who was promoted to General Officer rank on 12 August. He nevertheless retained overall responsibility for the Regiment, a fact which perhaps made the vacant post of Colonel of limited appeal to any ambitious officer. A Colonel Lavoignet, who was named the following day to succeed him, very quickly exchanged with Colonel Boussel de Courcy, who never played any real role with the Regiment.

General Castagny, who was campaigning just south of the U.S.–Mexico border, and was very aware of the ex-Confederate influx, was told to recruit among them if possible, then send them to San Luis Potosi, where they would sign engagement papers for three – rather than five – years. To sweeten the pot, they would be promised a grant of land at the end of their service.[28] In the event, however, only one volunteer came forward, and he wanted to be allowed to sign on for a 'trial period' of six months, which was refused.[29]

In the *Terres Chaudes* the decision was made to reinforce the small garrison at Cotaxtla and Lieutenant Berge sent twenty additional Sudanese under Lieutenant Salih Hijazi from Paso del Macho on 12 August. They had barely arrived when a party of some two hundred guerillas from Cocuite raced into town. The garrison retired to a secure place, got their mountain gun into action and sent word back to Berge and to Sous-Lieutenant Bosler, the Foreign Legion officer commanding at La Soledad. Bosler despatched an advance party of twenty Sudanese to strengthen the Cotaxtla contingent and wired for reinforcements from the Egyptian Battalion's headquarters at Veracruz. He was sent fifty men and was able to head south with a force large enough to scare off the guerillas.[30]

Troops were constantly sailing for France, some with regiments which were gradually being withdrawn from Mexico, others with men on leave or at the end of their service. Despite all precautions, *vomito negro*, contracted while waiting to embark, sometimes went with them. When Saint-Maurice sailed on the *Allier* at the beginning of July there were several deaths before the ship cleared the Gulf of Mexico. On 15 August, while returning to France, Camerone survivor Sergeant Karl Shaffner, Chevalier of the Legion of Honour, died on board ship and was buried at sea.[31]

Jeanningros had established himself in Monterrey with the 2nd Battalion of the Regiment Etranger and was observing the number of Confederates crossing from the United States into Mexico. Up to this time they had tended to be individuals, pairs or small groups of soldiers, but now a new dimension appeared in the form of the thousand-plus command of General Joseph O. Shelby of Missouri.

'Fighting Jo' had moved his cannon, arms, ammunition and supply train from Arkansas into Texas and crossed the U.S.–Mexico border at Eagle Pass. He sank his tattered Stars and Bars battle flag in the Rio Grande before reaching the Mexican side at Piedras Negras. For his part, Shelby would have been disposed to take service under Juarez, but when he gave his officers and men an opportunity to choose between joining the Empire or the Republic the majority chose Maximilian. So Shelby sold his cannon, muskets and powder to Republican Governor Biesca at Piedras Negras for $16,000 and pushed south towards Monterrey, meeting on the way a pair of northbound deserters from the *Osterreichische Freicorps*, who were heading for Texas, and several times having to fight brigands at river crossings.[32] Expecting that the news of his sale of weapons and munitions to the *Juaristas* would have preceded him,[33] Shelby prepared for an uncertain reception from Jeanningros at Monterrey. On the outskirts of the city the Confederates halted and former Governor Thomas C. Reynolds, who spoke French, prepared a bold letter, which Rainy McKinney and John Thrailkill, riding with a flag of truce, took into town.

It read:

> General: I have the honour to report that I am within one mile of your fortifications with my command. Preferring exile to surrender, I have left my own country to seek service in that held by His Imperial Majesty, the Emperor Maximilian. Shall it be peace or war between us? If the former, and with your permission, I shall enter your lines at once, claiming at your hands that courtesy due from one soldier to another. If the latter, I propose to attack you immediately.
>
> Very respectfully, yours,
JO. O. SHELBY.[34]

Jeanningros is said to have read the letter and told the emissaries: 'Tell your General to march in immediately. He is the only soldier that has yet come out of Yankeedom.'[35]

Shelby brought his men into town, Jeanningros had them billeted, and that evening gave a dinner for the officers. Among them was Colonel John N. Edwards, a former newspaperman who had been Shelby's Adjutant for much of the late war. The talk at the table was largely of battles, of Algeria, the Crimea, the Italian Campaign and the War between the States, and the wine flowed freely. Eventually, Shelby asked a question about the statesmanship of Maximilian.

> 'Ah! the Austrian; you should see him to understand him,' [*Edwards quoted Jeanningros as saying*]. 'More of a scholar than a king, good at botany, a poet on occasions, a traveller who gathers curiosities and writes books, a saint over his wine and a sinner among his cigars, in love with his wife, believing more in manifest destiny than drilled battalions, a good Spaniard in all but deceit and treachery, honest, earnest, tender-hearted and sincere, his faith is too strong in the liars who surround him, and his soul is too pure for the deeds that must be done. He cannot kill as we Frenchmen do. He knows nothing about diplomacy. In a nation of thieves and cut-throats, he goes devoutly to Mass, endows hospitals, laughs a good man's laugh at the praises of the blanketed rabble, says his prayers and sleeps the sleep of the gentleman and the prince. Bah! his days are numbered; nor can all the power of France keep his crown upon his head, if, indeed, it can keep that head upon his shoulders.'[36]

Jeanningros told Shelby that he should take his command to Mexico City, where Maximilian – and to some extent Bazaine – would decide whether or not to take them into the Mexican Imperial Service, and would listen to Shelby's ideas about raising a large force of American ex-soldiers for the defence of the Empire. After various adventures, he and his command reached the capital and had an interview with the Emperor, at which Bazaine was present, but they found no employment, and no support for Shelby's plan. Maximilian had decided that he would use diplomacy with the United States to obtain recognition, rather than force to defeat Juarez. The best that Shelby could obtain for his men was a land grant near Cordoba, and a number of the ex-Confederates settled there in agricultural pursuits around the settlement they called the Carlota Colony.

In Paris, Napoleon III, avidly poring over the reports and maps brought to him by Minister of War Randon, was looking to the future, particularly to the possibility that the United States, flushed with victory, and with a large standing army not yet demobilized, might decide to aid Juarez, or invade Mexico – with or without him – in an effort to enforce the Monroe Doctrine.

> If the United States wants to invade Mexico, the only plan to follow would be to evacuate the border areas and to hold a central core [*the Emperor advised Bazaine in August 1865*]. Then it would be necessary for them to wear themselves out by long, hard marches over an uninviting barren country ... Do not try to occupy all of the area but sacrifice some in order to save more; boldly abandon all that you cannot advantageously occupy, and mass your troops instead of scattering them.[37]

Bazaine had already been considering just such a strategy and ordered Jeanningros to turn Monterrey over to the Mexican Imperial Army and withdraw his 1st and 2nd Battalions to Saltillo. Lieutenant-Colonel Colonna d'Ornano took the 5th Battalion first to Tula, which he fortified, then went on to Victoria, which was being threatened by the Republicans.

The decision to create a *Compagnie franche Montee* for the Foreign Legion had been very successful, so in September it was decided to do the same for the *Tirailleurs Algeriens*, and then to create a similar forty-five-man unit for the Egyptian Battalion. The intention was to provide these traditional infantry formations with the means to better patrol in the *Terres Chaudes* and give chase to the guerillas, who were becoming increasingly bold.

On 7 October a former prisoner-of-war named Sotomayor, who had been pardoned and freed by Emperor Maximilian, led some two hundred guerillas in a bloody attack on the railway, derailing a train at seven o'clock in the morning at Arroyo de Piedras, between La Purga and La Soledad. A Sergeant and Corporal of the Guadeloupe Engineers were accompanying a large payroll, guarded by Legionnaire Vanderbendt. Lieutenant Friquet of the Martinique Engineers and two of his men were also on the train, along with a French Army Sergeant named Loubet, several other soldiers and some civilians. Having killed the train's driver, the guerillas robbed the passengers, separated the civilians from the military, and then shot nine soldiers out of hand, including Friquet, one of his men, Sergeant Loubet and Vanderbendt.

The Foreign Legion's Sous-Lieutenant Bosler sent word of the outrage from La Soledad to Veracruz, before setting off with a small force in pursuit of Sotomayor's band. He succeeded in scattering them, but not before they had killed one of the Martinique Engineers with the party and wounded nine others. An hour after midnight Sous-Lieutenant Baron of the Foreign Legion left Veracruz by train with fifty Sudanese, eighteen Mexican Imperial Cavalry under Colonel Figuerero and ten Sappers from the Martinique Engineers. Joining Bosler's little force, they set out on the trail of the guerillas, and caught up with them at seven o'clock the following morning. A group of fifteen mounted Sudanese charged the enemy at the ravine of Las Palmas and Bosler and his men, following closely, poured such a withering fire into the guerillas that they fled. The surviving Martinique Sapper from the train derailment subsequently recognized a Mexican who had taken part in the attack. He was tried by court martial in Veracruz and shot.[38]

There were still clashes between French and Mexican troops in and around Jalapa and Huatusco and in a minor one, the details of which are now lost, Lieutenant-Colonel Manuel Marrero was killed. The story of kindness of the Marrero family to the dying Sous-Lieutenant Maudet after the Combat of Camerone was well known in the French Expeditionary Corps, and Marrero's body was taken to Huatusco by two – unfortunately unidentified – French officers on 24 October and delivered to his sister, Dona Juana.[39]

On the night of 23/24 November travellers coming from Monterrey reported to Jeanningros that Escobedo had attacked the Imperial forces, largely taken the town and forced the garrison to withdraw to the citadel, where they were besieged. Despatched ahead of a larger relief column, Battalion Commander de La Hayrie put one hundred and fifty men in wagons normally used to transport supplies and rushed them in the direction of Monterrey. They arrived on the outskirts of the city at five o'clock in the morning, left the wagons and advanced on foot. The element of surprise was on his side and Escobedo initially made plans to retreat, but soon realized how few men were under de La Hayrie's command. The Republicans rallied, and things would have gone badly for the attackers had not Escobedo been warned of the approach of the main force. Saussier, commanding a detachment of the Foreign Legion Mounted Company, had pushed his men to cover two hundred and thirty-five kilometres (one hundred and forty-six miles) in thirty-two hours of forced marches and immediately set out after the retreating Escobedo, catching up with his rearguard and killing one hundred and twelve of them, before returning to Monterrey. De La Hayrie had come through the ordeal with only five men wounded, including Lieutenant Louis Bastidon, who at the age of seventeen had passed through Saint-Cyr at the same time as Zede, served in Italy then volunteered to go to Mexico with the Regiment Etranger.[40]

Early in December one hundred and eighty men of Captain Vigneaud's 4th Battalion took to the field as part of a column which included sixteen *Chasseurs a Cheval* and forty men of the Mexican Imperial Cavalry. A rapid march by the horsemen, accompanied by thirty-five mounted Voltigeurs, brought them into contact with the enemy, resulting in a dozen being killed and the capture of a hundred horses and mules. The 5th Battalion was then sent to Tule and orders came for them to establish a series of posts to protect the road from there to Tampico.

22
Disaster at Santa Isabel

The year 1865 was the apogee of the successes of the French Army in Mexico. From the beginning of 1866 theirs was largely a story of one stalemate or defeat after another – some military, most political – and early in the year it became clear that the days of the French Intervention were numbered. It had become unpopular in France, not only with Napoleon III and the various Ministers in the Government, who resented the continuing costs, but with the public, as the number of soldiers' deaths grew, both in battle and from disease. Even so, it would be twelve months before the actual departure of all of Marshal Bazaine's Expeditionary Corps – including the Foreign Legion.

Parisian newspaper and magazine readers, who had been given a relatively positive diet of how the war was going, began to hear the other side of the story in the closing months of 1865 when they had an opportunity to read what life had really been like in the *Terres Chaudes*. A new book called *Les Bivouacs de Vera Cruz a Mexico, par un Zouave*,[1] the first of the war memoirs to appear, was soon known to be the work of Captain Jean Jacques Jules Lafont, who had gone to Mexico as a Lieutenant in the Zouaves and subsequently transferred into the 36th Regiment of the Line. As no report of the Combat of Camerone appears to have been published in French newspapers or magazines at the time, it is probable that the eight-page account in the book was the first intimation that French and German readers – as the book was also published in Leipzig – had that the Foreign Legion had been engaged in a major military action in the Regiment's early days in Mexico. On the heels of *Bivouacs*, the magazine *Revue des Deux Mondes* published a lengthy two-part article by Count Emile de Keratry called 'La *Contre-Guerilla* Francaise au Mexique,' and he would later put them together as a book.[2]

Colonel Dupin returned to Mexico with the blessing of Napoleon III in January, but Bazaine did not welcome him back. He simply put the *Contre-guerilla*, comprising men of twenty-two nationalities, under Douay, who made use of them in the north. '[Dupin's] troop was perfectly designed for the task which it had been assigned – hunting guerillas,' Zede remarked. He believed that their Infantry were particularly effective, as they were largely made 'soldiers liberated from the army in Mexico who had acquired a taste for the country'. The majority, he added, 'were ex-soldiers of the Legion'.[3] French ex-soldiers and foreign-born adventurers made up the 1st Squadron of Cavalry, while the 2nd Squadron was drawn from time-expired members of the *Tirailleurs Algeriens*.[4] The pay was good, some thirty piastres a month, worth about one hundred and fifty French francs. Effective and hard-hitting, the *Contre-guerilla* was certainly rough. 'One cannot claim that each nation sent its most praiseworthy representatives,' Dupin admitted. 'If this force had marched through the boulevards of Paris, one would have thought it was an ancient band of thieves exhumed from the back streets of the city.'[5]

The Regiment Etranger began the year with the 1st and 2nd Battalions at Saltillo with Jeanningros, the 3rd, brought up to strength again, and 5th at San Luis Potosi with Lieutenant-Colonel Colonna d'Ornano, the 4th at Matehuala and the 6th, which was still recruiting in France. On 24 January, Colonel Boussel de Courcy, whose command of the regiment had been little more than nominal, exchanged positions with Colonel Pierre Guilhem of the 90th of the Line.[6]

Napoleon III now began giving serious thought to repatriating the French Expeditionary Corps, but was still adhering to the terms of the Convention of Miramar as far as the Foreign Legion was concerned.

> The longest time I can give for the repatriation of the army corps, which must be done in stages, is the beginning of next year [*he told Bazaine in a letter in mid-January*]. I should like for the evacuation of Mexico not to compromise the power of the Emperor. So take steps to organize a firm Foreign Legion and the Mexican army.[7]

The following month he was suggesting that the Austrian and Belgian 'Legions' should be dissolved, with chosen men being absorbed into the Regiment Etranger and strong recruiting efforts made among the Mexicans, in an effort to create a force of around fifteen thousand, who would be paid by France until the evacuation of the Expeditionary Corps.[8]

Even at this late date Bazaine was endeavouring to create the semblance of an infrastructure and the need for a telegraph link between Queretaro and San Luis Potosi was acute. The previous year a contractor who went to the United States with funds to buy wire had decamped. His successor proved to be incompetent. Bazaine took the view that the Foreign Legion could certainly do the work. Some officers personally advanced the money to buy wire and Captain Francois Charrier, Lieutenant Frederic Dally and Sous-Lieutenant George de Heckeren were given the job of erecting the telegraph line. Men with the required skills were transferred into the 6th Company of the 3rd Battalion to create a specialist team and they began work in February. Even before going into the mountains to cut the trees for the poles which would be needed, Charrier heard of a convoy of supplies being sent to a guerilla group and set out to capture it, covering eighty-four kilometres (fifty-two miles) in twenty-four hours and seizing the convoy. It took his command until the end of May, often fighting off wandering guerilla bands, to string two hundred and forty-one kilometres (nearly one hundred and fifty miles) of wire connecting San Luis Potosi with Querertaro and make sure that the telegraph worked properly. They spent the next four months protecting the line from Republican depredations.[9]

Jeanningros soon moved back to Monterrey with the 1st Battalion, leaving de Brian, who had been transferred from the 3rd Battalion to the 2nd, at Saltillo, which he left early in February on hearing that a guerilla leader named Geronimo Trevino was threatening the town of Parras. His second-in-command was Captain Cazes, now Adjutant-Major of the 2nd Battalion. Once the presence of the four

Companies of the 2nd had forced Trevino to leave the area, de Brian was told to remain at Parras and organize a local *Gendarmerie*.

He was also specifically ordered by Jeanningros not to attempt to campaign outside the town. Unfortunately, like Colonel Montagnac at Djemmaa-Ghazaouet more than two decades earlier, when he heard that the enemy was within striking distance, he was tempted beyond the realms of good sense. Just as Montagnac's disobedience to orders precipitated the affair at Sidi Brahim, which decimated the *Chasseurs d'Orleans*, de Brian's very similar act of disobedience precipitated a disaster for the Foreign Legion, in which a single military action accounted for almost a third of the regiment's total deaths in battle during their four years in Mexico.

Word reached Parras on 28 February that Trevino and twelve hundred horsemen had been joined by another Republican group of seven hundred men at the Hacienda de Santa Isabel, about fifteen kilometres (a little more than nine miles) north of Parras. To de Brian this was a matter of outrage, as much an affront to his sense of honour as anything else, and despite the fact that his four Companies were all under strength he decided to take battle to the Mexicans. As he dared not leave Parras undefended he left the 5th Company there under Lieutenant Bastidon, who was still recovering from his wound of the previous year. De Brian would march on Santa Isabel with the Company of Voltigeurs under Lieutenant Ravix, the 3rd Company under Captain Moulinier and Sous-Lieutenant Royaux and the 4th commanded by Lieutenant Schmidt and Sous-Lieutenant Moutier, a total of one hundred and eighty-five officers and men, who would be supported by members of the newly-created Mexican *Gendarmerie*.

The French too often suffered from the same kind of arrogance about the fighting abilities of its enemies that caused problems for British, U.S., Italian and Spanish armies opposed by indigenous peoples in Africa or the Americas. Lieutenant-Colonel Adrien de Tuce, now promoted and transferred to the 12th *Chasseurs d'Afrique*, quoted a letter written by an officer named Ferdinand Millet to his mother, complaining: 'Our captain instead of letting us charge the Mexicans, remained planted there, and we missed a fine business, as we were eighty horsemen, and there were only five hundred *chinacos* before us'.[10] Nor was it only the officers who suffered from this arrogance, as Legionnaire Amiable would write: 'We always said that ten of ours can fight fifty of these bandits, and usually give them a good thrashing.' He went further, saying: 'The Mexican is afraid of gunfire. When he shoots, he turns his head. One of their volleys discharged at 30 feet never frightens you. If one is hit, it's just bad luck',[11] which may have been true of some of the townsmen turned National Guardsmen, but was not of the guerilas of the North, who lived by their guns.

De Brian was an experienced and battle-hardened officer who should have known better. Saint-Maurice, who had come to know him well during the Oaxaca Campaign, said that he had authored 'several manuscripts on tactics and military history',[12] but, if so, he forgot all about theory, as opposed to practice, and compounded his disobedience to orders by a failure to seek whatever Intelligence might have been had locally about the Hacienda de Santa Isabel. It seems certain that he should have been able to learn much from Maximo Campos, the Sous-Prefect of Parras, who agreed to go into the field with him.

The Foreign Legion column set out from Parras with seven other officers and one hundred and seventy-seven men after dark on 28 February. They were accompanied by Dr. Rustegho and his ambulance, and by two hundred and fifty foot soldiers and one hundred and fifty horsemen of the *Gendarmerie* under Campos. By three o'clock in the morning they were eight hundred metres (about half a mile) from the Hacienda de Santa Isabel and de Brian divided his men into three groups, the Voltigeurs on the left, the 4th Company on the right and the Mexican foot soldiers and horsemen in the centre, with the 3rd Company to their rear, as a reserve. As soon as it began to get light he ordered the advance and the men scrambled to their feet and moved forward.

The hacienda, which was dominated by a small hill, was a large adobe building, with walls in some places twenty feet high and a flat roof. Trevino's riflemen on the top of the building began firing on the advancing French force, while others opened up from the hill, and things began to go wrong almost at once. A deep *barranca* blocked the advance of the Voltigeurs, causing them to have to move to the right and the men ceased to be Squads, Sections and Companies, jumbled up with Campos' troops and the 3rd Company. It was obvious that the marksmen on the hill must be evicted and the Legionnaires charged in a frontal attack and began scrambling upwards. Dr. Rustegho had his ambulance rushed forward to a position against the front wall of the hacienda as the Legionnaires surged up the slope.

De Brian was badly wounded before he had climbed far, but the other officers and Legionnaires pushed on. Lieutenant Schmidt was mortally wounded and Sous-Lieutenant Royaux killed. Captain Cazes, with fifty or sixty men kept climbing and soon saw the Mexicans beginning to fall back to the far side of the hill. Suddenly, from the hacienda, came a voice crying out several times in French: 'Retreat!' The Legionnaires stopped, looked puzzled, then broke off firing and began to descend. At this moment Trevino ordered into action almost a thousand horsemen he had hidden behind the hacienda. As they swept out into the open the mounted Mexican *Gendarmerie* decided that they would rather fight another day, wheeled their horses around and fled, leaving the Legion and Campos' foot soldiers to face whatever was to be offered.

Many of the ninety-odd Legionnaires coming down from the hill were killed and those on the ground in front of the hacienda were ridden down by Trevino's horsemen. Cazes fell and Lieutenant Ravix, isolated and alone, fought with his revolver and sabre until he was cut down. The wounded de Brian, who was being carried away by Sergeant Racle of the 3rd Company, was surrounded by a bunch of horsemen. Racle had only his bayonet and they were soon overwhelmed. Captain Moulinier formed a tiny square with four Voltigeurs and they were quickly despatched. Dr. Rustegho was hacked to death by a French deserter named Albert. Late of the 62nd Regiment – with whom, ironically, de Brian had come to Mexico – he was probably the man who had been heard shouting 'Retreat!' from the hacienda. Sous-Lieutenant Moutier was wounded and captured.

Sergeants Desbordes and Fiala of the Company of Voltigeurs and a Fusilier named Degeorges rallied about seventy men and descended into the *barranca* hoping to escape, but had not gone far when it turned into a dead end. The Mexicans gathered on the brink, firing down. When driven from the lip by the accurate return fire of the Legionnaires, they resorted to tumbling rocks on them. Eventually, Desbordes surrendered.

By half past seven in the morning the battle was over – and the Voltigeurs and the 3rd and 4th Companies virtually annihilated. The casualties were one hundred and two dead, including seven officers, and eighty-two prisoners, forty of them wounded. The overall cost of de Brian's disobedience was even higher because of the dead, wounded and prisoners among Campos' *Gendarmerie*. The sole escapee was Captain Cazes' Orderly, who made it back to Parras to spread the alarm the following day.[13]

Just after dawn on 2 March several Mexican riders dashed into Parras on lathered horses. The little town was held by Bastidon's 5th Company, only forty-four strong, and twenty-six members of the Baggage Train. The riders reported that de Brian and his entire command had been wiped out, but Bastidon at first refused to believe them. Soon, however, other riders began coming in with the same story, as well as news that large numbers of guerillas were approaching the town. Sending a man to Saltillo to raise the alarm, Bastidon had water, wood, flour, salt, several sheep, and forage for them, taken into the stone church and prepared to make a stand. He had decided, he said later, 'to fight to the last man'.

By eight o'clock the guerillas began arriving, first an estimated fifteen hundred men on horses and on foot, then another three hundred and fifty horsemen. The town was surrounded by noon and a Mexican with a white flag delivered a written surrender demand. It was signed by the aide-de-camp of 'General' Jesus Gonzalez Herrera. Bastidon rejected it and fighting broke out at once.

'When told to surrender, we responded with renewed energy,' said Corporal Abel Huart later.[14]

The initial attack lasted for three hours, and was followed by a second surrender demand, this one signed by Herrera himself. 'If "General" Herrera wants to take us prisoner, he will have to come and take us,' Bastidon responded. When, several hours later, a third emissary tried to deliver another surrender demand, Bastidon shouted to him: 'Go back! Go and tell your general that if he sends another messenger I shall open fire on him!'[15]

The attack began again, and while there were many Mexican targets, the Legionnaires' ammunition was limited, so they made every shot count.

Legionnaire Amiable was with the Mounted Company at Saltillo when Bastidon's rider arrived. Saussier immediately assembled four Companies of the 2nd Battalion, the Mounted Company and an Artillery section with mountain guns and was ready to move out by mid-afternoon. The siege at Parras was well into its fourth day when, halting for the night of 5 March, Saussier sent an Indian with a message telling Bastidon that he would arrive the following day. By the time his column had Parras in sight 'General' Herrera, warned of their coming, had withdrawn.

In a letter to Jeanningros written on 7 March, Saussier spoke of the 'formidable position' of Santa Isabel, mistakenly listed Sous-Lieutenant Moutier as being among the dead, and commended Bastidon for his defence of Parras.[16]

Amiable and the Mounted Company were sent to Santa Isabel to act as a burial party.

The spectacle before our eyes was awful [*he recalled*]. We buried at least 200 of our Legion . . . We dug ditches three metres deep and four metres across and put twenty cadavers in each. Several had already been buried; their hair and parts of their clothes came out of the earth. It stank. The ground in many places was full of dried blood, which formed large pools. I was sick for several days.[17]

Huart never forgot the fight at Parras, and forty years later still considered that it had been 'an honour' to have been there, although he felt that the defenders had been poorly treated afterwards. 'As a reward for our actions, we were told that we would be promoted into one of the Elite Companies, of Voltigeurs or of Grenadiers, but we never were,' he said. 'We were forgotten.'[18]

De Brian was faulted in the official reports for disobeying orders and going out after Trevino, but J.F. Elton, an English officer who spent time with the French in Mexico, remarked that it was generally felt to be 'hardly meet to question the acts of those who die bravely in the forefront of the battle'.[19]

The wounded prisoners were initially fairly well treated by the Mexicans, and the unwounded ones moved to a prisoner-of-war camp at Mapimi, in Comanche territory, but close to the U.S. border. Once there, Sergeant of Voltigeurs Fiala engineered a daring mass escape. He had signed his first engagement in 1844, been through all the campaigns – wounded in the Crimea in 1855 and awarded the *Medaille Militaire* – and went to Mexico with the 2nd Battalion. In his twenty-second year in the Foreign Legion, he was probably the regiment's oldest Sous-Officier in Mexico. First gaining the confidence of the guards, Fiala and his men bided their time. When an opportunity presented itself they dashed away from the camp, crossed the border into the U.S. and made their way to Brownsville, Texas. From there they took a ship to Veracruz and presented themselves at the Foreign Legion Depot. Colonel Guilhem promoted Fiala to the rank of Adjutant and Bazaine decorated him with the Cross of the Legion of Honour.[20]

In the *Terres Chaudes* the two original battalions of the Foreign Legion had done their work in tropical downpours. In the South the four battalions had faced desolate barren, rock-strewn country. Now, in the North, five-battalions strong, they traversed virtual deserts, always short of water, guarding convoys, chasing guerillas, covering enormous distances in record marching time, conditions which reminded the ever-dwindling number of old-timers of Southern Algeria.

Chaplain Lanusse, who had been in Mexico for even longer than the Regiment Etranger, and who had marched with Bazaine, the Foreign Legion and several other regiments across a large part of Mexico, neatly summed up the various campaigns as 'a struggle against the climate and the privations, against sickness and forces which were always superior in numbers and in their knowledge of the country'.[21]

In March, near Monterrey, Achilli, now a Captain and leading a mixed force of the Mounted Company on mules and a group of Mexican Auxiliaries, made a forced march, covering ninety kilometres (fifty-six miles) in thirteen hours and surprised two hundred and fifty enemy horsemen near Santiago, killing thirty of them in a running fight.[22] Just eight days later Captain Ballue set out with a force of Legionnaires, accompanied by detachments from the *Bat d'Af*, the 12th *Chasseurs d'Afrique* and Mexican Auxiliaries, and marched in the direction of the hacienda of General Negrete, but returned to base after a clash with Republican outposts.

Commandant Charles Clemmer was at Matehuala with three hundred men of the 5th Battalion and a hundred Imperial troops when Escobedo descended on the town with several thousand men. Word was sent to San Luis Potosi, where de La Hayrie quickly assembled the 3rd Battalion and four Companies of the 5th. They left at six o'clock in the morning of 27 March for what was normally considered to be a ten-day march. De La Hayrie pressed on, with regular stops every hour, little sleep and his men eating as they marched. Just after noon four days later they were shelled by Republican guns going through a pass sixty-six kilometres (forty-one miles) from Matehuala, and several were killed or wounded. They marched all night and covered the last section at a rate of some six kilometres an hour, reaching their destination, bayonets fixed and ready to fight the following day. Astonished that help had come so fast from so far, Escobedo withdrew.

'My tongue hung down to my feet,' Legionnaire Amiable remembered.[23]

A correspondent for the *New York Herald*, visiting Paso del Macho in early April, wrote disparagingly of it as little more than a wide spot in the road, where a traveller's 'troubles' began if prior arrangements had not been made for a seat on the *diligence* to Mexico City.[24] Perhaps he was the same *Herald* correspondent who had talked some months earlier to Chief Construction Engineer Lyons, and had been told: 'The work [to be done] on this line surpasses in magnitude and the difficulties to be overcome any other railroad in the world. As an instance of the energy with which the enterprise is being pushed, I may state that the road between Mexico [City] and Puebla alone will require about thirty thousand tons of railroad material, nearly the whole of which is [to be] brought from England and hauled up from Vera Cruz over roads which only those who have visited Mexico can know or describe'.[25]

The first men of the new 6th Battalion of the Regiment Etranger reached Veracruz on 25 April. They were on the road to Mexico City when, four days later, Bazaine announced what would be a sensible but unpopular consolidation of the three Legions – French, Austrian and Belgian – together as a single Division of two Brigades, a variation on Napoleon III's idea of two months earlier. The Regiment Etranger formed the 1st Brigade and the Austrians and Belgians the 2nd.[26]

In mid-year came another disaster, when a mixed force of Austrians and Mexican Imperial Army troops was overwhelmed while escorting a convoy near Camargo, across the border from Rio Grande City. The merchants and importers of Matamoras had been begging for strong escorts for two convoys of supplies for the business communities of Mier and Monterrey. Eventually, General Mejia assembled what he believed was a strong enough force to deter attacks. The convoy was to travel as a single entity from Matamoras to Mier under the protection of General Rafael Olvera with sixteen hundred Mexican Imperial Army troops, supported by three hundred members of the *Osterreichische Freicorps*. The portion of the convoy destined for Monterrey would be met at Mier by a predominantly Foreign Legion force, who would then take it southwards to its destination.

On 14 June the convoy was attacked by an enemy force estimated at five thousand, led by General Escobedo himself, and accompanied by a large number of American filibusters, former Confederate soldiers and recently discharged Union troops. At the height of the battle two battalions of Olvera's Imperial troops deserted to Escobedo's side, turning the tide and forcing the surrender of the other Imperials and the Austrians. A number of them were killed out of hand after surrendering, but more than a thousand were taken prisoner, among them Austrian-born Baron Max von Alvensleben, who had fought for the Union in the American Civil War and had joined the *Osterreichische Freicorps* early in the year.[27] Escobedo's spoils included eight cannon and three hundred wagon loads of goods valued at two million piastres.[28]

Even the iron constitution of Jeanningros gave in sometimes and he had put Lieutenant-Colonel de Tuce of the 12th *Chasseurs d'Afrique* in command of the column which was to travel from Monterrey to Mier to meet the convoy and escort it back. Vilmette's 1st Battalion of the Regiment Etranger, and Saussier's 2nd were joined by both the *Compagnie franche a Pied* and the *Compagnie franche Montee*, as well as a Squadron of de Tuce's *Chasseurs d'Afrique*, a detachment of the Belgian Volunteers and another from the Mexican Imperial Army. They marched into Mier on 18th June and found the town essentially deserted. There they learned of the fate of the convoy at Camargo four days earlier, and it was soon clear why the residents of Mier had decamped. Goods in shops and storehouses showed clearly that even if the population of the town had not actually participated in attacking French-protected convoys, they had at the very least benefitted from the goods and supplies which had been taken by force of arms.

Thirsty Legionnaires and other soldiers found much liquor, both imported and local, as well as French military equipment, which must have been taken from dead soldiers. Something then happened which snapped the normal discipline of the 1st and 2nd Battalions, which were considered the most solid, and still retained many Legionnaires who had been in Mexico since March 1863. Looting broke out and shops and private homes were pillaged. Legionnaire Amiable was there, did his share of looting and said that even officers were involved.[29] The U.S. border was close and eighty-nine Legionnaires decamped, either because they were afraid of punishment or were simply tired of the war. Amiable was not among them. When de Tuce and the other officers were able to restore some semblance of order they started back for Monterrey. The whole affair, even if partly understandable, was nevertheless a sorry blot on the regimental escutcheon.

As a result of the affair at Camargo, and the fact that Escobedo now had supplies in abundance and had replenished his treasury, Mejia decided to withdraw the Mexican Imperial Army from Matamoras. Moreover, guns were streaming across the border from the United States, both officially and unofficially, including, it appears, some of the new rapid-firing Gatling guns, which had been developed too late to be a factor in the American Civil War. Military historians have reported that their first use in warfare was in the Franco-Prussian War of 1870–71. In fact, the bloodthirsty Escobedo made effective use of them in his campaigns and has the doubtful distinction of being the first general to take automatic weapons into the field.[30]

In Europe, the Prussians were on the move again. The wily President-Minister Otto von Bismarck, seeking to extend both Prussia's influence and land mass, announced his intention of annexing the Duchies of Schleswig-Holstein, which Prussia and Austria had jointly seized from Denmark two years earlier. Austria immediately declared war and the Italians, seeing possibilities for further unification of their country, sided with Prussia in what became known as the Seven Weeks' War. Napoleon III remained neutral. Indeed, as Minister of War Randon remarked to Bazaine in a letter, France did not really know which side to favour.[31] On 3 July, at Sadowa, in Bohemia, the Prussians crushed the Austrian Army.

Even at this late point in the Intervention, Napoleon III was apparently still prepared to adhere to the Convention of Miramar as it related to the Foreign Legion.[31] Instructions were given for the raising of 7th and 8th Battalions, to bring the strength up to eight Battalions of Infantry, two Squadrons of Cavalry, two batteries of mountain guns, a Company of Engineers and a Transport Company.[32]

In Mexico City, taking advantage of the fact that Bazaine was out of the capital undertaking a military assessment of the situation in the North, Maximilian seized the opportunity to send Carlota to France to make a personal plea to Napoleon III. Her imminent departure was leaked to the French High Command by Charles de Barres, Editor of *L'Estafette*, and Bazaine's secretary sent a coded telegram to the Commander-in-Chief.[33] As it was impossible to prevent the trip, it was decided to rob it of its secrecy and a notice was inserted in the *Moniteur officiel* to the effect that the Empress was going to Europe to discuss 'the interests of Mexico and [the] settlement of various international questions'. Accompanied by her retainers, who included Maximilian's friend Charles de Bombelles, Carlota sailed from Veracruz on the Compagnie Generale Trans-atlantique's steamer *L'Imperatrice Eugenie* on 13 July.

23

The Last Farewell in Mexico

Captain Charles Blin had been looking for a war for eleven years when he finally had a chance to go to Mexico with a detachment of new troops for the 6th Battalion of the Regiment Etranger in the Summer of 1866. He had graduated from Saint-Cyr amost eleven years earlier and been posted to the 10th Regiment of the Line. It was a month after Sebastopol fell, and, having missed that war, Blin had been trying unsuccessfully to find another to get into ever since. After failing to obtain a transfer into any regiment being sent to take part in the Italian Campaign in 1859, he had tried vainly to find a regiment with whom he could go to China the following year. Despite much effort expended over almost four years, he had been unable to effect a transfer into any Mexico-bound regiment, but had not given up trying. Eventually, his perseverance paid off when he made contact with Captain Gabriel Menard de Chauglonne, who had helped to establish the Foreign Legion's Mounted Company and was now on sick leave in France. He had been replaced by Captain Henri Cartier d'Aure and was not anxious to return to Mexico, so was very happy to find someone to take his place. The necessary transfer documents were completed and approved.

Blin counted himself fortunate to be going overseas at last. He commanded one hundred and twenty men of the 6th Battalion of the Foreign Legion and sailed from St. Nazaire aboard the Compagnie Generale Trans-atlantique's steamer *La France* on 16 July. They put in at St. Thomas in the Danish Virgin Islands and Havana, Cuba, on the way to Mexico. Empress Carlota, who was going in the other direction on the *L'Imperatrice Eugenie*, also put in at Havana and St. Thomas, but she did not leave the ship. Both Blin and the Empress, in their different ways, were going to fight for Mexico, he as a soldier sent to sustain what had already been achieved, she as a mendicant to Napoleon III, begging for his continued support. Clearly, their respective ships passed each other somewhere in the Atlantic. Everything was new and exciting for Blin, and he had asked his parents to preserve his letters so that he would later have a record of his activities.[1]

On 10 August, *La France* arrived at Veracruz, carrying an assortment of soldiers from various regiments, some returning to Mexico after sick leave, and Captain Blin and his Legionnaires. He lunched with Sous-Lieutenants Baron and Gonzalez, both still serving with the Egyptian Battalion, then assembled his men, issued ammunition and marched them to the railway station to join other soldiers waiting to take the train to Paso del Macho.

The troops were commanded by a Captain of Zouaves named Voisin, and the journey hot but uneventful, until, after passing through La Soledad, several carriages were derailed close to the bridge over the Rio Jamapa. If the guerillas responsible had hoped for easy pickings they were disappointed. So many soldiers piled off the train and took up defensive positions that the would-be attackers simply melted away unseen. Voisin instructed Blin to get the majority of the men into the carriages at the front of the train, which had stayed on the rails and were still attached to the engine, and move out, while he remained behind with the derailed carriages and sixty soldiers.

A Company of the 6th Battalion, commanded by Lieutenant Charles Bablon, was manning the post at Paso del Macho. Blin thought better of the place than had the correspondent from the New York *Herald* four months earlier, finding a lively group of traders. Ex-Confederate General Jo Shelby had established a freight line between there and Mexico City, and frequent visitors included ex-General T.C. Hindman, who had opened a law office in Cordoba, close to the photographic studio operated by former Chief Justice Oldman of Texas. There was much contact with the men engaged in agricultural pursuits at the Carlota Colony. Blin bought himself a horse and led his men out the following day, through Chiquihuite, which had been abandoned, and on to Potrero, where they spent the night. Next day they reached Cordoba, where Captain Louis Morhain of the Regiment Etranger introduced Blin to the fruit drink *tepache*, which had so tickled the palate of the French-Canadian Saint-Maurice at Camerone almost two years earlier.[2]

Morhain was able to tell Blin that five of the six Foreign Legion battalions were being moved to Matehuala, while the 6th had its Headquarters at San Luis Potosi. At this point, the 1st was commanded by Vilmette, the 2nd by Saussier, the 3rd by Clemmer, the 4th by Koch, the 5th by Le Cacher de Bonneville and the 6th by Choppin-Merey.[3]

There was very little love lost between the three 'Legions' – French, Belgian and Austrian – and having them brigaded together had not improved relations very much. Foreign Legion officers often existed in testy relations with regular French Army officers and some of the Belgian officers were rather pretentious minor nobility. Compounding this prickly situation, Colonel Van der Smissen had been vocal about the 'deplorable' Foreign Legion desertions at Mier in June and Captain Ballue, now serving with the 6th Battalion at San Luis Potosi, hit back with some disparaging remarks about the courage, or lack of it, of Belgian officers, and suggested that they should be banned from the mess. In response, twenty-one Belgians sent their cards to a like number of French – mostly Foreign Legion – officers.[4] Battalion Commander Choppin-Merey was new to the regiment and the battalion and was perhaps resented, leading to a breakdown in discipline among the officers. No duels were fought as a result of this unfortunate exchange, and a potential crisis was averted when the more experienced Le Cacher de Bonneville was transferred from the 5th to the 6th and the 1st, 2nd and 5th Battalions were moved to San Luis Potosi.[5] Relations with the Austrians were not a great deal better, as their officers also often stood on the supposed dignity of their noble titles and their soldiers were generally young and untried. Moreover, news of their defeat at Camargo in mid-June, though against enormous odds, and in the face of the defection of two battalions of their Mexican allies, had been contemptuously received by officers of the Regiment Etranger, to whom surrender was an anathema.

The road from Corboba to Orizaba was still bad, but Blin marched his column into town on 16 August and the Commanding Officer seized the opportunity to attach some men of the *Bat d'Af,* including some military prisoners, to his column. They reached Mexico City[6] on 1 September. Major Joseph de Mallaret was in command at the Regiment Etranger's headquarters at the Bethleem Barracks. Blin found lodgings for himself at the Hotel Iturbide, where he met the regiment's Pay Officer, Captain Charles Pierret, who was in virtually permanent residence, along with a short-term guest, Captain Joseph Laurent. From them he learned that Colonel Guilhem was at San Luis Potosi directing the regiment's operations, and that Lieutenant-Colonel Colonna d'Ornano was in the field.[7]

The day before Blin's arrival, Marshal Bazaine had completed his plans for the withdrawal of the French forces from the inhospitable North. He had told Emperor Maximilian early in the month that this was made necessary because 'the people have no sympathy at all for the new order of established things; and the country does not offer enough resources to maintain a garrison sufficient to keep order and assure security.' The plan, he explained, would involve pulling out of the North and establishing a 'frontier' along a jagged and imaginary line running west from Tampico on the Gulf Coast. 'We are now able to reinforce the southern areas and thus, you might say, set up a new line of northern frontiers, solid and easy to guard, with a veritable arid, barren desert separating this line from the lands evacuated'.[8] It was essentially the plan suggested by Napoleon III many months earlier. Bazaine was rather more blunt in his advices to General Douay, telling him that towns and cities north of the 'frontier' would have to depend on the Mexican Imperial Army and their own resources, or make whatever peace they could with the *Juaristas,* as it was his intention to gradually pass responsibility to the Imperial generals for holding even this 'frontier', while withdrawing French troops, first to Mexico City and ultimately to the coast.[9]

Empress Eugenie called upon Empress Carlota at her Paris hotel on 10 August. The women were guarded with each other. The following day, Carlota called on Napoleon III at the Tuileries. Over the next few days she imperiously summoned Minister of War Randon and other French Ministers to her hotel, but they could promise her nothing. Napoleon III visited her at the hotel on 20 August. Carlota got nowhere with pleading, cajoling or even threatening. There were tears, too, but France, said its Emperor, would quit Mexico. He hoped that her husband could hold onto his throne, but was not prepared to expend any more money or send any more soldiers to make sure that he did. The first transatlantic cable link had reached Mexico City via New York on 13 August, and Maximilian had celebrated it by sending telegrams to Napoleon III and Queen Victoria. Now Carlota used it to advise him: 'All is useless.'

Apart from the lives and French treasure which the Mexican adventure had cost France, Napoleon was concerned about the rising might of Prussia. Under the Treaty of Prague, signed on 23 August, Austria gave up all rights to Schleswig-Holstein and allowed Prussia to annex four German States. Italy, as Prussia's ally, received the Austria Province of Venetia. The German Confederation, to which both Austria and Prussia had belonged, was abolished, and Austria would be shut out of the North German Confederation which Bismarck was planning. The

Emperor of the French had rather hoped that France might receive Mainz and part of Bavaria as a reward for having remained neutral in the Seven Weeks' War. Bismarck not only declined to make his hope a reality, but had also made it clear that Prussia viewed with disfavour Napoleon III's half-formed ideas about incorporating Belgium and Luxembourg into France. The outcome of the war had caused a profound shift in the balance of power in Europe, and far-seeing Frenchmen – even their Emperor – recognized a new reality between European nations.

In Mexico City, the Regiment Etranger was short of officers, and Major de Malleret needed to find some to accompany Captain Blin as he moved up country. Sergeant Mori, the regiment's famous prince and priest, hero of the Kabyle Campaign of 1857, and the Italian one of two years later, was now Sous-Lieutenant Charles Mori-Ubaldini,[10] and he was detailed to join Blin and his Legionnaires in a column marching to Queretaro under the command of Captain Jacques Barutel. De Malleret also obtained permission for a non-Legion officer, Sous-Lieutenant de Bru of the 5th Regiment of the Line, to accompany him.

> The column had a large number of *Clarions* and very few *Tambours* [*Blin would write later*]. Among them there was a decorated young soldier who caught my attention. He was one of the survivors of the Combat of Camerone. My memories of him have remained with me ever since.[11]

Tambour Lai was now serving with the 6th Battalion and marched with Blin and his Legionnaires to Queretaro. Their arrival on 15 September was reported to Guilhem by the telegraph. Jeanningros commanded the garrison, which included three Companies of the 6th Battalion. The Mounted Company, which had been gradually growing for some time, had reached a strength of one hundred and twenty-four men, one hundred and twenty-one horses and four mules, and had just been expanded and reorganized into two more formal Cavalry-style Squadrons. The 1st Squadron was commanded by the former Mounted Company commander, Captain Cartier d'Aure, and the 2nd by Captain Laurent. Each Squadron now had four officers and one hundred and forty-nine horses and men.[12] Both were on post at Queretaro. So was the Company of Engineers, comprising three officers, one hundred and twenty-two men and twenty-three mules. The Foreign Legion Artillery, also at Queretaro, numbered about four hundred men and five hundred mules and comprised a battery of three sections of mountain guns and three sections of field artillery.

Blin was surprised to find himself the senior officer of the 6th Battalion at Queretaro and Guilhem ordered him to take command of the entire Detachment and had him appointed to the 1st Division's War Council. In selecting one of the three Companies, Blin became its only *titulaire*, as the Lieutenant was on detached service and the Sous-Lieutenant on sick leave. Jeanningros lent him de Bru of the 5th of the Line, with whom he had come to Queretaro, and he soon learned the strengths of his Sous-Officiers.

> I had eight Sergeants [*he would recall in his memoir*]. A Swede, Fonsberg; a

> Prussian, Kopf, 22 years in the Legion; another, a former banker, Soultzener, forty years old but full of energy and activity. The Quartermaster Sergeant's name was Guernon, the Sergeant-Major Laine. Never had I been so well served. The men, like the Sous-Officiers and Corporals, were intelligent, self-sufficient, competent in everything.[13]

The 81st Regiment of the Line was the first to set out for the coast in the second half of September, but the rainy season had started and the movement of troops along the Orizaba Road was particularly difficult. Bazaine ordered the regiment held at Orizaba for the time being, and they were still there when General Henri Castelnau passed through on his way to Mexico City.

He had been named as Napoleon III's personal emissary, but given vague instructions, which inevitably caused much gossip. It was believed, correctly, that most of his efforts were to be directed at trying to persuade Emperor Maximilian to abdicate, but there was also an unlikely rumour that he was empowered, if needs be, to remove Bazaine from his command. Castelnau listened to pro-Empire, Church and ultra-Conservative elements, and to members of the Officer Corps who were jealous of the Marshal. Douay was noted for writing anti-Bazaine letters home, some of which reached Napoleon III, and Baraguey d'Hilliers was known to be in the Douay camp. Certain other officers had expressed dissatisfaction over the way in which the campaign was being conducted, and others again, who had graduated from Saint-Cyr or the *Ecole Polytechnique*, felt they were infinitely better qualified than a man who had learned the art of war fighting Arabs and Kabyles in Algeria and who was applying some of these techniques against the *Juaristas*. Little of what Castelnau did, or reported to Napoleon III, was not known to Bazaine, who rarely bothered to formally notice these matters.

> I cannot deny my humble origin [*he would remark in a letter later*]. No doubt it is because I have risen from the common people and the ranks that the envious pursue me, especially since my promotion to be Marshal; the officers who come from the special schools cannot forgive me.[14]

While Bazaine had temporarily halted the actual withdrawal of troops, he continued to plan for the orderly retirement of the forces under his command, and Guilhem was moving the Regiment Etranger around like pieces on a chessboard. Soon after two Companies arrived in Queretaro from Arroyo Sarco, Blin received orders to move his own Company to San Luis Potosi, but was recalled before reaching his destination. Vilmette's 1st Battalion was in the field with four hundred and fifty men, the Mounted Company, some of the Foreign Legion's Engineers and two mountain guns. On 15 October they surprised the enemy at Huichapan, killed thirty of them and captured fifty horses and a quantity of weapons. Captain Honore Rouvere, who had been patrolling ahead of the main column, and a Legionnaire with him, were wounded. Vilmette then moved south. Blin and his men were sent out in the direction of Huichapan eleven days later, when a strong *Juarista* force was reported to be on the move again, but after two days of marching learned that the enemy had left the area and were ordered to move to San Juan del Rio, where they spent three largely inactive weeks.

The Commander-in-Chief issued a Communique to all his commanders, telling them to remind the citizenry that a State of War still existed and that anyone found damaging, stealing from or otherwise interfering with telegraph lines or railway property would be subject to trial by court martial.[15] The Marshal's responsibilities also required that he assist and generally oversee in the creation of the Mexican armed forces, and by mid-October he was able to report that the Mexican Imperial Army now consisted of twenty-two infantry battalions and ten cavalry regiments, plus two Companies of *Gendarmerie* and some Artillery and Engineers. Together with the six thousand eight hundred and eleven members of the Austrian-Belgian 'Legion', this totalled just over twenty-four thousand men.[16]

In late October it became known in Mexico City that Empress Carlota, after her interviews with an unsympathetic Napoleon III, was showing signs of a mental breakdown. The dismal news came in the form of a telegram from his friend Charles de Bombelles. Perhaps for the first time, the Emperor of Mexico began thinking seriously about abdication. At the beginning of November, after having his personal effects and papers boxed for shipping, he left Mexico City, but went only as far as Orizaba. There, with a bodyguard of members of the *Osterreichische Freicorps*, he closeted himself with non-French advisers for a month, trying to decide whether to abdicate and leave Mexico or remain as Emperor.

On 1 December he announced his intention of returning to Mexico City and to continue as Emperor until a 'national congress gathered on the largest and most liberal basis' could meet to decide whether the country should remain as an Empire or return to being a Republic. He also appointed a Conservative Cabinet, which included Generals Leonardo Marquez, Miguel Miramon and Tomas Mejia, refused to deal with Bazaine and had as little to do with any Frenchmen as possible. Bazaine left him to his own devices and worked on the withdrawal of the French Army from the imaginary 'frontier' in the face of ever more aggressive acts by the Mexican Republican Army and their guerilla allies.

Despite the Convention of Miramar, and all that had gone before in planning and strategizing, the French evacuation was now to include the Foreign Legion. Bazaine had sought Randon's opinion as to whether they should be parts of his planning, and was holding them in readiness for either departure or for incorporation as part of the Mexican Imperial Army. When word came from the War Minister it was unequivocal.

> I have on several occasions studied the situation of the Foreign Legion [*Randon wrote*]. As I see it, the Treaty of Miramar, which had admitted the possibility of a stay of several years – this Treaty of Miramar, I say, seems to me to have been set at naught for a long time, and it seems that there can be no doubt as to the fate that must be reserved for it [the Foreign Legion], to wit, its repatriation at the same time as your other troops.[17]

Then, two weeks later, having heard rumours that Maximilian might abdicate, Randon wrote to Bazaine again.

> You ask me whether the Foreign Legion should be evacuated? [*he said*]. There is no doubt of it, since the Convention of Miramar has become a dead letter, so dead that it is likely though not certain that the Emperor Maximilian will have left Mexico before us.[18]

The logistics for effecting a smooth departure for the French Expeditionary Corps had been formidable. The wharf at Veracruz was felt to be too weak to handle the volume of departing troops and a large sum of money was needed to make repairs.[19] The railway tracks, too, were in a dilapidated condition, requiring considerable expenditure to put them in a fit state for the constant to-ing and fro-ing of trains which would be necessary.[20] Bazaine also had to enter into negotiations concerning the exchange of prisoners, in an effort to free a number of French, Belgian and Austrian troops held by the Republicans.[21]

At least he did not have to negotiate over the Foreign Legion prisoners taken at Santa Isabel. Sergeant Fiala's daring prison break with his men had solved the situation for those who were not wounded and the Mexicans had already returned those of the wounded who had survived. They had passed under the control of several Republican commanders, including Cortina, and Sous-Lieutenant Moutier would say later that there were times when they were badly treated, been poorly fed and were barefoot and in rags. On one occasion a Republican general told them that if they did not join the *Juaristas* they would be shot within twenty-four hours. They refused 'in a single voice', which impressed even Cortina, who remitted the sentence.[22] Eventually, after more than ten months, their captors put Moutier and the remaining thirty Legionnaires on board the steamer *Phlegeton* and sent them to Veracruz.[23]

Nor did Bazaine have to worry about some of the Austrian prisoners taken by Escobedo in the battle at Camargo. Lieutenant Baron Von Alvensleben, who had been one of them, had escaped from a prison camp, crossed into the United States, then led a daring raid on Matamoras to free a number of his compatriots held by the Republicans, returning with them to Veracruz.[24]

Bazain's Communique of mid-October featured later in negotiations with Porfirio Diaz concerning a cessation of hostilities if the French were allowed to withdraw along the Orizaba Road unmolested. Warnings were issued at the same time that the French would attack any Republican force which came within two days' march of any of the departing columns.[25]

The Army was taking with it as much as it could carry, including the heavy artillery, moved by wagons, which sometimes unavoidably had to cross the railway track between Paso del Macho and La Tejeria. There was occasional damage, which resulted in delays while sleepers were replaced, but overall the withdrawal was orderly and problem free. A huge tented hospital compound had been established at La Soledad and the railway line was guarded by the Egyptian Battalion, while Dupin's *Contre-guerilla* patrolled the roads and visited the villages within striking distance of the Orizaba Road. The Mexican Republican Army in the South generally adhered to the agreement between the French and Diaz, but the various guerilla bands were another matter.

The Regiment Etranger withdrew in three separate stages, the 1st Battalion, eight hundred men under Vilmette, was still in the field, continually pushing south. They received orders to proceed to the coast, but on the way to investigate reports of a large concentration of guerillas in the country around Tepeji. On mountain roads, in a blinding rainstorm, the Legionnaires laboured to move the two mountain guns and many wagons of food, munitions and baggage, often mired down in a sea of mud. On 11 December fifty men of the Foreign Legion Cavalry, with the guns, made unexpected contact with the enemy, some of whom were sniping from trees. Captain Barutel sustained a severe wound in the arm as he and Lieutenant Francois Glassier ran the two pieces of artillery up onto a small hill and opened fire, even though they could not see their quarry.

> As the first shot was fired, we saw the bandits toppling out of the trees, hurling shouts of anguish and rage [*Legionnaire Amiable remembered*]. Nothing can give a true idea of that scene, nor of the noise the detonation produced in the valley. One would have thought that the mountain was crumbling, and the cries of terror reverberating from all parts were taken up by a thousand human voices.[26]

Then, from a protected rocky area, came the sound of trumpets, first one, then two, then three, derisively playing French military marches, indicating the presence of deserters among the guerillas. Vilmette arrived with the main column and, seeing veteran Captain Dubosq, Lieutenants Rajaud and Etienne and Sous-Lieutenant Blank readying their men for a bayonet charge, the guerillas melted away into the rain and the fastness of the mountain. Vilmette had four dead and nine wounded – including Amiable – so took his men into the nearby village of Monte Alto. Installing the guns in front of the church, he had the wounded attended to and sent a rider north to report his predicament.

Surrounded by guerillas, the 1st Battalion spent a cold, wet night and in the morning Vilmette decided to fall back on Tepeji. A Squadron of *Chasseurs de France*, rapidly sent from Mexico City, found them there and helped clear the area so that they could all extricate themselves.[27] Vilmette was told to head for Veracruz and Legionnaire Amiable and the others wounded at Monte Alba were left at the field hospital at La Soledad as the battalion went on to the coast.

While Vilmette was making his first contact with the guerillas in the mountains, Sous-Lieutenant de Heckeren and fifty men of the Foreign Legion Cavalry were riding north from Tepeji to Mexico City with despatches for Bazaine. The senior Sous-Officier was Camerone survivor Karl Magnin, who had earned the *Medaille Militaire* for his defence of the southeastern breach at the Hacienda de la Trinidad and was now a Sergeant. Unaware that there were guerillas in the area, the detachment was taken by surprise when it came under fire as it approached Cuautitlan. De Heckeren led his men into the village, but quickly saw that they were likely to be surrounded. Although severely wounded, he was able to withdraw under fire and made a run for the Hacienda del Parral, which offered better protection. Sending one of his men for help, he forted up in the building and prepared to stand siege.

Memories of Camerone must have raced through the mind of Sergeant Magnin as he organized the defence, much responsibility falling on him as de Heckeren's wounds were hastily dressed. From seven in the evening until past midnight de Heckeren and the forty-nine men of the Foreign Legion Cavalry sustained a concerted attack from five hundred under the guerilla leader Fragoso, who only withdrew at the approach of a relief force under Captain Morhain and Sous-Lieutenant Maston.[28]

The 2nd Battalion of the Regiment Etranger left Mexico City, followed a few days later by the 3rd and 4th Battalions. The 5th and 6th would be the last to depart, and while de Heckeren's stand at Parral was essentially the last Foreign Legion battle in Mexico, minor skirmishes and police actions were still fairly common in the 'frontier' area. Blin, for example, saw, in these last days of the Intervention, the only real action of his seven months in Mexico. On 20 December he was sent with two Companies of the 6th Battalion and a Squadron of Foreign Legion Cavalry on 'a little operation' against guerillas in the direction of the village of Iskla. The Cavalry, ranging ahead, quickly overwhelmed the Mexican outposts, but left their own foot soldiers far behind.

> After thirty hours of marching [*Blin recalled*], our men, weighed down by their heavy sacs, arrived just in time to fire several volleys as two or three hundred of the band fled as fast as they could from the locality.[29]

He returned to Queretaro in time for the general withdrawal. The ships chartered to take the Expeditionary Corps home had been arriving at Veracruz and French regiments were held at Orizaba, so that the capacity of each ship could be telegraphed, at which time approved detachments would then begin to make their way to Paso del Macho to take the train to the coast. On 20 January the Belgian Volunteer Corps embarked at Veracruz. The following day the *Osterreichische Freicorps* was embarked. Some of its officers, including Lieutenant Baron Max von Alvensleben, had elected to stay in Mexico with their countryman the Emperor, and watched grimly as General de Thun took ship. 'His departure called forth extreme bitterness among the officers of the Imperial Legion,' he would say later.[30]

Blin and the 5th and 6th Battalions left Mexico City for Veracruz on 29 January, forming the guard for a convoy taking wives, civilians and their possessions, including the family of Marshal Bazaine.[31] The Commander-in-Chief remained behind, tying up administrative loose ends and issuing a series of Orders of the Day commending the regiments under his command. On 31 January it was the turn of the Regiment Etranger, and, in a wide-ranging overview of its role in the Expeditionary Corps, he made special mention of Camerone:

> The Regiment Etranger preserves the memory of Captain Danjou and the Sous-Lieutenants Maudet and Vilain and of the 62 brave men who, after a cruel struggle of 12 hours, despite having fired their last cartridges and made more than 300 of their adversaries pay the price, believed it was useless to submit and charged with the bayonet fixed, ready to die for the honour of their flag.[32]

Just after midnight on 3 February, deep in the *Terres Chaudes* at La Soledad, shots were heard coming from the direction of Camaron. The Regiment Etranger's Mounted Company and a Squadron of *Chasseurs de France* headed west at once, passed through Palo Verde and surprised stragglers from a group of eight hundred guerillas, who were reportedly planning to descend on Veracruz via the northern road. A dozen were captured and taken back to La Soledad. Within hours they were tried, and nine of them convicted of being found in arms against the French. The other three convinced their captors that they had been taken from their villages by force, so were each given fifty lashes with a rope and released. The convicted nine were executed by Dupin and the *Contre-guerilla* and their bodies left hanging by the road as a warning.

Bazaine issued his final Proclamation o the Mexican people the same day and left Mexico City on 5 February, going into camp just five kilometres (about three miles) away. He wrote a last letter to Maximilian, urging him to abdicate and join the withdrawing forces, but his messenger, tartly told that the Emperor would not receive the letter, was turned away. Bazaine had been extremely critical when President Juarez abandoned the capital in June 1863, leaving it without any form of civilian authority or law enforcement, so had made arrangements to stay in the area until informed that General Marquez of the Mexican Imperial Army had taken control. Once this was done, Bazaine moved on, caught up with Blin's convoy[33] and reached Puebla on 10 February.

Determined to reach Paris ahead of Bazaine, Castelnau took the *diligence* from Puebla to Veracruz to catch the French mailboat, while the Commander-in-Chief checked all the defences of the city prior to handing it over to Imperial troops. While there he received word that Marquez had unleashed a reign of terror and victimization in Mexico City, and at once telegraphed French Ambassador Alphonse Dano, asking him to once again urge Maximilian to join him for safe passage out of Mexico. The telegram arrived some hours after the Emperor had left to join his Imperial troops at Queretaro. Bazaine went on to Orizaba, then left the column under the command of Castaguy and headed east with a small group to oversee the evacuation at Veracruz. The 1st Battalion of the Regiment Etranger had already reached the coast, and the fourteen officers and five hundred men embarked on the *Pomone* on 18 February. The forty-five officers and nine hundred and seventy-nine men of the 2nd Battalion boarded the *Var* three days later.

Jeanningros was with the 5th and 6th Battalions. Leaving Captain Paul Lafontaine in the Hospital de San Jose de Gracia in Orizaba, they passed through Cordoba, marched on past the abandoned camp at Chiquihuite and arrived at Paso del Macho. Sick men were put on the train and sent ahead to the hospital at La Soledad, but Jeanningros had decreed that the main column should march to La Soledad, so they went on down the Orizaba Road, reaching Camerone on 25 February.

'During one of our last marches in the *Terres Chaudes* we reached Camerone on our way to camp at Palo Verde,' Blin recalled in his memoir. 'General Jeanningros was present. We formed a square around the grave of the Legion. The General said a few words of farewell.'[34]

Officers and soldiers of the Legion [*Jeanningros intoned*]. I have halted you here to say a last farewell to our brave companions in arms[,] dead on the field of honour. They fought[,] 60 against 2000; their heroic action will pass into posterity in the annals of our military pages in Mexico. They are dead on this foreign soil for the honour and the glory of our beautiful France. They died bringing order and civilization to this remote land. Honour to you, brave officers and soldiers; we bid you farewell, farewell Captain Danjou, farewell our brave comrades, your memory will never be effaced from our hearts and one day, if France and our Emperor have need of us, we will, like you, vanquish or die.[35]

The memory of Camerone was more poignant for some than for others. It is not known if any of the survivors were present, but Lieutenant Adolphe Gans, the sole remaining officer of the 3rd of the 1st, who had been too sick to accompany his men on the ill-fated reconnaissance, was there, and was deeply affected by the proceedings.

'During the ceremony I found myself standing close to Lieutenant Gans,' said Blin. 'He was desolate, and said to me in an emotion-charged voice: "My place should have been there." Then we marched past the grave, with the flag lowered'.[36]

It is not clear how the grave was marked at the time. Sous-Lieutenant Maine, who would certainly have stopped at Camerone on his way to the coast, later spoke of 'a broken column entwined with a garland of laurel leaves' with the inscription: 'Their glory and duty'.[37]

The two battalions went on to Palo Verde, camped for the night, then marched on to La Soledad. Blin sold his horse, and took the train to Veracruz. Less than twenty-four hours later guerillas tried to burn the trestle bridge over the Rio Jamapa, but the timber was still green, and wet from the rains, and the minimal damage was quickly repaired by French Engineers. The Foreign Legion Cavalry and the *Contre-guerilla* left La Soledad to hunt for the culprits and Dupin reportedly caught and hanged several of them. The 3rd and 4th Battalions were in Veracruz when the 5th and 6th arrived. On 27 February a total of forty-seven officers and one thousand one hundred and forty-nine men from the 3rd and 4th embarked on the *Tarn*, while the Regimental Headquarters staff and the 5th and 6th Battalions boarded the *Aveyron*, a total of fifty-two officers and one thousand one hundred and twenty-nine men.

In Blin's luggage was a silver-handled sabre, which he had been told had once belonged to President Juarez,[38] some Aztec manuscripts given to him by a Professor of Antiquities and the Cross of a Chevalier of the Legion of Honour once worn proudly by Camerone survivor *Tambour* Lai.[39] There is no clue as to how in came into Blin's possession. It seems unlikely that Lai would have sold it or given it away, so it may be that the little drummer, with whom Blin had marched and fought in the North, died during the campaign.

Bazaine himself oversaw the final evacuation. The Egyptian Battalion boarded *La Seine* on 12 March, the same ship which had brought them to Mexico more than four years earlier. Sous-Lieutenant Gabriel Baron of the Foreign Legion, who had been their leader, mentor and guide for so much of their time in the *Terres*

Chaudes, went with them, first to Toulon, then Paris, and finally to Alexandria, where he was personally thanked by the Khedive and made an officer of the Order of Majidiyya.[40]

The Commander-in-Chief, with his small son and pregnant wife, also embarked on 12 March, going aboard the *Souvereign*. Unlike Mexico City, Puebla, Orizaba and Cordoba, where troops of the Mexican Imperial Army took over as the French left, it was troops of the Mexican Republican Army who were closing in or Veracruz. Even so, the French fleet remained close to the Isla de los Sacrificios to ensure an orderly change of authority. General R. Benavides, arriving on the outskirts of the city on 15 March, saw seventeen French ships riding at anchor,[41] but they left as soon as he had entered Veracruz and taken control. Perhaps it was troops under Benavides, or more likely guerillas with them, who, in the euphoria of seeing the hated French leave, desecrated the grave of the 3rd of the 1st at Camaron. Nobody knows for sure.

'The monument was destroyed by an unknown and sacrilegious hand when the Republican regime was restored,' Captain Sebastian I. Campos, who had fought the French at Camerone, would write later. '[It was done by] someone who certainly knew of the unyielding patriotism represented by the remains of those heroes who succumbed and were vanquished in loyal combat'.[42]

Sailing for home, the Regiment Etranger counted its losses.

It had commenced the campaign with one hundred officers, of whom sixteen died from one cause or another in the just less than four years that the regiment was in Mexico. Many others resigned, or were transferred out on promotion. Only thirty-one of the original hundred – including Saussier, Zede and Giovanninelli, all future generals – were still with the regiment at the end of the campaign. More and more officers had come into the regiment, of course, as additional Battalions were created. Captain Lafontaine, who had been left in hospital in Orizaba, died there. Lieutenant-Colonel Emile Colonna d'Ornano died on board the ship as it was returning to Algeria, and two other officers would die within a few days of landing.

In all, the campaign in Mexico cost the French Expeditionary Corps five thousand, three hundred and forty-nine officers and men, of whom just over one third came from a single source: the Regiment Etranger. It lost thirty-one officers – nineteen killed in combat and twelve dead of diseases – and three hundred and twenty-eight Sous-Officiers and men, who died in combat or of wounds received. A staggering one thousand, five hundred and eighty-nine succumbed to diseases of one kind or another, mostly *vomito negro*. Total losses: one thousand, nine hundred and forty-eight.[43]

24
Fighting for France

Marshal Achille Bazaine took his Army back to a France which provided no welcoming pageantry, or parades or banquets. General Charles Thoumas said that the Commander-in-Chief successfully disengaged and evacuated twenty-eight thousand six hundred and ninety-three men,[1] but there was no official thanks for it, no flags or bunting in the streets of Toulon, or of Paris, no cheering crowds. The truth was that the Mexican Expedition had been long, expensive in lives, a drain on the national treasury and ultimately unpopular with the politicians. Only the public lauded Bazaine because he had been careful with soldiers' lives, and the Emperor was privately warm.

The Regiment Etranger's eight battalions – six of infantry, and the two comprising the two Squadrons of Cavalry, two batteries of Artillery and the Engineering company – trickled back into Mers-el-Kebir. The 1st and 2nd arrived on 26 March, with Colonel Pierre Guilhem and the Headquarters Company landing four days later. In his baggage was the articulated wooden hand of Captain Danjou.[2] Captains Ernest Munier and Nicolas Brout came ashore sick and were dead within a matter of days of returning from Mexico. Less than a week after his arrival Guilhem found himself faced with presiding over a massive regimental reorganization, following an Imperial Decision of 4 April ordering the reduction of the Regiment Etranger to three battalions, each with eight Companies.[3]

By 26 April all the battalions had landed and been distributed to various garrison towns around Algeria and the cutbacks in personnel began. Commandant Gustave Saussier – promoted to Lieutenant-Colonel – left the regiment after a seventeen-year career to join the 29th of the Line, and subsequently to command the 41st. Lieutenant Charles Zede transferred out after ten years. Sous-Lieutenant Philippe Maine's records – backdated to a day before the Imperial Decision – show that he was made up to Lieutenant on 3 April, undoubtedly the intention being to give him a little more status and pay when he transferred into the 119th of the Line ten days later.[4] They were just three of the eighty-four officers re-assigned to other regiments of the French Army, along with three hundred and eighty-seven Sous-Officiers and Corporals.

Word reached France that Emperor Maximilian had been captured, then executed by the Mexicans on 19 June, along with Generals Miguel Miramon and Tomas Mejia. The compassionate Chaplain Lanusse was moved to travel to Brussels to see ex-Empress Carlota,[5] but in Algeria the news was of little more than academic interest. Of much more concern was Colonel Guilhem's departure in August. Promoted to General, he handed over to Colonel Deplanque, who transferred in from the 7th of the Line and arrived just in time to oversee further cuts. These sent two hundred and seventy-four French-born Legionnaires into the 92nd of the Line and annulled the Acts of Engagement of nine hundred and fifty-two foreigners who had less than a year to serve. Chaplain Lanusse went off to his third war, travelling to Italy again with a French Expeditionary Corps, and was present in November at the defeat of Guiseppe Garibaldi at Mentana, ending his bid to topple the Papal State.[6] Dupin had dropped a rank to Major when Napoleon III reintegrated him into the French Army and was dead within a year, rumour said as a result of poisoning.

The slimmed-down Regiment Etranger went back to its normal role of policing Algeria, building roads and establishing strongpoints. Famine stalked the land and men lived on little more than biscuits in the isolated blockhouses and forts. Cholera broke out. In Paris, there was more post-war tinkering and on 22 January 1868 an unpopular Imperial Decision was handed down putting an end to the *Compagnies d'elite* – the Grenadiers and Voltigeurs – and creating *Deuxieme Soldats* – Second Class Soldiers – meaning new recruits and unpromotable Old Sweats, and *Premier Soldats* – First Class Soldiers – those earmarked for possible promotion to Corporal and above.[7] A little more than a year later, on 31 March 1869, came a more popular decision, with the Battle Honour OAJACA 1865 being approved for the Regimental Standard.[8]

Military artist Jean-Adolphe Beauce was still creating his Mexican Expedition paintings. His canvas 'The Last Hour of Camerone,' which the Canadian soldier-observer Faucher de Saint-Maurice had seen him working on in his Mexico City studio in the early Summer of 1865, had not been completed when the French evacuated the capital, and ultimately the country. Now, at his leisure, Beauce had resumed work on it. The finished painting, re-titled 'Le fin du combat' – 'The end of the battle' – caused more than a minor ripple in the Summer of 1869 when shown in the Salon in Paris.[9] Beauce depicted Sous-Lieutenant Maudet, at the head of the tiny bunch of survivors, advancing into the courtyard sword in hand. Various critics liked the overall thrust of the painting, but thought it unlikely that Maudet would have come out of the ruins of the old barn with his sword, asserting that after firing his last cartridge he would, like his men, have gone in with the bayonet, as, in fact, Regnault, Maine and Fritz had said was the case. A more fundamental criticism was that the uniforms were wrong, the soldiers depicted as Grenadiers, rather than Fusiliers. Nevertheless, the very striking and evocative painting was immediately bought by the State.

Soldiers who had fought in Mexico, civilians who had held posts at the Court of Maximilian and Carlota, and assorted historians, were busy bursting into print, providing publishers in France, Belgium and Austria, as well as Germany and England, and as far away as the United States, with the inevitable rush of war diaries, reminiscences, memoirs, autobiographies and official and semi-official histories which follow any war.

Accounts published in Belgium were quite numerous, beginning with Count Emile de Keratry's *L'Empereur Maximilien, son elevation et sa chute, apres les documents inedits par le Compte Emile de Keratry* in 1867. It was published the same year in Leipzig, and appeared in English as *The Rise and Fall of the Emperor Maximilian. A Narrative of the Mexican Empire, 1861–67. From Authentic*

Documents two years later. Among the other books was *Souvenirs d'un officier belge, 1864–66* by Emile Walton, a Lieutenant in the 2nd *Chasseurs a Pied* of the Belgian Volunteer Legion, who had visited Camerone, whose memoir was published in 1868, and *Le Mexique et la Legion belge 1864–67* by Captain Claude J. Des Loiseau of the Carabiniers, another visitor to Camerone, published in 1870.

British publishers were quick off the mark, too. An English-language edition of the memoirs of Austrian-born Baron Max von Alvensleben, who had served as a Lieutenant in the Mexican Imperial Army, was published in London in 1867 as *With Maximilian in Mexico*, and *With the French in Mexico* by J.F. Elton, a British officer who had been loosely attached to the French forces, came out the same year, and was also published in the United States. *The Court of Mexico*, a memoir by Countess Paola Kollonitz, former a lady-in-waiting to Empress Carlota, also appeared from a London publisher the following year.

Perhaps because the Mexican Expedition had been unpopular, French publishers anticipated a smaller reading public and were slower to react, but Emmanuel Domenech's two-volume *Histoire du Mexique. Juarez et Maximilien* was published in 1868. The author of two earlier books on Mexico, he had been Chaplain to the French Army, and Director of the Press for Maximilian. Count de Keratry's memoir *La Contre-Guerilla Francaise au Mexique (Souvenirs des terres chaudes)* appeared the following year.

The national disputes, muscle-flexing and wars of mid-19th-century Europe were invariably about territorial gain or loss, or fears on one country's part about the supposed expansionist ambitions, or actual intent, of another. The Crimean War was fought partly because Russia had invaded the Danubian Provinces of the Ottoman Empire, and Britain and France believed that the Russians had designs on Turkey itself. Both wanted to keep the Tsar's navy out of the Mediterranean. Sardinia-Piedmont joined the Allies because it wanted to make powerful friends for its ultimate hopes of unifying Italy. Napoleon III helped them in the 1859 struggle against Austria, and for his trouble added Nice and Savoy to his own country's landmass. France had stood on the sidelines in 1864 when Prussia and Austria took Schleswig and Holstein from Denmark, and had remained neutral – and unrewarded – two years later when Prussia went to war with Austria and defeated Emperor Franz Joseph's army.

Bismarck had then embarked on building up the Prussian Army and armaments, excluded Austria from the North German Confederation he brought into being in 1867, and looked for an opportunity for a war which would definitively lock the small South German States into William I's domain. The pieces he needed began to fall into place because of a revolution in Spain in 1868. In due course, he proposed Prince Leopold of the House of Hohenzollen – of which William I of Prussia was a member – as the new King of Spain. This required the approval of Napoleon III, who withheld it. As Leopold was an officer in the Prussian Army, and France may legitimately have been fearful of having a potential enemy on its southern border, in addition to one to the east, Napoleon III's position seemed reasonable, even if there were suspicions that approval was withheld as a way of getting back at Prussia. William I agreed that Leopold's name should be withdrawn, and that should have been the end of the matter, but then the Emperor of the French wanted an undertaking that no Hohenzollen would ever be King of Spain, and sent his Ambassador, Vincente Benedetti, to make the demand. Not unnaturally, the King of Prussia, then in his Summer retreat at Ems, saw this as an insult. On three occasions he refused to see the French Ambassador and sent a report to Bismarck, who recognized it as the moment he had sought. He made public what became known as 'The Ems Dispatch', but changed his monarch's words to have it appear that France's diplomat had come as some kind of mendicant beggar and had been smartly shown the palace door.

Napoleon III was livid. The Council of State met on 14 July – the French national holiday, when jingoism and wine are always in abundance – and decided that the country's honour had been offended. The National Assembly supported this view the next day and France declared war on Prussia on 19 July. There was some surprise in Paris when the South German States proceeded to make common cause with Prussia and the North German Confederation. A French Army of three hundred thousand found itself facing a Prussian Army four times as large, but over-confident Frenchmen nevertheless swarmed into the streets shouting 'To Berlin! To Berlin!' The Emperor himself took to the field with his troops.

The German offensive was launched on 6 August. Prussians and Bavarians steam-rollered their way into Alsace and Lorraine, destroying the French Army as they went. Marshal MacMahon was defeated at Worth. Chaplain Lanusse was in the field again[10] and by mid-month Marshal Bazaine and one hundred and eighty thousand men had been essentially bottled up in the fortress of Metz. Small battles gave the French some minor victories, but did nothing to change the war, and the Prussians gradually tightened their siege lines. The Regiment Etranger was still in Algeria, but the Zouaves and *Tirailleurs Algeriens* had already been in action against the Prussians. With Napoleon III in the field with his Army, Empress Eugenie issued an Imperial Decree on 22 August authorizing the formation of a 5th Battalion of the Regiment Etranger, to take in the numerous aliens rallying to the French flag 'for the duration' of the war.[11]

Some Camerone survivors were still in the Regiment Etranger, others in regular French Army regiments.

Hippolyte Kunassec was serving in the 57th of the Line, which, like the other French units, was hard pressed by the enemy. Promoted from Fusilier to Voltigeur after being returned to the French lines in July 1863, he had received the *Medaille Militaire* and made Corporal a month later, but his two-year enlistment had been coming to an end and he did not re-engage. By November he was back in Paris, once again a civilian, but in July 1864 went back into the Army, signing on with the 57th Regiment for seven years. By 1867 he was a Sergeant, and now he would soon once more be a prisoner-of-war.[12]

The former Corporal Maine had left the Regiment Etranger as a Lieutenant in 1867 to transfer into the 119th of the Line, but, ever-restless, had stayed with them only some fourteen months before transferring into 3rd *Infanterie de Marine* on 25 November 1868. He had gone with them to Cochin-China, but left Saigon on 10 March 1870, at the end of his tour of duty, arriving at Toulon on 30 April, the seventh anniversary of the Combat of Camerone, a date which may not have been lost on him.[13]

Accompanied by MacMahon, Napoleon III set out to relieve Metz, but at

Sedan, northeast of Paris, was engaged on 1 September by Prussian forces under the personal command of William I. MacMahon was wounded early in the fighting and the French suffered huge losses. The *Division de Marine* – the *Division Bleue*, four Infantry Regiments and three Artillery Batteries, commanded by General Vassoigne – had thirty-five officers killed and seventy wounded, along with two thousand six hundred and fifty-five other ranks. Less than a hundred men under Battalion Commander Lambert forted up in a house in Bazeilles, made a desperate last stand and fought for ten hours against overwhelming odds.

When the last cartridges had been fired, bayonets were fixed and Lambert led the handful of survivors through the door and into the yard. Captain Lissignolo of the Bavarian Infantry had served eight years in the Regiment Etranger. Who can say if the Combat of Camerone was in his mind as he ran between the besiegers and the besieged, and used his sabre to knock up the barrels of his men's rifles?.[14]

The following day, with three thousand dead and fourteen thousand wounded, the French surrendered. Along with the Emperor and MacMahon, the Prussians counted thirty-nine generals among the more than one hundred thousand prisoners, who included Sergeant Kunassec and Lieutenant Maine. Chaplain Lanusse was there, of course, ministering to the soldiers as they were marched away as prisoners-of-war. In Paris, Napoleon III's son was declared Emperor, with Eugenie as Regent. This Third Empire lasted three days, then the monarchy was toppled and the newly-proclaimed Third Republic began peace negotiations. The Prussians were besieging the city, and soldiers were being killed every day – including General Guilhem, late Colonel of the Regiment Etranger, on 9 September – but the peace terms were considered too humiliating. Leon Gambetta, the new Minister of Justice, staged a dramatic escape from Paris in a balloon, established himself at Tours, declared a dictatorship and began raising an Army of 30 Divisions.

Many French soldiers escaped from the Prussians, including Lieutenant Maine, who got away after only fifteen days of captivity. He was promoted to Captain on 23 September, and, with his regiment shattered, was put in charge of a company of *Franc-Tireurs* – unattached, free-ranging sharpshooters – operating out of the old *Infanterie de Marine* base at Rochefort. Later he was made a temporary Lieutenant-Colonel in command of *Mobiles* attached to the Army of the Loire. Kunassec also escaped from his captors, made his way back to French-held territory and was put into the 90th of the Line.[15]

The fourteen hundred 'for the duration' men of the newly-raised 5th Battalion of the Regiment Etranger did their training – without weapons – at Tours. Their Commanding Officer was Major Victor Joseph Arago, a graduate of Saint-Cyr who had served in the Crimea, Algeria and Italy. Among the volunteers was Prince Peter Karageorgevitch of the Serbian Royal Family, who had studied at Saint-Cyr in the early 1860s and signed 'for the duration' under the name of Kara. (More than thirty years later he would be King Peter of Serbia.) It was already known that on 22 September orders had been sent to Algeria for the despatch of two battalions of the Regiment Etranger, each a thousand strong – from which all German elements were to be excluded[16] – and in the meantime, the 5th Battalion became part of the 15th Army Corps under General de la Motterouge.

On 10 October, facing General von der Tann's 1st Bavarian Corps, the 22nd

Prussian Infantry Division and two cavalry divisions, de la Motterouge decided to retire across the River Loire. The next day the 5th Battalion made a stand at the village of Bel-Air-Les-Aides, outside Orleans. Arago was killed during the afternoon and the men fell back on the suburb of Bannier. There was desperate and unrelenting fighting, a bloody contest for every inch of ground, and by the time the Bavarians and Prussians had taken the town the 5th Battalion had lost some eight hundred men and the survivors were trying to slip through the enemy lines to rejoin the main French forces. Kara escaped disguised as a miller, but many were captured.[17]

In Algeria, the Regiment Etranger, because of its heavy German make-up, had encountered great difficulty in raising two battalions of the required strength. Along with the Germans, men believed likely to be physically unable to withstand a Winter campaign, were transferred into the 3rd and 4th Battalions, and the 1st and 2nd Battalions, eventually only fourteen hundred and ninety strong, commanded by Colonel Deplanque, landed at Toulon on the very day the 5th Battalion was in action at Bannier. Taken by train to Bourges, they were joined on the 19 October by the tattered survivors of that bloodbath.[18]

General d'Aurelle de Paladines, who had replaced de la Motterouge, was ordered to retake Orleans. Chaplain Lanusse was with this new Army of the Loire.[19] Prussian General von der Tann had been authorized to evacuate the city and fight in the countryside if faced with a French force of substantially superior numbers. The two sides met in battle at Coulmiers on 9 November. Among the enemy officers facing the section of the 15th Army Corps which involved the Regiment Etranger was Captain Ernest Milson von Bolt of the Prussian Hussars. Serving simply as Sous-Lieutenant Milson, eight years earlier he had been the first of the Regiment Etranger's officers in Mexico to be mentioned in an Order of the Day, and had then received the Cross of a Chevalier of the Legion of Honour. Now he was a senior Staff Officer with von der Tann. Watching through his telescope as the French advanced, Milson recognized the Regiment Etranger, moving forward steadily as *La Musique* play the stirring march Monsieur Wilhelm had composed prior to their departure for Mexico. It now had a name – *Le Boudin*, meaning blood sausage – and would come to be adopted as the Foreign Legion's anthem. Many of the Legionnaires were wearing their *Expedition du Mexique* medals – among them Belgian-born Camerone survivor Felix Brunswick, Chevalier of the Legion of Honour, and now holding the rank of Sergeant. Word filtered back later that, on recognizing his former comrades of the Regiment Etranger, Milson von Bolt ordered the Prussian artillery to cease firing and withdraw from the sector.[20] At any rate, Coulmiers, where the Regiment Etranger distinguished itself with a bayonet charge, was a French victory, the defeated Prussians leaving two thousand prisoners in French hands, and Orleans was evacuated two days later.

On 28 October came the shattering news that Bazaine, bottled up in Metz since August, his troops and the townspeople facing starvation, had capitulated, with a hundred and thirty thousand men and fourteen hundred guns. Milson von Bolt was again on hand, this time as a Staff Officer to his cousin, Prince Frederic-Charles, and visited the officer prisoners. General du Barail would recall later that 'with much good grace' he offered his assistance to 'officers he had known' in Mexico, but they 'all declined' his overtures.[21] Among those known to Captain von

Bolt was General Pierre Jeanningros, now commanding a Brigade of the Imperial Guard. He had already incurred Prussian displeasure by refusing to surrender his Regimental Standard and other banners to his captors. 'Our flags have been torn up on my orders, the staffs and the Eagles sawed up, and the pieces distributed among my two regiments,' he declared. 'The flags of my Brigade will not be going to Berlin.'[22] Captain von Bolt also knew Lieutenant-Colonel Saussier, who had similarly refused to hand over his Regimental Standard, led his officers in signing a statement of objection, then given both to Marshal Leboeuf, making their surrender his responsibility. Saussier had also declined to be paroled, declaring that it was his intention to escape. He subsequently did so – twice – and returned to France to fight again before the war was over.[23]

The capitulation of Metz freed two hundred thousand Prussian troops to conduct the war elsewhere and the French Government of National Defence now created an Army of the East. Colonel Deplanque was promoted to General and handed over command of the Regiment Etranger to Colonel de Curten. Then, in the mad disorganization of the French Army, de Curten was also made up to General, his place being taken by Battalion Commander Canat, who was promoted to Lieutenant-Colonel. The Regiment Etranger, now reduced to about a thousand men, began a retreat from Orleans on 4 December and was joined a week later at Chapelle-Saint-Ursin by a group of Irishmen who had come to France ostensibly to form an Irish Ambulance Brigade, but ended up offering their services as soldiers, which may, in fact, have been their original intention.

Led by an embryo soldier-of-fortune named Martin Waters Kirwan, they reported themselves to Canat, who decided to keep them together as the 8th Company of the 5th Battalion, where they became known as *La Compagnie Irlandaise*.[24] Regimental records indicate that Kirwan's command comprised himself, a Sous-Lieutenant, six Sous-Officiers, eight Corporals, a Trumpeter and seventy-six men. Kirwan's own account has his unit made up of himself, Lieutenant Patrick Cotter, Sous-Lieutenant Frank M'Alevey, a Dr. Macken, nine Sous-Officiers, eleven Corporals and seventy-six men, making a round total of one hundred.[25]

M'Alevey, the former Corporal in the 1st Company of the 1st Battalion in Mexico – was remembered by Kirwan as being very popular with the regiment. 'Sunshine or shower, feast or famine, M'Alevey was always the same jovial, joyous fun-maker; occasionally flirting, but ever the essence of wit, good humour, and joviality,' he said. 'His jokes generally went round the regiment.'[26]

Almost two thousand young Breton volunteers were drafted into the Regiment Etranger and, as part of the Army of the East, the 1st, 2nd and 5th Battalions, each now a thousand strong, were packed into trains in bitter weather and sent eastwards towards Besancon. They were on the move for days, with few supplies and no heat, spending Christmas Day at Vierzon, before being sent on to Clarval.[27]

After supper around their campfire on the evening of 16 January 1871, with a march to Montbeliard due to begin at midnight, the normally jovial Sous-Lieutenant M'Alevey grew thoughtful, telling Kirwan, Cotter and Dr. Macken: 'I was just thinking of a circumstance that happened in 1863, when I was in Mexico, and when I lost the dearest of my comrades; and who knows whether we four shall ever see another night together in this world?' Encouraged by the others, he talked about Captain Danjou, his special friend Sergeant Marie Morziki, of watching the men of the 3rd Company of the 1st Battalion march away from Chiquihuite, his own presence with Jeanningros' relief column, and of burying of the bodies at the Hacienda de la Trinidad.

> Since then [*M'Alevey told his companions*], I have stepped over the dead and dying on many a battlefield, and have seen men shoot one another down amid the horrid din of artillery, but the sight was not half so horrible or terrifying as the silent dead of Camerone.[28]

At Montbeliard the Regiment Etranger was thrown against the Prussians. Kirwan was wounded on the first day, M'Alevey on the second,[29] and the unequal struggle between the entrenched and well-provisioned Prussians and the ragtag, half-starved French ended in stalemate, the last battle of the Franco-Prussian War. In Paris, meanwhile, the victorious Prussians were attending to some housekeeping, and on 18 January, while the Army of the East was fighting at Montbeliard, William I of Prussia was at the Palace of Versailles, having himself crowned as the German Emperor. Besieged since October, the city was being starved into submission, and Bismarck and Jules Favre signed an Armistice ten days later. It did not apply to the Army of the East, who fought on for another six weeks.

The Regiment Etranger, the 39th Regiment of the Line – with whom they were brigaded – and the 44th Regiment *de Marche*, commanded by Lieutenant-Colonel Pascase Achilli, formerly of the Regiment Etranger in Mexico, bore the brunt of a number of skirmishes and firefights. Achilli refused to allow his men to join in the general French retreat and was killed at Cluze. Chaplain Lanusse, serving once more with General Bourbaki, was with him as most of what was left of the Army of the East slipped over the border into Switzerland to sit out the rest of the war in internment camps.[30] Following the general acceptance of the Armistice, the French demobilization began and orders came for the Regiment Etranger to discharge all the 'for the duration' volunteers and all soldiers whose service had commenced in 1863. In four days four hundred and fifteen men were demobilized,[31] including Kirwan's *Compagnie Irlandaise*, with the exception of Lieutenant Cotter, who elected to remain in the Foreign Legion.[32]

As well as land concessions and financial compensation, Prussian demands had included a victory march through the centre of Paris and to this the citizens objected. Revolutionaries seized the city, raised the Red Flag, set up the Commune, mobilized the National Guard and defied the French Government. MacMahon was ordered to take the city with his Army of Paris and on 27 March the sixty-six officers and one thousand and three men still remaining in the Regiment Etranger, accompanied by the 39th of the Line, set off for the capital to join the troops being sent against the Communards. Chaplain Lanusse, serving with his fourth Army in nine months, was on hand to minister to those in need.[33] The fighting in the streets of Paris was bloody and thankless, and cost many military lives, as well as those of at least twenty-five thousand Communards.

Captain Maine had his Legion of Honour decoration upgraded in rank from Chevalier to Officer on 5 May 1871 and, with the *Infanterie de Marine* still recruiting and reforming, went out to West Africa the following month on detached service, to take command of one of the eight Companies of the Battalion of the *Tirailleurs Senegalese*.[34]

President Louis Adolphe Thiers, who headed the new French government, and Bismarck signed the Treaty of Frankfurt on 10 May. It gave Prussia millions of francs in reparations, as well as most of Alsace and part of Lorraine. Now that it was formally over and their job completed the Regiment Etranger left Paris on 11 June, embarked at Toulon, disembarked at Mers-el-Kebir and were back in barracks at Mascara eleven days later.[35] The war had cost the French one hundred and fifty-six thousand dead and one hundred and forty-three thousand wounded, the Germans twenty-eight thousand dead and one hundred thousand wounded.

'In 1863 it was the body that bled,' remarked Chaplain Lanusse, who took up an appointment as Chaplain at the *Ecole Speciale Militaire* at Saint-Cyr on 10 August. 'In 1870 it was the heart which bled.'[36]

In the absence from Algeria of the 1st and 2nd Battalions, the largely German 3rd and 4th Battalions had acquitted themselves well. Because he was a German-speaking Swiss, Captain Henri-Guido Kauffmann, who had been a Headquarters Officer with Colonel Jeanningros in Mexico, had not been sent to France, as his linguistic skills were expected to be needed in Algeria. Many of the Germans who had volunteered 'for the duration' had been shipped across the Mediterranean and put into Kauffmann's 6th Company of the 4th Battalion. Training went well, perhaps because he had himself started as a common Legionnaire, perhaps because of the calibre – and possibly prior military training – of many of the 'durationists'.

In April 1871, while the 1st and 2nd Battalions were in Paris battling the Communards, a French column under the overall command of Lieutenant-Colonel des Meloizes was detailed to undertake an Observation Mission towards the border with Morocco. Trouble was not expected, as the strong column was made up of two Squadrons of *Chasseurs de France*, a Squadron of Spahis, three companies of indigenous irregular infantry and two light mountain guns, as well as Kauffmann's 6th Company of the 4th Battalion, many of whose two hundred and eighteen men had never been under fire. The column was divided in order to cover more ground and when Kauffmann moved into open country near Magourah he was attacked by a vastly superior force of enemy cavalry. The rapid fire of his men forced the enemy to break off the attack and turn their attention to the French irregulars, and in driving them off, the Captain of the Spahis and one of the Captains of the *Chasseurs de France* were killed.

Kauffmann established an unorthodox square, formed on three sides by his 6th Company and on the fourth by the cavalry, placing himself, the *Clarion* and the mountain guns in the centre. He succeeded in moving towards a piece of high ground in the middle of the plain. The enemy, now estimated at about two thousand, attacked the right side of the square with cavalry and the left with infantry. Once again they were driven off with heavy losses. The 6th Company had been well and truly blooded and stayed with the Observation Column until mid-June, when they reached Tlemcen, at roughly the time that the 1st and 2nd Battalions returned to Algeria from France. Kauffmann received a sword of honour from his Commanding Officer and the men of the 6th Company presented him with a souvenir of the engagement.[37]

25
Claiming the Regiment's Heritage

The Regimental Standards of the French Army and the Eagles atop the staffs were Napoleonic and Imperial, and consequently found no favour with those who now ran the Third Republic. A Circular dated 5 July 1871 ordered the immediate destruction of the Eagles and the incineration of the Regimental Standards and their staffs,[1] and Colonel Joseph de Mallaret, who had been a Major in Mexico and had taken command of the Regiment Etranger the previous January, moved to comply. As ordered, the staff and Eagle were sent promptly to the arsenal at Mascara. The Regimental Standard, however, was another matter. It had been at Magenta with the 2nd Etranger . . . it was the one which Standard-Bearer Maudet had carried so proudly onto the deck of the *Saint-Louis* when the Regiment Etranger departed for Mexico . . . it had been at Chiquihuite while its custodian was fighting at Camerone.

There has been some mystery about what happened to it.

General Paul Grisot, Colonel of the Foreign Legion from September 1883 to October 1886, and interested enough in its past to co-author a detailed history, ought to have been in a position to know, and he said that the Regimental Standard had been 'placed in the regimental library'.[2] By the same token, the history-minded Colonel Zeni, who held the same post from March 1891 to April 1895, and re-organized the regiment's collection of battle trophies, might also be thought to be a reliable source. Yet he told a journalist from *Le Sud-Oranais* that the Regimental Standard had been sent to des Invalides in Paris[3] in 1869 – which was obviously incorrect, as there had been no thought of its destruction until mid-1871. Historian and military flag expert Jean Brunon, who began his research on the flags of the Foreign Legion in the 1920s, and continued it for many years, finally became convinced that the Regimental Standard had indeed been incinerated, as ordered, by the *Service de l'Artillerie* in Oran.[4]

There is no dispute, however, about the fate of the staff and the Eagle. They were sold to a curio dealer by the arsenal at Mascara for no more than the scrap value of the metal, and it was only by the merest chance that, months later, Sous-Lieutenant Jules Kelbel of the Foreign Legion chanced upon them while browsing amongst bric-a-brac in a shop in Oran. He bought them for six francs and took them back to Sidi-bel-Abbes, where de Mallaret quietly put them away among the various military souvenirs.[5] As there was no immediate move to replace the Regimental Standard, de Mallaret devised a 'Provisional' one by adapting a simple Tricolour. The words REGIMENT ETRANGER were embroidered on the white centre panel[6] and there were no Battle Honours. It had to suffice the regiment for almost a decade.

Benito Juarez died of heart attack on 16 July 1872, leaving the way open for his old comrade Porfirio Diaz to gain control of the Presidency of Mexico. Marshal Jacques Randon, who had been France's Minister of War at the time of the Mexican Intervention, died the same year, as did Marshal Elie-Frederic Forey, the original Commander-in-Chief of the French Expeditionary Corps.

In the wake of the Franco-Prussian War, as is usual with a national defeat, there was a perceived need for someone to blame. Bazaine, as a common soldier who had attended no military school, and had risen through the ranks of the Foreign Legion to become a Marshal of France, became a convenient scapegoat for the aristocratic officers who had long begrudged him his position. Roundly denounced as responsible for almost every lost battle of the war, not just the capitulation at Metz, Bazaine demanded a Court of Inquiry, believing it would clear his name. Instead, early in 1872, it found him guilty, as did the National Assembly. President Adolphe Theirs, who admired Bazaine, and would undoubtedly have seen fair play, had resigned and Marshal MacMahon had replaced him.

Chaplain Lanusse refused to blame Bazaine for the capitulation,[7] but was one of very few people who spoke out. Underestimating the feeling against him within the military, Bazaine pressed for a court martial. It opened at Versailles on 6 October 1873 and ended predictably: 'The Council unanimously condemns Francois-Achille Bazaine to death and military degradation.' MacMahon quietly commuted the sentence to life imprisonment and Bazaine was shipped off to an island fortress offshore from Cannes in the South of France to serve his time. On 9 August 1874, he escaped, lowering himself some hundred metres (more than three hundred and twenty feet) down a cliff on a rope made of bedsheets and luggage straps. Madame Bazaine was waiting for him in a rowing boat, from which they transferred to a larger vessel and headed for Italy. Later in the year he made his home in Spain, where he had served four decades earlier in the Carlist War.[8] The officers of the Regiment Etranger, whatever they may have felt individually about Metz, could not help but admire the daring of their old commander.

The story of the unfortunate Maximilian and Carlota exerted a continuing fascination for Victorian readers and British interest had not yet been satiated. J.J. Kendall's *Mexico Under Maximilian* came out in 1871 and W. Harris Chynoweth's *The Fall of Maximilian, late Emperor of Mexico* the following year. In France, because of the defeats of the Franco-Prussian War, the Mexican Expedition – where there had at least been some victories – began to have reader appeal. Prince George Bibesco's *Le Corps Lorencez devant Puebla, 5 mai 1862* – though certainly an account of a defeat, rather than a victory – was published in Paris in 1872. Gustave Leon Noix's *L'Expedition du Mexique 1861–67, Recit politique et militaire*, based on primary source documents, was published in Paris in 1874. Narcisse-Henri-Edouard Faucher de Saint-Maurice's French-language memoir *Deux ans au Mexique* – the first book to use the Regiment Etranger's spelling of Camaron as Camerone – was published in Montreal the same year.[9]

Work on the Veracruz-to-Mexico City railway – now known simply as The Mexican Railway, rather than The Imperial Mexican Railway, for obvious reasons – had begun again after the French departed, and a book – *History of the Mexican Railway* by Gustavo Baz and E.L. Gallo – was published in Spanish in 1874 and in

English two years later. The authors, consumed with nationalistic fervour, remarked that the site of the station at 'El Camaron' was memorable in Mexican history as being the place where 'a few pickets of the national guard of Cordova and Huatusco . . . surprised a detachment of French troops and completely destroyed them'.[10]

More military changes were in the wind and in March 1875 the Regiment Etranger, under that name, ceased to exist, being redesignated the Legion Etrangere, having four battalions, each of four companies.[11] No new Regimental Standard was immediately forthcoming, and the Foreign Legion, which has always marched to its own drummer, continued using their 'Provisional' embroidered Tricolour, emblazoned with the name REGIMENT ETRANGER, for another five years.

Beauce's painting 'The end of the battle' had long since disappeared into the maw of the State when he died on 13 July 1875, but in October the Combat of Camerone received a public airing when former Captain Auguste Ballue – late of the 5th Company of the 1st Battalion and now a member of the Chamber of Deputies – wrote a semi-fictional two-part story for *Lectures du Soir*, a magazine much read in military circles. It was called 'Souvenirs du Mexique – Cameron' and featured two fictitious Indians, young lovers, the woman a messenger for the French Army, the man an *arriero* – wagoneer – working with the constant convoys of French supplies moving through the *Terres Chaudes* between Veracruz and besieged Puebla.

Despite the storyline being fictitious, Ballue was at pains to assure his readers of the solid foundation of time, place and events. At the end of the first article he declared that, militarily, 'these details are strictly factual,' and at the end of the second one wrote: 'In recalling this memoir of a feat of arms which will serve as a model and as an example, we are certain, without a shadow of a doubt, of the simple truth on the part of the purely military aspects of the story.'[12] The illustrations by de Vierge were very striking, although they depicted the fight at the Hacienda de la Trinidad as having taken place in a far more substantial building than had actually been the case.

So painful were the memories of the Combat of Camerone for some of those who had actually lived through it – unlike Ballue, who had been on the periphery – that they refused to speak about it. Any written depositions taken by Commandant Regnault when he debriefed the twenty Camerone survivors who had returned to the French lines – and Chaplain Lanusse believed that there were some[13] – do not appear to have survived, and although a number of the men of the 3rd of the 1st remained in the Regiment Etranger/Legion Etrangere none of them seem to have been asked to set down their memories.

Captain Philippe Maine waited fifteen years before speaking of the battle, only agreeing to talk about it after he retired from the Army, apparently invalided out following a breakdown of his health. He had served with the *Tirailleurs Senegalese* from 23 July 1871 to 3 April 1873 and then returned home to resume service with the 3rd *Infanterie de Marine*. More than half a lifetime of soldiering in France's wars, much of it spent in unhealthy tropical climes, had impaired his health. On 30 September 1874 he had been 'temporarily' taken off the active list due to 'infirmities', and the meticulous clerk making up his Service Record noted that he had been carried on the strength of the regiment for three years, one month and twenty days before being finally retired with a pension on 19 January 1878. He was only forty-eight years old, but his military career as a ranker in four different regiments had taken him to the Crimea, Algeria, Italy and Mexico. As an officer – in four regiments and a semi-military force – he had served in Mexico, Cochin-China, France and Senegal.[14]

Maine returned to his birthplace at Mussidan, which had featured so vividly in his hallucination during a lull in the fighting at Camerone, and went into business for himself, agreeing a few months later to talk about the battle to Lucien-Louis Lande, who was writing a book about military life. Maine's firsthand account of the battle, planned as a chapter for Lande's book, caught the attention of the Editor of the *Revue des Deux Mondes*. Publication rights were negotiated and it ran as an article in mid-July, under the title 'Camaron: Episode de la Guerre du Mexique.' Because of its eyewitness nature, it became, for historians, the seminal article on the battle – and, unfortunately, provided certain scraps of misinformation which have come down through the years as the story of the Combat of Camerone has been told and retold, not the least of them being the statement that Danjou had lost his left hand during the Crimean War.[15] Not attributed to Maine, but clearly picked up somewhere else by Lande, was the additional mis-statement that Danjou's wooden hand had been found 'among the debris' of the battle. It was apparently Maine's understanding that the grave of his comrades of the 3rd of the 1st was properly marked and that 'the Government of Mexico pays for its upkeep',[16] but it is unclear where he had learned this.

Clearly, the article brought back memories for many people at the time, including the Editor of the *Memorial de la Loire*, who was moved the following month to recall in print his own presence in Orizaba when the first Camerone survivors were brought in by Colonel Dupin and his men.[17]

Lande's *Souvenirs d'un Soldat* – featuring Maine's recollections, in a chapter called 'La Hacienda de Camaron: Episode de la Guerre du Mexique' – appeared later in the year and was quite successful. It included an excellent artist's rendering of the Orizaba Lancers' attack on the first square formed by *La Compagnie Danjou* west of the Hacienda de la Trinidad. However, the illustration purporting to be of the hacienda itself was extraordinarily imaginative. In the foreground – representing the small Indian village – was a group of brush tepee-style dwellings, and the building itself was depicted as having walls at least six metres (almost twenty feet) high, and a dome surmounted by a cross.[18]

The fact that Marshal Randon had given personal and immediate approval for CAMERONE 1863 to become a Battle Honour for the Regiment Etranger six months after the affair at the Hacienda de la Trinidad meant that it was a *fait accompli*. In 1878, when the bureaucratic work which went into the creation of new Regimental Standards for the French Army began again, it was decided that only four Battle Honours would be permitted. CAMERONE was re-approved for what had now become the Legion Etrangere, along with SEBASTOPOL, KABYLIE and MAGENTA.[19] On the reverse side was the motto: VALEUR ET DISCIPLINE and the new Standard was presented at a ceremony on 14 July 1880.

When Battle Honours were being considered for the *Chasseurs a Pied* at the same time, the name of their most glorious stand, thirty-five years earlier, was not even among them. However, a War Office functionary with a good memory pencilled it on the proposal document and SIDI BRAHIM 1845 was adopted.[20]

In 1881 Faucher de Saint-Maurice, who had been an Observer with the French forces at Oaxaca, entered politics in his native Quebec, becoming the Member of Parliament for Bellechasse, a post he held for nine years. He had been remembering and reviewing his days in Mexico and produced a small book called *Notes pour servir a l'histoire de Maximilien*, which he re-issued in a second edition eight years later. Perhaps drawing on his memories of the Bazaine-founded Mexican Society for Geography and Statistics, Saint-Maurice was instrumental in establishing the French-language section of the Royal Society of Canada.[21]

The 3rd Company's fight at Camerone was certainly alive and well in military circles and was featured pictorially in the definitive two-volume *Types et Uniformes de l'Armee Francaise* by Edouard Detaille and Jules Richard, published in 1885. Detaille was the reigning Official Artist to the Army and his painting, called 'Les derniers survivants de l'hacienda de Camerone' – 'The last survivors of the Hacienda of Camerone'[22] – was dramatic. Purists, however, pointed out that the Fusiliers were shown wearing traditional blue-grey greatcoats, rather than their actual dark blue tunics, and questioned the depiction of Maudet firing a revolver at the on-coming Mexicans as his last few companions load their rifles for the final shot and prepare to go in with the bayonet. It was pointed out that while Maudet – like Danjou and Vilain – would certainly have had a sidearm, its use would have been restricted by the amount of ammunition he carried, which would have been exhausted long before the final moments of the battle. The painting, however, was greatly liked and subsequently much reproduced.

Despite the existence of several partial histories of the Foreign Legion, and the numerous first-person accounts of more than half a century of campaigns, a need was felt for a full-scale history. The void was filled in 1888 with a book co-authored by a former senior officer of the Foreign Legion and one still serving with the 2nd Etranger. Colonel Paul Grisot, transferred in from the 88th Regiment of the Line, had become Commanding Officer of the single regiment Legion Etrangere in September 1883. He had been given the task of splitting it in two, creating the 1st and 2nd Regiments Etrangers, in yet another reorganization fifteen months later. He had assumed command of the newly-created 1st Etranger on New Year's Day 1885 and served for almost two years before being promoted to General and handing over to Colonel Wattringue. Lieutenant Ernest Coulombon was a serving officer with the 2nd Etranger and their jointly-authored book, *La Legion Etrangere de 1831 a 1887*, quickly became a classic. They readily admitted to drawing heavily on Comte Paul de Choulot's *Souvenirs pour servir a l'histoire du 1er Regiment de la Legion Etrangere*, and complained, as other historians would almost a century later, that the *Journals de Marche* of the various regiments, while replete with detail, tended to make dull reading, lacking colour and verve. Grisot and Coulombon's use of documents was as prodigious as their spelling of proper names was often appalling. Despite being written more as an Annals than as a Narrative History, it rapidly came to be regarded as the 'bible' of the Foreign Legion's first fifty-six years, and, while subsequently superseded, still cannot be surpassed.[23] They described the Combat of Camerone as 'one of the most glorious pages of the Foreign Regiments, one of the most brilliant in the records of the French Army'[24] – and for some inexplicable reason reported that Danjou had lost his right hand, which could easily have been checked by examining the genuine article among the regiment's treasures.

Perhaps it was the impetus of the publication of the Grisot/Coulombon book that gave Colonel Wattringue, coming to the Foreign Legion from the 3rd Regiment of the Line, the push he needed to begin seriously organizing a *Salle d'Honneur* – Hall of Honour, an embryo regimental museum – at Sidi-bel-Abbes. Almost from the time he had taken command of the 1st Etranger in October 1886 he had been wondering what to do with the assorted trophies and military bric-a-brac constantly arriving with officers and battalions returning from overseas tours of duty. After 1883 these had included many items from French Indo-China, particularly Tonkin, where the Foreign Legion had spearheaded the taking of a number of large and small towns from local warlords and their Chinese-backed allies, the so-called 'Black Flags'.

The 1st Battalion of the 1st Etranger, along with two battalions of *Tirailleurs Algeriens*, had made up a *Regiment de Marche* to go to Tonkin in 1883. Corporal Minnaert, a Belgian in the Third Company, at the beginning of a long and illustrious career in the regiment, had distinguished himself at the capture of Sontay at the end of the year, and of Bac-Ninh in 1884, as the French began to solidify their positions and gain control.

In late December, Black Flags, supported by Chinese regulars, laid siege to an old Chinese fort at Tuyen Quang on the Claire River. It was manned by the 1st and 2nd Companies of the 1st Etranger, a detachment of Foreign Legion Sappers – a total of three hundred and ninety men – a Company of *Tirailleurs Tonkinese* some two hundred-strong, and several Artillerymen, a total of just less than six hundred soldiers of France. The Chinese were building up their forces as the year turned and actual fighting began on 16 January 1885. At its height it involved at least ten thousand Chinese and Black Flags, and the siege continued until 3 March, when a relief column fought its way through. By that time the senior Foreign Legion officer and fifty-six Legionnaires were dead, and all the junior officers and one hundred and eighty-eight Legionnaires wounded. On 4 March, almost as the relief column arrived, Captain the Vicompte de Borelli was reconnoitering the ground outside the now ruined fort when a Chinese rifleman reared up out of the grass. As Fuslier Victor Catteau had done with Sous-Lieutenant Maudet at Camerone, Borelli's Orderly, Legionnaire Thiebald Streibler, the son of a former Foreign Legion Sapper, threw himself in front of his officer and fell with a bullet in his chest. De Borelli's men captured a multi-coloured silk flag, which he sent back to Sidi-bel-Abbes.

Had it not been for Camerone, Tuyen Quang would undoubtedly have been the Foreign Legion's most celebrated battle, with details easier to substantiate, as there were many survivors. Among them was Sergeant-Major Edward Husband, Paris-born of an English father and a French mother, who was commissioned as Sous-Lieutenant for his actions in the battle, and who left the Foreign Legion in 1896 as a Captain, and went on to become a Brigadier-General in the First World War. Several firsthand accounts of the siege at Tuyen Quang were published, de Borelli wrote an epic and widely-quoted poem called 'To My Men Who Are Dead'[25] and a number of surviving Legionnaires were still serving with the regiment more than twenty years later.

Still an exile, Marshal Bazaine died in modest circumstances in Madrid in 1888 and the same year Colonel Wattringue laid the foundation stone for the *Salle d'Honneur* at Sidi-bel-Abbes. The building work was, naturally, undertaken by Legionnaires, and the ceiling was painted with somewhat allegorical military scenes by one of them named Hablutzel. A Captain Cousin executed several battle paintings, including a Camerone one called 'Le Fin' – 'The End'. By this time Captain Danjou's articulated hand sat on a red velvet cushion inside a glass-sided mahogany casket, elaborately carved and proably the work of some cabinet-maker Legionnaire. Assorted memorabilia was taken out of storage boxes and displayed,[26] as was de Borelli's silk flag from Tuyen Quang.

The *Salle d'Honneur* had not been open long when visited by Frederic Martyn, an Englishman who would make the most of his five years in the Foreign Legion, fighting in Tonkin and Dahomey, as well in Southern Algeria. He had some advantages, as not only did he speak French and German, but he had been both an officer and a ranker in the British Army. Down on his luck in Paris, despondent, and more or less on a whim, he joined the Foreign Legion near the end of 1889, giving his name as 'Fred Brown'. Sent by train to Marseille, he spent some days at Fort St. Jean, which was used as an assembly point for Foreign Legion recruits and other soldiers of the *Armee d'Afrique*, then sent across the Mediterranean to Oran. Once in Sidi-bel-Abbes he was shown round the new regimental museum with his intake, just as 'every newly joined legionary was taken to visit it in order that he might be impressed by the feats of arms of his predecessors'.

> The 'Hall of Honour' is in a well-kept enclosure, walled off from the rest of the barracks, and is approached by a broad flight of steps [*Martyn wrote in his book about serving under the French flag*]. It is a very large room, with a painted ceiling, the work of a legionary, and the walls are literally covered with portraits of officers and men who have distinguished themselves, and with canvasses of stirring scenes in the Legion's history. The Adjutant-Major, who was acting as showman, drew our special attention to one of the pictures bearing the title 'The End,' and with soldierly feeling told us the story of the incident it commemorates – surely one of the most gallant feats of arms the world has ever known . . . In a glass case, under the picture, was the artificial hand of Captain Danjou.[27]

After telling the story of *La Compagnie Danjou*, which Martyn remembered in broadly accurate detail, the Adjutant-Major – with slight exaggeration – remarked: 'This grand act of devotion was not in vain, for while the Third of the First was keeping that two thousand two hundred men employed the convoy got safely through,' and he enjoined the recruits: 'Soldiers of the Legion, remember the third Company of this regiment and Camaron when it comes to your turn to fight.'

Martyn said he was 'profoundly impressed by what I had seen,' and by the story of Camerone. His friend and fellow recruit, a Russian nobleman and former Tsarist officer, serving under the name of Petrovski, exclaimed: 'What a regiment! What men!' and Martyn commented: 'I think that I was a much more valuable asset to France when I came out than when I went in'.[28] Within a matter of weeks he and Petrovski were on their way to Tonkin with the latest draft of Legionnaires.

By this time Military Chaplain Lanusse had been at Saint-Cyr for almost two decades, teaching and ministering, and, ever interested in military history, had expended much time producing accounts of varying lengths about his nation's heroic feats of arms. Although he had been in Italy with the victorious French Army in 1859, and had struggled through the confusions and defeats of the Franco-Prussian War, there is no doubt that Lanusse's mid-1862 to early-1867 service in Mexico with the French Expeditionary Corps had been the high spot of his military life.[29] Now, at the age of seventy-two, his position at the nation's premier military school somewhat less demanding, and himself generally considered to be 'the doyen of Military Chaplains of France',[30] he was writing furiously, sometimes sprinkling his texts with the kind of patriotic breast-beating he judged would motivate his officer cadets. Lanusse was also a talented illustrator and calligraphist and Boyer d'Agen, a journalist friend, visiting him in his little first-floor office, found the priest-soldier tucked away among his reports, documents and part-completed essays.

> His cross on his chest, his medals and decorations are displayed in boxes – 'I am covered in them!' he remarked happily – in his modest priest's room, where each of the civil and military ribbons is properly displayed, but the walls are bare, and the room simply furnished [*d'Agen wrote*]. Here and there are boxes full of manuscripts on parchment, each page dazzling with illuminations. Here is a library, with yet more manuscripts . . . none of which have been published, and perhaps never will be.[31]

If Mexico was 'his' war, Lanusse had made the Combat of Camerone 'his' battle, a matter of consuming interest from the moment he first heard of it while with the French troops besieging Puebla. He had taken the trouble to talk to the officers most concerned and to seek out and interview participants, and had twice visited the Hacienda de la Trinidad with one or more of the men of the Regiment Etranger who had fought there and survived. Always the enthusiast, Lanusse considered Camerone to have been been a 'glorious battle, destined to take first rank in military annuals, beside the greatest feats of arms'.[32] His one regret was that the grave of the 3rd of the 1st was not properly marked. 'I have thought more than once that I should write to our Minister of War, for him to talk with the Mexican Government about erecting a monument so that our sixty heroes will never be forgotten,' he said.[33] Utilizing his memory, and the notes he had taken of discussions, Lanusse had written the story 'on parchment with illuminations' – as he put it – in the manner of the monks of old. It was then handsomely bound, its cover made of metal, encrusted with semi-precious stones and engraved.

> It was one of those situations which cries out for parchment or bronze [*Lanusse enthused to General Alexis de La Hayrie in a letter in 1889*]. I have lavished gold and the most beautiful colours on those who so furiously gave their blood. I have been to the scene of the battle, and since that time have made a special study of it.[34]

D'Agen, who handled the opus with some awe, spoke of 'the incomparable opulence of this manuscript, on the cover of which I read the title engraved on metal and dotted with precious stones'.[35] He asked Lanusse if he intended to publish it, or any of his other works.

'Publish them?' the Chaplain exclaimed in surprise. 'Oh. No! The School, when I die, will perhaps conserve these chronicles as a souvenir of the Chaplain who devoted much time to the chalice and to the pen.'[36]

A friend in the Chamber of Deputies subsequently asked Lanusse to 'take the sumptuously bound book to the Library of the Chamber', where it was on show for a month and received an award from the Minister of Public Education. It was then displayed in the Ministry of War's section at the Universal Exposition of 1889. Lanusse told de La Hayrie that he planned to dedicate it 'to Generals Jeanningros and Saussier'.[37]

Now the General Commanding the 12th Infantry Division of the 6th Army Corps, de La Hayrie was aware of the success enjoyed by Lanusse's illuminated Camerone manuscript, and had quite probably seen it at the Exposition. Then he learned that Minister of War de Freycinet was engaged in overseeing from afar an ambitious plan to create a memorial to the French troops who had died in the two assaults of Puebla, and that Blanchard de Forges, France's Ambassador to Mexico, was deeply involved in the on-site arrangements. He also heard that, unconnected with the Puebla memorial, consideration was being given to a request from Edouard Sempe, the French Consul in Veracruz, for the provision of a proper marker for the grave of the men of *La Compagnie Danjou* at Camerone.[38]

De La Hayrie had been in Mexico almost from the beginning of the Intervention, serving the Zouaves and the *Tirailleurs Algeriens* before becoming a Battalion Commander with the Regiment Etranger. Of a certainty he had known the officers of the 1st Battalion who had been most immediately concerned with the events surrounding the battle, and may even have had an opportunity to talk to Camerone survivors. He was familiar with the overall military and geographical situation and felt that he had quite enough material to write a small book. He devoted part of the Summer of 1889 to working on the project and then sent the manuscript to Chaplain Lanusse for his comments. De La Hayrie felt that 'the defence of Camaron was without doubt the most heroic feat of arms of the age',[39] and Lanusse, noting that they were 'very much of the same idea' about the events at the Hacienda de la Trinidad, returned the manuscript with a most enthusiastic covering letter. 'Your story is perfect,' he told de La Hayrie,[40] who promptly took his little book to the printer.

For reasons that are not entirely clear today, the authorship of *Combat de Camaron, 30 avril 1863* was not showm.[41] However, as the first four pages comprised the endorsement letter from Lanusse, the identity of the writer of the remaining twenty-four pages can hardly have been really in doubt. The device, of course, enabled the unidentified author to declare that he had received the details of the battle from 'a former officer of the Legion'. This equally anonymous source had got them firsthand 'from the mouths of several survivors of the struggle, who, taken prisoner by the enemy, had been exchanged several months later'.[42] Internal evidence suggests that the Lande/Maine account in the *Revue des Deux Mondes* of eleven years earlier was among de La Hayrie's sources, and he almost certainly got many details from Saussier – Military Governor of Paris since 1884 – Jeanningros and Ballue. The 'former officer of the Legion' was therefore probably a collective, including himself.

Overall, the twenty-eight page booklet, which was dedicated to Saussier, told the story fairly accurately. Unfortunately, however, because de La Hayrie's short work was the first to be devoted to Camerone, and because of his reputation, it came to be seen as definitive, and over the years his errors concerning the hand of Captain Danjou, and the number of men of the 3rd of the 1st who died in captivity, were taken as incontrovertible facts.[43] Although demonstrably wrong, these mistakes were faithfully copied by others and became part of the lore of the Combat at Camerone. Additionally, nationalistic pride led de La Hayrie to claim that the last five men left fighting were Sous-Lieutenant Maudet, 'a Corporal and two French Legionnaires and a Prussian Legionnaire',[44] which would have been news to the survivors, for while Maine was certainly French, and Wensel was a Prussian, Catteau and Constantine were both Belgians.

De La Hayrie's timing was right, as there was a resurgence of interest in the Mexican Campaign. Ernest Louet, who had visited the exiled Marshal Bazaine in Madrid and obtained access to some of his documents for a major history of the Intervention, had died shortly after he began work on his book. Later, Paul Gaulot worked with the documents and the Paris publisher Paul Ollendorff brought out *Reve d'Empire* in 1889, and followed it with *L'Empire de Maximilien* the following year and *Fin d'Empire* a year later, describing the three-volume history as 'The Truth about the Mexican Expedition, based on unedited documents collected by Ernest Louet, Chief Paymaster to the Expeditionary Corps'.[45]

Despite his earlier expressed disinterest in having his work published, now that de La Hayrie's little booklet was in print, along with the first volume of the Gaulot/Louet trilogy, Chaplain Lanusse began having second thoughts about simply burying his own account of Camerone in the archives of Saint-Cyr. He enlisted the aid of his journalist friend d'Agen, who on 11 November 1890 delivered a public lecture concerning the military life and peacetime writings of the Chaplain of Saint-Cyr. Much praise was lavished on Lanusse's many unpublished literary pieces, and they were fulsomely commended to the attention of Minister of War de Freycinet.[46] The lecture was then published in two parts in the influential journal *Le Gaulois*,[47] a useful piece of promotional puffery which seemingly worked wonders. Just six months later Lanusse had a book contract from the house of Marmon et Flammarion,[48] which had a good track record as publishers of militaria.

Described as 'the first volume of a series',[49] *Les heros de Camaron: 30 avril 1863* appeared in the Summer of 1891. Lanusse had eventually decided to dedicate it solely to Saussier, rather than jointly to Jeanningros and Saussier, as had been his original intent. His rousing Dedication began: 'You carry a sword. I carry a cross. That is how we have found ourselves on the same battlefields; you to show your soldiers the road to honour, I, to give a benediction and show them the way to Heaven.'[50] There was much more in the same vein over the next twelve pages, as he almost fawningly reviewed Saussier's career, and reminisced about the several places in Mexico and elsewhere that their paths had crossed.[51] D'Agen contributed a rambling twenty-five-page Preface, which had little to do with the book, not much to do with Lanusse, next to nothing with Camerone and even mis-stated the number of men involved as sixty-three, rather than sixty-five.[52] General Forey's Order of the Day announcing the promotion of Maine and the gallantry awards to eleven other Camerone survivors, and Marshal Randon's letter to Jeanningros giving approval to the name CAMERONE as a Battle Honour, took up six pages near the back of the book,[53] and a reprinting of d'Agen's adulatory biographical article on Lanusse from *Le Gaulois* occupied a further twenty-six pages.[54] Clearly, most of the eighty pages taken up by the Dedication, the official letters and d'Agen's two lengthy pieces was 'make-weight', as the famed hand-written illuminated manuscript, when reduced to the cold reality of print, ran to only two hundred and thirty-two pages of the three hundred and twelve page book. Unfortunately, Lanusse copied de La Hayrie, who had copied Lane and Maine, concerning Captain Danjou's hand, giving further circulation to errors which became part of the myth.[55] There were no illustrations, d'Agen explained, but 'the cover gives an idea of these illuminations, by borrowing some precious designs from Abbe Lanusse',[56] and the publisher produced fifteen numbered special presentation copies, printed on Japan paper.[57] Despite some shortcomings, *Les heros de Camaron* was a worthy effort, and Lanusse received congratulatory letters from a number of people, including President M.F. Sadi Carnet, General Saussier, Colonel Gillet of the 2nd Regiment Etranger in Saida and author Roger de Beauvoir.[58] Replete with solid information, though eccentrically organized and somewhat rambling, it has been largely ignored by historians, perhaps because it is necessary to sift through so much chaff to find the grains of wheat. Most unfortunately, it is not known if the vaunted original illuminated manuscript which started it all still exists.[59]

In the meantime, Ambassador de Forges in Mexico City and Consul Sempe in Veracruz had made much progress towards the erection of a proper memorial at Camerone. A public subscription was being taken up with the support of Minister of Foreign Affairs Ribot and Minister of War de Freycinet. The amount to be expended was set at five thousand gold francs, which would cover the provision of a flat marble gravestone, suitably inscribed. It would be positioned at a slight angle, so as to be higher at the top than at the foot, and would be enclosed within a waist-high wrought iron fence, with a small access gate at the foot of the gravestone. It was agreed that any shortfall in the public subscription would be made up by funds from the War Ministry's *Service de Sante-Tombes*, and that an allowance of three piastres a month – a maximum of one hundred and fifty francs a year – would be set aside to pay a local person from the village to tend the grave.[60]

The Nacastle twin planted beside the grave by a nameless Legionnaire in 1863 had grown into a huge tree, but while its branches cast shade over the grave, its roots were destroying it and employees of the railway company constructed a new brick-lined vault some five metres (just over sixteen feet) to the east of the original grave and re-interred the remains of the men of *La Compagnie Danjou* in two large mahogany chests.[61] In a letter dated 11 June 1892 Ambassador de Forges notified his Minister in Paris that the necessary work had been completed.[62] Not long after the war memorial at Puebla had been dedicated, in the presence of President Porfirio Diaz himself, the much more modest gravestone for those who had died in the Combat of Camerone was solemnly dedicated.

The inscription, in Latin, said it all:

> THEY WERE HERE LESS THAN 60
> OPPOSED BY A WHOLE ARMY
> ITS MASS CRUSHED THEM
> LIFE RATHER THAN COURAGE
> ABANDONED THESE SOLDIERS OF FRANCE
> ON APRIL 30 1863
>
> IN THEIR MEMORY
> THIS MONUMENT IS PLACED
> BY THEIR COUNTRY
> IN THE YEAR 1892[63]

Somebody with a greater understanding of history and occasion than of artistic draughtsmanship and perspective produced a watercolour – elongated and out of scale – showing the gravestone and the wrought iron fence surrounding it. The now huge Nacastle tree casts its shade from the left-hand side and there are a number of small – very un-Mexican, very European-style – houses in the middle distance.[64] The painting was sent to Sidi-bel-Abbes and quite properly given a proud place in the *Salle d'Honneur*.

Colonel Wattringue was gone by then, having handed over command to Colonel Barburet in early 1890. He had stayed only some thirteen months before being replaced by the energetic Colonel Zeni. During the four years that he commanded the 1st Etranger he was very busy, as was the Foreign Legion. A tough campaign in Dahomey (now Benin) in West Africa in 1892 – in which Legionnaires Martyn and his friend Petrovski, and also Corporal Minnaert, took part – led to the acquisition of many new trophies.

The town of Mussidan recognized retired Captain Philippe Maine as an honoured son by erecting a plaque in the town hall and naming a street after him. Unfortunately, he was clearly a better soldier than he was a businessman, and his endeavours were not met with much success. The best known survivor of Camerone died on 27 June 1893, and was buried in the town of his birth.[65]

It had been Wattringue's intent that the *Salle d'Honneur* should be for the entire Foreign Legion, but Zeni's interests were more narrowly focused. He took the view that the home of the 1st Etranger was at Sidi-bel-Abbes and that the *Salle d'Honour* there should reflect the glories of the regiment.[66] He divided up the trophies and memorabilia, sending the military mementoes of the 2nd Etranger to their headquarters at Saida, where they established their own *Salle d'Honneur*, which diminished the significance of the Sidi-bel-Abbes collection.

A journalist from *Le Sud-Oranais* visited it in 1894 and it is clear from his article that Zeni's *Salle d'Honneur* was substantially different from the one conceived and brought into being by Wattringue and visited by Martyn and Petrovski, among others. The glass case containing Danjou's articulated hand was no longer on the small table below Captain Cousin's painting 'The End', as one of the first things which caught the reporter's eye were portraits of 'a captain and a sous-lieutenant', and 'a bizarre object, set on velvet', among a gallery of paintings of such famous officers as Marshal de Saint-Arnaud and Generals Saussier and Delebecque.

> We are in the presence of a glorious relic [*he wrote*]. It is the articulated hand of Captain Danjou, who led the heroes at Camaron; the day after the combat where the valiant officer succumbed with his company, this hand was retrieved from the field of battle and carefully preserved. The portraits placed above it are those of Captain Danjou and Sous-Lieutenant Vilain. They well deserve this place of honour.[67]

Cousin's painting – described as depicting 'an officer and five or six legionnaires still fighting in an outbuilding against hordes of Mexicans' – was prominently displayed beside another painting showing an incident during the siege at Tuyen Quang. Zeni's *Salle d'Honneur* also featured the silk banner captured from the Black Flags at Tuyen Quang, and the reporter noted that the display was dominated by 'a flag surmounted by the Imperial Eagle, in gold, with its wings spread', indicating that it had been affixed to the staff topped by the Imperial Eagle of the old Regiment Etranger of the Mexican Campaign, rescued from the Oran curio shop almost twenty years earlier. The reporter wrote of three large albums of 'inestimable value', containing pictures of 'the heroic officers who in more than sixty years had led the Legion in various parts of the world.' He also saw the painting of the 1892 grave, writing of 'a watercolour of the monument erected two years ago, in Mexico, at the farm at Camaron, where Danjou, Vilain and their valorous soldiers perished,' and noted: 'The countryside is barren; only a large tree, reminiscent of the weeping willow of Sainte-Helene, broods over the grave with its shadow.'[68] There was obviously no mention of Maudet, as none was made by the reporter.

The reporter apparently asked if there were any Camerone survivors at Sidi-bel-Abbes, and was told that 'the last one died here nearly a dozen years ago'.[69] As the Combat of Camerone had been fought more than three decades earlier, this was hardly surprising, though, in fact, survivor Hippolyte Kunassec was still very much alive and serving with the 2nd Etranger at Saida. The reporter did manage to find a number of Tuyen Quang survivors – the siege had taken place only nine years earlier – including Sous-Lieutenant Burel, who had received the Cross of the Legion of Honour while in the ranks, Adjutant Schal, who had been a Corporal at the time, and Sergeant Poser, who had been a simple Legionnaire.

The next Colonel of the 1st Etranger, Comte Georges de Villebois-Mareuil, who had come to the Foreign Legion from the 67th Regiment of the Line, took over from Zeni in April 1895. He arrived in Sidi-bel-Abbes a matter of days after another special *Regiment de Marche*, made up of men of the 1st and 2nd Etrangers, had departed for Madagascar, in the far off Indian Ocean. Among Villebois-Mareuil's first acts was to present the Cross of the Legion of Honour to Sergeant Minnaert, the hero of Sontay, Bac-Ninh, and the Dahomey Campaign, as well as another in Guinea and the Ivory Coast. A novelist and military theorist, Villebois-Mareuil knew he was earmarked for promotion, but fearing garrison life, and a desk in a barracks in France, expended much effort in begging to be sent to Madagascar to join his men. It was not to be, and when notified of his promotion he resigned his Commission, leaving the Army with mixed feelings and the Foreign Legion with 'incurable regret not to have led them under fire'.

He was no longer Colonel of the 1st Etranger when his lengthy general article on the regiment was published in the *Revue des Deux Mondes*[70] in mid-April 1896. Overall, his article attracted considerable attention at the time, and was to be frequently quoted in the coming years, though perhaps as much because of the prominence of the author, and the prestige of the magazine, as for the actual content. In writing of the Mexican Campaign, Villebois-Mareil clearly drew heavily on the Lande/Maine account in the same magazine eighteen years earlier, and spoke of 'the immortality of Camerone', and calling it 'one of the most brilliant feats of arms' in the annals of the French Army.[71]

Expectations that *Les heros de Camaron* would be the 'first of a series' of Lanusse books did not materialize. Boyer d'Agen had counted two hundred and sixty of the priest-soldier's manuscripts – of varying lengths – at the Universal Exposition of 1889, and saw more than three hundred when he visited Lanusse in his study at Saint-Cyr.[72] Possibly Marmon et Flammarion was daunted by the sheer size of the collection, and there had also been some disappointment that *Les heros de Camaron* had not received recognition from the Acadamie Francaise, which would undoubtedly have helped sales. When, in late November 1896, the Academie awarded Lanusse its first *Prix de Vertue*, it was for his exemplary seventy-eight years on this earth. Journalist Jean de Niville, writing in *l'Actualite*, noted that it was given 'for long and devoted military service', but 'perhaps also a little' for *Les heros de Camaron*, which had told the story of 'a feat of arms oft referred to in our military annals, and which, with Mazagran and Sidi Brahim, forms a trilogy worthy of Homeric times.'

> Chaplain Lanusse has told the story in terms which are both simple and moving at the same time, and with the eloquence of a man who has seen that of which he speaks [*de Niville wrote*]. He well understands that it is possible to write – with detail and personal reminiscences – of this epic Combat at Camaron, where fewer than a hundred soldiers of the Legion Etrangere covered themselves with glory before they died. The Academie Francaise has recognized him for another thing, his long and devoted services which excite admiration, but this forcefully focuses attention on his book and, it is to be hoped, will give it even greater success.[73]

26

The Last Survivor, the First Celebration

Sergeant Hippolyte Kunassec was in his twenty-fifth consecutive year in the Foreign Legion when he signed on for a final two-year engagement in 1897. Actually, the Camerone survivor had served a total of twenty-seven years with the regiment, an initial two-year stint, followed by an eight-year break, and most of even that had been in soldiering.

Kunassec – the Foreign Legion's spelling of his Austrian artist father's surname of Kuwasseg – had been nineteen when he signed a two-year engagement with the 2nd Etranger on 18 November 1861. He went to Mexico with the Regiment Etranger as a member of the 3rd Company of the 1st Battalion, fought at Camerone, was captured, then was part of the first prisoner exchange in July 1863. Becoming one of the four survivors promoted to Voltigeur, he made Corporal on 6 August and was one of the six who received the *Medaille Militaire* by Marshal Forey's Order #195 of 30 August.

He did not sign a second engagement, returning to Paris at the end of 1863, but the following year enlisted for seven years with the 57th Regiment of the Line. Kunassec made Sergeant in 1867, the year the Regiment Etranger came back from Mexico, and was captured by the Prussians three years later during the Franco-Prussian War. Escaping, he made his way back to the French lines, and, as his regiment was smashed and scattered, saw the war out as a member of the 90th Regiment of the Line.

Re-engaging in the Regiment Etranger in 1872, Kunassec had a roller-coaster career, rising to Sergeant six times, and being broken to the ranks on five occasions,[1] finally serving with the 2nd Etranger at Saida.

The same year, author Roger de Beauvoir, who had been one of the first to congratulate Chaplain Lanusse on the publication of *Les heros de Camaron*, brought out his own book, *La Legion Etrangere*, a full-scale history of the Foreign Legion. Like Lanusse, he dedicated his book to General Gustave Saussier and chose to tell his story in episodic narrative form, rather than – as had been the case with Grisot and Coulombon – virtually as an Annals. De Beauvoir provided a rattling good story and his handsomely-produced book featured work by a number of well-known illustrators, portraits of officers and men, and vigorous drawings of the events described. It contained the first published likeness of Captain Danjou, an unsigned line drawing clearly based on the photograph which had been made at Oran before he sailed for Mexico. Perhaps it had been among the photographic collection mentioned by the reporter from *Le Sud-Oranais* three years earlier, but if so, the picture must have been borrowed and not returned, as no photograph of Danjou was found among the Foreign Legion's collections by those hunting for one more than thirty years later. Another line drawing, this one signed by illustrator Lefebvre, was published as being of Sous-Lieutenant Maudet, but was actually from a photograph of Sous-Lieutenant Vilain. The illustrations dealing with Camerone, executed by Henri Doldier, had unrivalled accuracy, style and panache, and stood the test of time so well that they were still being used as illustrations in Foreign Legion articles and books three-quarters of a century later.[2]

In 1899 Kunassec finished his last engagement. Only fifty-six, but worn out by a lifetime of soldiering, he may well have been correct in believing that he was the last Camerone survivor. Some had died, still serving in the Foreign Legion in the early 1880s, while the whereabouts of those who had returned to civilian life were unknown, so Kunassec was certainly the last known survivor.

As he was saying goodbye to the regiment which he had called his own for twenty-seven unbroken years – and an actual total of twenty-nine – a young Sous-Lieutenant arrived in Sidi-bel-Abbes, on his way to join the 2nd Etranger, at the beginning of his own military career. The two men were briefly introduced. Lieutenant Abel Clement-Grandcourt left the Foreign Legion in 1905, but retained his interest in it, writing articles for military magazines, and a book on Morocco,[3] and many years later, as the distinguished General Clement-Grandcourt, enjoyed recalling that he had met the last serving Camerone survivor.[4]

The right-wing former Colonel Villebois-Mareuil, now a civilian, involved himself in politics, wrote prodigiously and supported the highly questionable guilty-of-treason verdict against Alfred Dreyfus on the grounds that even if he was innocent, the honour of the French Army was too important to sully by admitting he had been wrongly convicted. Villebois-Mareuil had a number of English friends, but considered England to be 'the hereditary enemy of France', and in late 1899 the French public and the officers and men of the Foreign Legion were interested to hear that he had gone to South Africa, to take up a military command with the Boers in their fight with the British. His new employers referred to him as 'Der Franse Kolonel' – 'The French Colonel' – and he was promoted to the rank of Combat-General before being killed in April 1900, fighting 'the hereditary enemy'.[5]

The early years of the century found the French pushing ever southwards into the Sahara – an area known as the Sud Oranais – and facing mounting opposition from desert warlords, and from the Moroccans across the scarcely-defined border. Things changed when Colonel Hubert Lyautey was placed in command of operations. A veteran of both Tonkin and Madagascar, an imperious soldier with a zeal for colonial expansion, and an enormous capacity for administration, he was promoted to General Officer rank and rapidly took the initiative.

On 31 October 1900, Sous-Lieutenant Marie Jules Victor Leon Francois arrived at Sidi-bel-Abbes, immediately after graduating at the top of his class at Saint-Cyr. Born on 9 April 1879, Francois soon met officers and men who had fought with the Foreign Legion in Tonkin, Dahomey, elsewhere in West Africa, Siam, Madagascar and, of course, Algeria. An enthusiast for all things connected with the Foreign Legion, Francois became a keen student of its history. There were even old Legionnaires who remembered the Mexican Expedition, with whom he could talk about Camerone. It is not impossible that he met ex-Sergeant Kunassec, who had retired the previous year, but was still living in Sidi-bel-Abbes.

Francois took part in a daring – and wholly unsanctioned by Paris – push into Morocco, when the French seized a small oasis and called it Colomb-Bechar, as if it were a place on the Algerian side of the frontier. He was in the area when Lyautey's troops occupied an oasis called Ras-el-Ain, also on the Moroccan side of the border, and called it Berguent, a place on no map, but now indisputably French-Algerian.

Perhaps it was the death of General Pierre Jeanningros, his old Commanding Officer, in 1902, which led ex-Sergeant Kunassec to think deeply about Camerone as the anniversary approached, and to send a letter to Colonel Bruneau of the 1st Etranger in Sidi-bel-Abbes.

> Among the glorious feats of arms of your brave regiment, the 30th April is a magnificent anniversary, principally for the 3rd Company of the 1st Battalion [*he wrote*]. I speak of the Combat of Camerone, which is wrapped in the folds of your glorious flag. This valiant Company, commanded by those brave officers Danjou, Maudet and Vilain, was decimated at Camerone on 30th April, 1863. Now I am old and infirm, but I think back to that time, when I was in the Legion and was a combatant there. On 30th April I raise my glass to the health of the heroic Legion and its Colonel.[6]

Bruneau, apparently moved by the sentiments, sent the letter to *Le Petite Journal* in Paris, which published it on the front page of their edition of 19 May 1902, accompanied by a photograph of Kunassec, a fine-looking old soldier, snappy with his clipped moustache, and sporting the *Medaille Militaire* and *Expedition du Mexique* medals on the lapel of his jacket.

A few weeks earlier, on 24 March, the decorating of the Regimental Standard of the 2nd *Tirailleurs Algeriens* with the Cross of a Chevalier of the Legion of Honour set in motion a train of events which would put the Foreign Legion very much in the public eye. Julien Saurel, a young journalist in Sidi-bel-Abbes, wondered why the Regimental Standard of the 1st Etranger had never been decorated in the same way.

He wrote at once to the headquarters of the Military Department of Oran, soliciting a Cross for the 1st Etranger, but received no reply. He tried again on 31 July, addressing a letter to the War Office in Paris. This time he received a response, but a negative one. Napoleon III had decreed, he was informed, that the Legion of Honour would only be bestowed on a Regimental Standard if an enemy flag had been taken in battle. The *Tirailleurs Algeriens* had captured a battle flag in an engagement in Mexico in 1863. As the Foreign Legion had never taken an enemy flag it was not eligible.

Saurel was not one to be stopped, writing a third letter on 11 October and addressing it directly to the Minister of War. He pointed out that Sergeant-Major Doze of the Foreign Legion had seized a battle flag during the siege of Constantine on 7 October 1837 and brought it back to the French lines. Further, he said, at Magenta, Sous-Lieutenant Callet, of what was then the 2nd Etranger, had seized an Austrian flag, but that in the confusion it had slipped from his hand and been snatched up by men of the 2nd Zouaves. In fact, Zede had seen them making off with it. Considering that Doze's feat was far less surrounded with possible controversy than Callet's act, Saurel felt sure that his plea would be well received.

The 2nd Zouaves, whose Regimental Standard had received the Cross of a Chevalier of the Legion of Honour for the Magenta exploit, denied any knowledge of Sous-Lieutenant Callet's involvement, and despite the fact that Doze's capture of the flag at Constantine had been well known throughout the *Armee d'Afrique*, and had been chronicled by Grisot and Coulombon, and in a number of military history books, the War Office said that nothing could be found in the archives to substantiate the claim. Anyway, Saurel was told, a Decree by Napoleon III in 1859 could certainly not be applied retroactively.

The matter might have ended there, had not the City Council of Sidi-bel-Abbes stepped in. They wrote to the Prefect of the Department of Oran, detailing the actions of the 1st Etranger during the previous several years of campaigning in the Sud Oranais and asking that the Legion of Honour be bestowed on the Regimental Standard not only 'in recognition of the brilliant exploits by the Legion Etrangere', but to recognize 'their great cooperation in expanding the colonizing work of France.'

The timing was fortuitous, as the government had just changed in France and incoming Minister of War Eugene Etienne was from Oran. He reviewed the request from the Councillors of Sidi-bel-Abbes and also the earlier correspondence. Aware that President Emile Loubet had visited Sidi-bel-Abbes in 1903, Etienne drew up a proposal that the Cross be bestowed in recognition of services over a much greater period than just the conquest of the Sud Oranais.

His proposal, dated 16 February, read:

Monsieur le President:

As a reward for the numerous exploits accomplished by the Legion Etrangere, everywhere France has had a need to plant the Flag of the Republic, in Tonkin as in Dahomey, in Madagascar as in the Extreme South of Algeria, and to recognize the acts of devotion, of courage and of abnegation which troops who are always on a war footing have rendered to the Nation in defence of our colonial domain, I have the honour to propose that you confer on the Legion Etrangere the insignia of the Legion of Honour and decree that the Flag of the 1st Regiment Etranger shall have the honour of carrying it. If you approve this proposition, I pray that you will attach your signature.

Eugene Etienne
Minister of War

Loubet supported the proposal and signed the necessary Decree[7] at once. It It was published in the *Journal officiel* the following day and Etienne at once telegraphed the decision to Mayor Bastide in Sidi-bel-Abbes.[8]

It had taken four years from Saurel's initial letter for the issue to be settled, and the actual decorating ceremony on 28 April 1906 went off very well. It was conducted in the presence of Colour Parties with the Regimental Standards of the

2nd Zouaves, the 2nd *Tirailleurs Algeriens*, the 2nd *Chasseurs d'Afrique* and the 2nd Spahis. Sidi-bel-Abbes' public buildings were festooned with Tricolours and blue-white-and-red bunting, as were many business houses and cafes, and at eight o'clock on the morning of 27 April Colonel Boutgourd and his officers led a delegation to the Foreign Legion Cemetery. In the afternoon the 1st Etranger marched through the town.

> At two o'clock, a grand parade had been organized by the Legionnaires and several of the city's various societies and organizations [Le Republicain *reported*]. The march was led by a detachment of Spahis, followed by a detachment of the Legion's Mounted Companies, brought in from Berguent to take part in the celebrations.

The following day, representatives of the Ministry of War, and the Governor-General of Algeria were joined by the Mayor and Councillors, and assorted notables from the region. At the top of the staffs of the Regimental Standards of the French Army is a silk decoration known as a *cravate*, to which medals awarded to the regiments are pinned.

> The revue marched past General Herson, commanding the Division of Oran [*said* Le Republicain]. Then, descending from his horse, he read the decree of the President of the Republic, affixed the Cross to the flag, touched the flagstaff with his sword and embraced and shook hands with the Standard-Bearer.[9]

Apparently, there had been at least some mention of Camerone and other notable battles in the speeches given at the ceremony. Joseph Ehrhart, who had joined the Foreign Legion after being prevented from re-enlisting in the regular French Army because of a poor service record, was impressed.

> When they blew the retreat, more than one Legionnaire had tears in his eyes [*he said later*]. I had been a Legionnaire for only a short time, [but] I was moved and my thoughts were all for those unknown men who had died so that this flag would always wave proudly.[10]

Seemingly, not every Legionnaire was quite so impressed. German-born Erwin Rosen, who had joined the Foreign Legion in 1905, was certainly in Sidi-bel-Abbes at the time of the decorating of the Regimental Standard, and may even have taken part in the parade, though he made no reference to it in the book he wrote after deserting the following year. He did mention, however, his curiosity about the *Salle d'Honneur*, and claimed to have bribed a fellow countryman to let him into the hallowed building to look around. In the dim light of the oil lamps, the Legion's treasured Camerone memento must have looked very real, for Rosen reported: 'A creepy souvenir of this fight lies on a little table in the *Salle d'Honneur* – an embalmed human hand. It is the hand of Captain Danjou' – severed, he breathlessly told his readers, by a sabre and picked up from beside the officer's dead body.[11]

Sous-Lieutenant Francois, in the meantime, had gone up one notch in rank and exchanged the burning desert of the Algerian-Moroccan border for the heat and humidity of Tonkin. He was commanding the small post of Ta-Lung, in the Second Military Territory, guarding the frontier track along the border with China, when he heard that the Regimental Standard of the 1st Etranger was to be decorated. Immediately noting the closeness of the date for the ceremony – 28 April – and the anniversary of Camerone two days later, Francois hit upon the idea of celebrating the presentation, and of telling his own Legionnaires the story of *La Compagnie Danjou* at the same time. It would not have been new to them, for all would have been through the *Salle d'Honneur* as recruits.

On the morning of 30 April the attention of the sentry manning the lookout tower at the Chinese military post of Thuy Cay, across the Song Bang Giang River from Ta-Lung, was drawn to further unusual activity at the tiny parade ground of the French military post. The day before, the Chinese had watched the French troops decorating their little bamboo-and-stone post with blue-white-and-red bunting and freshly-cut foliage, and had decided that it must be for some kind of celebration. Now the Chinese officer examined the French post through his field glasses.

The Tricolour hung limply at the flagpole, and he could see the detachment of men of the 1st Etranger drawn up on parade. He was not especially concerned. The bloody fighting in Tonkin between the French and the Chinese-backed Black Flags pirates had essentially died down several years before. Certainly, there were still occasional outbreaks, when some warlord, seeking food or loot or women, attacked a 'pacified' village and was pursued by locally-based French troops, but mostly the Chinese and the French, ensconced in their respective posts, merely watched each other across border rivers and streams, or demarcated lines. Like most Foreign Legion officers commanding isolated frontier posts, Francois spent much of his time finding work to keep his men busy. Usually it was short patrols, minor improvements to the post, or gardening.

The Chinese watched with interest as the men of the Foreign Legion paraded at 9:00 a.m., kitted out in their dress uniforms, and saw Francois walk slowly along the line, meeting the eyes of each Legionnaire in turn. Then, standing before them, he drew his sword.

'At my command, you will present arms to your flag, Chevalier of the Legion of Honour, just as if it was in front of you,' he told them. He snapped to attention: 'Present . . . arms!'

Then Francois re-told the story of the 3rd of the 1st, and how it had earned the Battle Honour of Camerone, which adorned their newly-decorated Regimental Standard.[12]

It was certainly the first time in more than four decades – since the first anniversary of Camerone and the service in the cathedral at Puebla in 1864, followed by the distribution of the *Expedition du Mexique* medals – that there had been an Official Remembrance.[13]

The extensive newspaper publicity relating to the events at Sidi-bel-Abbes struck various chords, and would certainly have caught the eye of the author of *Les heros de Camaron*, but the Chaplain of Saint-Cyr – ecclesiastically elevated to

Monseigneur seven years earlier – had died, full of honours and memories, the previous 27 October, in his eighty-eighth year.[14] A new edition of Paul Gaulot's three-volume work of 1889–91 came out as *L'Expedition du Mexique, 1861–1867* in mid-1906, putting the campaign back into the public eye.[15] Former Corporal Abel Huart in the 2nd Battalion of the Regiment Etranger in Mexico, stirred his audience with vivid images and ringing phrases at a lecture he gave in Orleans. 'Captain Danjou, [Sous-]Lieutenants Vilain and Maudet, and you Sous-Officiers and soldiers who sleep your last sleep in a foreign land, you will live eternally in our memories, surrounded by a brilliant halo,' he declaimed. 'Glory is the sunshine of the dead.'[16] He had, he said proudly, 'presented arms at the monument to Camerone'.[17] While it does not appear that an annual Camerone celebration was started as a result of the year's official activities in Sidi-bel-Abbes and unofficial one in Tonkin, the idea certainly piqued the interest of former Foreign Legion officers now serving in other regiments, and with the Old Comrades Associations of former Legionnaires, some of whom had served with Camerone veterans.

After French civilians were killed in Morocco in 1907 it became clear that a French takeover of Morocco would soon take place. By January 1908 an expeditionary force, landed at Casablanca, had grown to almost ten thousand men and the Conquest of Morocco began. General Charles Zede died during the year. He was known to have compiled his memoirs, and those who were more interested in the old Mexican Campaign than in the new Moroccan one wondered when they would be published. The ancient but disorganized Kingdom of Morocco became a French Protectorate, and the Foreign Legion was actively involved from the beginning, in saving the lives of French nationals in Fez in 1911, in seeing Lyautey installed as Resident General the following year, and in the on-going war. In the event, it would be a quarter of a century before Zede's writings would see the light of day, appearing just as twenty-five years of fighting in Morocco was coming to an end.

Clearly, at least some small locally-sponsored Camerone Day celebrations – on the pattern pioneered in Tonkin by Lieutenant Francois – were held in various places at the behest of like-minded officers over the next few years. General Jean-Pierre Hallo, interviewing an elderly former Foreign Legion officer named Ravet, was told that the 2nd Etranger commemorated Camerone in 1912, and that 'the meal was exceptional and at the morning parade the story of the Combat of Camerone was read aloud'.[18]

The same year the Federation of Societies of Former Legionnaires of France and the Colonies launched a monthly magazine called *La Legion Etrangere* which featured historical material as well as news of the veterans' organizations.[19] It more or less coincided with the publication of a book with the lively title of *Les Mysteres de la Legion etrangere* by journalist and author Georges d'Esparbes. By *Mysteres* d'Esparbes meant 'Mysterious Men,' rather than simply 'Mysteries,' and there is certainly no doubt that the Foreign Legion had some very unusual members between the mid-1880s and the outbreak of the First World War. However, whether they were anywhere near as exotic and 'mysterious' as d'Esparbes would have had his readers believe is highly arguable.

While working on a newspaper series just before the century turned he had seen a list of the former professions claimed by men engaging in the Foreign Legion in 1885 and 1898, and had come to the conclusion that they, like the names the men assumed, were largely fictitious. To d'Esparbes this must mean they were masking interesting middle- and upper-class individuals who had decided to get away from their pasts, and he thought the men 'mysterious'. Unfortunately, much of his 'research' was done in the bars of Sidi-bel-Abbes and the talkative Legionnaires of the 1st Etranger, delighted at the prospect of free drinks, told him what they thought he wanted to hear. The red wine of Algeria had become an inseparable part of the Legionnaires' lives. Know colloquially as *pinard*, it was cheap enough for even their penurious existence, contributing as much conviviality to their lives as drunkenness. Alcoholism became something of a problem in the garrison towns of the foreign regiments, but a blind eye was generally turned to it, providing a man could carry out his duties the following day. D'Esparbes' newspaper series was a success and he spun it off into a book, *La Legion etrangere*, which Paris publisher Flammarion put out in 1900. Officially, the Foreign Legion thought that 'a little too much imagination' on the part of the author 'diminished the value of the book'.[20] It made only a relatively slight literary ripple at the time, though some local wits began referring to the 1st Etranger as 'The 1st Mysterious'. Then, just before the First World War, *La Legion etrangere* was republished as *Les Mysteres de la Legion etrangere*,[21] with line drawings by talented illustrator Maurice Mahut, which the Foreign Legion brass thought were 'excellent'. True, part-true or false, there is absolutely no doubt that this second – re-titled – edition of the book greatly influenced the public perception of the Foreign Legion and of the men who served in it.

Aristide Merolli was an Italian middle-class professional bored with civilian life, who joined the Foreign Legion in 1910, and eventually rose to the rank of Captain, a fitting candidate for d'Esparbes' definition of 'mysterious'. He remembered attending Camerone Day celebrations in 1913 and 1914, which involved a retelling of the story, followed by a big meal, sports events and much drinking.[22]

When war broke out in August 1914 the usual heavily German make-up of the 1st and 2nd Etrangers, along with the numbers of serving Austrians and Turks, gave the French food for thought about using them in the war in Europe. Yet with thousands of foreigners in France clamouring to join the French Army something had to be done. Each of the two regiments already had a *Regiment de Marche* serving in Morocco and the decision was made to create new ones for the war in Europe. The redesignated 1st *Regiment de Marche* of each of the two regiments, made up of nationals of the Central Powers and others who had reason to fear the possibility of capture by the enemy, would stay in Morocco. The 2nd *Regiment de Marche*, and any subsequent ones which might be raised, would be part of the Allied forces in France.

The three-battalion 2nd *Regiment de Marche* of the 1st Etranger, raised in France, was joined by a fourth battalion from Algeria, as was the three-battalion 2nd *Regiment de Marche* of the 2nd Etranger. Certain long-serving German, Austrian and Turkish Legionnaires had volunteered to fight the Central Powers, even though they knew that capture by the enemy would mean certain death. A three-battalion 3rd *Regiment de Marche* of the 1st Etranger was also brought into being. Many of the foreign volunteers, who signed on 'for the duration of the war', were intellectuals or men of upper middle-class backgrounds, including the Rockwell brothers, Paul and Kiffin, from Atlanta, Georgia. Invalided out of the Foreign Legion on health grounds after the first Winter in the trenches, Paul Rockwell remained in France to be near his brother and joined the French Army's War Propaganda Department. He would subsequently write a definitive book about the American volunteers, some of whom were graduates of Harvard, Yale and other Ivy League academic institutions.[23] However, also among the seventy or so American 'durationists' were many men from varied and far more modest backgrounds, including Greek-born Nick Karayinis, who had joined his uncle in New York while still a lad, and helped him run a downtown fruit-stand. Among the true elites was Prince Karaman Khan Nazare-Aga, the son of the Persian Ambassador to France. The *Regiments de Marche* into which these disparate elements were put, became sometimes uneasy amalgamations of foreign volunteer 'durationists' and veteran Legionnaires from North Africa, who often resented the newcomers. However, the war was a great leveller.

A *Regiment de Marche d'Afrique en Orient* was sent from Algeria to Gallipoli early in the war and subsequently served in Serbia, and a 4th *Regiment de Marche* of the 1st Etranger, an all-Italian unit built around sons and grandsons of Guiseppe Garibaldi, the 'Great Liberator' of the previous century, saw much action before being disbanded in March 1915 and its personnel released to join the Italian Army. Almost all the British subjects also left to be incorporated into the British Army and there was further haemorrhaging as groups – the Belgians, Poles and others – were released to serve in their own armies as they entered the war against the Central Powers.

The Foreign Legion became part of the Moroccan Division – which included the Zouaves, the Spahis and the *Tirailleurs Algeriens* – of General Philippe Petain's 33rd Corps. The 2nd of the 1st sustained huge losses attacking Hill 140 in the Battle of Artois on 9 May 1915. Among them was a young Corporal named Zinovi Pechkoff, the adopted son of Russian writer Aleksei Peshkov – better known by his pen name of Maxim Gorki – who was serving with 'D' Battalion. Pechkoff's upper right arm was smashed by machine-gun bullets and doctors amputated it. For him the war was over, but he would later return to the Foreign Legion and become one of its most successful and admired Company Officers in Morocco.

The 3rd *Regiment de Marche*, which had seen little action, was disbanded in July and its men absorbed into the 2nd. Both Foreign Legion *Regiments de Marche* suffered heavy casualties in the Summer of 1915, before being withdrawn from the front. General Lyautey arrived in France and reviewed the Moroccan Division at Chaux-la-Chappelle on 30 July, calling for those who had served under him in Africa to be brought to him. David Wooster King, one of the American 'durationists' who was present, later recalled that 'cynical, hard-bitten Legionnaires returned to the ranks, shoulders back and eyes shining'.[24] They were reviewed again on 13 September near Belfort and received their Regimental Standards from President Raymond Poincare. By order of General Joseph Gallieni, the Minister of War, they bore the motto HONOUR AND COUNTRY instead of the regular

VALOUR AND DISCIPLINE. The following month Poincare, accompanied by King George V and the Prince of Wales, again reviewed the Moroccan Division.[25]

By now it was being realized that the losses of the *Regiments de Marche* had been so enormous that the only sensible thing to do was to form a single regiment, which was done on 11 November 1915 under the name of the *Regiment de Marche de la Legion Etrangere* – the RMLE – destined for future glory. A week later the Regimental Standard of the 2nd of the 2nd was laid up, so the RMLE inherited the traditions, honours and the Regimental Standard of the 2nd of the 1st. The regiment was involved in some of the great – and hugely wasteful – battles of the Summer of 1916, then kept out of the front lines, recuperating and being brought back up to strength, until April 1917. It bled profusely again at Auberive and lost its commanding officer, Lieutenant-Colonel Duriez. At the end of the month, on the anniversary of Camerone, he was replaced by an extraordinary officer who had first joined the Foreign Legion eighteen years earlier, and whose total dedication would earn him the name of 'Father of the Legion' and 'Premier Legionnaire of France'.

Lieutenant-Colonel Paul Rollet was the son of an officer who had fought in the Franco-Prussian War, and had later been Professor of Geography at Saint-Cyr. Born on 20 December 1875, young Rollet graduated from Saint-Cyr in 1896 and joined the 91st Infantry Regiment. In December 1899, soon after being promoted to Lieutenant, he transferred into the 1st Etranger at Sidi-bel-Abbes and after three years in Southern Algeria, was selected to join the *Regiment de Marche de Madagascar*. He returned to Algeria in 1905.

Then began a period of very hard service with the 1st Etranger's Mounted Companies, fast moving strike forces of two Legionnaires to one mule, capable of covering long distances and taking battle to 'dissident' tribes, often with the advantage of surprise on their side. The principle was the same as that of the Mounted Company in Mexico, but the reality was more efficient. Rollet asked nothing of his Legionnaires in the 3rd Mounted Company that he could not do himself and was much esteemed. Promoted to Captain in 1909, he took part two years later in the relief of Fez and the rescue of besieged French and foreign nationals, and in three years of almost constant movement, he and his 3rd Company had fought their way across Morocco in a series of eighteen battles.

Back in Sidi-bel-Abbes in May 1914, Rollet watched the ominous signs of the coming war, and, fearful that the Foreign Legion would be left in North Africa, demanded and obtained a transfer into the 31st Infantry Regiment serving in France. He was only with them for a matter of months after war broke out, then transferred into the 331st Infantry Regiment and saw two years of action in the Argonne, on the Somme and on the Aisne.[26]

Short of stature, with a neatly-trimmed beard, Rollet was something of an eccentric. He had long abandoned regulation boots for rope-soled canvas shoes, sometimes treated with boot-blacking to make them less conspicuous. He never wore a shirt, preferring his uniform next to his skin, and disguised the fact by wearing a celluloid collar and cuffs attached to elastic. Rollet also hated tin helmets and wore his kepi at all times, going into battle armed only with a pink parasol, which he used to wave his troops forward, as well as to hold aloft to pinpoint his own position for them.

Among the outstanding officers Rollet found already serving in the RMLE was Captain Fernand Maire of the 3rd Battalion, a hard-drinking dandy, who curled his moustache upwards, distained a pistol belt because it spoiled the hang of his uniform and went into action armed only with a cane. He took great pride in being a second-generation Legionnaire, and in the fact that his father had served in the *Brigade Etrangere* in the Crimea, been a Sergeant-Major in Italy – he was beside Colonel de Chabriere when he was killed at Magenta – and had been commissioned in the field in 1866, while serving with the 62nd Regiment of the Line in Mexico. A few months younger than Rollet, Maire had been a Sous-Lieutenant and Lieutenant in an infantry regiment and had transferred into the 2nd Etranger just before the war.[27] The two men had never met, but liked each other on sight.

'He fell upon us like a meteor,' Maire would say. 'Small, thin, nervous, a lined face from which shone, beneath thick arching brows, two transparent blue eyes . . . He suddenly restored to us a strong odour of Africa.'[28]

On 14 July, for the first time since war had broken out, there was a Bastille Day Parade in Paris and Rollet and Maire took a Foreign Legion contingent to the nation's capital. The Colour Party included the Greek-American 'durationist' Nick Karayinis, who had been wounded in 1915, cited in Regimental Orders and awarded the *Croix de Guerre* in 1916 and cited again in the Orders of the Day after Auberive.[29] President Poincare hung a yellow and green *fourragere* – lanyard – in the colours of the ribbon of the *Medaille Militaire*, on the Regimental Standard.

> Saturday, July 14, 1917, the *Regiment de Marche de la Legion Etrangere* received the just recompense due to its striking bravery [*the* Bulletin of the French Army *reported*]. Five times cited in the Orders of the Army, it saw itself awarded before any other troop the yellow and green *fourragere*. Its immortal glory has been proclaimed over the face of the earth.[30]

On 27 September, fresh from the battlefield at Verdun – where Karayinis had been cited for the third time in Army Orders and awarded the *Medaille Militaire*[31] – the Moroccan Division was reviewed by Petain, now Commander-in-Chief of the French Army. After reading out the six citations in Army Orders which the regiment had by now earned, Petain pinned the Legion of Honour to the *cravate* of the Standard and hung a scarlet *fourragere*, the colour of the ribbon of the decoration, on the staff, telling the Legionnaires: 'You have not ceased in your victories. I will not cease, either, until I invent new rewards for you.'

Despite having lost the Portuguese, Czechoslovakians and Armenians, who had left to join their national armies, the RMLE distinguished itself at Hangard Wood in April 1918 and at Soissons the following month. From 27 August to 16 September the Foreign Legion was engaged in what would turn out to be the last act of the war, the assault on the supposedly impregnable Hindenburg Line. Just before the bitter fighting, where gas was used against them, and at times the combat became hand-to-hand, Rollet had welcomed an old friend, Major Nicolas, back to the regiment. A member of the Royal Family of Montenegro, he had graduated from Saint-Cyr and served in an infantry regiment until transferring into the 1st Etranger in 1905. Like Rollet, he had left the Foreign Legion at the outbreak of war, and had served with the 101st and 124th Infantry Regiments before transferring into the RMLE.[32]

Cited once again in Army Orders, the regiment took up a position at Saulxures-les-Nancy, actually on the soil of Lorraine, which had been seized by the Germans in the Franco-Prussian War almost half a century before. On 29 October the RMLE went into the trenches around Champenoux, ready for a massive push into Lorraine, to seize the stronghold of Metz and inflict the final defeat. The attacks would begin on 11 November, the third birthday of the RMLE, and all was in readiness. Then came the news that the Germans had surrendered and an armistice been signed. The war was over and just six days later the Moroccan Division was given the honour of being the first in their sector of the front to advance into the rest of Lorraine.

Former Legionnaire Paul Ayers Rockwell, who was now attached to French Grand Army Headquarters as an official war correspondent for the *Chicago Daily News*, was with General Daugan when the Moroccan Division entered Chateau-Salines to be greeted by an ecstatic population, with the women in national costume, makeshift Tricolours flying everywhere and men wearing blue-white-and-red cockades on their hats.

> Colonel Rollet, his breast covered with medals and his sword drawn, rode at the head of his Legionnaires [*Rockwell wrote*]. Behind him came the Legion's band and the Legion's battle-flag ... On arriving where General Daugan and his staff were on horseback, Colonel Rollet dismounted, and, taking the Legion's flag, held it while the Legionnaires filed past. The spectators crowded near as the volunteer fighters of every race, creed, and social condition, representing five-score countries, and whose exploits are renowned throughout the world, went by ...
>
> The be-medalled Legionnaires marched by proudly erect, with that look in the eye which only comes with the consciousness of duty well performed. In the ranks were perhaps fifty survivors from 1914 ....[33]

Among them, Rockwell saw the Persian Prince Nazare-Aga, now a many times decorated Captain.

> When the last company of Legionnaires had passed, General Daugan approached and kissed the Legion's flag [*Rockwell reported*]. Immediately Colonel Rollet was surrounded by a throng of women and children and men, who embraced the banner with reverence and affection. The Legion's band began playing *La Marseillaise* and the refrain was taken up by a group of old men, some of them veterans of the War of 1870.[34]

The RMLE took part in the Victory Parade in Paris and, for the first and last time in his life, Rollet wore a tin helmet as the Foreign Legion swung down the Champs Elysses to the strains of *Le Boudin*. The 'for the duration' Legionnaires were demobilized in February 1919 and the following month the RMLE returned to

North Africa. Its nine citations in Army Orders, one less than the *Regiment d'infanterie coloniale du Maroc*, made it the second most decorated regiment in the French Army.

The first *Croix de Guerre*, to mark the Battle of Artois, had been pinned on the *cravate* of the Regimental Standard of the 1st *Regiment de Marche* of the 1st Etranger by President Poincare when he presented the banner to the regiment on 13 September 1915. When the 1st and 2nd *Regiments de Marche* had been merged into the RMLE on 11 November 1915, the new unit inherited the Regimental Standard of the 2nd of the 1st and received a *palme* – equal to a second *Croix de Guerre* – in January 1916, to mark the battle at Naverin Farm, as well as a second *palme* which would have been awarded to the now disbanded 2nd *Regiment de Marche* of the 2nd Etranger for its action at Souain. A third *palme* was awarded in August 1916 for the RMLE's assault at Belloy-en-Santerre and a fourth one in May 1917 for the battle of Auberive.

By an Order of the Army dated 5 June 1916 the Regimental Standard had received a *fourragere* in the colours of the *Croix de Guerre* and by another Order, dated 26 June 1917, it received a yellow and green *fourragere*, the colours of the *Medaille Militaire*, the first regiment of the French Army to be so honoured. On 27 September 1917 the Legion of Honour was pinned to the *cravate* and six weeks later, on 3 November, the scarlet *fourragere* was bestowed by Petain. The *cravate* received another *palme* in September 1917 for action at Cumieres and three more in 1918, for Hangard Wood in July, Montagne de Paris in October and Laffaux in November.

The same month Marshal Petain made good on his promise of the previous year to create something special for the Foreign Legion. The *fourrageres* in the colours of the *Croix de Guerre* and the Legion of Honour were exchanged for a unique double *fourragere*, combining the colours of the ribbons of both. Finally, on 30 August 1919, after it had returned to Algeria, the *Medaille Militaire* was pinned to the *cravate* of the Regimental Standard of the RMLE, where it joined the other medals and two non-French ones: the Grand Cross of the *Ordre de la Tour et l'Epee de Portugal* and the *Medaille des Volontaires Catalans*.

In total, the Regimental Standard was adorned with a double *fourragere*, combining the colours of the Legion of Honour and the *Croix de Guerre 1914–1918* – one of only two regiments to have been so honoured. The RMLE was also one of only five regiments to have been awarded the *Medaille Militaire* and one of nineteen decorated with the Legion of Honour.[35]

27

The Ascent of Colonel Paul Rollet

No Camerone celebrations appear to have been held during the First World War, at least, if there were, nobody thought to mention any in the various books of reminiscences – or in the collections of private letters of dead Legionnaires published later by families in their memory – which appeared in its wake.

A general re-organization of the Foreign Legion took place over the next four years, much of it aimed at providing the military manpower needed for the pacification of 'dissident' tribes in Morocco. They had been largely held at bay by the Germans, Austrians and Turks serving in the *Regiments de Marche* of the 1st and 2nd Etrangers during the the war. Fortunately, in this reshaping, the Foreign Legion had a friend in a high place.

General Jules Mordacq, who had been a Lieutenant in the Foreign Legion in Tonkin in the last years of the previous century, had written a book of reminiscences,[1] and also a military study of the 1859 Campaign against the Beni-Snassen,[2] was now Cabinet Secretary to Prime Minister Georges Clemenceau. As early as June of 1919 he was talking about the possibility of the Foreign Legion becoming not merely several infantry regiments but a full Division, with its own Cavalry and Artillery arms.[3] Rollet, at the time, was all for the Foreign Legion leaving Algeria completely, and becoming totally Morocco-based, but the War Ministry thought otherwise. The 1st Etranger at Sidi-bel-Abbes became the basic intake camp and administrative headquarters for the entire Foreign Legion, while the 2nd Etranger left Saida in Algeria to take up garrison duties at Meknes in Morocco, and the RMLE remained under its own name for the time being.

The embryo plans for a regiment of cavalry caused re-thinking about the names of the regiments of foot soldiers and the decision was taken to add the word Infantry to any new regiments and to phase it in for existing ones.

So when, on 15 November 1920, a new entity was brought into being, specifically for service in Morocco, it became the 4th *Regiment Etranger d'Infanterie* – 4th REI. Created from elements of the 1st Battalion of the 1st Etranger, it initially trained at Meknes, before moving to its new garrison at Marrakesh in southern Morocco. By a complicated system of 'affiliations' it was somehow determined that the 3rd Company of the 1st Battalion of the new regiment was the lineal descendant of *La Compagnie Danjou*.[4]

Less than two weeks later, on 30 November, the motto of VALEUR ET DISCIPLINE, which had traditionally been on their Regimental Standards, was changed to HONNEUR ET FIDELITE, henceforth to appear 'on the Flags and Standards of all the existing Corps of the Foreign Legion and of those which may subsequently be created'.[5] The words somewhat echoed the historic *Regiment Suisse* de Diesbach (1689–1792), whose banners had proclaimed FIDELITATE ET HONORE.[6]

On New Year's Day 1921 the RMLE, commanded by Rollet, was reconstituted as the 3rd *Regiment Etranger d'Infanterie* – 3rd REI – and three weeks later took up garrison duties in Fez to counter local unrest. The planned 1st *Regiment Etranger de Cavalerie* – 1st REC – was brought into being, with headquarters at Sousse in Tunisia, and on 20 June 1922 the 1st Regiment Etranger became the 1st *Regiment Etranger d'Infanterie* – 1st REI. All the regiments – or elements of them – would be involved in fighting the Rif tribesmen of Abd el-Krim, who twice bested the Spanish Army in partitioned Morocco before moving against the French, and then in the final 'pacification' of Morocco.

As the Commanding Officer of the 3rd REI it soon became clear to Rollet that the pre-war Legionnaire was a very different man from the post-war one. Comparatively few members of the Officer Corps and only a small number of the Sous-Officiers and Corporals of pre–1914 had survived the carnage of the Western Front, and not many of the surviving Old Sweats had re-engaged.

Many of the post-war recruits were former soldiers who had found that they liked fighting. Some had been recent enemies of the French. Yet the majority were young and unemployed, hungry men, for whom the Foreign Legion represented the prospect of regular meals. The Germans tended to be highly politicized, refugees from the post-Treaty of Versailles unrest in their homeland, while a large number of the Russians, usually older men, were ex-Tsarist officers, or the survivors of the White Russian Armies of Wrangel and Kolchak, chased out by the Bolsheviks.

Particularly during 1920 and 1921 desertions were a real problem for all of the Foreign Legion regiments and Rollet was not alone in believing that an *esprit de corps* was the key to inculcating these diverse soldiers with a sense of regimental pride. The story of Camerone appealed to him. Possibly he made a 'connection' between the 3rd Company of the 1st Battalion in Mexico and his own pre-war service with the 3rd *Compagnie Montée* of the 1st Etranger, another '3rd of the 1st'. Then, too, he had assumed command of the RMLE on the fifty-fourth anniversary of the Combat of Camerone. Other senior officers were also interested.

It was a time of the ascendancy of high profile officers of proven ability and sturdy independence of spirit. Rollet, Maire and Nicolas were referred to as *Les Mousquetaires* – 'The Musketeers'. Then there was Battalion Commander de Corta, who had spent most of the war as a prisoner of the Germans and was now a colourful fighting soldier, who took regimental musicians on his campaigns and often had them play jazz music late into the night, and a Swiss nobleman, Baron Albert de Tscharner, who had joined the RMLE in 1916 and stayed on after the war. There were also outstanding Company Officers, like Prince Aage of Denmark and Zinovi Pechkoff.

Aage, cousin to England's King George V, and also related to most of Europe's nobility, was the great-grandson of King Louis-Philippe, founder of the Foreign Legion. He had joined in 1922, after a bank failure wiped out his fortune, and would see hard fighting in the Rif War of the 1920s, make a good career under the Tricolour of France, and write two books about his service in the Foreign Legion.[7]

Pechkoff, after losing his right arm as a Corporal in May 1915, had taken his discharge. In the aftermath of the Russian Revolution he was with the anti-Bolshevik armies in Siberia and the Crimea, and after returning to France and becoming a French citizen, returned to the Foreign Legion as an officer. An admired company commander in the campaigns against Abd el-Krim, Pechkoff was several times wounded, would write a book about his experiences and eventually become a soldier-diplomat.[8]

All liked the idea of celebrating Camerone – and, to a lesser extent, other Foreign Legion battles – and some small localized celebrations appear to have been held as early as 1922. Rollet began developing Camerone Day as an annual holiday for the 3rd REI, with a parade, then a day of rest for the Legionnaires, and some extra wine. Former Sergeant-Chef Sterm recalled to General Hallo, himself a former Foreign Legion officer, that on Camerone Day 1924 'the 2nd *Compagnie Montee* at Sefrou stood down the guard overnight [and] distributed an extra quarter litre of wine, which caused some chaos in the Company!'[9] Rollet had developed for the 3rd REI a Camerone Day parade and extra rations of food and drink. It became the envy of the other foreign regiments, because, at this point, the amount of notice taken of Camerone, whether or not the story of *La Compagnie Danjou* was told, and the degree of celebrating permitted, depended on the regiment, the battalion, sometimes even the Company. Yet it would not be long before the concept would be formally taken up at the official level.

The same year the 3rd REI received a new Regimental Standard, this one emblazoned with the new approved Foreign Legion motto of HONOUR AND FIDELITY. Rollet had sought six Battle Honours for the Regimental Standard, which had inherited the traditions of his beloved RMLE, but by the time they had been agreed by the governing bureaucracy he was no longer in command. Nevertheless, approval was given for: CAMERONE 1863, ARTOIS 1915, CHAMPAGNE 1915, LA SOMME 1916, LES MONTS-VERDUN 1917, PICARDIE 1918 and VAUXAILLON 1918. At the end of the Rif War the Battle Honour MAROC 1925–1926 was added, and the *cravate* was decorated with the *Merite Militaire Cherifien*. Rollet, who never gave up, eventually also obtained approval for SOISSONNAIS 1918.

An Englishman, Adolphe Richard Cooper, at the end of a rambunctious second engagement in the Legion, was doing light duties at Sidi-bel-Abbes at the time, awaiting his discharge at the end of his five-year contract. He was given an assortment of clerking and administrative tasks, had a good deal of spare time for other activities, and, having an interest in history, made it his business to spend as much time as possible in the *Salle d'Honneur*. Cooper's first hitch in the Foreign Legion – at the age of fifteen, under the name of Cornelis Jean de Bruin – had taken him to Gallipoli with the *Regiment de Marche d'Afrique en Orient* to fight the Turks, and he was excited to find his citation for the first *Croix de Guerre* to be awarded. He enjoyed reading about the Foreign Legion's nine decades of fighting. Naturally, he looked for what there might be on the Combat of Camerone and found some records.

I took out of the file a roll which had the texture of parchment [*Cooper said many years later*]. On it was written in a neat hand all the names of the officers, NCOs and men who took part in the battle. It started with that of Captain Danjou, then Vilain and Maudet, the other officers, followed by those of the men. On another well-written parchment was the story of the battle itself . . .[10]

On 3 March, 1925, Lieutenant-Colonel Rollet handed over command of the 3rd REI. His place was soon to be taken taken by Lieutenant-Colonel Francois, who, as a young Lieutenant, had held the first Camerone Day in Tonkin nineteen years earlier. He had gone on to command a battalion of the 2nd Etranger there before returning to North Africa.

Rollet was under orders to take command of the 1st REI at Sidi-bel-Abbes in September, a six-month break – including a period of leave – which would give him leisure to think more about Camerone and *esprit de corps*, and also to begin to formulate ideas for the celebration, six years in the future, of the 100th Anniversary of the Foreign Legion. He left Morocco for Algeria.

Finding civilian life less appealing than he had expected, Adolphe Richard Cooper had rejoined the Foreign Legion. This time he reversed his given names, becoming Richard Adolphe Cooper, so as to start afresh with a clean sheet. While being rushed to Morocco with the 6th Battalion of the 1st REI in late April, to counter a threat to Fez posed by Abd el-Krim, he saw Rollet in Sidi-bel-Abbes. The Legionnaires were taken by a series of trains to Taza and then began marching. They knew they would be serving alongside the 3rd REI, so naturally looked forward to being part of the Camerone Day festivities. However, by the time they reached Sidi Abdullah the crisis at Fez had deepened and they were taken to the ancient city in Army trucks, arriving in the evening of 29 April, and finding that the celebrations had been drastically scaled down.

Normally, Cooper said, the day would have begun 'with a parade', at which 'the officer in charge of the unit reads details of the battle.' The extra food and drink was appreciated by the Legionnaires, and it was also a moving occasion.

> I have seen old seasoned soldiers standing to attention whilst listening to the story of the battle being read . . . and if you look well you will see tears gathering in their eyes, [*he recalled years later*]. It is such things that make the strength of the Legion.[11]

Pechkoff's company, which had also been marching from Taza to Fez, planned to celebrate Camerone Day in camp. They halted in the evening of 29 April, expecting two days of rest.

> In the morning after a calm night of sleep the Legionnaires went to bathe and to wash their clothes in the creek near by [*Pechkoff wrote later*]. Perfect serenity reigned in the camp. The smoke from the kitchen fires was rising into the sky. The men at the creek were playing, singing, splashing water on one another. Those who remained in the camp were writing letters. The non-commissioned officers were sitting on empty wine cases in the tent of

the canteen. Perfect relaxation ... peace ... Everyone had forgotten the fatigue of the last days, forgotten the dangers passed, and those awaiting them in the future.[12]

The noisy arrival of a motorcycle messenger disturbed the otherwise idyllic scene. Orders were given to break camp at once and the men hurriedly packed their gear and piled into a convoy of Army trucks which arrived for them. Fez was being seriously threatened and they arrived in the city as the day's truncated Camerone celebrations were getting under way.

> The reminder of this splendid episode of its history [*Pechkoff said*], coming as it did on the eve of a great struggle, evoked in the Legion a spirit of intense pride and a determination to outdo itself in the forthcoming encounter.[13]

Cooper said that he and the other men 'were naturally very upset' at having to forego 'the Legion's annual holiday' because of the advance of 'dissident' forces under Abd el-Krim.[14]

In Sidi-bel-Abbes, Rollet, the soon-to-be Colonel of the 1st REI, had arranged with the man he was to replace, Colonel Boulet-Desbarreau, to commemorate Camerone Day with a modest parade, and a photograph exists of him with a bemedalled Colour Party and the Regimental Standard.[15] Shortly afterwards he left Algeria and crossed the Mediterranean to Marseille to visit Jean Brunon, owner of one of the nation's finest private militaria collections, who had a special interest in the Foreign Legion.

Rollet, who was familiar with Brunon's background, knew that he and his brother, Raoul, had begun collecting militaria as young boys, gradually amassing an outstanding collection of flags, medals, uniforms, weapons, helmets, badges, photographs, prints, diaries, historical documents and other memorabilia, even before they were into their twenties. He also knew that both brothers had joined the Army to fight the Germans, that Raoul Brunon had been killed in action in 1917, and that Jean Brunon, returning home to Marseille, had been touchingly determined to preserve his brother's memory, doing so with what became known as the *Collection Raoul et Jean Brunon*.

Rollet was fifty and Brunon thirty when they met, but their dedication to the Foreign Legion, the one as its 'Father', the other as an enthusiastic non-serving acolyte, was mutual. Brunon's interests were wide, including Florence in the mid-16th century, the Army at the time of the French Revolution, Napoleon's Grenadiers and the Charge of the Light Brigade at Balaclava. He would publish material on all of them over the years, as well as on other topics, but his speciality was the Foreign Legion.

The two men met with Pierre Benigni, the forty-seven-year-old Official Painter to the Army, a former student of military artist Edouard Detaille who had created the painting 'The last survivors of the Hacienda of Camerone' for his 1885 book on the French Army. The three men discussed plans for the Foreign Legion's Centenary Celebrations in 1931 and Rollet spoke of his hopes for the production

The Ascent of Colonel Paul Rollet

of a book on the first one hundred years. It was agreed that Brunon would oversee the work and that Benigni would undertake a series of paintings. Rollet told his companions that he intended to mark the Centenary on 30 April – which would be the sixty-eighth anniversary of the Combat of Cameron – rather than on 9 March, the actual birthday of the Foreign Legion, and emphasized that the proposed book should make an especial effort to highlight the battle.

Once he took command of the 1st REI in September, Rollet had the time and the means to begin to turn his plans into reality. His enthusiasm for Cameron was supported by his fellow *Mousquetaires*, and he had a very staunch ally in Lieutenant-Colonel Francois, who had replaced him as Commanding Officer of the 3rd REI.

The most distinguished former Foreign Legion officer in Sidi-bel-Abbes was retired Lieutenant-Colonel Pierre Forey, who lived within walking distance of the Quartier Vienot and made it a point to pass by every day, receiving a proper salute from the sentries. The great-nephew of General – then Marshal – Elie Forey, who had led the French Expeditionary Corps in Mexico, Pierre Forey was born in 1860 and enlisted in the Army at the age of nineteen. He transferred into the 1st Etranger as a Sergeant in 1884 and almost at once joined a draft for Tonkin, where his actions earned him a commission as a Sous-Lieutenant two years later. After his first tour in Tonkin, Forey served in Algeria, took part in a short-lived campaign in Siam in 1893, came home, then returned to Indo-China in 1897. He did several tours in Tonkin, where, as a Captain, he narrowly escaped death when a bullet was deflected after hitting the centre of the cross of his Chevalier of the Legion of Honour decoration.

Following service in the Sahara, Forey took part in the French conquest of Morocco as Battalion Commander of the 1st *Regiment de Marche* of the 2nd Etranger for three years, beginning in 1909, leading a mixed force of Legionnaires and Zouaves. He went to the Dardanelles with the *Regiment de Marche d'Afrique en Orient* in 1915, then campaigned in Serbia, ending his thirty-five-year Legion career as Lieutenant-Colonel commanding the 1st Etranger from September 1918 until his retirement a year later.[16]

Rollet recruited him as President of the Celebrations Committee, an excellent choice, as he had been in virtually every theatre of war where the Foreign Legion had served between 1884 and his retirement in 1919, except for Madagascar and the Western Front.

Unfortunately for the French, the successes of Abd el-Krim, first against the Spanish, and then against the French, had been an encouragement for anti-French feelings in Lebanon and Syria, but things had begun to settle down when, unexpectedly, the Druzes reacted to bungling by the authorities and raised the standard of rebellion. The 5th Battalion of the 4th REI was camped outside a small village called Messifre on 16 September 1925 when their 1st Company received a heliograph message that some three thousand heavily armed Druzes were heading in their direction. Battalion Commander Kratzert conferred with Captain Landriau of the 4th Squadron of the 1st REC, whose horses were under guard in the town.

In the pre-dawn light the Druzes began hitting the series of strongpoints which comprised the Foreign Legion's position, coming in human waves to overwhelm the defenders. The fighting continued for hours and the defensive positions might have been finally overrun by a combination of superior Druze numbers and a shortage of ammunition on the part of the defenders, had not several aircraft flown in low to drop bombs on the attackers, inflicting more confusion than damage, but sufficient to throw them off guard, and make them fairly easy prey for the hastily summoned 16th *Tirailleurs Algeriens*. The defenders lost all of the 4th Squadron's horses, and had forty-seven dead – twenty-five of them cavalrymen – and eighty-three wounded, including twenty-four cavalrymen.

Just two months later Landriau, his Squadron now reduced to a mere one hundred men, was stationed in the old Crusader fort of Raschaya, on the Lebanese side of Mount Hermon, sharing the duties with a Squadron of Tunisian Spahis and another of Lebanese *Gendarmerie*. On 19 November, an REC patrol under young Lieutenant Paul Gardy was attacked by marauding Druzes. He lost three men when their horses bolted, but was able to hide his wounded with Maronite Christians, and make it back to the fort with the remains of his troop the following morning. The battle began in mid-afternoon, by which time the Druzes has massed almost four thousand men for the assault. The Commanding Officer, Captain Grancher of the Tunisian Spahis, was killed on the third day of the siege and Landriau took over. The last of six carrier pigeons were sent with a plea for reinforcements. Squadron Sergeant-Major Gazeaux and many cavalrymen were dead. Reconnaissance aircraft had flown overhead, and Lieutenant Gardy had led a bayonet charge which drove the Druzes from the fort, but all of the horses were dead and the remaining men down to fifteen shots each. Landriau was preparing to *faire Camerone* in a bayonet charge when a relief column arrived and drove the Druzes off. Landriau had lost fifteen men and had forty wounded, but the now horseless 4th Squadron was still functioning.

The story of Camerone had taken solid root with the 1st REC, as it had with the Foreign Legion infantry regiments, and Sous-Lieutenant Jacques Weygand, son of General Maxime Weygand, was told it in the officers club at Sousse, in Tunisia, when he arrived to join the regiment, the narrator being a young Lieutenant. When the story was done the Colonel spoke.

'*That* is the Legion,' he said. 'It is something that officers who have the honour to serve in it must never forget. After these, who were very great . . . others picked up the torch and passed it on to us. It is our duty to hold it as high as they did.'[17]

Messifre and Rachaya were the kind of battles that made Rollet rejoice in his beloved Foreign Legion, but there was more death than glory in Morocco, where Abd el-Krim was proving unexpectedly difficult to defeat.

Legionnaire Max Durer, a Dutchman serving as a bandman with the 2nd REI at Meknes, had vivid memories of Camerone Day celebrations of 1926. The day before, his White Russian friend Ivan Stefanovsky briefed him on what to expect.

'Usual morning duties, of course, but as light as we can make them,' Durer was told. 'Half an hour of drill, instead of an hour. An extra good meal as midday . . . Just think of it – freedom, entire freedom to go fourth, arm-in-arm, to enjoy ourselves. I shall dance tomorrow. I must show you how we dance in Russia.'

Apparently, the Legionnaires were allowed to add things to the special meal of blood sausage, and Durer's friends had done just that. Under his plate he found a few copper coins. 'That's your change, Durer,' Stefanovsky told him. 'We've sold your clothes, *petit*. You are the host. To your health' – and he and the three others at the table – Brunnen, a German, Verich, a Serb, and Morin, a man from the South of France, raised their glasses.

> There was little I could do for the moment but laugh, and eat my share of the black pudding [*Durer recalled later*]. Well primed to celebrate the fete of the Legion, I did not lag far behind the others when we sallied forth at about five o'clock to taste the pleasure of Meknes.

Their adventures included a visit to a shop and bar where his friends had sold Durer's kit, and another to a dubious cabaret, where Stefanovsky gave an exhibition of Russian dancing. The afternoon ended in a brawl with the Arab patrons. Such things were common on Camerone Day, Durer said: 'the bars and cafes were full all day and did a roaring trade . . . These parties always ended up in a free fight.' Usually they were with Arabs, but not always. 'Like Anglo-Saxon sailors, legionaries will fight among themselves where there is no one else to fight with,' Durer said. His group returned to the barracks in time for roll call, continued drinking, and the next morning 'we all felt the usual after-effects'.[18]

Lyautey, now a Marshal of France, had done his best with the men at his disposal and named General Daugan – who had reviewed Rollet's RMLE in Lorraine in 1918 – as Supreme Commander of all forces in Morocco. Even so, there were still too few men to contain Abd el-Krim and the tribes loyal to him, and eventually, the French Government recognized the seriousness of the situation and committed two full Infantry Divisions. Lyautey was over seventy years old and believed that once Abd el-Krim was defeated it would need a younger man in time of peace. He asked to be retired and returned to France. Marshal Petain arrived and began working in concert with the Spanish. Backed by artillery, armoured vehicles and spotter aircraft – which, owing to the rugged terrain, were only effective part of the time – Petain set about crushing the enemy, using more Foreign Legion and French Infantry troops than had ever been seen in North Africa. Commanding Officers, Battalion Commanders, even Company Officers, now took *fanions* – the equivalent of pennants or guidons – into the field as rallying points for their troops. Harried by both European nations, and with once-loyal tribes drifting away from his banner, Abd el-Krim finally surrendered on 26 May 1926 and, accompanied by wives and retainers, was sent into comfortable exile in the island of Reunion in the Indian Ocean. Georges-R. Manue, who served in the Foreign Legion in Morocco between 1921 and 1926, subsequently authored well-received books about his service, among them *Tetes brules: cinq ans a la Legion* and *La retraite au desert. Recit*.[19] The Rif War as such was over, but the final 'pacification' of 'dissident' tribes would take another seven years of fighting.

In his plans to mark the Centenary in a truly appropriate way Rollet conceived the idea of erecting a massive *Monument aux Morts* – a Cenotaph – on the parade ground of the Quartier Vienot. It would take both time and money, but, meanwhile, the popularity of the annual Camerone Day celebrations was growing among the regiments in Algeria and Morocco, and what would become the basic formula for the *Fete de Camerone* was gradually being institutionalized. By the late 1920s the celebrations were well established, and keenly anticipated by Legionnaires. Henri Pouliot, a French-Canadian who joined the Foreign Legion at the age of nineteen, and later wrote a book about his experiences in Algeria and Morocco, which was published in the Centenary Year, remembered the celebrations as high spots in his five years, and provided a good picture of how they had become established by the end of his service.

> Camerone is a glorious memory, a special date, and it is to remind Legionnaires of the wonderful feat of arms by their predecessors that this fete is celebrated [*Pouliot wrote*]. The 'Forgotten Ones' rejoice and pass the day eating and drinking and remembering this great deed of the past ... A grandstand and an obstacle course are constructed; flags and *fanions* float joyously in the air and on the roofs of barracks; everything is washed, cleaned, polished; offices, barrack-rooms and canteens are decorated with greenery and many flowers.
>
> Awakening, the notes of the trumpets fill the morning with fantastic sound; the air is filled with fifes and trumpets and *Le Boudin* is heard on all sides. The music is heard in the barrack-room where 'les messieurs' (the Legionnaires) savour their chocolate and devour truly appetizing fritters. The number of cooks has been quadrupled and their cleanliness is commendable. At eight o'clock there is a liberal distribution of sausage, bread, ham and white wine, which is greatly appreciated, and helps to stimulate the vigour and enthusiasm of the troops.
>
> The parade takes place, superb, magnificent, impeccable, brilliant in its precision and executed to perfection. Then, in the midst of an almost religious silence, the Adjutant advances solemnly, his uniform immaculate. He reads, in a strong and vibrant voice, which excites the soldiers, the *Recit de Camerone*. It raises pride and explains the spirit of the Legionnaires who fought this marvellous battle, and similar ones. It speaks without false vanity, and it is pleasant to feel that we are encouraged to be their worthy successors. After a short break comes the tour of the Captain. He makes a short address to the men, truly heartfelt, with elegant phrases, but simple, without big words, without artificial style and without affectation, understood by all and capable of going right to the heart. He speaks briefly of the Legion – the best infantry in the world! – giving the names of the dead in the valorous exploits of the past year, and ends his tour with a sincere cry ... giving it all his soul: '*Vive la Legion!*'... Then it is time for the soupe, the numerous plates and dishes loudly welcomed, as are the buckets containing generous amounts of 'divine pinard' – the great passion of the Legionnaire – which are greeted on arrival with grateful exclamations and shouts. At ten o'clock come the games, which take place in the presence of some pretty girls, sparking secret thoughts of ardour ... The fete continues throughout the night, punctuated by the sound of Russian and German melodies ... emotion, dances and chants like *Le Boudin*.[20]

Cooper, whose second engagement in the Foreign Legion ran from 1919 to 1924, and third from 1925 to 1930, also witnessed the development and formalization of Camerone celebrations at a crucial time.

> There is one day in the year when the whole Legion has a holiday and on that day, after morning parades and a banquet, every man can do whatever he likes and whatever he does do there is no punishment [*he reported*]. This day is April 30th, the anniversary of one of the Legion's earliest and greatest exploits . . . this story is read to all the soldiers of the Legion wherever they are stationed, in every barracks and camp and every outpost, from headquarters to the loneliest part of the Sahara and the men are exhorted to live up to that tradition. I cannot explain the strange thrill it gives a man of the Legion to hear that old story. It seems to go all down one's spine and I have seen hardened old soldiers weep as they stood on parade listening to it for perhaps the tenth time or more . . . Then there is a great feast. The menu could not be beaten in the best restaurant in the world. If any company has not enough money the men will forfeit their pay in order to contribute. After luncheon there is freedom. And the next day is really a holiday, too, for everyone has to recover![21]

Thanks to the efforts of a number of fiction writers – notably P.C. Wren, with his 1924 novel *Beau Geste*, set in about 1906, its several sequels and his other Foreign Legion stories – the world's best known and 'romantic' group of soldiers continued to exercise a certain magic on the minds of the public. It mattered not that Rollet liked neither the novels nor their subsequent Hollywood manifestations, the Foreign Legion was always of interest, and became even more intriguing to readers through the autobiographical books by serving officers like Pechkoff, Aage and American 'durationist' David Wooster King, whose 1927 book *L.M. 8046* was reissued three years later as *And Ten Thousand Shall Fall*.[22] Then came two books – *The Legion of the Damned*[23] and *With the Foreign Legion in Syria*,[24] by an American, Bennett J. Doty, and a Welshman, John Harvey – respectively an Infantryman and a Cavalryman – who had fought in the Foreign Legion in Syria and deserted together. In 1929 came another First World War story, *One Man's War* by Bert Hall and John J. Niles. The subtitle – 'The Story of the Lafayette Escadrille' – though not the text, overlooked the fact that Hall had been in the Foreign Legion before he became a flyer.[25]

Their success tempted American 'durationist' Paul Ayers Rockwell to venture into print in 1930 with a chronicle of the lives and deaths of his fellow American 'for the duration' volunteers, and he thought to comment briefly on Camerone.

> If the United States had not been so torn and disrupted during the early [eighteen] sixties, such names as Cajacca [Oaxaca], Santa Ysabel (sic), and Camaron might not ring so unfamiliarly on American ears [*Rockwell wrote*]. Camaron especially deserves to be rescued from oblivion. For unflagging courage in a desperate struggle against overwhelming odds, this fight should stand in the front ranks in annals of American warfare, alongside such

battles as The Alamo and Custer's last stand in the Valley of the [Little] Big Horn.[26]

With the exception of Harvey's and Rockwell's books, all had found both British and American publishers and some had been translated into French. Harvey's *With the Foreign Legion in Syria* – a magazine serial in the United States – also appeared in a Hebrew-language edition and was translated into Swedish.[27] Other manuscript reminiscences of the Foreign Legion were being considered by publishers in England, the United States and Germany.

Rollet assigned Captain Paul Rollin of the 1st REI to write the text of the proposed Foreign Legion Centenary History and Brunon began to provide him with information from the *Collection Raoul et Jean Brunon*. They soon discovered that between them they could come up with very little which actually documented the story of *La Compagnie Danjou* and the Combat of Camerone, and the resources of the *Salle d'Honneur* were of limited value.

G.-Jean Reybaz, a Swiss former Legionnaire, helped spread the word about the coming Centenary Celebrations with an article[28] called 'Pour le centenaire de la Legion: la Legion Etrangere au front (1915)', which appeared in the *Revue des Deux Mondes* in February 1930. Later in the year it became known that Legionnaire Schneidarek, serving in the 2nd REI, had been a General in the Army of Czechoslovakia,[29] the sort of fact which always supported the kind of mythic perception of the Foreign Legion in the eyes of outsiders.

The pre-war magazine *La Legion Etrangere* was resurrected[30] in January 1931, drawing much of its material from Brunon's personal archives, and with artist Benigni as a member of the Editorial Committee. It provided an efficient way to get the word about the Centenary out to Old Comrades' Associations, and if Rollet had reason to anticipate some disappointments with the book project he certainly had no cause for concern about the rest of the Centenary activities he had so meticulously planned.

28
The Centenary of the Foreign Legion

While serving in Tonkin in 1927 Major Fernand Maire had taken the opportunity to visit the old fort at Tuyen Quang, where the Foreign Legion had lived and died during the six-week siege in early 1885. Cleaning up the overgrown cemetery necessitated moving some of the graves, and several of them were found to contain a few Mexican coins, showing that at least a few of the dead Legionnaires had served in Mexico. However, as far as is known, none of them had been Camerone survivors, a number of whom were certainly serving in the Foreign Legion, but were almost certainly still in Algeria at the time. Maire erected a small stone monument in the cemetery and returned to Algeria with a few of the coins for the collection of the *Salle d'Honneur*.[1]

When he reached Sidi-bel-Abbes he learned of Rollet's idea for a *Monument aux Morts*, and was told that bringing this into being would be his especial responsibility. The Monument was to take the form of a platform, on which would rest a plinth, topped by a massive bronze globe, which would be guarded by four statues of Legionnaires in period uniforms. The parade ground would become a Court of Honour and the actual Monument, approached by a *Voie Sacre* – Sacred Way – would represent the Living of the Legion saluting the Dead of the Legion.

Rollet had been informed by Paris that no money could be made available from official sources, so he sought other ways to raise what he needed. Monsieur Aka, the Director of *La Musique*, had not only created a truly stellar military band, but had also formed a one-hundred-piece symphony orchestra. Both gave regular concerts in the Place Carnot in Sidi-bel-Abbes and these became a useful source of funds. They were also sent on tours and their earnings went into the general fund for the Monument.[2]

Some years earlier high quality onyx had been found close to the village of Oued-Chouly, some sixty-five kilometres (forty miles) from Sidi-bel-Abbes. The quarry had been abandoned, but Rollet obtained permission from Governor-General Cardes to re-open it and extract sufficient onyx for the Monument. Much of the heavy work fell to the Sappers and Pioneers of the 1st REI. A thirty-man detachment first built several kilometres of useable track from the quarry to a main road, then skilled volunteers with experience in stone-cutting and monumental masonry moved in under the direction of Corporal Glass to begin the actual quarrying.

Maire, promoted to Lieutenant-Colonel, visited the site on several occasions to check up on the quarrying work, but was more immediately involved at the Quartier Vienot, where the Sappers and Pioneers were using five hundred cubic metres (five hundred and forty-seven cubic yards) of concrete to provide a solid rectangular foundation for the Monument, which would be nine metres (twenty-nine-and-a-half feet) long, by seven metres (almost twenty-three feet) wide and three metres (nearly ten feet) high. The last trucks bearing the huge onyx blocks rumbled into Sidi-bel-Abbes a few days after the preliminary work was finished and on 8 October 1930 the actual foundation stone was formally laid by Lieutenant-Colonel Forey at a small ceremony.[3]

In the meantime, at the Paris studio of sculptor Charles Pourquet, work was in progress on four larger-than-life bronze figures depicting Legionnaires during important periods of the regiments' existence. The sculptor based three of his figures on illustrations[4] which Maurice Mahut had done for George d'Esparbes' 1912 book *Les Mysteres de la Legion etrangere* and the fourth on photographs of Legionnaires in the trenches of the Western Front during the First World War.

The Legionnaire of the King Louis-Philippe era was armed with an 1822 model fusil and represented the Conquest of Algeria. The Legionnaire of the Second Empire, with an 1842 model fusil, represented those who fought in the Crimea, Italy and Mexico. It was later claimed that the face of the Legionnaire, adorned with an 'Imperial' beard, was that of Captain Danjou, but unless it was taken from the line drawing in de Beauvoir's 1897 history, this seems unlikely, as the Foreign Legion at that time had no clear idea of how the hero of Camerone had looked.

The third Legionnaire, armed with an 1874 Gras rifle, represented the expeditionary forces sent to such places as Tonkin, Formosa, Dahomey, the French Soudan and Madagascar, and there was no argument about the statue's heavily-bearded face, which was that of a legendary officer named Paul Brundsaux. The fourth Legionnaire, with his tin hat and 1916 model rifle, represented the various *Regiments de Marche* of the 1st and 2nd Etrangers, who were amalgamated to form Rollet's *Regiment de Marche de la Legion Etrangere*.

Each of the figures, destined to stand on guard at a corner of the *Monument aux Morts*, was nearly three metres (almost ten feet) tall. Some seven tonnes of bronze went into the statues, large bronze garlands for each of the four sides of the plinth and the bed of bronze laurel leaves on which the globe would be placed. The only words on the Monument would be: *La Legion Etrangere a ses Morts 1831–1931* – The Foreign Legion to its Dead 1831–1931.

Rollet did not seek donations from the many Old Comrades Associations, instead urging the veterans to save up so that they could attend the actual Centenary Celebrations, where they would be made very welcome. Various organizations, some Sidi-bel-Abbes businesses and the city fathers of several Algerian towns made donations, but the majority of the six hundred thousand francs needed came from the Legionnaires themselves. Each year for four years every man, from the Colonel down to the most recent recruit, gave up a day's pay, and the names of the thirty thousand contributors were on a list which would be sealed in the base of the Monument.[5]

The great bronze globe arrived from France in two halves. Before it was put into position, Legionnaires skilled in metalwork etched in the borders of the fifteen countries where the Foreign Legion had shed its blood.

A single gold star for Camerone was placed in southeastern Mexico.

The plinth on which the globe would rest was ready and, once it had been carefully moved into position, the hand-polished onyx facing blocks were put in place. On 10 March 1931 Maire reported to Forey's Centenary Committee that everything was ready.

'Its purpose is not to embellish a military barracks,' Maire would say later. 'It is destined to be the symbol of the Corps which gave asylum to those who were in need of a refuge.'[6]

Of course, there were annoyances. In 1926 a decision had been made in Paris that no more than eight Battle Honours should appear on Regimental Standards and that dates should be shown for the campaigns. The 1st REI had received a Regimental Standard marking their participation in the Crimean War, in the Kabyle Campaign, Italy, Mexico, French Indo-China, Dahomey-Morocco, Madagascar and the First World War campaign at Gallipoli and in Serbia. Rollet had disagreed with the dates inserted by the Directorate of Artillery for some campaigns and was able to obtain agreement that these could be changed in time for the Centenary Celebrations. The Regimental Standard was sent to Paris, where it was felt that the silk was too weak to support the new wordings and a totally new one was prepared.

When it was returned to Sidi-bel-Abbes it was magnificent. The Battle Honours were shown as SEBASTOPOL 1855, KABYLIE 1857, MAGENTA 1859, CAMERONE 1863, EXTREME-ORIENT 1884–1885, DAHOMEY-MAROC 1892–1907–1925, MADAGASCAR 1895–1905 and ORIENT 1915–1917. There was just one snag: Instead of the correct motto of HONOUR AND FIDELITY it bore the words HONOUR AND COUNTRY. Rollet was livid. The whole premise of the Centenary Celebrations was predicated on the fact that the Foreign Legion was a corps of foreigners, and now the new Regimental Standard spoke of Country. He sent it back to the Artillery with appropriate comments. A corrected Regimental Standard was received in short order.

'The Premier Legionnaire of France' was promoted to the rank of General and the unique post of Inspector-General of the Foreign Legion was specially created, giving him an unparalleled oversight for all the regiments.[7] He handed over command[8] of his beloved 1st REI to his comrade Colonel Nicolas on 26 March.

Captain Rollin and Jean Brunon had laboured mightily on the manuscript for the proposed Centenary History, but their hopes of finding much on Camerone had been swiftly dashed. The 'roll which had the texture of parchment' containing 'all the names of the officers, N.C.Os and men who took part in the battle', which Legionnaire Cooper had examined in 1924, and the 'well-written parchment' giving 'the story of the battle itself',[9] had seemingly disappeared by the time they began their research five years later. The collection of officers' photographs which had been seen by the reporter from *Le Sud Oranais* in the early 1890s also appears to have been missing.

The scarcity of material meant that of the ten pages given over to the Mexican Campaign just less than two dealt with Camerone, while three were given over to pictures of officers, though not of Captain Danjou, as there was no photograph of him in the Foreign Legion Archives. In telling the story of Camerone the authors were forced to get by with an innocuous paragraph from Grisot and Coulombon's *La Legion etrangere de 1831 a 1887*,[10] to which they had added some remarks about

Camerone from Colonel Georges de Villebois-Mareuil's 1896 article in the *Revue des Deux Mondes*.[11]

Pierre Benigni provided two artistic contributions to the story of Camerone: '*Le Serment*' – 'The Oath' – depicted Danjou, in the room in the northwest corner of the Hacienda de la Trinidad, extracting a promise from his men to fight to the death. The '*Charge du sous-lieutenant Maudet*' was based on a painting by Hungarian-born Legionnaire E. Nagy and showed the last members of the 3rd of the 1st, led by Maudet, a sword in hand, bursting into the courtyard to sell their lives as dearly as possible.

Nevertheless, the highly anticipated book, entitled *Le Livre d'Or de la Legion Etrangere, 1831–1931 – The Golden Book of the Foreign Legion, 1831–1931* – was published as planned, and had a foreword by Marshal Louis Franchet d'Esperey.[12] It was a stirring tale of a century of fighting on four continents – Africa, Europe, Asia and America – and in due course would be awarded the *Prix Therouanne* and the *Prix Gobert* by the Academie Francaise. Brunon contributed the chapter which dealt with the Foreign Legion's many Regimental Standards, then spun it off into a small book in its own right called *La Voite de Gloire: Histoire des Drapeaux de la Legion Etrangere (1831–1931)*, which was published the same year.[13]

Naturally, every regiment of the Foreign Legion was to be represented at the Centenary Celebrations, as well as delegates from many of the associations of former Legionnaires. Details of the activity at Sidi-bel-Abbes travelled slowly to the more isolated outposts in Algeria and Morocco, but from the snippets of information they received Legionnaires and officers gathered that Rollet was up to something very special.

Sous-Lieutenant Weygand, serving with the 1st REC at Bou-Denib, on the edge of the Sahara, recalled that stories were constantly circulating that Rollet, assisted by Nicolas, was 'planning something to make the hard faces of his old companions light up with pride.'

> Knowing these two indefatigable men and the tremendous resources at their disposal, no one was surprised at the fantastic rumours that reached Bou-Denib [*Weygand, recalling the excitement, wrote twenty years later*]. [E]very letter from the *Tell* made the outpost Legionaries cherish the hope of being included in the delegation to the celebrations at Bel-Abbes. For each Squadron or Company was to send an officer, sergeant, and a few men selected for their long service and good conduct to represent their comrades and bring the tale back to the others on their return.

In the meantime, elaborate plans were being made for the local Camerone festivities. At Bou-Denib the 1st REC had a majority of Russian troopers and the celebrations were likely to be more colourful than usual, said Weygand, as 'all units of the garrison were present at the same time, a circumstance unprecedented in the memory of any Legionary in this front-line post.'

> Under the chairmanship of a sporting captain the moving spirits of the games were given every encouragement to display their talents [*he recalled*].

> There were to be horse- and donkey-races, a mule gymkhana, a circus, displays of skill of one kind or another, a play, orchestral music, and singing – a varied and somewhat overloaded programme. As usual Epaindieff [a Legionnaire from the Caucasus] and his companions were preparing for a Cossack display, always a popular event, in spite of the danger to the horses' legs. Finally, the Mounted Company had acquired in the last draft the *fakir* of the Legion. On parade the man was no more exotic than his native Aubervilliers, but his performance was excellent. After some experiments in cataleptic rigidity which were child's play for him he finished with a genuine crucifixion which left the spectators gasping.

Greatly to his surprise and pleasure, Weygand found himself selected as the officer to represent No. 1 Squadron of the 1st REC at the Centenary Celebrations. His *Croix de Guerre* on his chest, and with the best items of his uniform in a portmanteau, he and his men joined a convoy to Colomb-Bechar and took the train to Oran, going on from there to Sidi-bel-Abbes.

> The railway station at Sidi-bel-Abbes is normally a quiet and deserted spot, but that day it was thronged [*Weygand said*]. Civilians, French or Algerian, formed a very small part of the noisy crowd of spectators on the platforms. Legionaries far outnumbered them. Some of these were delegates from outlying units; the rest, who laid hold of them as soon as they stepped off the trains, were members of a formidable reception committee... A third category, also visitors, stood a little to one side. They were dressed as civilians, but there was something either old-fashioned or unexpected about their clothes. Bavarian hats, Spanish or Mexican bell-bottomed trousers, Tyrolese embroidered jackets, Russian blouses, contrasted oddly with less intriguing garments. The common denominator was the row of ribbons on every jacket, often including the *Croix de Guerre* or the Legion of Honour. The faces too were the faces of soldiers; they awoke suddenly to alertness when the buglers on duty at the station sounded a call. These were the veterans of the Legion. To celebrate the Centenary it was not enough for the Legion to invite only those then serving in its ranks; those who had contributed to its glory in the past were to be associated with its ceremonial triumph... They came from Rio de Janeiro and Caracas, from Berlin and Hamburg, from Prague, Geneva, Belgrade, and Stockholm. There were Turks, Italians, and Roumanians... and under the racial characteristics of each, under the fair colouring of the Saxon or the Asiatic brown, behind the long face of the Nordic and the heavy cheek-bones of the Slav, the same light shone through the unblinking stare of the German or the hot, quick eyes of the Spaniard.

'*Merde*,' remarked a member of Weygand's detachment to his officer. 'The whole bloody First Mysterious is here!'

> Every train was crowded with ghosts [*Weygand remembered*]. They arrived,

tired by their long journey and a little shaken, after all, to find themselves on the platform where they had detrained twenty or thirty years before with the draft from Fort Saint Jean; for a moment they could only stand and stare. Then, as the strangeness passed away, they turned to brush the dust off one another, and automatically checked their ties and waistcoat buttons. There were few mutual recognitions, few hearty greetings between the groups. The *bourgeois* in each had got the upper hand, and was distrustful of the company which his other self had kept; he preferred to steer clear of those whom that disreputable person had called friends. There were other barriers: some of these comrades of long ago were the enemies of yesterday. The empty eye-socket, the hand crippled in 1914, these might be the work of an old comrade of the Legion, ill met in no-man's-land in Champagne or on the bloodstained slopes of Gallipoli.

Delegates from twenty-seven Old Comrades Associations visited Sidi-bel-Abbes for the celebrations and these veterans found many changes since they had last been there, one of them being what Weygand described as the 'largest swimming bath in Oran Province, which had been planned by a well-known architect, now a Legionary'.

Once an hour the sounds of a march crashed out outside the station – a detachment of the band come to play in the latest arrivals [*he said*]. The briscards [old soldiers] fell in behind the gleaming instruments; collapsible poles were screwed together and the Colours of the Associations uncased; as the little procession marched off towards the town to the strains of *Boudin* . . . [I]t is a long way from the station to the Quartier Vienot, and marching is thirsty work; so from time to time the band halted in front of one of the brasseries patronized by Legionaries. The Colours went back into their shiny black casings; and while the bugle band returned to the station to escort later arrivals the veterans leaning on the bar carried on the good work of consolidating old acquaintance. An hour or two later they were irradiated with anisette and good-fellowship, when the blare of the band returning on its endless shuttle service made them pick up their bundles. With Colours once more uncased, the old pilgrims of tradition and glory fell in behind the detachment as it passed and picked up the step. Their own had by now become a little uncertain.[14]

Sidi-bel-Abbes had been the scene of grand occasions before. Napoleon III had visited in 1865, and twelve years later there had been celebrations for the inauguration of the railway line between the city and Oran. President Emile Loubet had visited in 1903. The decorating of the 1st Etranger's Regimental Standard three years later had been another major celebration, as had the visit of President Alexandre Millerand, who even fitted in a visit to the *Salle d'Honneur* while touring French North Africa in 1922, but the Centenary Celebration was the biggest thing Sidi-bel-Abbes had ever seen.

Marshal Louis Franchet d'Esperey represented the President of France, and was accompanied by an entourage of Generals, including Theveny and Vandenberg, who had commanded Legionnaires in Morocco before and during the First World War. The Governor-General of Algeria was there with a gaggle of lesser officials. Brigadier-General Stanley-Ford, the Military Attache in the U.S. Embassy, had come from Paris. Colonel P.T. Etherton, formerly Consul-General in Chinese Turkestan, represented the British Government. Colonel Lestock Reid, a noted explorer and big game hunter, had arrived from somewhere in Africa, Colonel Kosik of the Army of Czechslovakia had come from Prague and Prince Louis II of Monaco – himself a former Foreign Legion officer – had crossed the Mediterranean.[15]

The British Army's representative was Captain Codrington of the Coldstream Guards, a fine-looking officer, whose soldierly bearing was apparently greatly approved of by Englishmen serving in the Foreign Legion, as one of them made a special point of mentioning him to British travel writer John Gibbons, who visited Sidi-bel-Abbes the following year. Gibbons said that an English Legionnaire, 'who I do not think will ever see England again', cheekily remarked that he had been 'very proud . . . of being English and of having such a decent-looking Officer to stand for our country and to teach the French how a soldier should look'.[16]

A special new metal badge had been designed for the members of the 3rd Company of the 1st Battalion of the 4th REI, the designated lineal successors to *La Compagnie Danjou*. Octagonal in shape, it was diagonally bisected, with the flames of the Legion's traditional grenade and the dates 1831 and 1931 in the green top segment. The figure four was on the 'body' of the grenade in the lower, red, segment, and under it the words CAMERONE 30 AVRIL 1863 and 3E CIE – 3rd Company.[17]

> [T]he Legion had decided to house all the visitors within its own walls, steeped in the old atmosphere [*Weygand recalled*]. Officers, Legionaries, and veterans combined meant some two thousand to house and feed without dislocating the life of the fifteen hundred men of the First Foreign normally stationed at Bel-Abbes.
>
> But the Legion always manages somehow: barrack-rooms were emptied of their occupants, who went under canvas in the training area; and after a thorough house-cleaning every guest had a bed that was at least better than anything in the *bled*. As for the cook-houses, they were large and efficient enough to cope with two meals a day for nearly four thousand. Coffee? Coffee is never short at Bel-Abbes, which boasts the largest coffee percolator in the world, the 'perco', which can produce hundreds of litres in an hour.[18]

The popular American travel writer Richard Haliburton, and his pilot, Moye W. Stephens, Jr., had flown up from Niger in French Equatorial Africa. They were 'exceedingly curious about this unique army, so highly acclaimed, so bitterly damned', Haliburton would say, and 'wished to find out for ourselves it if were as colourful and as controversial as the story-books painted it . . . [So] the Legion's capital, *en fete*, seemed to us a proper place to begin'.[19]

At 8:30 on the morning of 30 April, with Colonels Nicolas and Richert, respectively of the 1st and 2nd REIs, and Lieutenant-Colonel Maire playing key rolls in the Celebrations, the massed regimental bands crashed out *Le Boudin* and the *Marseillaise*, and for the very first time the articulated wooden hand of Captain

Danjou in its wood-and-glass casket was ceremoniously carried from the *Salle d'Honneur* and presented in front of the *Monument aux Morts*.

Then Marshal Franchet d'Esperey, his gold and blue baton in his hand, the white feathers in his hat fluttering in the breeze, stepped forward to speak.

> Foreign troops under the French flag, the soul of the Legion and of that which is French, and I see the evidence of it in the anniversary today, that of the Combat of Camerone, of 30 April 1863.
>
> The thing which symbolizes this commemoration is the tradition of sacrifice without hope, simply for the honour of arms and fidelity to a promise which had been given. And this tradition which the Foreign Regiments make the object of their veneration, is it not also the same for our national sensibilities? We leave to others the easy way of commemorating victories. In our History, so rich in triumphs and in conquests, those which our people piously remember as the most worthy are the ancient resistances, the desperate assaults, the sacrifices, alas too often useless. Alesia, Roncevaux, le bucher de Rouen, Sidi-Brahim, the bayonet charges: here are the pinnacles of French emotion and the themes preferred by our poetry.
>
> The Legion, victorious on so many fields of battle, has chosen as the date for your annual fete, the anniversary of the day when, in an obscure Mexican farm, sixty Legionnaires fought to the death against two thousand enemies. It is under the aegis of the grand name of Camerone that you have wished, Legionnaires, to put the commemoration of a hundred battles and glories. You have proclaimed in the face of the world that for soldiers worthy of the name, a task performed and the rigorous execution of orders have found their own recompense and are not in need of the sanction of success. . .[20]

Finally, with all the Foreign Legion's Regimental Standards waving in front of it, Lieutenant-Colonel Forey formally presented the *Monument aux Morts* to General Rollet, who committed it to an honour guard of the 1st REI.

> On the dark sphere fifteen gold patches blazed out, showing the countries where foreign volunteers had shed their blood for France [*young Weygand remembered*] – fifteen golden plaques, representing a small fortune, subscribed by the Legionaries out of their pay.[21]

Then it was over, to Weygand 'an epic, shimmering in the sun, names echoed on the Colours assembled at it foot.'[22] At a banquet later in the day, the Governor-General spoke about the Foreign Legion, not forgetting to mention the English, Scottish and Irish soldiers who had served in its ranks, and in the evening there was a pageant called 'A Hundred Years of War', featuring stirring scenes from the past: Algeria, 1831–47; Spain, 1835–39; the Crimea, 1854–55; and Italy, 1859. 'Mexique 1863–67' featured the final charge at Camerone, based on Benigni's painting 'The Charge of Sous-Lieutenant Maudet.' Then came France, 1870–71; Dahomey, 1893; Madagascar, 1895–1905; Tonkin, 1884–1900 – depicting the Siege at Tuyen Quang; Morocco, 1907–1914; France, 1914–18; Morocco,

1925–26; and Syria, 1921–25 – depicting the stand at Messifre.

A handsome programme for the six days of events had been produced by the Foreign Legion.[23] The Old Comrades Association in Algiers had published another, well supported by advertisements from local bars and restaurants, as well as by Shell, Citroen and Courvoisier brandy, as well as by Gordon's Gin and Johnnie Walker.[24]

> [B]etween the exhibitions, shows, and ceremonies prepared for them the visitors had not an idle moment [*Weygand said*]. There was a march-past every day. March-past of the bands of the four Foreign Regiments, who one evening gave a concert with eight hundred performers. March-past of the Training Companies, recruits of all ages, kinds, and colours, eager to show that they would soon be worthy of their forerunners. March-past of the special troops – sappers, with their broad leather aprons, cavalry, armoured cars, gunners, signals. March-past of the delegates from the units in the desert, five hundred officers and men picked for long service and gallantry . . . Finally, march-past of the veterans, with their forest of Colours and banners, a cloud of colour fluttering over a still more diversified host. Each day was marked by some ceremony too – the opening of the swimming-pool, a visit to the *Salle d'Honneur*, a play.[25]

To writer Haliburton, who had an incurable urge to be always on the move, enough was enough, for he had become a little jaded. The 'pageants, concerts and speeches offered us one very pleasant picture of the Legion,' he remarked. 'But this was by no means the customary, typical picture'.[26] He was 'glad when the celebrations had come to a close'. He and Stephens flew directly to Fez and later took a bus into the mountains to visit a small military post at Rich.[27] Weygand made ready to return to Bou-Denib, not without some trepidation, as a visit from Inspector-General Rollet was in the offing. 'Just before leaving Bel-Abbes the officers from Southern Morocco were summoned to the General's office to learn that he would be coming to visit their units next week,' Weygand recalled, adding, ominously: 'He would inspect them in detail.'[28]

The events in the Quartier Vienot had been the high spot of the Centenary Celebrations, but Rollet and Nicolas had not forgotten the Legionnaires serving in the field, and not lucky enough to have been chosen to represent their units at Sidi-bel-Abbes. It had been an extraordinary celebration there, but, stretching all the organizational resources to the limit, gastronomic extravaganzas were sent even unto the uttermost part of Rollet's domain.

> We lunched off: hors d'oeuvres (six varieties); clear soup; fresh lobster on ice and salad; roast pork or roast beef; roast, fried or boiled potatoes; cauliflower or green peas; trifle; dessert; cheese (any variety known) and biscuits; coffee and liqueurs [*recalled Corporal Arthur L. Martin, an Englishman serving with 1st REI at Ain Sefra, on the northern edge of the Sahara*]. 'Vin rose' and white wine were served with the meal. It was certainly an exceptional occasion (the Legion Centenary), but it was also an exceptional feat to supply such a meal to a garrison of over one thousand men in a desert![29]

29
Voices from the Past

The Centenary celebrations had created unparalleled international interest in the Foreign Legion and special articles appeared in newspapers and magazines in England and the United States, as well as in many European countries. The widely-read news and feature magazine *The World Today* carried a story on the regiments by Francis Dickie,[1] and *World's Work* had one by popular American author Alice Williamson,[2] who had first visited Sidi-bel-Abbes in 1913, while collecting material for a Foreign Legion novel she was writing.[3] John Gibbons, the English travel writer and First World War veteran, similarly visited Algeria in 1932, gathering material for a book. While he did not receive any official assistance in Sidi-bel-Abbes, various officers helped him unofficially, and a Lieutenant, with an English-born Legionnaire on hand as interpreter, gave him a tour of the *Salle d'Honneur*.

'I copied down at random the first notice I came to,' Gibbons wrote in his entertaining book *The Truth About the Legion*, published the following year. It read: 'To Sous-Lieutenant Maudet and Five Legionnaires, sole survivors of the Sixty-Two of the Company of Captain Danjou who for Eight Hours Fought off Two Thousand Mexicans'.[4] Apparently the details of the battle were not given to Gibbons – perhaps the translator's knowledge was not up to it – and the 'notice' was clearly not close to the casket containing Captain Danjou's articulated hand. Failing to make the connection, and not having it explained to him, Gibbons, an otherwise fairly careful reporter, was wholly confused about what he was told concerning the Foreign Legion's most precious relic, writing: 'Somewhere in that Hall of Honour there is a Hand; it originally belonged to a Legion Captain and he lost it in the Crimea and it got cut off in Hospital and found its way to Bel-Abbes here in Africa. Then when he came out of hospital he had an artificial hand made and still went on being a Legion Officer and still went on fighting'.[5]

The Swiss-born Legionnaire Jean Reybaz, who had written about the Foreign Legion in a Centenary article two years earlier, now came out with a greatly expanded work with the d'Esparbesesque title of *Le 1er Mysterious: souvenirs de guerre d'un legionnaire suisse*.[6] It was the talk of the Sidi-bel-Abbes when Colonel Frank E. Evans of the U.S. Marine Corps arrived there in July. It was his second visit, the first having been made two years earlier, not long after returning to the United States after a three-year stint as Commanding Officer of the *Gendarmerie d'Haiti* during the American occupation of the Caribbean country. On the first occasion he had been fascinated by the Foreign Legion and had written several articles about it.[7] Now he was back, with credentials from the U.S. Navy Department, which he presented to Colonel Nicolas, seeking an appointment as an Observer in the forthcoming campaign against Berber 'dissidents' in Morocco's High Atlas.

He had described Captain Danjou's hand after his first visit to the Quartier Vienot, remarking: 'One of the most striking relics that is housed by the Legion in its beautiful *Salle d'Honneur* at Sidi-bel-Abbes is the artificial hand, built of leather and steel (sic) of Captain Danjou.' Evans had been a journalist before he joined the 1st Wisconsin Infantry Volunteers in 1898, at the outbreak of the Spanish-American War. He had been granted a Commission in the U.S. Marine Corps two years later and served in the Philippines and Panama in the early years of the century and then in France during the First World War. He wrote well, even vividly, of things he had personally experienced, but tended to be careless with historical facts, identifying *La Compagnie Danjou* as the 3rd Company of the 3rd Battalion of the 1st Regiment of the Foreign Legion. He thought that Danjou had lost his right hand, rather than his left – which is odd, considering that he had actually seen it – referred to 'Cameronne,' and reported that the hand had been 'carried out by his three gallant men from that death-house'.[8] Evans visited the *Salle d'Honneur* a second time during his mid-1932 visit to the Quartier Vienot.

> By far the most interesting installation at Sidi-bel-Abbes is the *Salle d'Honneur*, a low one storied building of fine proportions, set in a garden rich with plants and flowers, shaded by giant eucalyptus trees [*he wrote in* The Leatherneck, *the magazine of the U.S. Marine Corps*]. Here, in its five rooms, is an amazing collection of trophies and loot, and the pictorial history of the Legion in its hundred-odd years of combat in strange corners of the world ... To the *Salle d'Honneur*, after a recruit has received his initial outfit, he comes under the tutelage of a veteran, to learn its history and its proud traditions. The *Salle d'Honneur*, with its haunting beauty, its shrine of all that the Legion holds dear, leaves its imprint for life on those privileged to see it.[9]

Evans was interested in everything. He thought it 'would be a fitting thing if it could be possible for the Marine Corps to build such a shrine', and was especially taken by the Golden Book, in which were inscribed the names – including those of sixty-nine Americans – who died in the ranks of the Foreign Legion during the First World War. He obtained permission to be an Observer during the coming Summer campaign in Morocco and wrote extensively about it, providing a sympathetic outsider's eye-witness account of the in-the-field operations.[10]

The early 1930s were a time of fortuitous events, coinciding with the presence in Sidi-bel-Abbes of several history-minded officers, who undertook archival research, published the results and endeavoured to enhance the collection of the *Salle d'Honneur*. The initial effort to organize regimental trophies and bric-a-brac into some kind of museum had been made by Colonel Wattringue back in 1888, roughly coinciding with the publication of Grisot and Coulombon's *La Legion Etrangere, 1831–1887*, the first real history of the Foreign Legion. Now, more than four decades later, and in the wake of the Centenary Celebrations and the publication of the *Livre d'Or*, a number of new efforts were about to be made to conserve the histories of the regiments.

Captain Danjou's hand, which had been such a focal part of the Centenary Parade, did not make a return appearance at the annual celebrations for several years,[11] even when there were special extra events, like Jean Brunon and Pierre Benigni being made Honourary Legionnaires on Camerone Day 1933. In the latter part of that year Colonel Nicolas, commanding the 1st REI, was delighted when Brunon's efforts resulted in Jean Danjou, nephew and namesake of the hero of Camerone, presenting the *Salle d'Honneur* with a copy of the photograph of his uncle prior to his departure for Mexico.[12]

The year had seen a number of important changes in the life of the Foreign Legion. Specifically, the Summer Campaign in Morocco had brought an end to the final round of hostilities between the French and the last remaining Berber holdouts in the Grand Atlas. Clearly the observance of Camerone Day was now well-established, even in the field. G. Ward Price, a senior Foreign Correspondent with the London *Daily Mail*, who joined the French Headquarters Staff at Rabat in August 1933 to cover this final campaign, thought to mention it in his account of the fighting, remarking: 'This, of all its fights, is the one the Legion remembers with most pride.'[13]

> This combat represents, in the eyes of the Legion itself, the supreme fighting achievement of the corps, and its anniversary is celebrated with great solemnity as the Legion's special festival [*Ward Price added*]. [It is] the most famous fight in all the Legion's history... an everlasting example of the gallantry that the Legion expects of her sons.[14]

Another man who had been interested in the final campaign in Morocco was writer Jean des Vallieres and his Foreign Legion book, *Sous le drapeau de la Legion etrangere: Les Hommes Sans Noms – Beneath the Flag of the Foreign Legion: The Men Without Names* – was very much in the vein of d'Esparbes' *Mysteres* of more than two decades earlier, further adding to the perception of the Foreign Legion as somewhat exotic.[15] Des Vallieres' phrase 'The Men Without Names' stuck, and would be remembered, and his book certainly did much better in France than Gibbons' *The Truth About the Legion* when it was published in England the same year.

In Sidi-bel-Abbes the 1st REI had unexpectedly found itself with a wealth of worthwhile building materials when the Municipal Council announced plans to demolish the four great stone gateways of the city, built in 1849, in order to make way for expansion. Nicolas, who was dying of cancer, volunteered his men to undertake the demolition work, providing that the regiment could keep the greater part of the stonework. This was then used for several projects, including the construction of a cinema, expansion of the prison, a new mess for the Sous-Officiers and additions to the *Salle d'Honneur*, a major building programme which would ultimately be his tangible and lasting monument.[16]

In September, fully twenty-five years after his death, the military magazine *Carnet de la Sabretache* began serializing the much-anticipated memoirs of the General Charles Zede. The title, 'Souvenirs de Ma Vie: Algerie, Italie, Mexique,' seemed to promise much, as he had joined the Foreign Legion in 1857, straight from Saint-Cyr, and served with them until their return from Mexico a decade later, going on to become a much-decorated General by the time of his death in 1908.

The year turned and the January issue of the magazine *La Legion Etrangere* created something of a sensation when it published – portrait-style – the *Salle d'Honneur*'s now prized photograph of Captain Danjou with an article on Camerone. Photographs of Sous-Lieutenant Vilain and of the former Corporal Maine – in the uniform of a Captain of *Francs-Tireurs* in 1870 – were also used. Almost inevitably, the the caption to Danjou's picture repeated the old canard that he had lost his left hand during the Crimean War, while the accompanying text included the astonishing statement that his articulated replacement had been personally retrieved from Camerone's post-battle carnage by Maine.[17]

Too ill to continue his command of the 1st REI, Colonel Nicolas handed over to his old friend Maire on 17 April and returned to France. The Camerone-related instalment of Zede's memoirs appeared in the *Carnet de la Sabretache* the following month[18] and the battle was referred to as one which any regiment would be proud to consider 'the most glorious in its annals'. It was, said Zede, 'a wonderful example of military duty, accomplished in all of its integrity.'[19]

He also described his chance meeting with ex-Corporal Evariste Berg, by then a Sous-Lieutenant in the Zouaves,[20] at the Hacienda de la Trinidad in the early Summer of 1864, remembering Berg as 'Berc'. Zede said he found him to be 'an intelligent eyewitness', though a 'cold-blooded character', and asserted that he had 'interrogated him minutely', and 'had every reason to think' that what Berg told him about the affair at Camerone was 'absolutely truthful'.[21]

From what he had heard from others, and learned from Berg, Zede said he had concluded that Captain Danjou had faced two choices when confronted by the Orizaba Lancers on the road west of Camerone: to make a fighting withdrawal, taking losses as he moved towards Saussier at Paso del Macho, or to seriously engage the Mexicans, and do as much damage as possible for the sake of the convoy, which he believed to be at least at La Soledad, if not already even at Palo Verde. The unknown factor, of course, was that he did not know that Colonel Milan had more cavalry and numerous infantrymen within striking distance.

> It was possible for him to escape, that is to save his detachment, but fail in his mission to assist the convoy [*Zede wrote*]. He did not hesitate; he recognized that the inn at Camerone was a solid point of support for the menaced convoy; he occupied it and answered the demand that they surrender with an oath to defend themselves to the death. Vilain and Maudet would be killed in their turn to keep the oath and rejected two surrender demands before the arrival of more than a thousand enemy infantry rendered their situation without hope. The soldiers, animated by the example of their leaders, did not waver for a moment, in spite of their horrible sufferings from hunger, thirst [and] heat, made even worse by the smoke. Because of their devotion, the convoy which was so anxiously awaited at Puebla was saved and arrived in good shape.[22]

After almost a decade of retirement, Marshal Lyautey died in the summer of 1934, but his praise of the Foreign Legion has always been remembered.

'In Tonkin, in Madagascar, in Southern Oran, in Morocco, where I had them under my command, I regarded the Legion as my *Garde*, in the old and traditional sense of the word, Imperial and Royal in the term,' he said. 'One cannot speak too highly of these admirable troops and the good fortune of France to have them in her service'.[23]

Nicolas was also fading fast. He returned to Algeria, and was promoted to General Officer rank just before his death on 24 November.[24]

Zede's memoirs were of great interest to Colonel Maire, who apparently had his own views about the Combat of Camerone. A notably tough officer, who had expected – and received – much from his men during the First World War and in Morocco, he was respected by them because he was not careless with their lives. Maire himself admired the bravery and sacrifice of Captain Danjou and his men, but was resentful of the circumstances which had brought about so many deaths.

> Concerning Camerone, the accounts by several 'Men of Letters' lay emphasis on the story of the movement of the bullion, rather than on the tragic death of the soldiers [*Maire told his 'ghost writer' and friend, Jean-Pierre Dorian, on one occasion*]. I have often thought that they are less than sympathetic to the picture of horror for the Man – the Men. Rather, they are applauding those who caused this carnage, stupidly, blindly, unintelligently – blusterers, who for their own glory in the history books, sacrificed sixty-two Legionnaires – sixty-two against two thousand...[25]

An odd comment, perhaps, as there was so much more than the three million gold francs – siege cannons, ammunition and food, for example – being moved from Veracruz to Puebla in the two convoys, but the task was certainly larger than should have been reasonably asked of the number of Legionnaires available. It is not difficult to see who Maire was excoriating. He admired Marshal Bazaine, who was not only a former Foreign Legion officer of proven courage, but had commissioned Maire's father in the field in Mexico in 1866. He blamed the Regiment Etranger's many early casualties on General – later Marshal – Forey, the first Commander-in-Chief, who did not really care for the regiment and had spoken of deliberately leaving the 'foreigners' in the *Terres Chaudes* in preference to Frenchmen, despite the fact that he knew from personal experience of the unhealthy conditions. Then, when the *vomito negro* struck, Forey had ignored requests for reinforcements, leaving the Legionnaires ailing and dying in the fever zone, yet still expecting the sickly half-strength partial regiment to do the job of a healthy whole one. Forey was well aware that his vital line of communications was poorly protected, but made no attempt to support it with further manpower, perhaps some of General de Maussion's 7th Regiment of the Line, for example, which was the other major part of the Reserve Brigade. Even so, it seems extreme of Maire to suggest that Forey could possibly have anticipated the affair at Camerone, and allowed it to happen for the sake of his own place 'in the history books'.

Maire's life as a Foreign Legion officer was chronicled by Jean-Pierre Dorian in *Souvenirs du Colonel Maire de la Legion Etrangere*,[26] published in 1939, but the comment on Camerone was not included, and did not appear until a new edition of the book forty-two years later. Maire, of course, was still a serving officer when the autobiography first appeared, and possibly he withheld his 'glory' remark out of respect for retired Lieutenant-Colonel Pierre Forey, great-nephew of Mexico's Forey, who still lived in Sidi-bel-Abbes and was in almost daily contact with his old regiment. Additionally, it is not clear whether Maire's comment was made to Dorian when the autobiography was originally being 'ghosted' in the late 1930s, and was deliberately left out, or whether it was new material, emanating from Dorian's extensive dealings with Maire between 1939 and his death in 1951. Whatever the case, by the time the comment was published in 1981, in a slightly different book called *Le Colonel Maire: Un Heros de La Legion*,[27] Maire and Forey were both long dead.

In the eight months that he commanded the 1st REI, Maire continued with the building work, and during this time Brunon persuaded Danjou's namesake nephew to also give the *Salle d'Honneur* a tunic which his uncle had not taken to Mexico with him.[28] Brunon then located A.M.J. Gorski, a nephew of Camerone survivor Leon Gorski, and arranged for him first to provide photographs of his late uncle's *Medaille Militaire* and *Expedition du Mexique*, and eventually to donate them to the *Salle d'Honneur*.[29] The Cross of the Legion of Honour won by *Tambour* Lai at Camerone was presented to the *Salle d'Honneur* by General Blin, Head of the *Service Historique de l'Etat-Major de l'Armee*, whose father, Captain Theophile Blin, had in some manner acquired his decoration.[30]

Maire handed over command of the 1st REI in November 1934, being replaced for less than three months by Colonel Debas, who had had an interesting career in the Legion, having twice commanded the 2nd REI, and then the 5th REI.[31] He handed over the 1st to Colonel Paul Azan, a veteran of the Foreign Legion's First World War fighting in Gallipoli, and an officer with a distinct historical bent. In 1925, Azan had written a biography of Abd-el-Kader, and four years later published *Conquete et pacification d'Algerie*, followed the next year by two books on France's generals in Algeria. When he assumed command of the 1st REI on 16 February 1935 he was just finishing *L'Armee d'Afrique, 1830 a 1852*, a detailed study of the campaigns which had occupied the Foreign Legion – and other regiments – from France's first days in Algeria until the eve of the Crimean War.[32] He at once began planning a new *Musee du Souvenir*.

In Paris, Brunon was continuing his research on the Foreign Legion's Regimental Standards, and quite unexpectedly turned up the original letter sent by Colonel Jeanningros to Marshal Randon in October 1863, seeking to have the name Camerone appear on the *Expedition du Mexique* medal then being planned, and to have Camerone approved as a Battle Honour. The letter had been filed among the records of the Directorate of Artillery in 1863 – understandably so, as it was officially their job to deal with matters relating to Regimental Standards – where it had lain, unseen and forgotten, for more than seventy years. Fortunately, Jeanningros had also provided a copy of the 'Report on the Affair of Camarone' which Commandant Regnault had sent to General de Maussion on 17 August

1863, after the debriefing of the Camerone survivors, and of Marshal Forey's Order #195 awarding the decorations and medals. Brunon's discovery of these seminal documents led to their publication[33] in his 1935 booklet *Camerone et l'Aigle du Regiment Etranger, 1862–1870*, in which appeared, for the first time, the full-length photograph of Danjou taken in Oran.

Even as the new *Musee* took shape, Azan was gathering material for what would become a forty-seven-page book called *La Legion Etrangere (1831–1935)*, intended for young officers posted into the Legion,[34] and he had found a kindred historical enthusiast in the person of Lieutenant Andolenko of the 1st REI. Captain Danjou's hand made its second public appearance[35] at Camerone Day in 1936, and would 'participate' in the three Camerone Days prior to the Second World War. The *Musee* was formally inaugurated and, along with the Danjou photograph and tunic, the medals of Lai and Gorski, and other Camerone memorabilia, Azan had acquired a sculpted bust of Danjou – and busts of other officers – and succeeded in increasing the number of photographs of officers killed in action from sixty-four to one hundred and forty-four. Andolenko was compiling a short historical work[36] to be called *La filiation des bataillons de la Legion Etrangere, 1831–1936*.

The same year Prince Louis II of Monaco, Marshal Franchet d'Esperey and General Maxime Weygand joined other military and civilian admirers of Brunon in an effort to financially underpin his work by establishing The Association of Friends of the Collection Jean-Brunon.

In 1937 Captain Marsol, arriving at Ouazazat in Morocco to take command of the 3rd Company of the 1st Battalion of the 4th REI, was excited to learn that it was considered to be the lineal descendant of *La Compagnie Danjou*. A man with an eye for visual effect as well as for history, Marsol set about creating a new badge for his Company, and came up with a design which would ultimately have a lasting impact on the whole Foreign Legion.

Within a diamond shape, he re-created the design of the ribbon of the *Expedition du Mexique* medal of 1864 – an eagle with a serpent in its beak and its claws, set against a red and green St. Andrew's Cross, on a white background. In the finished item the word CAMERONE appeared above the eagle's head in gold letters, with *3e* – 3rd – beside the right wing and *Cie* – *Compagnie* – beside the left. It was very striking, and the early badges manufactured by Drago carried on the reverse the words on the 1892 Camerone gravestone in Mexico.[37]

The British soldier-writer Patrick Turnbull, who spent much of the 1930s travelling in Algeria and Morocco, visited Ouazazat that year and met some of the Legionnaires stationed there, a typical aglomeration of Czechs, Germans, a Dane or two, and other nationalities.[38] Turnbull also travelled to Tinghir and there met Lieutenant Alexander Djincheradze, a Georgian Prince, who was second-in-command of the 1st REC Squadron based at Bou Malem, who invited him to visit the desert outpost. He subsequently spent several months there,[39] meeting, among other people, a fellow Briton named Jim Forsdyke, a former British Cavalry officer, now a *Marechal des Logis* – Sergeant – in the 1st REC, just completing his tenth year of service and very happy with it.[40]

While Turnbull was enjoying the hospitality of the 1st REC at Bou Malem, a Foreign Legion officer detached to work in the Archives of the *Service Historique* in

Paris under the supervision of General Blin, quite providentially discovered another seminal Camerone document: Colonel Jeanningros' hurriedly-written post-battle Report to General Forey, dated 4 May 1863, sent after returning to Chiquihuite after the burial of the dead at Camerone.[41]

Inspector-General Rollet was also in Paris, lobbying the Ministry of War for funds to restart the magazine *La Legion Etrangere*, which he had carefully nurtured for more than five years, but which had been forced to suspend publication for financial reasons. Along with historical articles on the Foreign Legion and individuals, and news concerning Old Comrades Associations, it had published, at the very least, an annual illustrated article about Camerone, though few of them had added much that had not appeared in print before, and the magazine had folded in 1936. Rollet was at his most persuasive and prevailed on the Ministry to provide funds to underpin a rebirth of the magazine, with the same name but with a new and more modern look. Edited by a Madame Frager, and undergoing two name changes, it would publish many interesting and valuable articles during its twenty-one-year life.[42]

The *Salle d'Honneur*'s new *Salle des Trophees* was inaugurated by General Georges Catroux, Commanding the 19th Army Corps – the *Armee d'Afrique* – on Camerone Day 1938. Now styled the The Hall of Honour of the Foreign Legion – rather than simply of the 1st Etranger – it contained additional interesting Camerone memorabilia.[43] Brunon's growing relationship with the Danjou family had led to a Madame Marest – described by him as Danjou's daughter, though no record of a marriage has been found – presenting her father's Commission as a Lieutenant in the 2nd Regiment of the *Legion Etrangere*, dated 9 June, 1855, along with his Crimean War nomination of 1856 for the Legion of Honour.[44] Colonel Azan, following up on his book of three years earlier for new Legion officers, had put together a rather more ambitious volume of one hundred and thirty-six pages called *Memento du Soldat de la Legion Etrangere*, to be given to all new recruits[45] and Andolenko – now a Captain – had authored *Une Visite aux salles d'honneur et au Musee de souvenir de la Legion Etrangere*,[46] which was published to coincide with the opening of the *Salle des Trophees*.

Legionnaire Charles Favrel, a Breton and a former journalist, who experienced his first Camerone Day that year, noted later that being chosen to read the *Recit du Combat de Camerone* was considered a great honour, but remarked that much was lost when the job was given to some veteran German Sous-Officier with limited language skills. 'His audience already does not understand correct French, [so] the incident has little importance,' Favrel commented. He felt that it was the monumental post-parade drinking which was remembered: '"Camerone?" they say shaking their heads, "Oh, la, la! What a drunk!"' Favrel was quite possibly correct about how some Legionnaires felt, but not all, and, anyway, he was apt to belittle Foreign Legion traditions, a born complainer as a matter of course, who grumbled about the epaulettes of the dress uniform, the leg puttees and the traditional blue waistband.[47]

Whatever Favrel's view of the presentation of the *Recit*, the refurbished and expanded *Salle d'Honneur* made a strong impression on an Englishman named Alfred Perrott-White, who was among the first intakes to visit it. He had served in the Royal Flying Corps between 1916 and 1919 and won the *Croix de Guerre*, joined a British cavalry regiment the following year and spent a decade in India, eventually being discharged because of ill health. Perrott-White had then knocked about the world for a couple of years, returning to London to become first a bus driver and later an instructor of bus drivers. He joined the Foreign Legion at the age of thirty-eight in mid-April 1938, telling the interviewing officer that he was doing so 'purely for the adventure' and giving his name as 'Eustace Richard'. By the time he arrived in Sidi-bel-Abbes the year's Camerone celebrations were over, but he was taken to the *Salle d'Honneur*.

> Within it was a wonderful museum of military glory [*he wrote later*]. Old battle flags that had floated in bloody battles against the savage Arabs, flags that had been carried in the Mexican and Spanish wars, and of course, many that had been carried in European wars. In addition there were also captured flags. The whole of one wall was covered with oil portraits of every commanding officer of the Legion since its inception, and facing them a great panel of rare wood on which was painted the names of all the officers killed. At the end of the *Salle* was another panel carrying the names of every legionnaire who had won a decoration for valour. Incidentally, I am very proud to know that my name is now upon it. Along the centre of the floor was a score or more of glass cases holding the decorations of dead legionnaires with accompanying citations . . .
>
> Before we left the building, we were all given a [copy of Colonel Azan's] book printed in French containing the complete history of the Legion. In the flyleaf each man's name was written in beautiful copper-plate handwriting. To my everlasting regret I lost my copy some time after, in the great retreat to Dunkirk.
>
> To a man of my military background walking in the museum was like another man's going to church. It seemed to lift me up, and from that moment onward I was fiercely jealous of the Legion's reputation.[48]

Some of the *Salle d'Honneur*'s new acquisitions were described in an article called 'De Camerone a Bel-Abbes' in the May issue of *La Legion Etrangere*, in which the history-minded Andolenko included the text of Jeanningros' 4 May 1863 letter and reported the latest Camerone memorabilia acquired for the *Musee*.[49]

A few months later another Englishman, John Yeowell, received the *Salle d'Honneur* tour. His father had been killed during the First World War, a few months before his son was born, and his mother had taken a job as the lady companion to the wife of a Brigadier-General, who paid for the boy's education. Instead of settling down, young Yeowell picked up work where he could as a film extra, did a bit of tramping, and was even a pavement artist for a time outside London's National Portrait Gallery. In 1937 he was briefly 'a soldier of conscience' with an Irish Brigade in the Spanish Civil War. In early September the following year, more or less on a whim, the twenty-year-old went to Paris to join the Foreign Legion, giving his name as 'John Jerningham' and passing through Fort St. Jean on his way to Sidi-bel-Abbes.

We now began our period of indoctrination, not a word they used in those days, but true nonetheless [*Yeowell recalled years later*]. It was to fill our heads with the traditions of the Legion. Much the same happens even today, I gather. One of the first things they do is to take you around the museum of the Legion, the *Salle d'Honneur* where the great battles of the past were described to us, along with the exploits of the heroes. We saw the captured battle colours, ancient swords, rifles and other relics. They gave us each a little book with our names inscribed inside, a rather cheap little book in French, which highlighted the Legion of the past. It really did work. Every day on the parade ground there was some kind of traditional activity going on with the Legion band playing all the trumpet calls which we had to memorize and which always ended with a performance of *Le Boudin*. It was all very moving. And the traditions of the Legion began to sink in.[50]

Yeowell often lay in his bed in the old barracks, thinking about the generations of Legionnaires who had done the same there for nearly a century. 'It does get to you,' he would say later. 'In a curious way you feel proud of that past, which, incidentally, gradually becomes your own past.'

The house in which Jean Danjou had been born in the town of Chalabre was still standing, and still owned by the family. His niece lived there[51] and on the wall of a room in the house was a medal case containing Danjou's decorations, flanked by prints of Edouard Detaille's 'The last survivors of the Hacienda of Camerone' and Pierre Benigni's 'The Oath'. Nearby was a plan of the walled corral where Danjou and his men had died.[52]

Inspector-General Rollet, continuing his efforts to highlight Camerone in any way he could, persuaded Chalabre's city fathers to change the name of the street in which the house stood, and then instructed Colonel Azan at Sidi-bel-Abbes to have a marble plaque made to fix to the outside wall of the house in what was now to be called the Rue du Capitaine Danjou. Azan was preparing to hand over command of the 1st REI at the time and the work was executed at the Quartier Vienot by a Legionnaire skilled in marble cutting.[53]

It read:

> On 15 April 1828 there was born in this house
> Captain DANJOU
> who on 30 April 1863 at CAMERONE (Mexico)
> at the head of 66 Legionnaires of the 3rd Company
> of the Regiment Etranger, resisted to the death
> the furious assaults of 2000 Mexicans.
> 3 Officers and 49 men were mortally wounded,
> but the enemy had 500 dead.
> Since then, every year, the Legion celebrates
> the glorious anniversary of Camerone,
> symbol of unequalled military virtue.

A ceremony marked the plaque's placement in 1939, and the story it told was certainly rousing stuff, but considering the number of Legionnaires said to have been involved, the number reported to have died, and the astonishing number of Mexican casualties claimed, it is clear that Azan, with his rigorous regard for historical truth, had not been around to see that correct figures were supplied to the monumental mason.[54]

General Blin of the *Service Historique*, having given *Tambour* Lai's Cross of a Chevalier of the Legion of Honour to the *Salle d'Honneur*, had been digging among his father's papers and located a personal reminiscence. It appeared in the May 1939 issue of *La Legion Etrangere* under the title of 'Au Mexique, avec la Legion Etrangere: Souvenirs du Capitaine Blin: July 1866-March 1867,' and provided, among other things, a brief vignette of Lai in the closing days of the French Intervention.[55]

The Summer was gloomy, as Adolph Hitler's armies threatened Europe and, though now fully retired, General Rollet, as peppery as ever, his chest ablaze with orders, decorations and medals, was on the platform at the Gare de Lyon in Paris to greet the Legionnaires commanded by Captain Dimitri Amilakvari, a Georgian Prince who had left his homeland in 1917 and been a Legion officer since 1924, as they arrived for the 14 July Bastille Day parade along the Champs Elysees.

Less than two months later the world was plunged into war.

30
Celebrating Camerone in Strange Places

As Europe had moved inexorably towards the Second World War a number of serving Legionnaires, who might otherwise have opted to become civilians, had decided to continue soldiering. Among them was Sergeant-Major Collard, a Belgian with more than four decades of service in the Foreign Legion to his credit, who was permitted to re-engage, even though he was seventy years old.[1] A true link with the past, Collard had been born in 1868, the year after the Regiment Etranger returned from Mexico, and had joined the Foreign Legion in 1906, the year that the flag of the 1st Etranger was decorated with the Legion of Honour and Lieutenant Francois held his Camerone Day remembrance in Tonkin.

A second *Regiment Etranger de Cavalerie* (2nd REC) was created in July 1939 and the Foreign Legion battalion serving in Syria was turned into the 6th *Regiment Etranger d'Infanterie* (6th REI), but planned new infantry formations were only on paper when war was actually declared on 3 September. The first of them came into being a month later as the three-battalion 11th *Regiment Etranger d'Infanterie* (11th REI), commanded by Colonel Maire. He had largely whipped it into shape by December, but age forced him to step aside in favour of Colonel Jean-Baptiste Robert just before Christmas, when it left Algeria for France. The three-battalion 12th *Regiment Etranger d'Infanterie* (12th REI) was formed in February 1940.

So, too, was the two-battalion 13th *Demi-Brigade de la Legion Etrangere* (13th DBLE), which was commanded by the aristocratic Hungarian-born Lieutenant-Colonel Raoul Magrin-Vernerey, a much-wounded and decorated officer, who had run away from home to join the Foreign Legion when he was not quite sixteen. Retrieved by his parents, he was subsequently sent to Saint-Cyr, graduating the very month that the First World War broke out. He joined the 60th Infantry Regiment and by war's end was a Captain, seven times wounded and eleven times cited for gallantry. In 1924, at the age of thirty-two, Magrin-Vernerey realized his boyhood ambition by transferring into the Foreign Legion and served successively with the 1st, 3rd, 2nd, 5th and 4th REIs.[2]

Ailing for some time, there had been no question of Prince Aage taking part in the war in Europe and he died of pleurisy in Taza, Morocco, at the end of February 1940. He was buried in Casablanca, though his body would later be moved to the Foreign Legion cemetery in Sidi-bel-Abbes.[3] Zinovi Pechkoff, who had been on Marshal Lyautey's staff in Morocco in the mid-1920s, and then served in Syria and Lebanon as Military Adviser to the French High Commissioner during the latter part of the 1930s, was making a career for himself as a soldier-diplomat.[4]

Prince Napoleon, the Bonapartist Pretender to the Throne of France, and the Count of Paris, nephew of Prince Aage and son of the Duc de Guise, the Orleanist

Pretender, both wished to serve their country, but were not permitted by law to set foot in France. Prince Napoleon, who was living in Switzerland, had written to Premier Edouard Daladier – who had himself served in the Foreign Legion – in early September 1939 offering his services. They were politely refused, so he took advantage of the confusion of war to slip across the border into France and was able to engage in the Foreign Legion in March, as 'Louis Blanchard', a 'for the duration' Swiss citizen.[5]

As thousands of foreigners flocked to the French cause a 21st *Regiment de Marche de Volontaires Etrangers* (21st RMVE) was raised, soon followed by similar regiments, numbered 22nd and 23rd.

The 13th *Demi-Brigade*, which would become the most famous of the Free French regiments fighting with the Allies, sent a number of men who knew how to ski to be put through mountain warfare training in the French Alps, and Legionnaire 'Blanchard' – Prince Napoleon – an accomplished skier, volunteered. His application, however, was refused on orders from above. The half-brigade went to France without him and soon found itself designated to be part of an Anglo-French-Free Polish force tasked with driving the Germans from northern Norway. They left Liverpool on the former luxury liner *La Ville d'Alger*, now converted into an armed troop carrier.

There had been no time for a Regimental Standard to be made and the flag they took with them was flown from a British cavalry lance rustled up at the last moment as they left Liverpool. Camerone Day came when the regiment was at sea. Lieutenant Pierre O. Lapie, a French parliamentarian attached to the 13th *Demi-Brigade* to prepare a record of the Norwegian operation, remembered the modest shipboard remembrance.

> To celebrate this occasion our English friends had loaded the Legion with gifts [*Lapie recalled*]. The Lord Mayor of Liverpool had given a gramophone, some ladies and various organizations had given books, cigarettes and souvenirs of all kinds. The men squatted around the machine-guns at nightfall against sandbags (a protection from wind if not from bullets), and listened with delight to a record of Schubert's 'Ava Maria', sung by Tino-Rossi . . . At dinner, in a room atrociously resplendent with red lacquer and cut-glass, stewards who had signed on for service in the East, shivering in their linen uniforms, served a mediocre meal.[6]

'My last April 30th was a bit different,' an officer named Delamaze remarked to Lapie. 'I was with my section in Upper Morocco, in the Hamada de la Dahura. We had such a terrific sandstorm that it brought down a flight of swallows in a heap. But we celebrated Camerone.'

Legionnaire Favrel was also Narvik-bound and John Yeowell was on his way to Norway on the *Monarch of Bermuda*, sailing from Glasgow, whose Lord Provost had made sure that the Foreign Legion had been well feted.

While the 13th *Demi-Brigade* was quietly marking Camerone Day at sea, the 11th REI was receiving its Regimental Standard at a small ceremony in the field, but in the haste to produce it the Battle Honour for Camerone had been left off.

The 12th REI celebrated Camerone at St. Maurice de Gourdans and officers persuaded Legionnaire Frederic O'Brady, a Hungarian actor and musician, to send for his singer girlfriend from Paris for a party.[7] The so-called 'Phoney War' was still on, but the real war broke out before a correction could be made for the Regimental Standard of the 11th REI, or ones produced for the 12th REI and the 21st, 22nd and 23rd RMVEs. The 21st celebrated Camerone just hours before it left the training camp at Barcares in the South of France. It perhaps did not amount to much of a ceremony, or was little understood, as Hungarian-born Sergeant Hans Habe, who later wrote one of the best accounts of service in the 21st RMVE, did not think to mention it.[8]

On 6 May 1940, while the 13th *Demi-Brigade* was fighting alongside British, Polish and Norwegian forces outside Narvik, the Paris edition of the *New York Herald Tribune* was reporting that sixty-four-year-old General Paul Rollet was furiously – and fruitlessly – demanding to be put back on the Active List for war service.

The 13th *Demi-Brigade* and their allies took Bjerkvik, then Narvik and chased the Germans almost to the Swedish border. It was the first Allied victory of the war, but events were moving swiftly and precipitated a withdrawal and their return to France. Individually, rather than collectively, the 11th and 12th REIs were soon in action. So were the three RMVEs and the 97th *Groupe Reconnaissance Divissionnaire* (GRD 97), raised from among the Foreign Legion's two Cavalry regiments.

The 11th REI was made up of veteran Legionnaires, and ex-Foreign Legion Reservists, among them Georges-R. Manue, who had been in Morocco in the early 1920s. The Germans attacked Belgium and Holland on 10 May and seventeen days later fell on the Maginot Line, dive bombing with Stukas, and attacking with tanks and infantry. The first day the regiment took heavy losses, most Companies being reduced to fifty per cent of strength. 'We held the Bois d'Inor for over a fortnight,' wrote Sergeant Manue, in an unpublished memoir now in the Foreign Legion Archives. Almost surrounded at Saint-Germain-sur-Meuse, Commandant Clement decided to burn the Regimental Standard, so that it would not fall into German hands. He soaked it in gasoline and Legionnaire Dedeker set it on fire, then signed Clement's attestation that it had been destroyed. The *cravate*, along with the *fanion* of the 1st Battalion, were taken by motorcycle to Colonel Robert. When ordered to retreat, the 2nd Battalion punched a hole in the encircling German line, losing its commander, nine other officers and one in ten of its men, so that the other two battalions could escape. When the regiment was surrounded again, the *cravate* and *fanion* were buried in the porch of the church at Crezilles.

> We were still firing when the 'Cease fire' sounded, and there wasn't a man who was not prepared to go on fighting with his bayonet alone, if needs be, should ammunition run out [*wrote Sergeant Manue*]. When at last it was all over, the same thought was on everyone's mind – 'We didn't let old Maire down.'

The 11th REI had been reduced from three thousand men to eight hundred, only four hundred and fifty of whom were still able to march. 'The regiment', said Manue, 'was still a coherent and combattant unit,' and it remained so, most of the survivors managing to stay ahead of the Germans as they moved south and eventually got back to North Africa.[9]

All the Foreign Legion regiments engaged in France suffered huge losses during June. The 12th REI was reduced from three thousand men to three hundred, and essentially ceased to exist, except as individuals and small groups trying to locate other French regiments, or as prisoners-of-war. Among them was a young officer, Lieutenant Albert Brothier, who would spend five years in captivity and more than two decades later, as Colonel of the 1st Etranger, play a pivotal role in the greatest internal crisis the Foreign Legion ever faced. The GRD 97 and the 21st, 22nd and 23rd RMVEs were similarly obliterated, and most of those who were not dead became prisoners of the Germans. The unwounded and uncaptured, pitiful remnants of all the regiments decimated in France, filtered back to Algeria as best they could.

The fall of France and the humiliating Armistice signed with Germany on 22 June led to the partitioning of the country into Occupied and Unoccupied Zones, and to the rise of the French government established at Vichy with First World War hero Marshal Philippe Petain as Head of State.

Perrott-White, who had gone to France with the 2nd REI, and won a second *Croix de Guerre*, had been captured at Dunkirk. A Polish comrade knew the country and the pair escaped from a train carrying them to a German prison camp. They carefully made their way south through the Occupied Zone for several weeks, but the Pole died when they were almost at Lyon, which was in the Unoccupied Zone. There Perrott-White was welcomed and sent back to North Africa.[10]

In his own efforts to join up, the Count of Paris had also managed to reach the French capital, and had been received by Premier Daladier's successor, Paul Reynaud. It had been agreed that he could join the Foreign Legion, engaging as 'Henry Orliac', a Geneva-born 'for the duration' Swiss citizen, and he had started his journey to Sidi-bel-Abbes on 6 June. Those who recognized him from newspaper photographs had been told they were 'mistaken', and he had initially settled in quite well. Then he heard that his father, the Duc de Guise, had died at his home in Morocco. Legionnaire 'Orliac' was now himself the Orleanist Pretender, which made for impossible complications. The Foreign Legion quietly released him. Legionnaire 'Blanchard' – Prince Napoleon – was also released from the Foreign Legion soon after the fall of France, but contributed his efforts to the rest of the war as a member of the French Resistance.[11]

Only the 13th *Demi-Brigade*, in small groups and individually, managed to escape to England. Those who chose to rally to the call of Brigadier-General Charles de Gaulle formed the nucleus of the Free French Foreign Legion under Colonel Magrin-Vernerey, who took the *nom de guerre* of 'Monclar' to protect his family in France. Among the twenty-eight officers who opted to stay on were Pierre Koenig and Dimitri Amilakvari and around nine hundred Legionnaires also elected to join the embryo Free French. The remainder were shipped back to Morocco.

In the wake of the German victories, the 11th and 12th REIs, along with the

GRD 97 and the 2nd REC, were disbanded. So was the 4th REI, but a 4th *Demi-Brigade* was formed and hurriedly sent to Senegal. Most of its members were men likely to be executed if they fell into the hands of the Germans. Largely through the efforts of General Alphonse Juin, the Foreign Legion succeeded in hiding many whose lives would have been forfeit if they had fallen into enemy hands. Some were sent to join the 5th REI in Indo-China, although problems with the Japanese were developing.

At war with China, the Japanese soon realized that munitions were passing through Tonkin to Generalissimo Chiang Kai-shek and the Chinese Nationalists. Indo-China was viewed as potentially a part of 'Greater Japan' and they forced General Georges Catroux, the French Resident, to close the frontier between Tonkin and China and accept a Japanese Control Commission to see that it stayed closed. When Petain and his Vichy Government learned of this Catroux was summarily dismissed. His replacement, however, signed an agreement with the Japanese on 30 August, giving them certain military facilities in Tonkin in exchange for recognizing French authority. The pact would have far-reaching consequences.[12]

Other Legionnaires from decimated regiments trickling back to Sidi-bel-Abbes were transferred into the 1st and 2nd REIs and the 1st REC, which the Germans allowed to remain in existence. The German Armistice Commission monitored the Foreign Legion carefully, combing the regiments for pro- and anti-Nazi elements, and extracted some pro-Nazis, who were put into a special labour unit, the 361st Afrika Regiment.

It was not easy to keep spirits up under the circumstances of neutrality forced on them by the Vichy Government and the prying eyes of the Armistice Commission, so the Foreign Legion seized every opportunity that presented itself for a ceremonial occasion or a celebration.

General Jules Francois, at the end of a long and active career, which had begun as a Sous-Lieutenant arriving at Sidi-bel-Abbes in October 1900, retired as Commanding Officer of the French Army in Morocco in August. After making his farewell rounds, which included visits to the 2nd and 3rd REIs, and the 1st REC in Morocco, he expressed a wish to salute the Regimental Standard of the 1st REI for the last time in front of the *Monument aux Morts* at Sidi-bel-Abbes. Arriving at the Quartier Vienot on 19 September, he was greeted by Colonel Henri Giraud of the 1st REI and representative detachments from all the remaining Foreign Legion regiments. The venerable Lieutenant-Colonel Forey was also there, at the head of a delegation of active and retired officers and Legionnaires, many of whom had served with Francois in one place or another during the previous forty years.

The man who had spontaneously held the first quasi-formal celebration of Camerone at a tiny post in northern Tonkin in 1906 was moved to tears as he took the salute, then praised the Legionnaires he had fought with in campaigns in Sud Oranais, Tonkin and Morocco before the First World War, then during it, 'under the orders of my old comrade Rollet,' and afterwards in Syria, Lebanon, Tonkin and Morocco.

I am therefore qualified to proclaim that our Legionnaires remain worthy of those who have gone before them [*Francois said*]. They proved it by their heroism and their spirit of sacrifice in the course of recent operations in France and Norway and one of their chiefs who launched his men into battle, once again winning resounding praise . . .

At the moment that I bow to my obligation to end my active service, I wished that my last military act would be to pay devout homage to our dead, and I include all the Legionnaires of 1940, wherever they are, and all former Legionnaires dispersed across the entire world.[13]

Francois gave the *Salle d'Honneur* a copy of an account of the first Camerone celebration called 'Le poste de Ta-Lung' – though he did not identify himself as the officer involved – and an autographed photograph of himself, on which he had written: 'Always a Legionnaire.'

General Maxime Weygand, the Vichy Government's Delegate-General, whose son had been an officer in the 1st REC in the late 1920s, spent much of his time visiting the various Foreign Legion units in North Africa, advising them to 'train ceaselessly, adapt all training to the evolution of modern technique in warfare, and above all maintain rigid traditional discipline based on the mutual respect existing between all ranks'.[14]

Rollet, still fruitlessly demanding to be put back into active service, died in German-occupied Paris on 16 April 1941 and was buried there,[15] but his body, like that of Aage, would later be reinterred in Sidi-bel-Abbes.

Considering his dedication, it is perhaps not surprising that Brunon had managed to keep the magazine *La Legion Etrangere* in existence – and the story of Camerone alive – even as the war progressed. He was operating in the Unoccupied Zone and the issue of May 1941 contained another reprinting[16] of his 'Camerone et l'Aigle du Regiment Etranger, 1862–1870.'

The war soon became very confusing for the Foreign Legion.

The 13th *Demi-Brigade* was pro-de Gaulle. The regiments in North Africa had been effectively neutralized by the Vichy Government's links with Germany and were passive and static. In Syria, the political leadership, and many senior Army officers – in the 6th REI and in other regiments – had decided to remain loyal to Marshal Petain as the legitimate leader of France. Abrasive and often haughty, General de Gaulle had never been personally popular in the Army. The Foreign Legion had served under Petain in the First World War and in Morocco, and a case could be made – and was – that de Gaulle was inciting mutiny by establishing Free French forces, but the decision to stand with Petain put the 6th REI squarely in the Vichy camp.

Now stiffened by a handful of new officers – including Sous-Lieutenants Pierre Messmer and Jean Simon – the 13th *Demi-Brigade* sailed from England with an Anglo-French naval force, heading for West Africa to install the Free French in colonies under Vichy control. Travelling with them was a young American, John F. Hasey, serving as a Sous-Lieutenant with the Free French Medical Transport Section. At Dakar in Senegal it was made clear that the local administration was loyal to Vichy. The convoy steamed away.

Hasey decided that he did not want to stay with what was, in fact, an

Celebrating Camerone in Strange Places   345

Ambulance Service, and effected a transfer into the Free French Foreign Legion.[17] After securing the greater part of French West Africa and French Equatorial Africa for the Free French, the 13th *Demi-Brigade* sailed round Africa to Port Sudan to take part in the campaign to drive the Italians out of Eritrea, on the Red Sea. There was much hard fighting alongside British, Australian and Indian troops, especially at the mountain fortress of Keren. The port city of Massawa was taken by the Foreign Legion on 8 April 1941 and the Italians surrendered. Camerone Day came just before the 13th *Demi-Brigade* was scheduled to move from Eritrea to the Middle East.

> More than 200 officers of [the] French and English armies and navies sat down to a banquet, and a telegram of good wishes was sent to the Vichy-French troops in [Algeria and] Morocco, home of the Foreign Legion [*Hasey would recall later*]. Although different in their allegiance, the Free French Foreign Legion could not ignore such a courtesy on that day. The party went well into the night. The soldiers of the Legion put on their own show for their own benefit and enjoyment and in a big open air Italian amphitheatre, and permitted officers to look on. For one day they could mimic their officers, lampoon and make sport of them; and some of the officers' faces were quite red. They sang parodies and risque songs, ribbed commanders, big and small, put on acts that repeated painful episodes in various commands, and made jokes of things that were ordinarily contemplated with military sanctimony. Even recent experiences outside Massawa became part of vaudeville skits.[18]

The 13th *Demi-Brigade* left Eritrea a few days later for Palestine, where it would wait until ordered to take part in an unhappy campaign in Syria against Vichy French military, including the 6th REI. It was resting at Quastina in Palestine on 11 May when Free French units marched to Buckingham Palace to receive their Regimental Standards. The one made for the 13th *Demi-Brigade* had come into being without any Foreign Legion input and the memories of non-Legion French officers had been poor. Brunon, who saw it later, noted, among other things, that the style of lettering was different, and that while Battle Honours for BJERKVIK (sic), NARVIK, KEREN and MASSOUA were shown, CAMERONE had been left off.[19] Arrangements were to be made for it to be sent out to the regiment in the Middle East.

When the British, Indians and Australians moved into Syria to face the Vichy-supporting French garrison the 13th *Demi-Brigade* had to do so without the formidable Colonel Monclar, who refused to be part of a campaign which would pit Frenchmen against Frenchmen. Koenig had risen fast and now held General Officer rank, so Monclar's place was taken by Lieutenant-Colonel Amilakvari. On 20 July, in the attack on Damascus, Sous-Lieutenant Hasey was hit in the throat, chest and arm. His fighting days were over. The Vichy French garrison surrendered soon afterwards and officers and men of the 6th REI were given the choice of joining the Free French or returning to Algeria. A handful of officers and less than a thousand men joined de Gaulle's forces. The others went back to France and then

North Africa, where their Commanding Officer, Colonel Fernand Barre, took command of the 1st REI at Sidi-bel-Abbes and the 6th REI was disbanded.

Former Foreign Legion Sergeant A.R. Cooper was now Second Lieutenant Cooper of Britain's Special Operations Executive and was landed on the Algerian coast as a saboteur in late June, 1941. He was the only British agent to undertake such a task, but was captured before he could initiate any action, and sent to the Laghouat Internment Camp on the fringes of the Sahara.[20] Somehow the Germans got to hear that the *cravate* and *fanion* belonging to the 11th REI had been hidden before the 'cease fire' and reports reached the Foreign Legion that serious efforts were being made to find them. It would clearly be only a matter of time before their hiding place in the church wall at Crezilles would be discovered, so 21 September 1941 a brave nurse, Madame Mefredy, travelled from the Unoccupied Zone to the Occupied Zone, retrieved the treasures from their hiding place, and returned safely to the Unoccupied Zone. They were then sent to Brunon in Marseille, who arranged for their return to Sidi-bel-Abbes.[21]

The Syrian Campaign had been short and bitter and after it the 13th *Demi-Brigade* moved to Homs and plans were made for the London-made Regimental Standard to be formally presented by General Catroux on 19 October. Amilakvari began to fear that it would not be received in time and asked French women resident in Cairo to also make one for the regiment. It featured the Battle Honours CAMERONE, BJERWICK 1940, NARVIK 1940, KEREN 1941 and MASSOUAH 1941. The Cross of Lorraine, the symbol of the Free French, was also embroidered on it. Both Regimental Standards arrived in time for Catroux's review, but Amilakvari chose what became known as the Cairo Flag – as opposed to the London Flag – for the ceremony.

'It is probable that the [Lieutenant-]Colonel, made his decision because the London Flag did not carry the inscription "Camerone" which figured on the Cairo Flag,' Brunon commented later.[22]

The 13th *Demi-Brigade* went back to North Africa and the following year survived an epic siege in the Western Desert, facing Rommel's Afrika Corps and his Italian allies at Bir Hakeim in Libya.[23] The regiment now numbered one thousand seven hundred and seventy-one men, organized into three battalions, each of four Companies. The British had been only able to equip the 2nd and 3rd Battalions as mechanized infantry by the time General Koenig's 1st Free French Brigade Group was needed to hold a desolate desert crossroads called Bir Hakeim – 'The Chief's Well'. Koenig's command was made up of the nine hundred and fifty-seven Legionnaires of the 2nd and 3rd Battalions – about a third of the total force – along with men of the *Infanterie de Marine* and troops from the South Pacific, Central and North Africa. A handful of British troops was present as anti-tank gunners.

Koenig took over Bir Hakeim on 14 February 1942, fortifying it with bunkers and deep trenches, while sending out columns to attack the Italians and Germans in the area. On 27 May the siege began with an Italian attack. Fearing his forward command post being overrun, Captain Morel burned the 5th Company's *fanion*, as did Captain Otte under similar circumstances. The enemy was beaten off. General Erwin Rommel had expected Bir Hakeim to fall easily, but it did not.

Surrender demands were rejected and Koenig told his men: 'The struggle will be long. You, will be victorious.'[24]

Among the officers whose names became indelibly linked with the defence of Bir Hakeim were Amilakvari and Captain Pierre Messmer. The fifteen-day siege ended in a desperate and daring breakout on 10 June, and some two thousand five hundred men of Koenig's command managed to reach the British lines. Koenig and Amilakvari escaped in a staff car. Captains Pierre Messmer and Andre Lalande, on foot and separated from their men, were lucky enough to be picked up by a Foreign Legion bren-gun carrier and carried to safety. Captain Jean Simon, who had lost an eye in Syria, crashed his truck into a trench full of German infantry, but got away in the confusion. Foreign Legion casualties had been relatively light during the actual siege, but the breakout was more costly, the 13th *Demi-Brigade* losing more than two hundred men, killed, wounded, captured or missing, which it could ill afford.

The regiment was then attached to General Bernard Montgomery's 8th Armoured Corps and Amilakvari was killed on 24 October at El-Himeimat, in a muddled off-centre-stage clash during the Battle of El-Alamein. He had once said: 'The only way for us foreigners to show gratitude to France for all she has done for us is to die for her,' and he met his obligation.[25]

Brunon continued publishing *La Legion Etrangere*, even as the Germans were preparing to march into the Vichy Government's Unoccupied Zone. When they did so, in November, at huge personal risk he moved the historic flags, standards and banners in his famous collection to a safe place, so that they would not fall into German hands and be taken to Berlin as trophies.[26]

Allied forces had landed in North Africa the same month and the Foreign Legion units in Morocco put up rather more than a token defence, sustaining considerable losses. Among the U.S. Army officers to land in Oran was Colonel David Wooster King, who had risen to the rank of Legionnaire 1st Class in the 2nd *Regiment de Marche* of the 2nd Etranger during the First World War. Now he was personally escorted to Sidi-Bel-Abbes, reviewed the troops and dined in the officers' mess.[27] Perrott-White, because he spoke English, was soon detached to the Americans in a liaison capacity.[28]

Among the other Americans who descended upon Sidi-bel-Abbes, attracted by the mystique of the Foreign Legion, was Ernie Pyle, the most famous of the American War Correspondents, who took a tour of the *Salle d'Honneur*.

> Around the walls stood case after case of Legion mementoes – old swords, flags, pieces of uniform, guns, bullets, decorations [*he told his readers*]. The walls were hung with hundreds of pictures of Legion members who had died gloriously. Life-sized wax figures standing around the walls of one room showed the dozen or so types of uniform worn by the Legion over the years. The museum wasn't wild or exotic as you might think. It was almost like a little section of the Smithsonian. A Belgian corporal acted as guide and gave a little Cook's-tour explanation of everything. Souvenir postcards and booklets were for sale. The Legion's most prized memento was, of all things, a wooden hand. In 1854 the Legion fought in the Russian Crimea, and in

that campaign a Captain Danjou had one hand shot off. He had a wooden hand made to replace it. The hand was of fine workmanship, the fingers were all jointed, and the thing looked almost lifelike . . .[29]

Pyle's heart was always in the right place, but he sometimes got the wrong end of the stick. Apart from his error about where Danjou lost his hand, he reported the Combat of Camerone as having taken place when '[a] tiny party of 115 Legionnaires barricaded themselves in a hacienda at the town of Camerone, and battled a force of four thousand Mexicans,' adding breathlessly: 'All but three of the Legionnaires were killed.' Pyle was quick, too, to note the seeming parallels with the siege of The Alamo. He also wrote of the Camerone Day celebrations: 'Captain Danjou's hand is brought out in its glass case and is displayed as a symbol of what the Legion means. It all seemed a little gruesome, but the Legion felt deeply about it.'

More knowledgeable wartime visitors to the *Salle d'Honneur* included Xavier and Louis Sol la Lande, the Mexico-born sons of a French Consul in Veracruz. In close contact with the French community there and in Mexico City, they knew a great deal about the French Intervention of eighty years earlier, but not very much about Camerone, which was a relatively short distance from their place of birth.[30]

Now that the forced-to-be-neutral, Vichy-controlled, North African arm of the Foreign Legion was back in the war on the side of the Allies, the 4th *Demi-Brigade* was brought back from Senegal and joined elements of the 1st REI in forming the 1st *Regiment Etranger d'Infanterie de Marche* (1st REIM). Cavalrymen gave up horses for trucks as the 1st REC was reorganized, and the 3rd REI was re-built from its Moroccan and Algerian garrisons. Once again its Regimental Standard, the much-decorated banner of the First World War *Regiment de Marche de la Legion Etrangere*, was going to war.

In the Allied effort to drive the Germans out of Tunisia both the 1st REIM and the 3rd REI were in action at the beginning of 1943, but the enemy deployed the 10th Panzer Division to keep them from the approaches to Tunis and they were badly savaged at Kasserine Pass, along with the U.S. Army units involved. The 3rd REI lost thirty-five officers and sixteen hundred men during January.

Worse still, they also lost their precious Regimental Standard, when a fast-moving German attack on 18–19 January, with armour and infantry, overran their fighting headquarters position. Oddly, the German and Italian commanders do not seem to have realized that they had in their possession not only the Foreign Legion's most decorated banner, but one which was known and revered throughout the French Army. A photograph of Axis officers with the cherished Regimental Standard appeared in the Italian newspaper *Corriere della Sera*,[31] but no real propaganda use was made of the capture, and it became merely a decoration in a meeting room in some buildings used as a field hospital.

The 13th *Demi-Brigade* returned to Sidi-bel-Abbes in 1943 and was not really welcomed by the reactivated formerly neutral regiments. The Free French Foreign Legion had seen action in Europe, Africa and Asia Minor and was naturally loyal to de Gaulle. The North African regiments, who had been forced to sit things out in North Africa, were understandably loyal to General Henri Giraud, a former

Colonel of the 1st REI, now commanding the 19th Army Corps, and de Gaulle's opponent in a struggle for power and recognition.

Allied efforts drove the Germans out of Tunisia and the captured Regimental Standard of the 3rd REI was supposed to have gone with them. Nazi propaganda chief Dr. Joseph Goebbels would have recognized its significance and have had a field day with it. However, in the mass confusion as the Germans pulled out, two French residents of Tunis succeeded in retrieving the banner from the back of a German ambulance. They returned it to Giraud, who restored it to the 3rd REI. At some point during the more than three months that it was in enemy hands somebody had removed the *cravate*, with the various medals pinned to it, and the coloured lanyards – the *fourrageres*. This is not a story which finds its way into official Foreign Legion histories and gung-ho heroic accounts, but a nameless somebody, in the interests of accuracy and completeness, provided the regimental archives[31] with an account called 'The Adventure of the Standard of the 3rd Etranger, Tunisia 19 January–12 May 1943.' It took part – without its *cravate* and *fourrageres* – in the celebration held in Tunis on 20 May to mark the defeat of the Axis Powers in North Africa.[32] Giraud refused to allow the Free French Foreign Legion to march with his 19th Army Corps, but this hardly troubled the 13th *Demi-Brigade*, who were quite happy to be with the men of the Britain's Eighth Army, at whose side they had fought many battles and engagements.

In July, the 3rd REI and the 1st REIM, along with men from the old 11th and 12th REIs were formed into a single *Regiment de Marche de la Legion Etrangere* (RMLE). In an effort to lower tensions between the Foreign Legion regiments, the designation 'Free French' was dropped at the end of the month, although the 13th *Demi-Brigade* retained – as it does to this day – its Cross of Lorraine badge and patches.

Designated as the 1st and 2nd *Bataillons de Legion Etrangere* (BLE), the 13th *Demi-Brigade* landed in Italy in April 1944. What had been the 1st Division of the Free French was now cosmetically called the *1e division de marche infanterie*. They fought well under the overall direction of General Juin, taking part in the liberation of Rome.

They went back to North Africa briefly, but on 16 August went ashore at Cavalaire on the coast of Provence as part in 'Operation Anvil.' They helped to liberate Toulon and then swung north, entering Lyon in early September. They were in Alsace in November.

The RMLE landed in France in late September 1944. Along with the 1st REC, commanded by Colonel Miquel, they became part of the 5th Armoured Division and headed for Alsace. They stormed Haricourt and Montbeliard in November, took Belfort, and were in battle around Strasbourg. The year turned and they and were joined by the 13th *Demi-Brigade* for the attack on Colmar. On 2 February a tank belonging to the 1st REC was the first to enter the city, with four dead Legionnaires on the back. It was the 13th *Demi-Brigade*'s last battle, as, reduced to a mere seven hundred men, they were withdrawn and sent into the French Alps, where they ended the war. The RMLE and the 1st REC continued on, took Stuttgart and had actually crossed the Danube into Austria when the armistice was signed. Now commanded by Colonel Jean Olie, elements of the RMLE and the

13th *Demi-Brigade*, commanded by Lieutenant-Colonel Bernard Saint-Hillier, took part in the Victory March through Paris on 18 June.

The Battle Honours approved for the Regimental Standard of the 13th *Demi-Brigade* were finally agreed as: BJERVIK-NARVIK 1940, KEREN-MASSOUAH 1941, BIR-HAKEIM 1942, ROME 1944, COLMAR 1945 and AUTHION 1945. The *cravate* was decorated with: the *Croix de la Liberation, Medaille de la Resistance, Croix de Guerre 1939–1945* with four *palmes*, *Croix de Guerre T.O.E.* with four *palmes*, the Norwegian *Croix de Guerre* with sword – the equivalent of a second medal – and a *fourragere* in the colours of the ribbons of the *Medaille Militaire* and the two types of *Croix de Guerre*.[33]

The Battle Honours approved for the RMLE were: DJEBEL-MANSOUR 1943, ALSACE 1944–1945 and STUTTGART 1945. The *cravate* was decorated with the *Croix de Guerre 1939–45* with three *palmes*, the *Croix de Guerre* for *Theatres d'Operations Exterieux (TOE)* with four *palmes*, the Flame of Unity Medal, awarded to the regiment by the President of the United States as a Distinguised Unit in the Rhine-Bavarian Alps campaigns, and a *fourragere* in the colours of the *Medaille Militaire* and the *Croix de Guerre TOE*.[34] Still commanded by Colonel Olie, it was subsequently transformed back into the 3rd REI.

In French Indo-China the 5th REI, which had been created in 1930, lived out their strange war, the soldiers in their garrisons, watching the Japanese build their own army to almost thirty thousand, while the French civilian administration, at least in theory, ran the country. It would end tragically, for once the War in Europe was over, and the Allies began winning the one in the Pacific, the Japanese feared an invasion of Indo-China.

On 9 March 1945 – the Foreign Legion's official one hundred and fifteenth birthday – invitations were sent to General Emile Lemonnier, the senior French officer in the Lang Son area, and his officers to attend a reception given by the Imperial Japanese Government. Formal toasts and pleasantries preceded dinner, but as the French officers filed into the dining room revolvers were produced by their hosts and they were told that they were prisoners. Lemonnier and Camille Auphelle, the French Resident, were presented with a surrender document and told to sign. They flatly refused. Taken to the Kilua grottoes, near the Chinese border, they were made to dig their own graves, then offered a final chance to sign the surrender document. When they again refused they were beheaded.

In Lang Son a hundred Legionnaires fought a whole Japanese regiment until their ammunition ran out. Marched into a courtyard, they were lined up against a wall, menaced by machine-guns. Their officer, Lieutenant Jean-Pierre Duronsoy, started to sing the *Marseillaise*. His men, Poles, Czechs, Germans, Greeks and others, took up the refrain. Then the Japanese fell on them with bayonets, swords, even pickaxes, and hacked them to death. Attacked by the Japanese at the citadel in Hanoi, a pair of Foreign Legion Sergeant-Majors emptied the cells of prisoners and fought until they were all overcome.

At Tong, northwest of Hanoi, headquarters of the 5th REI, General Marcel Alessandri, who had commanded the regiment until the end of 1940, knew that he had but one choice: to get the two thousand French troops out of Tonkin at once. He disbanded his local Tonkinese soldiers, notified his officers to be ready to move, and told them that there was no transport available. So they would march, west first, then north to cross the Chinese border, more than eleven hundred kilometres (seven hundred miles) through wicked country. The 5th REI had no Colonel and no Battalion Commanders, so the three battalions were commanded by Captains.

Ambushed many times along the way, the Foreign Legion made a fighting withdrawal, as the Japanese hit them whenever they could, falling on them in jungle clearings and at river crossings. At Meos Pass on 28 March Captain Jules Gaucher's battalion covered the other two battalions and charged Japanese guns. Every clash cost Foreign Legion lives, but the battalions struggled on. At a place called Dien Bien Phu, desolate except for an unused airstrip, some three thousand Japanese tried to encircle the French troops, but they broke through and headed north. On 2 May a thousand Legionnaires crossed the Tonkin–China frontier into Yunnan Province. Then they marched on for another four hundred and eighty kilometres (three hundred miles), reaching Tsao-pa on 15 June.

There they found sanctuary and help from Chiang Kai-shek's Nationalists. They also found an old friend, Zinovi Pechkoff. After the fall of France, he had travelled to London, joined de Gaulle and the Free French and had been sent to the United States for what amounted to a propaganda tour. He had then gone to South Africa as the Free French liaison officer on the staff of General Jan Christian Smuts. Promoted to General Officer rank, he had then been sent to China as the Free French liaison officer to the Nationalist Chinese Government. In this role he was able to rally resources to alleviate the suffering of the Foreign Legion and other French troops who crossed into China, and who must now wait out the war.

Brunon had metamorphosed the magazine *La Legion Etrangere* into *Vert et Rouge: Revue de la Legion Etrangere* in 1944 and in this new manifestation kept the story of Camerone alive by publishing the old Lande/Maine article of 1878 under the title of 'Le combat de Camerone: vu par le Caporal Maine' in May 1945, the month the war ended.[35]

Initially, peace agreements gave Tonkin to Nationalist China and Annam and Cochin-China to Britain, which was glad enough to see the French return. The old 2nd REI, which had ceased to exist in 1940, was re-born in 1945, first as the *Regiment de Marche de la Legion Etrangere en Extreme-Orient*, then, on New Year's Day 1946, once again as the 2nd REI, and made ready to depart for Indo-China, the first of the Foreign Legion's regiments, newly-formed or old-established, to face the Viet Minh fighters of Ho Chi Minh and General General Vo Nguyen Giap in the coming eight years. The 13th *Demi-Brigade* was also sent out to Indo-China. The so-called Cairo Flag, which had been with them for so much of the Second World War, was laid up in Sidi-bel-Abbes before the regiment's departure and the London Flag went with it to the Far East. On 8 February, Gaucher, now a Battalion Commander, marched what remained of the 5th REI to the Chinese border and crossed back into Tonkin.

The Camerone Day celebration in Sidi-bel-Abbes in 1946 was especially poignant, the first to be held since the end of the war. All the 'Musketeers' were gone, Rollet and Nicolas dead, Maire and de Corta retired and back in France, de Tscharner in his native Switzerland. Magrin-Vernerey – Monclar – was now Commanding General of all French Forces in Algeria. The most distinguished of the old-time Foreign Legion officers was the long-retired Lieutenant-Colonel Pierre Forey, still resident in Sidi-bel-Abbes. Colonel Louis Gaultier, who commanded both the 1st REI and the *Depot Commun des Regiments Etrangers* – the administrative arm of all the foreign regiments – suggested that the frail old soldier might like to carry the hand of Captain Danjou in the Camerone Day Parade, an invitation accepted with alacrity.

As a man who had first gone to Indo-China sixty-two years earlier as a young Sergeant of the Foreign Legion, there was some irony in the fact that Forey should officiate in this manner at a time when the regiments were getting ready to participate once more in campaigning there. At the age of eighty-six, it was his last official duty.[36]

In June came bad news from Saigon. Captain Faucon of the 13th *Demi-Brigade*, with a half company of men, leaving their trucks on hard ground, had descended into a swamp during a relatively routine sweep patrol near Tay-Ninh. Suddenly flushing out a vastly superior force, and surrounded on three sides by a hard-to-see foe, Faucon realized that their only chance was to get back to the trucks, and, equally, that his men could only do this with a sacrificial rear guard giving them covering fire.

'Fall back!' he told his Legionnaires. 'Me, I'm going to *faire Camerone.*'

Adjutant Struszyna and two Legionnaires remained with their officer. Struszyna fired the machine-gun until his ammunition ran out, then used his pistol. Each Legionnaire kept a last shot for himself. Hit three times, the Adjutant fell, then the two Legionnaires. The men who had reached the trucks dispersed the enemy with machine-gun fire, then went back to look for Faucon, Struszyna and the two Legionnaires. They found the Adjutant and the two men, surrounded by some sixty enemy dead, but there was no sign of Faucon, who had been wounded, captured and carried away. He soon made an attempt to escape, was re-taken and then beheaded.[37]

This firefight, the first of many to come, was still fresh in the minds of the officers and men of the Foreign Legion when they turned out to bury Lieutenant-Colonel Forey in Sidi-bel-Abbes a few weeks later.

31
Camerone at Dien Bien Phu

General Magrin-Vernerey – the legendary Monclar – following in the footsteps of the even more legendary Rollet, became Inspector-General of the Foreign Legion in 1948, and at once began planning visits to the regiments serving in Algeria, Morocco, Madagascar and Indo-China. On the other side of the Atlantic a chance event occurred mid-year which would have a far-reaching effect on the status of Camerone in the Foreign Legion's psyche.

While serving as a soldier-diplomat with France's Permanent Mission to the United Nations in New York, Colonel Marcel J. Penette, who had been an officer with the Foreign Legion for three years, had cause to visit Mexico. He knew of the wartime visit to Sidi-bel-Abbes by the brothers Xavier and Louis Sol la Lande and squeezed enough time out of his schedule to visit Veracruz, then travel inland to pay homage at the grave of the 3rd of the 1st at Camerone, a personal pilgrimage still vivid in his memory almost thirty-five years later.

> I was deeply shocked by what I saw at this historic place, by the contrast between the idea of the remembrance of Camerone, which all Legionnaires understand, and the sad reality of what I saw [*Penette told me in 1982*]. The metal fence round the grave was sometimes used to tether animals and was loose and broken in several places. The gate was jammed and impossible to open and all the metal was rusty. There were little lumps of earth all over the gravestone, the bricks at the base were coming loose and grass was pushing up through the crevices. The old guardian appointed by the French Government had died a long time before, at a great age, and had not been replaced. It was only by good luck that, three years previously, the grave had not been destroyed to permit the expansion of a road. The big tree had disappeared. In short, the monument of 1892 was in a pitiful state. Everything indicated abandonment and desolation. It had been totally forgotten.[1]

At the time, the most he was able to do was to make arrangements through the French Embassy in Mexico City to have the grave cleaned up and kept in a respectable condition. Saddened, Penette went back to New York, and in the coming months began to dream a dream of perhaps one day providing a better and more fitting monument, but it would be fifteen years before he would see his wish become at least partly a reality – and a lot of Foreign Legion blood would have been shed by then in support of France's ever-shifting colonial policies in Southeast Asia and North Africa.

The parades and pomp of the *Fete de Camerone*, the *Recit* and the spirit and tradition of the Combat, were now as well established in the post-war Foreign Legion as in the pre-war one, though, in a world which had changed forever, the impact – or sometimes lack of it – of the story and the ceremonies depended very much upon the individual Legionnaire. It inspired some men in a very real way, and even when it did not it certainly punctuated their years of service, even more than Christmas.

In many ways, Colin John, an Englishman and former Captain in the Royal Artillery, was a classic Foreign Legion recruit of the post-war years, militarily inclined, socially unsettled, a rolling stone. He had served with the Eighth Army in North Africa, and been near Bir Hakeim in 1942 when the 13th *Demi-Brigade* was making its stand. After the war he had walked out on his wife and children, unsuccessfully tried his hand at journalism and playwriting, lived with, then abandoned, a girl in France, and another in Holland, and drunk too much and too often. In the autumn of 1948 he was in France, working on the translation of a travel book. Taking stock of himself in Strasbourg, he decided that he was 'a failure'.

He then walked almost a thousand kilometres (some six hundred miles) from there to the South of France in the course of a month, without any real idea of why he was doing so. In a small town, the proprietor of a hotel in which he had stayed the previous year listened to his woes, then told him: 'In Marseille is the recruiting section of the Legion. If I have diagnosed your illness aright, that's going to be the best place for you for the next five years.' John had his passport and British Army papers with him and told the recruiting Sergeant-Major: 'I'm fed up with civilian life. I like Army life. I happened to be in France, and I was broke. So I came along here.' Exhibiting a startling lack of originality he engaged under the *nom de guerre* of 'John Smith', nationality Irish, and was undergoing training in the Corporals *peleton* – training section – at the Camp de Chasseurs near Saida in April 1949 when his first Camerone Day rolled around.

> This battle, unimportant in itself and in its material consequences, has been commemorated ever since by the Legion as the supreme example of bravery, sacrifice, and fidelity to the sworn word [*John would write later*]. It is marked every year, wherever units of the Legion happen to be, by massive parades, with music and all the usual pomp and ceremony, the awarding of decorations, speeches by high-ranking officers, and all the gaudy display and pageantry dear to the hearts of the military-minded.
>
> Our *peleton* was to take a leading part in the parade; so we spent the three days before the 30th in marching, counter-marching, presenting arms, and executing eyes left and eyes right, so that we should give a faultless performance on The Day. Our gaiters had to be painted a perfect white, and we were shown how to put on the blue waist-sash and the huge red epaulettes which are the traditional parade dress of the Legion. We washed and re-washed our white *couvre-kepis*...
>
> After the ceremony at the main barracks on the morning of the 30th, we marched the two kilometres (a mile and a quarter) back to the Camp de

Chasseurs, where a huge meal was awaiting us, together with wine in abundance.[2]

By early evening John's three best friends were in the guardhouse, one for insulting the Sergeant of the Guard, one for damaging government property when an Arab donkey threw him through a window, and the third for remonstrating with the Sergeant-Chef who was apprehending the window-breaker. 'The principle applied was that we could get as drunk as we liked and do what we liked, short of causing material damage, so long as we remained inside the camp,' John said later. 'If we wanted to go into town, we had to be properly dressed and reasonably steady on our legs.' He had drunk comparatively little, so went with another friend to a military-approved brothel. The evening ended in a fight, and John wound up in the guardhouse with his three friends. 'For us the feast of Camerone for the year 1949 was at an end,' he remarked. 'We were all released at dawn the next morning, for offences committed on the day of Camerone, unless they be of a most serious nature, are never punished.'

The Foreign Legion, taking advantage of the fact that many of those signing engagements had been paratroops, often with the German Army, had added a 1st *Bataillon Etranger de Parachutistes* (1st BEP) to its manpower arsenal in July 1948, followed by a 2nd Battalion (2nd BEP) in November, and they had soon been in action in Indo-China, and would become an indispensable adjunct to operations against the Viet Minh.

All the traditions of the Foreign Legion had, of course, also gone to Indo-China, and Leslie Aparvary, a Hungarian serving in the Second Section of the 2nd Company of the 1st BEP, experienced his first Camerone in northern Tonkin, while John was enjoying his in Algeria.

Aparvary, a veteran of the German Army, had fled his post-war home in Hungary, believing that the Secret Police were on his tail, joined the Foreign Legion in late June 1948 and been posted to Tonkin less than four months later. Weeks of service guarding convoys had earned him a break, and he was pulled out of the firing line and sent to Lang Son for Camerone.

> The company enjoyed a twelve-course dinner followed by wine, and its effects became apparent within a matter of hours [*he recalled later*]. The carousing finished late at night and all was quiet. I was on guard duty, for hardly a man besides myself was able to stand.[3]

The edict of Napoleon III that the names of Danjou, Vilain and Maudet should be engraved in gold letters on the walls of l'Hotel des Invalides in Paris was at last obeyed – albeit eighty-six years late. At the initiative of General Blanc, Director of the *Musee de l'Armee*, and Colonel Gaultier, who was still commanding the *Depot Commun des Regiments Etrangers* at Sidi-bel-Abbes, the Emperor's wish was, at least in part, obeyed. On 6 August 1949 General Catroux unveiled a marble plaque set in a wall on the ground floor of the Court of Honour, in the *Galerie de l'Orient* in the presence of Blanc and Gaultier. However, it bore only Danjou's name, not those of Vilain and Maudet, but – unlike the plaque placed on the wall of the

Danjou family house at Chalabre a decade earlier – it had the merit of being essentially accurate.

TO THE MEMORY
OF OFFICERS AND LEGIONNAIRES
WHO UNDER THE ORDERS OF CAPTAIN DANJOU FACED ODDS OF
FORTY-TO-ONE
DURING TEN HOURS ON 30 APRIL 1863 AT
CAMERONE
'LIFE RATHER THAN COURAGE
ABANDONED THESE SOLDIERS OF FRANCE'.[4]

The defeat of Chiang Kai-shek's Nationalist Chinese by Mao Tse-tung's People's Army in China provided Ho Chi Minh and General Giap with huge amounts of weaponry, a safe place to train and hundreds of Chinese instructors. Consequently, the ever-escalating war in Indo-China took a serious turn for the worse from late 1949. Giap was strong enough to challenge the French from across the China–Tonkin border and unleashed massive attacks on convoys and posts along Colonial Route 4. Dong-Khe fell, was retaken and fell again. At the end of September 1950 Lieutenant-Colonel Pierre Charton of the 3rd REI was ordered to abandon Cao Bang and withdraw to Lang Son with his Legionnaires and Moroccan *Tirailleurs*. General Marcel Alessandri, who knew the country and conditions well, was opposed to the withdrawal, but the new Commander-in-Chief, General Marcel Carpentier, insisted on it, devising a plan which called for Charton to pull out of Cao Bang and rendezvous with what was known as Task Force Bayard, which included the 1st BEP, for the final withdrawal to Lang Son.

A flurry of muddled messages, orders and instructions not given, others countermanded, then countermanded again, added to a confused operation, as Charton and his men, encumbered by many civilians, were attacked by the Viet Minh. Other Viet Minh savaged the Bayard Group and the 1st BEP in dreadful country, full of precipitous gorges and ambush points. During one attack on the 3rd REI – in an act reminiscent of Catteau and Maudet at Camerone and Streibler and de Borelli at Tuyen Quang – Sergeant-Chef Schoenberger threw himself in front of Charton and was mown down by a Viet Minh sub-machine gun. The difference was that while Maudet was mortally wounded, and de Borelli unscathed, Charton was both wounded and captured.[5]

The 1st BEP was cut to ribbons and ceased to exist as a coherent unit. Legionnaire Janos Kemencei, a Hungarian, would report later that several men proposed that they should *faire Camerone*, but the idea was rejected. 'With what fortifications and what munitions?' Kemencei asked rhetorically, as they lacked both a suitable defensive position and sufficient ammunition to make a serious stand.[6] Instead, the three Captains of the 1st BEP, each with a compass and the remnants of their Companies, disappeared into the jungle. Days later, Captain Pierre Jeanpierre, a veteran of the Syrian campaign of 1941, the French *Maquis* and the Nazi death camp of Mauthausen, staggered into That Khe with what remained of his command – two officers and twenty-one men. Kemencei was not among them, having been taken prisoner. In the military panic among the brass in Hanoi orders were given for Lang Son to be evacuated, which was untidily done and control of Colonial Route 4 passed into the hands of the Viet Minh.

In Algeria, in September of the same year, Colonel Jean Olie, late of the RMLE and 3rd REI, was named to head the new *Groupement Autonome de la Legion Etrangere* (GALE), the new name for the Foreign Legion's administrative arm at Sidi-bel-Abbes. Casting around for a fitting badge for the unit, instead of designing a new one he adopted the one with the Mexican Eagle created by Captain Marsol in 1937 for his 3rd Company of the 1st Battalion of the 4th REI. It proved popular, and was preserved five years later when the GALE itself was dissolved. At the same time the 1st *Regiment Etranger d'Infanterie* was losing the word *Infanterie* in its title and its new Commanding Officer, Colonel Raberin, decided that the GALE badge should be adopted as the official insignia of the renamed regiment.[7]

In August 1950, following North Korea's invasion of South Korea, France agreed to contribute an infantry battalion to the United Nations Expeditionary Force then being assembled for what was being euphemistically referred to as a 'Police Action'. General Magrin-Vernerey, Inspector-General of the Foreign Legion, immediately volunteered to command the thousand-strong *Batallion Francais*. Happily reverting to the rank of Lieutenant-Colonel, and re-assuming his *nom de guerre* of 'Monclar', he took his all-volunteer mixed force of men from the Foreign Legion, the Colonial Infantry, regular French Army regiments, Army Reservists and former French Resistance fighters to South Korea in late November. Attached to the 23rd Regiment of the U.S. 2nd Division, they were quickly involved in the bitter fighting. The 1st and 3rd Companies singularly distinguished themselves by a costly but spectacular bayonet charge at Wonju on 10 January 1951, as the U.N. Forces, trying to throw the North Koreans back across the demarcated border at the 38th Parallel, fought a series of actions in terrible weather. On 1 February the 3rd Battalion of the U.S. 23rd Regiment and the 3rd Company of the *Bataillon Francais* were heavily engaged by Chinese troops employing their terrifying 'Human Wave' tactic to overwhelm their foes by sheer weight of numbers, regardless of the cost, at a place called Twin Tunnels.

> The enemy arrived, bringing with them not only their personal armament but that of their Headquarters [*Monclar would say in his Official Report*]. The Commandant L[e].M[ire] gave orders to hold out at any cost ... Two Sous-Officiers of the Legion then threw their kepis in the air and shouted: '*Faire Camerone*'.[8]

Monclar reached retirement age that year and was named Governor of des Invalides in Paris.

Camerone Day 1951 was remembered by Colin John, now a Sergeant-Instructor at Sidi-bel-Abbes, and two other English-born Legionnaires, Henry Ainley and Adrian Liddell-Hart, very different men, in different circumstances, one also at Sidi-bel-Abbes, the other at Saida. All three were older than the average Foreign Legion recruit of the day.

John, who spoke good French and passable German, was thirty-nine and had completed the Corporals *peleton*, followed it with one for Sergeants, and – much to his chagrin – then been retained to conduct recruit training with the GALE. Colonel Olie had made it quite clear that he needed his Sergeant-Instructors, and that any chance they had of going to Indo-China, or elsewhere, rested entirely on how well he could get along without them and still meet training commitments. As a Sous-Officier, John's experiences on his third Camerone Day were understandably very different from those of Corporal-in-training Ainley or Legionnaire 2nd Class Liddell-Hart.

> The parade and march past the Colours had just finished, and the Colonel was getting together with his officers and NCOs to drink a glass or two with us, in the best traditions of the Legion, before going on to lunch [*John recalled*]. When there was complete silence in the room, he began to speak[:] '. . . [T]he Legion's destiny remains unchanged. And, let pessimists say what they will to the contrary, the character of the Legionnaire has not changed either. At the present time in Indo-China, isolated, heroic actions are being fought every day of the week.'[9]

Then, praising the Sous-Officiers as 'the very stuff of the Legion, without whom the whole organization and discipline would collapse', the Colonel enjoined them: '[T]oday is Camerone. I'm not going to tell you not to get drunk, because I know perfectly well that most of you are half-drunk already. So I'll just say, don't get too drunk. I lift my glass to the memory of Camerone, to the corps of Sous-Officiers, and – *a la Legion!*'

Elsewhere on the Quartier Vienot, Old Etonian Ainley, the namesake son of the famous British actor, and serving under a *nom de guerre*, was a member of the Corporals *peleton*. He had joined the Legion as an idealist. After coming down from Oxford he had gone round the world on a Finnish windjammer and, when war broke out, served in the Merchant Marine and the Royal Navy, until demobilized in 1943 for medical reasons. A spell working on a deep sea trawler was followed by one stage-managing in London's West End and in 1947 he became the French Correspondent for a London newspaper. At the age of thirty-two, in November 1950, driven, he said, 'by a mixture of misguided idealism and general disgust with everybody else's inertia about Communism', he turned up in Sidi-bel-Abbes and joined the Foreign Legion. Thinking back on his first *Fete de Camerone*, Ainley felt that the celebration had become 'the equivalent of the feasts of slaves in Roman times'.

> [T]he 29th April and 1st May had been added in order to let the Legionnaires work up steam for and get over the ill effects of the 30th's orgy [*he remarked*]. Apart from a ceremonial parade in which we all had to take part, we had three clear days in which to do anything we liked without fear of disciplinary measures being taken.[10]

Ainley and a friend unwisely beat up a couple of Corporals – for which they were not charged, but paid dearly later – a German bully got knifed by one of his victims, and three members of the Corporals *peleton* deserted.

Adrian Liddell-Hart, another Old Etonian, and also one with a Second World War seagoing background, was undergoing his initial Foreign Legion training at Saida at the time. The son of the noted British military analyst and historian Sir Basil Liddell-Hart, he had been a Royal Navy officer on a corvette and a destroyer during the war, taken part in Combined Operations and had been stationed for a time in North Africa. After losing a bid to become a Member of Parliament, he had worked in Berlin with the United Nations, and taken another unsuccessful run for Parliament, before deciding to join the Foreign Legion under the name of 'Peter Brand'. Already being eyed by his superiors as a less-than-satisfactory trainee Legionnaire, the twenty-eight-year-old Liddell-Hart was busy making life more difficult for himself by refusing to be fitted into the Foreign Legion's disciplinary mould, and went into town the morning of Camerone Day with a friend.

> By a convenient coincidence, the Legion, the Communist Party and the Catholic Church celebrate consecutively [*he wrote later*]. On the 30th April there was a big parade in honour of Camerone followed by an elaborate meal with champagne and liqueurs for everyone and a fair in the afternoon... [W]e returned late for the dithyramb on the Battle of Camerone... On the morrow the Communists and others held a demonstration in the town to mark May Day. To avoid trouble we were confined to barracks with nothing to do but sleep off the effects of Camerone. The next day we recovered from an inoculation – followed by Ascension Day.[11]

The Concise Oxford Dictionary of Current English defines a 'dithyramb' as an 'inflated poem, speech or writing' – or, presumably, story – which seems indicative of Liddell-Hart's general contempt for the regimental traditions. Anyway, it would be his one and only Camerone Day, as he was posted to Indo-China, as a member of the 1st REC, did his soldiering in the swamps and marshes of the Mekong Delta, and proved so unsatisfactory that the Foreign Legion released him in January 1952, after just less than a year's service. Ainley got his chance to fight in mid-September, serving in Cochin-China and Annam, until invalided out after three years' service. John, by agreeing to re-engage for an additional six months, was included in a draft for Indo-China, but broke his leg and missed going out to the Far East with his best friend. By the time he landed in Saigon in March 1952 the friend was long dead, and John was sent up-country to Tonkin to join a Transport Company in Hanoi.

In France, Brunon was managing to keep the Foreign Legion magazine alive – though under a slightly different name, *Vert et Rouge: Traditions et Souvenirs Militaires* – and publishing regularly. 'Camerone: Le Temoignage d'un Caporal survivant,' which appeared in May 1951, was drawn from General Zede's account of his meeting with the former Corporal Berg in the early Summer of 1864.[12] Brunon was excited when Jean-Adolphe Beauce's Camerone painting 'The end of the Battle' – bought by the nation in 1869, and unseen since – was discovered in storage in the *Musee de Tours* the following year and presented to the Foreign Legion. It became a prized acquisition for the *Salle d'Honneur* in Sidi-bel-Abbes. Enthusiasm aside, Brunon critiqued it pertinently.

> Although it does not conform exactly to strict reality, the artist's imaginative composition is of major interest[,] because Beauce had certainly seen the hacienda at Camerone [*Brunon wrote*]. The types of Mexicans are perfectly shown, [but] the Legionnaires are depicted in capotes, not in tunics, [and] all are Grenadiers, although there were only Fusiliers in the 3rd Company of the [1st Battalion of the] Regiment Etranger.[13]

On Camerone Day 1953 the Legionnaires serving in the *Bataillon de Coree* sent greetings to their comrades in Algeria: 'We are all in heart with the Legionnaires at Sidi-Bel-Abbes and more particularly with our brothers in Indo-China'.[14] In late October 1953, as the Korean War was ending at the conference table rather than on the battlefield, they were transferred to Tonkin, but few of them lasted long. Many of the battle-hardened veterans had survived bloody actions at Twin Tunnels, Chipyong-Ni and Putchaetul, where their Pioneer Company had been annihilated. They had lived through the battles of Punch Bowl and Creve-Coeur in 1951, and the Iron Triangle, T-Bone and Arrow Head – where the Pioneers had again been wiped out – the following year. In Tonkin they rapidly fell in clashes with the Viet Minh.

Promoted to Sergeant-Chef, Colin John managed to effect a transfer into active service with the 3rd REI and was sent into Laos, which the French feared was a target for the Viet Minh. When his unit was withdrawn, after a long and trying march they reached the valley of the Nan Yum River in northwest Tonkin and arrived at Dien Bien Phu, which the French had decided to fortify as a strategic point, where it could not only block any Viet Minh movement towards Laos but also be used as a base for more general operations against them. Colonel Christian de Castries, a cavalry officer with a reputation for fast-moving strikes against the enemy, was given overall command, as it was anticipated that it would be a base for forays against the Viet Minh, not the scene of a static defensive post under siege.

The site had been seized by an air drop of the 1st BEP the previous November, and construction at once began on a series of unconnected strongpoints around the old Japanese-built airstrip. It was described as an 'entrenched camp'. Anticipating it as merely an operations base, the dugouts were little more than roofed foxholes, rather than the deep and shellproof bunkers which would turn out to be needed. Lying in a bowl surrounded by hills, Dien Bien Phu could only be serviced by air, but despite warnings, most of the armchair soldiers in Hanoi declared that Giap had neither heavy guns, nor the means to move them, so would be unable to threaten the encampment.

The Nan Yum River ran north-to-south down the centre of the valley, with a road called RP41 running roughly parallel for much of the way. The series of dug-in defensive bases were given girls' names – Gabrielle, Beatrice, Anne-Marie, Dominique, Huguette, Eliane, Claudine and Isabelle – and were manned by Legionnaires from the 1st BEP, the 2nd REI, 3rd REI and the 13th *Demi-Brigade*, as well as fighting men from virtually every arm of the French Union, including Lieutenant-Colonel Marcel Bigeard's tough Colonial Paratroops, Algerian and Moroccan *Tirailleurs*, Senegalese and Vietnamese Paratroopers and T'ai auxiliaries.

During the first ten days of March 1954 there were sporadic incidents with patrols, occasional shots fired at strongpoint Beatrice, held by the 3rd Battalion of the 13th *Demi-Brigade*, and a few shells landed on or near the airstrip. Nobody knew that under the cover of the jungle's tree canopy Giap was assembling fifty thousand men and batteries of 75 mm and 105 mm guns. As he was near the end of his engagement, Sergeant-Chef John was flown out of Dien Bien Phu towards the end of the second week of the month, bound for Hanoi, then Sidi-bel-Abbes and his discharge. On 12 March, by official count, there were two thousand nine hundred and sixty-nine Legionnaires at Dien Bien Phu, out of a total garrison of ten thousand eight hundred and fourteen. The next day saw the beginning of what would become one of the seminal battles of the 20th century, heralding the end of French rule in Southeast Asia, even the end of the French Empire as it had been known,[15] and would for the Foreign Legion add a new dimension to the meaning and significance of the *Fete de Camerone*.

The Battle of Dien Bien Phu began at precisely half past five in the evening of 13 March, with the massive pounding of Beatrice by 105 mm guns. Lieutenant-Colonel Gaucher, survivor of the 5th REI's fighting withdrawal to China in 1945, and now commander of the 3rd Battalion of the 13th *Demi-Brigade*, was mortally wounded in one of the first salvos. Other officers with him were killed or seriously wounded, but his Chief of Staff, Major Michel Vadot, barely scratched. Then came the sweeping waves of Viet Minh, some with plastic charges and Bangalore torpedoes to destroy the barbed wire entanglements. Faced by two regiments of the 312th Viet Minh Division, the Legionnaires were gradually overwhelmed by sheer numbers and fanaticism, until, in the early hours of the 14 March, calling down their own artillery fire on their position, the remnants slipped away.

The next day the same Viet Minh tactics were used against the *Tirailleurs Algeriens* in Gabrielle. The battle lasted all night and by dawn the Viet Minh held the stronghold. The 1st BEP fought their way in and retook the position, but Colonel de Castries – who would soon be promoted – gave orders that it be abandoned. The paratroops retired, bringing out the remnants of the *Tirailleurs*. On 17 March the Anne-Marie stronghold was heavily bombarded and the T'ai auxiliaries broke and fled. The position was then occupied by a company of the 1st BEP.

When Lieutenant-Colonel Maurice Lemeunier heard in Hanoi that Gaucher was dead he insisted that, as the Legionnaire with the longest experience in Indo-China, he be sent to Dien Bien Phu. He had never made a parachute jump, but hurled himself out of a Dakota at night and made it safely to the ground. He was one of several hundred novice Foreign Legion parachutists who would join their comrades in the coming weeks in what those involved – but not the desk-bound in Hanoi – were gradually coming to feel was a doomed garrison.

The airstrip, the very lifeline for Dien Bien Phu, became dangerous due to anti-aircraft fire and shelling in daylight hours as early as 15 March, but daring pilots kept flying in, bringing in supplies and taking out the worst of the wounded, then switched to night flying. On 27 March the night shelling was so heavy that a Dakota coming to evacuate wounded men was forced to abort its landing and flee. On board was a French Air Force nurse, Genevieve de Galard, who considered that she had not completed her mission and insisted on returning the following day. Once on the ground, her plane was hit and crippled. Trapped in the 'entrenched camp' with its defenders, she made her way to the underground hospital, a veritable charnel house, where Major Paul Grauwin and a small team of medical personnel were working round-the-clock on every type of wound imaginable.

Following the initial attacks there had been a break of almost two weeks. Giap had suffered enormous losses and was short of ammunition, but while he waited for more men and munitions he was quietly tightening his noose around Dien Bien Phu. The 1st BEP managed to clear the Viet Minh from the road which ran south to Isabelle, but on 30 March the battle began again. Heavy shelling, followed by massed waves of Viet Minh infantry, became the pattern. Attacks were followed by counter-attacks on positions already made untenable by Viet Minh shelling.

Isabelle, the most southerly of the defensive positions, some five kilometres (three miles) down the valley, sat astride both the river and the road, and was held by the 3rd Battalion of the 3rd REI, a battalion of *Tirailleurs Algeriens* and a Moroccan *Goum*, with a battery of 105 mm guns and a number of small tanks. It had been under regular harassing fire while the Viet Minh began digging trenches, but now Giap focused serious attention on it, with what seemed to be a never-ending series of shelling, followed by infantry attacks. Yet the bastion held.

Giap, once again with huge losses, called off his assaults, only to restart them on 6 April. The 2nd BEP dropped into Dien Bien Phu three days later. Dominique and Eliane, held by Algerians and Moroccans, fell on the night of 22–23 April. Paratroopers of the 2nd BEP assaulted a portion of Eliane, now known as Eliane 1, which changed hands several times before the paratroops managed to secure it, but suffered so many casualties that the 1st and 2nd BEPs were merged into a single *Bataillon de Marche* BEP. The coming of the monsoon turned the dust into mud and ooze. By the end of the month the Viet Minh had occupied the airstrip and of the sixteen thousand men of the French Union forces who had been engaged in battle since 13 March only three thousand able-bodied soldiers remained in the central position and another twelve hundred at Isabelle.

The *Fete de Camerone* fell on the forty-third day of the siege. Legionnaires hoped that Hanoi would send them some *Vinogle*, a canned, jelly-like wine concentrate – nicknamed 'Tiger's Blood' – supposed to be diluted one part concentrate to two parts water, but often drunk neat.

On Eliane 2 – which the Viet Minh called Hill 5 – Captain Coutant's company of the 1st Battalion of the 13th *Demi-Brigade* uneasily shared a shattered hill of opposing trenches and foxholes, almost within grenade-throwing distance of each other.

Legionnaire Wagner, Coutant's Orderly, greeted his officer: 'It's Camerone Day, Captain,' served him a steaming cup of coffee and presented him with a full package of cigarettes. When asked how he had managed it, Wagner replied: 'By muddling through, Captain.' Coutant's junior officers arrived to pay their respects. He read the *Recit de Camerone* and they exchanged toasts with mugs containing a few drops of *Vinogle*, saved especially for the occasion. A little later Legionnaire Frohlich arrived breathlessly with news.

'Captain, a package of *Vinogle* has come down in front of the position, on the Viet Minh side,' he reported.

'So what?' asked Coutant. 'You're not going over there.'

'No, but I thought it a pity ... particularly since the Viet Minh are like us – nothing to drink,' Frohlich said wistfully.

'Okay,' said Coutant. 'Bring up a machine-gun and stop anyone getting near that package.'

Throughout the day, four Legionnaires kept watch on the *Vinogle*.[16]

In the Command Post of the 13th *Demi-Brigade* Lieutenant-Colonel Lemeunier, the most senior Legionnaire at Dien Bien Phu, read the *Recit* over a radio hook-up, which could be heard throughout the entire camp. Then, immaculate in his full dress uniform, he created four Honourary Legionnaires of the regiment. General de Castries and Lieutenant-Colonel Pierre Langlais of the 3rd REI were made Honourary Corporals. Lieutenant-Colonel Bigeard of the Colonial Paratroops and nurse Genevieve de Galard became Honourary Legionnaires 1st Class.

The ceremony called for a Legionnaire to present himself as 'godfather' of the individual to be honoured and the Orderly of Major Vadot, now Chief of Staff to Langlais, stood as 'godfather' for Nurse de Galard. She told him: 'If we ever get out of this alive, I'll buy you a bottle of champagne no matter where we meet' – and it was a promise she would keep. The Camerone 'feast' consisted of tinned beef and rice and a tiny piece of cheese, washed down with a glass of *Vinogle*.[17]

From a loudspeaker, seemingly on the Viet Minh-held Beatrice, came a falsetto voice: 'Why continue to fight?' it asked. 'Why do what the Legionnaires did at Camerone – get yourselves massacred?'

> In Bel Abbes and elsewhere it's Camerone day – and we, poor sods, we haven't even got any concentrated wine for the occasion [*Sergeant Kubiak of the 1st Battalion of the 13th* Demi-Brigade, *who had survived the attack on Beatrice, wrote in his diary*]. The Viets have set up loud speakers and, in between peppering us, are calling on us to surrender if we don't want to be wiped out 'as at Camerone.' In reply we begin to sing '*Le Boudin*,' the refrain being liberally interspersed with the mot de Cambronne. Believe it or not, morale is high.[18]

There was no *Vinogle* to be had in the battered and still smoking ruins of Claudine. Commandant Coldeboeuf of the 1st Battalion of the 2nd REI wrote in the daily *Journal*: 'A Camerone without wine or blood sausage'.[19] So the battalion, along with Lieutenant Erwan Bergot's 1st Foreign Legion Heavy Airborne Mortar Company, and Legionnaires in other scattered fortified outposts and rain-soaked trenches, celebrated Camerone as best they could, with perhaps a piece of cheese and an extra cigarette or two, and getting by with a drink made from powdered lemons and oranges.

Down the valley at Isabelle, Colonel Andre Lalande himself sung *Le Boudin* over the loudspeaker system and two chaplains – the Reverend Pierre Tissot, the only Protestant cleric at Dien Bien Phu, and Father Guidon, a Catholic priest – both trapped in Isabelle when the road north to the main entrenched camp was cut by the Viet Minh, were made Honourary Legionnaires 1st Class.[20]

After dark on Eliane 2, the Viet Minh attempted a sortie to retrieve the *Vinogle*. They were driven back with machine-gun fire. Sergeant Chef Soos, realizing that his men were becoming obsessive about the *Vinogle* – and it was now realized that there were several packages – and suggested to Captain Coutant that he 'organize what he could not prevent'. It seemed like good advice and Coutant consulted his platoon commanders. 'If we don't go and get them, someone is going to make a bloody fool of himself,' he said. Volunteers were called for. Practically the entire Company stepped forward, but only six were chosen.

Covered by their comrades, they slipped into no man's land at ten o'clock that night, sliding from tree stump to tree stump and shell hole to shell hole, one group to create a diversion, the other to grab the precious packages. At the shrill of a whistle the diversionary team hurled grenades at the slits of the Viet Minh blockhouses, then set off plastic charges with explosives found on the dead bodies of enemy 'human bombs' killed in the earlier fighting. The other group grabbed the *Vinogle*. All six Legionnaires returned unscathed and Coutant's Company, and such members of other Companies as could be reached, toasted the memory of Captain Danjou and the Combat of Camerone.

The message General de Castries sent to Hanoi spoke of a successful raid by members of Coutant's Company, resulting in the destruction of Viet Minh blockhouses, with the loss of ten of the enemy. The official communique reported: '1st Battalion of 13th *Demi-Brigade* raided Viet Minh works south of Eliane 2. Two blockhouses totally destroyed and one damaged.'[21]

Ex-Sergeant-Chef John arrived in Paris 'just in time to celebrate April 30th at the Legion's base at Fort de Vincennes' and marked 'a sad Camerone' with his comrades. 'At least eight battalions of the Legion were doomed, and we knew it, though we tried not to admit it,' he said later.[22]

In the valley of the Nan Yum, the Viet Minh, after celebrating 1 May as International Labour Day, attacked again. An Algerian battalion making a sortie from Isabelle was cut off and all but annihilated, and two days later Huguette and Claudine were engaged by six Viet Minh battalions from Giap's 308th 'Iron Division'. The next forty-eight hours were even worse for the defenders and the end came on 7 May.

De Castries, reluctant to attempt a breakout, which he believed would probably fail, and would almost certainly mean the butchering of the wounded left behind, advised Hanoi that he would surrender. The Legionnaires clinging to what remained of Claudine planned to make a dash for Isabelle, but as they prepared to leave Sergeant Kubiak 'heard our battalion commander swearing like a trooper'. He turned in the direction of the officer's gaze and 'saw a white flag fluttering over the General's H.Q.' It was the end, but in a last desperate act of defiance, the Legionnaires opened up on the Viet Minh, mowing them down, but taking casualties themselves, including Kubiak.[23]

At five o'clock in the afternoon it was almost all over. Captain Capeyron of the

3rd Company of the 1st Battalion of the 13th *Demi-Brigade*, realized that he should destroy the Company flag. The word *Fidelite* had just been consumed by the flames from the quickly kindled fire when Viet-Minh soldiers arrived. An officer shouted: 'Hands up!' Capeyron did not obey quicly enough and several enemy soldiers kicked him from behind. His Legionnaires started forward.

'Don't move,' Capeyron told them quietly. 'It's too late.'[24]

The Legionnaires of Major Clemencon's 1st Battalion of the 2nd REI cut up the Battalion Flag, each taking a piece and hiding it. Over the coming months of Viet-Minh captivity dying men handed their precious piece of flag to whoever was nearest to them and, incredibly, almost three quarters of it eventually found its way back to Sidi-bel-Abbes, where loving hands painstakingly pieced it together like a jigsaw puzzle and eventually put it in a frame.[25]

The 1st BEP was once again reduced to a mere handful, just as they had been after the Cao Bang debacle of less than four years earlier. Legionnaire Kemencei, captured after Cao Bang and then released, was at Isabelle and said later that the Legionnaires discussed making a last stand 'to preserve the honour of the Legion'. Yet, he added significantly, they also discussed the incompetence of the military leadership in Hanoi, which had placed them at Dien Bien Phu in the first place. They decided, he said, that the armchair generals in their air-conditioned offices far from the fighting were 'unworthy to command the men who have the misfortune to serve under their orders'. Anyway, they reasoned 'a decimated army is not worth much, and battles are won with the living'.[26]

Now a civilian, Colin John reached London the same day. The next morning he saw the newspaper headlines: DIEN BIEN PHU FALLS. ISABELLE FIGHTS ON. He bought the French newspapers *Le Figaro* and *Le Monde*. A man in a pub said to him: 'Aren't you jolly glad not to have been there?' 'Not particularly,' John replied,[27] and in the book he wrote about his life in the Foreign Legion he speculated: 'I might go back and sign on for another spell'[28] – but, as far as is known, he did not do so.

Isabelle did, indeed, 'fight on', Colonel Lalande advising Hanoi by radio that he would attempt a breakout. Separate parties of Legionnaires slipped out of the wreckage of the strongpoint, some disappearing forever, others facing withering Viet Minh fire. Astonishingly, of the roughly six hundred Legionnaires who surreptitiously left Isabelle, about a hundred actually succeeded in melting into the jungle, and, weeks later, reduced to a handful, crossed into Laos.[29] Behind them their comrades were either dead or prisoners, as, facing the inevitable, Lalande had surrendered in the early hours of 8 May.

The news reached Sidi-bel-Abbes later that same day and Colonel Paul Gardy at once convened a parade at the Quartier Vienot.

'Dien Bien Phu has just been taken,' he informed the serried ranks of Legionnaires. 'We are assembled here to do homage to the sacrifice of those who have fallen in this epic struggle. We shall now present arms to the Colours which have vanished in battle.'

Then he intoned the roll of units which had disappeared: The 2nd and 3rd Battalions of the 13th *Demi-Brigade* . . . The 2nd and 3rd Battalions of the 3rd REI . . . The 1st Battalion of the 2nd REI . . . The 1st and 2nd BEPs. There were others, too, small specialist units, like the Mixed Mortar Companies of the 3rd REI and the 5th REI, and an assortment of mechanics, cooks and secretaries from other regiments, who had parachuted without training into the 'entrenched encampment'.

The Last Post was sounded.

In the ruins of Dien Bien Phu the severely wounded Sergeant Kubiak became one of the four thousand Legion prisoners divided into small groups and sent off on a terrible eight hundred-kilometre (five hundred-mile) march to Viet Minh prison camps. He would later be repatriated, but would die in a few years, having been permanently disabled as a result of his privations. General de Castries and Colonel Lalande and Lieutenant-Colonels Langlais and Bigeard were made to parade back and forth while Soviet and Viet Minh camera crews recorded their defeat.

There was perhaps some irony in the fact that the May issue of Brunon's magazine *Vert et Rouge: Traditions et Souvenirs Militaires* was on the presses as Dien Bien Phu fell. It contained an article by Captain Oudry called 'Camerone (30 avril 1863),' an overview of much of the then extant scholarship concerning the battle of ninety-one years earlier.[29]

On 24 May the Viet Minh permitted the evacuation of eight hundred and eighty-five of the most seriously wounded, among them Sergeant-Chef Beres, a Hungarian, who five days earlier had painfully dragged himself into a Viet Minh command tent to retrieve the *fanion* of the 4th Company of the 1st Battalion of the 13th *Demi-Brigade*, which he had seen there earlier. It had been captured in the assault on Beatrice and Beres hid it on his person and it went with him when he was evacuated to Laos.[30]

The French and the Viet Minh signed a cease fire in Geneva in late July and agreed on a prisoner exchange. Exhaustive research by historian Bernard Fall concluded that only about three thousand men – including the eight hundred and eighty-five evacuated in late May – returned to France from Viet Minh captivity. Of the sixteen thousand five hundred and forty-four men engaged at Dien Bien Phu about three thousand died in the battle. (The Viet Minh had seven thousand nine hundred dead and some fifteen thousand wounded.) Around ten thousand French Union troops perished on the 'death march' to the Viet Minh prison camps, or in the camps themselves, in a three-month period[31] and the last dozen Legionnaires were not freed until 1959.

From 1945 to 1954 the Foreign Legion lost three hundred and nine officers, one thousand and eighty-two Sous-Officiers and nine thousand and ninety-two other ranks[32] – along with thirty thousand wounded – in Indo-China. Of the six thousand three hundred and twenty-eight captured in that period only two thousand five hundred and sixty-seven returned alive.

Lieutenant Erwan Bergot of the 1st Foreign Legion Airborne Heavy Mortar Company at Dien Bien Phu has written about the men of what was known as Prisoner Convoy #42. Of four hundred men marched away from the smoking ruins of the broken fortress, ninety-two had died on the gruelling trek to the prison camp. Another ninety-two succumbed to wounds, disease and malnutrition. More than three months later, seventy-three survivors set off on another march, this time to be turned over to the French at the river port of Vietri.

On 30 August their Viet Minh guards rested them for a day by some venerable ruins overlooking the Claire River. There was not much left of the old brickwork, as the place had been used for bombing practice, but a Legionnaire found a stone obelisk, surrounded by a small fence. It was the monument erected by Colonel Maire in 1927 to the memory of Sapper Sergeant 'Bobby' Bobillot and those who had fallen in the siege at Tuyen Quang. The Viet Minh guards – deliberately or otherwise – had built their latrine right beside the monument.

Legionnaire Margot, a Swiss, realized that they were at the site of the old fort. His comrades gathered round: Sergeant Ballestracci, who had parachuted into Dien Bien Phu a few days before the end, the Polish Corporal Plewa, Gimber-Rus of the 1st Foreign Legion Airborne Heavy Mortar Company, who had lost an arm in battle, and Ennen, a German reduced to skin-and-bones in the prison camp. Margot, whose hair had turned white though he was only thirty-five, dug back in his memory to tell his comrades what he could remember having read about the events which had taken place there sixty-nine years earlier. When he had finished his story, the tattered remnants of Prisoner Convoy #42 – Swiss, Spaniards, Germans, Italians, Poles and others, Legionnaires all – left with nothing but their lives and regimental pride, rose as one man and took up guard positions around the obelisk.

On that day, no Viet Minh, despite threats, was permitted to use the latrine, and had to go elsewhere to perform their bodily functions.[33]

32
A Bitter Homecoming

In North Africa a new era was coming. Independence was in the air, as the French Protectorates of Tunisia and Morocco sought nationhood. It was not unexpected, but to the French the timing was of the essence, so Independence demands were deemed contentious, and underground political movements sprang up in both countries, pitting French forces against 'dissidents'. Algeria, however, was constitutionally part of Metropolitan France.

An Englishman named John Townsend got his tour of the *Salle d'Honneur* in April 1954, on his very first morning at Sidi-bel-Abbes. He must have seemed an ideal prospect for the Foreign Legion. In 1941 he had joined the Merchant Navy, been Radio Officer on ships making the U-boat-threatened Murmansk and Archangel runs and survived being torpedoed. In September 1944, as a member of a Royal Engineers group attached to the Parachute Regiment, he had taken part of the drop on Arnhem, then stayed in the post-war Army, qualifying as a draughtsman, until 1953.

Rousted out of bed at four-thirty in the pre-dawn, given a cup of coffee and a chunk of dry bread, and sent to the camp barber for a very short-back-and-sides, Townsend and his intake were then conducted through the *Salle d'Honneur* by a young French lieutenant.

> You will hear this story every year on Camerone Day, the 30th April, just as the soldiers of the Legion before you have heard it every year for almost a hundred years [*Townsend quoted their guide as saying*]. It will always be told by the youngest officer on the station, and you will be assembled to hear it wherever you are serving, in France, the deserts of North Africa or the jungles of Indo-China... The spirit these men showed at Camerone was the spirit which made the Legion great, the most feared fighting force in the world. Today the name of Camerone is embroidered on our Colours. When you follow those Colours into action, you will be expected to acquit yourselves with the same courage as Captain Danjou and his men in the face of danger'.[1]

The 1st Etranger was the only Foreign Legion regiment in North Africa at the time and it had been necessary to create specific *Regiments de Marche* to undertake the various assignments. Sent to Tunisia with the 3rd *Regiment de Marche*, Townsend soon attempted to desert with a true Foreign Legion misfit, Old Etonian and playboy Michael West de Wend Fenton. Townsend was caught and charged with 'attempted desertion while on active service', but leniently treated.[2] Unfortunately, he saw nothing wrong in sending articles about the Foreign Legion's operations to the *Manchester Evening News*, which caused him to fall afoul of the *Deuxieme Bureau*, the French Secret Service. Arrested in February 1955, and accused of passing secrets to a foreign power, Townsend ended up being sentenced to be shot, and spent thirty-four days in the death cell at Sidi-bel-Abbes before being unexpectedly released, then expelled after just one year's service.[3]

The wealthy friends of Legionnaire Fenton, who had joined the Foreign Legion in May 1954 in the wake of Dien Bien Phu, urged a former British officer named Michael Alexander to try to help him 'escape' – meaning desert.[4] Alexander, who had first seen the Foreign Legion in action at Bir Hakeim in 1942, crossed and re-crossed Algeria by car, trying to locate Fenton. At one point he and a female companion were in Sidi-bel-Abbes, seeking information on the Legionnaire's whereabouts, and visited the *Salle d'Honneur*. It should perhaps come as no surprise that he had a rather jaundiced view of it.

> We entered through the *Porte d'Honneur* into a hall lined with dummy legionnaires in uniforms of various periods, the British-type battle-dress of our guide making a poor showing against the flowing blue coat with red epaulettes, and baggy trousers of a more romantic age [*Alexander wrote later*]. Patterns of swords and bayonets looked like exploding fireworks on the walls of the *Voie Sacre*, down which we passed to the beflagged *Temple des Heros*, with its faded photographs and sad relics of soldiers who had died in battle, then, already surfeited, we hurried through the *Salle des Trophees et des Batailles*, the *Musee du Souvenir*, the *Salle des Combats Anciens*, [and] the *Salle des Combats Recents*...[5]

After many hundreds of motoring miles, Alexander located Fenton and his 'escape' was arranged by sea from Oran to Lisbon in February 1955, about six weeks before Townsend, his erstwhile companion in the attempted desertion in Tunisia, was booted out. By this time there was 'dissidence' in Algeria as well, and it would be a long and bloody war. The likes of Townsend and Fenton were best out of it, as it would call for extraordinary stamina and dedication by Officers, Sous-Officiers and Legionnaires.

The first whiff of war had come in November 1954, when nationalist Algerians raised the standard of revolt, and unleashed a wave of terrorism against the French, the locally-born *Pied Noir* community, some of whose members had been there for several generations, and pro-French Algerians.[6] The rebellion would gradually be organized under the National Liberation Front (FLN) and its National Liberation Army (ALN). Initially, the 1st Etranger bore the brunt of the military action, but the other Foreign Legion regiments gradually returned to North Africa. The 2nd REI and 4th REI went to Morocco, the 3rd REI to Algeria. So did the 13th *Demi-Brigade* and, finally, the 5th REI, though it did not return until February 1956. The 1st REC was sent from Indo-China to Tunisia in January 1956, but France's days were numbered there and the country advanced to Independence later in the year, although a French presence remained at the leased naval base at Bizerta. Morocco also attained Independence in 1956, although the 4th REI did not leave the country until the following year.

The 1st and 2nd *Bataillons Etranger de Parachutistes* were re-raised and reconstituted at regimental strength as the 1st and 2nd *Regiments Etranger de Parachutistes* – 1st and 2nd REPs – and became the cutting edge of anti-terrorism fighters, the 1st REP based at Zeralda, the 2nd REP at Philippeville. When members of the FLN were given sanctuary in newly-independent Morocco and Tunisia, the French erected, mined and wired electrified fences – *barrages* – on the borders, as much to keep the 'dissidents' in, where they might be dealt with, as to keep reinforcements out, preventing cross-border strikes as much as possible. The introduction of helicopters gave the 1st and 2nd REPs, and the French and Colonial Paratroops, a flexibility of movement, and even men from the infantry regiments of the Foreign Legion were sometimes flown into action.

Under the leadership of Lieutenant-Colonel Pierre Jeanpierre, a Legion officer since 1936 and a survivor of the campaign in Syria, the French *Maquis* and the Nazi concentration camp at Mauthausen, the 1st BEP racked up more successes and more medals than any other regiment. Jeanpierre was one of the handful of BEP survivors of both the 1950 debacle at Cao-Bang in northern Tonkin, and of Dien Bien Phu four years later. He commanded the 1st REP in the 1956 Anglo-French Suez Intervention and later rooted out FLN terrorists in a major operation in Algiers. In two years the regiment accounted for some two thousand 'dissidents', though at a cost to themselves of one hundred and twenty-three dead and three hundred and fifty wounded, to become the elite unit of the Foreign Legion.

On 29 April 1958 two FLN groups, each thought to be about four hundred strong, broke through the Tunisian *barrage* and the 1st REP was rushed by truck and jeep to give battle. Unable to get back through the wire the terrorists were discovered at dawn, entrenched on a wooded hill.

> The companies moved up to the attack [*wrote a French reporter covering the operation*]. In line, automatics at the hip, the Legionnaires advanced under heavy fire from a couple of dozen light machine-guns. Pushing on slowly and deliberately, the Legionnaires cleaned up the first of the FLN trenches. Halting only to throw a grenade, they moved forward again, to the accompaniment of shouts of 'Camerone!' Before they could get to grips, the FLN broke, trying to escape individually or else to go to ground in some dense thicket or tumble of scrub-covered boulder[s] . . . Four and a half hours of scattered combat and the last of the rebels had fallen. It was a good haul, and a triumph for Colonel Jeanpierre, the regimental commander . . . 192 rebels killed, 8 prisoners, 43 light automatics, 76 rifles . . . an excellent start to Camerone Day.[7]

Jeanpierre, who drove himself as hard as he drove his men, exulted in the fact that this was the first time in ninety-five years that the Foreign Legion had actually been engaged in battle on the anniversary of Camerone.

> The goal of a Legionnaire is the supreme adventure of combat, at the end of which is either victory or death [*he told young Sergeant Albert 'Bobby' Dovecar after the skirmish*]. What matters is the action, the combat which places you

on a different plane from the rest of the herd. Cameron, 1863, was like that: victory or death.[8]

There had been six French Governments since 1954 and in May the Army revolted and demanded that General Charles de Gaulle take power. At the end of the same month Jeanpierre was killed when his helicopter was hit by ground fire while spotting for 'dissidents' in what should have been little more than a routine operation. His funeral was a highly emotional affair, with oaths sworn by some of his officers to die rather than see Algeria become independent. De Gaulle became Prime Minister on 1 June and flew to Algeria, kneeling at Jeanpierre's grave and proclaiming '*Algerie Francaise*', giving the *Pieds Noirs* – the *colons* – and the Army the belief that the rebels had only to be defeated for a return to the *status quo*. Yet even at this moment events were beginning to take shape which would put the Foreign Legion at the heart of a political disaster which would threaten its entire future.

In October, while still Prime Minister, de Gaulle extended a peace offer to the FLN, but it was rejected and a new wave of terror was unleashed. While the Foreign Legion, French and Colonial paratroops and regular French Army units were fighting a hard and dirty war against the ALN – the nationalists' military arm – in the mountains, the war in the cities against the FLN, its political masters, had been essentially won by a succession of initiatives waged under the overall direction of General Jacques Massu and implemented by Air Force General Maurice Challe.

The Army soon had further cause for concern, because by September de Gaulle was talking about a referendum on the future of Algeria, which would posit Independence, integration with France or a Federal State in association with France. General Challe, who was conducting the war, was outraged, writing: 'One does not propose to soldiers to go out and get killed for an imprecise final objective.'[9] When General Massu was quoted in a West German magazine as saying that he and his officers would 'not execute unconditionally the orders of the Head of State' he was promptly recalled, dressed down and sent to a new command in eastern France.

Challe was forced to send in men from two paratroop regiments to disperse a *Pied Noir* demonstration in Algiers on 24 January 1959. When the local *Gendarmerie*, moving against them, was fired on and showered with homemade bombs, the 1st REP, under the orders of Battalion Commander Henri Dufour, made no attempt to help them. The officers of the 1st REP were now almost totally politicized and during the five-day uprising Captain Pierre Sergent urged Dufour to let the regiment join the insurrectionists. He refused, but negotiated an agreement under which the *Pieds Noirs* were allowed to march away, with their weapons, and were accorded military honours by the 1st REP.

British-born journalist and foreign correspondent Geoffrey Bocca, who had first encountered the Foreign Legion on the eve of their move into southern Europe during the Second World War, was in Algiers at the time of Camerone Day in 1959, thought it 'the most stirring in years'.

Down the rue Michelet the Legion marched, behind fife, trumpet and drum, in kepis of white and kepis of red, blue and gold, in blue sashes, white belts, green ties and epaulettes of red and green [*he wrote*]. The Legion paras wore green berets and vividly mottled jumping dress which made them look like leopard men.

The pioneers with their huge beards, leather aprons and gleaming battleaxes resembled the early Saxon marauders of our history books, and were just as fierce. They were followed by the educated dandies of the Sahara Company, the *gendarmerie* of a million square miles of desert and oasis, wearing kepis with flapping puggarees, flowing cloaks and baggy Arab trousers. These were the guardians of the peace among the southern oases, at Air Sefra, Ghgardaia, Touggourt. All were Legionnaires.

Their boots crashed on the road, to the slow time of music that was almost drowned by the cheers of the *colons* crowding the sidewalk . . . On the terrace of the Hotel Saint George, Legion and para officers toyed with Scotch and soda, wiggled their toes and stretched bones which were luxuriously weary from the *bled*. Happily they watched twilight creep over Algiers. It was a breathtaking sight. The city with its magnificent harbour, the new skyscrapers trying their way upward, while squealing flights of swallows wheeled and disappeared into the red setting sun. Life was good. War was good.

Edith Piaf had just dedicated her latest hit record to the Legion, '*Non, je ne regrette rien*'.[10]

Things, in fact, were not nearly as rosy as Bocca saw them. Many officers, especially in the 1st REP, had began to question their loyalty to a political leader who appeared to be on the brink of selling out the Foreign Legion, the *Pieds Noirs* and French-supporting Algerian Arabs. General Gardy, now Inspector-General of the Foreign Legion, was on hand the day after Camerone to install newly-promoted Lieutenant-Colonel Dufour – who had begun his Foreign Legion career as far back as 1934, under the redoubtable Maire – as Commanding Officer of the 1st REP. At the ceremony Gardy took it upon himself to change the wording of the traditional instruction to the Legionnaires. Instead of telling them to conduct themselves 'in the interest of the service, the execution of military regulations and the respect for the laws', he told them to behave 'in the interests of the Foreign Legion'.[11]

Captain Sergent would soon be telling Dufour, that 'only a revolution' could 'reverse the course of events'.[12] Sergent would be a leader in the attempted putsch of April 1961, but even his extremism paled beside that of Lieutenant Roger Degueldre and, at a lower level, Sergeant 'Bobby' Dovecar and Corporal Claude Tenne.

A situation was gradually developing over which the individual Legionnaire would have no control, but which would be pivotal to the futures of the various regiments, and which in the short term would threaten the very existence of France's foreign regiments, though none of this was clear at the time. There was a war to be fought, and it appears that in the rush to train recruits for combat missions Legionnaires were hurried through Sidi-bel-Abbès, and sent for training at Saida or Mascara, without being given what had once been an almost obligatory tour of the *Salle d'Honneur*. Certainly, two of the three Legionnaires who set down their memories of Cameron Day 1960 failed to mention any such tour, while the third made merely a passing reference to knowing of its existence.

James William Worden, a former Royal Air Force officer, who had flown many wartime missions in the Western Desert, joined the Foreign Legion at the end of 1959. A Belfast man, Lou 'Paddy' Riley, who had flown in Wellingtons with Worden, was already serving and encouraged him to join, even though he was thirty-six years old. He would eventually spend seven years in the Foreign Legion – and say he wished it had been fifteen – serving in both the 3rd REI and the 2nd REP.

> I first heard the account of the Battle of Cameron while standing rigidly to attention and presenting arms on the main Legion parade ground at Sidi-bel-Abbès, watching the wooden hand of Captain Danjou, which had been picked up after the carnage, being carried with reverence by a veteran Adjutant [*Worden would say later*]. I could not help noticing that despite the black patch over an empty socket where an eye had once been, tears were running down his cheeks.[13]

The parade, said Worden, was an event 'whose impact had a lasting effect on the rest of my Legion service'.[14] The Adjutant who carried Danjou's articulated hand was a veteran of Dien Bien Phu, where he had lost his eye, though Worden – who had obtained special permission to step out of the parade formation to take photographs of him – considered that 'he was a damn sight better marksman than most Legionnaires with two eyes'.[15]

Simon Murray, who had joined the Foreign Legion in Paris on 22 February 1960, was doing his basic training at Mascara at the time. He was nineteen years old, an ex-public school boy, and came from a long military background. His great-great-grandfather, great-grandfather, grandfather and father had been officers in noted British regiments and his brother was an officer in the Scots Greys. Young Murray ultimately rose to the rank of Corporal-Chef in the 2nd REP and kept a notebook during his Legion service.

> Cameron Day is approaching... [*he noted in his Diary two days before the event*]. The Legion goes mad on Cameron Day. Officers and NCOs do all the corvee, including serving the food. There will be side-shows and a parade of floats through the town. There will even be a bullfight. It is apparently a carnival of carnivals and frantic preparations are under way for all the many events.

The reality lived up to its advance billing.

> It was a day of great celebration – extra food, and very good food, and masses to drink [*Murray reported in his Diary*]. A grand performance was

given in the town stadium of bullfighting, cycle racing, snake charming, and a mock Battle of Camerone which would have done credit to any Hollywood film set. This evening has produced mass intoxication . . .[16]

A rather different view was given by Peter Reeves, a Dutchman who had joined the Foreign Legion in Paris ten days before Murray. He was in his mid-thirties, by his own admission both amoral and light-fingered, and, as he told it, had left a job in America, fallen out with his family in Holland and been robbed by a prostitute in Paris. His time at Sidi-bel-Abbes was short and busy. 'I never went to the museum although I was quartered near it,' he said. 'I never seemed to have the time.' Someone compared Camerone to the siege of The Alamo, which had preceded it by twenty-seven years, then it was off to Saida for training.

> During the first week of basic training we had been told, to the point of tedium, of the Legion battle so zealously commemorated each April 30th [*Reeves would say later*]. I felt that Captain Danjou's men were blood brothers of the simpletons at The Alamo. Both tales were of ludicrous mass suicide. But what the hell! Almost a hundred years later we could enjoy a big bash, because a handful of our predecessors had been willing to die for the highly touted honour of the Legion. *Mort pour la France* – and all that shit.
>
> Decorations were put up. The kitchen was busy getting supplies. Many of the local merchants donated fine food and wines. Cases of shrimp, lobster, fowl and cheeses, and truckloads of wine were brought in and stored in a huge refrigerated room.
>
> Then Camerone arrived.
>
> The celebration began at midnight with a gargantuan feast and for two consecutive days the Legionnaire was king. Officers served the Legionnaires. No one had to salute. All gates were opened and anyone with up to a fifteen-day prison sentence was pardoned.
>
> There were a few exceptions to all this freedom, however. Our Company was given guard duty and although we enjoyed the day tremendously we were not allowed outside the gate. We would have given anything in order to go into town because the town belonged to the Legion on Camerone. There were parades but the paraders did not take the matter seriously. They were anxious to get back to all the fun.
>
> Everything was free. It was not possible for a Legionnaire to buy a beer. As soon as he entered a bar or restaurant every colonist in the place was eager to offer him food and drink, more than he could possibly hold. In the eyes of the colonists, during Camerone, the Legionnaire could do no wrong. We were loved like brothers during those two exuberant days.
>
> Unfortunately, I was not able to take full advantage of this celebration of Camerone in 1960. Since I had joined the Legion in Paris I had not been allowed to go out in town anywhere.[17]

The military plotting, which had initially been more talk than action, now moved into a new phase, much of it going on in Spain, where General Raoul Salan,

France's most decorated soldier, and a former Commander-in-Chief in Algeria, lived in retirement and entertained *Pied Noir* extremists. They talked of a rebellion to force de Gaulle to recognize *Algerie Francaise*, and even of secession. Dufour of the 1st REP contacted General Andre Zeller, a retired Chief of Staff of the Armed Forces, with a hare-brained plan for the regiment to capture the French Delegate-General, head of the civil government, as it marched past the reviewing stand in Algiers on Bastille Day. This was to be coordinated with the capture of de Gaulle and his Ministers by the troops marching down the Champs Elysées in Paris. The unhappiness of Foreign Legion officers and long-serving other ranks new no bounds. Algeria they felt, belonged not only to the *Pieds Noirs* and the Algerian Muslims, but also to them. Sidi-bel-Abbes was their home. Their dead were buried there. They were fighting, and to a large degree winning, a dangerous and bloody war.

Pierre Messmer, veteran of Eritrea, Syria and Bir Hakeim, a true hero of the 13th *Demi-Brigade* during the Second World War, and now France's Minister of Defence, visited Algeria, hopping by helicopter from regiment to regiment – especially those of the Foreign Legion – telling them: 'Your duty is clear. Win the war on the ground and have confidence in General de Gaulle.' He was soon made to appear either a knave or a fool – though he was neither – when, on 4 November, de Gaulle went on French television talking about Independence for Algeria.

In an unexpected way the funeral of ten men of the 1st REP was the catalyst for rebellion. Belonging to Captain Sergent's No. 1 Company, they had fallen in a vicious firefight when a helicopter landed a detachment under Lieutenant Daniel Godot on an exposed hill position, unaware that it was surrounded by rebels. Calling for covering fire from the helicopters, once the error had been realized, probably reduced further losses and the detachment was evacuated as dusk was falling.

'It is not possible that your sacrifice was in vain,' said their Commanding Officer, Dufour, in his funeral oration at Zerelda on 14 November. 'It is not possible that our compatriots in the metropole remain deaf to our cries of anguish.' The Chaplain for the 10th Parachute Division, Father Delarue, added his own thoughts during the service: 'You have come from every nation in Europe where people still love liberty, to bring freedom to this country. Yet you die at a time when, if we believe the speeches we hear, we no longer know why we die.'[18]

Dufour's remarks cost him his job. He was relieved of his command and ordered to return to France. Instead, he went to ground in Algeria, taking the Regimental Standard with him, fully conscious that without it his successor, Lieutenant-Colonel Maurice Guiraud, would not be able to formally take command.

De Gaulle was to visit Algeria in December and many plots were afoot, none of them coordinated, because the anti-de Gaulle, anti-Independence, pro-*Algerie Francaise* factions were multi-layered and distrustful of each other – united, to the extent that they were, only by a determination to keep Algeria part of France. At least three groups of *Pied Noir* extremists had plans to assassinate de Gaulle. The FLN had the same thought in mind. Captain Sergeant was conspiring with Air Force Chief of Staff General Edmond Jouhaud and the Commanding Officers of the 14th and 18th *Regiments de Chasseurs Parachutistes* (RCP) with a woolly plan to take advantage of a planned *Pied Noir* demonstration. From his hideout Dufour contacted Colonel Albert Brothier of the 1st Etranger and asked him to help in a plot to kidnap de Gaulle when he visited Sidi-bel-Abbes. He was surprised at the negative reply.

The 1st REP was part of the 10th Paratroop Division, the 2nd REP part of the 25th, and Brothier, of all the Colonels of the Foreign Legion, had the best understanding of the emotions of the officers of the two parachute regiments, as they had been inter-linked since the gory days of Tonkin and Dien Bien Phu. The son of a gendarme, Brothier had been a young Lieutenant in 1940 in the 12th REI and spent five years in a German prisoner-of-war camp, joining the 13th *Demi-Brigade* in Indo-China in 1946. The terribly mauled 1st *Bataillon Etranger de Parachutistes* (BEP) was dissolved in January 1951, then reconstituted in mid-March under the command of Captain Darmuzai. Brothier led it as a Battalion Commander in 1952, Captain Guiraud in 1953, Captain Elie Denoix de Saint-Marc in 1954, then Battalion Commander Jeanpierre later that year. He saw it reconstituted as the 1st *Regiment Etranger des Parachutistes* in 1955. Brothier, by now a Lieutenant-Colonel, took over command the following year, beginning a musical chairs command pattern: Jeanpierre again in 1957, until his death the following year, then Brothier again, followed by Dufour, then Guiraud. Darmuzai, who had led the 1st BEP in 1951, was now a Lieutenant-Colonel, and had succeeded Colonel Lefort as Commanding Officer of the 2nd REP the previous March. Moreover, Colonel Georges Masselot, who commanded the 18th *Regiment de Chasseurs Parachutistes*, had served with Brothier as a Lieutenant in the 12th REI in 1939–40 and been Battalion Commander of the 2nd BEP in 1954.

De Gaulle got a sense of the Army's feelings during his December visit, which was punctuated by massive *Pied Noir* demonstrations against him. Dufour surfaced again – with the 1st REP's Regimental Standard – and was posted to Germany, and de Gaulle took steps to replace more junior officers whose loyalty he doubted, especially those of the 1st REP. Some, like Sergent, grudgingly went back to France, but continued plotting. Degueldre, who had become a real *Algerie Francaise* zealot, deserted when he was transferred to the 4th REI, went underground and helped to found the terrorist *Organisation Armee Secrete* (OAS).

The year turned and now Generals Salan, Jouhaud and Zeller were plotting in earnest, talking of a putsch, and holding many clandestine discussions with the Right-wing leadership of the *Pied Noir*. Support was expected from the 1st and 2nd REPs, the two Foreign Legion Cavalry regiments, the two RCP paratroop regiments and a dragoon regiment. There was even talk of a parachute drop on Paris to depose de Gaulle. When Challe was unexpectedly pulled out of Algeria and sent to a NATO command, he resigned his Commission and soon became the fourth plotter. Surprisingly, former Inspector-General of the Foreign Legion General Paul Gardy became the fifth.

'When we march, the whole Legion will march with us,' he blithely told his fellow conspirators.[19]

Yet it was infinitely more complicated than that. Although many die-hard Foreign Legion officers, mostly in the 1st REP, but also in some other regiments, as well as in the Colonial and French Parachute regiments and some Regular Army units, were strong supporters of any movement which would keep Algeria as part of Metropolitan France, open rebellion against the government – treason, in short – was a huge step. In some ways the dilemma was similar to that faced by the 6th REI in Syria in 1941 – to remain loyal to the Head of State, however wrong he might be felt to be, or to throw discipline out of the window and come out in open rebellion.

Guiraud of the 1st REP went on sick leave early in April 1961, leaving the regiment commanded by Major Denoix de Saint-Marc, at that point not involved with the plotters, but aware that something was afoot. Sergent, having taken sick leave while in France, was already back in Algiers when Challe and Zeller arrived clandestinely on 20 April. The following evening Saint-Marc was personally requested by Challe to join a putsch to ensure that Algeria remained French, and to force de Gaulle to resign. He agreed, on his terms – that no *Pieds Noirs* be involved, nor quasi-Fascists, and that the putsch be as bloodless as possible. Assigned to lead his old Company, Sergent headed a convoy of trucks racing from Zerelda to Algiers, bluffed his way into the Pellisier Barracks and seized control. Other groups quickly occupied the office of the Delegate-General – the seat of the civil government – the radio station and key buildings. Several General Officers and some senior civil officials were arrested and sent under guard by air to In-Salah, on the edge of the Sahara.

Colonel Georges Masselot of the 18th REP was despatched to arrest General Pouilly, the Military Commander in Oran. From the putschists' point of view, he was not the best man to have sent. Pouilly's son had been killed while serving under Masselot's command, and Masselot's son killed while under Pouilly. Admitting that he was wholeheartedly committed to the putsch, Masselot told Pouilly that he would take not personal action against him and left.

At seven o'clock in the morning on 22 April a radio broadcast announced that the Army had taken over and that '*Algerie Francaise* is not dead.' With just fifty officers and little more than three thousand men the plotters had gained control of the key positions in Algiers and the surrounding areas at the cost of a single life. They had neglected, however, to seize the telephone exchange and Paris immediately knew what had happened.

It soon became abundantly clear that the support which the architects of what became known as the 'Generals' Putsch' had expected was not going to materialize. There was no help to be had from soldiers in Oran, Constantine or Bone. In Tizi-Ouzou, in eastern Algeria, General Jean Simon, a veteran of the Syrian Campaign and Bir Hakeim, and also a former Colonel of the 3rd REI, learned of the putsch from one of his officers and immediately telephoned Army Headquarters in Algiers.

When Colonel Brothier of the 1st Etranger heard what was happening he summoned his officers.

'The Legion is foreign by definition and will not intervene in a purely French quarrel,' he told them bluntly.[20] To telephoned questions from the Colonels of other Foreign Legion regiments he responded: 'We cannot take the risk of seeing the Germans fire upon Frenchmen. The putsch is a French affair; it is unthinkable that foreigners should become mixed up in it.'[21]

After telling the same thing to a highly agitated General Gardy, who had hurried to Sidi-bel-Abbes hoping to drum up support for the putsch, Brothier sent two Companies of the 1st Etranger to support General Pouilly in Oran. He also had the Foreign Legion's radio band hooked into Radio Oran, so that broadcasts from the putschists could be heard in eastern Algeria.

'You'll have to get rid of me before the *Demi-Brigade* gets involved in sedition,' Colonel Vaillant told his own officers.[22]

The 2nd REP was at Camp Pehau, not far from their home base of Philippeville, the day after the coup. Lieutenant-Colonel Darmuzai had forbidden his officers to become involved in the putsch, but was now nowhere to be found. His second-in-command, Major Cabiro, was present when the men were rousted out near midnight and piled into trucks to drive some five hundred kilometres (three hundred miles) to Algiers.

> First thing in the morning we drove to the airport and our role became immediately clear [*Legionnaire Murray wrote in his Diary*]. We were to occupy the airport, which was held by French marines, and they weren't having any of it. So we were given wooden batons, heavy, with sharp points, and in one long line we slowly eased into the marines, pushing them forward like bolshie rams. They frequently turned and attacked with aggression. This was met in many cases with savage beatings and it became a sad and shoddy business. Marine officers were pushed around by our officers – there were scenes of officers yelling at each other with questions of loyalty and accusations of traitor and so on. [Lieutenant] L'Hospitallier bust his baton on the head of one of the marines. Gradually they were herded out of the airport premises and we were in control of the base from which we will apparently make the drop on Paris.[23]

33
End of an Era

In the French capital de Gaulle met briefly with Louis Joxe, his new Minister for Algerian Affairs, telling him he had 'all powers', and with General Jean Olie, the new Chief of Staff of the Armed Forces, who was flying with Joxe to Algeria. Olie, particularly, was no doubt heading south with a heavy heart. He had commanded the *Regiment de Marche de la Legion Etrangere* with distinction from March 1945 until the end of the Second World War, overseen its re-transition into the 3rd REI, then gone on to command the *Groupement Autonome de la Legion Etrangere* five years later, so this was going to be an unhappy return to his old haunts. The two men went to the airport and flew off to Algeria, not knowing what they might find.

They landed at Oran, visited General Pouilly, who declared his loyalty, but said he did not know how long he would remain at liberty, then flew to Telergma, near Constantine. From there they went to Bone, then back home. Challe had learned of their visit and exulted in the fact that they had returned to France.

'General Olie is in flight!' he told his fellow putschists.

In fact, Olie and his party had left Telergma just ahead of a para column converging on the airfield. General Salan arrived from Spain to join the conspirators, but his connections with *Pied Noir* extremists and the OAS made him a liability as far as many of the undecided senior officers, still deciding which way to jump, were concerned.

In Paris, de Gaulle had declared a State of Emergency and ringed the National Assembly with tanks. Then, dressed in the uniform of a Brigadier-General, he went on television calling on Frenchmen, and especially soldiers, to ignore any orders given by those involved in the 'Generals' Putsch'. It tipped the scales and decided many of the fence-sitters. As a former Air Force General, Challe was dismayed when the pilots of the fleet of transport aircraft flew their planes out of Algeria, ending any thoughts of a parachute drop on Paris. The French Navy declared their intention to defend the port of Mers-el-Kebir and a French cruiser was offshore. General Pouilly flew from Oran to Algiers to confront Challe. He was forthright in his denunciation of disloyalty, and for his trouble was arrested and sent to join the other prisoners at In-Salah.

By 25 April the putch was over, though die-hards like Captain Sergent were all for fighting on. In the event, Generals Salan, Zeller, Jouhaud and Gardy fled, as did Sergent, Lieutenants Degueldre and Godot and a number of other officers. Challe was planning to surrender. Challe went to Zerelda and was joined there later in the day by Saint-Marc and the 1st REP. The following morning they found the camp surrounded and an officer came in to arrest Challe. Saint-Marc turned out a guard of honour for him as he was led away, a prisoner of the State, headed for France and a trial.

The 1st REP was to be disbanded and the Legionnaires were told that they would be assigned to different regiments. Saint-Marc, bareheaded and without his medals, reviewed them one last time on their parade ground, formally turned the regiment over to Lieutenant-Colonel Guiraud, who had been recalled from leave, then surrendered himself. Before quitting Zerelda the 1st REP destroyed the furniture in their barracks, blew up their ammunition magazines, then piled into trucks to be taken to Sidi-bel-Abbes. They left singing Piaf's *Non, je ne regrette rien*, but many – including Sergeant Dovecar and Corporal Claude Tenne – never reached their destination, dropping off a truck in the dark and disappearing. Some soon surfaced again as part of the murky *demi-monde* of Separatist terrorism as members of the OAS, which came to specialize in bombings and assassinations. In the confusion following the failed putsch, men deserted from all the Foreign Legion regiments, some making for home, others for the OAS.

The Dutchman Reeves, who had trained as a Medical Orderly, was among the many disillusioned Legionnaires. 'The approach of Camerone did not generate much excitement [and] I could not envision it being celebrated under the present circumstances,' he said later. He was quite right, as he soon heard that 'it had been officially decided that there would be no feast this year'.[1] It was also announced that the Foreign Legion would not take part in the traditional Bastille Day Parade along the Champs Elysées in Paris. Only Legionnaires on 'special errands' were permitted to leave barracks by themselves. Reeves had regularly been running such 'special errands', going into town to have dressings for the infirmary sterilized, and on 27 April he used this freedom to desert, and headed for Oran.

The same day Murray's 3rd Company was piled into trucks and sent back to their base at Philippeville, but made to camp on a nearby hillside. 'It was probably feared that we would also blow the place to pieces,' he remarked. 'From what we can gather from the snatches of radio broadcasts and newspapers, the Legion is being cited as the root of all the trouble. We are to be the scapegoats for the rest of the French army.'[2] Darmuzai, who had warned his officers not to become involved in the putsch, then made himself scarce, went to France in its wake and was soon named as Commanding Officer of the 25th Parachute Division. The Legionnaires remained under canvas within sight of their barracks.

> Today was *La Fete de Camerone* and surely the most sober environment for Camerone since 1863 – prisoners of our camp in the wood halfway up the mountain overlooking Philippeville, our home town [*Murray grumbled in his Diary*]. No passes were issued so we just sat in misery on the hill and guzzled the extra food and beer that was issued to cheer our sinking spirits.[3]

Minister of Defence Messmer, who had flown to Algiers, presided over the dissolving of the mutinous 14th and 18th *Regiments de Chasseurs Parachutistes*, then went to Sidi-bel-Abbes, where, on Camerone Day, a disconsolate Guiraud watched as orders were dictated dissolving the 1st REP. Police and troops were out combing the towns and countryside for deserters, but the only one caught that day was Reeves, who was taken back to Saida.[4] Messmer went back to Paris to temporarily suspend recruiting for the Foreign Legion, and, more importantly, to try to persuade de Gaulle that enough was enough, that there was neither necessity nor good sense in disbanding the entire Foreign Legion, perhaps gently reminding him that the 13th *Demi-Brigade*'s stand at Bir Hakeim nineteen years earlier had given the then leader of the Free French the credibility he had so desperately needed at the time.

Lieutenant-Colonel Maurice Chenel, a veteran of Dien Bien Phu, and recently qualified as a paratrooper – though he had never commanded an airborne regiment – took command of the 2nd REP on 3rd May, and two days later helicopters swooped down on Murray's 3rd Company in the field, seized Cabiro and Captain Branca and carried them off while their men stood at attention and watched them go.[5]

A few days later, in Sidi-bel-Abbes, Brothier assembled the Sous-Officiers and Coroprals of the now defunct 1st REP. '[He told] us that the Foreign Legion had no business in intervening in a politico-military conflict,' recalled Janos Kemencei, who had fought in both the 1st BEP and the 1st REP, but had been seconded to training duties some time earlier. 'He was applauded by almost everyone.'[6]

On the last day of the month, working under the direction of Lieutenant Deguedre, Sergeant Dovecar, Corporal Tenne and Legionnaire Herbert Petri – deserters all – took four civilian OAS men with them and murdered Roger Gavoury, Police Commissioner for Algiers. By the time they were arrested in October they had helped Degueldre and his so-called Delta Commando terrorist group wreak havoc as an assassin and a controller of assassins. In Paris, Generals Salan, Jouhaud and Gardy were sentenced to death *in absentia*. Generals Challe and Zeller each received fifteen years in prison and Major Saint-Marc ten. The Colonels of the 14th and 18th RCPs drew eight years each, while nine Captains and two Lieutenants were given suspended sentences of from one to two years.

Legionnaire 1st Class Jim Worden had been with the 2nd Battalion of the 3rd REI near the Tunisian frontier when the putsch got under way. After it, the battalion was rushed westward to Zerelda to take over what was left of the camp of the departed 1st REP. Worden and his Section spent some days outside the camp guarding the girls of the regimental brothel, then headed back east to more combing of the countryside for rebels. On Bastille Day, just as they sat down to a celebratory meal, word came that the battalion was going to cross the frontier into Tunisia to defend the leased naval base at Bizerta, which had been attacked by the Tunisian Army. Worden and a Sergeant were left behind, as they were scheduled for training courses. The battalion returned three weeks later.[7]

Promoted, Colonel Brothier handed over the 1st Etranger to Colonel Vaillant in late August, and the war went on, while the politicians talked and negotiated and the purges of officers involved in the 'Generals' Putsch' continued. On 5 September, Murray's Lieutenant, Lhopitallier, who had led the 3rd Company against the Marines at Algiers airport, was withdrawn from the regiment and sent back to France.[8] New officers, often young and arrogant, anxious to throw their weight about, were posted into the various Foreign Legion regiments. 'We'll tame all of you, the anti-Gaullists, OAS and all that,' one of them shouted at the veteran Kemencei in a bar.[9]

Completing his annual 'Report sur la morel' on 21 November, Vaillant felt called upon to remark that although the former Sous-Officiers and Corporals of the former 1st REP were 'sensitized to the maximum, they have a special spirit', and he adroitly summed up the situation not only in his own regiment, but in all the others of the Foreign Legion.

> The successive spectacle of generals arrested by their subordinates, then junior officers tried and thrown out of the army for having executed the orders of their superiors has profoundly troubled the spirit of discipline [*he wrote*]. As far as the Legion is concerned, the dissolution of the 1st REP, the momentary suspension of recruitment, then its difficult reinstitution, and finally the impression that the Legion was made the scapegoat of this affair by the atmosphere of distrust and general suspicion of which it is the object, all this has provoked bitterness and a defensive reaction which consists of enclosing itself in the attitude of an outcast.[10]

In the meantime, the Foreign Legion remained on the alert, and fighting in the hills, while a referendum on Algeria's future was being organized. It invited a 'Yes' or 'No' vote on the question of whether France should give up Algeria and allow the country to move to Independence, and resulted in a 'Yes' victory. A cease-fire was announced in March 1962 and Independence was around the corner. The *Pieds Noirs* departed from Algeria in droves and the FLN, no longer a government-in-exile in Tunisia, returned to Algeria and unleashed their fury on those of their countrymen who had supported France, particularly those who had served in the Army. The OAS, its strength beefed up by the presence of the Foreign Legion deserters, unleashed another reign of terror.

The 2nd REP was based near Constantine and time and energy were devoted to preparations for Camerone Day, which would be the last one before Independence, perhaps the last one ever, as it seemed unlikely that there would be any place for the Foreign Legion in the Algeria of the future. Stalls were set up, a Spanish Legionnaire named Nalda offered to be the matador at a bullfight, and local bookmakers got busy.

> We had a big parade this morning [*Simon Murray wrote in his Diary*]. Lots of brass arrived and we were inspected by a four-star general. Senior officers from regular army units in the area came with their wives to see how the Legionnaire animals lived. The main event, the bullfight, got under way just after lunch in front of a huge crowd. The bullring was surrounded by bales of straw, behind which the crowd was pressed four deep. Nalda was dressed immaculately and after several vodkas he eventually staggered into the ring. A roar went up from the crowd and the bull promptly charged. Nalda panicked and, having seen the bull, I didn't blame him. Twenty Spaniards leapt into the ring to save the honour of Spain and attacked the bull with bottles, brooms and pickaxe handles. The bull went berserk and charged headlong through the straw bales and was last seen going for its life down the main street of the village of Telergma.[11]

Murray and a friend broke camp and hitchhiked into Constantine, where they were approached by an OAS recruiter. When they got back to their camp they found that the Legionnaires had wrecked Telergma. Murray was promoted to Legionnaire 1st Class shortly afterwards.

Reeves had been sent to the Disciplinary Company at Colomb-Bechar on 15 July 1961 for his desertion attempt, and, if his account of the goings-on there is even half-true, he was lucky to survive. He suffered a heart attack early in 1962 and was sent to Sidi-bel-Abbes in mid-April for a determination on his case. It was recommended that he be given a Dishonourable Discharge and he was awaiting for the necessary paperwork when Camerone Day came round.

> It was all but totally disregarded [*he would say later*]. Television cameras recorded the last Camerone of the Legion in Sidi-bel-Abbes. A handful of smartly uniformed Legionnaires marched for the cameras. There were almost no spectators. They all knew it was really the end of the Legion, [almost] a century after the first Camerone. This one was just as futile, but one which would only be remembered because it was the last. Even at that it would be remembered by very few men. The Legion might possibly struggle on to the bitter end but the fact remained that it was no longer needed – anywhere.[12]

Reeves was discharged six weeks later, at a time when Paris, indeed all France, was a-buzz over the trials of OAS terrorists. Dovecar and his immediate associates had been captured the previous October and Degueldre in early April. Dovecar, Tenne and Petri, along with four civilians, were charged with the murder of Algiers Police Commissioner Gavory, and it no doubt took great courage for Colonel Brothier to take the stand to speak on behalf of the three Legionnaires he had once commanded. What they had done could not be excused, but he sought to explain how some Legionnaires at least could be led astray by the 'devotion of the men to their officers'.

> It is from them that they find the structure and the balance that civilian life did not give them [*he explained*]. Thus, they transfer all their attachments and affection to their officers, for they have no critical sense. In their officers they will forgive everything, even the most extravagant actions.[13]

Dovecar was sentenced to death, along with civilian OAS member Claude Piegats, who was said to have provided a gun for the attack on Gavoury. Tenne and Petri were jailed for life. As the sentences were announced, Tenne indicated that he wished to speak: 'I ask the court to grant me the favour of dying with my Sergeant,' he said. When his request was refused, he ripped the medals from his chest and hurled them to the floor. Dovercar and Petri followed suit. The remaining three civilians were given lighter sentences. Captain Pierre Sergent, on the run from the law himself, but a master of disguises, formulated a plan to rescue the condemned man from the death cell, but it proved impossible and Dovecar was executed by firing squad on 7 June. His last words were: '*Vive La Legion!*'

General Gardy was also still on the run, and eventually reached South America, but Generals Jouhaud and Salan were arrested. Although already sentenced to death *in absentia*, they were tried by a specially established High Military Tribunal. Jouhaud was sentenced to death, but his leader, Salan, tried and convicted some six weeks later, was given life imprisonment, which forced de Gaulle to commute Jouhaud's sentence. The High Military Tribunal was immediately scrapped, and replaced by a Military Court of Justice, whose first job was to try Degueldre. When he was executed by firing squad he was singing the *Marseillaise*. Sergent and other Foreign Legion *Algerie Francaise* adherents, and some OAS assassins remained at large.

France had salvaged few concessions from the Independence talks with the FLN: a lease on the naval base at Mers-el-Kebir, with the Foreign Legion to be part of the defence and security arrangements connected with it; control of nuclear testing sites near Colomb-Bechar and of oil drilling in the Sahara. So then began a period of almost gypsy-like existence for the various Foreign Legion regiments. The 2nd REP moved to Bou Sfer, as part of the security force for Mers-el-Kebir. The 2nd REC was disbanded in July and its effectives absorbed into the 1st REC, which was based at Mers-el-Kebir. The same month the 4th REI was sent to Touggourt to guard the oil fields and in October the 2nd REI was moved to Colomb-Bechar to join the 5th REI as part of the Sahara Military Sites Command. The 3rd REI – minus one Company of near time-expired men – departed for Diego-Suarez at the northernmost tip of Madagascar and the 13th *Demi-Brigade* was despatched to French Somaliland in the Horn of Africa.

The 1st Etranger remained in Sidi-bel-Abbes for the time being, charged with closing down the 'Mother House' of the Foreign Legion. The Camp de la Demande at Aubagne, an old and rundown military property, sixteen kilometres (ten miles) from Marseille, originally built as a rest camp for German sailors during World War II, was to be their new home.

At Puyloubier, thirty-two kilometres (twenty miles) from Aubagne, was *La Domaine Capitaine Danjou*, the regiments' home for aged and infirm Legionnaires, a two hundred-and-forty-hectare farm and vineyard, cared for by the residents and the source of the specially-bottled wine served in messes. The *Domaine* was the modern-day successor to several similar former institutions, including the *Maison des Invalides* established after the First World War at a chateau bought for the purpose by the Persian Captain Nazare-Aga of the RMLE and presented to his old regiment.

The treasures of the *Salle d'Honneur*, crate after crate of swords and trophies, pictures and archives, were packed and shipped to Puyloubier. In leaving Algeria the Foreign Legion was also saying goodbye to its dead, buried at Sid-bel-Abbes, the city it had created out of a wilderness, and in scattered cemeteries or lonely graves. On 29 September the coffins of General Paul Rollet, Prince Aage of Denmark and Legionnaire Heinz Zimmerman were exhumed in the presence of the Hand of Captain Danjou, carried in its wood-and-glass casket by Adjutant Janos Kemencei.[14] The coffins were sent to Puyloubier for reburial.

Corporal Jim Warden was stationed nearby with the Company of the 3rd REI which had not gone to Madagascar, and it was his unit which received the three coffins for reburial in the little cemetery. The new graves for Rollet and Aage, Worden recalled, were dug by volunteers, 'many of whom had not only known them both but served under them'.

> Legionnaire Zimmerman, an ordinary Legionnaire who did not aspire to greatness, served for twenty years and died in his sleep [*Worden would write later*]. He is the Legion's Unknown Soldier except that we know who he is and we also know who he represents: all Legionnaires who have died in obscurity in the Legion. We provided the labour for the digging of the graves and the provision of the honour guard. I claimed the privilege of digging the grave of Zimmerman for myself, although as a Corporal I should have been supervising and not labouring. But this was not a labour of toil but a labour of love and respect.

Worden's Company inevitably drew guard duty at Puyloubier, and were dolly-ragged by the veterans, who – though knowing full well that the 3rd REI had done more than its share of fighting in Algeria – pretended to see them as 'nothing more than novice recruits'. Virtually every Foreign Legion campaign and battle of the preceding four decades – and more – was represented in the medals worn by the Puyloubier veterans, who included Russian-born Captain Vladimir Solomirsky. As a Lieutenant he had led men of the 3rd Squadron of the 1st REC in a brilliant cavalry charge at Tizi Outine in Morocco on 20 September 1925, and it was considered an honour to buy him a beer. 'You had to put your name on a list and await your turn,' said Worden.[15]

At Sidi-bel-Abbes the final winding down continued. The great bronze globe on the *Monument des Morts*, and the onyx slabs used as facing for the plinth on which it rested, were carefully taken apart, packed and shipped across the Mediterranean, to be stored. History-minded officers remembered a condition laid down by Captain de Borelli when he gave the *Salle d'Honneur* the silk flag captured at Tuyen Quang in 1885, and at dusk on 24 October the men of the 1st Etranger fell-in for a ritual incineration.

> In the heart of the Caserne Vienot, itself more than a century old, the seven hundred men who would leave the following day, gathered with their Colonel [and] their officers for the last evening [*wrote former Legionnaire Georges-R. Manue, who had gone to Sidi-bel-Abbes to be present*]. At the centre of the parade ground, an officer read the poem, known to all, which Captain de Borelli had written for his Legionnaires who had died in Tonkin in the struggle against the Black Flags. The voice strong – a mixture of anger and emotion – it broke at the last verse: 'It is your Captain who thinks of you and who counts his dead.' Then a Legionnaire very carefully spread on the ground a many-coloured piece of silk. It was a flag taken by [de] Borelli's men in battle and which the Captain had given to the *Musee du Souvenir*, with a stipulation which had always been felt to be unnecessary, because such an eventuality had been considered absurd: if the Legion left Bel-Abbes, the flag was to be burned. It burned brightly now, in an absolute

silence, and seven hundred faces showed the same sorrow. When the flames died down, the torches of a hundred men, lit from the embers, crackled at this moving scene.[16]

Colonel Vaillant arrived in Marseille with the majority of his men two days later and went straight to the Camp de la Demand, and the few Legionnaires who had remained behind marched out of the Quartier Vienot for the last time on 13 November. Left behind in Algeria and Morocco were the 2nd, 4th and 5th REIs and the 1st REC and 2nd REP, depressed by sterile guard duty and road-building, and there would be little change in the coming months. New plans for the deployment of the Foreign Legion were being developed in Paris, but they would take time to put into effect.

Near the end of 1961 Colonel Brothier had written: 'The oldest veterans of the Legion who have for forty years traversed with it many depressing periods, are still able to see beyond the present situation and believe that the Legion will find its place by having the necessary resilience to cross over a difficult period'[17]. Now, near the end of 1962, it seemed this might be true.

> General Lefort, the Inspector-General of the Legion, reviewed his old regiment today and gave us information that might turn out to be that which will save us from insanity [*Murray wrote in his Diary on 10 December*]. The regiment is to undergo a massive metamorphosis designed to make us the crack unit of the French army, ready to participate in combat operations that may arise in the seventies and eighties. If we do not do this, it is likely that we will eventually disappear as a regiment. The French requirement for ground troops now that they have lost Indo-China and North Africa is going to be considerably less, and the axe will fall on those units that are the least useful. Hence the regiment is going to set about training up special sections in underwater combat, demolition, guerrilla warfare, night fighting, special armaments. We will be trained to operate tanks and armoured vehicles, we will be taught to ski and mountaineer, we will become familiar with submarines, we will be sent on survival courses and we will become a highly skilled and dexterous force for multipurpose capability. In addition it has been decided that the regiment will improve its P[ublic] R[elations] and we will enter a team for the French army pentathlon and the French shooting championships in the coming year. This is all terrific stuff. At last someone has come forward with a directive on where we are going. The message has been well received. Morale has in one stroke been given a gigantic shot in the arm. We're back in business. Somebody thinks we can do more than just build bloody roads all day. Suddenly the mountain of the next two years diminishes, there is a feeling of moving forward again.[18]

34
General Penette Dreams a Dream

On 30 April 1954, while Captain Coutant's men of the 13th *Demi-Brigade* at Dien Bien Phu were plotting ways to retrieve the cases of *Vinogle* in no man's land, on the other side of the world former Foreign Legion officer Marcel Penette, now Military Attache to France's embassies in Washington, D.C., and Mexico City, was leading what he called 'a sort of pilgrimage' to the grave of the 3rd of the 1st at Camerone.

As Colonel Penette, he had been Military Attache at France's Permanent Mission to the United Nations in New York when he visited Camerone for the first time in 1948. Now he was General Penette, and was still grieving over the condition in which he had found the grave six years earlier. He would always say that as a former Foreign Legion officer the Combat of Camerone spoke forcefully to him, touching his military emotions in three very special ways.

> The first is fidelity to the mission, regardless of the cost [*he explained*]. Surrounded since morning, without any possibility of being relieved, the 65 Officers, Sous-Officiers and Legionnaires of Captain Danjou fought on until evening, until there were just three men standing, simply because honour demanded it, refusing to surrender while they still had weapons. The second is the wonderful example of humanity on the part of our adversary, the Major and doctor Francisco Talavera, who, after having directed his National Guard battalion all day in a hard and murderous assault, returned, after the last shot was fired, to his medical vocation and tended our wounded with the same care as his own.
>
> The third is the international origins of this group of heroes. A class at Saint-Cyr was designated 'Centenary of Camerone.' The Foreign Legion, in acknowledgement of military virtue, adopted this day and part of another and made the anniversary of 30 April 1863 its official annual fete. On that date, in countries all over the world, associations of former Legionnaires – gathered in fraternity and comradeship – celebrate the memory, reinforce their bonds of friendship and reaffirm the ideals of 'Honour and Fidelity' which motivated them while serving under our Tricolour. It also goes beyond the limits of our frontiers, the fame of 'Camerone,' the French spelling of the name of the modest Veracruz village of Camaron, is today known and revered in all parts of the world.[1]

In 1948 Penette had been very surprised to find that few members of the French expatriate community in Mexico City had any idea where the hamlet of Camaron

– Camerone – was located, even if they were vaguely aware that the Foreign Legion had fought a battle there almost a century before. True, it had been renamed Villa Adalberto Tejeda twenty years earlier, but the railway station retained – as it still does today – the name Camaron.

Penette had interested a number of people in Mexico City in the story of Camerone and after being promoted in 1953 began planning to have 'a pilgrimage' to the grave of the 3rd of the 1st on Camerone Day the following year. On the appointed day Penette and the handful of friends who accompanied him gathered round the wrought iron fence which protected the grave on the railway station platform. It was very, very close to the tracks and they held onto their hats as trains rushed by.

It was a time when the newspapers were full of stories about the siege at Dien Bien Phu, heightening interest in the French Army in general and the Foreign Legion in particular. Penette had already found several people interested in his idea of erecting a new monument, notably Captain Jean Castaignt, a French Army Reserve Officer resident in Mexico. An indefatigable researcher, Castaignt had brought several of his Mexican friends into the growing circle of Camerone enthusiasts, including Lieutenant-Colonel Daniel Sousa, who was a lawyer by training and a descendant of the wealthy textiles merchant Manuel Sousa, at whose Jalapa house Colonel Francisco de Paula Milan had planned his campaign against the French more than two weeks before the Combat of Camerone. Carlos Lascurain y Zulueta, President of the Municipality of Jalapa, and Captain Louis Hallard, also a French Army Reserve Officer, were early supporters. Louis and Xavier Sol la Lande of Veracruz, who had visited Sidi-bel-Abbes during the Second World War, were other interested adherents to the cause.

Penette also met Manuel Gonzalez y Montesinos, whose grandfather, after whom he had been named, had been President of Mexico between 1880 and 1884. On his mother's side, he was the grandson of a Colonel Montesinos, who had fought the French at Puebla in 1863, and subsequently spent two years as a prisoner-of-war in France. Penette was astonished to learn that the elderly Gonzalez y Montesinos had joined the Foreign Legion during the First World War, served under Colonel Rollet in the *Regiment de Marche de la Legion Etrangere*, been wounded three times and decorated with the Legion of Honour.

Over the next few years the annual 30 April 'pilgrimage' to Camerone became something of a tradition and further interest was sparked when Louis Sol la Lande located Milan's grave in Crypt No.15 in the old cemetery at Jalapa.[2] He had been promoted to the rank of General Officer after the French Intervention and had died in 1884. Descendants of Dr. Francisco Talavera, who had led the National Guard of Cordoba at Camerone, then given medical attention to the wounded, Mexican and French alike, were located.

Penette retired from the French Army in 1958 and decided to make his home in Mexico. He and Castaignt began collecting material on Camerone and soon expanded their research into a full-scale historical project aimed at telling the story of the Regiment Etranger and its role in the Mexican Expeditionary Corps between 1863 and 1867. There was comparatively little material in print: some forty-four pages in Grisot and Coulombon's 1887 history of the Foreign Legion, a few pages in the first edition of *La Livre d'Or de la Legion Etrangere*, some reminiscences about particular aspects of the campaign by serving Foreign Legion officers, books dealing with their experiences by three Legionnaires, brief mentions of the Regiment Etranger in the military memoirs of several contemporary non-Foreign Legion officers, even briefer ones in overall histories of the French Intervention and a smattering of articles in obscure and long out-of-print magazines and journals.

Their interest coincided with the publication of a second edition of the *Livre d'Or*, the timing apparently related to France's withdrawal from French Indo-China four years earlier.[3] Now elevated to Honourary Corporal-Chef of the Foreign Legion, Brunon was again involved, this time with former Legionnaire and author Georges-R. Manue, who had served in Morocco in the 1920s and with the 11th REI in 1940 and written about his military adventures. He contributed the new *Livre d'Or*'s material for the years 1934–45. The third co-author was ex-Foreign Legion officer Captain Pierre Carles, now with the *Service Historique de l'Armee de Terre* at Vincennes. Brunon authored the seven pages of text concerning Camerone, this time writing that the final charge had been made by Sous-Lieutenant Maudet, Corporal Maine and three Legionnaires, one fewer than stated in the 1931 edition. It was also incorrectly stated that two officers and twenty-two Legionnaires died in the Hacienda de la Trinidad, that nineteen Legionnaires died in captivity, and that only twelve were exchanged for Mexican prisoners-of-war.

In Marseilles, after 118 issues, under its several names, what had finally become *Vert et Rouge: Traditions et Souvenirs Militaires*, ceased publication the same year,[4] though it would be superseded by the Foreign Legion's own magazine, *Kepi blanc*, which has annually kept the story of Camerone alive with assorted original articles, and related reprints and insights.

Penette and Castaignt realized that their book was clearly going to be a labour of love. They knew that Mexico's military archives were closed to historians and researchers, but Penette hoped that being in Mexico City, and in a position which gave him access to very senior Mexican military people, would enable them to obtain access to contemporary records. For a while this seemed likely, as a group of Mexican military historians and academics announced plans for serious research on the French Intervention, with the intention of publishing the results in time for the Centenary in 1962.

Yet, despite this seemingly positive atmosphere, in the long run Penette and Castaignt actually gained very limited access to official Mexican records, and much of the specifically local material was located through the efforts of Castaignt, Louis Sol la Lande and Sousa. A great deal of the research had to be done in French military archives. The *Service Historique de l'Armee de Terre* was a major source, and fortunately the Foreign Legion's Archives in Sidi-bel-Abbes proved to have more on the overall campaign than they had been able to provide merely on Camerone for Brunon and Rollin in the late 1920s.

Castaignt, searching church records in Huatusco, pinpointed the grave of Sous-Lieutenant Maudet in the grounds of the historic Spanish Colonial church, known as the 'Viejo Iglesia' – Old Church – which had been seriously damaged by an earthquake in 1920. Although the structure had been badly weakened, it was twenty-two years before a decision was taken to pull it down and build a new church. Castaignt and Sousa examined records showing that on 12 May 1943 workmen had found the old grave that contained the remains of Sous-Lieutenant Maudet, eighty years and four days after he was buried.

A priest had been present when the coffin was opened and most of the remains crumbled away when touched. The exception was the skull, on which a few strands of blond hair were seen, before they turned to powder on being exposed to the air. Curiously, for Maudet had been wounded in the thigh and hip, the priest noted a fracture in the skull, such as might have been made by a bayonet or a sabre. The kepi was relatively intact, as was Maudet's sword, medals and the slightly-corroded gilt buttons on his uniform. The colours of the Tricolour ribbon which had been placed across his chest were still recognizable, with the gold letters spelling out *Gloria a las Armas Francia* still readable. The crucifix which Dona Juana Marrero de Gomez had placed in his hands was found, as was the little glass bottle. The stopper had deteriorated and humidity had damaged the slip of paper it contained, but the words '*murio el 8 May 1863 Francia*' were just legible.

The priest had made an inventory of the contents of the coffin, which was then stored until the new church would rise from the foundations of the old, at which time Sous-Lieutenant Maudet was re-buried at the foot of one of the columns in the nave. On 14 May 1959, Lieutenant-Colonel Sousa marked the grave with a rectangular marble plaque,[5] which read, in Spanish:

> Here lies Sous-Lieutenant Clement Maudet,
> of the Foreign Legion of France,
> who died in Huatusco, 8 May 1863,
> of wounds received in the
> Combat of Camaron on 30 April 1863

Early in 1960, with the support of his friends, Penette began actively exploring the idea of setting up a non-profit charitable and benevolent organization, which would be the legal entity to undertake the proposed erection of a monument to the dead of Camerone. There was enthusiastic support from General Jean Olie, Chief of Staff to President de Gaulle, General Paul Gardy, who had succeeded Olie as Commanding Officer of the *Groupement de la Legion Etrangere* and was now Inspector-General of the Foreign Legion, and feelers put out to a gaggle of General Officers in France, all of them ex-Legionnaires, produced favourable responses from Generals Pierre Koenig, Raoul Magrin-Vernerey – Monclar – and Zinovi Pechkoff. Marshal Alphonse Juin also endorsed the idea, as did General Maxime Weygand and General Miquel, who had commanded the 1st REC from 1943 until the end of the Second World War.

The Camerone Association was registered in Mexico City on 25 July 1960 by a group of twenty-seven French, Mexican and foreign nationals. The six-man executive was headed by Penette as President and Captain Louis Hallard as Executive Vice-President. Castaignt, designated as the Association's Historian, shared the post of Secretary General with Louis Sol la Lande. Andre Kuhn and Andre Lesur were, respectively, Secretary and Treasurer[6] and Manuel Gonzalez y

General Penette Dreams a Dream

Montesinos and Xavier Sol la Lande were among the Founding Members.

It was felt that the Association's aims would be helped by having the blessing of the President of France, and undoubtedly Minister of Defence Pierre Messmer, as an old Legionnaire, and already supportive of the Association's plans, had a considerable hand in selling the idea to the Head of State. Olie clearly also played a major role, and it was he who signed the letter conveying de Gaulle's blessing.[7] This enabled Colonel Francois Pepin-Lehalleur, who was occupying Penette's former position as Military Attache at France's embassy in Mexico City – and, like him, was a former Foreign Legion officer – to officially assist The Camerone Association. Encouraging letters of support were received from Prince Napoleon and the Count of Paris, both of whom had served briefly in the Foreign Legion at the beginning of the Second World War.[8]

The project, which became known as 'The Legionnaires Monument', now began to take on a life of its own. Minister Messmer was identifiably supportive, and Minister of Veterans Affairs and Victims of War Triboulet was also brought into the picture. Admiral Galleret, the Commissioner General of Monuments of Wars and the Resistance – *Monuments des Guerres et de la Resistance* – promised an annual budgetary appropriation for the upkeep of the proposed Monument and to also provide funding to build a house for a custodian.

General Koenig brought together thirty-two prominent people in a Committee of Patronage and within forty-eight hours received three cheques, each for a million Old Francs. The first came from Georges Pompidou on behalf of the Banque Rothschild, and the second from the Comte de Vogue, President and Director General of Sainte-Gobain. The third was from a donor who – perhaps in the best traditions of the Foreign Legion – requested anonymity. There were many other individual donations, too. For example, Guy de Berc, Director of the Compagnie Generale Trans-atlantique in New York, sent a thousand U.S. dollars directly to Penette.

As the plans called for The Camerone Association to acquire Mexican land on which to build 'The Legionnaires Monument', permissions had to be given by the Ministry of Foreign Relations, the State of Veracruz and the Municipality of Villa Adalberto Tejeda. These permissions were being sought in the early part of 1961 and the approval of the Ministry of Foreign Relations was actually being drafted when the world heard of the 'General's Putsch' in Algeria, an event which cast a pall of gloom over the Association, as there was much speculation that the Foreign Legion might be legislated out of existence. Fortunately, this did not happen and the various permissions were granted during the year.[9] The Association hoped to have the Monument fairly close to where the battle had actually been fought, but several pieces of public land offered by the Municipality were considered to be too small, while others were felt to be too far away. So the Association began looking at possible privately-owned sites and eventually, on 14 December, found a very suitable location. 'It respected the tradition, since it was beside the little river where Dr. Francisco Talavera tended the French wounded on the evening of 30 April, 1863,' Penette would explain later. Negotiations were opened with the owner, David Alarcon Barradas, a descendant of the Alarcon family, which had owned the Hacienda de la Trinidad at the time of the battle. The Camerone Association began the year 1962 with a great deal of hope and on 18 February agreed to buy ten hectares of land from Alarcon Barradas at three thousand pesos (about twelve hundred francs) each.

However, unknown to them, a situation was building which would seriously impact their plans. They were aware, of course, that the Mexicans were planning elaborate celebrations for the Centenary of the *Cinqo de Mayo*, their victory over General Lorencez's forces at Puebla on 5 May 1862. What they did not know was that the Government of Mexico had requested the return of several banners seized in June 1863, when Puebla finally fell, and which were kept at des Invalides in Paris as battle trophies. Unfortunately, the very month that the land deal for 'The Legionnaires Monument' was being finalized, the French Ambassador was politely telling the Mexican Government that the banners would not be returned. Immediately, what Penette would call 'The Affair of the Flags', became a serious problem.

'This resulted in a coldness in our relations with the Mexicans, and an uncertainty about the Camerone Celebrations,' he would say later.

The Association had selected architect Vladimir Kaspe, a Manchurian-born naturalized French citizen, long resident in Mexico, to design the Monument. French-trained, and holder of the *Grande Medaille* of the Society of Architects, he seemed to fit the bill very well, and Penette provided him with guidelines which expressed the Association's thinking. Kaspe's instructions were that the Monument should be simple, but dignified and imposing, capable of withstanding the vicissitudes of its location – the region is earthquake-prone – and, because of occasional prolonged droughts, should not overly rely on vegetation, either trees or flowers. Kaspe presented his drawings in March and they were unanimously accepted by his clients. Faustino Ortiz Garcia of Cordoba was contracted as the builder.

When the Combat of Camerone had been fought, the small dam north of the Orizaba Road was in ruins, and it was near it that Dr. Talavera had established his field hospital. The dam had subsequently been repaired to provide water for the hamlet, but was destroyed again during the revolutionary upheavals of 1910 and had never been fixed. The Municipality of Villa Adalberto Tejeda was enthusiastic about the idea of the Camerone Monument and when delays occurred in obtaining a fully valid land survey, and clear title to the Alarcon Barradas property, the Association suggested that their contractor could usefully expend some time repairing the old dam. On 14 May the work was commenced and by the end of the month three bulldozers were moved to the site of the Monument, to begin clearing land. Clear title was completed on 18 June and construction began in earnest.[10]

Penette, together with the Association's Secretary and Treasurer – Andre Kuhn and Andre Lesur – travelled to Paris the following month to discuss architect Kaspe's drawings with General Koenig and with General Morel, a veteran of Bir Hakeim and former Commanding Officer of the 13th *Demi-Brigade*, who had succeeded General Gardy as Inspector-General of the Foreign Legion. Their approval was immediate, followed by endorsement by Minister of Defence Messmer. A small model, made by Horio Tanasescu, was left in Paris to be part of a planned Foreign Legion exhibition at des Invalides to mark the Camerone

Centenary the following year, after which it would be given to the Foreign Legion for the Museum which it was hoped would be built at Aubagne.

Contractor Ortiz Garcia had his own problems, as virtually all the building materials – largely stone and cement, but marble, too, at a later date – had to be brought in by train. Even water had to come in by tanker cars, and in August the project became more costly when rolling stock space needed for hauling freshly-harvested sugarcane caused an increase in freight rates for the materials required for the Monument. The dam was completed in September at a cost of sixty-two thousand pesos – about twenty-five thousand francs – and, as well as helping the hamlet, would also solve the contractor's water problem and he began concentrating efforts on the Monument site.

Penette and Castaignt's book on the Regiment Etranger was published – in Spanish, of course – under the title of *La Legion Extranjera en la Intervencion Francesca*[11] later in the year, and was awarded a medal by the *Sociedad Mexicana de Geografia y Estadistica*. Central to it was the story of the Combat of Camerone and the authors had been able, from Mexican sources – mostly personal memoirs and State, rather than Federal, records – to gather some never-before-published snippets, not just about the Regiment Etranger's side of the battle but about the Mexican side, as well.

As progress was made on the Monument, the Foreign Legion began formulating its elaborate plans for the Camerone Centenary at its new home at the Camp de la Demand at Aubagne – which the men of the 1st Etranger were busily transforming – at des Invalides in Paris and at Camerone itself. Certain supercilious members of the French Army, perhaps jealous of all the activity, were heard to belittle the battle as a mere skirmish, and to scoff that the Foreign Legion, in a public relations exercise, was boosting it out of all proportion to its significance even to the Mexican Expedition, let alone to overall military importance. Other regiments, they said, had their own tales of glory, and special days – and had documentation to back up the stories. The Foreign Legion still had very little actual contemporary documentation to back up the saga of *La Compagnie Danjou*, and such criticisms always touched a raw nerve.

Therefore, when Lieutenant-Colonel Carles, working on records at the *Service Historique de l'Armee de Terre*, discovered General Ernest de Maussion's glowing report of his Inspection of the Regiment Etranger on 25 September 1863 – less than five months after Camerone – there was some excitement. The men of the 3rd Company of the 1st Battalion, de Maussion had said, 'immortalized the flag and its Regiment in sustaining at Camaron a heroic struggle of 62 against 1,800', and, although the Regiment Etranger had not had an opportunity 'to measure itself against the enemy at Puebla', they could console themselves 'with the thought that the Combat of Camaron will forever remain one of the most glorious episodes of the campaign in Mexico.' The Inspecting General had concluded: 'In the face of such an example, of what is such a Regiment not capable?'[12]

> The remarks expressed in these reports on troops were generally understood to reflect the sentiments of the Inspector [*Carles, hastening to communicate his documentary find, wrote enthusiastically to Brunon*]. Even at this early date

we see the impact of the exceptional aspects of the affair at Camerone for the men of the Expeditionary Corps in Mexico. This proves that Camerone is not a publicity invention of the modern Legion.[13]

Towards the end of the year The Camerone Association was horrified to learn that Veterans Affairs Minister Triboulet had unilaterally decided to have the graves of all French soldiers in the eastern part of Mexico relocated to Camerone. They protested vigorously, and began to marshal their forces against the idea, but the French Government ruled against it as far too costly.

The work continued apace and as of the early part of January 1963 the contractor had forty-eight workers engaged in construction at the Monument site and The Camerone Association began to believe it might be possible to have it completed in time for dedication in the second half of April. They also came to an agreement with the descendants of Dr. Francisco Talavera that a special mausoleum should be built at the Camerone Monument to house his remains. Born in Puebla on 21 September 1822, he had died in Cordoba on 9 February 1893 and was buried there, and his descendants had been very amenable to having his grave relocated.

Then came a bombshell. Fernando Lopez Arias, the new Governor of the State of Veracruz, who had taken office the previous December, suddenly announced that his predecessor's approval for the Monument to be constructed had been given without proper authority, and that he intended to cancel the authorization and seek an order for all construction work to cease.

Hiding its anger, the Association reacted temperately, saying that any such action would be contrary to all normal usage, and protested that the work was too far advanced for any cancellation to be either fair or reasonable. It was suspected that the Governor was merely using 'The Legionnaires Monument' as a means of distracting public opinion away from important and contentious local issues. They also pointed out that by taking this extreme step the Governor would be depriving his own State of an opportunity to recognize Dr. Talavera as one of the real heroes of the Mexican Republican Army during the French Intervention. However, in the meantime, the Governor's objections and threats seemed serious enough for General Koenig to decide that no further monies from the Camerone Memorial Appeal should be transferred to Mexico until the situation was clarified.

The Association still perceived a 'coldness' on the part of many Mexican Federal and State officials over 'The Affair of the Flags' and sent President de Gaulle a brief on the matter, setting out all sides of the controversy. It so happened that President Lopez Mateos of Mexico was at that very moment on an official visit to France. Not privy to the behind-the-scenes diplomacy and political niceties, the Association noted with satisfaction the news that de Gaulle had accepted an invitation to pay a return official visit to Mexico the following year. As a result, there was no more meddling over the Camerone Monument by the Governor of Veracruz, at least for the time being.

While all this was going on, there occurred in Paris a little footnote to a footnote of history which had a sidebar interest in the story of Camerone. Genevieve de Galard, the French Air Force nurse who had been made an Honourary Legionnaire

1st Class on Camerone Day at Dien Bien Phu, was out driving with her husband when she spotted Major Vadot's Orderly, her Legionnaire 'godfather', walking along a street. They stopped the car and, after an embrace, she was happy to make good on her promise of nine years earlier to buy him a bottle of champagne in the – then seemingly unlikely – event that they both survived the siege.[14]

As the weeks went by, The Camerone Association had to agonizingly come to terms with the fact that the Monument could not be completed in time for the Centenary, so efforts were made to at least have it as 'finished'-looking as possible, more like a Cenotaph than a construction site. The Foreign Legion had had disappointments before, and was used to muddling through, usually managing to successfully disguise the fact and turning a necessity into a virtue. So plans were made with the French and Mexican armies, and with the politicians – both French and Mexican – all pulling together, to bring off a Dedication, rather than an Inauguration, an event which would be fitting, if not definitive. It was agreed that the ceremonies should take place ten days before the actual anniversary of Camerone, so as to enable serving officers and men of the Foreign Legion to return to their bases in France and elsewhere in time for regimental celebrations.

> On the 5th and 6th of April 1963, the old 1892 gravestone was raised with great care, happily without damage [*Penette would say later*]. The old funeral chamber was opened in the presence of some officials and many sympathizers. Victor Perez Duran, a notary public from Cordoba, represented the Government of the State of Vera Cruz at the exhumation, and with others took a detailed inventory of the remains collected. Two galvanized iron containers had been prepared. The remains originally buried in two mahogany chests were reverently put into the containers. Louis Sol la Lande made sure that he personally positioned the lids, sealed them with pliers, then soldered them shut.[15]

Captain Castaignt represented French Consul-General Durieux. Paul Soubic, President of the Association of Former Combatants, was among those present, as were Angel Batiz, Ramon and Ignacio Molina Enriquez. Jacques de Choulot, whose grandfather had fought in the *Brigade Etrangere* in the Crimean War, and Raul Sempe Montalvo, grandson of French Consul Edouard Sempe, who had overseen the creation of the 1892 monument, were particularly interested spectators. Penette had put a handful of the debris from each of the mahogany chests into a small canvas bag before the galvanized containers were soldered up by Sol la Lande. They were then taken to the Monument and lowered into their new resting place. The old gravestone had been cleaned and was placed on a litter and left on the platform of the Cameron railway station, where it would remain until the delegation from Paris arrived.

35
Danjou's Hand Goes Back to Mexico

The articulated wooden hand of Captain Jean Danjou returned to Mexico on 18 April 1963, safe in its wood and glass casket and accompanied by Rene Danjou, the last surviving member of the family. They had travelled from Paris with the Foreign Legion's forty-strong Official Party, led by General Olie, leaving Orly Airport the previous day and breaking their journey in the Azores and Bermuda.[1]

A great deal of thought had gone into the make-up of the Official Party, which included writer Georges-R. Manue, author of books and articles about his service in the Foreign Legion, and co-author of the 1958 edition of the *Livre d'Or*, who was present in a dual capacity. In his reportorial account of the '*Pelerinage a Camerone*' – 'Pilgrimage to Camerone' – he explained that 'the Colonels of the two oldest regiments, the 1st and 2nd Etrangers, represented the Legion of today, two retired Colonels that of yesterday.'

Those of the 'Legion of Today' were Colonel Vaillant of the 1st Etranger, who was also a former Commanding Officer of the 13th *Demi-Brigade*, and Colonel Romet of the 2nd REI. The 'Legion of Yesterday' was represented by Colonel Louis Gaultier – who had commanded the *Regiment de March de la Legion Etrangere* in late 1944 and early 1945, before handing over to the then Colonel Olie, and had then commanded both the 1st REI and the *Depot Commun des Regiments Etrangers* at Sidi-bel-Abbes – and by Colonel Charles Jacquot, who had commanded the 3rd REI in 1950–51 and then spent three years as Commanding Officer of the 2nd REI.

These were dedicated long-serving Foreign Legion officers – the true believers – and Gaultier and Jacquot would be using their presence on the delegation to prepare a firsthand report on the ceremonies at the Camerone Monument for their soon-to-be-published history of the Foreign Legion.

It had also been decided that that there should be participants from both the First and Second World Wars – 'two former officers of the Legion, one for the soldiers of '14–'18, the other for those who, in '40–'44, served under the grenade,' as Manue put it. Leon Nicolai, a former Tsarist officer who had served with Rollet's *Regiment de Marche de la Legion Etrangere*, and was now President of the Society of Former Legionnaires in the United States of America, had flown down from San Francisco to represent the Legionnaires of the First World War, and Manue himself had accepted 'the honour of going on the pilgrimage' to represent the Legionnaires of the Second World War.[2]

The delegation was somewhat multi-layered, with both military and diplomatic representatives, among them General Lefort, a former Commanding Officer of the 2nd REP, who had replaced General Morel as Inspector-General of the Foreign

Legion, Counsellor de la Fourniere of the Ministry of Defence, and General Jean Compagnon, Military Attache at the French Embassy in Washington, a group certainly diverse enough to keep French Ambassador Raymond Offroy busy, and also his Military Attache, Colonel Pepin-Lehalleur. Lieutenant-Colonel Victor Manuel Ruiz of the Mexican Army's 2nd Bureau had been assigned to act as Olie's aide-de-camp.

Other senior Foreign Legion officers, past and present, had been included to represent the various Foreign Legion regiments. Colonel Thevenon was a former Commanding Officer of the 2nd REI, Colonel Laimay had succeeded Jacquot as Commanding Officer of the 3rd REI in 1951, and Lieutenant-Colonel Nougues was scheduled to take command of the 5th REI the following month. The casket containing Captain Danjou's hand had been entrusted to the care of Captain Camus.

Additionally, there were twelve Sous-Officiers – including Adjutant-Chefs Della Rosa and Egel and *Clarion* Sergeant-Chef Esperou – drawn from the various regiments. Secretary-General Arakelian represented the *Association des anciens officiers combattants de l'armee francaise a titre etranger*, and there was a press corps, including journalists from *Paris Match*, Agence France Presse, *Le Figaro*, the Associated Press, *France-Soir* and the *Service cinematographique de l'Armee*.

The Camerone Association was represented by its Founder and President, General Penette, Executive Vice-President Captain Hallard, Historian and Co-Secretary-General Captain Castaignt and member and First World War veteran Manuel Gonzalez y Montesinos.

Present on their own accounts were three former Legionnaires. The Georgian Prince Major Alexander Djintcheradze, much admired by the English Legionnaire A.R. Cooper, who had served under him in Morocco in the mid-1920s – and who had hosted the British soldier-writer Patrick Turnbull at Bou Malem a decade later – had travelled down from New York. Former Legionnaire Francois Slistan arrived from Chicago and Laszlo Pataky, who in 1952 had written a book[3] about his service with the 13th *Demi-Brigade*, flew up from his home in Guatemala.

The Official Party set off early on 19 April for Puebla, riding in rather luxurious air-conditioned buses. They laid a wreath at the Franco-Mexican military monument in the French Cemetery and then went to visit the statue of General Ignacio Zaragoza, where a Mexican bugler sounded '*Aux Morts*' – the 'Last Post' – as another wreath was laid. There was a visit to the museum at Fort Lorenzo, which Manue called 'a sanctuary of Mexican patriotism', but although he liked 'the very well done dioramas reconstructing the Battle of Puebla', he considered that much of the museum seemed to be 'without passion'. Colonels Gaultier and Jacquot thought the museum rather poor on all fronts, but were interested in some 80 mm light mountain guns made in France in 1903, about which they could learn nothing.

The Generals, Colonels, some of the Sous-Officiers and the Directors of The Camerone Association were then taken to City Hall, where they were made Honourary Citizens of Puebla, and the Mayor was given a Camerone Centenary souvenir medallion featuring Captain Danjou. The Mexican national anthem was played, followed by the *Marseillaise* and the *Marche Lorraine*, which Manue, Gaultier and Jacquot all thought were excellently rendered.

Afterwards they went to the Hotel Lastra, where they found that those who had not been invited to City Hall were in full control, pounding a piano and giving lusty voice to *Le Boudin* and the *Chant of the 1st REC*, which contains the line: 'He has served with Honour and Fidelity in the 1st Foreign Cavalry.' The party left soon afterwards for Orizaba to spend the night, moving on early in the morning of Saturday, 20 April, to Huatusco.

There a rude surprise awaited them. The air-conditioned luxury buses were staying where they were and the remaining forty-eight kilometres (almost thirty miles), down into the humid *Terres Chaudes*, was to be travelled over an unmade track in Mexican Army trucks. Manue was amused as the senior officers and diplomats, in their neatly pressed uniforms and suits, clambered into the backs of the trucks. He wondered when they had last used that mode of transport. Gaultier and Jacquot were told that the region was not particularly safe, being subject to occasional depredations by bandits, and were doubtless glad of the many isolated Army posts and checkpoints scattered along the rough road.

At Villa Adalberto Tejeda – Camaron – they were met by the Mayor, Rafael Molina Enriquez, and by Carlos Talavera, descendant of Dr. Francisco Talavera, the soldier-doctor of the Combat of Camerone. Wreaths were laid at plinths in memory of Independence heroes Miguel Hidalgo and Jose Maria Morelos.

'Camaron is a very poor and dusty village,' Gaultier and Jacquot would write later. 'Its streets are traversed by horses and carts far more frequently than by automobiles. A few large Flamboyants provided perches for the 'zopilotes', a kind of sad carrion-eater, but the vegetation was very sparse.'

On the railway station platform, beside the old grave of the 3rd of the 1st, the 1892 marble gravestone was waiting to be taken to the new Monument. *Clarion* Sergeant-Chef Esperou sounded '*garde a vous*' and the litter bearing the slab was lifted for its journey. It was an occasion of great emotion, with an eight-man pallbearer party, and looking back later, those who reported on the matter had different memories concerning their identities.

Penette remembered them as having been himself, General Lefort, Colonels Vaillant and Romet, Manuel Gonzalez y Montesinos, Rene Danjou and Adjutant-Chefs Egel and Della Rosa. Manue recalled the pallbearers as General Lefort and 'five officers and sous-officiers, the Mayor of Camerone and the descendant of Captain Danjou.' Colonels Gaultier and Jacquot said the gravestone was escorted by Penette, Lefort, Rene Danjou and 'several Legionnaires, former and active'. These four eyewitnesses had different memories of the participants, and Lieutenant-Colonel Louis Garros, who was not present, was given to understand that the two Sous-Officiers were Adjutant-Chefs Schacht and Torne-Sistero. *Kepi blanc*, in a later report, agreed that Schacht and Torne-Sistero were the two Adjutant-Chefs involved, along with General Lefort and Colonels Vaillant and Romet and Gonzalez y Montesinos, added General Olie and Counsellor de La Forniere of the Ministry of Defence, but left out Penette and Rene Danjou.[4]

In the grand scheme of things, it probably does not matter who escorted the gravestone to its new location. It was sufficient that it reached its destination safely and was there lowered reverently into its new position.

The overall Monument, of course, was still unfinished, but Manue thought the 'grandeur' and 'simplicity' were right for the occasion. A detachment from the 13th Infantry Regiment of Veracruz was drawn up on parade, with quite a large crowd present, Gaultier and Jacquot subsequently mentioning 'the representatives of many French and Mexican organizations, with their flags . . . and the entire population of the village.'

Captain Camus stepped forward and laid the casket containing Captain Danjou's wooden hand on the gravestone.

'The emotion was intense,' Gaultier and Jacquot would write later. 'It was the defining moment of the pilgrimage, the unforgettable spark between the ghosts of the Legionaires which had been there for a hundred years, and the hearts of the delegation, who bore witness by their presence to the living thoughts of every Legionnaire in the world.'

General Penette spoke on behalf of The Camerone Association. Then General Olie, in ringing phrases – reminiscent of the words of Colonel Pierre Jeanningros at the grave of the 3rd of the 1st in February 1867 – spoke in the name of the Foreign Legion.

'The veneration of the dead, of those killed in battle, knows no frontiers, no oblivion,' he said. 'In the face of the supreme sacrifice of the soldier, the notion of enemy is erased. It is their example that we are obligated, very modestly, to emulate if we must.'

Mayor Molina Enriquez spoke on behalf of the village, wreaths were laid and Colonel Laimay read the *Recit de Camerone*. A firing party from the 13th Infantry fired a salvo over the grave and Esperou sounded *Aux Morts*. The Mexican bugler responded. The Absolution was given by Bernault de Salaignac, curate to the French Parish in Mexico, himself a former Military Chaplain, and by the local priest. They then conducted Communion, assisted by a Protestant clergyman. The Mayor and the local priest had both spoken in Spanish, 'a language which we did not comprehend,' Manue said – but which made the Foreign Legion party think of the men of the 3rd of the 1st who had heard Colonel Milan haranguing his troops just before the final assault at the hacienda.

General Lefort then conferred the *Medaille Militaire* on Adjutant-Chefs Egel and Della Rosa and presented insignia to Captains Castaignt and Hallard of The Camerone Association, making them Honourary Legionnaires 1st Class, in recognition of their efforts in bringing the idea of the Camerone Monument to fruition.

The Official Party then moved to the – still empty – marble tomb for Dr. Talavera. A wreath was laid, a salvo fired, and Ambassador Offroy spoke of the events of 30 April 1863. Manue noted that the soldier-doctor's great-grandson, Carlos Talavera, was moved to tears as he shook hands with Captain Danjou's great-great-nephew, Rene, in front of the tomb.

The ceremony over, the Mayor invited the Official Party to his home for a wash and refreshments. Gaultier and Jacquot remembered 'the beer and cold drinks', and that girls from the village served 'the famous 'Camaron,' delicious crayfish with long pincers, who had given their name to the stream and the village, along with olives and a dry and strong cheese.' As their shyness evaporated, Manue heard the girls whispering breathlessly together: 'These are the Legionnaires!'

Then it was over and the Official Party clambered once more into the Mexican Army trucks and bounced their way back along the rough road to Huatusco. There they rejoined their air-conditioned buses and set off for Veracruz, arriving near midnight. Awakened early the following morning by the sounds of bugles, drums and marching men, they saw Mexican soldiers and Marines parading at a monument near the Hotel Emporia. It was a Mexican feast day, but the Foreign Legion delegation had other things to do. Boarding several launches, they cruised along the outer walls of the old Fort San Juan d'Ulloa, and then went to the Isla de los Sacrificios, where so many French soldiers, including Legionnaires, had been buried after succumbing to the dreaded *vomito negro*. A wreath was laid at the monument erected to the French dead.

Back in the city, they were entertained at a reception given by Dr. Raul Sempe Montalvo, grandson of the man who had overseen the erection of the 1892 Monument. Consul Edouard Sempe's official garb – a long coat, with the Legion d'Honneur on it, a bicorne hat and a sword – were displayed in the main room and Dr. Sempe spoke about how his ancestor had been able to prevent violence against the small resident French community after Marshal Bazaine's Expeditionary Corps left Mexico in early 1867, and of his role in marking the grave at Camerone twenty-five years later. General Olie replied. Gaultier and Jacquot were moved, saying that the words of the two men 'went right to the hearts of all of us'.

The Official Party then set out for Mexico City, driving through the late afternoon and evening and finishing the four-hundred-and-fifty kilometre (two hundred and eighty-mile) journey well into the night. Yet they were up early the following morning – 22 April – to accompany Olie as he laid a huge wreath, with a blue-white-and-red ribbon saying *L'Armee Francaise*, at the Independence Memorial. An informal visit to the home of Military Attache Pepin-Lahalleur was followed by a formal reception at the residence of Ambassador Offroy.

There General Penette presented General Lefort with the small canvas bag containing earth and fragments which he had taken from the grave of the 3rd of the 1st earlier in the month, when the contents were being placed in the galvanized containers to be moved to the Camerone Monument. The bag, said Penette, was to be given to the planned Foreign Legion Museum.

The delegation arrived back in Paris on 25 April, loaded with souvenir sombreros and other tourist knick-knacks and going their separate ways, the serving officers and Sous-Officiers heading back to their regiments in Corsica, Djibouti and Madagascar. Manue said he recognized 'some joyous impatience among those of our comrades who would be returning to their garrisons for 30 April', anxious to tell about their visit to Camerone. Colonels Gaultier and Jacquot had to now rapidly write up their account of the Dedication of the Camerone Monument to complete their ambitious three-volume work – a full-scale history of the Foreign Legion, called *Honneur et Fidelite: C'est La Legion* – which was due for publication later in the year, lavishly illustrated with vivid line drawings and paintings by Louis Fregier.[5]

The main Centenary Celebrations were to be staged in Paris and at Aubagne, and there would be commemorations wherever the Foreign Legion was based, though for obvious political reasons nothing especially elaborate had been planned for those stationed in Algeria.

Lieutenant-Colonel Chenel saw his role as to keep the 2nd REP out of trouble, and once Independence had come, and the regiment had moved to Bou Sfer, there was initially construction work and road building until the new plans for the 2nd REP had been announced by General Lefort the previous December. Legionnaire Murray was now engaged in practice as a member of a Foreign Legion team involved in the French national shooting championships, and the way he told it, Camerone Day at Bou Sfer did little more than mark another milestone in his service: 'Routine now,' he reported in his Diary. 'Sideshows, chariot races, jousting, boxing and drinking.'[6]

A special Centenary publication – *Camerone 1863–1963* – had been issued by the *Service Information de la Legion Etrangere*[7] and *Kepi blanc* had published articles on places visited by men of the Regiment Etranger in Mexico in 1863 and on the building of the Camerone Monument, illustrating both with photographs by Castaignt.[8] The *Federation des Societes d'Anciens de la Legion Etrangere* put out a publication called *Centenaire du Combat de Camerone*[9] and Jean Brunon, as might have been expected, had made a special effort, authoring a small book titled simply *Camerone*, which brought together much of what he had learned during years of research.[10]

General Koenig officiated at the Centenary Celebrations at des Invalides, where the Regimental Standard of the First World War's 2nd *Regiment de Marche du 2nd Etranger* took pride of place. It is kept at the *Musee de l'Armee*, concurrently mounting an exhibit on the Foreign Legion which included the model of the Camerone Monument that Penette had left with Koenig in July of the previous year.[11]

General Olie, Captain Camus, as custodian of Danjou's hand, and Manue did not linger in Paris, as they needed to be at Aubagne in plenty of time for the celebrations, which were to get under way on the evening of 29 April with an elaborate *son et lumiere* – sound and light show – at an open air theatre nearby.

Manue found the Camp de la Demande completely changed, transformed into a new Quartier Vienot.

> The Spring in Provence, a little late this year, gave to the country a charm and freshness . . . [*he wrote*] The camp covered a very large area where big clusters of trees hid the living quarters . . . The direction of the roads was dictated by the nature of the forest. They were gracefully winding and were edged with flowers. In the heart of the estate, the *Voie Sacree* of Bel-Abbes had been reconstructed step by step, fitting in with the features of the land. When finished the monument stood, as it had at Bel-Abbes, on an immense rectangular parade ground. The bronze globe on which were engraved the places where the Legion had fought glistened in the sun, giving an added charm to the foliage. The statues which guarded it were of the Legionnaires of the major epochs of 1831 to 1931. The overall effect was truly noble, set against its background of wooded mountains.[12]

At the *son et lumiere*, held in the presence of Defence Minister Messmer, the stage was surmounted by a huge sign reading: **LEGIO PATRIA NOSTRA**.

> The public had come in large numbers from all around, and also from Marseille [*Manue wrote*]. [In the] shadows, the notes of the *Clarions* and the drums of the *Tambours* were made majestic by the projectors surrounding the actors in ten sketches representing the great battles of the Legion, from Magenta to Mexico, from Tonkin to Morocco, those of the War of '14–'18 and of '39–'45 and those of Indo-China and Algeria. The stirring commentary was given in language and image which was always emphatic . . . and the audience of children, young women, Legionnaires, workers and people from the neighbourhood, listened with lumps in their throats, thrilled by the exploding of bombs and the gusts of wind, and responded with pride and frenzied applause.[13]

Manue considered the parade at the new Quartier Vienot on the morning of Camerone Day, 30 April, to have been a triumph.

> The parade unfolded regally, the movements near perfection [*he wrote*]. At the front were the Sappers, their aprons in the traditional white leather of their predecessors in the Imperial Army. They surrounded an Adjutant carrying in its glass casket the wooden hand of Captain Danjou. The rhythm of *La Musique*, the elongated strides of the march, the swinging of the arms. There was nothing mechanical in the gait, but the power of the majesty of the Roman Legions which I always think of, gathering round their eagles, the *Tertia Augusta of* Mauritania, who constructed roads and cities and whose footprints were the Legion's natural setting. . . The afternoon of the 30th, they played host to their friends in a superlative funfair, with numerous games and kiosks, and many games of chance. The camp belonged to them and they blushed with pleasure over the many compliments they received.[14]

Manue forgot to mention that one special touch: in its new position the *Monument aux Morts* faced south – towards Algeria.

'The last shot is fired, we are back to zero,'[15] an officer remarked to him, and, writing immediately afterwards, Manue pursued the thought: 'The Centenary of Camerone marked – one could say – the beginning of a new era for the Legion. It had moved away from its despair. This had given it confidence and opened up new horizons.'[16]

He was correct, of course, even if it was not immediately apparent. Recruitment was down and in the very month of the Camerone Centenary, only sixteen men signed engagement papers – the smallest number for any month in the past twenty years – while long-serving Legionnaires were leaving. Adjutant Kemencei retired in August after seventeen years of service,[17] and the Foreign Legion was being very selective with its intake.

When seventeen-year-old Jon Swain engaged, a blind eye was blinked at his age, but not about his stated ambition to become a journalist. Midway through his training an officer of the Deuxieme Bureau bluntly told him in an interview: 'No journalists here!' and he was summarily released from his contract. He went on to become a noted foreign correspondent and author, his Indo-China-set book *River of Time*[18] being filmed as 'The Killing Fields'.

Canadian-born author Charles Mercer travelled to Puyloubier and visited the chapel where 'among other mementoes of the past, stand Legion regimental Colours, splendid with honours, but growing dusty in the dim light that flows through stained glass windows', while they waited to be moved to the yet-to-be-built Museum at the Quartier Vienot. Mercer then went to Aubagne. The *Voie Sacre* and the *Monument aux Morts* were there, of course, but it was only half the story. The troops were actually living in broken-down buildings scattered around the camp, tucked away out of sight.

> Dilapidated-looking wooden barracks scattered among the brush along dusty tracks housed squads of Legionnaires [*Mercer reported*]. There was an air of impermanence about the camp that Summer that reflected the mood of uncertainty and restlessness in the Legion.
>
> [There are] plans for a new and better installation rising from the brush and decrepit barracks it [has] inherited. The plan is on paper, in cardboard models, in the minds of many Legionnaires.

'It will happen, you have my word on it,' his officer guide told him. 'I can't say when. Maybe 1965 or 1966. But it will happen. It will be just like this...'. He gestured to the models.[19]

The Legion was still restructuring and, with the lease on the nuclear testing sites running out, plans had been made for the 5th REI to be redeployed to French Polynesia in the South Pacific. In June the regiment sent a detachment from Colomb-Bechar to Tahiti and another left for Mururoa in September. The 5th Mixed Pacific Regiment (5th RMP) – Legionnaires and French Army Engineers – came into being, with Lieutenant-Colonel Nougues as Commanding Officer, on 1 October, a month later the 5th REI was formally disbanded, the new 5th RMP inheriting its traditions and Regimental Standard.

In Mexico, The Camerone Association was pressing ahead with its plans. Penette and Gonzalez y Montesinos, who had succeeded him as President of the Association, came to hear that France's new Minister of Veterans Affairs and Victims of War – Minister Sainteny, successor to Minister Triboulet – had resuscitated his predecessor's idea of relocating all French military graves in eastern Mexico to Camerone. The proposal was subsequently dropped again. State Governor Lopez Arias was once more taking a keen – and not always very welcome – interest in the Monument, and The Association spent much time dealing with him. Finally, at a meeting with the French Ambassador on 28 November, he gave his approval, and, seeking some political mileage, he urged that it be completed during his term of office.

The other irritant to harmonious Franco-Mexican relations over the Camerone Monument was removed early in 1964, when 'The Affair of the Flags' was finally settled. The French returned three Mexican banners captured at Puebla in 1863, doing so on 5 March, just eleven days before President de Gaulle began his official visit to Mexico.

Work continued slowly on the Monument. In truth, it had never really stopped, but The Camerone Association had sought to keep a low profile while contention over the flags, and problems with the Governor of the State, had had the potential to cause difficulties. Now that these obstacles had been removed work moved forward on the overall physical structure.

The part of the Monument calling for trees and shrubs was in the hands of Jacques de Choulot, to whom the job was not just a job. His great-grandfather, the Comte Paul de Choulot, had joined the Foreign Legion as a Sous-Lieutenant in 1842 and served for fifteen years. As the Lieutenant of the 1st Etranger's Company of Voltigeurs he had stormed the heights of the Alma and taken part in the siege of Sebastopol, being twice wounded, promoted to Captain and decorated with the Legion of Honneur, then leaving to become a Lieutenant-Colonel in a Regiment of the Line in 1857. Cypresses and flowering bougainvillea were planted at the Monument, and it pleased landscaper de Choulot to think that his grandfather and Captain Danjou, although in different regiments of the *Brigade Etrangere*, must have known each other.

Mexican officialdom tends to love statues and Governor Lopez Arias was especially keen on them. As he had now given his blessing to the Monument project, he was determined to have a say in the planning, but many of his ideas ran contrary to the thinking of both The Camerone Association and the Foreign Legion. Consequently, Penette was to say later: 'Deciding on a decorative motif symbolizing Franco-Mexican friendship was laborious.' The Association rejected a suggestion that the Monument should feature statues of Captain Danjou and Colonel Milan, Penette and Gonzalez y Montesinos, gently explaining that this would be 'too personalized'. An idea for statues of a Mexican soldier and a French soldier shaking hands was turned down, because there was already one in the French Cemetery at Puebla. Then a suggestion was put forward concerning statues of a Mexican Militiaman and a Foreign Legionnaire. This was rejected as being 'a little too allegorical'.

Eventually, it was agreed that a wall should be built slightly behind the head of the gravestone and that large bronze plaques of both the Mexican Eagle and the Eagle which had adorned the flagstaff of the Regiment Etranger during the Mexican Expedition should be affixed to it. Between the two Eagles would be the words VIRTUTI MILITARI – MILITARY VIRTUE – in large bronze letters. A well-known Mexican sculptor, Juan Olaguibel, was commissioned to make the two bronze Eagles, which were to be fully one-point-eight metres (almost six feet) tall. Artisans at Puyloubier made a mould of the Eagle of the Regiment Etranger – the same Eagle that had been rescued from the Oran junkshop almost a century earlier – and shipped it to sculptor Olaguibel. These further delays forced the Association to face the fact that there was no way that everything could be ready, as had originally been hoped,[20] for a full-scale Inauguration of the Monument in 1964.

By contrast, work on the Quartier Vienot at Aubagne continued rapidly. It was believed that the climate of the South of France would be suitable for subtropical trees and some flamboyant saplings were sent to Aubagne by landscaper de Choulot. A stone from the old wall of the Hacienda de la Trinidad was recovered and sent to Puyloubier, along with the wrought iron fence which had surrounded the 1892 grave. It was re-erected in the Foreign Legion cemetery, where Rollet, Aage and Zimmerman were buried,[21] and where other Legionnaires would be interred in the coming years. Minister of Defence Messner had finally been able to authorize expenditure for a Foreign Legion Museum and visited Aubagne on Camerone Day 1964 to formally lay the foundation stone. A less happy event concurrently taking place was the dissolving of the 4th REI, which had been guarding the Sahara oil fields at Touggouart since July of 1962.

At Bou Sfer, where the 2nd REP was still ensconced, the concerns about ostentatious ceremonies ensured that Camerone Day was about the same as the previous year for Murray, now a Corporal-Chef. '[It] went quietly by,' he noted in his Diary. 'We had the usual stands and everybody got drunk and that was about it.'[22] It would be his last, as his engagement would end early the following year.

It was rather more memorable for Worden, who had transferred into the 2nd REP the previous September and was now also a Corporal-Chef. He had just received from Paris a long-playing record called 'Camerone', which, somewhat to his surprise, instead of being about the battle, had turned out to be the story of the fall of Dien Bien Phu. Perhaps because he was himself a veteran of the Second World War, and was older than the majority of Legionnaires with his length of service and rank, Worden enjoyed a certain familiarity and relationship with the senior Sous-Officiers that would have been denied to most of his contemporaries. Consequently, on the eve of Camerone Day he felt emboldened to invite three veteran Sous-Officiers, all of whom had been at Dien Bien Phu ten years earlier, to listen to the record with him. It was an extremely emotional experience for all four men. Indeed, Worden was so moved by it all that '[I] volunteered myself the dirtiest job in the Legion on Camerone Day, as corporal of the guard,' he said later, remembering the surprise and delight of the man he replaced.[23]

Later in the year the first detachment of the 2nd REP left Bou Sfer for Calvi in Corsica, which was destined to become the regiment's new home. Lieutenant-Colonel Robert Caillaud, who had assumed command in May 1963, was another of the alumni of Dien Bien Phu, an experienced paratroop officer with big plans for his regiment and the connections and backing to make them happen. The other Foreign Legion regiments were still scattered about the world, some of them in places where leases were fast running out, others where it had been agreed they should not remain.

On 9 June 1964 General Raoul Magrin-Vernerey – Monclar – of the 13th *Demi-Brigade* and the Free French Forces, was buried as he had lived, among his Legionnaires. Governor of des Invalides for the past two years, he was the holder of virtually every French military decoration and civil honour, and of gallantry medals from Britain and the United States. The funeral took place at des Invalides, in the presence of President de Gaulle, Minister of Defence Messmer and other political and military dignitaries. A battalion of the 1st Etranger, complete with its Regimental Standard and *La Musique*, and under the personal command of Colonel Vadot, who had fought with the 13th *Demi-Brigade* at Dien Bien Phu and commanded the 4th REI in 1961, was in attendance.[24]

In Mexico, Captain Castaignt, the Historian of The Camerone Association, died, but Governor Lopez Arias finally gave official approval of the plans for the

Camerone Memorial in a letter to the French Ambassador dated 7 August 1964. Early the following year Gonzalez y Montesinos relinquished the Presidency of the Association to Dr. Efren Marin, but it was not until the second half of 1965 that all phases of the Monument were completed and arrangements could be made for a definitive Inauguration in mid-December.

There was considerable excitement when General Olie advised that he would once again be available to travel to Mexico.[25] The delegation, he informed The Camerone Association, would be much smaller than the one for the Dedication in April 1963, and would actually be led by General Koenig, who would be the personal representative of Minister of Defence Messmer. The other members of the delegation would be General Miquel, who had led the 1st REC from late 1943 until the end of the war, Colonel Vadot of the 1st Etranger, who was the Foreign Legion's longest-serving *Chef de Corps*, and Captain Gomez Urtizberea of the 1st Etranger, the longest-serving officer. They would be accompanied by Admiral Galleret, representing the Minister of Veterans Affairs.

The Official Party arrived on 13 December and was met by French Ambassador Jacques Vimont and representatives of The Camerone Association: General Penette, Gonzalez y Montesinos and Dr. Marin, respectively the first three Presidents of the Association, along with Executive Vice-President Hallard. Colonel Miguel Rodriguez Iturralde of the 26th Military Zone of Veracruz represented the Army of Mexico.

Courtesy calls and the inevitable cocktail parties and receptions occupied the evening and most of the next day, but early in the morning of 15 December the formal party arrived at Villa Adalberto Tejeda – Camaron/Cameron – where they were greeted by the new Mayor, Antonio Couttolenc Espinosa. As before, wreaths were laid at the plinths to Hidalgo and Morelos, and Koenig also laid one at a small pyramid-shaped cairn, which had been erected in the main street and in which Governor Lopez Arias had plans to relocate the remains of General Milan. The delegation had been joined by Carlos Talavera, who had come from Cordoba, and they all paused at the tomb of his soldier-doctor ancestor, whose remains had already been re-interred.

General Olie must have been most pleasantly surprised to see the changes made since his first visit more than two-and-a-half years before. The whole area of the monument had been flag-stoned and enclosed with a waist-high stone wall. At the head of the actual grave was a white stone wall, to which were affixed the two bronze Eagles, with the words VIRTUTI MILITARI prominent between them. The gravestone itself was now surrounded by a bronze border and the green-white-and-red Mexican flag fluttered from a flagpole to its right and the blue-white-and-red Tricolour of France to the left. The trees had taken root well.[26]

Members of The Camerone Association, French and Mexican nationals interested in the story of Camerone, and about half the population of Villa Adalberto Tejeda, were present, and as the Official Party arrived at the graveside a detachment of the 13th Infantry Regiment of Veracruz, who had officiated at the Dedication, presented arms.

A wreath of red and green was placed at the foot of the grave. Ambassador Vimont spoke for France and Couttolenc Espinosa for the Municipality.

Camerone Association President Marin had been delayed en route so Hallard read his brief remarks. Then Koenig stepped forward to read the Inaugurating Message from Minister Messmer.

> It was a little more than a century ago, the 30th April 1863, at six o'clock in the evening, very close to here, that a Colonel of the Mexican Army accorded the honours of war to the few Legion survivors of a desperate battle [*Messmer had written*]. And, in the very place where the Monument you have come to inaugurate now stands, the Mexican officer rendered aid to the wounded of the 3rd Company of the 1st Battalion of the Foreign Legion.
>
> Today again, the Mexicans are at your side to honour the memory of those who died with Honour and Fidelity. And the Mexican soil offers them, in the place of their sacrifice, a grave worthy of their heroism.
>
> So it is that in the lofty cult of military virtues, the adversaries of the past are the friends today, recognizing each other as brothers in arms.
>
> Nothing is needed to exalt Camerone, nor the unsurpassed men who fought here. The name, which is embroidered in letters of gold on the flags and standards of the Foreign Regiments, as it is graven in our memory, remains the symbol of the spirit of sacrifice. This monument offers a tangible remembrance of the heroes who lie beneath these stones in their last sleep.
>
> The Army of France is associated with this commemoration of Camerone, and with all those, Mexicans, French and veterans of the Foreign Legion, who are here together.
>
> Today, no less than yesterday, I do not forget that I have had the honour of fighting with you, in the ranks of the Foreign Regiments. I would like to be at Camerone at this time, and I have asked the representative of my Ministry to express my personal sentiments.[27]

Dr. Marin had arrived while Messmer's message was being read. He now accompanied Koenig and Ambassador Vimont to the white back wall of the Monument, where the bronze Eagles, flanking the words VIRTUTI MILITARI, were affixed. Beneath the Eagles, in French and Spanish, respectively, was carved HOMAGE TO THE COMBATANTS OF CAMERONE, and between them the dates: 30-IV-1863, 30-IV-1963. As the soldiers presented arms, the General, the Diplomat and the Doctor stood first in front of the Mexican Eagle, then in front of the Eagle of the Regiment Etranger. Then Hallard addressed the crowd, making a brief speech about the trials, tribulations and triumphs which had been faced by The Camerone Association in its efforts to make Penette's dream of the Monument a reality.

'There was a cathedral-like silence as these words were heard, showing that they touched even the hardest of hearts,' Penette said later.

The Camerone Association had arranged for the manufacture of a limited edition of copies of the Eagle of the Regiment Etranger. The first one was to be given for the Foreign Legion Museum, the second to the *Federation des amicables d'anciens legionnaires* and Koenig received the third. The others were presented to people who had played decisive parts in bringing the Camerone Monument into being.

In a manner of speaking, the statue-loving Governor Lopez Arias had the last word, because some time later, when a secondary school was built not far from the Camerone Monument, a statue – by Juan Olaguibel – of Colonel Francisco de Paula Milan, waving his sword in the air, was erected in the main street. No matter. The Camerone Monument had been well planned and well built. It suffered no damage eight years later when a major earth tremor shook the region.[28]

'It survived in all its glory, undisturbed by the buffeting of the elements' said Penette, with obvious satisfaction – adding: 'Like the legendary Legion itself.'

36
A New Beginning

The unidentified Foreign Legion officer who in the summer of 1963 had shown writer Charles Mercer models and plans for the reconstruction of the Camp de la Demand at Aubagne had cautioned: 'I can't say when.' He had tentatively suggested: 'Maybe 1965 or 1966' – and turned out to be pretty close in his time estimate. Work on the Foreign Legion Museum had gone ahead as part of the general building programme, which continued throughout 1964 and 1965 and into 1966. In the early months of the new year Colonel Vadot of the 1st Etranger oversaw the gradual moving of the Foreign Legion's treasures from their temporary home at Puyloubier to be cleaned, properly curated and selected for display. The Quartier Vienot was now completed, from the *Voie Sacre* and the *Monument aux Morts*, to the administrative buildings, messes and barracks – and the Museum. It was inaugurated by Minister of Defence Messmer and General Koenig on 29 April 1966, the eve of the Feast of Camerone.[1] Messner took the parade salute the next day.

What had once been the elegant *Salle d'Honneur* at Sidi-bel-Abbes, with its various specially-dedicated rooms, had been recreated in museum-style, a world-class facility, as the *Musee de la Legion Etrangere*, housed in a two-storey building, entered through a flag-bedecked hallway leading to the *Salle d'Honneur* and the Crypt.[2] The floor of the *Salle d'Honneur* is of green marble, with a carpet of paler green in the centre, under a long table. The walls are red, one of them dominated by Jean-Adolphe Beauce's painting 'The end of the battle', flanked by a portrait in oils of Captain Jean Danjou.

The Crypt, illuminated by hidden lighting, is reached through an arched doorway, and a cross, lit from below, is let into the green marble floor. Up to waist height are glass cases displaying many of the Foreign Legion's laid-up Regimental Standards, while above them, picked out in gold on the wood-panelled walls, are the names of the nine hundred and seven officers who have died on active service, starting with that of Lieutenant Cham, killed in Algeria in May 1832.

At the centre of the end wall, flanked by panels with the names of officers killed in the Second World War, is a single panel, unadorned except for a small two-tiered shelf. The wood-and-glass casket containing the articulated hand of Captain Danjou rests on the top shelf. Below it, now in a priceless Roman urn of the IIIrd Augusta period, is the debris taken from the 1892 grave of the 3rd of the 1st, and given to Inspector-General Lefort by General Penette after the Dedication of the Camerone Monument in 1963. Beneath the panel, in one of the many glass-fronted cases containing flags and other memorabilia, is the bronze Eagle from the staff of the Regiment Etranger.[3]

The *Salle des Campagnes*, reached by a flight of stairs, is divided into ten individual sections, and has aisles of glass-cased exhibits of weapons and badges, photographs, medals and decorations. There are life-sized models of Legionnaires in period uniforms, and the walls are decorated with prints and weapons.

A number of Camerone-related items are displayed in the section on the Mexican Expedition. They include the tunic and medals of Captain Danjou, and the photograph he had made before going to Mexico, oil paintings of Sous-Lieutenants Vilain and Maudet, the watercolour of the 1892 grave and a sword stick which once belonged to Corporal Maine. There is also a photograph of Dona Juana Marrero de Gomez and a fragment of the cross she put in Sous-Lieutenant Maudet's hands when he was buried, some stones from the Hacienda de la Trinidad, the sabre and Lefraucheux revolver which belonged to Captain Pharaon Van den Bulcke – a Fusilier at Camerone, commissioned later in the 20th Regiment of the Line – and a diorama of the Combat of Camerone executed for Brunon by Madame Fernande Metayer.

Other mementoes of the Mexican Expedition include Marshal Bazaine's kepi and his Grande Cross of the Order of Notre-Dame de Guadaloupe, a bust of Colonel – then General – Pierre Jeanningros and the diploma for his *Medaille du Mexique*, the medals and service documents of Sous-Lieutenant Lucien Bosler – who succeeded Maudet as Standard-Bearer of the Regiment Etranger – the sabre which supposedly belonged to President Benito Juarez, and Mexican scenes by the Swiss artist Sous-Lieutenant Henri-Guido Kauffmann.

Vadot, who had overseen so much of the transition of the Camp de la Demande into the new Quartier Vienot, handed over command of the 1st Etranger mid-year, being replaced by Colonel Chenel, who had managed the difficult job of keeping the 2nd REP from attracting hostile attention following the 'General's Putsch' of 1961. This would have been an equally appropriate moment for Georges-R. Manue to have been speaking – as he had three years earlier – of 'the beginning of a new era for the Legion', for such it was. Moreover, after more than five years of an almost nomad-like existence, the various regiments were making preparations to settle into new homes, several of them in France, for the first time in the history of the Foreign Legion.

General Zinovi Pechkoff, the last of the old-time Company Officers from the Rif War and Syria, companion of '*Les Mousquetaires*', soldier and diplomat, lived long enough to see the Foreign Legion coming back into its own, dying on 26 November, at the age of 82. He had been in Japan after the surrender in 1945, and had later been sent to Formosa to break the news to Generalissimo Chiang Kai-shek and the Nationalist Chinese that France intended to give formal recognition to Chairman Mao Tse-tung and the People's Republic of China. Pechkoff retired in 1950, almost on the eve of the Korean War. Although ranked as a General of the Army Corps, he had decreed that his tombstone, in the Russian Cemetery of Sainte-Genevieve-des-Bois, should simply read: 'The Legionnaire Zinovi Pechkoff'.[4]

The quick action of Colonels Brothier and Vaillant, and the 'insider' influence of Minister of Defence Messmer and Chief of Staff Olie – with a combination of arguments emphasizing both emotion and pragmatism – had saved the Foreign

Legion from suffering the full wrath of President de Gaulle in the wake of the 'General's Putsch'. Messmer remained as Minister of Defence until 1969, became Minister of State for France's Overseas Departments and Territories under President Georges Pompidou in 1971 and was himself Prime Minister of France from 1972 to 1974. During this time, crucial to the re-shaping of the Foreign Regiments, the far-seeing forward planning of General Lefort and, at a lower level, of the Colonels and Lieutenant-Colonels of the various regiments, turned them into a fighting force essential to the military commitments and interests of France.

Lieutenant-Colonel Robert Caillaud, who assumed command of the 2nd REP at the end of May 1963, was another of the alumni of Dien Bien Phu, an experienced paratroop officer with big plans for his regiment and the connections and backing to make them happen. American writer Howard R. Simpson, who had been a war correspondent and then a diplomat in Indo-China, spent a great deal of time with the 2nd REP while gathering material for his book *The Paratroopers of the French Foreign Legion*. He reported that Caillaud had 'drawn on his knowledge of foreign special operations forces, including the British Special Air Service (SAS) to develop his plans.'

He envisaged, said Simpson, a regiment in which 'each of the four combat companies would have specialized skills and tasks: 1st Company: Intelligence gathering, operations behind enemy lines, deep penetration patrols; 2nd Company: mountain warfare, including formation of ski scouts; 3rd Company: amphibious operations, including sub-aqua infiltration, combat swimmers; and 4th Company: mine warfare and sniping.'

'This was a revolutionary concept at the time,' Simpson commented.[5]

Caillaud's contacts, some of them going back to his cadet days at Saint-Cyr, were called on to help, as funds – as usual – were scarce. The French Navy and the *Chasseurs Alpins* gave assistance, advice and sometimes equipment. The French Army made parachute training facilities available and men were sent on rotation for courses. Caillaud commanded the regiment for two years and by the time he left the way had been cleared for the 2nd REP to become an integral part of the 11th Paratroop Division, an always-on-call member of the French Rapid Action Force. In June 1967 it finally left Algeria for its new base at Calvi in Corsica and the ground work laid by Caillaud provided a solid foundation on which his successors were able to build.

During the course of the year, the *Musee de l'Armee* in Paris, after extensive negotiations with Jean Brunon for the acquisition of the extraordinary *Collection Raoul et Jean Brunon*, brought the matter to a successful conclusion. The *Collection*, which encompasses the story of French arms from 1700 to 1918, became the foundation for the *Musee de l'Emperi*, housed in the refurbished chateau of the same name, in Salon-de-Provence. Brunon, in his early seventies, was named as Honourary Curator, with his son, named Raoul for his late uncle, as Curator.[6]

Many French regiments were dissolved – and one of the casualties was the 2nd REI, though this turned out to be only temporary – and the Colonels of the Foreign Legion maintained a very low profile, hoping to keep their regiments intact.

The 1st REC finally left Mers-el-Kebir on 17 October 1967 to move into its new base at the Quartier Labouche at Orange, north of Aubagne. In November, the 3rd REI detached a Company from Diego Suarez to the strategically-important Comoro Islands, which straddle the Mozambique Channel between Madagascar and the African coast. It was officially designated the *Detachment de Legion Etrangere des Comoros* (DLEC).

Yet another political crisis rocked France in May 1968, when students took to the streets in massive protests against the policies of de Gaulle. The Army stood firmly with the government. General Jacques Massu, who was commanding French troops in Germany, is believed to have used some leverage to broker an amnesty for those who had been convicted for their parts in the 'Generals' Putsch' of seven years earlier. Among them was former Inspector-General of the Foreign Legion Paul Gardy.

In April 1969 the Foreign Legion was in action again, when men of the 2nd REP and a *Compagnie Motorise de la Legion Etrangere*, drawn from various regiments, were flown into the landlocked former African colony of Chad, as France responded to a request for help under the terms of a military pact. It was the first combat mission since the Foreign Legion left Algeria, and would be the forerunner of many in the coming years, involving a number of the regiments, and on New Year's Day 1971 a new entity was created as the 61st Mixed Engineers Battalion – Legion (61st BMGL). It had its origins in the 21st Company of the 61st Battalion of Engineers.

At Aubagne, the Camerone Day celebrations were bigger and more elaborate than ever, with full pomp and ceremony, bearded Sappers, *La Musique* and visiting dignitaries. On Camerone Day 1970 the casket containing Captain Danjou's hand was carried by Captain Gomez Urtizberea, the oldest serving Foreign Legion officer, who had gone to Mexico for the Inauguration of the Monument in 1965, and the following year it was carried by Adjutant Gustave Schuvetz, a Russian who had been wounded at Meos Pass in Tonkin on 28 March 1945, more than a quarter of a century earlier, in the 5th REI's fighting retreat to China.

The 2nd REI was re-raised in September 1972, based at Corte and Bonifacio in Corsica and given two distinct roles: 'Training and Instruction' and 'Rapid Intervention'. On 25 August 1973 the 3rd REI left Madagascar for French Guiana, to take on responsibilities for guarding the European Space Agency's new 'Ariane' rocket site at Kourou, securing the borders with Brazil and Suriname and creating a formidable jungle training school, whose facilities have since been utilized by specialized units of the British, Dutch, U.S. and other armies. The DLEC, originally a Company of the 3rd REI, remained in the Comoro Islands and when, three years later, residents of the island of Mayotte decided not to move to Independence with the other islands, the unit's name was changed to the *Detachment de Legion Etrangere de Mayotte* (DLEM). In 1984 it was enrusted with the Regimental Standard of the long-disbanded 2nd *Regiment Etranger de Cavalerie*.

Brunon, Manue and Carles were again involved when a third edition of *Le Livre d'Or* came out in 1976, this time at the instigation of the publishing house of Charles-Lavauzelle, who had been responsible for the second edition. The section on Camerone scarcely differed from its predecessor, but Carles contributed the material on the 1954–1962 Algerian War and the Legion's departure for France, while the period 1962–1976 was chronicled by Battalion Commander Guibert-Lassalle, *Chef de Section Information et Historique de la Legion Etrangere*.[7]

The same year the Instruction Group of the 2 REI left Corsica, going first to Puyloubier, then to Orange and finally, on 1 September 1977, setting down roots at Castelnaudary, in the shadow of the Pyrenees, adopting the name *Regiment d'Instruction de la Legion Etrangere*. Continuing with the re-shaping of the Foreign Legion, on 1 June 1980 it would be transformed into a re-constituted 4th Regiment Etranger – the word *Infanterie* being dropped – inheriting the flag and traditions of the former regiment and becoming the training regiment for the Foreign Legion. The 'Rapid Intervention' section of the 2nd REI remained in Corsica for another six years, then moved to a new base at the Quartier Vallongue, near Nimes, west of Marseille, where it was developed into a highly trained fighting regiment and a key component of France's Rapid Action Force.

The 13th *Demi-Brigade* was ensconced in French Somaliland, carrying out patrols along the borders with Ethiopia and the Somali Democratic Republic (SDR), and helping to contain the rebel *Front de la Cote des Somalis*. When Somalia and British Somaliland had united in 1960 to become the SDR the new government had stated its intention of incorporating neighbouring French Somaliland, despite the fact that its citizens had voted to remain an Overseas Territory of France. On 3 February 1976 rebels from the *Front* hijacked a school bus carrying the children of French military personnel and made for the border with the SDR. Brought to a halt – and a stand-off – within yards of the frontier, the rebels demanded the release of their jailed comrades, the restoration of weapons seized in operations against them, the departure of all French security forces and immediate Independence for French Somaliland. Marksmen from the 2nd REP, who were in the country on a training exercise, and from the 13th *Demi-Brigade*, ended the terrorist act in a shoot-out, in which all the rebels, and, unfortunately, two of the children, were killed. French Somaliland moved on to Independence the following year as the Republic of Djibouti. It is still the home of the 13th *Demi-Brigade*, to which a squadron of the 1st REC is permanently attached, and other units, notably the 2nd REP, undertake tours of duty there.

The Foreign Legion's intervention in Zaire – the former Belgian Congo – two years later was a full-fledged military operation. The natural resources-rich Shaba Province, once known as Katanga, had rebelled against the national government following Independence in 1960, a secession bid which was bloodily suppressed. On 13 May 1978 Shaba Province was invaded from across the border with Angola by more than a thousand of the exiled irregular Katangan troops from the *Front de Liberation Nationale Congolais*, who seized the mining town of Kolwezi, taking many African and European hostages. Belgium began readying a relief force in Brussels, but France moved faster.

As the most combat-ready unit of the 11th Paratroop Division, six hundred and fifty men of the 2nd REP were flown from Corsica to the Zairean capital of Kinshasa, where they were to be provided with air drop capability. To save weight they had been told to leave their own parachutes at home, as they would be provided with U.S.-made equipment in Zaire. Unfortunately, fixtures and fittings on the parachute harnesses were different from their own, and adjustments had to be made with string and baling wire so that the men of 2nd REP would arrive on the ground with their weaponry. There would be two drops, some two-thirds of the paratroops going direct to Kolwezi, with the remaining third being dropped at Kamina, two hundred and fifty kilometres (a hundred and fifty miles) away, to join them later. There was insufficient airlift capability, which meant that eighty men were packed into the planes, sixteen more than the recommended maximum.

The initial drop of four hundred and five men of the 2nd REP on 19 May, despite some organizational difficulties, was successfully carried out, and the Legionnaires secured the town, located and freed some hostages and were joined by their two hundred and thirty-three second drop comrades the next day. The French had not been told that Zairean paratroops had secured the Katanga airstrip two days earlier, but the Belgians knew and their troops simply landed there. The 2nd REP was essentially in control when the Belgians arrived and it then transpired that the two groups of paras had been given different objectives. The Belgians were merely to evacuate Belgian citizens and other expatriates, while the 2nd REP was to scour the surrounding area for rebel soldiers, who were retreating towards the Angolan border, and await the arrival of a multinational African force. Their work completed, the 2nd REP was withdrawn. They had sustained losses of five dead and twenty wounded, but reviewing the totality of the operation, and accepting the various logistical and communications problems as having been a learning experience, the regiment's performance in 'Operation Leopard' was considered to have been outstanding, and marked their full acceptance as a Rapid Intervention Force of proven ability. At the same time, another crisis in Chad created the need for 'Operation Tacaud', which involved the 2nd REI and the 1st REC, who provided rotating detachments for almost two years.[8]

Rene Danjou, the last surviving member of the family, died in 1980, willing Captain Danjou's case of medals to the Foreign Legion Museum, where it joined the tunic[9] which namesake nephew Jean Danjou had presented to the *Salle d'Honneur* in 1934. A few months later former 1st REP officer Pierre Sergent, who was becoming known for his historical writings on the Foreign Legion – as opposed to his earlier autobiographical ones – brought out *Camerone: La Campagne heroique de la Legion etrangere au Mexique*, a campaign history rather than a specific work on the Combat of Camerone.[10] During his research he had heard of a file in the Austrian State Archives containing letters exchanged between France's Marshal Bazaine and Austria's General de Thun, which showed that Captain Danjou's articulated hand had been carried away from Camerone as a trophy, and bought by an Austrian officer from a Mexican rancher some two years later. This information was not well received by some Foreign Legion officers when Sergent made it public, as it was contrary to the mythic story of Danjou and Camerone.

The Foreign Legion's Sesquicentennial – 150th Anniversary – was in 1981 and Brunon, who was now very frail, was pleased that the house of France-Empire, who had published his book *Camerone* in 1963 for the Camerone Centenary, wanted it updated to tie in with the Sesquicentennial.[11] He was also involved in organizing a fourth edition of the *Livre d'Or* the same year,[12] the authors were again shown as himself, Manue and Carles. Adjutant Chef Tibor Szecsko, the Curator of the Foreign Legion Museum, covered the period 1976–81. In an article in a Special Edition of the *Revue Historique des Armees*, Carles wrote that the *Livre d'Or* has 'no pretensions other than to conserve the memory of the great moments' of the Foreign Legion.[13]

Brunon died the following year at the age of eighty-seven.[14] So the last of the great authorities on Camerone was gone, but the need for the Foreign Legion to underpin French interests and military alliances was not.

On 19 August 1982 men from the 2nd REP were sent to Lebanon as part of 'Operation Epaulard', a United Nations multinational force, tasked with assisting in the evacuation of the leader of the Palestine Liberation Organization and some of his men. The job completed, they departed on 13 September, but continuing civil strife caused a second multinational force to return to West Beirut in May of the following year. Elements of the 1st Etranger, 2nd REI, 4th Etranger and the 1st REC were involved in operations, which cost the lives of five Legionnaires of the 2nd REI. 'Operation Manta' took the 2nd REP, 2nd REI and 1st REC back to Chad the same year.

While it is not unusual to mark the anniversaries of events in terms of decades, or multiples thereof, it is difficult to determine the reason that the French Post Office decided to mark the one hundred and twenty-first anniversary of the Combat of Camerone. Perhaps they were too late off the mark to commemorate the one hundred and twentieth anniversary? More likely, as the year 1984 was the thirtieth anniversary of the fall of Dien Bien Phu, it may have been thought worth celebrating the men of the Foreign Legion – with which Dien Bien Phu had particularly strong associations – but through an earlier battle, rather than a much more recent one.

Whatever the reason, artist Jean Delpech was commissioned to design a Camerone postage stamp. Born in Hanoi in 1916, he had studied both there and in Paris and had joined the French Army at the outbreak of the Second World War. Released in 1940, after service in Alsace and Champagne, he had returned to his art studies and two years later, when threatened with being taken by the Nazis for forced labour, went underground and fought with the Resistance, using his artistic talents to manufacture documents and passes for covert operations against the Germans. After Paris had been liberated he joined the magazine *L'Armee francaise au combat*, then established himself as both a commercial artist, designing stamps and theatrical backgrounds, and as a more orthodox one, his work gracing several museums and many private collections.

Inspired by Benigni's painting 'The Oath', depicting Danjou swearing to fight '*jusqu'a la mort*', Delpech produced a striking postage stamp, with a stylized modern-day Legionnaire on the left hand side. The black, red and green three francs ten centimes Camerone stamp – the twentieth issued by the post office that year – and the mandatory First Day Covers so beloved by philatelists, went on sale at des Invalides and at Aubagne on Camerone Day, with general release[15] to all post offices on 2 May.

On 1 July a brand new Foreign Legion regiment came into being. The joint French Army-Legion Batallion, the 61st BMGL, had been disbanded in 1982, but now came back into existence as the 6th *Regiment Etranger de Genie* (6th REG), a highly specialized combat engineering regiment, seen as the successor – regimentally, but certainly not in focus – to the short-lived 6th REI, which had fought the Allies in Syria. Briefly reformed in 1949, it had again been dissolved in 1955. Now it was reborn as a fully operational rapid reaction regiment, based in south-central France.

British-born freelance photo-journalist John Robert Young, who had made much of his name in Canada, realized that the Foreign Legion was 'becoming increasingly aware that the public gaze is more closely focused upon it, now that it is based within metropolitan France.' He appealed directly to President Francois Mitterand for permission to create a photo-essay of the modern Foreign Legion, and once approval was given set about photographing Legionnaires wherever they were serving. The resulting book, *The French Foreign Legion*, which was published late in the year, had the subtitle 'The Inside Story of the World-Famous Fighting Force' and contained two hundred and fifty-one illustrations, some from Foreign Legion and other archives, but almost two hundred of them the fruit of Young's fifty thousand-mile journey and three hundred rolls of film.[16] His sparkling pictures were supplemented with an historical text by former Foreign Legion officer Erwan Bergot, who has become a well-known writer on his old corps and on other French military matters.

Looking at the military effect of the Combat at Camerone, rather than just at the battle, Bergot summed up, without exaggeration, what it had meant to the overall campaign in Mexico.

> Captain Danjou's men had kept their word to the end [*he wrote*]. By their bitter resistance, they had forced Milan's troops, first to reveal themselves, and then to become tied down in a day-long battle. The 3rd Company [of the 1st Battalion] of the Foreign Regiment had saved the convoy. Their sacrifice had made possible a French victory at Puebla.[17]

Young's photographs included a section on the Foreign Legion Museum, with interior shots of the crypt, and coverage of Camerone Day at Aubagne.

> It is during this yearly act of remembrance that, at Aubagne, the wooden hand of Capitain Danjou, in its glass casket, is paraded before the Legion [*he wrote*]. The presentation of the hand symbolizes the spirit of the Legion's brotherhood. They come to Aubagne each year from all parts of the world, these ex-Legionnaires and their families. For them it is a pilgrimage. In returning to their 'Mother House' in Provence, Legionnaires relive their glorious past. After the parade, it is party time for the Legion. Wives, sons, daughters and girlfriends mingle with the 'old sweats' from Algeria and Indo-China – general and legionnaire alike. They drink Legion wine from the vineyards of Puyloubier, sing Legion songs, consume plates of salad, garlic-sausage and ham. Children lick chocolate ice-cream, drink fizzy lemonade, play games of chance, and throw fluffy balls at rows of tins. The 'family' is having a great picnic. For the Legion, Camerone Day provides the opportunity to demonstrate that it is one of the finest fighting units in the

world. At Aubagne, several hundred guests, from all parts of the community, are treated to a day of celebrations, following the traditional reading of the historical battle in distant Mexico. With a splash of colour, with marching, singing and music, the men of the Legion entertain their guests in the proudest military tradition. Bearded pioneers, wearing leather aprons and shouldering gleaming axes, contrast with the rows of Legionnaires standing to attention along the Sacred Way . . .[18]

In French Polynesia, the 5th Mixed Pacific Regiment – 5th RMP – created in 1963 and made up of Legionnaires and French Army Engineers, had constructed sites in Tahiti, Mururoa, Hao and Rapa, facilitating France's nuclear testing programme five years later. By 1976 it was based at Mururoa, with detachments in Tahiti and several small atolls, and in July 1985 became a wholly Foreign Legion regiment again, reborn as the 5th Regiment Etranger.

The youngest of the regiments, the 6th *Regiment Etranger de Genie* (6th REG), was not quite three years old when in 1987 its Sapper and combat engineering specialists were sent to Africa to take part in 'Operation Epervier', yet another Chad operation, serving with members of the 2nd REP, 2nd REI and 1st REC.

37
Camerone and the Foreign Legion Today

In the last decade of the twentieth century the Foreign Legion became very much the work horse for French military commitments overseas. The greater part of the French Army is made up of short-term conscripts, meaning that foreign assignments, particularly those involving defence pacts between France and many of her former colonies in Africa, fall on that part of her military machine which is made up of professional soldiers.

In May–June 1990 the 2nd REP and 2nd REI each supplied a Company for 'Operation Requin', when European hostages were seized during political disturbances in Gabon and by September the 2nd REI was in Saudi Arabia for the run-up to the Gulf War. They were joined by men from the 1st Etranger, 2nd REP, 1st REC and 6th REG in 'Operation Daguet' as the year turned and France contributed two thousand five hundred Legionnaires for the United Nations multinational force.

The year was a busy one, with elements of the Foreign Legion involved in 'Operation Baumier' in the Republic of Congo Brazzaville, 'Operation Verdier' in Togo and 'Operation Godoria' in Djibouti.

Another excellent pictorial essay appeared during the year under the title *The Making of a Legionnaire* by Peter Macdonald. He took many of the pictures himself and supplemented them with archival photos, producing a book which was part-history, part contemporary reportage.

> The spirit of Camerone permeates the whole Legion and is purposely indoctrinated into recruits from day one [*Macdonald wrote*]. This spirit breeds bravery, loyalty to one's comrades and the Legion, and the ability to carry out orders in the face of overwhelming odds. These are the virtues which the Legion hopes to inculcate in the thousands of adventurous spirits who arrive each year at its recruiting centres.[1]

From 1992 elements of the 2nd REP, 2nd REI, 1st REC and 6th REG were continuously involved in the United Nations' UNPROFOR operations in Bosnia, which were replaced by NATO's IFOR and SFOR missions in the former People's Republic of Yugoslavia, and the 2nd REI and 1st REC contributed men for United Nations' operations in Cambodia.

The French photo journalist Yves Debay has frequently photographed the Foreign Legion under conditions of peace and war and his book *The French Foreign Legion Today*, published in 1992, provided an excellent thumbnail sketch of each of the regiments, and also of their traditions.

> The 1st REI (sic) celebrates Camerone Day with lavish care and pomp [*Debay wrote*]. Camerone stands as the very symbol of devotion beyond the call of duty. On 30 April, Camerone is celebrated in all garrisons, but with greater emphasis at the home of the Legion. The vigil, an account of the combat, and a re-enactment precede the festival. In Aubagne, the highlight of the evening ceremony takes place on the 'sacred way' when a Legionnaire carries Captain Danjou's wooden hand to the cenotaph . . . The day after the celebration, '*tradition oblige*,' officers serve the men the morning coffee.[2]

The following year the 2nd REP and 13th *Demi-Brigade* were involved in 'Operation Oryx' as part of the United Nations' UNOSOM II operation in Somalia. In 1994 Legionnaires of the 13th *Demi-Brigade* were briefly in Yemen as part of both 'Operation Diapason I' and 'Operation Diapason II', and later in the year men of the 2nd REP, 2nd REI and 13th *Demi-Brigade* took part in the important 'Operation Turquoise', with the United Nations' MINUR II mission during the genocide in Rwanda.

At the Camerone Day Parade at Aubagne that year, the hand of Captain Danjou was most fittingly carried by former Foreign Legion officer Pierre Messmer, who had played such a seminal role as a politician in saving and re-moulding his old corps.

The *Detachment de Legion Etrangere de Mayotte* had conducted 'Operation Oside' in the Comoro Islands in 1989 and in 1995 mounted 'Operation Azalee' there to oust a group of soldiers of fortune who had seized control of the capital city.

The Foreign Legion had participated in 'Operation Barracuda' in the Central African Republic in 1979 and the 2nd REP was back there late in 1996 for 'Operation Almandine II', and then became involved in a larger scale engagement in the Republic of Congo Brazzaville.

The 2nd REP had been in the former French colony, across the Congo River from Zaire, along with British, Belgian, U.S. and Portuguese troops in 'Operation Pelican I', in case the civil war there made it necessary to evacuate foreign nationals. Intervention in Zaire was not required, but suddenly the Foreign Legion found itself involved in protecting expatriates in Brazzaville, when the government began fighting two rival militia groups loyal to its political opponents, and eventually, in 'Operation Pelican II', in which elements of the 1st REC and the 2nd REI were also involved.

Debay covered many of the decade's deployments in his book *French Foreign Legion Operations 1990–2000*, and also photographed and wrote about Camerone Day at Aubagne.

> For the Legion, Camerone remains the ultimate example of duty, loyalty, and the fulfillment of the mission at any cost [*he wrote*]. . . . the greatest ceremonial takes place at the 1er R[egiment] E[tranger] depot at Aubagne, where a solemn parade and a generously lubricated feast are attended by thousands of former officers and legionnaires from all over the world.[3]

Debay has also specifically chronicled the operational role of the 2nd REP in a magnificent pictorial book called *The 2e REP: French Foreign Legion Paratroopers*, complete with black-and-white archival photos of their very beginnings as the 2nd Foreign Paratroop Battalion.[4]

In the new millennium the Foreign Legion has been involved several times in the Ivory Coast, and as this book was being completed one hundred and forty men of the 3rd REI were being flown to Haiti to join other French troops and soldiers from Canada, the U.S. and Chile, as peacekeepers in the wake of civil unrest and the fall of yet another government.

The Foreign Legion, from an all-time high of thirty-four thousand in Indo-China, and twenty-six thousand in Algeria, in now a lean and highly proficient fighting force of just over eight thousand men, and can afford to turn away all but the most promising would-be recruits.

How the story of Camerone and *La Compagnie Danjou* has impacted on some of those who have been accepted since the mid-1970s can be gauged by what six of them – four Englishmen, a Canadian and an American, three deserters and three who completed their contracts – have written in their books about the Foreign Legion.

The story apparently made no impression at all on Barry Galvin, who, failing to be accepted for the British Army, engaged in the Foreign Legion in 1974, and was given the name Bas Gordon. After increasingly turbulent military service in Chad, Djibouti and Mayotte, he deserted from Corsica with the help of his mother in August 1976. In the book she authored – to which he contributed – Camerone features merely as part of the history the Foreign Legion.[5]

Martin Chadzynski, a Polish-born naturalized American, ran away from his home in the United States to join the Foreign Legion in November 1977. Serving under the name of Mark Chalmers, his trip to the Museum at Aubagne had a considerable impact on him – 'I felt as though I was walking back through history,' he said – and the visit to the crypt awed him even more. He looked at the Hand of Captain Danjou as a Sergeant-Chef with a flair for the dramatic told the story of Camerone.

> Silence gathered around us [*Chadzynski recalled later*]. The light bathing the sacred relic seemed to give life to the carved wooden hand... 'Ever since that day,' our Sergeant-Chef said, 'the Legion solemnly remembers the date and honours the men who fought and died there.' His look travelled slowly from man to man in our group. 'May you represent the Legion as well and as bravely wherever you may be called to duty in the service of *la Legion Etrangere*'.

Chadzynski did his training at Castelnaudary, and got through it, before first unsuccessfully deserting, then invoking the fact that he was still only seventeen – under age – when he joined, and obtaining a discharge after four months of service.[6]

Christian Jennings was another young Englishman who had failed to get into the British Army. A Territorial Army parachutist, he joined the Foreign Legion – keeping his own name – in the summer of 1984. Like Chadzynski, he was impressed by the Museum and the crypt at Aubagne.

> We went down into the crypt where the wooden hand of Capitaine Danjou lay in a glass case [*Jennings wrote later*]. It was the focal point of the room, and whenever visiting dignitaries and military authorities came to visit Aubagne they would be taken down to the crypt where they would stand and salute the hand... I walked over and stood respectfully in front of Capitaine Danjou's false limb. It was made of dark wood and looked ljke a graceful gorilla's paw. As a military museum it was very interesting, but as an insight into the ways of thinking of the French Foreign Legion it was invaluable. It contained all the mementoes of an organization for which pain and suffering (military and personal) became virtues, because they were experienced in the cause of the Legion and ultimately the cause of France. It was a cross between military masochism and romantic delusion, and was almost impossible to understand unless one could grasp the complete picture... I had yet to be disillusioned. Basic training and a posting to a Regiment lay ahead, all of it an unknown quantity, and my enthusiasm was so manifest because everything that lay in front of me was so foreign.

Castelnaudary was overcrowded, so Jennings did his basic training at Orange, home of the 1st REC, and was then posted to the 2nd REP in Corsica, where training began all over again. He wanted to make good, but too much Kronenbourg beer, and a sloppy attitude – resulting in beatings from Corporals and Sergeants – marked him down as unlikely to succeed. He would do a tour of duty in Djibouti – where he made an unsuccessful desertion attempt – be put on an aborted draft for Chad, volunteer to go to French Guiana, and then finally make a run for it in April 1986, when sent to Marseilles for dental treatment, and given a leave pass to Paris.[7]

The fact that twenty-five-year-old Bill Parris had spent five years in the R.A.F. Regiment might have been expected to have somewhat prepared him for his sojourn in the Foreign Legion. Retreating from a broken marriage, he signed his engagement papers in October 1986, and was given the name Peter Parker. During his first days at Aubagne he often looked at a large building on the compound, and was taken there just before leaving for basic training.

> On the side of the building was a huge Legion banner with the words *Legio Patria Nostra*, the Legion is our Homeland, emblazoned on it [*Parris would recall*]. Without having to be told, I somehow knew this was a special place. It had the ambience of a cathedral. A silence, observed only for the most revered places, was conversely almost shouting at me about how fortunate I was even to be allowed near this monument. This building was the Legion museum, a hallowed place, where centuries of courage and acts of supreme bravery performed by past Legionnaires were honoured, immortalized and remembered. I felt proud and humbled to be there.

They were admitted by a Sergeant, who conducted the tour, his 'respect and admiration for his task' obvious. Speaking in both French and English, Parris thought he told his stories 'in the careful way that an old man might talk to his grandson.'

> We all listened in respectful silence [*said Parris*]. He spoke of men and deeds he could only have heard or read of, but it was clear that he was in awe of the men who had taken part in those historic Legion actions. We saw battle honours, captured enemy regalia, photographs and medals awarded to past Legionnaires, obviously left to the museum in order to keep them in the family. The history of the Legion was unfolding before us, and it was awesome and thrilling: just to be in this glorious place added to my motivation to be even a tiny part of the Legion, to be spoken of in the same breath as these fearsome warriors.

Then they were shown 'the most special shrine – the articulated, severed wooden hand of *Capitaine* Danjou, displayed in a case within the Chapel of Remembrance', and told the story of *La Compagnie Danjou* and what they had done at the Hacienda de la Trinidad.

> Camerone became an inspiring symbol of the Legion's fighting spirit [*Parris remarked*]. The message from Camerone is simple: a fight to the death against overwhelming odds is central to the Legion's tradition and each Legionnaire knows he will lay down his life should the brigade demand it. Soldiering means combat and combat could very well result in death. Why enlist if this simple truth is not understood? It was a marvellous piece of psychology to show us this place just before we were due to leave for Castelnaudary.

Part way through their training, Parris and some of his comrades were told by their officer, Lieutenant Colomb, that they would be going to the *Domaine Capitaine Danjou* at Puyloubier to carry out *corvee* duties and talk to the old Legionnaires.

'Learn about the Legion's battles, their victories and defeats,' Colomb told the little group. 'They are your victories and defeats also. Speak to the men who have fought, veterans who have survived horror on the battlefield and who have built the Legion's fearsome reputation, for these men are also our family now, they are still Legionnaires and your comrades.'

> The hills surrounding Domaine Capitaine Danjou were covered in vines and tall, wrought-iron gates opened onto a tree-shaded courtyard where we disembarked the truck [*Parris remembered*]. There was a huge manorial building which housed the administrative offices . . . A mood of tranquility permeated the place.

He and another English Legionnaire talked to a former German Army paratrooper named Karl, who had joined the Foreign Legion in 1946 and served in Indo-China and Algeria. When they were leaving, he told them: 'Enjoy this life you have chosen. Serve with honour and be proud.' They then visited the graves of General Rollet, Prince Aage and Legionnaire Zimmerman. 'I felt that the privilege had been all mine,' Parris said.[9]

He completed his training and was posted to the 2nd REP, where marches and parachute training occupied him fully until 30 April and 1987's *Fete de Camerone*.

Camerone Day is marked with respect and enthusiasm by all ranks [*Parris said*]. Individual regiments may have slightly differing ways of celebrating the day, depending on the *Chef du Corps*, but the main theme remains basically the same.

Roles are reversed, throughout the *quartier*. The most junior Legionnaire, the newest to the Section, is granted the honour of being *caporal de jour*. It is he who decides on the allocation of the various duties to be performed that day, and it is he who leads the Section onto La Place Darne, the parade square ... All cleaning duties normally performed by Legionnaires, even cleaning the showers and toilets, would be executed by the NCOs and officers. It is all completed with great humour and good grace.

The day began when the Sous-Officiers brought us lowly Legionnaires breakfast in our rooms. Coffee, croissants and pastries were taken at leisure instead of coarse bread being gulped or rammed down our throats so as not to be late for parade. After breakfast, the Sous-Officiers had to start corvee, as directed by the *caporal de jour*. It was all taken in good heart and is a tradition warmly welcomed by both Legionnaires and NCOs.

Although the day was one of festivity and jubilant spirits, we were still soldiers and some things had to be done, come what may. Physical fitness was as much of a tool of our trade as deft confidence with any weapon we had to handle. Thus we had a quick ten kilometre run before we got down to enjoying ourselves ... After the run there was a parade and we were inspected by high-raking officers. I was a little surprised to notice that they were from the regular French Army; it is considered an honour for a serving officer to be invited by their Legion counterparts to inspect Legionnaires. Some come on attachment and it is thought to be a good career move for ambitious men, for if they can command Legionnaires, they can command anyone. Perhaps they were merely curious and maybe some of them just wanted to see how this day was celebrated.

Parris had been vaguely aware that arrangements for Camerone Day were under way for months, but the rigorous training programme for new recruits to the 2nd REP had made them oblivious to the activity.

Permanent barracks open their doors to outsiders for the day, which happens only rarely [*he said*]. Some members of the public, mostly tourists, do enter the *quartier* and gaze at this secret world into which they have been invited ... Only the hardest-looking and best-dressed Legionnaires are called upon to perform the guard that day; even more care than usual being taken in preparing their *tenue de garde*, so that they and the Legion look their immaculate best...

The preparations included the construction of display stands, side-shows such as games of skill and chance, and the erection of huge marquees around the camp. Everyone was dressed in spotless, best uniform; snowy white kepis covered our shaven heads and men appeared to grow in stature as they swaggered around the camp ...

The weather was glorious, the sun beating down from cloudless blue skies, as former Legionnaires and their families – 'still part of the brotherhood and not forgotten, especially on this sacred day,' said Parris – mixed with serving officers and men, and with civilian guests.

> The whole scene was reminiscent of a hospital fund raiser, not home to a fearsome fighting unit [*Parris thought*]. The Tricolour fluttered in the cooling breeze coming off the Mediterranean. Alongside the flag was the Legion ensign, its green and red colour dazzling in the sunshine. In the centre of this flag was the Legion emblem, the exploding grenade.

The tradition of abundant food and drink was upheld.

> Copious amounts of food, wine and Kronenbourg were consumed by all in a wonderfully relaxed and friendly environment [*Parris said*]. It has been known for Legionnaires in jail on Camerone Day to be freed, dependent on the nature of their crime, and to have their transgression struck from the record. This is a form of amnesty if you like, in remembrance of our comrades who gave their lives at Camerone all those years ago.[10]

The next morning, 'heavily hung-over', Parris was told that he was being sent to French Guiana to take part in a course at the Jungle Commando Warfare School – which he hated. It was his first overseas posting, and would be followed by a combat mission – 'Operation Noroit' – in Rwanda in 1990, when the 2nd REP was tasked with protecting French nationals during a political flare-up. He was honourably discharged at the end of his five-year engagement.

Simon Jameson, an Englishman, and Evan McGorman, a Canadian, both wrote books about joining the Foreign Legion – not autobiographies as such, but 'How To' books – and included remarks concerning Camerone Day. Jameson was a member of the 1st REC and saw service in the Gulf War. McGorman, who had completed four years with the Royal Canadian Horse Artillery when he joined the Foreign Legion in 1989, served in the 2nd REP and did tours of duty in Chad and Djibouti, as well as exchanging his kepi for a blue beret as a member of the Foreign Legion detachment in Sarajevo, as part of the U.N. Peacekeeping Mission in the former Republic of Yugoslavia.

Jameson's experience of Camerone Days with the 1st REC at Orange were not dissimilar to those of Parris with the 2nd REP in Corsica. He was impressed that former Legionnaires 'come to relive their past and to pay homage to their family', and considered that the parading of the wooden hand of Captain Danjou 'epitomizes the spirit of the French Foreign Legion'.

> The preparation for the festivities normally begins months in advance [*he said*]. Stands are built, games are devised, marquees erected. The day is not just for Legionnaires but also for a select number of family and friends of the Legion. It is the one day of the year that the Legion opens its doors to outsiders.
>
> The day begins with the roles reversed in every section of the Quartier. *Le*

> *Legionnaire le plus jeune* (the most recent Legionnaire to join the Section) becomes the *Caporal du Jour* for the day. It is he who allocates the corvee duties, and marches the Section onto *La Place d'Armes*. And it is the Sous-Officers and the Officers who do the corvee. They will clean the toilets, the showers, the corridors – every job normally allocated to the Legionnaires. The day will initially start with the Sous-Officiers bringing the *Petit dejeuner* to the Legionnaires in their rooms. They will serve the Legionnaires their *cafe* and bring their *croissants* (pastries). After which they will start the corvee as directed by the *Caporal du Jour*. The tradition is warmly welcomed by the Legionnaires and no-one is offended.
>
> Each regiment may run the day differently[,] according to the wishes of the respective *Chef du Corps*. It may start with a run, ending with whiskey and black pudding and Legion songs. On returning to the Quartier there is a parade by the Legionnaires in full *Tenue de Parade*, followed by the festivities which have been so carefully prepared. Much wine is drunk and food consumed. It is a relaxed day and enjoyed by all.[11]

McGorman believed that the Combat of Camerone had 'bestowed upon the Legion the reputation of an indomitable fighting force in the face of overwhelming odds.' He liked the homely touch, too, writing: 'A nice little feature about Camerone is the quaint custom of being served breakfast in bed by your officers and NCOs. In upholding this tradition they bring you coffee, hot chocolate, croissants, bread, and all the trimmings to start your day off right. It's not exactly a continental breakfast but it is an agreeable diversion.'

He also liked the fact that 'activities also involve an opportunity for the general public to come on base and view displays of modern military equipment and Legion history as well as film and video presentations,' and remembered with pleasure a Camerone Day during an overseas tour.

> While in Abeche, Chad, for one Camerone our Company invited several local officials, dignitaries, and missionaries into camp to dine and take part in the celebrations [*McGorman recalled*]. Of course, having gone to the trouble of preparing a certain amount of pageantry, we'd have looked pretty stupid without an audience with whom we could share it all.[12]

Former British soldier and author Lieutenant-Colonel Patrick Turnbull, M.C., who had spent some months with the 1st REC in Southern Morocco in the late 1930s, and written one of the best popular histories of the Foreign Legion a quarter of a century later, was among the many regular non-Foreign Legion visitors to Aubagne for Camerone Day for a number of years prior to his untimely death. Those ex-Legionnaires who attend the *Fete de Camerone* put the lie to the florid stories told in newspapers and books by deserters – men who have gained fame or notoriety by 'escaping' from the terrible Foreign Legion. So does the fact that there are active Old Comrades' Associations in France, Germany and other European countries, and even beyond. In 1931, following the Foreign Legion Centenary Celebrations in Sidi-bel-Abbes, thirty veterans' organizations formed an umbrella group called the *Union des Societes d'Anciens Legionnaires*. In 1957, with more than one hundred and seventy veterans' organizations in existence, the *Union* changed its name to the *Federation des Societes d'Anciens de la Legion Etrangere*.

John Yowell of the 4th REI and then the 13th *Demi-Brigade*, remained with the Foreign Legion after the Narvik campaign and was involved in liaison between the British and the newly-established Free French Legation in London. He joined the British Army in 1941 and saw action in several theatres of the war, including Burma, being demobbed in 1949, taking a job with the Ministry of Agriculture, and working with them until his retirement.

Long before that he had become Secretary of the Foreign Legion Association of Great Britain. Jim Worden of the 3rd REI and 2nd REP succeeded Yowell, with the title of Secretary General. For some years the President was a serving British Army officer, Colonel – now Brigadier – Anthony Hunter-Choat, OBE, formerly Sergeant Tony Choat of the 1st REP and later of the 1st Etranger. He subsequently became the Association's Secretary General, with John Duckmanton serving as President. Each year, on either 30 April, or a day close to it, the Foreign Legion Association of Great Britain – formally *L'Association amicale des anciens combattants de la Legion etrangere de Grande-Bretagne* – stages a Camerone Day Parade in front of the statue of Marshal Ferdinand Foch (1851–1929) in Grosvenor Gardens, near London's Victoria Station. Foch, an important French military theorist, as well as a fighting general, commanded both French and British troops at Ypres in 1915 and in the Battle of the Somme the following year, and was Supreme Allied Commander in 1918, becoming a Marshal of France soon afterwards. The Camerone Parade in London features the *Recit de Camerone* and a trumpeter – sometimes provided by the Brigade of Guards – to sound *Aux Morts*, and is attended by the Military Attache of the French Embassy, and sometimes his counterparts from other embassies.

The May issue of *Kepi blanc*, the Foreign Legion's monthly magazine, always reports on the Camerone Celebrations of the various regiments, as well as those of the many Old Comrades Associations around the world.

There seems to be little doubt that the example of the men of *La Compagnie Danjou* inspired not only the French forces at the time, but also their Belgian allies. Indeed, the fact that there were fourteen Belgians in the Combat of Camerone – almost a quarter of the effectives – and that three of them were among the last six men standing, caused a leading Belgian military historian to bewail the fact that the Belgian Army did not themselves mark the Camerone Centenary. Albert Duchesne, the Conservateur of the *Musee Royal de l'Armee et d'Histoire Militaire* in Brussels, in a letter to the *Carnet de la Fourragere*, wanted to know 'why the anniversary was not marked in some proper way by this country's Army?'[13]

In Mexico, retired Brigadier-General Luis Garfias Magana has raised much the same point on a number of occasions. His writings on Camerone – sometimes a little marred by national pride, to the possible detriment of some historical accuracy – have provided considerable information on the battle from the Mexican perspective. Despite the annual observances at the Camerone Monument, he feels that more notice should be given to the events which took place at the Hacienda de la Trinidad.

> This battle is an important part of the military tradition of the French Army [*Garfias Magana has written*]. It deserves to also form a part of the Mexican

Army's historical military tradition. To the French it represents valour and sacrifice taken to its ultimate limits. To the Mexicans it represents the defence of their most valued ideals: the defence of their homeland. If today those Legionnaires of France deserve their place in the memory of the French Army, then those part-time and anonymous soldiers deserve honourable remembrance by today's Mexican Army. This battle, beyond a shadow of a doubt, had many singular aspects, and is deservedly remembered in France. In Mexico we believe that those who died in that action should be remembered as well in a reverent way. If for France April 30th 1863 is a worthy day for homage, then may it also be for us, because a group of anonymous Mexicans, simple men from small towns, were those who, in those difficult hours for our country, gave the only thing they could – their lives.[14]

So the story of *La Compagnie Danjou*, and what it did at Camerone lives on. The shadows of Danjou, Vilain, Maudet and the men of the 3rd of the 1st, hover over all, and will do so as long as there is a Foreign Legion.

In the process of establishing Camerone as the central event in the Legion calendar, Rollet demonstrated his command of Legion psychology [*wrote U.S. historian Douglas Porch*]. Camerone established the cult of sacrifice, of heroic death in battle. And while evoking heroic moments in the history of the regiment is hardly unique to the Legion, the power of its message is probably unequalled. Camerone and the hand of Danjou exercised a powerful effect in a Legion recruited among the disoriented, men who verbalized little and responded best to visual symbols.[15]

Perhaps the meaning of Camerone to the Foreign Legion, and to Legionnaires, can best be illustrated in the words of a vigorous Colonel who went on to become a General, a long-serving Sicilian Sous-Officier and a lowly British Corporal-Chef.

Speaking to his Sous-Officiers in Sidi-bel-Abbes on Camerone Day 1951, the veteran and much admired Colonel Jean Olie put it this way:

It is a festive occasion, and rightly so [*he said*]. It is also a sad occasion, and rightly so. It is sad because we remember the sacrifices made by our predecessors[,] in the name of our inflexible motto, *Honneur et Fidelite*. And it is right that we should think for a moment of our comrades fallen on many battlefields before and since Camerone, in all parts of the world where the Legion has fought and is fighting still. For the story of Camerone is simply this: that against overwhelming odds a handful of men, tactically defeated, fought on, faithful to the vow they had made, to the bitter end.[16]

Early in 1963, some four months after the Foreign Legion had left Algeria, author Geoffrey Bocca, sat talking with Sergeant-Chef LaBella, a Sicilian, in a cafe in Ajaccio in Corsica. Bocca had been impressed watching the Foreign Legion march through Algiers on Camerone Day 1959, and had reported on the war against the Algerian Nationalists. He and LaBella had known each other for a long time, and the drinks were flowing. The Sergeant-Chef had served in Indo-China and as well as Algeria. The Foreign Legion was his home and always would be. 'I am a Legionnaire for life,' he said, and he had bought into the myths and mystique in the tradition of d'Esparbes' '1st Mysterious' and de Vallieres' 'Men Without Names'. He had made it his world – *Legio Patria Nostra*. After a while, the talk turned to the upcoming celebrations for the Centenary of Camerone.

'Why make such a thing of it?' Bocca asked. 'You can't find it in the history books. It was a completely insignificant action. Outside the Legion no one has ever heard of it. Courage and sacrifice to the last man is not uncommon among soldiers, in the Legion and out of it. Furthermore, you lost it. Can't you do better than that?'

There was a pause, while LaBella perhaps considered whether to answer Bocca or hit him, and chose the former.

> The appeal of Camerone to a Legionnaire is as natural as instinct [*he said patiently*]. He reaches out to it in his own heart, because it is part of his own pain. It is the great reminder to the Legionnaire that the sand is always blowing in his eyes, the battleground is always ill-chosen, the odds are too great, the cause insufficient to justify his death, the tools at hand always the wrong ones. And above all, nobody cares whether he wins or loses, lives or dies. Camerone gives the Legionnaire strength to live with his despair. It reminds him that he cannot win, but it makes him feel that there is dignity in being a loser ... The Legion is alone in the world, surrounded by enemies. Camerone is the expression of our desolation. Do not belittle it .[17]

Overstated? Yes. True? Essentially – even if only partly so – and General Paul Rollet, 'The Premier Legionnaire of France', would have been proud of Sergeant-Chef LaBella.

Corporal-Chef Jim Worden, seven years in the Foreign Legion, echoed some of Bocca's questions, yet summed it up this way:

> The fact is, Camerone is more than a day of celebration and tradition, it is almost a credo to both legionnaires and ex-legionnaires. It is an absolute requirement to understand why it is that this day above all others is the one most celebrated by the Legion. Why should a tiny battle in Mexico on 30 April 1863, at a place that no one has ever heard of, mean so much to the Legion, especially as this was a battle that had been lost? The fact is, that this was an outstanding example of what the Legion is about – *never surrender* – and what it would stand for in the future. That is why it is still celebrated with such reverence.[18]

Perhaps the last words on the Combat of Camerone should go to retired Foreign Legion Colonels Louis Gaultier and Charles Jacquot, veterans of many campaigns, men who had seen it all and done it all.

'Camerone and those who fell there!' they would say.[19] 'The end of a Company? No! On the contrary, in the blood and the mayhem, a place in the world – and at the same time a consecration. This was the birthplace of those who would be called "The Men Without Names".'

Appendix

The 3rd Company of the 1st Battalion of the
Regiment Etranger – 30 April 1863

It was the belief of Corporal Evariste Berg that by listing those who were alive and in Mexican captivity on 1 May 1863 it would be possible for Colonel Pierre Jeanningros to compare it with the Company roster, and to know which members of the 3rd Company of the 1st Battalion had died at the Hacienda de la Trinidad.

At the time, nobody prepared a full list of those killed, wounded and taken prisoner, although Commandant Eloi Regnault, as Interim Commanding Officer of the Regiment Etranger, attempted something of the kind in mid-August. No contemporary account names all of the Legionnaires who fought at Camerone.

General Marcel J. Penette produced the first complete roll call of the sixty-two Legionnaires who marched out of Chiquihuite with Danjou, Vilain and Maudet just after midnight on 30 April 1863. He published it in his co-authored book *La Legion Extranjera en la Intervencion Francesca* in 1962. (Pierre Sergent in *La Campagne heroique de la Legion etrangere au Mexico*, published eighteen years later, provided a roll call of surnames, but included Fusilier Fursbaz twice, making it appear that sixty-six men had been involved.) Adjutant-Chef Tibor Szecsko, Curator of the Foreign Legion Museum, confirmed and/or corrected the spellings of the names in Penette's roll call for Jean Brunon's Foreign Legion sesquicentennial edition of *Camerone* in 1981.

Berg had provided the names of thirty-nine Legionnaires and a man 'we don't know' – the critically wounded Fusilier Van den Meersche – who were in captivity with him at La Joya. Regnault's report of 17 August 1863, named forty-six Legionnaires, living and dead, for whom he could account. (He did not mention eight of the men who were with him at Cordoba.) Corporal Philippe Maine mentioned twelve of his comrades in his telling of the battle, and Fusilier Friedrich Fritz named twenty. By cross-checking Penette's roll call with Berg's letter, Regnault's report, and the accounts of Maine and Fritz, it is possible to determine what happened to whom, and at what point, in the initial skirmishes, the actual battle and, to some degree, the aftermath.

The Roll Call

1. **Captain Jean Danjou**: Adjutant-Major, 1st Battalion. Born 15 April 1828 in Chalabre, France. Served in Algeria, the Crimea and Italy. Chevalier of the Legion of Honour. **Killed at Camerone, 30 April 1863.**
2. **Sous-Lieutenant Clement Maudet**: Standard-Bearer of the Regiment Etranger. Born 8 July 1829 in St. Mars d'Outille, France. Served in Algeria, the Crimea and Italy. *Medaille Militaire*. **Died at Huatusco on 8 May 1863, of wounds received at Camerone.**
3. **Sous-Lieutenant Jean Nicholas Napoleon Vilain**: Acting Pay Officer, 1st Battalion Officer *titulaire* of 3rd Company. Born 3 August 1836 in Poitiers, France. Served in Algeria, the Crimea and Italy. Chevalier of the Legion of Honour. **Killed at Camerone.**
4. **Sergeant-Major Henri Tonel**: French. **Killed at Camerone.**
5. **Sergeant Jean Germeys**: Belgian. Served in Algeria, the Crimea and Italy. Chevalier of the Legion of Honour. **Died at Huatusco on 11 May 1863, of wounds received at Camerone.**
6. **Sergeant Marie Morziki**: French-born son of self-exiled Polish officer. Served in Algeria. **Killed at Camerone.**
7. **Sergeant Alfred Palmaert**: Belgian. Survived Camerone. *Medaille Militaire*. **Died of dysentery at Cordoba on 20 August 1863.**
8. **Sergeant Karl Schaffner**: From Berne, Switzerland. Served in Italy. Survived Camerone. Chevalier of the Legion of Honour. **Died on board ship returning to France on 15 August 1865.**
9. **Corporal Evariste Berg**: Born 13 February 1834 in St. Benoit, Reunion (Isle Bourbon), Indian Ocean. Served in *Artillerie de Marine* and 1st Zouaves before going to Mexico with the Regiment Etranger. Survived Camerone. Re-Commissioned in Zouaves. **Killed in duel at Cordoba on 11 June 1864.**
10. **Corporal Adolfi Delcaretto**: Born in Algeria. **Died at Huatusco on 13 May 1863, of wounds received at Camerone.**
11. **Corporal Aime Favas**: Swiss. **Killed at Camerone.**
12. **Corporal Karl Magnin**: Austrian. Survived Camerone. *Medaille Militaire*.
13. **Corporal Philippe Maine**: Born 4 September 1830 in Mussidan, France. Served in Zouaves, *Chasseurs a Pied* and *Infanterie Legere d'Afrique* before going to Mexico with the Regiment Etranger. Chevalier of the Legion of Honour. Survived Camerone. Commissioned in Regiment Etranger. Later transferred to the 119th Regiment of the Line, then the 3rd *Infanterie de Marine*, fought in the Franco-Prussian War, went to West Africa on attachment to the *Tirailleurs Senegalese*, and ended his service with the 3rd *Infanterie de Marine*. **Died on 27 June 1893 in Mussidan.**

Appendix

14. **Corporal Heindrich Pinzinger**: A Bavarian. Served in Algeria, the Crimea and Italy. Survived Camerone. Chevalier of the Legion of Honour.
15. *Tambour* **Casimir Lai**: Born Cagliari, Sardinia. Italy. Survived Camerone.   Chevalier of the Legion of Honour. **Probably died campaigning in Northern Mexico, 1866.**

Fusiliers of the 3rd Company

16. **Jean Baas**: Belgian. **Died in Jalapa on 4 August 1863, of wounds received at Camerone.**
17. **Aloysio Bernardo**: From Asturias, Spain. **Killed at Camerone.**
18. **Natale Bertolotto**: Born 23 December 1839 in Toulon, France, to Italian parents. **Killed at Camerone.**
19. **Claude Billod**: French. **Died at Huatusco on 11 June 1863, of wounds received at Camerone.**
20. **Anton Bogucki**: **Died on 1 May 1863, at La Joya, of wounds received in the withdrawal to the Hacienda de la Trinidad.**
21. **Felix Brunswick**: Belgian. Served in Algeria and Mexico. Survived Camerone. Served in Franco-Prussian War. Chevalier of the Legion of Honour.
22. **Nikolas Burgiser**: **Killed at Camerone.**
23. **Georg Catenhusen**: **Killed at Camerone.**
24. **Victor Catteau**: Belgian. **Killed at Camerone.**
25. **Peter Conrad**: **Killed at Camerone.**
26. **Laurent Constantin**: Belgian. Survived Camerone.
27. **Constant Dael**: Belgian. **Died at Huatusco on 11 June 1863, of wounds received at Camerone.**
28. **Therese-Francois Daglincks**: Belgian. Survived Camerone.
29. **Hartog De Vries**: From Amsterdam, Holland. Survived Camerone.
30. **Peter Dicken**: German. **Killed at Camerone.**
31. **Charles Dubois**: **Killed at Camerone.**
32. **Friedrich Friedrich**: **Killed at Camerone.**
33. **Friedrich Fritz**: A Wurttemberger. Served in Algeria, the Crimea and Italy. Survived Camerone. Chevalier of the Legion of Honour.
34. **Georg Fursbaz**: **Killed at Camerone.**
35. **Aloys Gaertner**: **Taken prisoner and disappeared.**
36. **Leon Gorski**: French-born son of exiled Polish officer. Survived Camerone. *Medaille Militaire*. **Died in Paris on 14 December 1864.**
37. **Louis Groux**: **Killed at Camerone.**
38. **Emile Hipp**: **Killed at Camerone.**
39. **Adolphe Jeannin**: **Taken prisoner and disappeared.**
40. **Hippolyte Kunassec**: Born 22 July 1843 in Villeneuve-Saint-Georges, France. Son of Austrian father. Survived Camerone. *Medaille Militaire*. Served with 57th and 90th Regiments of the Line in the Franco-Prussian War. Re-engaged in Regiment Etranger 1872. Retired 1899. **Still alive 1902.**
41. **Hans Kurz**: **Died at Huatusco on 28 May 1863, of wounds received at Camerone.**
42. **Felix Langmeier**: **Killed at Camerone.**
43. **Friedrich Lemmer**: **Taken prisoner and disappeared.**
44. **Jean-Baptiste Leonard**: Belgian. Survived Camerone.
45. **Louis Lernoud**: **Killed at Camerone.**
46. **Edouard Merlet**: **Taken prisoner and disappeared.**
47. **Joseph Rebers**: Survived Camerone. *Medaille Militaire*. **Died of dysentery in camp, 1 October 1863.**
48. **Johann Reus**: German. **Killed at Camerone.**
49. **Ludwig Rohr**: Bavarian. **Died at Huatusco on 25 May 1863, of wounds received at Camerone.**
50. **Hermann Schifer**: **Taken prisoner and disappeared.**
51. **Josef Schreiblich**: Survived Camerone. *Medaille Militaire*.
52. **Hans Seffrin**: **Taken prisoner and disappeared.**
53. **Joseph Segers**: Belgian. **Taken prisoner and disappeared.**
54. **Daniel Seiler**: **Killed at Camerone.**
55. **Jean Timmermans**: Belgian. **Died at Huatusco on 15 May 1863, of wounds received at Camerone.**
56. **Pharaon Van den Bulcke**: French, from Lille. Survived Camerone. Later Commissioned in the 20th Regiment of the Line.
57. **Josef Van den Meersche**: Belgian. **Died on 1 May 1863, at La Joya, of wounds received in the withdrawal to the Hacienda de la Trinidad.**
58. **Henri Vandesavel**: Belgian. **Killed at Camerone.**
59. **Luitpol Van Opstal**: Belgian. Survived Camerone. **Died of cancer at Orizaba 23 March 1864.**
60. **Jean-Baptiste Verjus**: French, from Paris. Survived Camerone.
61. **Gottfried Wensel**: Prussian. Served in Algeria, the Crimea and Italy. Survived Camerone. Chevalier of the Legion of Honour.
62. **Karl Wittgens**: **Killed at Camerone.**
63. **Nicolas Zey**: **Taken prisoner and disappeared.**

Others Fusiliers Present

64. **Ulrich Konrad**: Orderly to Captain Danjou. Belonged to the 5th Company. **Taken prisoner and disappeared.**
65. —— **Holler**: Mystery man. **Taken prisoner and disappeared.**

The 16 captured before reaching the Hacienda de la Trinidad

Van den Meersche	Bogucki	Kurz	*De Vries*	Merlet	*Verjus*	Segers	*Van Opstal*
Van den Bulcke	Seffrin	Gaertner	Lemmer	Jeannin	Schifer	Holler	Zey

(**Died of wounds.** *Returned to French lines.* Taken prisoner and disappeared.)

The 49 men inside the Hacienda de la Trinidad

Danjou	Vilain	*Maudet*	Tonel	Morziki	Favas	Bernardo
Bertolotto	Burgiser	Conrad	Catteau	Catenhusen	Dicken	Dubois
Fursbaz	Friedrich	Groux	Hipp	Lernoud	Langmeier	Seiler
Wittgens	Reus	Vandesavel	*Germeys*	Dael	Rohr	*Timmermans*
Baas	Billod					
Delcaretto	Palmaert	Schaffner	*Lai*	*Pinzinger*	Fritz	Wensel
Rebers	Schreiblich	Maine	Berg	Magnin	Brunswick	Gorski
Kunassec	Constantin	Leonard	Daglincks	Konrad *		

(**Killed in Hacienda.** *Died of wounds.* Returned to French lines. * Disappeared.)

Killed in Hacienda: Officers – 2. Other Ranks – 21

Captain Jean Danjou   Sous-Lieutenant Jean Vilain   Sgt.-Maj. Henri Tonel
     Sergeant Marie Morziki   Corporal Aime Favas

Aloysio Bernardo	Natale Bertolotto	Nikolas Burgiser	Victor Catteau
Georg Catenhusen	Peter Conrad		
Peter Dicken	Charles Dubois		
Friedrich Friedrich	Georg Fursbaz		
Louis Groux	Emile Hipp		
Felix Langmeier	Louis Lernoud		
Johann Reus	Daniel Seiler		
Henri Vandesavel	Karl Wittgens		

Died of Wounds and Buried near La Joya

Fusiliers Josef Van den Meersche and Anton Bogucki died on 1 May and were buried in graves on the bank of the Rio Chiquito.

Wounded Who Died Later *

Sous-Lieutenant Clement Maudet, 8 May 1863.

Sergeant Jean Germeys, 11 May.   Corporal Adolfi Delcaretto, 13 May.
Fusilier Jean Timmermans, 15 May.   Fusilier Constant Dael, 23 May.
Fusilier Ludwig Rohr, 25 May.   Fusilier Hans Kurz, 28 May.
Fusilier Claude Billod, 11 June.   Fusilier Jean Baas, 4 August.

(* All died at Huatusco, except for Baas, who died at Jalapa.)

Source Notes

Preface

1. [General Jules Francois], 'Le poste de Ta-Lung', manuscript given to the Service Information et Historique de la Legion Etrangere by its author in 1940. He does not identify himself as the young officer, merely tells the story of the commemoration of Camerone – Archives of the Legion Etrangere, hereafter cited as A.L.E. – and quoted in General Jean-Pierre Hallo, Monsieur Legionnaire (Limoges: Charles-Lavauzelle 1994), 223.
2. Jean Brunon, Paul Rollin and Pierre Benigni, Le Livre d'Or de la Legion Etrangere, 1831–1931 (Paris: Frazier-Soye 1931). Preface by Marshal Louis Franchet d'Esperey. The seven-page chapter on the Mexican Campaign, 119–25, contains photographs of several Foreign Legion officers, but not of Captain Danjou, as none could be found. Brunon would be involved in researching, writing and/or publishing the three subsequent editions of The Golden Book of the Foreign Legion.
3. Colonel Pierre Jeanningros, Commanding Officer, Veracruz and the Terres Chaudes, to Marshal Jacques Randon, Minister of War, Paris, Letter #454, 1 October 1863 – Collections of the Service Historique de l'Armee du Terre, Chateau de Vincennes, France. Hereafter cited as S.H.A.T.
4. 'Report on the Affair of Camerone' – Commandant Eloi Regnault, Interim Commander, Regiment Etranger, Cordoba, to General Ernest de Maussion, Commanding the Reserve Brigade, Orizaba, 17 August 1863 – S.H.A.T.
5. Colonel Pierre Jeanningros, Commanding Officer, Regiment Etranger, Chiquihuite, to General Elie-Frederic Forey, Commander-in-Chief, Corps Expeditionnaire du Mexique, Headquarters, Cerro San Juan, 4 May 1863 – S.H.A.T.
6. Louis-Lande, L. [Lucien-Louis Lande]. 'Camaron, 30 avril 1863: Episode de la guerre du Mexique', Revue des Deux Mondes, 28 (15 July 1878), 444–67. Hereafter cited as Lande/Maine, 'Camaron.' The statement – 451 – that Danjou had lost his hand in the Crimean War is attributed to Maine, but the claim – 466 – that the hand was found after the battle is not a direct quote from him. Article reprinted as 'Le combat de Camerone: vu par le Caporal Maine', Vert et Rouge: Revue de la Legion Etrangere (May 1945), 8–14.
7. Lande, Lucien-Louis, Souvenirs d'un soldat (Paris: Societe Francaise d'Imprimerie et de Librairie 1878), 199–235. The chapter is called 'La Hacienda de Camaron: Episode de la Guerre du Mexique'. The errors concerning Danjou's hand are, of course, repeated: wounded in the Crimea, 210, his hand found at the scene of the battle, 235. The book was made up of four articles which Lande had written for the Revue des Deux Mondes between 1871 and 1878. He had served in the Infanterie de Marine during the Franco-Prussian War, and had won the Medaille Militaire. He died in 1880, but his book was republished (Paris: Lecene, Oudin 1893), with an Introduction about the author by Emile Faquet. An abridged edition, containing only two of the four stories, was subsequently published as La Hacienda de Camaron: Episode de la guerre du Mexique (Paris: Societe Francaise d'Imprimerie et de Librairie [Collection Lecene et Oudin] n.d.).
8. Anonymous [attributed to General Alexis de La Hayrie]. Le Combat de Camaron, 30 avril 1863 (Lille: Imprimerie Danel 1889). Danjou wounded in the Crimea, 12; his hand found after the battle, 23. Hereafter cited as [de La Hayrie], Camaron.
9. Lanusse, L'Abbe [Jean Efrem]. Les heros de Camaron: 30 avril 1863. (Paris: Marmon et Flammarion 1891). Preface and Historical Notes by Boyer d'Agen. Danjou wounded in the Crimea, 19 and 208; his hand found after the battle, 208.
10. General Charles Zede, 'Souvenirs de ma vie. Algerie, Italie, Mexique', Carnet de la Sabretache, no.370 (May–June 1934), 217. Reprinted as 'Camerone: Le Temoignage d'un Caporal survivant', Vert et Rouge: Traditions et souvenirs militaires (May 1951), 14.
11. Jean Brunon, Camerone et l'Aigle du Regiment Etranger 1862–70 (Marseille: Imprimerie Meridionale 1935), 16–24. Republished as Jean Brunon, 'Camerone et l'Aigle du Regiment Etranger, 1862–1870', Carnet de la Sabretache, no.81 (March/April 1936), 97–113; and Jean Brunon, 'Camerone et l'Aigle du Regiment Etranger 1862–1870', La Legion Etrangere (May 1941), 12–18.
12. Captain Oudry, 'Camerone (30 avril 1863)', Vert et Rouge: Traditions et souvenirs militaires (May 1954), 16. Actually, Oudry knew very little about Captain Danjou, saying that he had been born in 1823 – rather than 1828 – and repeating the statement that he had lost his hand in the Crimean War. He also bewails the 'fact' that the list of Camerone participants was 'unhappily incomplete', and can only give the names of the three officers and twenty-nine of the men, which seems to confirm that materials known to have once been held by the Foreign Legion Archives had 'disappeared' over the years.
13. See Appendix.
14. Pierre Sergent, Camerone: La Campagne heroique de la Legion Etranger au Mexique (Paris: Fayard 1980), 373–76; and Pierre Sergent, 'Du nouveau sur le combat de Camerone', Revue Historique des Armees, no.1 (1981), 86–88.

Source Notes 433

15. Adjutant Chef Tibor Szecsko, Legion Archivist, cited in Douglas Porch, *The French Foreign Legion: A Complete History of the Legendary Fighting Force* (New York: HarperCollins 1991), 680, n.34.
16. R.W. Thompson, *An Echo of Trumpets* (London: Allen & Unwin 1964), 139.
17. Jean Brunon and Georges-R. Manue, *Le Livre d'Or de la Legion Etrangere 1831–1955* (Paris-Limoges: Charles-Lavauzelle 1958). Foreword by Marshal Adolphe Juin. The chapter on the Mexican Campaign had grown to thirteen pages – 67–79 – with a better telling of the Combat of Camerone occupying 69–76, and relevant illustrations, including one of Captain Jean Danjou.
18. Patrick Turnbull, *The Foreign Legion* (London: Heinemann 1964). Subtitle: 'A History of the Foreign Legion'. The section on the Mexican Campaign occupies pages 56–69, and the account of Camerone pages 59–65.
19. Colin Rickards, 'Another 'Alamo' ', *Frontier Times* [Austin, Texas], 43, no.1 (December 1968-January 1969), 10–11 *et. seq.*
20. *El Heraldo* [Mexico City], 16 May 1863; *El Siglo Diez y Nueva* [Mexico City], 17 May 1863.
21. General M[arcel] Penette and Captain J[ean] Castaingt, *La Legion Extranjera en la Intervencion Francesca* (Mexico City: Publicaciones Especial del Primer Congresso Nacional de Historia para el Estudio de la Guerra de Intervencion 1962).
22. Jean Brunon, *Camerone* (Paris: Editions France-Empire 1981), 205. Hereafter cited as Brunon, *Camerone* [1981], to differentiate it from the first edition, published eighteen years earlier.
23. Lieutenant-Colonel Pierre Carles, 'Survol de l'histoire du sous-officier de la Legion etrangere 1831–1981', *Revue Historique des Armees*, no.1 (1981), 24. Special Issue on 'La Legion Etrangere 1831–1981'.
24. M[artin] W[aters] Kirwan, *Reminiscences of the Franco-German War, by Captain Kirwan, Late Captain Commanding the Irish Legion During the War of 1870-71* (London: Simpkin 1873; Dublin: W.B. Kelly 1873). Re-published as *La Compagnie Irlandaise: Reminiscences of the Franco-Prussian War* (Montreal: Dawson Brothers 1878). Many of the specific details of the actual battle – in which he was not involved – are incorrect, though more probably the result of Kirwan's bad memory than of M'Alevey's errors. Hereafter cited as Kirwan/M'Alevey, *Compagnie Irlandaise*.
25. [Narcisse-Henri-Edouard] Faucher de Saint-Maurice, *Deux ans au Mexique* (Montreal: Duernay Freres et Dansereau 1874).
26. Carles, 'l'histoire du sous-officier', 24.
27. Douglas Porch, Monterey, California, to Author, 5 March 2002.
28. Samuel Gibiat, Division of the Conservateur du Patrimoine, S.H.A.T., to Author, 18 April 2002.
29. Jack Autrey Dabbs, *The French Army in Mexico 1861–1867: A Study in Military Government* (The Hague: Mouton & Co. 1963). Based upon the archives of Marshal Bazaine, this excellent study is largely drawn from the professional and personal papers accumulated over a period of years by the Marshal while he was in exile in Spain. After his death in 1885 they were rescued by Jesus Zenil, Mexico's Ambassador to Spain, who had them in his possession in Vienna at the time of his own death. Ignacio Mariscal, Mexico's Minister of Foreign Affairs, arranged for them to be taken to Mexico City in December 1906. Historian Genaro Garcia selected and translated a number of the documents and had them published in a multi-volume series under the title *Colection de Documentos ineditos o muy raros para la historia de Mexico* (Mexico City: Libreria de la Vda. de Ch. Bouret 1908–1910). The Bazaine Archives (BA) formed part of the huge Genaro Garcia Collection, which was acquired by the University of Texas. The BA, with texts in both French and Spanish, consist of twenty-six volumes, of two hundred folios each. In writing *The French Army in Mexico*, Dabbs, a Professor in the Department of Modern Languages at the A. & M. College of Texas, studied the whole period of the French Intervention, especially the books of personal reminiscences by soldiers and officials at the court of Emperor Maximilian, inter-relating them, where necessary, with documents and letters from the BA, both published and unpublished. Surprisingly, considering that Bazaine always retained a place in his heart for the Foreign Legion, his alma mater, there is no mention of the Combat of Camerone, nor of Colonel Francisco de Paula Milan in the vast collection of materials – Jack Autrey Dabbs, Austin, Texas, to Author, 11 September, 1984.

Chapter 1 – 'A Legion of Foreigners'

1. LOI – Qui authorise la formation d'une legion d'etrangers en France et de corps militaires composes d'indigenes et d'etrangers, hors du territoire continental – 9 March 1831; ORDONNANCE DU ROI – relative a la formation de la Legion etrangere – 10 March 1831; INSTRUCTION – Pour l'admission dans la Legion etrangere, en execution de l'ordonnance royale de 10 March 1831 – 18 March 1831. All the early official documents, Decrees and Orders which governed the creation and operation of France's foreign regiments from 1831 can be found in Lieutenant-Colonel [Paul Emile Gustave] Morel, *La Legion etrangere, recueil de documents concernant l'historique, l'organisation et la legislation speciale des regiments etrangers* (Paris: Librairie Chapelot 1912). While serving as a Captain in the Foreign Legion, Morel, signing himself G.M, wrote articles for *France Militaire* in 1899, 1901 and 1903 and a study called 'La Legion etrangere et les troupes coloniales' for the *Journal des Sciences militaires* in 1902. It was published as a book in Paris by Chapelot the following year. In compiling the detailed bibliography which accompanied his collection of documents, Morel was assisted by Captain Boutmy of the 1st Etranger, author of a brief history of the Foreign Legion a decade earlier: Captain Boutmy, *Le Petit historique de la Legion Etrangere* (Bel-Abbes: Presses du 1er Etranger 1902).
2. General [Paul] Grisot and Lieutenant [Ernest] Coulombon, *La Legion etrangere de 1831 a 1887* (Paris: Berger-Levrault 1888), 10–11. Hereafter cited as Grisot/Coulombon, *Legion etrangere*.
3. Grisot/Coulombon, *Legion etrangere*, 18–19.
4. Philip Guedalla, *The Two Marshals: Bazaine, Petain* (London: Hodder and Stoughton 1943), 27.

5. ORDONNANCE DU ROI – Portant que la Legion etrangere cessera de faire partie de l'armee francaise – 29 June 1835.
6. ORDONNANCE – Qui prescrit la formation d'une nouvelle Legion etrangere composee d'etrangers, sous la denomination de Legion etrangere – 16 December 1835; EXECUTION – De l'ordonnance qui prescrit la formation d'une nouvelle Legion composee d'etrangers – 2 January 1836.
7. Anthony Clayton, *France, Soldiers and Africa* (London: Brassey's Defence Publishers 1988), 211; Francis Pulszky, *The Tricolor on the Atlas; or, Algeria and the French Conquest* (London: T. Nelson and Sons 1854), 357–58. Much of this book was drawn from the writings of Bavarian naturalist Dr. Morotz Wagner. Pulszky supplemented and updated Wagner's information with details from the official *Blue Book*, published under Imperial Authority in 1853 and called *Tableau de la Situation des Establissements Francais dans l'Algerie, 1850–52*; Laurence Trent Cave, *The French in Africa* (London: Charles J. Skeet 1859), 163–64. Cave, a member of the Royal Geographical Society, was a former officer in the 5th Regiment and visited Algeria in 1853 to obtain firsthand material for his book. He reports one hundred and forty-three Frenchmen as having faced 'from twelve to fourteen thousand attackers'.
8. Clemens Lamping and M.A. de France, *The French in Algiers*. Translated by Lady [Lucy] Duff Gordon. Part I: *The Soldier of the Foreign Legion* by Clemens Lamping. Part II: *The Prisoners of Abd-el-Kader; or, Five Months' Captivity Among the Arabs* by Lt. M.A. de France. (London: John Murray 1845), 86–87. Lamping heard that there were one hundred and fifty *disciplinaires*, and misspells Lelievre's name as Lievre and the scene of the struggle as Fort Massagran. He also thought that in terms of numbers of attackers the affair had been 'somewhat exaggerated by the French newspapers'. His brief account of the fight is given in a letter he wrote from nearby Mostaganem in October 1840. When he returned to Oldenburg, Lamping published his reminiscences in two volumes, but only the first was translated into English.
9. ORDONNANCE DU ROI – Qui divise la Legion etrangere en deux regiments dont elle determine la composition – 30 December 1840.
10. Cave, *French in Africa*, 181–82; Brunon, *Camerone* [1981], 103.
11. Le Comte Guy de Miribel, *Memoires du Marechal de Mac Mahon, Duc de Magenta* (Paris: Plon 1932), 178–81.

Chapter 2 – Sidi Brahim – A Cautionary Tale

1. Wilfrid Blunt, *Desert Hawk: Abd el Kader and the French Conquest of Algeria* (London: Methuen 1947), 202–15, contains a good account of the affair at Sidi Brahim. The *Chasseurs a Pied* had been raised by a ROYAL ORDINANCE dated 28 September 1840. Their name was changed to *Chasseurs d'Orleans* by an ORDINANCE dated 19 July 1842.
2. Colonel Jean Defrasne, 'Avec Mac-Mahon . . . A l'origine des *chasseurs a pied*', *Revue Historique des Armees*, no.4 (1981), 106–07.
3. Count P[aul] de Castellane, *Military Life in Algeria* (London: Hurst and Blackett 1853), I, 236–37.
4. Dossier Clement Maudet, No. 5Y3 15 577 – S.H.A.T.
5. Dossier Clement Maudet, No. 5Y3 15 577.
6. Dossier Clement Maudet, No. 5Y3 15 577.
7. Edouard Collineau, 'Notes et souvenirs du General Collineau', *Carnet de la Sabretache*, no.288 (March–April 1924), 172.
8. The affair at Zaatcha became a major issue in France, debated in the National Assembly, and important enough to rate extensive contemporary coverage in four issues of the pictorial magazine *L'Illustration*. An overview is to be found in Charles Boucher, 'Le siege de Zaatcha', *Revue des Deux Mondes* (1 April 1851), 70–100, and the unfortunate commander, who was forced into retirement the following year, set down his own version in [General] E[mile] Herbillon, *Relation du siege de Zaatcha* (Paris: J. Dumaine 1863). Porch, *Foreign Legion*, 90–117, offers an excellent analysis of both the reasons for, and the actions at, Zaatcha.
9. Dossier Clement Maudet, No. 5Y3 15 577.
10. General F.C. du Barail, *Mes Souvenirs* (Paris: Plon 1894–96), I, 367–68; Jomard, 'Travaux archeologiques du Colonel Carbuccia', *Moniteur universel* (25 April 1851), republished as a pamphlet (Paris: Panckoucke 1851); Macquet, *Notice sur la legion etrangere. Expedition de la petite Kabylie (1851) aux ruines de Lambese* (Namur: Rouvroy 1853). A Belgian, Macquet later served in the 2nd Etranger in the Crimea and wrote about it: *Correspondence d'un soldat belge en Crimee* (Tournay: Flamme 1858).
11. Roger de Beauvoir, *La Legion Etrangere* (Paris: Firmin-Didot 1897), 18.
12. Collineau, 'Notes et souvenirs', 172. He need not have worried, as he went on to rise through the military hierarchy and died in China as a General of Division – Grisot/Coulombon, *Legion etrangere*, 123.
13. Grisot/Coulombon, *Legion etrangere*, 111.

Chapter 3 – The First Foreign War

1. Dossier Jean Danjou, No. 5Ye 15 583 – S.H.A.T.
2. Dossier Jean Danjou, No. 5Ye 15 583. Brunon, *Camerone* [1981], 116–17, provides biographical material he received through his considerable contacts with Danjou's daughter, Mme. Marest, and namesake nephew, Jean Danjou, in the 1930s.
3. Dossier Jean Danjou, No. 5Ye 15 583.
4. Dossier Jean Danjou, No. 5Ye 15 583.
5. Grisot/Coulombon, *Legion etrangere*, 116.
6. Dossier Clement Maudet, No. 5Y3 15 577.
7. Dossier Clement Maudet, No. 5Y3 15 577.
8. Order de la Division, No.19, 22 May 1854, quoted in Grisot/Coulombon, *Legion etrangere*, 118.
9. Dossier Jean Vilain, No. 5Ye 15 575 – S.H.A.T.
10. Dossier Jean Vilain, No. 5Ye 15 575.
11. Dossier Jean Vilain, No. 5Ye 15 575.
12. Dossier Jean Vilain, No. 5Ye 15 575 gives his date of arrival as 26 November.
13. DECRET IMPERIAL – Relatif a la formation d'une seconde Legion etrangere – 17 January 1855.
14. Comte P[aul] de Choulot, *Souvenirs pour servir a*

l'histoire du 1er regiment de la Legion etrangere (Paris: Dumaine; Bourges: J. Bernard 1864).
15. Marquis Louis de Massol, *France, Algerie, Orient* (Versailles: Beau 1860).
16. Dossier Clement Maudet, No. 5Y3 15 577.
17. Dossier Clement Maudet, No. 5Y3 15 577.
18. Dossier Jean Vilain, No. 5Ye 15 575.
19. Dossier Jean Danjou, No. 5Ye 15 583.
20. It has been claimed that Corporal Vilain was awarded the Meritorious Service Medal by the British for his actions on 18 June – Tony Geraghty, *March or Die: France and the Foreign Legion* (London: Fontana/Collins 1987), Appendix II, 395. Geraghty writes: '... Lieutenant Jean Nicolas Napoleon Vilain, at the time of his death on 30 April 1863, wore on his breast *three* decorations for bravery: *Chevalier de l'Order de la Legion d'Honneur*, gained at Solferino on 17 June 1859; the *Medaille d'Or* won during the battle of Magenta, [4 June] 1859 and the British Meritorious Service Medal, granted by Queen Victoria for his services rendered to the British during the Assault of (sic) Malakoff, Sebastopol on 18 June 1855.' This appears to be extremely unlikely, for a number of reasons. The Meritorious Service Medal, instituted in 1845 – Geraghty mistakenly says 1849 – was given, and very rarely, to selected Non-Commissioned Officers in the British Army for long and meritorious service – H. Taprell Dorling, *Ribbons and Medals* (London: Osprey 1983), 84–85, and Anonymous, *Medal Yearbook 2002* (Honiton, [Devon]: Token Publishing 2002), 202. Details of the awarding of the Meritorious Service Medal are in Record Group WO 101 at the Public Record Office at Kew and the names of recipients were published in the *London Gazette*, often many months after the awards were made. The indexes to the publication for 1855, 1856 and 1857 fail to show any such award being made to Corporal Vilain. In fact, no awards of the Meritorious Service Medal were made in that period – Lesley Smurthwaite, Department of Uniforms, Badges and Medals, National Army Museum, London, to Author, 28 August 2002. Exception can also be taken to Geraghty's quoted statement on numerous other grounds: Vilain was a Sous-Lieutenant – not a Lieutenant – in 1863; the Battle of Solferino was fought on 24 June – not 17 June – 1859 and Vilain had no part in it, as the 1st Etranger had remained in Milan after the Battle of Magenta, twenty days earlier, in which he had been badly wounded; the British did not assault the Malakoff on 18 June 1855, it being an entirely French affair; the *Brigade Etrangere* was not involved in any of the fighting, and the British attack was on the Great Redan.
21. Dossier Evariste Berg – S.H.A.T.
22. Dossier Philippe Maine, 3rd *Regiment d'infanterie de Marine* – S.H.A.T. As this was Maine's last regiment, it is his most complete military document, with details of his assorted service, campaigns and decorations, transcribed from his previous documents.
23. Dossier Jean Danjou, No. 5Ye 15 583.
24. Dossier Jean Vilain, No. 5Ye 15 575.
25. Dossier Jean Vilain, No. 5Ye 15 575.
26. Dossier Jean Danjou, No. 5Ye 15 583.
27. Dossier Clement Maudet, No. 5Y3 15 577. He had re-engaged on 6 July 1855.
28. Dossier Jean Danjou, No. 5Ye 15 583. A photograph of the certificate accompanying the decoration is published in Captain Andolenko, 'De Camerone a Bel-Abbes', *La Legion Etrangere*, no.9 (May 1938), 8.
29. A photograph of the Crimean Medal – with 'clasps' for the battles of the Alma and Inkermann and the siege at Sebastopol – awarded to Sous-Lieutenant Philippe Jaudon, Standard-Bearer of the 1st Regiment of the Foreign Legion 1855–56, is published in Brunon, *l'Aigle*. Jaudon served in the Foreign Legion as a Lieutenant and a Captain in Mexico. Not all of the medals for the French had the year 1854 on them and many individual recipients added their own specially-made 'clasps' for the battles of Traktir, Tchernaia, Mer d'Azoff and/or Malakoff. – E.C. Joslin, *British Battles and Medals* (London: Spink 1988), 128.
30. Dossier Jean Danjou, No. 5Ye 15 583.
31. Dossier Clement Maudet, No. 5Y3 15 577.
32. DECRET IMPERIAL – Qui licencie 1er et 2e legions etrangeres et cree 2 regiments etrangers – 16 April 1856; RAPPORT – A l'Emperor sur la reorganisation des troupes etrangeres au service de la France – 16 April 1856 – signed by Marshal Jean-Baptiste Vaillant, Minister of War.

Chapter 4 – Tempering the Steel

1. Dossier Jean Danjou, No. 5Ye 15 583.
2. Brunon/Manue/Carles, *Livre d'Or* (1981), 404, n.2.
3. Ghislain de Diesbach, *Service de France* (Paris: Emile-Paul 1972), 274; Captain [Gabriel] De Diesbach de Torny, 'Notes et Souvenirs 1862–1867.' Unpublished manuscript, A.L.E.
4. Dossier Jean Vilain, No. 5Ye 15 575.
5. E[douard] Perret, *Recits Algeriens* (Paris: Bloud et Barnal 1887), II, 130.
6. Grisot/Coulombon, *Legion etrangere*, 235–37; Brunon/Manue/Carles, *Livre d'Or* (1981), 61–62.
7. Jean Brunon, Georges-R. Manue and Pierre Carles, *Le Livre d'Or de la Legion Etrangere, 1831–1976* (Paris-Limoges: Charles-Lavauzelle 1976), 62. Additional material by Battalion Commander Guibert-Lassalle, *Chef de Section Information et Historique de la Legion Etrangere*.
8. Zede, 'Souvenirs', *Carnet* 366, 435 and 438–39.
9. Brunon, *l'Aigle*, 11.
10. Dossier Jean Danjou, No. 5Ye 15 583.
11. The 2nd Etranger travelled to Genoa via Oran and Toulon and landed on 12 April. The 1st Etranger, coming from Corsica, landed on 26 April.
12. Carles, 'l'histoire du sous-officier', 28, n.4.
13. Grisot/Coulombon, *Legion etrangere*, 248.
14. Grisot/Coulombon, *Legion etrangere*, 249.
15. *Journal de Marche* of the 2nd Etranger, quoted in Patrick Turnbull, *Solferino: Birth of a Nation* (London: Robert Hale 1985), 108.
16. Zede, 'Souvenirs', *Carnet* 368, 46.
17. Dossier Jean Vilain, No. 5Ye 15 575.
18. Zede, 'Souvenirs', *Carnet* 368, 46.
19. Zede, 'Souvenirs', *Carnet* 368, 45.
20. Zede, 'Souvenirs', *Carnet* 368, 48-50.
21. Miccilas Kamienski, *Le mort d'un soldat* (Paris: n.p. 1960), 14. His reminiscences had been post-humously published ninety-nine years earlier: Miccilas Kamienski, *Souvenirs* (Paris: Librairie nouvelle 1861).

22. Zede, 'Souvenirs', *Carnet* 368, 51.
23. Jean Efrem Lanusse was born on 2 January 1818 at Tonneins-Dessous, the son of Jean Lanusse, a former soldier of Napoleon, and his wife Rosalie Clairac. His mother died before he was a year old and he grew up hearing the stories of military glory from his father and his old comrades. The young man entered the seminary at Agen and after Ordination was appointed Vicar of Saint-Pierre de Tonneins – Colonel Allain Bernede, 'Monseigneur Jean Lanusse: Sa Vie en Anecdotes', 3–4, Dossier l'Abbe Lanusse, *Musee du Souvenir*, Ecole Speciale Militaire de Saint-Cyr, Coetquidan, France. Lanusse's given names were Jean Efrem and there is evidence that he did not use the first name, except when merely using initials, as J.E. His correspondence was always signed Efrem Lanusse – L'Abbe Jean Efrem Lanusse Collection, Author's Archives.
24. Dossier Jean Vilain, No. 5Ye 15 575; Grisot/Coulombon, *Legion etrangere*, 253.
25. Dossier Clement Maudet, No. 5Y3 15 577.
26. Grisot/Coulombon, *Legion etrangere*, 253.
27. Grisot/Coulombon, *Legion etrangere*, 257.
28. Turnbull, *Solferino*, 120–50; Grisot/Coulombon, *Legion etrangere*, 257–62; Brunon/Manue/Carles, *Livre d'Or* (1981), 92–94.
29. Bernede, 'Monseigneur Lanusse', 5.
30. Quoted in Guedalla, *Two Marshals*, 87
31. Grisot/Coulombon, *Legion etrangere*, 261.
32. Dossier Jean Vilain, No. 5Ye 15 575.

Chapter 5 – Doldrums in Algeria

1. Grisot/Coulombon, *Legion etrangere*, 264; Louis Meziere, *Un soldat d'Afrique: le colonel Mathieu Butet* (Tours: Imprimerie Menard 1909).
2. DECRET IMPERIAL – Relatif aux engagements et rengagements dans les regiments etrangers – 30 June, 1859; DECRET IMPERIAL – Qui donne au 1er regiment etranger la meme organisation qu'au 2e regiment – 14 October 1859.
3. Dossier Jean Vilain, No. 5Ye 15 575.
4. Dossier Clement Maudet, No. 5Y3 15 577.
5. Grisot/Coulombon, *Legion etrangere*, 267.
6. Grisot/Coulombon, *Legion etrangere*, 267.
7. Grisot/Coulombon, *Legion etrangere*, 267.
8. Grisot/Coulombon, *Legion etrangere*, 221–22.
9. Dossier Jean Vilain, No. 5Ye 15 575.
10. 'Inspection of the 1st Etranger' by General Ulrich, 6 August 1861 – Xb778 S.H.A.T.
11. 'Inspection of the 2nd Etranger' by General Deligny, 6 August 1861 – Xb778 S.H.A.T.
12. Carles, 'l'histoire du sous-officier', 29.
13. Grisot/Coulombon, *Legion etrangere*, 266.
14. Kirwan/M'Alevey, *Compagnie Irlandaise*, 77–78.
15. Kirwan/M'Alevey, *Compagnie Irlandaise*, 188.
16. DECRET – Qui licencie le 1er regiment etranger – 14 December 1861.
17. SUSPENSION – Des engagements volontaires dans le regiment etranger – 16 December 1861.
18. DECRET – Qui licencie le 1er regiment etranger – 14 December 1861.
19. Grisot/Coulombon, *Legion etrangere*, 271.
20. A former classmate of Walker, Henry A. Crabbe, could not learn from what had happened to others of his ilk, and led yet another filibustering expedition into Sonora. It ended with a firing squad in April 1857. Walker himself avoided Mexico when he again sought territorial acquisitions, moving his area of activities to the Republic of Nicaragua – on several separate occasions – and then to the Republic of Honduras, where, in September 1860, he met the same fate as Raousset-Boulbon and Crabbe. There is an enormous amount of literature on these filibusters. Edward S. Wallace, *Destiny and Glory* (New York: Coward-McCann 1957) and Joseph Allen Stout, Jr., *The Liberators: Filibustering Expeditions into Mexico, 1848–1862* (Los Angeles: Westernlore Press 1973) provide good general overviews.
21. *El Moniteur Republicano*, 2 December 1861; *Siglo* 3 December, 1861.
22. *Siglo*, 17, 18 and 19 December 1861.
23. *Siglo*, 15 January 1862.
24. *Siglo*, 25 January 1862.
25. *Siglo*, 23 February 1862.
26. *Siglo*, 10 March 1862.
27. Quoted in Penette/Castaignt, *Legion Extrangera*, 19, and Sergent, *Camerone*, 14.

Chapter 6 – 'Let's go to Mexico!'

1. De Beauvoir, *Legion Etrangere*, 66; Brunon/Manue, *Livre d'Or* (1958), 68.
2. Quoted in Turnbull, *Foreign Legion,* 59.
3. Saint-Maurice, *Deux ans*, 77–78.
4. Lanusse, *Les heros*, 33.
5. During the Mexican War of 1847–48 the hamlet was still known as Temexcal – or a variation of that name, sometimes Temezcal. It appeared on U.S. Army maps as Temaseal – R.S. Ripley, *The War With Mexico* (first published in 1849; facsimile reprint New York: Burt Franklin 1970), II, map titled 'Route from Vera Cruz to Mexico' published between pages 54–55.
6. Lanusse, *Les heros*, 34.
7. *Siglo*, 27 March 1862.
8. *Siglo*, 13 April 1862.
9. *Siglo*, 20 March 1862.
10. *Siglo*, 29 March 1862.
11. *Siglo*, 20 April, 1862
12. *Siglo*, 24 April 1862, Supplement 465.
13. Gustave Leon Niox, *L'Expedition du Mexique 1861–67. Recit politique et militaire* (Paris: Librairie militaire du J. Dumoine 1874), 144–45.
14. *Siglo*, 6 May 1862.
15. Paul Gaulot, *Reve d'Empire: La Verite sur l'Expedition du Mexique d'apres les documents inedite de Ernest Louet, payeur en chef des Corps Expeditionnaire* (Paris: Paul Ollendorff 1890), 78–79. Almonte issued this Proclamation on 15 June.
16. Noix, *L'Expedition*, 156–71. The *Cinco de Mayo* is still a national holiday in Mexico.
17. Niox, *L'Expedition*, 179.
18. Brunon, *l'Camerone et l'Aigle*, 12.
19. Sergent, *Camerone*, 456. Sergent's fruitless search for the Petition took him to the National Archives of France for Napoleon III's papers, and the Archives of S.H.A.T. for records from the War Ministry or the Division of Oran and the Sub-Division of Sidi-bel-Abbes, as well as to the A.L.E. at Aubagne. Grisot/Coulombon, *Legion etrangere*, 272, are certainly mistaken in saying that the Petition was sent to the Emperor 'at the end of the year' – 1862 – as

Source Notes

Faidherbe's rebuke was dated 28 July. It seems that the news, on 19 July, that the 81st Regiment of the Line was to go to Mexico triggered the Petition, which was clearly signed only a few days later.
20. Lieutenant [Edmond] Campion, 'Deux ans au Mexique, 1863–1865'. Archives du Ministere de la Defense Nationale, Paris. Unpublished 232-page manuscript, written in 1868. Hereafter cited as Campion, '. . . au Mexique.'
21. General Deligny, Commandant of the Division of Oran, Message No.490, *Livre Algerie* H 299, No.3 – S.H.A.T.
22. Diesbach, 'Notes et Souvenirs', August 1862.
23. Anonymous, *Veillee de Camerone 1958* (Sidi-bel-Abbes: Presses du 1st Regiment Etranger 1958), 9.
24. Grisot/Coulombon, *Legion etrangere*, 272. Grisot, after examining Foreign Legion documents in the 1880s – which apparently no longer exist – wrote that Deligny had 'taken due note of the views of the Regiment and would convey them strongly to the Minister of War.'
25. Abel Huart, *Souvenirs de la Guerre du Mexique 1862–1867* (Orleans: Auguste Gout 1906), 4. This booklet, the text of a speech given by Huart to the Societe d'Agriculture, Sciences, Belles-Lettres et Arts d'Orleans more than four decades after the events, had the subtitle of 'Le Combat de Camerone 1st May (sic) 1863 [and] The Capture of Puebla 17 May 1863.' It appears that the old soldier refreshed his memories about the Combat of Camerone, and got the may date, from a new edition of Gaulot's book, published as *L'Expedition du Mexique (1861–1867). D'apres les documents et souvenirs de Ernest Louet, Payeur en chef du Corps Expeditionnaire* (Paris: Paul Ollendorff 1906, for the Societe d'Editions Litteraires et Artistiques), 110.
26. Noix, *L'Expedition*, 209.
27. Diesbach, 'Notes et Souvenirs', November 1862.
28. Dossier Evariste Berg – S.H.A.T. The service statistics are contained in Berg's file, and much biographical information is to be found in the assorted papers of the Council of Inquiry – Jean-Paul Pinard, Paris, to Author, 1 February 1984 – which determined his unsuitability to hold a Commission in the 1st Zouaves.
29. Brunon, *Camerone* [1981], 123–24.
30. Quoted in Sergent, *Camerone*, 119, but not sourced.
31. Dossier Philippe Maine.

Chapter 7 – 'I leave, resolved to do my duty'

1. Dossier Philippe Maine.
2. Dossier Evariste Berg.
3. General Deligny, Commandant of the Division of Oran, to Colonel Faidherbe, Commandant of the Sub-Division of Sidi-bel-Abbes, 15 January, 1863 – *Livre Algerie* H 301 – S.H.A.T.
4. Grisot/Coulombon, *Legion etrangere*, 272–73.
5. Dossier Jean Vilain, No. 5Ye 15 575.
6. Dossier Clement Maudet, No. 5Y3 15 577; Zede, 'Souvenirs', *Carnet* 370, 217; Zede, 'Temoignage', 13.
7. Raymond Guyader, 'Le Legionnaire de 1860–1867', *Kepi blanc*, no.434 (April 1984), 35–36; Raymond Guyader, 'L'Officier Legion de Camerone', *Kepi blanc*, no.457 (April 1986), 36–37. Guyader notes that, while dress often met general regimental demands, many slight variations were worn, and apparently unofficially condoned. Brunon, *Camerone* [1981], 80–81. Only two examples of a Legionnaire's 'basquine' are known to exist. Brunon acquired one for the *Musee de l'Emperi*. The other is in the Belgium's *Musee Royal de l'Armee* in Brussels.
8. *Annuaire militaire de l'Empire Francaise pour l'annee 1863 publiee sur les documents communiques par le Ministre de la Guerre* (Paris: Berger-Levrault 1863), 410, Chapter XI – Infanterie, 'Regiment Etranger, 1863'.
9. Brunon, *Camerone et l'Aigle*, 10.
10. Brunon, *Camerone et l'Aigle*, 10.
11. The photograph, obtained from Danjou's family in the early 1930s by historian Brunon, was first published, portrait-style, in Anonymous, 'Les Heros de Camerone,' *La Legion Etrangere*, no.37 (January 1934), 129, then as a full-length photo in Brunon, *Camerone et l'Aigle* the following year. The caption to the portrait-style picture claimed that Danjou had lost his right hand in the Crimea.
12. Lande/Maine, 'Camaron', 454. An eve-of-departure photograph taken of Sous-Lieutenant Diesbach has the same studio background set-up.
13. Quoted in Sergent, *Camerone*, 20–21.
14. Kirwan/M'Alevey, *Compagnie Irlandaise*, 181–82.
15. Grisot/Coulombon, *Legion etrangere*, 273.
16. Campion, '. . . au Mexique'.
17. Grisot/Coulombon, *Legion etrangere*, 273.
18. Anonymous, *Marches et Chants de la Legion Etrangere* (Aubagne: Les Presses de Kepi Blanc 1984), 19. 'Eugenie' is the regimental song of the 1st Regiment Etranger.
19. Brunon, *Camerone* (Paris: France-Empire 1963), 58.
20. Kirwan/M'Alevey, *Compagnie Irlandaise*, 182–83.
21. *Le Monde Illustre*, 8 March 1862, published an artist's drawing of the on-deck entertainment. Sergent, *Camerone*, reproduces the illustration as being of the Regiment Etranger's 'Crossing of the Line' activities, although the figures are clearly sailors and men of the *Tirailleurs Algeriens*.
22. Jean et Raoul Brunon, 'D'Une Rive a l'Autre de l'Atlantique par les Antilles, Mexique 1861–1867', *Revue Historique de l'Armee*, no.3 (August 1967), 127–35, provides a good general account of the voyages of French regiments to Mexico.
23. Brunon *Camerone* [1981], 48.
24. Captain Jean Danjou to one of his several brothers – unnamed – 4 March, 1863. A copy of the letter, presented to the *Collection Raoul et Jean Brunon* by the late officer's namesake nephew, was provided to the Author by Jean Brunon.
25. Diesbach, 'Notes and Souvenirs', March 1863.
26. Kirwan/M'Alevey, *Compagnie Irlandaise*, 183–84.
27. Anonymous, 'La Legion etrangere', *La revue d'linfanterie*, no.524 (1 May 1936), 810. This Special Issue on the Foreign Legion contained an 'Index bibliographique sommaire des publications concernant la Legion Etrangere', compiled by Colonel P. Guinard.
28. Quoted in Brunon, *Camerone* [1981], 60.

Chapter 8 – Into the Terres Chaudes

1. Richard Hill and Peter Hogg, *A Black Corps d'Elite* (East Lansing: Michigan State University Press 1995). Subtitle: 'An Egyptian Sudanese Conscript

Battalion with the French Army in Mexico, 1863–1867, and its Survivors in Subsequent African History'. This is the definitive work on this unit – actually of half-battalion strength.
2. Colonel Yves Salkin, 'La contre-guerilla du colonel du Pin au Mexique (1863–1865)', *Revue Historique des Armees*, no.1 (1977), 29; Raymond Sereac, 'La *Contre-Guerilla* du Colonel du Pin', *La Legion Etrangere* (November–December 1943), 20–25. Contemporary records spell this officer's name as both Dupin and, less frequently, du Pin. His predecessor, de Stoecklin, sometimes appears as Stoeklin.
3. Brunon, *Camerone* [1981], 105; Sergent, *Camerone*, 71–72.
4. Compte E[mile] de Keratry, 'La Contre-Guerilla Francaise Au Mexique: Souvenirs des Terres Chaudes', *Revue des Deux Mondes*, 59 (1 October 1865), Part I, 695–96. Part I of this article, 691–737, was called 'La Guerre de Partisans dans l'Etat de Vera-Cruz'. Part II appeared in 61 (1 February 1866).
5. Salkin, '. . . du Pin au Mexique', 33.
6. General Charles Thoumas, *Recits du guerre 1862–1867: Les Francais au Mexique* (Paris: Bloud et Barral n.d.), 122.
7. De Keratry, 'Contre-guerilla,' 717–18, and Hill/Hogg, *Corps d'Elite*, 42, are incorrect in stating that it occurred on 6 April.
8. This was Legionnaire 8952 – name not given – and he was the first of nineteen deserters during the month of April. They fled individually, or with a friend, although eleven deserted collectively on 17 April. These deserters appear to have all been from the 2nd Battalion, based at La Tejeria, which was close to the coast, which offered the possibility of getting away by ship to the United States or elsewhere. The desertions were gleefully reported by *Sieglo* on 31 March, 13, 15, 17 and 24, 25 and 27 April 1863.
9. Kirwan/M'Alevey, *Compagnie Irlandaise*, 90–91.
10. Diesbach, 'Notes et Souvenirs', April 1863.
11. Kirwan/M'Alevey, *Compagnie Irlandaise*, 184.
12. [Jean Jacques Jules Lafont], *Les Bivouacs de Vera Cruz a Mexico par un Zouave* (Paris et Liepzick: Jung Treuttel 1865), 8–9.
13. Kirwan/M'Alevey, *Compagnie Irlandaise*, 184.
14. Lanusse, *Les heros*, 30–31.
15. Lande/Maine, 'Camaron', 448–49.
16. Lanusse, *Les heros*, 28.
17. Lanusse, *Les heros*, 55.
18. Lanusse, *Les heros*, 94-98.
19. Lanusse, *Les heros*, 83.
20. Lanusse, *Les heros*, 40.
21. [Lafont], *Bivouacs*, 60–61.

Chapter 9 – 'A good Company ours, the 3rd of the 1st'

1. Diesbach, 'Notes et Souvenirs', April 1863.
2. Kirwan/M'Alevey, *Compagnie Irlandaise*, 184–85.
3. Lande/Maine, 'Camaron', 447.
4. Archive de Cancelados de la Secretaria de la Defensa National, Mexico City.
5. Charles Blanchot, *Memoires, L'Intervention Francaise au Mexique* (Paris: Emile Nourry 1911), I, 328–31.
6. Colonel Francisco de Paula Milan, La Joya, to General-in-Chief Miguel Blanco, Fort San Lorenzo, near Puebla, 30 April 1863 – Brigadier-General Jesus de Leon Toral, *Historia Documental Militar de la Intervencion Francesca en Mexico* (Mexico City: S.M.G.E., 1962), 188.
7. Lanusse, *Les heros*, 70 and 196.
8. *Historique de la Contre-Guerilla*, quoted in Brunon, *Camerone* [1981], 111–13.
9. Quoted in Brunon, *Camerone* [1981], 35–36.
10. Diesbach, 'Notes et Souvenirs', April 1863.
11. Diesbach, 'Notes et Souvenirs', April 1863.
12. Guyader, 'L'Officier Legion', 37.
13. Zede, 'Souvenirs', *Carnet* 370, 219; Zede, 'Temoignage,' 14.
14. A[uguste] Ballue, 'Souvenirs du Mexique – Cameron', *Lectures du Soir*, 42 (Musee des Familles, October and November 1875), 312–18 and 335–40. Reprinted as Captain Auguste Ballue, 'Camaron', *Kepi blanc*, no.271 (May 1965), 20–37. The illustrations included two of Sous-Lieutenant Henri-Guido Kauffmann's original paintings from Mexico.
15. Ballue, 'Cameron', 318.
16. Ballue, 'Cameron', 318.
17. Kirwan/M'Alevey, *Compagnie Irlandaise*, 185.
18. Lande/Maine, 'Camaron', 447.
19. Lande/Maine, 'Camaron', 447. Maine said that they were armed with the Minie carbine and sabre-bayonet, but his memory played tricks on him, as at this point in the Mexican campaign only the Companies of Voltigeurs had this weapon, and the Fusiliers of the Companies of the Centre – of which the 3rd Company was one – were armed with the 1857 Fusil.
20. Lande/Maine, 'Camaron', 447. Despite Maine's assertion, it is arguable as to whether or not Frenchmen were in a majority in the 3rd Company. At this late point in time, even the names of around forty members of the company are not known, simply because they were on the sick list, and did not fight at Camerone. Of the sixty who did, the birthplaces of only about a third are known. Some were certainly French. Others – like Gorski and Morziki – were the French-born sons of non-French fathers. Others again were certainly foreign born. The surnames of the men who fought at Camerone are known, even if not much else about them, and many of them are not French names.
21. Holler is Corporal Berg's spelling of this man's name. It also appears in Legion records as Haller and Heller, no first name given, and with nothing to otherwise identify him. General Penette failed to learn anything substantive about him and calls him 'Legionnaire X' – Penette/Castaingt, *Legion Extranjera*, 135, n.12.
22. *El Heraldo*, 16 May 1863.
23. Sergent, *Camerone*, 131, identifies the muleteer by name, and says that Dominguez was also responsible for looking after Captain Danjou's horse. All the evidence, however, seems to indicate that Danjou marched with his men, rather than rode, and I believe that Sergent is mistaken about the horse.

Chapter 10 – 'We will amuse the enemy'

1. Brunon, *Camerone* [1981], 130.
2. Lande/Maine, 'Camaron', 448.
3. Lande/Maine, 'Camaron', 449.

Source Notes

4. Lande/Maine, 'Camaron', 449–50.
5. Brunon, *Camerone* [1981], 176.
6. Lande/Maine, 'Camaron', 450.
7. Sergent, *Camerone*, 130, mistakenly identifies the wounded man as [Peter] Conrad.
8. Lande/Maine, 'Camaron', 451.
9. *El Heraldo*, 16 May 1863. This post-battle letter written by Corporal Berg to Colonel Jeanningros provided many of the details concerning the Combat of Camerone.
10. Lande/Maine, 'Camaron', 451–52
11. *El Heraldo*, 16 May 1863.
12. Lande/Maine, 'Camaron', 451.
13. Lande/Maine, 'Camaron', 451.
14. Lande/Maine, 'Camaron', 452.
15. Sebastian I. Campos, *Recuerdos Historicos de la Ciudad de Veracruz y Costa de Sotavento del Estado* (Orizaba: n.p. 1893), II, 70. Writing thirty years later, Campos' memories of events were vivid, but his details poor, as he reported that one hundred men of the Regiment Etranger's 2nd Battalion were involved, and also that the battle was fought on 4 May 1863.
16. *El Heraldo*, 16 May 1863. Berg listed the injuries sustained by the men of the 3rd of the 1st who were prisoners-of-war.
17. Fusilier Van den Meersche was not mentioned by Berg, but was among the sixteen men wounded and captured at this time.
18. Lande/Maine, 'Camaron', 451–53.
19. Lanusse, *Les heros*, 109.
20. Lande/Maine, 'Camaron', 453. Fritz also believed that 'the bayonet terrified them' – Lanusse, *Les heros*, 152.
21. Lande/Maine, 'Camaron', 453.
22. *El Heraldo*, 16 May 1863.
23. Lande/Maine, 'Camaron', 453. Morziki is incorrectly spelled as Morzicki.
24. Campos, *Recuerdos*, 70–71; Penette/Castaignt, *Legion Extranjera*, 25, n.23.
25. Lande/Maine, 'Camaron', 459.
26. Zede, 'Souvenirs', *Carnet* 370, 220; Zede, 'Temoignage', 15.
27. Penette/Castaingt, *Legion Extranjera*, 27. Research by Penette, Castaignt, Daniel Sousa of Huatusco, Louis Sol la Lande of Veracruz and others in the early 1960s established these men as the most prominent guerilla leaders involved. Penette and Castaignt, using published Mexican sources, also list a number of other guerilla leaders known to have been active in the region.
28. Lande/Maine, 'Camaron', 454.
29. Zede, 'Souvenirs', *Carnet* 370, 220; Zede 'Temoignage,' 15.
30. Lande/Maine, 'Camaron', 487. The evidence seems to be, at least at that point, Milan's regular cavalry outnumbered the mounted guerillas.
31. Penette/Castaingt, *Legion Extranjera,* 123. Lande/Maine, 'Camaron', 454, and Brunon, *Camerone* [1981], 145, incorrectly call him Laisne.
32. Lande/Maine, 'Camaron', 454.
33. Lanusse, *Les heros*, 129.
34. Lande/Maine, 'Camaron', 451.
35. Lande/Maine, 'Camaron', 455–56.
36. *El Heraldo*, 16 May 1863.
37. Lande/Maine, 'Camaron', 454.
38. *El Heraldo*, 16 May 1863. This painting, executed in the late 1920s for *Le Livre d'Or de la Legion Etrangere*, the regimental history published for the Foreign Legion's Centenary, is the property of the Museum of the Foreign Legion at Aubagne, France.
39. Lanusse, *Les heros*, 130.
40. Lande/Maine, 'Camaron', 455.
41. Lande/Maine, 'Camaron', 455.
42. *El Heraldo*, 16 May 1863.
43. Lanusse, *Les heros*, 136.
44. 'Report on the Affair at Camerone' – Commandant Eloi Regnault, Interim Commander of the Regiment Etranger, Cordoba, to General Ernest de Maussion, Commanding the Reserve Brigade, Orizaba, 17 August 1863 – S.H.A.T.
45. *El Heraldo*, 16 May 1863. This was when things were fresh in his memory. Diesbach, 'Notes et Souvenirs', May 1863, was mistaken when he said that 'Danjou fell with a bullet in the brain.'
46. Lande/Maine, 'Camaron', 455.
47. *El Heraldo*, 16 May 1863.
48. Lande/Maine, 'Camaron', 455.
49. Lausse, *Les heros*, 134.
50. Lande/Maine, 'Camaron', 455.
51. Campos, *Recuerdos*, 72.
52. Lanusse, *Les heros*, 140. Proper names were not Lanusse's forte and, quoting Fritz, he set them down as Schumasser for Schreiblich and Bauss for Baas. He also said that Fusilier Leonard (Leonhard) was killed, which was not the case, as he was one of the last men standing. Fusilier Lernoud was killed at this point, and it is probable that Lanusse misheard Fritz, or could not subsequently read his own notes.
53. Lande/Maine, 'Camaron', 455–56.
54. Lande/Maine, 'Camaron', 456.
55. Lande/Maine, 'Camaron', 454.
56. Lande/Maine, 'Camaron', 456.
57. Campos, *Recuerdos*, 75, remarkd that the Mexicans were at a disadvantage in facing the Foreign Legion at Camerone.
58. Brigadier-General Luis Garfias M[agana], *La Intervencion Francesca en Mexico* (Mexico City: Panorama Editorial for Secretaria de la Defensa Nacional 1981), 84–85.
59. Garfias M[agana], *Intervencion*, 85. This is certainly open to challenge, as Juarez was able to receive guns from the United States, many of them coming via California, moved southwards to Mexican ports on the Pacific Coast. He had found it possible to buy twenty-five thousand rifles even after the American Civil War broke out – *El Moniteur Republicano*, 2 December 1861 and *Siglo* 3 December 1861. The whole question of weapons reaching Mexico from the United States, especially after the Summer of 1865, is examined in detail in Robert Ryal Miller, 'Arms Across The Border: United States Aid To Juarez During the French Intervention in Mexico', *Transactions of the American Philosophical Society*, New Series, 63, Part 6 (December 1973).
60. Lande/Maine, 'Camaron', 457.
61. Brunon, *Camerone* [1981], 148.
62. *El Heraldo*, 16 May 1863.
63. Lande/Maine, 'Camaron', 456.
64. Lanusse, *Les heros*, 144.
65. Lande/Maine, 'Camaron', 457.
66. Lande/Maine, 'Camaron', 457.
67. Lande/Maine, 'Camaron', 457.
68. Lanusse, *Les heros*, 150.
69. Lande/Maine, 'Camaron', 461.

Chapter 11 – 'Jusqu'a la mort!'

1. Campos, *Recuerdos*, 71–72.
2. Lande/Maine, 'Camaron', 457.
3. Campos, *Recuerdos*, 72.
4. Lanusse, *Les heros*, 151.
5. Lanusse, *Les heros*, 152.
6. Lande/Maine, 'Camaron', 457.
7. Campos, *Recuerdos*, 72.
8. Lande/Maine, 'Camaron', 458.
9. Lanusse, *Les heros*, 153–54. The names of Corporal Delcaretto – who was critically wounded, not killed – and Fusiler Hipp are spelled correctly, the others mis-spelled as Langmayer [Langmeier], Weinsein [Wittgens] and Daylink [Daglincks].
10. Lande/Maine, 'Camaron', 458.
11. *El Heraldo*, 16 May 1863.
12. Lanusse, *Les heros*, 154–55.
13. Lanusse, *Les heros*, 153–54.
14. Lande/Maine, 'Camaron', 458.
15. Lanusse, *Les heros*, 156. These men's names, given as Rebores and Brunswick, should have been Rebers and Brunswick. Fritz incorrectly remembered that Corporal Pinzinger – given as Puizenger – was hit at this time.
16. *El Heraldo*, 16 May 1863.
17. Lanusse, *Les heros*, 134.
18. Lande/Maine, 'Camaron', 458.
19. Lande/Maine, 'Camaron', 458.
20. *El Heraldo*, 16 May 1863.
21. By comparing Corporal Berg's list of the seriously wounded, as opposed to slightly wounded, it was possible to determine who was sent on to La Joya, and who was retained for treatment at the field hospital near the dam.
22. Lande/Maine, 'Camaron', 458.
23. Lande/Maine, 'Camaron', 459.
24. Lande/Maine, 'Camaron', 462.
25. Lanusse, *Les heros*, 142.
26. Lande/Maine, 'Camaron', 459.
27. Lanusse, *Les heros*, 160.
28. Lanusse, *Les heros*, 158–59. Diesbach, 'Notes et Souvenirs', May 1863, talked to several Camerone survivors and wrote: 'The wounded and dying suffered tortures from thirst. It was impossible to given them any relief in their agony. Some even drank their own blood.' Turnbull, *Foreign Legion*, 60–64, mistakenly identified Diesbach as being in the 5th Company of the 2nd Battalion.
29. Lanusse, *Les heros*, 156.
30. Lande/Maine, 'Camaron', 461.
31. *El Heraldo*, 16 May 1863.
32. Lanusse, *Les heros*, 163.
33. Lanusse, *Les heros*, 162–64.
34. Lanusse, *Les heros*, 175.
35. Lanusse, *Les heros*, 165.
36. Lanusse, *Les heros*, 175–76.
37. Lande/Maine, 'Camaron', 460.
38. Campos, *Recuerdos*, 72.
39. Garfias M[agana], *Intervencion*, 86, reports his death, but refers to him as 'Captain Juan Canesco of the Perote guerilas.' Penette/Castaignt, *Legion Extranjera*, 27, in their list of prominent guerila leaders in the area, describe him as Juan Canesco from El Izote. It seems probable that he was with the National Guardsmen from there when he was killed.
40. Lanusse, *Les heros*, 178.
41. Lande/Maine, 'Camaron', 459.
42. Lande/Maine, 'Camaron', 460.
43. Lande/Maine, 'Camaron', 460. Maine spells this Fusilier's name as Bartolotto and said that he was Spanish. This is clearly an error by either Maine or Lande. Bertolotto was born in Toulon, France, on 23 December 1839, the son of a Sardinian sailor and his Piedmontese wife. Fusilier Aloysio Bernardo, who was killed in the corral, probably early in the afternoon, was a Spaniard from Asturias.
44. Lanusse, *Les heros*, 168–69.
45. Lande/Maine, 'Camaron', 460.
46. Lanusse, *Les heros*, 169.
47. Lande/Maine, 'Camaron', 460.
48. Lanusse, *Les heros*, 170.
49. Lande/Maine, 'Camaron', 460; Fritz, mentioning this 'new summons to surrender', commented that it drew 'no response' – Lanusse, *Les heros*, 170.
50. Zede, 'Souvenirs', *Carnet* 370, 222; Zede, 'Temoignage', 15.
51. *El Heraldo*, 16 May 1863.
52. Lanusse, *Les heros*, 171–72.
53. Lanusse, *Les heros*, 171–72. Magnin's name is mis-spelled as Mequin. Berg said later: 'We threw down our arms, believing that we had done what was required for the honour of the flag and for the glory of the regiment.' – *El Heraldo*, 16 May 1863.
54. Lanusse, *Les heros*, 173–74.
55. Campos, *Recuerdos*, 74.
56. Lande/Maine, 'Camaron', 460.
57. Lande/Maine, 'Camaron', 461.
58. Lanusse, *Les heros*, 174–75.
59. Lande/Maine, 'Camaron', 462.
60. Lande/Maine, 'Camaron', 462.
61. Lande/Maine, 'Camaron', 462.
62. Lanusse, *Les heros*, 178.
63. Lanusse, *Les heros*, 178–79.
64. Lanusse, *Les heros*, 179.
65. Lande/Maine, 'Camaron', 463.
66. Lande/Maine, 'Camaron', 462.
67. Lanusse, *Les heros*, 179.
68. Lanusse, *Les heros*, 179–80.
69. Lanusse, *Les heros*, 180–81.
70. Lande/Maine, 'Camaron', 462.
71. Lanusse, *Les heros*, 180–81.
72. Lande/Maine, 'Camaron', 463–64.
73. Lanusse, *Les heros*, 180.
74. Lande/Maine, 'Camaron', 464.
75. Lanusse, *Les heros*, 182–84. In telling of this moment fifteen years later Maine does not mention having asked for Cambas' agreement that they had done all that could be reasonably expected of them, reporting: 'We will surrender,' I responded, 'if you will allow us to retain our arms and our equipment, and if you promise to help and take care of our wounded Lieutenant' – Lande/Maine, 'Camaron', 463.
76. Lanusse, *Les heros*, 184.
77. Lande/Maine, 'Camaron', 463–64.
78. Lanusse, *Les heros*, 182–84.
79. Lanusse, *Les heros*, 186–87.
80. Lanusse, *Les heros*, 186–87.
81. Lande/Maine, 'Camaron', 464.
82. Lanusse, *Les heros*, 186–87.
83. Lanusse, *Les heros*, 188.
84. Campos, *Recuerdos*, 75.
85. Lande/Maine, 'Camaron', 464–65.
86. *El Heraldo*, 16 May 1863.
87. Sebastian I. Campos, *Operaciones militares del*

Estado de Veracruz y de la Costa de Stavento (Mexico City: n.p. 1891), quoted in Turnbull, *Foreign Legion*, 64.
88. Lanusse, *Les heros*, 189.

Chapter 12 – The Aftermath

1. Colonel Pierre Jeanningros, Commanding Officer, Regiment Etranger, Chiquihuite, to Commander-in-Chief, General Elie-Frederic Forey, Headquarters, Corps Expeditionnaire du Mexique, Cerro San Juan, 4 May 1863.
2. Kirwin/M'Alevey, *Compagnie Irlandaise*, 188.
3. Jeanningros to Forey, 4 May 1863.
4. Kirwin/M'Alevey, *Compagnie Irlandaise*, 186.
5. Jeanningros to Forey, 4 May 1863.
6. Jeanningros to Forey, 4 May 1863.
7. Kirwan/M'Alevey, *Compagnie Irlandaise*, 186.
8. Kirwan/M'Alevey, *Compangnie Irlandaise*, 187. Lai's Commanding Officer noted that he had 'a sabre cut to the hand and a bullet in the chest' – Jeanningros to Forey, 4 May 1863.
9. Brunon, *Camerone* [1981], 163; [de La Hayrie], *Combat*, 22.
10. Jeanningros to Forey, 4 May 1863. In point of fact, the estimate must have come from Vilain or Maudet, as Danjou had been killed prior to the arrival of the Infantry.
11. Kirwin/M'Alevey, *Compagnie Irlandaise*, 187.
12. Lanusse, *Les heros*, 209–11. Lanusse almost certainly received the account directly from Lai.
13. Jeanningros to Forey, 4 May 1863.
14. Kirwan/M'Alevey, *Compagnie Irlandaise*, 188.
15. Jeanningros to Forey, 4 May 1863.
16. Kirwan/M'Alevey, *Compagnie Irlandaise*, 188.
17. It is on display in the Foreign Legion Museum – Anonymous, *Musee de la Legion Etrangere: 150 Ans de Campagnes* (Aubagne: Presses de *Kepi blanc* 1981), 46.
18. Kirwan/M'Alevey, *Compagnie Irlandaise*, 188.
19. As Captain Sebastian Campos had been sent to La Joya to alert Milan to the fact that the 3rd of the 1st was forted up in the Hacienda de la Trinidad, use of the phrase 'I left with the cavalry' was either dissimulation, or intended to convey that, as Commanding Officer, he had ordered the reconnoitering to be carried out.
20. Not entirely true, as the Foreign Legion had, with great difficulty, made a few holes in the east wall, and the Mexicans subsequently brought crowbars and picks to break the walls of the hacienda and the outside wall.
21. Clearly a misunderstanding, as Danjou and Vilain fought until killed and Maudet participated in the final charge.
22. Another misunderstanding, a confusion of Danjou's rank as a Captain and his administrative post as Adjutant-Major of the Regiment Etranger.
23. Milan did not know that *Tambour* Lai had survived.
24. 'Troop class' referred to the National Guardsmen. It was to Milan's advantage not to mention the heavy losses of the guerillas. In fact, the official Mexican version generally ignores even their participation in the battle.
25. If he did, this document may be somewhere in the Mexican Military Archives, which are not open to researchers. It is possible that Milan did not provide a list, as the author of an important military study of the Intervention, who had access to some of the surviving Mexican records, was only able to report that 'an undetermined number of Mexican soldiers' died at Camerone – Garfias Magana, *Intervencion*, 86.
26. Colonel Francisco de P. Milan, La Joya, to General-in-Chief Miguel Blanco of the Central Brigade, Fort San Lorenzo, near Puebla, 30 April 1863 – quoted in De Leon Toral, *Historia Documental*, 188–89.
27. *El Heraldo*, 16 May 1863.
28. These graves, on land belonging to Pasqual Lagunes, a relative of David Alarcon, a descendant of the family which owned the Hacienda de la Trinidad, were located in the late 1970s by Captain Jean Castaingt, a French Army Reserve officer living in Mexico, but he was unable to learn the names of the Legionnaires buried in them.
29. The actual count of men killed at Camerone, or who died of wounds after it, is: two officers and twenty-one men killed, two wounded men died in the Mexican field hospital the day after the battle and one officer and eight men died of their wounds between 8 May and 4 August – a total of thirty-four. A mid-August report set the casualties at two officers and twenty men killed, with one officer and seven men dying of their wounds later, for a total of thirty – Commandant Eloi Regnault, Interim Commander, Regiment Etranger, Cordoba, to General Ernest de Maussion, Commanding the Reserve Brigade, Orizaba, 17 August 1863. De La Hayrie, writing in 1889, said that two officers and twenty-two men died in the battle and one officer and eight men after it, a total of thirty-three – *Combat*, 23. This figure was repeated in Zede, 'Souvenirs', *Carnet* 370, 219, and Zede, 'Temoignage', 14.
30. De Keratry, 'Contre-guerilla', 720.
31. Colonel Pierre Jeanningros, Paso Ancho, to General Ernest de Maussion, Orizaba, 2 May 1863 – S.H.A.T.
32. Regnault to de Maussion, 17 August 1863.
33. *Siglo*, 16 May 1863.
34. Campion, '. . .au Mexique.'
35. Campion, '. . .au Mexique.'
36. Campion, '. . .au Mexique.' Sergent, *Camerone*, 167–70, quotes several pages of conversation from Campion's manuscript memoir.
37. Brunon, *Camerone* [1981], 174.
38. Campion, 'au Mexique'.

Chapter 13 – 'A brilliant military page for the Regiment'

1. Jeanningros to Forey, 4 May 1863.
2. Campion, '. . . au Mexique'.
3. *Historique de la Contre-guerrilla*, entry for 3 May 1863, quoted in Captain Raymond Sereac, 'Apres Camerone: Comment la Contre-guerrilla du Colonel Dupin s'efforca de venger les heros de la Legion,' *Pages de l'Empire francaise: la Legion Etrangere*, no.30 (April–May 1962), 8–9.
4. De Keratry, 'Contre-Guerrilla', 720.
5. Campion, '. . . au Mexique'.
6. Kirwan/M'Alevey, *Compagnie Irlandaise*, 189.
7. Diesbach, 'Notes et Souvenirs,' May 1863.
8. Kirwan/M'Alevey, *Compagnie Irlandaise*, 189.

9. Campion, '. . . au Mexique'.
10. [de La Hayrie], *Combat*, 23–24. No doubt the wording reported by de La Hayrie was similar, but use of the name Legion Etrangere seems suspect, as Regiment Etranger would almost certainly have been used. Brunon, *Camerone* [1981], 167, gives the same wording, apparently another 'derivative' error traceable to de La Hayrie'. Over the next three years visitors to Camerone would note several temporary grave markers, with various forms of words on them. A typographical error in de La Hayrie's booklet gives the date of the battle as 20 April.
11. A reporter for the semi-official publication *Le Sud-Oranais*, in an article on the *Salle d'Honneur* at Sidi-bel-Abbes, circa 1894, described the gravesite at Camerone, and was told that the tree shading the gravestone had its own history. 'It was planted by the soldiers . . . at the tomb of their companions in arms' – quoted by de Beauvoir, *Legion Etrangere*, 149. Oudry, 'Camerone', 27, wrote: 'The Legionnaires planted a weeping willow.' The tree was subsequently identified as a Nacaste, a corruption of Guanacaste (*Enterolobium cyclocarpum*)– General [Marcel] Penette, *Histoire du Memorial de Camerone* (Paris: Privately Printed 1976), 6, n.10. It has a flat, spreading crown, and is often much wider than it is tall.
12. Jeanningros to Forey, 4 May 1863.
13. Campion, '. . . au Mexique.'
14. Lanusse, *Les heros*, 222.
15. Jeanningros to Forey, 4 May 1863.
16. Jeanningros to Forey, 4 May 1863.
17. Jeanningros to Forey, 4 May 1863. The story of the Brigadier of the *Chasseurs d'Afrique* is told in Lanusse, *Les heros*, 36–37.
18. Huart, *Souvenirs*, 8. His otherwise generally accurate account of the Combat of Camerone covers pages 5 to 9 and was probably obtained from survivors and other men of the 1st Battalion.
19. *Siglo*, 8 May 1863.
20. Penette/Castaignt, *Legion Extranjera*, 29, n.28. Details concerning Maudet's last days at Dona Juana's home in Huatusco were provided to the authors by her grandson, Alberto Gomez. There is a photograph of 'Mama Juana' in the Foreign Legion Museum.
21. General-in-Chief Miguel Blanco, Fort San Lorenzo, to Minister of War and Marine Ignacio Comonfort, Pensa Cola, 7 May 1863 – Toral, *Historia Documental*, 189.
22. Blanchot, *Memoires*, I, 344.
23. Blanchot, *Memoires*, I, 344–45.
24. Noix, *L'Expedition*, 279.
25. *Siglo*, 8 May 1863.
26. Lieutenant-Colonel Daniel Sousa, 'The Grave of Sous-Lieutenant Clement Maudet', report prepared by at the request of Captain Jean Castaignt of The Camerone Association. Printed in Sergent, *Camerone*, 462–63. [Captain Jean Castaignt], 'Huatusco conserve pieusement le souvenir et les restes d'un Officer de la Legion Etrangere', *Kepi blanc*, no.157 (May 1960), 73. Castaignt also authored an interesting and well-illustrated article on Huatusco and its links with the Regiment Etranger – 'Huatusco, petite ville du Mexique ait partie de l'histoire legionnaire', *Kepi blanc*, no.157 (May 1960), 68–73. Along with his photographs, the magazine used one of the paintings by Sous-Lieutenant Henri-Guido Kauffmann.
27. Penette/Castaignt, *Legion Extranjera*, 26.
28. General Order of the Army, 10 May 1863 – Grisot/Coulombon, *Legion etrangere*, 279; [Lafont], *Bivouacs*, 60; section republished as Captain Lafont, 'Le Pueblito de Camerone', *Vert et Rouge: Revue de la Legion Etrangere* (May 1949), 34.
29. Minister of War Ignacio Comonfort, In the Field, to General-in-Chief Miguel Blanco, Fort San Lorenzo, 12 May 1863 – Toral, *Historia Documental*, 190.
30. Noix, *L'Expedition*, 279.
31. Penette/Castaignt, *Legion Extranjera*, 26.
32. Penette/Castaignt, *Legion Extranjera*, 133. The hospital of St. Vincent was destroyed during the Revolution of 1910.
33. It has not been possible to determine when Berg's letter appeared in the Jalapa *Independiente*, as it seems that few copies of the newspaper of this period have survived – Patrick Shannon, Head of Interlibrary Lending, Microfilm Collection of the Doe Library, Berkeley Library, University of California at Berkeley, to Author, 7 October 2002. However, items from the *Independiente* were widely published elsewhere. Neither the A.L.E. nor S.H.A.T. has a copy of Berg's letter, and it seems likely that it never reached Jeanningros, though the Foreign Legion certainly knew of it, and what it said, from the various newspapers who published it.
34. *El Heraldo*, 16 May 1863. The paper also published the brief account of the battle which had appeared in *Siglo* eight days earlier.
35. *Siglo*, 17 May 1863.
36. *Siglo*, 17 May 1863.
37. The Author has seen the relevant issues of *El Heraldo* and *Siglo* – though not *El Monitor Republicano*. Sergent, *Camerone*, 176, apparently saw one published version of the letter which contained the statement: 'Sergeant-Major Tonel was remarkable for his coolness right up to the moment when he fell mortally wounded; but the one who earned the right to the greatest admiration by all was Sergeant Morziki. I am carrying out his last wish and ask that you tell Sergeant Bernard that, two minutes before he was killed, Morziki sent him a last farewell.' Berg was not in the shed in the southwest corner of the courtyard, but could have been told by survivors – Maine, Fritz, Wensel, Constantine, Leonard and others – about Morziki's last message to his friend.
38. Brunon, *Camerone* [1981], 93.
39. Grisot/Coulombon, *Legion etrangere*, 275; Penette/Castaignt, 22, n.17.
40. U.S. historian Douglas Porch was told that the French publication *L'Illustration* had devoted 'a large article to the battle with an engraving in its 18 July 1863 issue' – Porch, *Foreign Legion*, 680, n.25. A careful search of *L'Illustration* failed to find the alleged story and illustration – Jean-Francois Chanal, Service de Reproduction, *Bibliotheque Nationale de France*, to Author, 22 January 2002. The *Bibliotheque* also checked a number of subsequent possible issues of *L'Illustration*, and fruitlessly examined several other pictorial publications of the period, including *Le Monde Illustre* – Chanal to Author, 25 February 2002.
41. *Leipzig Illustrirte Zeitung*, 25 July 1863. In the

engraving, mounted Mexicans and foot soldiers attack Zouaves outside a two-storey building, while other Zouaves shoot down on them from the roof. The Author is grateful to Tom Gillmore of the Mary Evans Picture Library for bringing the existence of this illustration to his attention.
42. Blanchot, *Memoires*, I, 289.

Chapter 14 – Dupin Gets a Free Hand

1. De Keratry, 'Contre-guerilla', 722.
2. Hill/Hogg, *Corps d'Elite*, 39.
3. Diesbach, 'Notes et Souvenirs', May 1863.
4. Diesbach, 'Notes et Souvenirs', May 1863.
5. Hill/Hogg, *Corps d'Elite*, 45–46. The authors quote from the autobiographical reminiscences of a senior Mexican prisoner-of-war: Lieutenant-Colonel Francisco de Paula Troncoso, *Diario de las operaciones militaries del sitio del Puebla en 1863* (Mexico City: n.p. 1909), 296–97.
6. Penette/Castaignt, *Legion Extranjera*, 133–34.
7. Lanusse, *Les heros*, 222–23.
8. Lande/Maine, 'Camaron', 454.
9. Lande/Maine, 'Camaron', 464.
10. Penette/Castaignt, *Legion Extranjera*, 134.
11. Sergent, *Camerone*, 192; Brunon, *Camerone* [1981], 175–76.
12. Penette/Castaignt, *Legion Extranjera*, 26.
13. Diesbach, 'Notes and Souvenirs', June, 1863.
14. Ballue, 'Cameron', 312.
15. Penette/Castaignt, *Legion Extranjera*, 134, citing Microfilm of French Military Archives held at the College of Mexico; De Keratry, an officer in the *Contre-guerilla*, makes no mention of the finding of Fusilier De Vries when writing of the raid on Tomatlan in his memoirs – De Keratry, 'Contre-guerrilla', 730–31; Bergot, *Foreign Legion*, 87, is mistaken in saying that Dupin found De Vries at Cueva-Pintada.
16. *Historique* of the *Contre-Guerilla* quoted in Brunon, *Camerone* [1981], 176–77; also quoted in Sereac, 'Apres Camerone', 10–11.
17. Hill/Hogg, *Corps d'Elite*, 39. Lieutenant Jean Lebre died on 21 July 1863.
18. *Historique* of the *Contre-guerilla*, quoted in Sereac, 'Apres Camerone', 11.
19. Lanusse, *Les heros*, 223.
20. Lande/Maine, 'Camaron', 467.
21. *Historique* of the *Contre-guerilla*, quoted in Sereac, 'Apres Camerone', 11.
22. Lanusse, *Les heros*, 45–46.
23. Brunon, *Camerone* [1981], 177–78, says that twelve prisoners were exchanged, and sets the timeframe as mid-July. Sergent, *Camerone*, 193, says that twenty men were exchanged, but that only sixteen of them were Camerone survivors, the other four – who he names – being men of the *Infanterie de Marine*. As it appears that four more men were turned over to the French shortly afterwards, this may be what Brunon meant by 'twelve', thinking it had been a single exchange. As another four men were returned shortly afterwards – making a total of sixteen – it may be what Sergent meant, also believing that they had all been exchanged at the same time. The *Historique* of the *Contre-guerilla* says of the prisoners: 'They told all about the bad treatment they had to suffer during their captivity' – quoted in Sereac, 'Apres Camerone', 11. This may be tellling, as the Camerone survivors did not speak of being poorly treated in their captivity. Other French prisoners-of-war sometimes did.
24. Lande/Maine, 'Camaron', 467. It seems probable that eight is the correct number, as only eight Legionnaires were promoted at the time.
25. *Memorial de la Loire*, August 1878, quoted in Sergent, *Camerone*, 193–94. The story says that Jeanningros 'later distributed the crosses and medals'. This is ambiguous, as the context implies 'later' to mean the same day. In point of fact, apart from the Cross of a Chevalier of the Legion of Honour bestowed earlier on *Tambour* Lai – no decorations or medals were even announced until six weeks later.
26. Dossier Philippe Maine, 21 July 1863. It is reasonable to believe that his companions were upgraded to the Elite Companies the same day.
27. Diesbach, 'Notes et Souvenirs', July 1863.
28. Kirwan/M'Alevey, *Compagnie Irlandaise*, 184.
29. Diesbach, 'Notes et Souvenirs', July 1863.
30. Adrien de Tuce, *Cinq ans au Mexique 1862–67* (Paris: Cahiers de la Quinzaine, n.d.), 65–66.
31. De Tuce, *Cinq ans au Mexique*, 68–69.
32. Only the date – 14 July – of the return of Corporal Maine and his seven comrades is known, but it is clear that the other twelve exchanged prisoners were back in Cordoba by mid-August.
33. Diesbach, 'Notes et Souvenirs', August 1863.
34. *Annuaire militaire . . . 1863*, 421.
35. Diesbach, 'Notes et Souvenirs', August 1863.
36. Hill/Hogg, *Corps d'Elite*, 40.
37. Diesbach, 'Notes et Souvenirs', August 1863.

Chapter 15 – 'Everyone did his Duty'

1. 'Report on the Affair at Camerone' – Regnault to de Maussion, 17 August 1863. Regnault used the spelling Camarone. A relatively small number of Legionnaires' names are also mis-spelled in the report: Tonnelle [Tonel], Morzicki [Morziki], Bartolotto [Bertolotto], Bockuki [Bogucki], Kurtz [Kurz], Burgeiser [Burgiser], Dagline [Daglincks], Kunaseck [Kunassec], Rebord [Rebers], Wittgens [Witgens] and Langmayer [Langmeier].
2. It has been claimed that Peter Dicken was an 'Anglo-Saxon' – Geraghty, *March or Die*, 71. James W. Ryan, *Camerone: The French Foreign Legion's Greatest Battle* (Westport, Connecticut: Praeger, 1996), 18, calls him Dickens and describes him an 'Englishman'. He was, in fact, a German.
3. Penette/Castaignt, *Legion Extrangera*, 134.
4. Regnault to de Maussion, 17 August 1863.
5. Penette/Castaignt, *Legion Extrangera*, 134.
6. Diesbach, 'Notes et Souvenirs', August 1863.
7. Marshal Elie-Frederic Forey, Commander-in-Chief, Corps Expeditionnaire du Mexique, Order of the Day #195, 30 August 1863, Mexico City - S.H.A.T. Forey uses the spelling Camaron, and, inevitably, a number of Legionnaires' names are mis-spelled: Gorsky [Gorski], Kunasseg [Kunassec], Rerbers [Rebers] and Schreiblick [Schreiblich]. The Author worked from Forey's original Order #195. It is reproduced in two sections in Brunon, *l'Camerone et l'Aigle*, 15–16 and 24–25, and follows the original, except for omitting Regnault's listing of the

forty-six members of *La Compagnie Danjou* for whom he could account. Lande/Maine, 'Camaron', 467, incorrectly dates Forey's Order #195 as 31 August. So does Lanusse, *Les heros*, 235–38, and he also 'improves' on it: Increasing Milan's forces to two thousand, and inaccurately reporting Forey as saying that the three officers died with twenty-nine soldiers (two more than the Commander-in-Chief's actual count) and that twenty-one others (to Forey's sixteen) were wounded, a total of fifty-three, to Forey's forty-six. Lanusse is equally careless with the names of those decorated: Cunassec [Kunassec], Schreiblick [Schreiblich], Rebares [Rebers], Weinseil [Wensel]. Grisot/Coulombon, *Legion etrangere*, 278–79, are even worse: Cunassec [Kunassec], Maquin [Magnin], Finzinger [Pinzinger], Schoeffner [Schaffner], Schreiblick [Schreiblich] and Riberes [Rebers]. Fusilier Catteau appears as Katau, and five lines later as Cotteau, while Fusilier Wensel appears as both Wenzel and Werhseil. Commandant Regnault's Name is spelled Reynault.
8. Order of the Day #195, 30 August, 1863.
9. Lande/Maine, 'Camaron', 467, citing the *Moniteur universel*, 9 August 1864.
10. Evariste Berg, *Releve de Services*.
11. Zede, 'Souvenirs', *Carnet* 370, 219; Zede, 'Temoignage', 14.
12. Dossier Philippe Maine, 21 July 1863.
13. Zede, 'Souvenirs', *Carnet* 370, 219; Zede, 'Temoignage', 14.
14. Lanusse, *Les heros*, 217.
15. [de La Hayrie], *Camaron*, 23, copied in Zede, 'Souvenirs', *Carnet* 370, 219. (He also copies de La Hayrie's incorrect spelling of Vilain as Villain.) The original edition of the *Livre d'Or* (1931) makes no attempt to deal with the number of survivors, but Zede's memoirs, published three years later, are given the stamp of authenticity in the three subsequent editions of the regimental history: Brunon/Manue, *Livre d'Or* (1958), 75; Brunon/Manue/Carles, *Livre d'Or* (1976), 107; Brunon/Manue/Carles, *Livre d'Or* (1981), 107.
16. The Foreign Legion Museum has the diploma for his *Medaille du Mexique* and his officer's sabre and Lefaucheux revolver – Anonymous, *Musee*, 46.
17. Napoleon III to Bazaine, #3 Biarritz, 29 September 1863 – BA, I, f. 97, cited in Dabbs, *French Army*, 65.
18. Dossier Philippe Maine, 14 September 1863; Penette/Castaignt, *Legion Extranjera*, 105.
19. Diesbach, 'Notes et Souvenirs', September 1863.
20. Lanusse, *Les heros*, 47.
21. Lanusse, *Les heros*, 48.
22. Lanusse does not date his visit to Camerone, but it had to be after Forey's Order #195 of 30 August 1863 and before the Regiment Etranger was pulled out of the *Terres Chaudes* in March 1864. The variables suggest late September 1863.
23. Cross-referencing the roster of the 3rd of the 1st makes it clear that Friedrich Fritz is the only Camerone survivor to answer the needs of Lanusse's three clues.
24. Lanusse, *Les heros*, 49.
25. Lanusse, *Les heros*, 50.
26. Lanusse, *Les heros*, 216. It is apparent that Lanusse either did not take a note, or was being careless, as the inscription would certainly have said Regiment Etranger, rather than Legion Etrangere.
27. Lanusse, *Les heros*, 49–50.
28. Lanusse, *Les heros*, 52–54. It may perhaps be guessed that Fritz spoke of 'the glory and grandeur' of the Regiment Etranger, rather than of France – which sounds more like the patriotic Chaplain Lanusse.
29. Lanusse, *Les heros*, 113–14. Fritz – or Lanusse – grossly exaggerates the number of Mexican Cavalry present at Camerone at this point in the action.
30. Lanusse, *Les heros*, 55.
31. Lanusse, *Les heros*, 130.
32. Lanusse, *Les heros*, 172–73.
33. Lanusse, *Les heros*, 164–65.
34. Lanusse, *Les heros*, 170–71.
35. Lanusse, *Les heros*, 222.
36. Lanusse, *Les heros*, 166.
37. Lanusse, *Les heros*, 185–86.
38. 'Inspection of the Regiment Etranger' by General Ernest de Maussion, Cordoba, 25 September 1863 – Xb 778, S.H.A.T.
39. Bazaine to Napoleon III, Mexico City, 25 October 1863 – BA, I, f. 173-75, quoted in Dabbs, *French Army*, 70.

Chapter 16 – 'The past will be the guide for the future'

1. Colonel Pierre Jeanningros, Commanding Officer, Veracruz and the *Terres Chaudes*, to Marshal Jacques Randon, Minister of War, Paris, Letter #454, 1 October 1863 – S.H.A.T. The letter is reproduced in Brunon, *Camerone et l'Aigle*, 13–14, Brunon, 'Camerone et l'Aigle', 14 and 17, and Brunon, *Camerone* [1981], 180, which also publishes a photograph of the letter. The same photograph also appears in Brunon/Manue, *Livre d'Or* (1958), between 74 and 75; Brunon/Manue/Carles, *Livre d'Or* (1976), 103; and Brunon/Manue/Carles, *Livre d'Or* (1981), 110. Lanusse, *Les heros*, 239, refers to the letter, but wrongly dates it 1 September 1863.
2. General Order #195, 30 August 1863. It is reproduced in Brunon, *Camerone et l'Aigle*, 14–15; Brunon, 'Camerone et l'Aigle', 14 and 17; and Brunon, *Camerone* [1981], 180.
3. Regnault to de Maussion, 17 August 1863. Reproduced in Brunon, *Camerone et l'Aigle*, 16–24, and Brunon, 'Camerone et l'Aigle,' 14–17. In neither case is the whole report quoted.
4. Penette/Castaingt, *Legion Extranjera*, 134.
5. *Historique* of the Egyptian Battalion, 3 and 4 October 1863 – G7, 124, S.H.A.T., quoted in Hill/Hogg, *Corps d'Elite*, 42–43; De Keratry, 'Contre-guerilla', 736–37; Grisot/Coulombon, *Legion etrangere*, 281–82, mistakenly say that the escort was provided by the 2nd Battalion of the Regiment Etranger. A contemporary artist's impression of the attack, published in *L'Illustration*, appears in Sergent, *Camerone*.
6. Diesbach, 'Notes et Souvenirs', October 1863.
7. *Historique sommaire du corps*, 31 October 1863, mss., A.L.E.
8. Grisot/Coulombon, *Legion etrangere*, 280.
9. Ballue, 'Cameron', 21.
10. Marshal Jacques Randon, Minister of War, Paris, to Colonel Pierre Jeanningros, Commanding

Officer, Veracruz and the *Terres Chaudes*, 4 November 1863 – S.H.A.T. The notation is clearly visible in photographs of the letter: *Livre d'Or* (1958), (1976) and (1981).
11. Randon to Jeanningros, 4 November 1863. The letter is reproduced in Brunon, *Camerone et l'Aigle*, 25–26; Brunon, 'Camerone et l'Aigle', 18; and Brunon, *Camerone* [1981], 181; Lanusse, *Les heros*, 239–40, also publishes the letter, changing it slightly, by substituting the word 'campaign' for the word 'expedition', and incorrectly dating it 4 October 1863, rather than 4 November 1863.
12. Marshal Jacques Randon, Minister of War, Paris, to General Achille Bazaine, Commander-in-Chief, Corps Expeditionnaire du Mexique, Mexico City, 4 November 1863 – S.H.A.T.
13. Marshal Jacques Randon, Minister of War, Paris, to 3rd Directorate of the Artillery, November 4, 1863 – General Correspondence of the Ministry of War – S.H.A.T. The letter is quoted in Oudry, 'Camerone', 28–29.
14. The Regimental Standard was ordered destroyed by the Government of the Third Republic's Circulaire of 5 July 1871 – Brunon, *Camerone et l'Aigle*, 27; Brunon, *Camerone* [1981], 182; and Brunon/Manue/Carles, *Livre d'Or* (1981), 400.
15. Campion, '. . . au Mexique.'
16. Bazaine to Napoleon III, 19 November 1863 – BA, II, f.325 and 370–71, cited in Dabbs, *French Army*, 70–71. It appears that the recruiting may not have been altogether successful, as it was later asserted that most them were former soldiers who had fought at Puebla and that they deserted *en masse* as soon as they could – Grisot/Coulombon, *Legion etrangere*, 280.
17. Campion, '. . . au Mexique.'
18. Abbe J.E. Lanusse, Aumonier, *Ecole Speciale Militaire*, Saint-Cyr, to General Alexis de La Hyrie, Commandant, 12th Division d'Infanterie, 6th Corps d'armee, 23 October 1889 – quoted in [de La Hayrie], *Combat*, iv.
19. Lanusse, *Les heros*, 56–58.
20. Lanusse, *Les heros*, 66.
21. Lanusse, *Les heros*, 50.
22. Lanusse, *Les heros*, 192–93. Sergent, *Camerone*, 80, says that Abbe de Ribens (given as Ribeins) is buried at Palo Verde. If so, it is surmised that his body was moved there when the station for the Imperial Mexican Railway was built at Camaron in mid-1864.
23. Grisot/Coulombon, *Legion etrangere*, 282–83.
24. Zede, 'Souvenirs', *Carnet* 371, 254.
25. Frederic Martyn, *Life in the Legion from a Soldier's Point of View* (London: Everett 1911), 267–68. The story, with minor embellishments, may very well be true, as there are many documented examples of unilateral actions by priests attempting to frustrate the French, and give individual support to Labastida's wishes.

Chapter 17 – An Illusive Enemy

1. Henri Spinner, *Les Souvenirs d'un vieux soldat* (Neuchatel: Messeiller 1906), 23. The first part of the book, 'A la Legion au Mexique', deals with his service in the Foreign Legion, the second, 'Dans les troupes papales', as a member of the Vatican's Swiss Guards. Previously published in German: Heinrich Spinner, *Algier, Meziko, Rom* (Zurich: Schroeter 1901). Subtitle: 'Schicksale eines Schweizers im fremden Kriegsdiensten'.
2. Grisot/Coulombon, *Legion etrangere*, 282–83.
3. Grisot/Coulombon, *Legion etrangere*, 282–83.
4. Porch, *Foreign Legion*, 137.
5. Diesbach, 'Notes et Souvenirs', February 1864.
6. Diesbach, 'Notes et Souvenirs', February 1864.
7. Zede, 'Souvenirs', *Carnet* 373, 55.
8. Zede, 'Souvenirs', *Carnet* 373, 55.
9. Unpublished manuscript Memoir by Charles-Louis Dupin – Archives of the Ministry of Defence, Paris – 1K 198, S.H.A.T.
10. Sereac, 'Contre-Guerilla', 20-25; Salkin, 'du Pin au Mexique', 31.
11. Dabbs, *French Army*, 98–99.
12. Dabbs, *French Army*, 102–04, deals with Bazaine's problems with Santa Anna.
13. Quoted in Sergent, *Camerone*, 247.
14. Diesbach, 'Notes et Souvenirs', February 1864.
15. Penette/Castaignt, *Legion Extrangera*, 135.
16. Grisot/Coulombon, *Legion etrangere*, 282-83.
17. Bazaine to Randon, #17, Mexico City, 27 April 1864 – BA, VII, f. 1344–1345, quoted in Dabbs, *French Army*, 230.
18. Zede, 'Souvenirs', *Carnet* 371, 256.
19. Spinner, *Souvenirs*, 23.
20. Grisot/Coulombon, *Legion etrangere*, 284–85, are mistaken in saying that Jeanningros did not return to Puebla until 6 June.
21. Spinner, *Souvenirs*, 23.
22. Zede, 'Souvenirs', *Carnet* 371, 261.
23. Zede, 'Souvenirs', *Carnet* 371, 261.
24. DECRET IMPERIAL – Qui cree un quatrieme bataillon dans le regiment etranger – 30 April 1864.
25. Randon to Jeanningros, 4 November 1863. Considering the early production of the medal, and the fact that it was specifically dated, the original intention may well have been to subsequently issue attachable 'clasps' for individual battles, as the British had done with the Crimean Medal. The fact that none were issued for the *Expedition du Mexique* medal was doubtless because, as the war dragged on, it became increasingly unpopular in France, and was seen as best forgotten. Otherwise, the campaigns involving Oaxaca – or, as the French spell it, Oajaca – Monterrey/Matamoras, and possibly Tampico, might have suggested themselves as suitable for commemoration.
26. *Historique sommaire du corps*, April 1864 – manuscript in A.L.E.
27. Zede, 'Souvenirs', *Carnet* 371, 764.
28. Zede, 'Souvenirs', *Carnet* 370, 221; Zede, 'Temoignage', 15.
29. Zede, 'Souvenirs', *Carnet* 371, 266.

Chapter 18 – The Emperor Arrives

1. Pierre Jeanningros to his wife, Louise, 24 May 1864 – quoted in Sergent, *Camerone*, 268–69. Bazaine, of course, subsequently married a Mexican woman and a number of French civilians also took Mexican wives.
2. Zede, 'Souvenirs', *Carnet* 371, 764.
3. Empress Carlota to Empress Eugenie, letter quoted in Joan Haslip, *The Crown of Mexico* (New York: Holt, Rinehart and Winston 1972), 242.

4. Blair Niles, *Passengers to Mexico* (New York: Farrar & Rinehart 1943), 128, quoting from Countess Paola Kollonitz, *The Court of Mexico* (London: n.p. 1868).
5. Carlota to Eugenie, in Haslip, *Crown*, 245.
6. Carlota to Eugenie, in Haslip, *Crown*, 248.
7. Kollonitz, in Haslip, *Crown* 247, quoting from Kollonitz, *Court.*
8. Diesbach, 'Notes et Souvenirs', May 1864.
9. Diesbach, 'Notes et Souvenirs', June 1864.
10. Henri Loizillon, *Lettres sur l'Expedition au Mexique publiees par sa soeur, 1862–67* (Paris: Ernest Flammarion n.d.), 236. (Nouvelle edition.) Letter to Mme. Cornu, 1 June 1864.
11. Zede, 'Souvenirs', *Carnet* 370, 219, and Zede, 'Temoignage', 14, reported that, not long after their meeting at Camerone, Berg was 'killed in a duel in Mexico by another Sous-Lieutenant named Tochon'. Penette/Castaignt, *Legion Extrangera*, 135, were able to confirm the place and date, but not the circumstances.
12. Gustavo Baz and E.L. Gallo, *History of the Mexican Railway* (Mexico City: Gallo & Co. 1876), 93. English translation by George F. Henderson. Originally published as Gustavo Baz and E.L. Gallo, *Historia Del Ferrocarril Mexicano. Riqueza de Mexico en la Zona del Golfo a la Mesa Central, bajo su aspecto geologico, agricola, manufacturero y comercial* (Mexico City: Gallo & Cie. 1874).
13. Bazaine to Randon, #17, 24 March 1864, in BA, VI, f. 1003; Bazaine to Carlos Corta, Commission for Finance, Mexico City, 18 April 1864, in BA, VII, f. 1256; Bazaine to Colonel Louis Doutrelaine, #372, 22 April 1864, in BA, VII, f. 1282, cited or quoted in Dabbs, *French Army*, 240.
14. Campion, '. . . au Mexique.'
15. Hill/Hogg, *Corps d'Elite*, 56–60. The authors are mistaken in saying that a hundred Austrian Volunteers were included in Marechal's force, as Austrian troops did not arrive in Mexico until late December.
16. Bergot, *Foreign Legion*, 84, n.1.
17. Sergent, *Camerone*, 258.
18. Spinner, *Souvenirs*, 38.
19. Campion, '. . . au Mexique'; Diesbach, 'Notes et Souvenirs', July 1864.
20. Pierre Jeanningros to his wife, Louise, 3 August 1864 – quoted in Sergent, *Camerone*, 308.
21. Grisot/Coulombon, *Legion etrangere*, 285–86.
22. De Keratry, 'Contre-Guerilla', 734.
23. Baz/Gallo, *Mexican Railway*, 93.
24. De Keratry, 'Contre-guerilla', 735.
25. De Keratry, 'Contre-guerilla', 735
26. De Keratry, 'Contre-guerilla', 736
27. De Keratry, 'Contre-guerilla', 737.

Chapter 19 – Bazaine Plans a Campaign

1. Un Carabinier [Narcisse-Henri-Edouard Faucher de Saint-Maurice], *Organisation militaire des Canadas: L'Enemie! L'Enemie!* (Quebec City: Typographie de Leger Brousseau 1862). The booklet's hoped-for anonymity was lost when the author sent a copy to Lieutenant-Colonel Boucher de la Bruere with the inscription: 'Hommage de l'auteur N.H.E. Faucher de Saint-Maurice.' *Cours de tactique* (Quebec City: Typographie de Leger Brousseau 1863). Gerard Parizeau, 'Faucher de Saint-Maurice: ecrivain, journaliste, depute, president de la section francaise de la Societe royale du Canada', (Ottawa: *Proceedings and Transactions of the Royal Society of Canada*), IV Series, 7 (1969), 207–30; Kenneth Landry, 'Faucher de Saint-Maurice, Narcisse-Henri-Edouard', *Dictionary of Canadian Biography*, (Toronto: University of Toronto Press 1975) XII, 308–09.
2. [Narcisse-Henri-Edouard] Faucher de Saint-Maurice, *De Quebec a Mexico souvenirs de voyage, de garnison, de combat et de bivouac* (Montreal: Duernay Freres et Dansereau 1874), in two volumes. The work was part of a four-volume set of de Saint-Maurice's writings: Volume I, *A la Brunante, Contes et recits*, a work of 347 pages, was a collection of short stories; Volumes II and III, *De Quebec a Mexico . . .*, totalling 507 pages, were travel reportage and his war experiences; and Volume IV, *Choses et autres*, 294 pages, was a series of articles and critiques of Canadian literature. J.-B. Berard, 'Etude litteraire: M. Faucher de St. Maurice', *Revue canadienne*, 11 (1874), 914–26. *De Quebec a Mexico . . .* was favourably reviewed by M. Coquille, Editor of the Paris newspaper *Le Monde*, which encouraged de Saint-Maurice to re-issue the second volume as *Deux ans au Mexique*, with Coquille's review forming the Introduction. The book was popular and several editions were published in Montreal: 1878, 1879 and 1880 – Lynn Lafontaine, National Library of Canada, to Author, 16 December 1999. Edition used: (Montreal: Librairie Saint-Joseph 1881).
3. Saint-Maurice, *Deux ans*, 17. The nickname piou-piou was applied to French infantrymen, in much the same way as their British counterparts were referred to as Tommy and Americans as G.I. Joe.
4. Saint-Maurice, *Deux ans*, 19. Clearly the bronze column seen by Chaplain Lanusse had gone, and Saint-Maurice's memory of the inscription on the grave is obviously in error. Regiment Etranger would have been there, rather than Legion Etrangere, and Maudet, of course, was a Sous-Lieutenant.
5. Saint-Maurice, *Deux ans*, 24.
6. Saint-Maurice, *Deux ans*, 33.
7. Saint-Maurice, *Deux ans*, 37.
8. Saint-Maurice, *Deux ans*, 36.
9. Grisot/Coulombon, *Legion etrangere*, 285.
10. Saint-Maurice, *Deux ans*, 41.
11. Saint-Maurice, *Deux ans*, 175.
12. Grisot/Coulombon, *Legion etrangere*, 284.
13. 'Inspection of the Regiment Etranger' by General Augustin Brincourt, 15 September 1864 – Xb 778, S.H.A.T.
14. Brunon, Jean, 'Camerone et l'Aigle du Regiment Etranger 1862–1870', *La Legion Etrangere* (May 1941), 18.
15. Spinner, *Souvenirs*, 126.
16. Grisot/Coulombon, *Legion etrangere*, 286.
17. Grisot/Coulombon, *Legion etrangere*, 285.
18. The political ramifications of raising the Belgian Volunteers is covered in Arnold Blumberg, 'The Diplomacy of the Mexican Empire, 1863–1867', *Transactions of the American Philosophical Society*, New Series, Volume 61, Part 8 (November 1971), 61-65. The story of their stay in Mexico has been told by their commander:

General Alfred Louis Adolphe Graves Van der Smissen, *Souvenirs du Mexique, 1864–1867* (Brussels: J. Lebegue 1892; Paris: Charles-Lavauzelle 1892), as well as by a historian: Albert Duchesne, *L'expedition des volontaires belges au Mexique 1864–1867: Au service de Maximilien et de Charlotte* (Brussels: Centre d'Histoire Militaire, Musee Royal de l'Armee 1967).
19. Captain Claude J. Des Loiseau, *Le Mexique et la Legion Belge, 1864–67* (Brussels: Imprimerie-Lithographic de J. de Cocq 1870), 24–25. Loiseau was told the story of the Combat of Camerone and of 'Captain Adjutant-Major d'Anjou' and his men, though he gathered that the battle lasted only some 'two or three hours'.
20. A number of Foreign Legion subalterns, often the most junior in their respective ranks, were detached to serve with the *Contre-guerilla*, the Egyptian Battalion or units of the Mexican Imperial Army for greater or lesser periods of time.
21. Des Loiseau, *Legion belge*, 25.
22. Emile Walton, *Souvenirs d'un Officier Belge au Mexique, 1864–1866* (Paris: Tomers 1868), 14 and 25. Walton got the details of the inscription wrong, writing that it said: 'Here lies the 4th Company of the 3rd Battalion of the Foreign Legion.'
23. Baz/Gallo, *Mexican Railway*, 94.
24. Headquarters Letter No. 8839, 27 November 1864 – Saint-Maurice, *Deux ans*, 71.
25. Saint-Maurice, *Deux ans*, 78. Lansquenet was a card game of German origin.
26. Saint-Maurice, *Deux ans*, 78.
27. Saint-Maurice, *Deux ans*, 101.
28. Saint-Maurice, *Deux ans*, 100.
29. Saint-Maurice, *Deux Ans*, 12.
30. Eugene Amiable, *Legionnaire au Mexique* (Brussels: Charles Dessart 1942), 52 and 98. Preface and Annotations by Louis Leconte, *Conservateur-en-Chef* of the *Musee Royal de l'Armee* in Brussels. Amiable was born in the town of Tirlemont in 1838 and joined the Foreign Legion in 1864. Leconte notes that care must be taken in using the book, because of inconsistencies and Amiable's carelessness with dates.
31. Saint-Maurice, *Deux ans*, 77.
32. Saint-Maurice, *Deux Ans*, 101–02.
33. Brunon, 'Camerone et l'Aigle', 18.

Chapter 20 – Oaxaca Falls

1. Saint-Maurice, *Deux ans*, 107.
2. Saint-Maurice, *Deux ans*, 119.
3. Sergeant, *Camerone*, 321–46, and Saint-Maurice, *Deux ans*, 104–51, have good accounts of the Oaxaca Campaign; other details from Grisot/Coulombon, *Legion etrangere*, 287–89, and De Beauvoir, *Legion Etrangere*, 86–87.
4. Saint-Maurice, *Deux ans*, 123–24.
5. Hill/Hogg, *Corps d'Elite*, 65–66.
6. Loizillon, *Lettres*, 274–300, no. lxv, from Morelia, to his sister, 6 February 1865.
7. Kirwan/M'Alevey, *Compagnie Irlandaise*, 91. Kirwan's memory was not helped by the fact that he was unfamiliar with the map of Southern Mexico.
8. Kirwan/M'Alevey, *Compagnie Irlandaise*, 93.
9. Kirwan/M'Alevey, *Compagnie Irlandaise*, 96.
10. Zede, 'Souvenirs', *Carnet* 373, 450.
11. Grisot/Coulombon, *Legion etrangere*, 289.
12. Kirwan/M'Alevey, *Compagnie Irlandaise*, 93–94.
13. Kirwan/M'Alevey, *Compagnie Irlandaise*, 93–94.
14. Spinner, *Souvenirs*, 155.
15. Sergent, *Camerone*, 346.
16. Saint-Maurice, *Deux ans*, 139.
17. Kirwan/M'Alevey, *Compagnie Irlandaise*, 94
18. Grisot/Coulombon, *Legion etrangere*, 289.
19. Zede, 'Souvenirs', *Carnet* 373, 455.
20. Louis Leconte, in his Preface to Amiable, *Legionnaire*, 13, expresses some doubts about Amiable having been a member of the Mounted Company.
21. Amiable, *Legionnaire*, 94 and 103–05.
22. Saint-Maurice, *Deux ans*, 145.
23. Kirwan/M'Alevey, *Compagnie Irlandaise*, 95. It is incorrectly stated by Kirwan that Docir escaped when the earthquake struck Puebla, but the earthquake occurred the previous October. It may well be, however, that the building in which Docir was kept had been damaged by the earthquake, making escape easier. Dupin's name is given as Dupau. De Beauvoir, *Legion Etrangere*, 86–87, tells, briefly, a similar story of treachery concerning a Prussian-born Corporal – name not given – who was also executed by firing squad. It is surmised that the men may have been one and the same.
24. The various aspects of the raising of the *Osterreichische Freicorps* is dealt with in Blumberg, 'Diplomacy', 64–65.
25. Biographical details on Lieutenant Gruber, Record Group Five, Belgish-osterreiche Freikorps [Belgian-Austrian Volunteer Corps], Kriegsarchiv [War Archives], Vienna. The Order of Guadaloupe was bestowed on 6 February 1865 – Dr. Rainer Egger, Osterreichisches Staatsarchiv [Austrian State Archives], Vienna, to Author, 30 December 1999, and Dr. Peter Broucek, Curator Record Group Five, Belgish-osterreiche Freikorps, to Author, 8 June 2002. Unfortunately, no photograph of Lieutenant Gruber has been found – Dr. Robert Rill, Picture Collection, Kriegsarchiv, to Author, 28 June 2002.
26. Zede, 'Souvenirs', *Carnet* 371, 258–59.

Chapter 21 – The Hand of Captain Danjou

1. Hill/Hogg, *Corps d'Elite*, 67–72.
2. Bazaine to Randon, 27 August 1865 – G7,2, S.H.A.T., cited in Hill/Hogg, *Corps d'Elite*, 78, n.14.
3. Hill/Hogg, *Corps d'Elite*, 72; De Keratry, 'Contre-guerilla', 735, mistakenly says that it was La Soledad which Napoleon III ordered renamed Villa Marechal.
4. DECRET IMPERIAL – Qui cree un cinquieme bataillon dans le regiment etranger – 5 April 1865.
5. Penette/Castaignt, *Legion Extranjera*, 26, n.12.
6. Du Barail, *Mes Souvenirs*, II, 375.
7. Saint-Maurice, *Deux ans*, 172.
8. Saint-Maurice, *Deux Ans*, 161. Grisot/Coulombon, *Legion etrangere*, 291, give 30 April as the date of Jeanningros' departure from Mexico City, which is certainly incorrect, as a major fire in the capital on 3 May killed several officers and men of different regiments. Saint-Maurice was there, helped as a firefighter, and was around for some days afterwards for various funerals – Saint-Maurice, *Deux ans*, 157-61.

9. Saint-Maurice, *Deux ans*, 165.
10. Saint-Maurice, *Deux Ans*, 177.
11. Saint-Maurice, *Deux ans*, 166–69.
12. Saint-Maurice, *Deux ans*, 176.
13. Saint-Maurice, *Deux ans*, 174–75.
14. Saint-Maurice, *Deux ans*, 173.
15. This painting is now in the Foreign Legion Museum – Anonymous, *Musee*, 46.
16. Bazaine to Vaillant, No. 30, 26 June 1864 – BA, IX, f. 1656, cited in Dabbs, *French Army*, 245.
17. Hill/Hogg, *Corps d'Elite*, 73.
18. Saint-Maurice, *Deux Ans*, 188.
19. DECRET IMPERIAL – Qui cree in sixieme batallion dans le regiment etranger – 8 July 1865.
20. NOTE MINISTERIELLE – Indiquant le lieu sur lequel doivent etre diriges les engages volontaires qui s'engagent pour servir dans le regiment etranger – 29 March 1865.
21. The medal was awarded on 13 April – Dr. Rainer Egger, Osterreichisches Staatsarchiv [Austrian State Archives], Vienna, to Author, 30 December 1999, and Dr. Peter Broucek, Curator Record Group Five, Belgish-osterreiche Freikorps, to Author, 8 June 2002. When Emperor Maximilian awarded the *Medaille du Merite Militaire* to several French soldiers the medals were forwarded to Bazaine, who immediately noted that the colours in the ribbon were identical with that of France's Legion of Honour. Anticipating objections from holders of the French decoration, Bazaine withheld distributing the medals pending specific approval by Minister of War Randon, and asked Emperor Maximilian to change the ribbon's colour combination – Bazaine to Randon, No.44, 8 June, 1864 – BA, IX, f. 1606, cited in Dabbs, *French Army*, 115.
22. General the Count de Thun, Commanding Officer of the *Osterreichische Freicorps*, Zacapoaxtla, to Marshal Bazaine, Mexico City, 22 July 1865 – file called (in German) 'The Artificial Hand of the brave Captain Danjou', Record Group Five, Belgish-osterreiche Freikorps [Belgian-Austrian Volunteer Corps], Kriegsarchiv [War Archives], in the Austrian State Archives in Vienna. The letter – and others relating to it – was discovered in 1979 by Professor Ferdinand Anders of the University of Vienna. Sergent, *Camerone*, 374; Pierre Sergent, 'Du nouveau sur le combat de Camerone', *Revue Historique des Armees*, no.1 (1981), 87.
23. Bazaine to General the Count de Thun, No. 344, Mexico City, 28 July 1865 – in file called 'The Artificial Hand of the brave Captain Danjou'; Sergent, *Camerone*, 376; Sergent, 'Du nouveau', 88.
24. Sergent, *Camerone*, 376.
25. Charles Loysel, Secretary to Emperor Maximilian, to Bazaine, 23 July 1865 – BA, XIII, f. 2534, cited in Dabbs, *French Army*, 140.
26. Grisot/Coulombon, *Legion etrangere*, 293–94.
27. DECRET IMPERIAL – Qui cree in sixieme batallion dans le regiment etranger – 8 July 1865.
28. Bazaine to Castagny, Mexico City, #414, 16 August 1865, – BA XIII, f. 2575, cited in Dabbs, *French Army*, 142.
29. Dabbs, *French Army*, 142.
30. Hill/Hogg, *Corps d'Elite*, 73.
31. Penette/Castaignt, *Legion Extranjera*, 134.
32. John N. Edwards, *Shelby's Expedition to Mexico, An Unwritten Leaf of the War* (Kansas City: Kansas City Times Book and Job Printing House 1872), 25. Edwards is generally accurate in his reporting of events, but sometimes exaggerates. Certainly, some of his statements about Dupin – 43–44 – are overdrawn. Later he became the chronicler of Shelby's Civil War activities, writing *Shelby and His Men, or the War in the West* in 1867.
33. While Jeanningros in Monterrey may well have heard of Shelby's sale of guns and munitions to the Republicans, it took some time for word of it to reach Mexico City: T. Wurtemberg, French Consul in Matamoras, to Bazaine, 14 November 1865 – BA, XV, f. 2862, cited in Dabbs, *French Army*, 150.
34. Edwards, *Shelby's Expedition*, 41.
35. Edwards, *Shelby's Expedition*, 41.
36. Edwards, *Shelby's Expedition*, 42.
37. Napoleon III to Bazaine, No. 19, Chalons, 17 August 1865 – BA, XIII, f. 2578, quoted in Dabbs, *French Army*, 142–43.
38. Hill/Hogg, *Corps d'Elite*, 75.
39. Penette/Castaignt, *Legion Extranjera*, 29, n.28. Information provided to the authors by Alberto Gomez, the grandson of Dona Juana Marrero de Gomez.
40. Grisot/Coulombon, *Legion etrangere*, 295–96; Sergent, *Camerone*, 391–93.

Chapter 22 – Disaster at Santa Isabel

1. [Lafont, Jean Jacques Jules]. *Les Bivouacs de Vera Cruz a Mexico, par un Zouave* (Paris et Liepzick: Jung Treuttel 1865), 53–60.
2. Compte E[mile] de Keratry, 'La *Contre-Guerilla Francaise Au Mexique: Souvenirs des Terres Chaudes*', *Revue des Deux Mondes*, 59 (1 October 1865). Part I, 'La Guerre de Partisans dans l'Etat de Vera-Cruz'. Part II appeared in 61 (1 February 1866). The two-part serial appeared in book form three years later: Count Emile de Keratry *La Contre-Guerilla Francaise au Mexique (Souvenirs des terres chaudes)* (Paris: Librairie Internationale 1869).
3. Zede, 'Souvenirs,' *Carnet* 373, 55–56.
4. Salkin, '. . . du Pin au Mexique', 39; Sereac, 'Contre-Guerilla', 20.
5. Charles-Louis Dupin. Unpublished manuscript Memoir – Archives of the Ministry of Defence, Paris – 1K 198, S.H.A.T.
6. Grisot/Coulombon, *Legion etrangere*, 299.
7. Napoleon III to Bazaine, No. 21, Tuileries, 13 January 1866 – BA, XVI, f. 3186, quoted in Dabbs, *French Army*, 159.
8. Napoleon III to Bazaine, No. 23, Paris, 16 February 1866 – BA, XVIII, f. 3484, cited in Dabbs, *French Army*, 162, n.6.
9. Grisot/Coulombon, *Legion etrangere*, 308; Bazaine to Douay, No.761, 2 December 1866 – BA, XXV, f. 4913, cited in Dabbs, *French Army*, 243, n.118.
10. De Tuce, *Cinq ans*, 121–22, quoting Millet's letter to his mother dated 9 December 1866, almost a year after the debacle at Santa Isabel, showing that some officers never learned. *Chinacos* was a slang term for the guerillas in the region.
11. Amiable, *Legionnaire*, 145.
12. Saint-Maurice, *Deux ans*, 146.
13. Grisot/Coulombon, *Legion etrangere*, 300–03; De

Beauvoir, *Legion Etrangere*, 88–89; Porch, *Foreign Legion*, 151–53; Penette/Castaignt, *Legion Extrangera*, 70–75. The most complete account of the action at Santa Isabel is to be found in Sergent, *Camerone*, 397–411. He went over the battleground and the records in considerable detail and reports that every year, on 1 March, a commemoration is staged at Santa Isabel by the Military Commander of the State of Coahuila. The *barranca* where the survivors sought refuge is known as *l'arroyo de los Franceses*.
14. Huart, *Souvenirs*, 25.
15. Penette/Castaignt, *Legion Extranjera*, 76–80; Commandant Saussier to Lieutenant Bastidon, 5 March 1866 and Lieutenant Bastidon to Commandant Saussier, 6 March 1866, quoted in Sergeant, *Camerone*, 405–09.
16. Saussier to Jeanningros, 7 March 1866, quoted in De Beauvoir, *Legion Etrangere*, 88–89.
17. Amiable, *Legionnaire*, 129–30. Obviously, the 'more than 200' burials included men of Maximo Campos' Mexican G*endarmerie* as well.
18. Huart, *Souvenirs*, 25.
19. J[ames] F[rederick] Elton, *With the French in Mexico* (London: Chapman and Hall 1867), 52. Elton, late of the 98th Regiment, had served in India and was travelling in Mexico. His account of the affair at Santa Isabel – 48–52 – which he visited soon after the battle, is essentially accurate, although he was told that the Legionnaires actually succeeded in fighting their way into the hacienda. He spells de Brian's name as de Briant. Elton subsequently became British Consul in Mozambique and an explorer in East and Central Africa.
20. On his retirement from the Foreign Legion a job was found for Fiala as Custodian of the Chateau at Pau in the Pyrenees – Sergent, *Camerone*, 413–15; Carles, '. . . histoire du sous-officier', 30, calls him Finala; Porch, *Foreign Legion*, 154.
21. Lanusse, *Les heros*, 16.
22. Grisot/Coulombon, *Legion etrangere*, 303.
23. Amiable, *Legionnaire*, 98.
24. New York *Herald*, 19 April 1866.
25. New York *Herald*, 19 November 1865. In 1868, the year after the French Intervention ended, the wooden bridge over the Rio Jamapa, west of La Soledad, was replaced with a wood and steel one and the following year work began to extend the railway from Paso del Macho to Atoyac, which was reached in 1870.
26. Grisot/Coulombon, *Legion etrangere*, 304.
27. Baron Max von Alvensleben, *With Maximilian in Mexico: From the Notes of a Mexican Officer* (London: Longmans, Green 1867), 50–69.
28. Grisot/Coulombon, *Legion etrangere*, 305–06; Gaulot, *Expedition du Mexique* (1906), II, 318–19.
29. Amiable, *Legionnaire*, 142.
30. Albert Hans, *La guerre du Mexique selon les Mexicains* (Paris: Berger-Levrault 1899), 8–9, cited in Dabbs, *French Army*, 172, n.51.
31. Randon to Bazaine, 30 June 1866 – BA, XXII, f. 4224–4226, cited in Dabbs, *French Army*, 171.
32. DECRET IMPERIAL – Portant creation d'un septieme at d'un huitieme bataillon dans le regiment etranger – 4 July 1866.
33. Bazaine's Secretary to Bazaine, Coded Telegram No. 445, Mexico City, 4 July 1866 – BA. XXII, f. 4254, cited in Dabbs, *French Army*, 174, n.59.

Chapter 23 – The Last Farewell in Mexico

1. [Charles Blin], 'Au Mexique, avec la Legion Etrangere (Souvenirs du Capitaine Blin – Juillet 1866–Mars 1867', *La Legion Etrangere* (1939), 6–12, is based on his letters and notes.
2. Blin, 'Au Mexique', 8–9.
3. Grisot/Coulombon, *Legion etrangere*, 313.
4. Amiable, *Legionnaire*, 151.
5. Grisot/Coulombon, *Legion etrangere*, 313.
6. Blin, 'Au Mexique', 10.
7. Blin, 'Au Mexique', 11. He mis-remembers Colonna d'Ornano as Cuneo d'Ornano.
8. Bazaine to Maximilian, 4 August 1866 – BA, XXII, f. 4387, quoted in Dabbs, *French Army*, 177, n.77.
9. Bazaine to Douay, No. 702, 31 August 1866 – BA, XXIII, f. 4505, cited in Dabbs, *French Army*, 180, n.93.
10. The Commission was dated 16 March 1865 – *Annuaire de l'armee 1867*, 396.
11. Blin, 'Au Mexique', 11.
12. P. Guinard, 'Cavaliers de la Legion etrangere au Mexique', *Carnet de la Sabretache*, no.389 (July–August 1937), 323, n.5; Raymond Guyader, 'L'Uniforme du Cavalier au Mexique 1864–1867', *Kepi blanc*, no.436 (June 1984), 34–35.
13. Blin, 'Au Mexique', 12.
14. Guedalla, *Two Marshals*, 126.
15. Bazaine *Circulaire*, No.2135, 15 October 1866 – BA, XXIV, f. 4702, cited in Dabbs, *French Army*, 204.
16. Bazaine to Minister of Justice, No. 702, 16 October 1866 – BA, XXIV, f. 4718–4719, cited in Dabbs, *French Army*, 204.
17. Randon to Bazaine, 30 November 1866 – BA, XXIV, f. 4901, quoted in Dabbs, *French Army*, 200, n.58.
18. Randon to Bazaine, 15 December 1866 – BA, XXV, f. 4959–4961, quoted in Dabbs, *French Army*, 200, n.59.
19. Bazaine to Minister of Public Works, No. 675, 21 March 1866 – BA, XIX, f. 3679, cited in Dabbs, *French Army*, 243, n.120.
20. Bazaine to Barron [Baron?], No. 2238, 31 December 1866 – BA, XXVI, f. 5031, cited in Dabbs, *French Army*, 207, n.106.
21. Bazaine to Douay, Telegram No. 766, 5 January 1867 – BA, XXVI, f. 5065; Castagny to Bazaine, Telegram, 6 January 1867 – BA, XXXVI, f. 5059, cited in Dabbs, *French Army*, 205, n.94 and n.95.
22. Saint-Maurice, *Deux ans*, 146, quoting Moutier in a letter to the Paris newspaper *Constitutionel*.
23. They arrived in Veracruz on 7 January 1867, in time for the French withdrawal – Penette/Castaignt, *Legion Extranjera*, 73, n.66.
24. Von Alvensleben, *With Maximilian*, 59–60.
25. Porfirio Diaz to Colonel [?], Oaxaca, 12 January 1867 – Emile de Keratry, *L'Empereur Maximilien, Son elevation et sa chute, apres des documents inedits par le Compte Emile de Keratry* (Leipzig: Duncker und Humblot 1867), 291. Published in English two years later as *The Rise and Fall of the Emperor Maximilian. A Narrative of the Mexican Empire, 1861–67. From Authentic Documents*.
26. Amiable, *Legionnaire*, 151.
27. Penette/Castaignt, *Legion Extranjera*, 90–91; Grisot/Coulombon, *Legion etrangere*, 314.
28. Penette/Castaignt, *Legion Extranjera*, 90–91; Grisot/Coulombon, *Legion etrangere*, 314–15.

29. Blin, 'Au Mexique', 12.
30. Von Alvensleben, *With Maximilian*, 232.
31. Blin, 'Au Mexique', 12.
32. Penette/Castaignt, *Legion Extranjera*, 95. Several other paragraphs are also quoted.
33. Blin, 'Au Mexique', 12.
34. Blin, 'Au Mexique', 12.
35. The original document, in Jeanningros' handwriting, is in the Foreign Legion Museum. It is headed: '1863. – Mexique. Combat de Cameronne, 60 against 2000. Farewell address by General Jeanningros, Commander of the Legion, in the presence of troops forming a square around the grave of the gallant men of the Legion, dead on the field of honour. 25 February 1867, two days before the evacuation of the French Army for France.' A photograph of the two-page document appears in the second, third and fourth editions of the *Livre d'Or* (1958), 81; (1976), 104; and (1981), 115.
36. Blin, 'Au Mexique', 12. Gans held the rank of Captain at the time of his death – Grisot/Coulombon, *Legion etrangere*, 236.
37. Lande/Maine, 'Camaron', 467.
38. The sword was presented to the *Salle d'Honneur* of the Legion Etrangere in Sidi-bel- Abbes by General Blin, a former Chief of the *Service Historique de l'Armee*, and the son of Captain Blin, and is now in the Foreign Legion Museum – Anonymous, *Musee*, 46, with photograph, 44.
39. *Tambour* Lai's Cross of a Chevalier of the Legion of Honour was also given to the *Salle d'Honneur* by General Blin – Brunon, *Camerone et l'Aigle*.
40. Hill/Hogg, *Corps d'Elite*, 118.
41. 'Report to the Minister of War and Navy on the siege and occupation of Veracruz, 5 July 1867,' quoted in De Leon Toral, *Historia Documental*, 791.
42. Sebastian I. Campos, *Operaciones militares del Estado de Vera Cruz y de la Costa de Stavento* (Mexico City, 1891), cited in Penette, *Histoire*, 5–6, and Penette, 'Memorial', 111. This was confirmed in a letter to Penette, dated 10 April 1958, from Dr. Eusebio Davalos Hurtado, Director of the National Institute of Anthropology and History in Mexico City, who wrote: 'The monument was destroyed not long after the military occupation ceased' – Penette, *Histoire*, 5, n.6, and Penette, 'Memorial', 123, n.5.
43. The total losses were one thousand nine hundred and forty-eight. Penette/Castaignt, *Legion Extranjera*, 97, note that an error in addition in Grisot/Coulombon, *Legion etrangere*, 316, has led to the Foreign Legion's Official Record repeatedly being inaccurately given for more than a century.

Chapter 24 – Fighting for France

1. General Charles Thoumas, *Recits du guerre 1862–1867: Les Francais au Mexique* (Paris: Librairie Bloud et Barral n.d.)
2. Among the many inaccurate stories about the hand of Captain Danjou is one by a certain Teodoro Labnadie, who in his old age told how he was taken to Sidi-bel- Abbes by his father, who was on a business trip to North Africa. There, Labnadie said, they met Corporal Emilio (sic) Berg, who had carried the hand back from Mexico – General Luis Garfias M[agana], 'Sucedio en Camaron', *Revista del Ejercito y Fuerza Aerea Mexicanos*, XVII, no.4 (April 1979), 9. Corporal Evariste Berg, of course, was killed in a duel in Mexico in June of 1864.
3. NOTE – Prescrivant que les engages volontaires pour le regiment etranger devront etre, a l'avenir, diriges sur Sidi-bel-Abbes – 8 February 1867; Morel, *Legion Etrangere*, 49; Grisot/Coulombon, *Legion etrangere*, 318–20.
4. Dossier Philippe Maine.
5. Bernede, 'Monseigneur Lanusse', 15. The tragic Carlota, her mind gone due to the pressures and loss of her husband, died in January 1927.
6. Dossier Jean Efrem Lanusse.
7. Morel, *Legion Etrangere*, 49. The decision, which applied to all Infantry regiments, was upheld by MINISTERIAL INSTRUCTION No.25 five days later – 27 January – and then by a MINISTERIAL DECISION, dated 29 February. The fact that there was so much official paperwork indicates that the move was distinctly unpopular; Brunon, *Camerone et l'Aigle*, 27.
8. Brunon/Manue/Carles, *Livre d'Or* (1981), 400.
9. Porch, *Foreign Legion*, 680, n.25.
10. Dossier Jean Efem Lanusse. He served with the Army of the Rhine from 29 July to 21 September, 1870.
11. DECRET IMPERIAL – Portant creation d'un cinquieme bataillon dans le regiment etranger – 22 August 1870; Grisot/Coulombon, *Legion etrangere*, 577.
12. Carles, '. . . l'histoire du sous-officier', 32.
13. Dossier Philippe Maine. A photograph of him as Captain of a Company of *Franc-Tireur* sharpshooters in 1870 was first published in Anonymous, 'Les Heros', 132. A photograph taken of Maine in 1871, perhaps just before departing for Cochin-China, shows him in the uniform of a Captain of the *Infanterie de Marine* – Brunon, *Camerone* [1981].
14. Brunon, *Camerone* [1981], 187–88. The gallant stand of the *Infanterie* and *Artillerie de Marine* at Bazailles was immortalized by artist Alphonse de Neuville in his painting 'Les dernieres cartouches', but it was not until eighty-three years later, in 1953, that BAZEILLES 1870 was approved for the Regimental Standards of their successors, the 1st, 2nd, 3rd and 4th Colonial Infantry and 1st Colonial Artillery.
15. Dossier Philippe Maine. *Le Petit Journal* [Paris], 19 May 1902.
16. Grisot/Coulombon, *Legion etrangere*, 327.
17. Auguste Boucher, *Recits de l'invasion: Journal d'un bourgeois d'Orleans pendant l'occupation Prussienne* (Orleans: H. Herluison 1871).
18. Grisot/Coulombon, *Legion etrangere*, 331–32.
19. Bernede, 'Monseigneur Lanusse', 9.
20. Geraghty, *March of Die*, 84. The Belgian government, fearful of being seen by Prussia to be violating its neutrality, had asked that Belgian 'for the duration' volunteers be sent to serve in Africa rather than France – Henry Dutailly, '1871. Au combat dans le Loiret', *Historia*, no.414 (2nd trimester 1981), 40. Special Issue: 'La Legion etrangere. 150e anniversaire.' The Regiment Etranger complied, but did not consider that the request applied to Belgians already serving under normal Acts of Engagement. Sergeant Brunswick and the other Belgians fought with their non-Belgian comrades in France.

21. Du Barail, *Souvenirs*, II, 263. Milson von Bolt was a Major when he retired.
22. Saint-Maurice, *Deux ans*, 78; De Beauvoir, *Legion Etrangere*, 66.
23. De Beauvoir, *Legion Etrangere*, 98–100; Lanusse, *Les heros*, xii–xiii.
24. Grisot/Coulombon, *Legion etrangere*, 337. The authors scathingly dismiss Kirwan – who actually seems to have been at the very least a competent Company Officer – as a 'journalist who spent his time sending stories to newspapers'. The Author has not found evidence of this, and it may be that they were confusing Kirwan with a certain Dyer Mac Adaras, an Irishman of a somewhat dubious reputation, who claimed to be able to raise an army of his countrymen to fight for France.
25. Kirwan/M'Alevey, *Compagnie Irlandaise*, 294–97, Appendix: 'Nominal Roll of The Irish Company', compiled 24 January 1871.
26. Kirwan/M'Alevey, *Compagnie Irlandaise*, 77–78. No *Etat des Service* can be found for M'Alevey by S.H.A.T. It seems possible, therefore, that he had been made an Acting Sous-Lieutenant in the field. On the other hand, as Grisot/Coulombon – *Legion etrangere*, 350 – point out, during the Franco-Prussian War 'the muster-rolls were badly maintained'.
27. Kirwan/M'Alevey, *Compagnie Irlandaise*, 180; Grisot/Coulombon, *Legion etrangere*, 343.
28. Kirwan/M'Alevey, *Compagnie Irlandaise*, 181.
29. Kirwan/M'Alevey, *Compagnie Irlandaise*, 294.
30. De Beauvoir, *Legion Etrangere*, 92–95; Jean Efrem Lanusse, *Etat des Services*. He was Chaplain to the Army of the Loire and the Army of the East from 22 September 1870 to 14 May 1871; Bernede, 'Monseigneur Lanusse', 12.
31. Grisot/Coulombon, *Legion etrangere*, 350.
32. Dossier Patrick Cotter – S.H.A.T. Commissioned a Sous-Lieutenant on 20 October 1870, he was promoted to Lieutenant on 3 August 1872 and Captain on 26 March 1880. Cotter was made a Chevalier of the Legion of Honour on 13 July 1881 and posted to Tonkin on 30 December 1883. He was killed in action on 24 March 1885.
33. Dossier Jean Efrem Lanusse. He was Chaplain to the Army of Paris from 15 May to 10 August, 1871; Bernede, 'Monseigneur Lanusse', 12.
34. Dossier Philippe Maine.
35. Grisot/Coulombon, *Legion etrangere*, 365.
36. Bernede, 'Monseigneur Lanusse', 8.
37. Grisot/Coulombon, *Legion etrangere*, 369–70; De Beauvoir, *Legion Etrangere*, 110–14. Kauffmann committed suicide during a fit of depression shortly afterwards.

Chapter 25 – Claiming the Regiment's Heritage

1. Brunon, *Camerone et l'Aigle*, 27; Brunon, 'Camerone et l'Aigle', 18; Brunon, *Camerone* [1981], 182; Brunon/Manue/Carles, *Livre d'Or* (1981), 400.
2. Grisot/Coulombon, *Legion etrangere*, 368, n.1.
3. *Le Sud-Oranais*, undated article c.1894, quoted in De Beauvoir, *Legion Etrangere*, 150.
4. Brunon, *Camerone et l'Aigle*, 27; Brunon, 'Camerone et l'Aigle', 18; Brunon, *Camerone* [1981], 182; Brunon/Manue, *Livre d'Or* (1958), 400.
5. Grisot/Coulombon, *Legion etrangere*, 368, n.1; Brunon, *Camerone et l'Aigle*, 27; Brunon, 'Cameron et l'Aigle', 18; Brunon, *Camerone* [1981], 182; Brunon/Manue/Carles, *Livre d'Or* (1981), 400. Brunon says that the price was five francs. Kelbel joined the Regiment Etranger on 4 December 1870.
6. A photograph of this 'Provisional' Regimental Standard appears in Brunon/Manue/Carles, *Livre d'Or* (1981), 402. It is preserved in the Foreign Legion Museum – Anonymous, *Musee*, 47.
7. Bernede, 'Monseigneur Lanusse', 15.
8. Guedalla, *Two Marshals*, 228–57.
9. [Narcisse-Henri-Edouard] Faucher de Saint-Maurice, *Deux ans au Mexique* (Montreal: Duernay Freres et Dansereau 1874). Edition used – the 5th, revised: (Montreal: Librairie Saint-Joseph 1881). The title of the book is misleading, as Saint-Maurice was actually in Mexico for just less than ten months – in other words, parts of two years – disembarking at Veracruz in September 1864 and re-embarking in June 1865.
10. Baz/Gallo, *Mexican Railway*, 93.
11. DECRET – Qui rend au regiment etranger son ancienne denomination de legion etrangere – 29 March 1875.
12. A[uguste] Ballue, 'Souvenirs du Mexique – Cameron,' *Lectures du Soir*, 42 (Musee des Familles, October and November 1875), 312–18 and 335–40. His attestations of the military accuracy of his story, 318 and 340; reprinted *Kepi blanc* #271 (May 1965), 19–37.
13. L'Abbe [Jean Efrem] Lanusse, *Les heros de Camaron: 30 avril 1863* (Paris: Marmon et Flammarion 1891), 46.
14. Dossier Philippe Maine.
15. L. Louis-Lande [Lucien-Louis Lande], 'Camaron, 30 avril 1863: Episode de la guerre du Mexique', *Revue des Deux Mondes*, 28 (15 July, 1878), 444–67. Apart from the errors concerning the hand of Captain Danjou, an obvious error on the part of Lande, though attributed to Maine, is the statement – 446 – that all three Battalions of the Regiment Etranger went to Mexico at the same time, and that the 3rd Battalion was left at La Soledad, while the 1st and 2nd went on to Chiquihuite. The article also incorrectly states – 467 – that four, rather than six, of the survivors received the *Medaille Militaire*.
16. Lande/Maine, 'Camaron', 467. Despite exhaustive research, the Author has not been able to confirm this.
17. *Memorial de la Loire*, undated article of August 1878, quoted in Sergent, *Camerone*, 193–94.
18. Lucien-Louis Lande, *Souvenirs d'un soldat* (Paris: Societe Francaise d'Imprimerie et de Librairie 1878). The introductory remarks to the chapter containing Maine's reminiscences – 'La Hacienda de Camaron: Episode de la Guerre du Mexique', 197–237 – are slightly different from those in the *Revue des Deux Mondes* article, but the errors are repeated.
19. Brunon/Manue/Carles, *Livre d'Or* (1981), 403.
20. Brunon, *Camerone* [1981], 187.
21. *Transactions of the Royal Society of Canada* (Ottawa: 1882–83), 1st Series, I, (1882–83), Section I, 13–19. In 1888 Faucher de Saint-Maurice took a trip to France, Algeria and Tunisia, which resulted in a book called *Loin du Pays:*

souvenirs d'Europe, d'Afrique et d'Amerique, which was published in two volumes, totalling 1016 pages, the following year. He died in 1897, leaving a large literary legacy – Paul de Cazes, 'Pour Faucher de Saint-Maurice', *Revue des deux Frances* (Paris: 1 October 1897), 22–24; Raoul Renault, 'Faucher de Saint-Maurice: son oeuvre', *Courier du Livre* (Montreal, April 1897); Ann M. Morris, Reference Department, The D.B. Waldon Library, The University of Western Ontario, London, Ontario, to Author, 13 December 1999.

22. E[douard] Detaille and J[ules] Richard, *Types et Uniformes de l'Armee Francaise* (Paris: Boussod et Valadon 1885–1889), a definitive two-volume work covering the years 1790–1885. [Jean Baptiste] Edouard Detaille (1847–1912) was the leading military artist of his day. He had seen battle in the Franco-Prussian War and the collection of military uniforms and artefacts he assembled for his paintings became part of the foundation collection of the *Musee de l'Armee* in Paris.

23. Grisot, General [Paul] and Coulombon, Lieutenant [Ernest]. *La Legion etrangere de 1831 a 1887* (Paris: Berger-Levrault 1888). The Mexican Expedition section occupies pages 271–316, with Camerone covered in pages 276–79.

24. Grisot/Coulombon, *Legion etrangere*, 276.

25. 'A mes hommes qui sont morts' – Captain de Borelli, *Nouvelle Review*, April 1887.

26. Anonymous, *Musee*, 47. The Author has not been able to trace Cousin's Camerone painting, 'The End'.

27. Martyn, *Life in the Legion*, 108.

28. Martyn, *Life in the Legion*, 110–11.

29. Lanusse left France for Mexico on 12 July 1862 and returned home on 5 April 1867 – Dossier Jean Efrem Lanusse.

30. *Le Gaulois*, 13 November 1890. Reprinted in Lanusse, *Les heros*, 253, 'Notes et Eclaircissments' by Boyer d'Agen, 20 June 1891.

31. *Le Gaulois*, 13 November 1890. The *Musee du Souvenir* at Saint-Cyr owns a photograph of Lanusse at work in his study which bears out d'Agen's description of both the spartan and cluttered aspects of the Chaplain's workspace.

32. Lanusse, *Les heros*, 45.

33. Lanusse, *Les heros*, 41–42.

34. L'Abbe Lanusse to General Alexis de La Hayrie, 23 October 1889 – [de La Hayrie], *Combat*, iii.

35. *Le Gaulois*, 13 November 1890 – Lanusse, *Les heros*, 245, d'Agen, 'Notes et Eclaircissments', 20 June 1891.

36. Lanusse, *Les heros*, 244.

37. Lanusse to de La Hayrie, 23 October 1889 – [de La Hayrie], *Combat*, iv and vi.

38. Penette, *Histoire*, p. n.7; Penette, 'Memorial', 111.

39. [de La Hayrie], *Combat*, 1.

40. Lanusse to de La Hayrie, 23 October 1889 – [de La Hayrie], *Combat*, iv and vi.

41. Anonymous [attributed to General Alexis de La Hayrie], *Le Combat de Camaron, 30 avril 1863* (Lille: Imprimerie Danel 1889). Introduction by L'Abbe E. Lanusse. It was probably the typesetter who consistently misread de La Hayrie's handwriting and mis-spelled Maudet as Mandet, but the author must be blamed for both Vilain and Milan being mis-spelled. Additionally, Dr. Talavera became Dr. Valvera and Fusilier Catteau became Cattant. Indicative of very careless proof-reading, Saussier became Saucier.

42. [de La Hayrie], *Combat*, 2.

43. [de La Hayrie], *Combat*, 23, 12 and 2.

44. [de La Hayrie], *Combat*, 20.

45. Paul Gaulot, *Reve d'Empire: La Verite sur l'Expedition du Mexique d'apres les documents inedite de Ernest Louet, payeur en chef des Corps Expeditionnaire* (Paris: Paul Ollendorff, 1890).

46. *Le Gaulois*, 22 December 1890 – Lanusse, *Les heros*, 268, d'Agen, 'Notes et Eclaircissments', 20 June 1891.

47. *Le Gaulois*, 13 November and 22 December 1890 – Lanusse, *Les heros*, 242–68.

48. Lanusse, *Les heros*, 269, d'Agen, 'Notes et Eclaircissments', 20 June 1891.

49. Lanusse, L'Abbe [Jean Efrem], *Les heros de Camaron: 30 avril 1863* (Paris: Marmon et Flammarion 1891), 269. Preface and Historical Notes by Boyer d'Agen.

50. Lanusse, *Les heros*, Dedication, vii.

51. Lanusse, *Les heros*, vii–xviii.

52. Lanusse, *Les heros*, Preface, xix–xliii, dated 1 June 1891. In his article in *Le Gaulois* d'Agen also twice refers to sixty-three *Tirailleurs*, rather than sixty-two Fusiliers and three officers – Lanusse, *Les heros*, 258 and 263, d'Agen, 'Notes et Eclaircissments', 20 June 1891.

53. Lanusse, *Les heros*, 235–41, 'Pieces Officielles'. Lanusse must have had a copy of Forey's General Order #195 of 30 August 1863, as he uses it – 235–38 – but unaccountably dates it 31 August. He refers – 239 – to Jeanningros' letter to Randon of 1 October 1863 – mis-dating it 1 September 1863 – and quotes Randon to Jeanningros – 239–40 – of 4 November 1863, but mis-dates it as 4 October 1863. It is disappointing to have to note that some of the figures given in Forey's Order #195 have been 'doctored' for effect.

54. Reprinted in Lanusse, *Les heros*, 242–68, d'Agen, 'Notes et Eclaircissments', 20 June 1891.

55. Lanusse, *Les heros*, 19 and 207–08. He also follows de La Hayrie's mis-spellings of Villain and Millan and the spelling of the names of the Legionnaires he mentions is also more often incorrect than correct.

56. Lanusse, *Les heros*, 18, n.1.

57. Lanusse, *Les heros*, Publisher's Note, opposite title page.

58. These and other letters are in 'Monseigneur Lanusse', Recueil de Souvenir Collection: General Saussier, 8 July 1891; De Beauvoir, [?] August 1891; Colonel Gillet, 15 November 1891; and President Carnot, 3 May 1893.

59. The whereabouts of this manuscript are unknown today – even if it still survives. In trying to locate it, the Author queried S.H.A.T., the A.L.E., the Library of the *Ecole Speciale Militaire* at Saint-Cyr and the *Bibliotheque Nationale* in Paris. Even its existence had escaped the attention of the librarians at these institutions. All were very interested to learn of it, but none held it in their Collections, or any ideas as to where it might have ended up.

60. Penette, *Histoire*, 5, n.7 and Penette, 'Le Memorial', 111.

61. Penette, *Histoire*, 5, n.7 and Penette, 'Le Memorial', 111.

62. Penette, *Histoire*, 5, n.7 and Penette, 'Le Memorial', 111. Penette was told that the railway company had charged the work to the Mexican Government, but

was unable to locate any records.
63. In Latin: The accepted French translation is: QVOS HIC NON PLVS LX ILS FURENT ICI MOINS DE SOIXANTE ADVERSI TOTIVS AGMINIS OPPOSES A TOUTE UNE ARMEE MOLES CONSTRAVIT SA MASSE LES ECRASA VITA PRIAM QVAM VIRTVS LA VIE PLUTOT QUE LE COURAGE M ILITES DESERVIT GALLICOS ABANDONNA CES SOLDATS FRANCAIS DIE XXX MENSI APR. ANNI MDCCCXIII LE 30 AVRIL 1863 IN MEMOPIAM A LEUR MEMORIE HOC MONVMENTVM CE MONUMENT A ELEVE SUIS PATRIA PONEBAT PAR LEURS PAYS ANNO MDCCCXCII DANS L'ANNEE 1892
64. Undated article from *Le Sud-Oranais*, c.1894, quoted in De Beauvoir, *Legion Etrangere*, 144–51. A photograph of the painting was published in *Vert et Rouge: Traditions et Souvenirs Militaires* (May 1951), 6, and also to accompany Albert Duchesne, 'Des Belges au combat de Camerone', *Carnet de la Fourragere*, XV, 2 (September 1963), 112.
65. Anonymous, 'Le Capitaine Maine', *La Legion Etrangere*, no.53 (May 1935), 7.
66. Anonymous, *Musee*, 47.
67. *Le Sud-Oranais*, quoted in De Beauvoir, *Legion Etrangere*, 147.
68. *Le Sud-Oranais*, quoted in De Beauvoir, *Legion Etrangere*, 148–49.
69. *Le Sud-Oranais*, quoted in De Beauvoir, *Legion Etrangere*, 150.
70. Comte [Georges Henri Marie Anne Victor] de Villebois-Mareuil, 'La Legion Etrangere', *Revue des Deux Mondes*, 134, no.4 (15 April 1896), 877–78. Colonel de Villebois-Mareuil assumed command of the 1st Etranger on 14 April 1895, and resigned from the French Army on 29 December the same year, after a distinguished military career. The article was written after he had returned to civilian life.
71. De Villebois-Mareuil, 'Legion Etrangere', 877.
72. *Le Gaulois*, 13 November 1890 – Lanusse, *Les heros*, 254, d'Agen, 'Notes et Eclaircissments', 20 June 1891.
73. Jean de Nivelle, 'L'aumonier de Saint-Cyr', *l'Actualite*, 28 November 1896.

Chapter 26 – The Last Survivor, the First Celebration

1. Carles, '... histoire du sous-officier', 32. Terms of Engagement were for five years, but veteran Legionnaires were permitted – and at Kunassec's age encouraged – to sign for shorter periods.
2. De Beauvoir, *Legion Etrangere*. The Mexican Expedition section occupies pages 66–97, with Camerone covered in pages 66–85.
3. C-G. [Captain Abel Clement-Grandcourt], 'La situation actuelle dans la Legion etrangere', *Bulletin du Comite de l'Afrique francaise* (October 1909), 336–38; 'Les Alsaciens-Lorrains et la Legion etrangere', *Feuilles d'histoire* (1 June 1910), 550–69; 'Le recruteur prussian', *Echo de Paris* (5 March 1911); Captain [Abel] Clement-Grandcourt, *Croquis marocains, sur la Moulouya* (Paris: Fournier 1912).
4. Brunon, *Camerone* [1981], 124.
5. *Le Figaro*, 8 April 1900; Roy Macnab, *The French Colonel: Villebois-Mareuil and the Boers, 1899–1900* (Cape Town: Oxford University Press 1975), 207.
6. *Le Petite Journal*, 19 May 1902. Kunnasec was quoted by the newspaper as describing himself as 'the youngest in the Company' at Camerone, which he was not, though he may have meant that he was the youngest to survive the battle, which could well have been the case, as he was some three months shy of his twentieth birthday at the time.
7. MINISTERIAL DECREE, Paris, 16 February, 1906; *Journal officiel*, 17 February 1906.
8. Lieutenant-Colonel Louis Garros, 'La Croix de la Legion d'Honneur au Drapeau du Ier Etranger (1906)', in 'La Legion: Grandeur at Servitude'. *Historama*, Series no.3 (November 1967), 45. This major magazine treatment of the Foreign Legion's story was subsequently turned into a book: Louis Garros, *Storia della Legione Straniera* (Rome: Edizioni Ferni Ginevra 1972).
9. *Le Republicain*, quoted in Anonymous, 'Sidi-bel-Abbes – Historique', *Kepi blanc* no.382 (September 1979), 8–9. Special Issue on Sidi-bel Abbes. The event was extensively covered locally, regionally and nationally: *Echo d'Oran*, 28 April 1906; the *Revue Nord-Africaine*, published in Algiers, dedicated its issues of 29 April and 6 May 1906 to the events at Sidi-bel-Abbes; 'La decoration du drapeau du 1er etranger', *Monde illustre*, 12 May 1906.
10. Joseph Ehrhart, 'Mes treize annees de Legion etrangere'. Unpublished manuscript, Part 1, A.L.E. Ehrhart mis-remembered being told that Camerone had been fought on '28 April, 1866'. On 9 March 1909 – the Foreign Legion's seventy-eighth birthday – the City of Milan presented the *cravates* of the Regimental Standards of the 1st and 2nd Etrangers with a gold medal struck to mark the Fiftieth Anniversary of the Italian Campaign.
11. Erwin Rosen [Erwin Carle], *In the Foreign Legion* (London: Duckworth 1910), 139.
12. [General Jules Francois], 'Le poste de Ta-Lung', manuscript presented to the *Salle d'Honneur* at Sidi-bel-Abbes by General Francois in 1940, A.L.E. The name of the young Lieutenant involved – himself – was not given, as he apparently wished more to record the occasion than to take the credit for having initiated it. General Jean-Pierre Hallo, *Monsieur Legionnaire* (Limoges: Charles-Lavauzelle 1994), 223.
13. Lieutenant Francois would make the Foreign Legion his career. He served in Sud Oranais, went to Tonkin with the 1st Etranger, commanded a Battalion of the 2nd Etranger there and entered the *Ecole Superieure de Guerre* in 1911.
14. 'Monseigneur Lanusse', Recueil de Souvenir Collection. The invitation to his funeral listed his many medals, awards and French, Mexican, Belgian, Spanish, Russian and Papal decorations.
15. Paul Gaulot, *L'Expedition du Mexique, 1861–1867* (Paris: Librairie Paul Ollendorff 1906). This edition was published for the Societe d'Editions Litteraires et Artistiques. The date of the Combat of Camerone is given as 1 May 1863.
16. Huart, *Souvenirs*, 5. Subtitle: 'Le Combat de Camerone 1 Mai (sic) 1863 La Prise de Puebla 17 Mai 1863'. He had written an earlier book, *D'une demission a une reinstallation ou trois anees*

d'entr'acte au Mexique et en Afrique (Orleans: Chez Georges Michau 1890). The statement in Gaulot, L'Expedition, 110, that the Combat of Camerone occurred on 1 May 1863, and was probably the cause of Huart giving the same incorrect date. Among his few errors of memory is his statement that Maudet was wounded near the beginning of the defence of the corral at the Hacienda de la Trinidad.

17. Huart, Souvenirs, 25.
18. Hallo, Monsieur Legionnaire, 223. General Hallo spent much of his military career in the Foreign Legion, so had excellent resources upon which to draw for his material.
19. La Legion Etrangere served as the Official Organ of the Federation of Societies of Former Legionnaires of France and the Colonies. The first issue was published on 30 April 1912 and the last – the 28th – on 1 August 1914.
20. George d'Esparbes, La Legion etrangere (Paris: Flammarion 1900). The Foreign Legion's view of it: Livre d'Or (1981), 497.
21. Georges d'Esparbes, Les Mysteres de la Legion etrangere (Paris: Flammarion 1912). Illustrated by Maurice Mahut; Livre d'Or (1981), 497.
22. Aristide Merolli, La grenade heroique: Avant la tourmente (Casablanca-Fez: Editions Moynier 1937), 307, 332. He also co-authored with Lieutenant Nadau, Une visite a la salle d'honneur (Sidi-bel-Abbes: Presses du 1er Regiment etranger 1930).
23. Paul Ayers Rockwell, American Fighters in the Foreign Legion 1914–1918 (Boston: Houghton Mifflin 1930). Kiffin Rockwell subsequently transferred into the French Aviation and was killed while flying over the German lines on 23 September 1916. His life was chronicled in Paul Ayers Rockwell, War Letters of Kiffin Yates Rockwell (Garden City, N.Y.: The Country Life Press 1925). Subtitle: 'Foreign Legionnaire and Aviator, France, 1914–1916'.
24. David Wooster King, L.M.8046 (New York: Duffield 1927), 68–70. Subtitle: 'An Intimate Story of the Foreign Legion'. Introduction by Hendrik Willem Van Loon. 'Durationist' Alan Seeger was also impressed by the review and wrote about it: Alan Seeger, Letters and Diary of Alan Seeger (New York: Charles Scribner's Sons 1917), 138–40. Prefatory Note and Conclusion [by] C.L.S. [Charles Louis Seeger].
25. The review was held on 26 October 1915 and two of the American 'durationists' left firsthand accounts – Edmond Genet, letter to his mother, 28 October 1915, quoted in Grace Ellery Channing (Ed.), War Letters of Edmond Genet (New York: Charles Scribner's Sons 1918), 104–05. Subtitle: 'The First American Aviator Killed Flying the Stars and Stripes'. Introduction and Conclusion by Channing. Prefatory Note by John Jay Chapman; Seeger, Letters and Diary, 174–75, Army Postcard to his Family, 27 October 1915.
26. Adjutant-chef Andre Gandelin, 'Le general Rollet, un homme de coeur, de caractere et d'ideal', Revue historique des armees, no.1 (1981), 121–41.
27. Jean-Pierre Dorian, Souvenirs du Colonel Maire de la Legion Etrangere (Paris: Albin Michel 1939).
28. Jean-Pierre Dorian, Le Colonel Maire: Un heros de la Legion (Paris: Albin Michel 1981), 136–37.
29. Rockwell, American Fighters, 10, 113, 186, 233 and 263.
30. Quoted in Rockwell, American Fighters, 263.
31. Rockwell, American Fighters, 277. After the United States entered the war Karayinis and three other American 'durationists' transferred into the Twenty-Third U.S. Engineers, where their fighting abilities and the medals they had earned were totally ignored. Karayinis and another man were made mail-carriers, one was given a job as a messenger and the other an office job – Rockwell, American Fighters, 312.
32. [Garros], 'Le General Nicolas', Historama, 152.
33. Rockwell, American Fighters, 343–44.
34. Rockwell, American Fighters, 344.
35. Brunon/Manue/Carles, Livre d'Or (1981), 409; Porch, Foreign Legion, 334.

Chapter 27 – The Ascent of Colonel Paul Rollet

1. Captain [J.J.J.] Mordacq, 'Pacification du Haut-Tonkin', Journal des Sciences militaires (February 1901). Subtitle: 'Historique des dernieres operations militaires, colonne du Nord'. The lengthy article was published as a small book by the Paris publisher Chapelot later the same year.
2. Commandant [J.J.J.] Mordacq, Tactique des grosses colonnes: expedition du Beni-Snassen en 1859 (Paris: Berger-Levrault 1906).
3. General Jules Mordacq, Le ministere Clemenceau. Journal d'un temoin (Paris: Plon 1931), III, 328. There was official resistance to the idea of a Cavalry arm for the Foreign Legion, but the 1st Regiment Etranger de Cavalerie came into being in 1921. Even stronger resistance to an Artillery arm, meant that none was created.
4. Christian Malcros, Insignes de la Legion Etrangere (Aubagne: Presses de la Legion Etrangere 1981), 11. For the raising of the 4th REI see: Anonymous, Historique du 1er bataillon formant corps du 1er Regiment etranger et du 1er bataillon du 4e Regiment de la Legion etrangere (Marrakech: Hebreard n.d. c.1922).
5. Brunon/Manue/Carles, Livre d'Or (1981), 404.
6. Brunon/Manue/Carles, Livre d'Or (1981), 404, n.2.
7. Aage was born on 10 June 1887 in Copenhagen. He had been a member of the Royal Danish Army, and was attached to the French Army at Metz in 1920–21, prior to joining the Foreign Legion. His two books cover operations in Morocco 1923–25 and the men with whom he served: H.H. Prince Aage of Denmark, A Royal Adventurer in the Foreign Legion (New York: Doubleday, Page 1927) – published in Britain as My Life in the French Foreign Legion (London: Everleigh Nash & Grayson 1928) – and H.H. Prince Aage of Denmark, Fire by Day and Flame by Night (London: Sampson Low, Marston 1937). Subtitle: 'With the Fighting Hermits of the African Desert. Memoirs of His Highness Prince Aage of Denmark'.
8. Pechkoff was born on 16 October 1884 in Ninji-Novgorod and lived in New Zealand, Italy and France with his adoptive father. He joined the Foreign Legion in 1914 and lost his arm in action the following year. He was with the White Russians in Siberia and the Crimea for a time. His blood

father, Jakob Sverdloff, was a close colleague of Lenin. Pechkoff became a French citizen in 1923. Zinovi Pechkoff, *The Bugle Sounds* (New York and London: Appleton 1926). Subtitle 'Life in the Foreign Legion'. Preface by Andre Maurois. The book was written while Pechkoff was recovering from wounds received in the fighting in Morocco.
9. Hallo, *Monsieur Legionnaire*, 223.
10. A.R. Cooper, *March or Bust: Adventures in the Foreign Legion* (London: Robert Hale 1972), 32. Cooper said that he took notes, which he subsequently lost – A.R. Cooper, Maidstone, Kent, to Author, 27 June 1984. His account of Camerone is littered with errors. Obviously, the documents he had handled in 1924 went missing at some point during the next five years. When historian Douglas Porch was doing his research in the A.L.E. for *The French Foreign Legion* in the 1980s he examined a file called 'Dossier Camerone', which promised more in its title than it provided in its contents. It was, Porch says, 'a small folder that had the notes of an interview from [Corporal] Maine, and a few brief biographies of some of the men involved in the battle.' He considered it to be 'nothing particularly extraordinary, except that it was the 'report' of the battle from someone who had lived it' – Douglas Porch, Monterey, California, to Author, 5 March 2002.
11. Cooper, *March or Bust*, 31–32.
12. Pechkoff, *Bugle*, 185–86.
13. Pechkoff, *Bugle*, 188.
14. A.R. Cooper and Sydney Tremayne, *The Man Who Liked Hell: Twelve Years in the Foreign Legion* (London: Jarrolds 1933), 157.
15. 'Les Drapeaux du 1er Regiment Etranger', *Kepi blanc*, no.431 (January 1984), Part 2, 32.
16. [Garros], 'Le Colonel Forey', *Historama*, 156.
17. Jacques Weygand, *Legionnaire* (London: George G. Harrap 1952), 33–34. Subtitle: 'Life with the Foreign Legion Cavalry'. Translated by Raymond Johnes. The author says: 'The events in this book are partly imaginary' and calls the central character – himself – 'Robert Vaudreuil'. Yet it is largely autobiographical, with a number of photographs of the 1st *Regiment Etranger de Cavalerie*. Weygand served with them for six years, 1925–31, then transferred to an indigenous Algerian unit, which led to a second book of autobiography: *Goumier de l'Atlas* (Paris: Flammarion 1954).
18. William Penderel, *Parade of Violence* (London: Selwyn & Blount 1937), 139–46, 136. Subtitle: 'True Story of [Max Durer] A Pacifist Destined to Fight'. Durer had joined the Foreign Legion in late 1924. He had been involved in the affairs around Fez the following April, when Camerone Day celebrations were truncated, so was seeing his first celebration in April 1926. He deserted after seven years of service.
19. G.-R. Manue, *Tres brules: cinq ans a la Legion* (Paris: Nouvelle Societe d'editions 1929). The book received an award from the Academie Francaise. Also: G.-R. Manue, *Sur les marches du Maroc insoumis* (Paris: Gallimand 1930) and G.-R. Manue, *La retraite au desert. Recit*, (Paris: A. Redier 1932).
20. Henri Pouliot, *Legionnaire* (Quebec City [Canada]: Privately Printed 1931; third edition 1937), 276–79. Subtitle: 'Histoire veridique et vecue d'un Quebecois simple soldat a la Legion Etrangere'.

Preface by Joan-Charles Harvey. Pouliot remembered Camerone as Cameroun.
21. Cooper/Tremayne, *Man Who Liked Hell*, 99–100. Cooper – or his co-author – also wrote: 'At Sidi Bel Abbes the regiment files past the wooden (sic) arm of Captain d'Anjou.' This was certainly drawn from reports of the 1931 Centenary Celebrations, as it does not appear that Danjou's hand was ever paraded during the Celebrations prior to 1931. It does not seem from Cooper's service records that he was ever in Sidi-bel-Abbes for a Camerone Day. There is evidence that he was unhappy with the job his co-author – a poet and novelist in his own right – made of the reminiscences, and always hoped that the book could be corrected and republished. Almost forty years later he presented his own version of some of the events described in the first book by writing a second one: Cooper, *March or Bust*.
22. David Wooster King, *And Ten Thousand Shall Fall* (New York: Duffield 1930).
23. Bennett J. Doty, *The Legion of the Damned* (New York: Century 1928). Subtitle: 'The Adventures of Bennett J. Doty in the French Foreign Legion, As Told by Himself'. Doty had been in the battle with the Druzes at Messifre.
24. John Harvey, *With the Foreign Legion in Syria* (London: Hutchinson 1928). Harvey had been with the Foreign Legion Cavalry in the battle at Raschaya.
25. Bert Hall and John J. Niles, *One Man's War* (New York: Holt 1929). Preface by Elliott White Springs.
26. Rockwell, *American Fighters*, 16.
27. Harvey, *Foreign Legion in Syria*. Hebrew-language edition: *Im Ligyon Hazarim Negad Ha-Druzin* (Tel Aviv: Mitspah 1930). Translated by A. Kriukin. *Med Framlingslegionen I Syrien* (Stockholm: Ahlstrom & Nordberg 1931). Translated by Helge Dahl.
28. G.-Jean Reybaz, 'Pour le centenaire de la Legion: la Legion Etrangere au front (1915)', *Revue des Deux Mondes* (1 Feb 1930).
29. Brunon, *Camerone* (1981), 19.
30. Rollet was behind the rebirth of *La Legion Etrangere*, once the Official Organ of the Federation of Societies of Former Legionnaires of France and the Colonies.

Chapter 28 – The Centenary of the Foreign Legion

1. These coins are now in the Foreign Legion Museum – Anonymous, *Musee*, 30.
2. Anonymous, 'Sidi-bel-Abbes – Historique', *Kepi blanc*, no.382 (September 1979), 15. Section called 'La musique de 1831 a nos jours'. Special issue on Sidi-bel-Abbes.
3. Anonymous, 'Sidi-bel-Abbes', 10.
4. Anonymous, 'Sidi-bel-Abbes', 11.
5. Anonymous, 'Sidi-bel-Abbes', 10.
6. Anonymous, 'Sidi-bel-Abbes', 10.
7. Brunon/Manue/Carles, *Livre d'Or* (1981), 491.
8. Brunon/Manue/Carles, *Livre d'Or* (1981), 485.
9. Cooper, *March or Bust*, 32. As late as 1954 the Foreign Legion had no idea of the names of all the men engaged at Camerone. The roll call they had, said Captain Oudry in an overview of the research to date, was 'unfortunately incomplete'. He could give only the names of the three officers and

twenty-nine men – Oudry, 'Camerone', 19.
10. Grisot/Coulombon, *Legion etrangere*, 275.
11. De Villebois-Mareuil, 'Legion Etrangere', 877.
12. Jean Brunon, Paul Rollin and Pierre Benigni, *Le Livre d'Or de la Legion Etrangere, 1831–1931* (Paris: Frazier-Soye 1931). Preface by Marshal Louis Franchet d'Esperey.
13. Jean Brunon, *La Voite de Gloire: Histoire des Drapeaux de la Legion Etrangere (1831–1931)* (Paris: Frazier-Soye 1931).
14. Weygand, *Legionnaire*, 184–88.
15. Brunon/Manue/Carles, *Livre d'Or* (1981), 451.
16. John Gibbons, *The Truth About the Legion* (London: Methuen 1933), 54.
17. Malcros, *Insignes*, 37.
18. Weygand, *Legionnaire*, 190.
19. Richard Haliburton, *The Flying Carpet* (Indianapolis: Bobbs-Merrill 1932). Edition used: (New York: Garden City Publishing 1932), 57.
20. Quoted in Brunon, *Camerone* (1981), 186.
21. Weygand, *Legionnaire*, 191.
22. Weygand, *Legionnaire*, 191.
23. *Programme: Centenaire de la Legion Etrangere, 1931–1931* (Sidi-Bel-Abbes: n.p., 1931) – copy in Richard Haliburton Collection, Library of Princeton University, Princeton, New Jersey.
24. *Centenaire de la Legion, 1831–1931* (Algiers: l'Amicale de la Legion Etrangere, 1931) – Haliburton Collection, Princeton University Library. The cover featured a drawing of Sergeant Minnaert, who was also featured among the various historical articles inside.
25. Weygand, *Legionnaire*, 191.
26. Haliburton, *Flying Carpet*, 57.
27. Moye W. Stephens, La Verne, California, to Author, 14 March 1986.
28. Weygand, *Legionnaire*, 192.
29. Lieutenant A.L. Martin, 'The Real Foreign Legion', *Army, Navy & Air Force Gazette*, LXXIV, no.3846 (5 October 1933), 807. Martin is described as 'lately Corporal 25292, 1st Regiment Foreign Legion'.

Chapter 29 – Voices from the Past

1. Francis Dickie, 'The Centenary of the Foreign Legion: The Famous French Force Holds High Festival in Sidi-bel-Abbes', *The World Today*, LVIII, no.1 (June 1931), 29–36.
2. Alice Williamson, 'A Century of the Foreign Legion', *World's Work*, 60 (May 1931), 53–56.
3. C.N. & A.M. Williamson, *A Soldier of the Legion* (New York: A.L. Burt 1914; London: Methuen 1914). This was a husband and wife writing team: Charles Norris Williamson (1859–1920) and Alice Muriel Williamson, nee Livingston, 1869–1933.
4. Gibbons, *Truth*, 53.
5. Gibbons, *Truth*, 55–56.
6. Jean Reybaz, *Le 1er Mysterious: souvenirs de guerre d'un legionnaire suisse* (Paris: Andre Barry 1932).
7. Colonel Frank E. Evans, 'They Know How to Die', *Marine Corps Gazette*, XVI, no.1 (May 1931), 5–10 *et. seq.*; Colonel Frank E. Evans, 'A Century of Combat', *Marine Corps Gazette*, XVI, no.2 (August 1931), 18–25 *et. seq.*; Colonel Frank E. Evans, 'The Making of a Legionnaire', *Marine Corps Gazette*, XVII, no.2 (May 1932), 7–16.
8. Evans, 'Century of Combat', 21.
9. Colonel Frank E. Evans, 'The French Foreign Legion, '*The Leatherneck* (June 1940), 11–12.
10. Colonel Frank E. Evans, 'The Legion in Morocco', *Marine Corps Gazette*, XVII, no.2 (August 1932), 25–30; Colonel Frank E. Evans, 'The French Campaign in Morocco', *Proceedings of the U.S. Naval Institute*, 60, no.1 (January 1934), 80–95. He also wrote a number of general articles on the Foreign Legion for mass circulation magazines during the 1930s. Evans rose to the rank of General, served in Hawaii and the mainland United States, retired in 1940, settled in Hawaii and wrote three more Foreign Legion articles for *The Leatherneck*. He died in Honolulu on 25 November 1941, seven days before the Japanese attack on Pearl Harbor, and his final article was published posthumously – Danny J. Crawford, Head, Reference Section, History and Museums Division, Department of the Navy, Washington, D.C., 1 February 1985.
11. Hallo, *Monsieur Legionnaire*, 223.
12. Anonymous, *Musee*, 46.
13. G. Ward Price, *In Morocco with the Legion* (London: Jarrolds 1934), 237. Price provides an excellent first-hand account of this final campaign, but his version of the Combat of Camerone is somewhat garbled.
14. Ward Price, *In Morocco*, 232, 236–37.
15. Jean des Vallieres, *Sous le drapeau de la Legion etrangere: Les Hommes Sans Noms* (Paris: Albin Michel 1933). The bibliography in the *Livre d'Or* (1981), 504, classifies the book as fiction. This author wrote two other books on the Foreign Legion: Jean de Vallieres, *Sa grandeur l'Infortune* (Paris: Albin Michel 1945) and Jean de Vallieres, *Et Voici La Legion Etrangere* (Paris: Andre Bonne 1963).
16. Anonymous, 'Sidi-bel-Abbes', 9.
17. Anonymous, 'Les Heros', 133.
18. General Charles-Jules Zede, 'Souvenirs de Ma Vie: Algerie, Italie, Mexique', began in the *Carnet de la Sabretache*, no.366 (September–October 1933), 426–41, and ended in no.374 (January–February 1935), 33–74. The Camerone material appears in no.370 (May–June 1934), 215–34.
19. Zede, 'Souvenirs', *Carnet* 370, 216; Zede, 'Temoignage', 15.
20. Zede, 'Souvenirs', *Carnet* 370, 223; Zede, 'Temoignage', 16.
21. Zede, 'Souvenirs', *Carnet* 370, 223; Zede, 'Temoignage', 16.
22. Zede, 'Souvenirs', *Carnet* 370, 223; Zede, 'Temoignage', 16.
23. Quoted in Brunon, *Camerone* [1981], 21.
24. Anonymous, 'Sidi-bel-Abbes', 24.
25. Jean-Pierre Dorian, *Le Colonel Maire: Un Heros de La Legion* (Paris: Editions Albin Michel 1981), 142.
26. Jean-Pierre Dorian, *Souvenirs du Colonel Maire de la Legion Etrangere* (Editions Albin Michel 1939), 62. Dorian was not involved in Fernand Maire, *Nouveaux Souvenirs sur la Legion Etrangere* (Paris: Fayard 1948).
27. Dorian, *Le Colonel Maire*. This edition contains a number of minor additions to the original text, of which the comment about Camerone is one. Maire, who was something of an egalitarian, may also have disapproved of Zede's emphasis on the

officers, rather than the men, in his memoirs.
28. Brunon, *Camerone* [1981], 118; Anonymous, *Musee*, 46.
29. A photograph of the Gorski medals was published in Brunon, *Camerone et l'Aigle*.
30. The sword that supposedly belonged to Benito Juarez which Captain Blin brought back from Mexico is in the Foreign Legion Museum – Anonymous, *Musee*, 46.
31. Debas, as a Battalion Commander led the 2nd REI from 25 July 1925 to 31 December 1926. He yielded command to Lieutenant-Colonel Geneau, but then, promoted to Lieutenant-Colonel, took command again on 1 July 1926, and held it until 9 May 1930. On 1 September 1930 he assumed command of the 5th REI and remained in the post until 5 April 1934. He became Colonel of the 1st REI on 22 November the same year and handed over to Colonel Azan on 15 February 1935.
32. Paul Azan, *L'Emir Abd el Kader* (Paris: Hachette 1925); Paul Azan, *Conquete et pacification d'Algerie* (Paris: Librairie de France 1929); and Paul Azan *L'Armee d'Afrique, 1830 a 1852* (Paris: Plon 1936).
33. Jean Brunon, *Camerone et l'Aigle du Regiment Etranger 1862–70*. Marseille: Imprimerie Meridionale 1935.
34. Lieutenant-Colonel Paul Azan, *La Legion Etrangere (1831–1935)* (Sidi-bel-Abbes: Presses du 1er Regiment Etranger 1935).
35. Hallo, *Monsieur Legionnaire*, 223.
36. Lieutenant Andolenko, *La filiation des bataillons de la Legion Etrangere, 1831–1936* (Sidi-bel-Abbes: Presses du 1er Etranger, 1937).
37. Malcros, *Insignes*, 38–39.
38. Patrick Turnbull, *The Hotter Winds* (London: Hutchinson 1960). Edition used (London: The Adventurers Club 1961), 108–110.
39. Turnbull, *Hotter Winds*, 127–27 and 155–68. Turnbull's knowledge of the Foreign Legion was limited. His brief telling of the Combat of Camerone – 133 – is garbled, but four years later, after extensive research in Paris and at Sidi-bel-Abbes, he wrote what up to that time was the best English-language Foreign Legion general history.
40. The Foreign Legion's spelling of Forsdyke was Fosdick. He was killed in 1940, serving in France as a member of the specially-raised Divisional Reconnaissance Group 97 – Turnbull, *Foreign Legion*, 178.
41. Andolenko, 'De Camerone', 6. A photographic print of the letter was provided for the *Salle d'Honneur* by General Blin.
42. Brunon, *Camerone* [1981], 211.
43. Andolenko, 'De Camerone', 6–8.
44. Andolenko, 'De Camerone', 8. The article includes a photograph of the Legion of Honour nomination, dated 16 April 1856.
45. Colonel Paul Azan, *Memento du soldat de la Legion Etrangere* (Sidi-bel-Abbes: Presses du 1er Regiment Etranger 1937).
46. Captain Andolenko, *Une Visite aux salles d'honneur et au Musee de souvenir de la Legion Etrangere* (Sidi-bel-Abbes: Presses du 1er Regiment Etranger 1938).
47. Charles Favrel, *Ci-devant legionnaire: La vrai legende de la Legion* (Paris: Presses de la Cite 1963), 45 and 58–59.
48. Alfred Perrott-White, *French Legionnaire* (Caldwell [Idaho]: Caxton Printers 1951), 65. The loss was most unfortunate, as it led to Perrott-White misremembering – 47 – Camerone as having involved two hundred Legionnaires in combat with three thousand Mexicans, fighting until there was only one French survivor. Camerone is called Cameroun.
49. Andolenko, 'De Camerone', 6–8.
50. Quoted in John Parker, *Inside the Foreign Legion* (London: Judy Piatkus 1998), 99. Subtitle: 'The Sensational Story of the World's Toughest Army'.
51. Brunon, *Camerone* [1981], 183.
52. Brunon, *Camerone* [1981], 118.
53. Brunon, *Camerone* [1981], 183. The text read:
Le 15 Avril 1828 naitre dans cette maison
le Capitaine DANJOU
qui le 30 Avril 1863 a CAMERONE (Mexique)
a la tete de 66 Legionnaires de la 3me Compagne du Regiment Etranger, resista jusqu'a la mort
aux assauts furieux de 2000 Mexicains.
3 Officers et 49 hommes furent mortellement frappes, mais l'enemi laissant 500 Cadavres.
Depuis, tous les ans, la Legion fete
le glorioux anniversaire de Camerone,
symbole de ses vertus inegalables.
54. A photograph of the plaque appears in Brunon, 'Camerone et l'Aigle', 13, and in Anonymous, 'Un Enfant de Chalabre: Le Capitaine Danjou', *Kepi blanc*, no.444 (February 1985), 46.
55. Blin, 'Au Mexique', 6–12. A photograph of Captain Blin accompanies the article.

Chapter 30 – Celebrating Camerone in Strange Places

1. Colin John, *Nothing to Lose* (London: Cassell 1955), 161. Collard completed forty-eight years of service in the Foreign Legion and died in 1954.
2. [Garros], 'Monclar', *Historama*, 148.
3. Aage died on 29 February, 1940 – [Garros], 'Le Prince Aage', *Historama*, 151.
4. [Garros], 'Le General Pechkoff', *Historama*, 152.
5. Adjutant Jerome Pelos, 'Les Volontaires de la Guerre 1939–1940', *Kepi blanc*, no.490 (May 1989), 25.
6. Captain Pierre O. Lapie, *With the Foreign Legion at Narvik* (London: John Murray 1941), 4–6. Translated by Anthony Merryn. Foreword by P.C. Wren.
7. Frederic O'Brady, *All Told* (New York: Simon and Schuster 1964), 188–90. Subtitle: 'The Confessions of Frederic O'Brady'.
8. 'Le 21eme Regiment de Marche de Volontaires Etrangers', *Kepi blanc*, No.490 (May, 1989), 40; Hans Habe, *A Thousand Shall Fall* (New York: Harcourt, Brace 1941). Hans Habe was the pen name of Budapest-born Janos Bekessy.
9. Georges-R. Manue, 'Vu du Rang', unpublished memoir in A.L.E., quoted in Turnbull, *Foreign Legion*, 176–77. Published as Georges-R. Manue, *Sous la grenade a sept flammes: Comment on a cree un corps d'elite, 1939–1940* (Paris: Sequana 1941). Also Georges-R. Manue, 'Rien n'est perdu. Le 11e de Legion au feu, mai–juin 1940', *Le Temps*, May and June 1942; Hugh McLeave, *The Damned Die Hard* (New York: Saturday Review Press 1973), 185–87; Anonymous, 'Le 11eme Regiment Etranger d'Infanterie' and Lieutenant-Colonel Claude Boudoux d'Hautefeuille,

'Souvenirs d'un Chef de Section au 11eme R.E.I. en 39–40', *Kepi blanc*, no.490 (May 1989), 30–34.
10. Perrott-White, *Legionnaire*, 63–67.
11. Prince Napoleon, 'Legionnaire Blanchard', *Kepi blanc*, no.490 (May 1989), 26–27; Bocca, *Legion*, 134–36; Pelos, 'Les Volontaires de la Guerre 1939–1940', 25.
12. The stories of the regular regiments of the Foreign Legion and the three Regiments of Foreign Volunteers involved in the Second World War are told, with varying degrees of detail and emphasis, in all the English language general histories of the Foreign Legion: Howard Swiggett, *March or Die* (New York: G.P. Putnam's Sons 1953), 150–62; Edgar O'Ballance, *The Story of the French Foreign Legion* (London: Faber and Faber 1961), 158–71; Charles Mercer, *Legion of Strangers* (New York: Holt, Rinehart and Winston 1964), 256–76. Subtitle: 'The Vivid History of a Unique Military Tradition – The French Foreign Legion'; Geoffrey Bocca, *La Legion!* (New York: Thomas Y. Crowell 1964), 127–45. Subtitle: 'The French Foreign Legion and the Men Who Made It Glorious'; Turnbull, *Foreign Legion*, 171–91; McLeave, *The Damned*, 176–98; John Laffin, *The French Foreign Legion* (London: J.M. Dent 1974), 118–25; Geraghty, *March or Die*, 172–226; Roy Anderson, *Devils, Not Men* (London: Robert Hale 1987), 67–82. Subtitle: 'The History of the French Foreign Legion'. Foreword by Colonel Anthony Hunter-Choat; and Porch, *Foreign Legion*, 441–504. A great deal on the 11th and 12th REIs, the GRD 97 and the 21st, 22nd and 23rd RMVEs is to be found in the multi-authored 'Les Volontaires de la Guerre 1939–1940', *Kepi blanc*, no.490 (May 1989), 24-48.
13. Anonymous, 'Le General Francois', *Vert et Rouge: Traditions et Souvenirs Militaires*, no.91 (April 1954), 26–27.
14. Brunon/Manue/Carles, *Livre d'Or* (1981), 248.
15. Rollet died on 16 April 1941 – [Garros], 'Le General Rollet', *Historama*, 147.
16. Brunon, 'Camerone et l'Aigle', 12–18.
17. John F. Hasey, *Yankee Fighter*, as told to Joseph F. Dineen (Boston: Little, Brown 1942). Edition used: (New York: Garden City Publishing 1944), 218–19. Subtitle: 'The Story of an American Officer in the Free French Foreign Legion'.
18. Hasey, *Yankee Fighter*, 256–57. The Feast of Camerone is said to have taken place on 15 April, meaning that either Hasey mis-remembered, or 'ghost writer' Dineen mis-dated, the event. Throat wounds made it difficult for Hasey to speak, and his right arm was in a sling, at the time that his story was given to Dineen. It is also possible that Camerone celebrations were held early, as the date of the 13th *Demi-Brigade*'s departure from Eritrea, while known to be imminent, was not actually settled until shortly before they left for the Middle East.
19. Brunon/Manue/Carles, *Livre d'Or* (1981), 414–15.
20. A.R. Cooper, *Born to Fight* (Edinburgh: William Blackwood 1969), 248–54. For Cooper's Special Operations Executive work in Algeria and Italy see: Captain Dick Cooper, *The Adventures of a Secret Agent* (London: Frederick Muller 1957).
21. The *cravate* and *fanion* were returned to Sidi-bel-Abbes in February 1942. Brunon/Manue/Carles, *Livre d'Or* (1981), 238–42 and 411–12. The *cravate* of the 11th REI is in the Foreign Legion Museum – Anonymous, *Musee*, 42.
22. Brunon/Manue/Carles, *Livre d'Or* (1981), 414–15. This Regimental Flag was with the regiment for the rest of the Second World War. The Battle Honours LIBYE BIR-HAKEIM 1942 and ITALY 1944 were subsequently added, and the flag led the 2nd Battalion of the 13th *Demi-Brigade* in the April 1945 Victory Parade in Paris.
23. Richard Holmes, *Bir Hacheim – Desert Citadel* (New York: Ballantine Books 1970). It took Koenig almost thirty years to set down his own account of the siege: General Pierre Koenig, *Ce Jour-la: Bir Hakeim* (Paris: Robert Laffont 1971).
24. Brunon, *Camerone* [1981] 22.
25. The exact words vary slightly, but the sentiment is the same: Turnbull, *Foreign Legion*, 181; McLeave, *The Damned*, 197.
26. Anonymous, 'Jean Brunon (1895–1982)', *Kepi blanc*, no.435 (May 1984), 40.
27. Bocca, *Legion*, 141–42.
28. Perrott-White, *Legionnaire*, 186–205.
29. Ernie Pyle, *Here Is Your War: The Story of G.I. Joe* (New York: Henry Holt 1943). Edition used: (Cleveland: The World Publishing Company 1945), 168–69. Pyle was killed by a Japanese sniper in the Pacific Campaign on 18 April 1945.
30. Penette, *Histoire*, 7, n.11.
31. Porch, *Foreign Legion* has a photograph of the Regimental Flag in enemy hands.
32. Anonymous, 'L'Aventure du Drapeau du 3e Etranger, Tunisie 19 Janvier–12 Mai 1943', – *Journal de Marche du 3e REI, December 1942/Avril 1943*, 12 – A.L.E.
33. Brunon/Manue/Carles, *Livre d'Or* (1981), 415–16.
34. Brunon/Manue/Carles, *Livre d'Or* (1981), 410–11.
35. Corporal Philippe Maine, 'Le combat de Camerone: vu par le Caporal Maine', *Vert et Rouge: Revue de la Legion Etrangere* (May 1945), 8–14. The illustrations include the highly imaginative drawing (11) of the Hacienda de la Trinidad and the excellent one of the Mexican cavalry attack on the 3rd of the 1st's 'square' (13) from Lucien-Louis Lande's 1878 book *Souvenirs d'un soldat*.
36. [Garros], 'Forey', *Historama*, 156. The old warrior died on 11 July 1946.
37. Brunon/Manue/Carles, *Livre d'Or* (1981), 294.

Chapter 31 – Camerone at Dien Bien Phu

1. General Marcel J. Penette, Paris, to Author, 7 July 1982.
2. John, *Nothing to Lose*, 141–43. The surname John was, in fact, a *nom de plume* for the purposes of his book – a second *anonymat*, in fact.
3. Leslie Aparvary, *A Legionnaire's Journey* (Calgary, Alberta: Detselig Enterprises 1989), 128. He was subsequently invalided out, lived in Paris and Brussels and then emigrated to Canada, where he worked in the oil industry in Calgary, Alberta.
4. Brunon, *Camerone* [1981], 183. A photograph of General Catroux laying a wreath at the foot of the plaque is published in [Garros], *Historama*, 35. The text on the plaque read:
A LA MEMOIRE
DES OFFICERS ET LEGIONNAIRES
QUE SOUS LES ORDERS DU CAPITAINE

DANJOU LUTTERER
UN CONTRE QUARANTE
PENDENT DIX HOURS LE 30 AVRIL 1863 A
CAMERONE
'LA VIE PLUTOT LE COURAGE
ABANDONNA CES SOLDATS FRANCAIS'
5. The story of the events along Colonial Route 4 has been ably told: Colonel Pierre Charton, 'RCA' Indo-Chine 1950 (Paris: Societe de Production Litteraire 1975). Subtitle: 'La Tragedie de l'evacuation de Cao-Bang racontee par un participant'.
6. Janos Kemencei, Legionnaire en avant! (Paris: Jacques Gracher 1985), 205–11. Preface by Pierre Sergent. Kemencei, by adding two years to his age, had succeeded in joining the Foreign Legion in 1946 while still only sixteen years old.
7. Malcros, Insignes, 11.
8. Official Report, 3rd Company at Twin Tunnels, 1 February 1950, quoted in Brunon, Camerone [1981], 11; Swiggett, March or Die, 230, identifies the NCOs as Sergeants Van der Borght and Fanconnet [Falconetti]. Both survived, though the 3rd Company suffered heavy losses. Sergeant Joseph Falconetti was killed on 26 September 1951.The story of the Bataillon Francais is told in Erwan Bergot, Bataillon de Coree (Paris: Presses de la Cite 1983). Subtitle: 'Les volontaires francais 1950-1953'.
9. John, Nothing to Lose, 176–77 and 180–81.
10. Henry Ainley, In Order to Die: With the Foreign Legion in Indo-China (London: Burke 1955), 19.
11. Adrian Liddell-Hart, Strange Company (London: Weidenfeld and Nicholson 1953), 70–71.
12. General Charles Zede, 'Camerone: Le Temoignage d'un Caporal survivant', Vert et Rouge: Traditions et Souvenirs Militaires, no.33 (May 1951), 12–16.
13. Brunon, Camerone [1981], 154, n.1. A good oversize reproduction – 31.75 cms x 19 cms (12.5 ins x 7.5 ins) – of Beauce's painting was published in Kepi blanc, no.423 (April 1983), 32–33.
14. Quoted in Swiggett, March or Die, xii.
15. The Battle of Dien Bien Phu has been extensively chronicled, several times by senior officers who survived it, though their books have not been translated into English. Among the best is Erwan Bergot, Les 170 jours de Dien-Bien-Phu (Paris: Presses de la Cite 1979), written by a former Lieutenant in the 1st Foreign Legion Airborne Heavy Mortar Company at Dien Bien Phu. Another insider's view comes from Paul Grauwin, Doctor at Dien Bien Phu (London: Hutchinson 1955). The best studies are: Jules Roy, The Battle of Dienbienphu (New York: Harper and Row 1965). Edition used: (New York: Carrol & Graf 1984); Bernard Fall, Hell In A Very Small Place (Philadelphia: J.B. Lippincot 1966). Subtitle: 'The Siege of Dien Bien Phu'. (Edition used: New York: Vantage 1968); and Howard R. Simpson, Dien Bien Phu (Washington: Brassey's 1994). Subtitle: 'The Epic Battle America Forgot'. All three had long connections with Indo-China – Roy as a soldier, Fall as an academic and Simpson as a diplomat and journalist – and extraordinary resources for gathering and telling their stories.
16. Bergot, Foreign Legion, 216–18.
17. Fall, Small Place, 348, and 476, n.14.
18. Quoted in Turnbull, Foreign Legion, 229. Kubiak's Diary is held by the A.L.E.

19. Fall, Small Place, 347, and 476, n.13.
20. Fall, Small Place, 290.
21. Bergot, Foreign Legion, 216–19; Fall, Small Place, 347.
22. John, Nothing to Lose, 277.
23. Sergeant Kubiak, 'Operation Castor . . . Verdun 1954', Kepi blanc (October 1962).
24. Roy, Dienbienphu, 280.
25. Laffin, Foreign Legion, 138.
26. Kemencei, Legionnaire, 291–92.
27. John, Nothing to Lose, 283.
28. John, Nothing to Lose, 10.
29. Captain Oudry, 'Camerone (30 avril 1863)', Vert et Rouge: Traditions et souvenirs militaires, no. 86 (May 1954), 16–29.
30. Le Monde [Paris], 25 May 1954; Fall, Small Place, 431.
31. Fall, Small Place, 438.
32. Brunon/Manue/Carles, Livre d'Or [1981], 389.
33. Bergot, Foreign Legion, 220–24.

Chapter 32 – A Bitter Homecoming

1. John Townsend, The Legion of the Damned (London: Elek Books 1961). Edition used: (London: The Adventurers Club 1963), 29–31.
2. Townsend, . . . the Damned, 51–57.
3. Townsend, . . . the Damned, 123–90.
4. Michael Alexander, The Reluctant Legionnaire (London: Rupert Hart-Davis 1956). Subtitle: 'An Escapade'.
5. Alexander, Reluctant Legionnaire, 85. The reference to the Voie Sacre is inaccurate. It was the approach to the Monument aux Morts which was the Voie Sacre, not a corridor in the Salle d'Honneur, as Alexander reports.
6. The best English-language accounts of the tumultuous events leading to the Independence of Algeria, are Alistair Horne, A Savage War of Peace: Algeria 1954–1962 (London: Macmillan 1977) and John Talbot, The War Without A Name: France in Algeria 1954–1962 (New York: Alfred A. Knopf 1980). There are good accounts, highlighting the Foreign Legion's role, in McLeave, The Damned, 244–87, Geraghty, March or Die, 253–307, and Porch, Foreign Legion, 565–617.
7. Quoted in Turnbull, Foreign Legion, 242.
8. Geraghty, March or Die, 272.
9. Horne, Savage War, 347.
10. Bocca, La Legion!, 233–34.
11. Kemencei, Legionnaire, 338–39.
12. Pierre Sergent, Ma Peau au Bout de mes Idees (Paris: Table Ronde 1967), 173.
13. Parker, Foreign Legion, 15.
14. James William Worden, Wayward Legionnaire (London: Robert Hale 1988), 59. Subtitle: 'A Life in the French Foreign Legion'.
15. Worden, Wayward, 55.
16. Simon Murray, Legionnaire (London: Sidgwick & Jackson 1978). Edition used: (New York: Times Books 1978), 40. Subtitle: 'An Englishman in the French Foreign Legion'. Diary entries for 28 April and 30 April 1960.
17. Peter Reeves/Hurk Davis, Legion of Outcasts: The Autobiography of Peter Reeves as told to Hurk Davis (Los Angeles: Holloway House 1968), 102–03. Reeves served from February 1960 to May 1962. His as-told-to reminiscences are billed

as the 'First startling expose of the incredible brutality and shame of the French Foreign Legion.'
18. Horne, *Savage War*, 299–504, and Talbot, *War Without*, 153–249, both cover the 'Generals' Putsch' and the *Organization Armee Secrete* in detail, and there are also a number of accounts in French, some by participants. The three books by former Foreign Legion officer Pierre Sergent are important sources: Sergent, *Ma Peau*; Pierre Sergent, *La Bataille* (Paris: Table Ronde 1968); and Pierre Sergent, *Je ne regrette rien – La poignante histoire des legionnaires parachutistes du 1er REP* (Paris: Librairie Artheme Fayard 1972).
19. McLeave, *The Damned*, 262.
20. McLeave, *The Damned*, 267.
21. Henri Le Mire, *Histoire militaire de la guerre d'Algerie* (Paris: Albin Michel 1982), 343.
22. McLeave, *The Damned*, 267.
23. Murray, *Legionnaire*, 137–38. Diary entry for 24 April 1961. Murray's spelling of names is not always correct. L'Hospitallier instead of Lhopitallier, Gabriot instead of Cabiro and Damusez for Darmuzai, are examples.

Chapter 33 – End of an Era

1. Reeves, *Outcasts*, 175.
2. Murray, *Legionnaire*, 140. Diary entry for 27 April 1961.
3. Murray, *Legionnaire*, 141. Diary entry for 30 April 1961.
4. Reeves, *Outcasts*, 179.
5. Murray, *Legionnaire*, 141–42. Diary entry for 3 May 1961.
6. Kemencei, *Legionnaire*, 336.
7. Worden, *Wayward*, 111–20; Horne, *Savage War*, 474–75. The French response to the Tunisian attack on the leased naval base at Bizerta earned them condemnation from the United Nations and hardened attitudes throughout the Arab world – *Report of the Committee of Enquiry into Events in Bizerta, Tunisia 18–24 July 1961* (Geneva: International Commission of Jurists 1961).
8. Murray, *Legionnaire*, 156. Diary entry for 5 September 1961.
9. Kemencei, *Legionnaire*, 338–39.
10. Colonel Vaillant, 1st Etranger, 'Report sur la morel', 21 November 1961 – A.L.E.
11. Murray, *Legionnaire*, 183–84. Diary entry for 30 April 1962.
12. Reeves, *Outcasts*, 311.
13. Quoted in Geraghty, *March or Die*, 284.
14. Kzmencei, *Legionnaire*, 344. In 1981, the review *Historama* devoted an issue to the 150th anniversary of the Foreign Legion. A photograph of page 10 shows Kemencei carrying the casket containing the Hand of Captain Danjou.
15. Worden, *Wayward*, 157–58 and 162. Solomirsky died on 20 March 1989 at the age of 94 – *Kepi blanc*, No.490 (May 1989), 56.
16. Georges-R. Manue, 'Pelerinage a Camerone', *Revue des Deux Mondes*, II, (1 June 1963), 354–55.
17. Colonel Vaillant, 1st Etranger, 'Report sur la morel', 21 November 1961 – A.L.E.
18. Murray, *Legionnaire*, 211. Diary entry for 10 December 1962.

Chapter 34 – General Penette Dreams a Dream

1. The definitive account of the founding and early days of The Camerone Association, and the many highs and lows it encountered in bringing the plans for the Camerone Monument to fruition, is to be found in General Marcel Penette, *Histoire du Memorial de Camerone*, a thirty-two-page typewritten booklet which he had privately printed in Paris in November 1976. He presented a signed copy to the Author in July 1982. (Cited as Penette, *Histoire*.) General Marcel Penette, 'Le memorial de Camerone', *Revue Historique des Armees*, no.4 (1981), 109–25 – cited as Penette, 'Memorial' – is a condensed, but slightly updated and revised, version of the *Histoire*. They provided the basic material for this chapter.
2. Penette, *Histoire*, 8.
3. Jean Brunon, Georges-R. Manue and Pierre Carles, *Le Livre d'Or de la Legion Etrangere, 1831–1955* (Paris-Limoges: Charles-Lavauzelle 1958). Foreword by Marshal Alphonse Juin.
4. Brunon, *Camerone* [1981], 211.
5. Sousa, 'The Grave of Sous-Lieutenant Clement Maudet'; [Castaignt], 'Huatusco', 73. A photograph of the grave marker accompanied the article.
6. Penette, *Histoire*, 9; Penette, 'Memorial', 115. The Presidents of The Camerone Association in its first fifteen years were: General Penette, Manuel Gonzalez y Montesinos, Dr. Efren Marin and Joaquin Talavera Sanchez.
7. General Jean Olie, *Chef de l'Etat-Major Particulier*, Paris, to General Marcel J. Penette, Mexico City, 29 August 1960. Reproduced in *Histoire*, 23.
8. Prince Napoleon, Paris, to General Marcel Penette, Mexico City, 29 August 1960; Comte de Paris, Paris, to General Marcel Penette, Mexico City, 10 October 1960. Reproduced in *Histoire*, 24–25. The law banning the two Pretenders from living in France had been repealed in 1950.
9. Ministry of Foreign Relations, 26 April, 1961; State of Veracruz, 6 November; Municipality of Villa Adalberto Tejeda, 10 November. The permissions from Foreign Relations and Villa Adalberto Tejeda are reproduced in *Histoire*, 27–29.
10. Much of the work in searching relevant land records was done by Colonel Francois Pepin-Lehalleur, the Military Attache at the French Embassy in Mexico City, Rafael Molina Enriquez, President of the Municipality of Villa Adalberto Tejeda – the equivalent of the Mayor – and lawyer Joaquin Talavera Sanchez in Mexico City.
11. General M[arcel] Penette and Captain J[ean] Castaingt, *La Legion Extranjera en la Intervencion Francesca* (Mexico City: Publicaciones Especial del Primer Congresso Nacional de Historia para el Estudio de la Guerra de Intervencion, 1962). It has never been translated into French.
12. 'Inspection of the Regiment Etranger' by General Ernest de Maussion, Cordoba, 25 September, 1863 – Xb 778, S.H.A.T.
13. Lieutenant-Colonel Pierre Carles, S.H.A.T., Vincennes, to Jean Brunon, Salon-de-Provence – Brunon, *Camerone* [1981], 207.
14. Fall, *Small Place*, 348, and 476, n.14, quoting an interview with Colonel Michel Vadot at Aubagne in August 1963.
15. Penette, *Histoire*, 15; Penette, 'Memorial', 117–18.

Chapter 35 – Danjou's Hand Goes Back to Mexico

1. Penette, *Histoire*, 16–17, and Penette, 'Memorial', 118–20, provide details of the Dedication of the Camerone Monument on 20 April 1963. These have been augmented by the detailed eyewitness two-part account 'Pelerinage a Camerone' by Georges-R. Manue, *Revue des Deux Mondes* (15 May 1963), 274–812, and (1 June 1963), 349–58, and a second equally full eyewitness account in *Honneur et Fidelite: C'Est La Legion* by Louis Gaultier and Charles Jacquot (Marseilles: Les Impressions Francaises 1963), III, 104–16.
2. Manue, 'Pelerinage', I, 277.
3. *Los Duros, Aventuras en la Legion Extrangera* by Laszlo Pataky (Managua, Nicaragua: Editorial Novedades 1952).
4. Penette, *Histoire*, 16; Penette, 'Memorial', 119; Manue, 'Peligrinage', II, 350; Gaultier/Jacquot, *Honneur et Fidelite*, III, 112; [Garros], 'Le Memorial de Camerone', *Historama*, 160; Anonymous, 'Ephemeride Legionnaire', *Kepi blanc* no.424 (April 1983), 53.
5. Louis Gaultier and Charles Jacquot, *Honneur et Fidelite: C'Est La Legion* (Marseilles: Les Impressions Francaises 1963).
6. Murray, *Legionnaire*, 227. Diary entry for 1 May 1963.
7. *Camerone 1863–1963* (Aubagne: *Kepi blanc* 1963).
8. Jean Castaignt, 'Mexique: Lieux frequentes par le R.E. en 1863' and 'Mexique: Les travaux en cours a Camerone' – with photographs of the new dam and of the model of the Monument – *Kepi blanc*, no.193 (May 1963), 20–21 and 22–23.
9. *Centenaire du Combat de Camerone, 1863–1963* (Paris: La Maison des Anciens Legionnaires de Paris 1963).
10. Jean Brunon, *Camerone* (Paris: France-Empire, 1963).
11. [Garros], *Historama*, 149, has a photograph of the parade, with Koenig taking the salute.
12. Manue, 'Pelerinage', II, 256.
13. Manue, 'Pelerinage', II, 254.
14. Manue, 'Pelerinage', II, 356.
15. Manue, 'Pelerinage', II, 357.
16. Manue, 'Pelerinage', II, 358.
17. Kemencei, *Legionnaire*, 344.
18. Jon Swain, *River of Time* (New York: St. Martin's Press 1997), 232–34.
19. Mercer, *Strangers*, 320–22.
20. Penette, *Histoire*, 17–19; Penette, 'Memorial', 120–21.
21. Anonymous, 'La Memorial de Camerone', *Kepi blanc*, no.428 (October 1983), 40.
22. Murray, *Legionnaire*, 277. Diary entry for 4 May 1964. Murray's five-year engagement ended in February 1965.
23. Worden, *Wayward Legionnaire*, 186. Worden left the Foreign Legion late in 1965 after sustaining a back injury while parachuting.
24. [Garros], 'Monclar', *Historama*, 149.
25. Penette, *Histoire*, 20–21, and Penette, 'Memorial', 122, provide details of the Inauguration of the Camerone Monument on 15 December 1965, as does [Garros], 'Le Memorial', *Historama*, 158–60.
26. Photographs of the Camerone Memorial can be found in Penette, 'Memorial', 121; Sergent, *Camerone*; Brunon, *Camerone* [1981]; Y.-J. Baubiat, 'Le Mexique et Camerone', *Kepi blanc*, no.428 (October 1983), 39.
27. [Garros], 'Le Memorial', *Historama*, 159–60.
28. Penette, *Histoire*, 21; Penette, 'Memorial', 122.

Chapter 36 – A New Beginning

1. *Camerone 1966* (Sidi-bel-Abbes: Presses du 1st Regiment Etranger, 1966). General Koenig died in September 1970, and fourteen years later, in connection with the commemorations for the fortieth anniversary of D-Day, he was posthumously named a Marshal of France.
2. Anonymous, *Musee*, provides a useful overview of the Museum.
3. Excellent colour pictures taken in the Crypt are to be found in Yves Debay, *The French Foreign Legion Today* (London: Windrow & Greene 1992), 45; and Anonymous, *Musee*, 5.
4. [Garros], 'Le General Pechkoff', *Historama*, 152.
5. Howard R. Simpson, *The Paratroopers of the French Foreign Legion* (Washington: Brassey's 1997), 39. Subtitle: 'From Vietnam to Bosnia'.
6. Anonymous, 'Le Musee de l'Emperi', *Kepi blanc*, no.435 (May 1984), 40.
7. Jean Brunon, Georges-R. Manue and Pierre Carles, *Le Livre d'Or de la Legion Etrangere (1831–1976)* (Paris-Limoges: Charles-Lavauzelle 1976). Material by Battalion Commander Guibert-Lassalle, Chef de Section Information et Historique de la Legion Etrangere.
8. Simpson, *Paratroopers*, 66–76, gives the best English-language account of the affair at Kolwezi. Geraghty, *March or Die*, 316–23, also deals with Kolwezi, and with the tangled activities in Chad, 314–15 and 323–28, and Chad is also covered in Anderson, *Devils*, 135–39.
9. Brunon, *Camerone* [1981], 118, n.1.
10. Pierre Sergent, *Camerone: La campagne heroique de la Legion etrangere au Mexique* (Paris: Fayard 1980).
11. Jean Brunon, *Camerone* (Paris: Editions France-Empire 1981).
12. Jean Brunon, Georges-R. Manue and Pierre Carles, *Le Livre d'Or de la Legion Etrangere (1831–1981)* (Paris-Limoges: Charles-Lavauzelle, 1981). Material by Adjutant Chef Tibor Szecsko, the Curator of the *Musee de la Legion Etrangere*.
13. Carles, '. . . l'histoire du sous-officier', 24.
14. Anonymous, 'Jean Brunon', *Kepi blanc*, no.435 (May 1984), 38.
15. 'Legion Etrangere: Couverture de l'encart philatelique', *Kepi blanc*, no.434 (April 1984), 3; 'Autour d'un Evenement Philatelique', *Kepi blanc*, no.435 (May 1984), 45; '*Kepi blanc* philatelie', *Kepi blanc*, no.436 (June 1984), 8.
16. John Robert Young, *The French Foreign Legion* (New York and London: Thames and Hudson 1984). Subtitle: 'The Inside Story of the World-Famous Fighting Force'. Introduction by Len Deighton. 'The History of the Legion' by Erwan Bergot.
17. Young, *Foreign Legion*, 10.
18. Young, *Foreign Legion*, 153 and 164.

Chapter 37 – Camerone and the Foreign Legion Today

1. Peter Macdonald, *The Making of a Legionnaire* (London: Sidgwick and Jackson 1991), 25.
2. Yves Debay, *The French Foreign Legion Today*

(London: Windrow & Greene 1992), 42–44. Translated by Jean-Pierre Villaume. Europa Militaria No. 10. Debay's photographs are outstanding. Unfortunately, the statement that the 3rd of the 1st had been 'attacked by 3,000 horsemen', and that Danjou's hand 'was found in the smouldering ruins' of the hacienda, mar the text. Debay did not deal with Camerone in his companion volume, *The French Foreign Legion in Action* (London: Windrow and Greene 1992). Translated by Jean-Pierre Villaume. Europa Militaria No. 11.

3. Yves Debay, *French Foreign Legion Operations 1990–2000* (Ramsbury, Wilts, U.K.: The Crowood Press 2000), 7. Translated by Hilary Hook. Edited by Martin Windrow. Europa Militaria Special 15. The canard about Danjou and the Crimea is repeated, as is the one about his hand being found 'amid the grim debris of battle'.

4. Yves Debay, *The 2e REP: French Foreign Legion Paratroopers* (Paris: Histoire et Collections 2002). Translated by Alan McKay.

5. Sadie Galvin, *Operation Sadie* (London: W.H. Allen 1977). Subtitle: 'How I Rescued My Son From The Freign Legion'.

6. Martin Chadzynski and Carli Laklan, *Runaway!* (New York: McGraw-Hill 1979), 81–82.

7. Christian Jennings, *Mouthful of Rocks* (London: Bloomsbury 1989), 34–35. Subtitle: 'Through Africa and Corsica in the French Foreign Legion'.

8. Bill Parris, *The Making of a Legionnaire* (London: Weidenfeld and Nicolson 2004), 43–45. Subtitle: 'My Life in the French Foreign Legion Parachute Regiment'.

9. Parris, *The Making* . . ., 97–100.

10. Parris, *The Making* . . ., 177–80.

11. Simon Jameson, *The French Foreign Legion: A Guidebook to Joining* (Plymouth, Devon: Salvo Books 1997), 76–77.

12. Evan McGorman, *Life in the French Foreign Legion* (Central Point, Oregon: Hellgate Press 2000), 157–58. Subtitle: 'How to Join and What to Expect When You Get There'.

13. Albert Duchesne, 'Des Belges au combat de Camerone', *Carnet de la Fourragere*, XV, no.2 (September 1967), 112.

14. Garfias M[agana], *Intervencion*, 82–91; Luis Garfias M[agana], 'Sucedio en Camaron', 4–9; and Luis Garfias Magana, 'Camaron', *Excelsior* (1 April 1990), 6–7.

15. Porch, *Foreign Legion*, 420.

16. Quoted in John, *Nothing to Lose*, 180.

17. Bocca, *Legion!*, 8–10. Yet Bocca wrote: 'The Legion looks after its own. In 1963, it flew a party of officers and Sous-Officiers to Mexico to the scene of the battle. A memorial commemorates it. It was such a little battle, fought so far away, for such a futile cause. How apt!' The Sergeant-Chef's name was not 'LaBella'. It was merely a common Sicilian one, chosen by Bocca for the purposes of the story.

18. Quoted in Parker, *Inside the Foreign Legion*, 15.

19. Gaultier/Jacquot, *Honneur et Fidelite*, III, 107.

Bibliography

Primary Sources Official Documents

LOI – Qui authorise la formation d'une legion d'etrangers en France et de corps militaires composes d'indigenes et d'etrangers, hors du territoire continental – 9 March 1831.

ORDONNANCE DU ROI – relative a la formation de la Legion etrangere – 10 March 1831.

INSTRUCTION – Pour l'admission dans la Legion etrangere, en execution de l'ordonnance royale de 10 March 1831 – 18 March 1831.

ORDONNANCE DU ROI – Portant que la Legion etrangere cessera de faire partie de l'armee francaise – 29 June 1835.

ORDONNANCE – Qui prescrit la formation d'une nouvelle Legion etrangere composee d'etrangers, sous la denomination de Legion etrangere – 16 December 1835.

EXECUTION – De l'ordonnance qui prescrit la formation d'une nouvelle Legion Composee d'etrangers – 2 January 1836.

ORDONNANCE DU ROI – Qui divise la Legion etrangere en deux regiments dont elle determine la composition – 30 December 1840.

DECRET IMPERIAL – Relatif a la formation d'une seconde Legion etrangere – 17 January 1855.

DECRET IMPERIAL - Qui licencie 1er et 2e legions etrangeres et cree 2 regiments etrangers – 16 April 1856.

RAPPORT – A l'Emperor sur la reorganisation des troupes etrangeres au service de la France – 16 April 1856.

DECRET IMPERIAL – Relatif aux engagements et rengagements dans les regiments etrangers – 30 June, 1859.

DECRET IMPERIAL – Qui donne au 1er regiment etranger la meme organisation qu'au 2e regiment – 14 October 1859.

DECRET – Qui licencie le 1er regiment etranger – 14 December 1861.

SUSPENSION – Des engagements volontaires dans le regiment etranger – 16 December 1861.

DECRET IMPERIAL – Qui cree un quatrieme bataillon dans le regiment etranger – 30 April 1864.

NOTE MINISTERIELLE – Indiquant le lieu sur lequel doivent etre diriges les engages volontaires qui s'engagent pour servir dans le regiment etranger – 29 March 1865.

DECRET IMPERIAL – Qui cree un cinquieme bataillon dans le regiment etranger – 5 April 1865.

DECRET IMPERIAL – Qui cree in sixieme bataillon dans le regiment etranger – 8 July 1865.

DECRET IMPERIAL – Portant creation d'un septieme et d'un huitieme bataillon dans le regiment etranger – 4 July 1866.

NOTE – Prescrivant que les engages volontaires pour le regiment etranger devront etre, a l'avenir, diriges sur Sidi-bel-Abbes – 8 February 1867.

DECRET IMPERIAL – Portant creation d'un cinquieme bataillon dans le regiment etranger – 22 August 1870.

DECRET – Qui rend au regiment etranger son ancienne denomination de legion etrangere, Versailles – 29 March 1875.

MINISTERIAL DECREE, Paris – 16 February, 1906.

Archival Collections

Archives of the Service Historique de l'Armee de Terre (S.H.A.T.), Chateau de Vincennes, France.

Livre Algerie H 299, no.3, Message no.490 – General Deligny, Commanding Officer, Division of Oran, to Colonel Jeanningros, Commanding Officer, Regiment Etranger, Sidi-bel-Abbes.

Livre Algerie H 301 – General Deligny, Commanding Officer, Division of Oran, to Colonel Faidherbe, Commanding Sub-Division of Sidi-bel-Abbes, 15 January, 1863.

'Inspection of the 1st Etranger' by General Ulrich, 6 August 1861 – Xb778.

'Inspection of the 2nd Etranger' by General Deligny, 6 August 1861 – Xb778.

'Inspection of the Regiment Etranger' by General Ernest de Maussion, Cordoba, 25 September, 1863 – Xb 778.

'Inspection of the Regiment Etranger' by General Augustin Brincourt, 15 September 1864 – Xb 778.

Dossier Jean Danjou, No. 5Ye 15 583.

Dossier Jean Vilain, No. 5Ye 15 575.

Dossier Clement Maudet, No. 5Y3 15 577.

Dossier Philippe Maine.

Dossier Evariste Berg.

Dossier Patrick Cotter.

Colonel Pierre Jeanningros, Paso Ancho, to Colonel Ernest de Maussion, Orizaba, 2 May 1863.

Colonel Pierre Jeanningros, Commanding Officer, Regiment Etranger, Chiquihuite, to Commander-in-Chief, General Elie-Frederic Forey, Headquarters, Corps Expeditionnaire du Mexique, Cerro San Juan, 4 May 1863.

Marshal Elie-Frederic Forey, Commander-in-Chief, Corps Expeditionnaire du Mexique, In the Field, General Order of the Army, 10 May 1863.

'Report on the Affair of Camarone', – Commandant Eloi Regnault, Interim Commander of the Regiment Etranger, Cordoba, to General Ernest de Maussion, Commanding the Reserve Brigade, Orizaba, 17 August 1863.

Marshal Elie-Frederic Forey, Commander-in-Chief, Corps Expeditionnaire du Mexique, Order of the Day #195, Mexico City, 30 August 1863.

Colonel Pierre Jeanningros, Commanding Officer, Veracruz and the *Terres Chaudes*, to Marshal Jacques Randon, Minister of War, Paris, Letter #454, 1 October 1863.

Marshal Jacques Randon, Minister of War, Paris, to Colonel Pierre Jeanningros, Commanding Officer, Veracruz and the *Terres Chaudes*, 4 November 1863.

Marshal Jacques Randon, Minister of War, Paris, to General Francois-Achille Bazaine, Commander-in-Chief, French Expeditionary Corps, Mexico City, 4 November 1863.

Marshal Jacques Randon, Minister of War, Paris, to 3rd Directorate of the Artillery, 4 November, 1863.

Archives de La Legion Etrangere (A.L.E.), Aubagne, France.

'Notes et Souvenirs 1862–1867' by Captain [Gabriel] De Diesbach de Torny. Unpublished manuscript.

'Mes treize annees de Legion etrangere' by Joseph Ehrhart, Unpublished manuscript, Part 1.

'Le poste de Ta-Lung', [by General Jules Francois]. Manuscript presented to the *Salle d'Honneur* at Sidi-bel-Abbes by General Francois in 1940.

Historique sommaire du corps, October 1863. Historique sommaire du corps, April 1864.

General Pierre Jeanningros, '1863. – Mexique. Combat of Cameronne, 60 against 2000. Farewell address by General Jeanningros, Commander of the Legion, in the Presence of troops forming a square around the grave of the gallant men of the Legion, dead on the field of honour. 25 February 1867, two days before the evacuation of the French Army for France.' '1863. Manuscript of two pages.

Anonymous, 'L'Aventure du Drapeau du 3e Etranger, Tunisie [,] 19 Janvier–12 Mai 1943,' *Journal de Marche du 3e REI, December 1942/Avril 1943.*

Colonel Vaillant, 1st Etranger, 'Report sur la morel,' 21 November 1961.

Miscellaneous

'Deux ans au Mexique, 1863–1865', by Lieutenant [Edmond] Campion. Unpublished 232-page manuscript, 1868. Archives of the Ministry of National Defence, Paris.

Charles Dupin. Unpublished Memoir. Archives of the Ministry of National Defence, Paris.

'The Artificial Hand of the brave Captain Danjou'. Record Group Five, Belgish-osterreiche Freikorps [Belgian-Austrian Volunteer Corps], Kriegsarchiv [War Archives], Osterreichisches Staatsarchiv [Austrian State Archives], Vienna.

'The Grave of Sous-Lieutenant Clement Maudet' by Lieutenant-Colonel Daniel Sousa, The Camerone Association, Mexico City.

Musee du Souvenir, Ecole Speciale Militaire de Saint-Cyr, Coetquidan, France.

Jean Efrem Lanusse, *Etat des Services*.

'Monseigneur Lanusse', Recueil de Souvenir Collection.

'Monseigneur Jean Lanusse: Sa Vie en Anecdotes' by Colonel Allain Bernede.

Author's Archives and Correspondence

General Marcel J. Penette Papers. Jean Brunon/Musee de L'Empri Papers.

The Camerone Association Papers. L'Abbe Jean Efrem Lanusse Collection.

General Frank E. Evans Collection. Correspondence – France.

Correspondence – Legion Etrangere. Correspondence – Mexico.

Correspondence – Austria. Correspondence – United States.

Correspondence – Canada. Correspondence – England.

Books

Aage, H.H. Prince of Denmark. *A Royal Adventurer in the Foreign Legion*. New York: Doubleday, Page 1927. Published in Britain as *My Life in the French Foreign Legion*. London: Everleigh Nash & Grayson 1928.

Ainley, Henry. *In Order to Die: With the Foreign Legion in Indo-China*. London: Burke 1955.

Alexander, Michael. *The Reluctant Legionnaire*. London: Rupert Hart-Davis 1956. Subtitle: 'An Escapade'.

Alvensleben, Baron Max von. *With Maximilian in Mexico: From the Notes of a Mexican Officer*. London: Longmans, Green 1867.

Amiable, Eugene. *Legionnaire au Mexique*. Brussels: Charles Dessart 1942. Preface and Annotations by Louis Leconte, *Conservateur-en-Chef* of the *Musee Royal de l'Armee*, Brussels, Belgium.

Andolenko, Lieutenant. *La filiation des bataillons de la Legion Etrangere, 1831–1936*. Sidi-bel-Abbes: Presses du 1er Etranger 1937.

Andolenko, Captain. *Une Visite aux salles d'honneur et au Musee de souvenir de la Legion Etrangere*. Sidi-bel-Abbes: Presses du 1er Regiment Etranger 1938.

Annuaire militaire de l'Empire Francaise pour l'annee 1863 publiee sur les documents communiques par le Ministre de la Guerre. Paris: Berger-Levrault 1863.

Annuaire militaire de l'Empire Francaise pour l'annee 1864 publiee sur les documents communiques par le Ministre de la Guerre. Paris: Berger-Levrault 1864.

Annuaire militaire de l'Empire Francaise pour l'annee 1867 publiee sur les documents communiques par le Ministre de la Guerre. Paris: Berger-Levrault 1867.

Anonymous [attributed to General Alexis de La Hayrie]. *Le Combat de Camaron, 30 avril 1863*. Lille: Imprimerie Danel 1889.

———. *Historique du 1er bataillon formant corps du 1er Regiment etranger et du 1er bataillon du 4e Regiment de la Legion etrangere* (Marrakech: Hebreard n.d. c.1922.

———. *Veillee de Camerone 1958*. Sidi-bel-Abbes: Presses du 1st Regiment Etranger 1958.

———. *Camerone 1863–1963*. Aubagne: *Kepi blanc* 1963.

———. *Centenaire du Combat de Camerone, 1863–1963*. Paris: La Maison des Anciens Legionnaires de Paris 1963.

———. *Camerone 1966*. Aubagne: Presses du 1st Regiment Etranger 1966.

———. *Musee de la Legion Etrangere: 150 Ans de Campagnes*. Aubagne: Presses de *Kepi blanc* 1981.

———. *Marches et Chants de la Legion Etrangere*. Aubagne: Les Presses de *Kepi Blanc* 1984.

Aparvary, Leslie. *A Legionnaire's Journey*. Calgary, Alberta: Detselig Enterprises 1989.

Azan, Lieutenant-Colonel Paul. *La Legion Etrangere (1831–1935)*. Sidi-bel-Abbes: Presses du 1er Regiment Etranger 1935.

Azan, Colonel Paul. *Memento du soldat de la Legion Etrangere*. Sidi-bel-Abbes: Presses du 1er Regiment Etranger 1937.

Barail, F.C. du. *Souvenirs du General du Barail*. Paris: Plon 1894–96. I and II.

Baz, Gustavo and Gallo, E.L. *History of The Mexican Railway*. Mexico City: Gallo & Co. 1876. Translated by George F. Henderson. Originally published as Baz, Gustavo and Gallo, E.L. *Historia Del Ferrocarril Mexicano. Riqueza de Mexico en la Zona del Golfo a la Mesa Central, bajo su aspecto geologico, agricola, manufacturero y comercial*. Mexico City: Gallo & Cie. 1874.

Beauvoir, Roger de. *La Legion Etrangere*. Paris: Firmin-Didot 1897.

Bergot, Erwan. *The French Foreign Legion*. London: Allan Wingate 1975.

———. *Les 170 jours de Dien-Bien-Phu*. Paris: Presses de la Cite 1979.

———. *Bataillon de Coree*. Paris: Presses de la Cite 1983. Subtitle: 'Les volontaires francais 1950–1953'.

Blanchot, Charles. *Memoires, L'Intervention Francaise au Mexique*. Paris: Emile Nourry 1911.

Blunt, Wilfrid. *Desert Hawk: Abd el Kader and the French Conquest of Algeria*. London: Methuen 1947.

Bocca, Geoffrey. *La Legion!* New York: Thomas Y. Crowell 1964. Subtitle: 'The French Foreign Legion and the Men Who Made It Glorious'.

Brunon, Jean. *La Voite de Gloire: Histoire des Drapeaux de la Legion Etrangere (1831–1931)*. Paris: Frazier-Soye 1931.

———, *Camerone et l'Aigle du Regiment Etranger 1862–70*. Marseille: Imprimerie Meridionale 1935.

———. *Camerone*. Paris: Editions France-Empire 1963.

———. *Camerone*. Paris: Editions France-Empire 1981.

Brunon, Jean, Rollin, Paul, and Benigni, Pierre. *Le Livre d'Or de la Legion Etrangere, 1831–1931*. Paris: Frazier-Soye 1931. Preface by Marshal Louis Franchet d'Esperey.

———, Manue, Georges-R. and Carles, Pierre. *Le Livre d'Or de la Legion Etrangere, 1831–1955*. Paris-Limoges: Charles-Lavauzelle 1958. Foreword by Marshal Alphonse Juin.

———, ——— and ———. *Le Livre d'Or de la Legion Etrangere, 1831–1976*. Paris-Limoges: Charles-Lavauzelle 1976. Material by Battalion Commander Guibert-Lassalle, Chef de Section Information et Historique de la Legion Etrangere.

———, ——— and ———. *Le Livre d'Or de la Legion Etrangere, 1831–1981*. Paris-Limoges: Charles-Lavauzelle 1981. Material by Adjutant Chef Tibor Szecsko, Curator of the Musee de la Legion Etrangere.

Campos, Sebastian I. *Operaciones militares del Estado de Veracruz y de la Costa de Stavento*. Mexico City: n.p. 1891.

———. *Recuerdos Historicos de la Ciudad de Veracruz y Costa de Sotavento del Estado*. Orizaba: n.p. 1893.

Chadzynski, Martin, with Laklam, Carli. *Runaway!* New York: McGraw-Hill 1979.

Channing, Grace Ellery (Ed.). *War Letters of Edmond Genet*. New York: Charles Scribner's Sons 1918. Subtitle: 'The First American Aviator Killed Flying the Stars and Stripes'. Introduction and Conclusion by Channing. Prefatory Note by John Jay Chapman.

Charton, Colonel Pierre. *'RCA' Indo-Chine 1950*. Paris: Societe de Production Litteraire 1975. Subtitle: 'La Tragedie de l'evacuation de Cao-Bang racontee par un participant'.

Cooper, A.R. and Tremayne, Sydney. *The Man Who Liked Hell: Twelve Years in the Foreign Legion*. London: Jarrolds 1933.

———. *Born to Fight*. Edinburgh: William Blackwood 1969.

———. *March or Bust: Adventures in the Foreign Legion*. London: Robert Hale 1972.

Cooper, Captain Dick. *Adventures of a Secret Agent*. London: Frederick Muller, 1957.

d'Esparbes, George. *La Legion etrangere*. Paris: Flammarion 1900.

———. *Les Mysteres de la Legion etrangere*. Paris: Flammarion 1912. Illustrated by Maurice Mahut.

Dabbs, Jack Autrey. *The French Army in Mexico 1861–1867: A Study in Military Government*. The Hague: Mouton 1963.

Debay, Yves. *The French Foreign Legion Today*. London: Windrow & Greene 1992. Translated by Jean-Pierre Villaume. Europa Militaria No. 10.

———. *The French Foreign Legion in Action*. London: Windrow and Greene 1992. Translated by Jean-Pierre Villaume. Europa Militaria No. 11.

———. *French Foreign Legion Operations 1990–2000*. Ramsbury, Wilts, U.K.: The Crowood Press 2000. Translated by Hilary Hook. Edited by Martin Windrow. Europa Militaria Special 15.

———. *The 2e REP: French Foreign Legion Paratroopers*. Paris: Histoire et Collections 2002. Translated by Alan McKay.

Des Loiseau, Captain Claude J. *Le Mexique et la Legion Belge, 1864–67*. Brussels: Imprimerie-Lithographic de J. de Cocq 1870.

Detaille, E[douard] and Richard, J[ules]. *Types et Uniformes de l'Armee Francaise*. Paris: Boussod et Valadon 1885–1889. II.

Domenech, Emmanuel. *Histoire du Mexique, Juarez et Maximilien, Correspondances inedites*. Paris: Librairie internationale 1868, II.

Dorian, Jean-Pierre. *Souvenirs du Colonel Maire de la Legion Etrangere*. Editions Albin Michel 1939.

———. *Le Colonel Maire: Un Heros de La Legion*. Paris: Editions Albin Michel 1981.

Duchesne, Albert. *L'expedition des volontaires belges au Mexique 1864–1867: Au service de Maximilien et de Charlotte*. Brussels: Centre d'Histoire Militaire, Musee Royal de l'Armee 1967.

Edwards, John N. *Shelby's Expedition to Mexico, An Unwritten Leaf of the War*. Kansas City: Kansas City Times Book and Job Printing House 1872.

Elton, J[ames] F[rederick]. *With the French in Mexico*. London: Chapman and Hall 1867.

Fall, Bernard. *Hell In A Very Small Place*. Philadelphia: J.B. Lippincot 1966. Subtitle: 'The Siege of Dien Bien Phu'.

Favrel, Charles. *Ci-devant legionnaire*. Paris: Presses de la Cite 1963.

Garfias M[agana], Brigadier-General Luis. *La*

Intervencion Francesca en Mexico. Mexico City: Panorama Editorial for Secretaria de la Defensa Nacional 1981.

Garros, Louis. *Storia della Legione Straniera*. Rome: Edizioni Ferni Ginevra 1972.

Gaulot, Paul. *Reve d'Empire: La Verite sur l'Expedition du Mexique d'apres les documents inedite de Ernest Louet, payeur en chef des Corps Expeditionnaire*. Paris: Paul Ollendorff 1889.

———. *L'Empire de Maximilien: La Verite sur l'Expedition du Mexique . . . Ernest Ernest Louet . . .* Paris: Paul Ollendorff 1890.

———. *Fin d'Empire: La Verite sur l'Expedition du Mexique . . . Ernest Louet . . .* Paris: Paul Ollendorff 1891.

———. *L'Expedition du Mexique (1861–1867). D'apres les documents et souvenirs de Ernest Louet, Payeur en chef du Corps Expeditionnaire*. Paris: Paul Ollendorff 1906, for the Societe d'Editions Litteraires et Artistiques.

Gaultier, Louis and Jacquot, Charles. *Honneur et Fidelite: C'Est La Legion*. Marseilles: Les Impressions Francaises 1963. I, II and III.

Geraghty, Tony. *March or Die: France and the Foreign Legion*. London: Grafton Books 1986.

———. *March or Die: France and the Foreign Legion*. London: Fontana/Collins 1987.

Gibbons, John. *The Truth About the Legion*. London: Methuen 1933.

Grauwin, Paul. *Doctor at Dien Bien Phu*. London: Hutchinson 1955.

Grisot, General [Paul] and Coulombon, Lieutenant [Ernest]. *La Legion etrangere de 1831 a 1887*. Paris: Berger-Levrault 1888.

Guedalla, Philip. *The Two Marshals: Bazaine, Petain*. London: Hodder and Stoughton 1943.

Haliburton, Richard. *The Flying Carpet*. Indianapolis: Bobbs-Merrill 1932.

Hallo, General Jean-Pierre. *Monsieur Legionnaire*. Limoges: Charles-Lavauzelle 1994.

Hans, Albert. *La Guerre du Mexicque selon les Mexicains*. Paris: Berger-Levrault 1899.

Hasey, John F. *Yankee Fighter*. As told to Joseph F. Dineen. Boston: Little, Brown 1942. Subtitle: 'The Story of an American Officer in the Free French Foreign Legion'.

Haslip, Joan. *The Crown of Mexico*. New York: Holt, Rinehart and Winston 1972.

Hill, Richard and Hogg, Peter. *A Black Corps d'Elite*. East Lansing: Michigan State University Press 1995. Subtitle: 'An Egyptian Sudanese Conscript Battalion with the French Army in Mexico, 1863–1867, and its Survivors in Subsequent African History'.

Holmes, Richard. *Bir Hacheim – Desert Citadel*. New York: Ballantine Books 1970.

Horne, Alistair. *A Savage War of Peace: Algeria 1954–1962*. London: Macmillan 1977.

Huart, Abel. *Souvenirs de la Guerre du Mexique 1862–1867*. Orleans: Auguste Gout 1906. Subtitle: 'Le Combat de Camerone 1 Mai (sic) 1863 La Prise de Puebla 17 Mai 1863'.

Jameson, Simon. *The French Foreign Legion: A Guidebook to Joining*. Plymouth, Devon: Salvo Books 1997.

Jennings, Christian. *Mouthful of Rocks*. London: Bloomsbury 1989. Subtitle: 'Through Africa and Corsica in the French Foreign Legion'.

John, Colin. *Nothing to Lose*. London: Cassell 1955.

Kemencei, Janos. *Legionnaire en avant!* Paris: Jacques Gracher 1985. Preface by Pierre Sergent.

Keratry, Emile de. *L'Empereur Maximilien, Son elevation et sa chute, apres des documents inedits par le Compte Emile de Keratry*. Leipzig: Duncker und Humblot 1867.

———. *La Contre-Guerilla Francaise au Mexique (Souvenirs des terres chaudes)*. Paris: Librairie Internationale 1869.

King, David Wooster. *L.M. 8046*. New York: Duffield 1927. Subtitle: 'An Intimate Story of the Foreign Legion'. Introduction by Hendrik Willem Van Loon. Reissued as *And Ten Thousand Shall Fall*. New York: Duffield 1930.

Kirwan, M[artin] W[aters]. *Reminiscences of the Franco-German War, by Captain Kirwan, Late Captain Commanding the Irish Legion During the War of 1870–71*. London: Simpkin 1873. Published as *La Compagnie Irlandaise: Reminiscences of the Franco-Prussian War*. Montreal: Dawson Brothers 1878.

[Lafont, Jean Jacques Jules]. *Les Bivouacs de Vera Cruz a Mexico, par un Zouave*. Paris et Liepzick: Jung Treuttel 1865.

L'Amicale de la Legion Etrangere, Alger. *Centenaire de la Legion, 1831–1931*. Algiers: Privately Printed 1931.

Lande, Lucien-Louis. *Souvenirs d'un soldat*. Paris: Societe Francaise d'Imprimerie et de Librairie 1878.

———. *Souvenirs d'un Soldat*. Paris: Lecene, Oudiin 1893. Introduction by Emile Faquet.

———. *La Hacienda de Camaron*. Paris: Societe Francaise d'Imprimerie et de Librairie [Collection Lecene et Oudin] n.d.

Lanusse, L'Abbe [Jean Efrem]. *Les heros de Camaron: 30 avril 1863*. Paris: Marmon et Flammarion 1891. Preface and Historical Notes by Boyer d'Agen.

Lapie, Captain Pierre O. *With the Foreign Legion at Narvik*. London: John Murray 1941. Translated by Anthony Merryn. Foreword by P.C. Wren.

Legion Etrangere. *Programme: Centenaire de la Legion Etrangere, 1931–1931* (Sidi-Bel-Abbes: 1931.

Le Mire, Henri. *Histoire militaire de la guerre d'Algerie*. Paris: Albin Michel 1982.

Liddell-Hart, Adrian. *Strange Company*. London: Weidenfeld and Nicholson 1953.

Loizillon, Henri. *Lettres sur l'Expedition au Mexique publiees par sa soeur, 1862–67*. Paris: Ernest Flammarion n.d.

Macdonald, Peter. *The Making of a Legionnaire*. London: Sidgwick and Jackson 1991.

McGorman, Evan. *Life in the French Foreign Legion*. Central Point, Oregon: Hellgate Press 2000. Subtitle: 'How to Join and What to Expect When You Get There'.

McLeave, Hugh. *The Damned Die Hard*. New York: Saturday Review Press 1973.

Malcros, Christian. *Insignes de la Legion Etrangere*. Aubagne: Presses de la Legion Etrangere 1981.

Manue, G.-R. *Tetes brules: cinq ans a la Legion*. Paris: Nouvelle Societe d'editions 1929.

———. *Sur les marches du Maroc insoumis*. Paris: Gallimand 1930.

———. *La retraite au desert. Recit*. Paris: A. Redier 1932.

———. *Sous la grenade a sept flammes: Comment on a cree un corps d'elite, 1939–1940*. Paris: Sequana 1941.

Martyn, Frederic. *Life in the Legion from a Soldier's Point of View.* London: Everett 1911.

Mercer, Charles. *Legion of Strangers.* New York: Holt, Rinehart and Winston 1964. Subtitle: 'The Vivid History of a Unique Military Tradition – The French Foreign Legion'.

Merolli, Lieutenant and Nadau, Lieutenant. *Une visite a la salle d'honneur.* Sidi-bel-Abbes: Presses du 1er Regiment etranger 1930.

Mordacq, General Jules. *Le ministere Clemenceau. Journal d'un temoin.* Paris: Plon 1931, III.

Morel, Lieutenant-Colonel [Paul Emile Gustave]. *La Legion etrangere: recueil de documents concernant l'historique, l'organisation et la legislation speciale des regiments etrangers.* Paris: Librairie Chapelot 1912. Bibliography by Captain Boutmy of the 1st Etranger.

Murray, Simon. *Legionnaire.* London: Sidgwick & Jackson 1978. Subtitle: 'An Englishman in the French Foreign Legion'.

Niles, Blair. *Passengers to Mexico.* New York: Farrar & Rinehart 1943.

Niox, General Gustave Leon. *Expedition du Mexique, 1861–1867. Recit politique et militaire.* Paris: Librairie militaire du J. Dumoine 1874.

O'Brady, Frederic. *All Told.* New York: Simon and Schuster 1964. Subtitle: 'The Confessions of Frederic O'Brady'.

Parker, John. *Inside the Foreign Legion.* London: Judy Piatkus 1998. Subtitle: 'The Sensational Story of the World's Toughest Army'.

Parris, Bill. *The Making of a Legionnaire.* London: Weidenfeld and Nicolson 2004. Subtitle: 'My Life in the French Foreign Legion Parachute Regiment'.

Pechkoff, Major Zinovi. *The Bugle Sounds.* New York and London: Appleton 1926. Subtitle: 'Life in the Foreign Legion', Preface by Andre Maurois.

Penderel, William. *Parade of Violence.* London: Selwyn & Blount, 1937. Subtitle: 'The True Story of [Max Durer] A Pacifist Destined to Fight'.

Penette, General Marcel. *Histoire du Memorial de Camerone.* Paris: Privately printed 1976.

———, and Castaingt, Captain J[ean]. *La Legion Extranjera en la Intervencion Francesca.* Mexico City: Publicaciones Especial del Primer Congresso Nacional de Historia para el Estudio de la Guerra de Intervencion 1962.

Perrott-White, Alfred. *French Legionnaire.* Caldwell, Idaho: Caxton Printers 1951.

Porch, Douglas. *The French Foreign Legion: A Complete History of the Legendary Fighting Force.* New York: HarperCollins 1991.

Pouliot, Henri. *Legionnaire.* Quebec City: Privately Printed 1931. Preface by John-Charles Harvey. Subtitle: 'Histoire veridique et vecue d'un Quebecois simple soldat a la Legion Etrangere.'

Price, G. Ward. *In Morocco with the Legion.* London: Jarrolds 1934.

Pyle, Ernie. *Here Is Your War: The Story of G.I. Joe.* New York: Henry Holt 1943.

Reeves, Peter and Davis, Hurk. *Legion of Outcasts: The Autobiography of Peter Reeves as told to Hurk Davis.* Los Angeles: Holloway House 1968.

Reybaz, Jean. *Le 1er Mysterious: souvenirs de guerre d'un legionnaire suisse.* Paris: Andre Barry 1932.

Rockwell, Paul Ayers. *American Fighters in the Foreign Legion 1914–1918.* Boston: Houghton Mifflin 1930.

Rosen, Erwin [Erwin Carle]. *In the Foreign Legion.* London: Duckworth 1910.

Roy, Jules. *The Battle of Dienbienphu.* New York: Harper and Row 1965.

Saint-Maurice, [Narcisse-Henri-Edouard] Faucher de. *De Quebec a Mexico: souvenirs de voyage, de garnison, de combat et de bivouac.* Montreal: Duernay Freres et Dansereau 1874, II.

Saint-Maurice, [Narcisse-Henri-Edouard] Faucher de. *Deux ans au Mexique.* Montreal: Librairie Saint-Joseph, 1881.

Seeger, Alan. *Letters and Diary of Alan Seeger.* New York: Charles Scribner's Sons 1917. Prefatory Note and Conclusion by C.L.S. [Charles Louis Seeger].

Sergent, Pierre. *Ma Peau au Bout de mes Idees.* Paris: Table Ronde 1967.

———. *La Bataille.* Paris: Table Ronde 1968.

———. *Je ne regrette rien – La poignante histoire des legionnaires parachutistes du 1er REP.* Paris: Librairie Artheme Fayard 1972.

———. *Camerone: La Campagne heroique de la Legion Etranger au Mexique.* Paris: Fayard 1980.

Simpson, Howard R. *Dien Bien Phu.* Washington: Brassey's 1994. Subtitle: 'The Epic Battle America Forgot'.

———. *The Paratroopers of the French Foreign Legion.* Washington: Brassey's 1997.

Spinner, Heinrich. *Algier, Meziko, Rom.* Zurich: Schroeter 1901.

Spinner, Henri. *Les Souvenirs d'un vieux soldat.* Neuchatel, Switzerland: Messeiller 1906.

Swiggett, Howard. *March or Die.* New York: G.P. Putnam's Sons 1953.

Talbot, John. *The War Without A Name: France in Algeria 1954–1962.* New York: Alfred A. Knopf 1980.

Thoumas, General Charles. *Recits du guerre 1862–1867: Les Francais au Mexique.* Paris: Bloud et Barral n.d.

Toral, Brigadier-General Jesus de Leon. *Historia Documental Militar de la Intervencion Francesca en Mexico.* Mexico City: S.M.G.E. 1962. Reprinted: Mexico City: Panorama Editorial for Secretaria de la Defensa Nacional 1981.

Townsend, John. *The Legion of the Damned.* London: Elek Books 1961.

Transactions of the Royal Society of Canada. Ottawa: 1882–83. 1st Series, I, Section I.

Troncoso, Lieutenant-Colonel Francisco de Paula. *Diario de las operaciones militares del sitio del Puebla en 1863.* Mexico City: n.p.1909.

Tuce, Adrien de. *Cinq ans au Mexique, 1862–67.* Paris: Cahiers de la Quinzaine, n.d.

Turnbull, Patrick. *The Hotter Winds.* London: Hutchinson 1960.

———. *The Foreign Legion.* London: Heinemann 1964.

Vallieres, Jean des. *Sous le drapeau de la Legion etrangere: Les Hommes Sans Noms.* Paris: Albin Michel 1933.

Walton, Emile. *Souvenirs d'un Officier Belge au Mexique, 1864–1866.* Paris: Tomers 1868.

Weygand, Jacques. *Legionnaire.* London: George G. Harrap 1952. Translated by Raymond Johnes. Subtitle: 'Life with the Foreign Legion Cavalry'.

Worden, James William. *Wayward Legionnaire.* London: Robert Hale 1988. Subtitle: 'A Life in the French Foreign Legion'.

Young, John Robert. *The French Foreign Legion.* New York and London: Thames and Hudson 1984. Subtitle: 'The Inside Story of the World-Famous

Fighting Force'. Introduction by Len Deighton. 'The History of the Legion' by Erwan Bergot.

Periodicals

El Moniteur Republicano [Mexico City], 2 December 1861
El Heraldo [Mexico City], 16 May 1863
El Siglo Diez y Nueva, 3 December 1861; 17 December 1861; 18 December 1861; 19 December 1861; 15 January 1862; 25 January 1862; 23 February 1862; 10 March 1862; 20 March 1862; 27 March 1862; 29 March 1862; 13 April 1862; 20 April 1862; 24 April 1862; 6 May 1862; 13 March 1863; 15 March 1863; 17 March 1863; 31 March,1863; 24 April 1863; 25 April,1863; 27 April 1863; 8 May 1863; 17 May 1863
Le Monde Illustre [Paris], 1862–63.
Leipzig Illustrirte Zeitung, 25 July 1863
Moniteur universel [Paris], 9 August 1864
National Review, April 1887 *Le Gaulois*, 13 November 1890
New York *Herald*, 19 November 1865
Le Gaulois, 22 December 1890
Le Petit Journal [Paris], 19 May 1902
Journal officiel, 17 February, 1906
Revue Nord-Africaine, 29 April, 1906
Revue Nord-Africaine, 6 May 1906
Echo d'Oran, 28 April 1906
New York Herald Tribune 6 May 1940
Le Monde [Paris], 25 May 1954

Articles

Capitaine Andolenko. 'De Camerone a Bel-Abbes', *La Legion Etrangere*, no.9 (May 1938).
Anonymous. 'Travaux archeologiques du Colonel Carbuccia', *Moniteur universel*, 25 April 1851; republished as a pamphlet (Paris: Panckoucke, 1851).
———. 'La decoration du drapeau du 1er etranger', *Monde illustre* (12 May 1906).
———. 'Les Heros de Camerone', *La Legion Etrangere*, no.37 (January 1934).
———. 'Le Capitaine Maine', *La Legion Etrangere*, no.53 (May 1935).
———. 'La Legion etrangere', *La revue d'linfanterie*, no.524 (1 May 1936). Special Issue on the Foreign Legion. Included: Colonel P. Guinard. 'Index bibliographique sommaire des publications concernant la Legion Etrangere'.
———. 'Le General Francois', *Vert et Rouge: Traditions et Souvenirs Militaires*, no.91 (April 1954).
———. 'Sidi-bel-Abbes – Historique', *Kepi blanc*, no.382 (September 1979).
———. 'Ephemeride Legionnaire', *Kepi blanc*, no.424 (April 1983).
———. 'La Memorial de Camerone', *Kepi blanc*, no.428 (October 1983).
———. 'Les Drapeaux du 1er Regiment Etranger', *Kepi blanc*, no.431 (January 1984), Part 2.
———. 'Legion Etrangere: Couverture de l'encart philatelique', *Kepi blanc*, no.434 (April 1984).
———. 'Jean Brunon (1895–1982)', *Kepi blanc*, no.435 (May 1984).
———. 'Le Musee de l'Emperi', *Kepi blanc*, no.435 (May 1984), 40.
———. 'Autour d'un Evenement Philatelique', *Kepi blanc*, no.435 (May 1984).
———. '*Kepi blanc* philatelie', *Kepi blanc*, no.436 (June 1984).
———. 'Un Enfant de Chalabre: Le Capitaine Danjou', *Kepi blanc*, no.444 (February 1985).
———. 'Le 21eme Regiment de Marche de Volontaires Etrangers', *Kepi blanc*, no.490 (May 1989).
———. 'Le 11eme Regiment Etranger d'Infanterie', *Kepi blanc*, no.490 (May 1989).
———. 'Le Capitaine Solomirsky', *Kepi blanc*, no.490 (May 1989).
A[uguste] Ballue. 'Souvenirs du Mexique – Cameron', *Lectures du Soir*, 42, Musee des Familles (October and November 1875).
Captain Auguste Ballue. 'Camaron', *Kepi blanc*, no.271 (May 1965).
Y.-J. Baubiat. 'Le Mexique et Camerone', *Kepi blanc*, no.428 (October 1983).
[Charles Blin]. 'Au Mexique, avec la Legion Etrangere (Souvenirs du Capitaine Blin – Juillet 1866–Mars 1867', *La Legion Etrangere*, (1939).
Arnold Blumberg, 'The Diplomacy of the Mexican Empire, 1863–1867', *Transactions of the American Philosophical Society*, New Series, 61, Part 8, (November 1971).
Captain de Borelli. 'A mes hommes qui sont morts', *Nouvelle Review* (April 1887).
Charles Boucher. 'Le siege de Zaatcha', *Revue des Deux Mondes* (1 April 1851).
Lieutenant-Colonel Claude Boudoux d'Hautefeuille, 'Souvenirs d'un Chef de Section au 11eme R.E.I. en 39–40', *Kepi blanc*, no.490 (May 1989).
Jean Brunon. 'Camerone et l'Aigle du Regiment Etranger, 1862–1870', *Carnet de la Sabretache*, no.81 (March/April 1936).
———. 'Camerone et l'Aigle du Regiment Etranger 1862–1870', *La Legion Etrangere* (May 1941).
Jean et Raoul Brunon. 'D'Une Rive a l'Autre de l'Atlantique par les Antilles, Mexique 1861–1867', *Revue Historique de l'Armee*, no.3 (August 1967).
Lieutenant-Colonel Pierre Carles. 'Survol de l'histoire du sous-officier de la Legion etrangere (1831–1981)', *Revue Historique des Armees*, no.1 (1981). Special Issue dedicated to 'Le Legion Entrangere 1831–1981'.
Captain Jean Castaignt. 'Huatusco conserve pieusement le souvenir et les restes d'un Officier de la Legion Etrangere', *Kepi blanc*, no.157 (May 1960).
[———] 'Huatusco, petite ville du Mexique ait partie de l'histoire legionnaire', *Kepi blanc*, no.157 (May 1960).
Jean Castaignt. 'Mexique: Lieux frequentes par le R.E. en 1863', *Kepi blanc*, no.193 (May 1963).
———. 'Mexique: Les traveaux en cours a Camerone', *Kepi blanc*, no.193 (May 1963).
Edouard Collineau. 'Un soldat de fortune. Notes et souvenirs de general Collineau', *Carnet de la Sabretache*, no.288 (March–April 1924).
Colonel Jean Defrasne. 'Avec Mac-Mahon . . . A l'origine des *chasseurs a pied* ', *Revue Historique des Armees*, No.4 (1981).
Francis Dickie. 'The Centenary of the Foreign Legion: The Famous French Force Holds High Festival in Sidi-bel-Abbes', *The World Today*, LVIII, no.1 (June 1931).
Albert Duchesne. 'Des Belges au combat de

Camerone', *Carnet de la Fouragere*, XV, No.2 (September 1967).
Henry Dutailly. '1871. Au combat dans le Loiret', *Historia*, no.414 (2nd trimester 1981), 40. Special Issue: 'La Legion etrangere. 150e anniversaire'.
Colonel Frank E. Evans. 'They Know How to Die', *Marine Corps Gazette*, XVI, no.1 (May 1931).
———. 'A Century of Combat', *Marine Corps Gazette*, XVI, no.2 (August 1931).
———. 'The Making of a Legionnaire', *Marine Corps Gazette*, XVII, no.2 (May 1932).
———. 'The Legion in Morocco', *Marine Corps Gazette*, XVII, no.2 (August 1932).
———. 'The French Campaign in Morocco', *Proceedings of the U.S. Naval Institute*, 60, no.1 (January 1934).
———. 'The French Foreign Legion', *The Leatherneck* (June 1940).
Adjutant-chef Andre Gandelin. 'Le general Rollet, un homme de coeur, de caractere et d'ideal', *Revue historique des armees*, no.1 (1981).
Lieutenant-Colonel Louis Garros. 'La Legion: Grandeur at Servitude', *Historama*, Series no.3 (November 1967).
Luis Garfias M[agana]. 'Sucedio en Camaron', *Revista del Ejercito y Fuerza Aerea Mexicanos* XVII, no.4 (April 1979).
Luis Garfias Magana. 'Camaron', *Excelsior* (1 April 1990).
P. Guinard. 'Cavaliers de la Legion etrangere au Mexique', *Carnet de la Sabretache*, no.389 (July–August 1937).
Raymond Guyader. 'Le Legionnaire de 1860–1867,' *Kepi blanc*, no.434 (April 1984).
———. 'L'Uniforme du Cavalier au Mexique 1864–1867', *Kepi blanc*, no.436 (June 1984).
———. 'L'Officier Legion de Camerone', *Kepi blanc*, no.457 (April 1986).
Jomard. 'Travaux archeologiques du Colonel Carbuccia', *Moniteur universel* (25 April 1851).
Kepi blanc. Multiple Authors. 'Les Volontaires de la Guerre 1939–1940', *Kepi blanc*, no.490 (May 1989).
Compte E[mile] de Keratry. 'La Contre-Guerilla Francaise Au Mexique: Souvenirs des Terres Chaudes', Part I. *Revue des Deux Mondes*, 59 (1 October 1865); 'La Guerre de Partisans dans l'Etat de Vera-Cruz', Part II, *Revue des Deux Mondes*, 61 (1 February 1866).
Sergeant Kubiak. 'Operation Castor . . . Verdun 1954', *Kepi blanc* (October 1962).
Captain [Jean Jacques Jules] Lafont. 'Le Pueblito de Camarone', *Vert et Rouge: Traditions et Souvenirs Militaires*, no.21 (May 1949).
Louis-Lande, L. [Lucien-Louis Lande]. 'Camaron, 30 avril 1863: Episode de la guerre du Mexique', *Revue des Deux Mondes*, 28 (15 July 1878).
———. [———]. 'Le combat de Camerone: vu par le Caporal Maine', *Vert et Rouge: Revue de la Legion Etrangere*, no.2, (May 1945).
Kenneth Landry. 'Faucher de Saint-Maurice, Narcisse-Henri-Edouard', *Dictionary of Canadian Biography*. Toronto: University of Toronto Press 1975.
Georges-R. Manue. 'Rien n'est perdu. Le 11e de Legion au feu, mai–juin 1940', *Le Temps*, May and June 1942.
———. 'Pelerinage a Camerone'. *Revue des Deux Mondes* (15 May 1963), and (1 June 1963).

Lieutenant A.L. Martin. 'The Real Foreign Legion', *Army, Navy & Air Force Gazette*, LXXIV, no.3846 (5 October 1933).
Robert Ryal Miller, 'Arms Across The Border: United States Aid To Juarez During the French Intervention in Mexico', *Transactions of the American Philosophical Society*, New Series, 63, Part 6 (December 1973).
Captain [J.J.J.] Mordacq. 'Pacification du Haut-Tonkin', *Journal des Sciences militaires* (February 1901). Subtitle: 'Historique des dernieres operations militaires colonne du Nord'.
Jean de Nivelle. 'L'aumonier de Saint-Cyr', *l'Actualite* (28 November 1896).
Captain Oudry. 'Camerone (30 Avril 1863)', *Vert et Rouge: Traditions et Souvenirs Militaires*, no. 86 (May 1954).
Prince Napoleon. 'Legionnaire Blanchard', *Kepi blanc*, no. 490 (May 1989).
Adjutant Jerome Pelos. 'Les Volontaires de la Guerre 1939–1940', *Kepi blanc*, no.490 (May 1989).
General Marcel Penette. 'Le memorial de Camerone', *Revue Historique des Armees*, no.4 (1981).
Prince Napoleon. 'Legionnaire Blanchard'. *Kepi blanc*, no.490 (May 1989).
G.-Jean Reybaz. 'Pour le centenaire de la Legion: la Legion Etrangere au front (1915)', *Revue des Deux Mondes* (1 Feb 1930).
Colin Rickards. 'Another 'Alamo', *Frontier Times* (Austin, Texas), 43, 1 (December 1968–January 1969).
Colonel Yves Salkin. 'La contre-guerilla du colonel du Pin au Mexique (1863–1865)', *Revue Historique des Armees*, no.1 (1977).
Raymond Sereac. 'Apres Camerone: Comment la Contre-guerilla du Colonel Dupin s'efforca de venger les heros de la Legion', *La Legion Etrangere*, no.30 (April–May 1942).
———. 'La Contre-Guerilla du Colonel du Pin', *La Legion Etrangere*, no.38, (November–December 1943).
Pierre Sergent. 'Du nouveau sur le combat de Camerone', *Revue Historique des Armees*, no.1 (1981).
Comte [Georges Henri Marie Anne Victor] de Villebois-Mareuil. 'La Legion Etrangere', *Revue des Deux Mondes*, 134, no.4 (15 April 1896).
Alice Williamson. 'A Century of the Foreign Legion', *World's Work*, 60 (May 1931).
General Charles-Jules Zede. 'Souvenirs de ma vie. Algerie. Italy. Mexique', *Carnet de la Sabretache*, no.366 (September–October 1933) to no.374 (January–February 1935).
———. 'Camerone: Le Temoignage d'un Caporal survivant', *Vert et Rouge: Traditions et Souvenirs Militaires*, no.33 (May 1951).

Secondary Sources

Aage, H.H. Prince of Denmark. *Fire by Day and Flame by Night*. London: Sampson Low, Marston 1937. Subtitle: 'With the Fighting Hermits of the African Desert. Memoirs of His Highness Prince Aage of Denmark'.
Anderson, Roy. *Devils, Not Men*. London: Robert Hale 1987. Subtitle: 'The History of the French Foreign Legion'. Foreword by Colonel Anthony Hunter-Choat.

Anonymous. *Medal Yearbook 2002*. Honiton [Devon], Token Publishing 2002.

Boucher, Auguste. *Recits de l'invasion: Journal d'un bourgeois d'Orleans pendant l'occupation Prussienne*. Orleans: H. Herluison 1871.

Castellane, Count P[aul] de. *Military Life in Algeria*. London: Hurst and Blackett 1853, I.

Cave, Lawrence Trent. *The French in Africa*. London: Charles J. Skeet 1859.

Choulot, Comte P[aul] de. *Souvenirs pour servir a l'histoire du 1er regiment de la Legion etrangere*. Paris: Dumaine; Bourges: J. Bernard 1864.

Clayton, Anthony. *France, Soldiers and Africa*. London: Brassey's Defence Publishers 1988.

Clement-Grandcourt, Captain [Abel]. *Croquis marocains, sur la Moulouya*. Paris: Fournier 1912.

Diesbach, Ghislain de. *Service de France*. Paris: Emile-Paul 1972.

Doty, Bennett J. *The Legion of the Damned*. New York: Century 1928. Subtitle: 'The Adventures of Bennett J. Doty in the French Foreign Legion, As Told by Himself.'

Dorling, H. Taprell. *Ribbons and Medals*. London: Osprey 1983.

Duff Gordon, Lady [Lucy] (Trans.). *The French in Algiers. Part I: Clemens Lamping, The Soldier of the Foreign Legion; Part II: M.A. de France, The Prisoners of Abd-el-Kader; or, Five Months' Captivity Among the Arabs*. London: John Murray 1845.

Galvin, Mrs Sadie. *Operation Sadie*. London: W.H. Allen 1977. Subtitle: 'How I Rescued My Son from the Foreign Legion'.

Habe, Hans. *A Thousand Shall Fall*. New York: Harcourt, Brace 1941.

Hall, Bert and Niles, John J. *One Man's War*. New York: Holt 1929. Preface by Elliott White Springs.

Harvey, John. *With the Foreign Legion in Syria*. London: Hutchinson 1928.

Herbillon, [General] E[mile]. *Relation du siege de Zaatcha*. Paris: J. Dumaine 1863.

Huart, Abel. *D'une demission a une reinstallation ou trois anees d'entr'acte au Mexique et en Afrique*. Orleans: Chez Georges Michau 1890.

International Commission of Jurists. *Report of the Committee of Inquiry into Events in Bizerta, Tunisia 18–24 July 1961*. Geneva 1961.

Joslin, E.C. *British Battles and Medals*. London: Spink 1988.

Kamienski, Miccilas. *Souvenirs*. Paris: Librairie nouvelle 1861.

———. *Le mort d'un soldat*. Paris: n.p. 1960.

Koenig, General Pierre. *Ce Jour-la: Bir Hakeim*. Paris: Robert Laffont 1971.

Laffin, John. *The French Foreign Legion*. London: J.M. Dent 1974.

Macnab, Rob. *The French Colonel: Villebois-Mareuil and the Boers, 1899–1900*. Cape Town: Oxford University Press 1975.

Macquet. *Notice sur la legion etrangere. Expedition de la petite Kabylie (1851) aux ruines de Lambese*. Namur: Rouvroy 1853.

———. *Correspondence d'un soldat belge en Crimee*. Tournay: Flamme 1858.

Massol, Marquis Louis de. *France, Algerie, Orient*. Versailles: Beau 1860.

Meziere, Louis. *Un soldat d'Afrique: le colonel Mathieu Butet*. Tours: Imprimerie Menard 1909.

Miribel, Comte Guy de. *Memoires du Marechal de Mac Mahon, Duc de Magenta*. Paris: Plon 1932.

Mordacq, Commandant [J.J.J.]. *Tactique des grosses colonnes: expedition du Beni-Snassen en 1859*. Paris: Berger-Levrault 1906.

O'Ballance, Edgar. *The Story of the French Foreign Legion*. London: Faber and Faber 1961.

Pataky, Laszlo. *Los Duros, Aventuras en la Legion Extrangera*. Managua, Nicaragua: Editorial Novedades 1952.

Perret, E[douard]. *Recits Algeriens*. Paris: Bloud et Barnal 1887?, II.

Pulszky, Francis. *The Tricolor on the Atlas; or, Algeria and the French Conquest*. London: T. Nelson and Sons 1854.

Ripley, R.S. *The War With Mexico*. New York: Burt Franklin 1970.

Ryan, James W. *Camerone: The French Foreign Legion's Greatest Battle*. Westport, Connecticut: Praeger 1996.

Saint-Maurice, N.H.E. Faucher de. *Cours de tactique*. Quebec City: Typographie de Leger Brousseau 1863.

Stout, Joseph Allen Jr. *The Liberators: Filibustering Expeditions into Mexico, 1848–1862*. Los Angeles: Westernlore Press 1973.

Turnbull, Patrick. *Solferino: Birth of a Nation*. London: Robert Hale 1985.

Thompson, R.W. *An Echo of Trumpets*. London: Allen & Unwin 1964.

Trent Cave, Lawrence. *The French in Africa*. London: Charles J. Skeet 1859.

Un Carabinier [Narcisse-Henri-Edouard Faucher de Saint-Maurice]. *Organisation militaire des Canadas: L'Enemie! L'Enemie!* Quebec City: Typographie de Leger Brousseau 1862.

Vallieres, Jean des. *Sa grandeur l'Infortune*. Paris: Albin Michel 1945.

———. *Et Voici La Legion Etrangere*. Paris: Andre Bonne 1963.

Van der Smissen, General Alfred Louis Adolphe Graves. *Souvenirs du Mexique, 1864–1867*. Brussels: J. Lebegue 1892; Paris: Charles-Lavauzelle 1892.

Wallace, Edward S. *Destiny and Glory*. New York: Coward-McCann 1957.

Index

Sub headings are in chronological order. Ranks only given when no first name.

Aage, Prince 309, 339, 384–5
Abd el-Krim 311, 313, 314, 315
Abd-el-Kader 24, 25, 26, 28, 28–9, 30; at Sidi Brahim and after 31, 32; surrender 33
Abrial, Jean 46, 102, 105, 178, 179
Acatlan, Mexico 205
Achilli, Pascase 90, 116, 172, 226, 256, 279
Ainley, Henry 357, 358–9, 359
Aka, Monsieur 319
Alba, Manuel 174
alcoholism 302
Alessandri, Marcel 350–1, 356
Alexander, Michael 369
Algeria 22; France and 22, 368; Foreign Legion in 22–4, 272, 280; war of independence 369, 370–1, 374–8, 379–82, 384
Almonte, Juan N. 77, 78, 176, 195, 198, 209
Alvarado, Mexico 104
Alvarez, Juan 194
American Civil War 73, 246
American volunteers, World War I 303
Amiable, Eugene 227, 236, 255, 258, 267
Amilakvari, Dimitri 338, 342, 345, 346, 347
Andolenko, Lt. 334, 336
Aparvary, Leslie 355
Arago, Victor Joseph 276, 277
Arakelian, Secretary-General 397
Armee d'Afrique 23, 26
Astolfi, Antoine 61
Atoyac, Mexico 104, 111, 179
Aubagne, Campe de la Demande, France 384, 393, 401, 403, 404–5, 409
Aubin, Auguste 180, 195, 196
Aubry, Auguste 45, 52, 64, 65
Auphelle, Camille 350
Austria: war in Italy 55–61; and Prussia 202–3, 259, 262–3, 274
Austrian Volunteer Corps (*Osterreichische Freicorps*) 224, 229, 236–7, 238–9, 240, 244–5, 257, 261, 268
Ayala, Jose 134, 136
Aymard, Alphonse 202, 218
Azan, Paul 333, 334, 335, 337

Baas, Jean 132, 155, 166, 171, 181
Bablon, Charles 261
badges: 3rd Company of 1st Battalion of 4th REI 325, 334;

GALE 357
Ballestracci, Sgt. 367
balloons, used for aerial observation 60
Ballue, Auguste 88; on Mexican Expedition 90, 111–12, 117–18, 119, 160, 256–7; illness 170, 182; disagreement with Belgians 261; writing about Camerone 283
Barburet, Col. 292
Barera, Valentin 55, 90, 112, 118, 182
Baron, Gabriel 231, 238, 249, 260, 270–1
Barre, Fernand 346
Barutel, Jacques 263, 267
Bastidon, Louis 250, 253, 255
Bat d'Af 24, 25, 26, 36, 231, 232
Bazaine, Francois Achille 25, 26, 27, 28; head of Arab Bureau 29, 33–4, 37; during Crimean War 42, 44, 48, 49; in Italy 56, 61; with Expeditionary Force to Mexico 78–9, 82, 96; and seige of Puebla 103, 113, 166–7, 169; enters Mexico City 172; and recruitment of Indian volunteers 185, 189–90, 195; Commander-in-Chief in Mexico 192, 193, 194, 195; first campaign 195–6, 196, 197, 198; on return to Mexico City 199, 202, 203, 205, 216, 218; and Scientific Commission 213; a Marshal of France 218; Southern campaign 222, 225, 229, 230, 231, 232, 233, 234, 235, 236; Northern campaign 237, 240, 241, 249, 251, 262; becomes maginalized 239; marriage 243–4; and discovery of Danjou's hand 245–6; and telegraph installation 252; reorganisation of Legions 257; and withdrawal from Mexico 264, 265, 268, 269, 270, 271; return to France 272; during Franco-Prussian war and after 275, 277, 282; death 287
Beauce, Jean-Adolphe 73, 196, 242–3; 'Last Hour of Camerone' painting 242, 273, 283, 359–60
Bedeau, Alphonse 26
Belgian Volunteer Legion 224–5, 236, 239, 257, 261, 268
Belgians at Camerone 426
Beni-Snassen rebels, Algeria 39–40, 63

Benigni, Pierre 130, 312, 318, 322, 330
Beres, Sgt.-Chef 366
Berg, Evariste 47, 83–4, 87, 93, 119; at Camerone 124, 129, 131, 140, 142, 143; after Camerone 148, 154–6, 177, 183; meeting with Zede 207–8, 331; in a duel 212
Berge, Lt. 243, 247
Bergot, Erwan 363, 366, 416
Bernard, Sous-Lt. 45, 46
Bernardo, Aloysio 93, 156, 161
Bernelle, Joseph 24, 25
Bertier, Gen. 196
Bertolotto, Natale 142, 145, 156, 161
Bertrand, Capt. 38, 45
Bigeard, Lt.-Col. 363, 366
Billod, Claude 93, 156, 171, 172, 181
Bir Hakeim, Libya 346–7
Bismarck, Otto von 202, 259, 262–3, 274, 275, 279, 280
Blanchot, Charles 113
Blanco, Miguel 166
Blank, Francois 215, 234, 267
Blin, Charles (Theophile) 260–1, 262, 263, 264, 268, 270, 333, 338
Bocca, Geoffrey 371–2, 428
Boechat, Capt. 193
Bogucki, Fus. 125–6, 139, 148, 155, 156, 181
Bontenaille, Sous-Lt. 192
Borgella-Houra, Jean-Baptiste 174, 180
Bosler, Lucien 179, 201, 247, 249
Bosnia 418
Bosquet, Pierre 38, 44, 47
Bou Sfer, Algeria 384, 405
Boulet-Desbarreau, Col. 312
Bourbaki, Gen. 36, 52, 279
Boutgourd, Col. 299
Bouzian (Arab leader) 35, 36, 37
Boyer, Napoleon 116, 195, 198, 199, 213
Branca, Capt. 381
Brandt, Fus. 52
Brayer, Col. 58
Brigade Etrangere (Crimean War brigade) 44–5, 47, 47–8, 48, 49
Brincourt, Augustin 114, 205, 215, 216, 222–3, 240, 241
Britain, and Mexico 70, 71, 72–3, 77
Brothier, Albert 342, 376, 377–8, 381, 383, 386

Brout, Nicolas 272
Brundsaux, Paul 320
Bruneau, Col. 297
Brunon, Jean 281, 330; collector of militaria 134, 312, 333–4, 334, 347; Honorary Legionnaire 330; and Foreign Legion magazine 344, 347, 351, 359; and *Musee de l'Emperi* 411; *Camerone* (book) 401, 414; and *Le Livre d'Or* 312–13, 318, 321–2, 389, 412, 414–15; death 415
Brunon, Raoul 312, 411
Brunswick, Felix 138, 156, 175, 183, 205, 277
Bugeaud, Thomas 25, 26, 27, 29
Burel, Sous-Lt. 293
Burgiser, Nikolas 156, 161
Bustamante, Anastasio 68, 69
Butet, Mathieu 58, 63, 64, 67, 68, 73–4

Cabiro, Maj. 378, 381
Cabossel, Charles 90; on Mexican Expedition 114, 117, 118, 158–9, 160, 162; illness 178, 182, 205
Cabrera, Luis 221
Caillaud, Robert 405, 411
Cairo Flag 346, 351
Callet, Sous-Lt. 58, 297
Calvi, Corsica 405, 411
Camargo, battle at 257–8, 261, 266
Camaron (Cámerone), Mexico 107–9, 388, 398; *Contre-guerilla* based at 216–18, *see also* Camerone, Combat at
Cambas, Angel Luciano 134, 147, 162, 171, 178
Cambodia 418
Camerone Association 390–3, 394, 395, 397, 400–4, 406, 407–8
Camerone, Combat at: 3rd Company scouting assignment 119–21, 122–4; the battle 124–35, 136–47; aftermath 147–9, 150–9, 160–3, 176; Jeanningros report on 163–5; newspaper reports of 158, 168, 168–9; prisoner exchange 174–5; Regnault's report on 181–2, 183; Forey's Order of the Day and 183–4; survivors 171, 172, 173, 175, 177, 184–5, 203, 223, 292, 296; visits to site 186–8, 196–7, 207–8, 220, 224–5; request for commemoration 191–2, 194, 333–4; first anniversary 206; pictures of 242, 273, 283, 285, 287, 293, 296, 322, 359–60; Bazaine on 268; visit during French withdrawal 269–70; desecration of graves 271; memorial at 289, 291–2; Foreign Legion Centenary and 313; plaque on l'Hotel des Invalides 355–6; Penette's visits to site 353, 387–8; Monument 390–3, 394, 395, 398–9, 403–4, 406–7;

items exhibited in museum 410; postage stamp 415; impact today 420–9; accounts of and writings on 283–5, 288–90, 290–1, 321, 331, 332, 389, 393, 401, 414, 416–17
Camerone Days: first in China 300; early 301–2, 302; developed by Rollet 310; 1920s 311–12, 314–15; increasing popularity 315–17; Foreign Legion Centenary year 322–7; 1930s 330, 334, 335; 1940s 340–1, 345, 351–2, 354–5, 355; 1950's 357–9, 360; at Dien Bien Phu 362–4; 1960's 373–4, 380, 382, 383, 405; Centenary 393, 400–2; modern 412, 419, 419–20, 423–4, 424–5, 426, 427–8
Campion, Edmond 79–80, 90, 157, 195, 196; entomological interests 213, 215
Campos, Maximo 253, 254
Campos, Sebastian I. 125, 127, 136
Camus, Capt. 397, 399, 401
Canat, Lt.-Col. 278
Canesco, Juan 142
Canrobert, Francois Certain: in Algeria 27, 33, 34, 36; during Crimean War 43, 44, 46; in Italy 56
Capeyron, Capt. 364–5
Capitan, Capt. 77
Carbuccia, Jean-Luc 35, 36, 37, 42
Carles, Pierre 389, 412–13, 415
Carlota, Empress of Mexico 203, 211–12, 259, 260, 262, 265
Carpentier, Marcel 356
Carteret–Trecourt, Simon 215, 216, 223, 232, 234, 235, 237, 240, 243
Castagny, Armand 56, 196, 218, 246–7, 269
Castaignt, Jean 388; and Camerone Association 390, 395, 397, 399; book on Regiment Etranger 388, 389, 393
Castelnau, Henri 264, 269
Catenhusen, George 156, 161
Catroux, Georges 335, 343, 346, 355
Catteau, Victor 93, 142, 145, 146, 156, 161
Cazarini, Col. 170
Cazes, Jean 64, 93; on Mexican Expedition 90, 94, 104–5, 114, 174, 179, 252; death at Santa Isabel 254
Cecciono family 88
Chad 412, 414, 415, 417
Chadzynski, Martin 420
Challe, Maurice 371, 376, 377, 379, 381
Cham, Lieutenant 23–4, 409
Chapdelaine, Lt. 31, 31–2
Chappell, Sous-Lt. 202
Charles X, King of France 22
Charrier, Francois 252

Charton, Pierre 356
Chasseurs d'Afrique 23, 24, 25, 94
Chasseurs a Pied 27, 30, 36, 82, 285
Chaussers d'Orleans 30–2
Chenel, Maurice 381, 401, 410
Chesneau, Charles 231, 232, 238, 239
Chiang Kai-shek 343, 356
China: Foreign Legion in 286–7, 300; World War II and after 342, 356, *see also* Indo-China
Chiquihuite, Mexico 98, 104, 110, 179
Choppin-Merey, Battalion Commander 261
Clement, Commandant 341
Clement-Grandcourt, Abel 296
Clemmer, Charles 257, 261
Cocuite, Mexico 231, 238, 243
Codrington, Capt. 325
Coffyn, Capt. 30, 31, 32
Coldebouef, Commandant 363
Collard, Sgt.-Maj. 339
Collineau, Edouard 27, 28, 33, 36, 37, 38, 39
Colomb, Lt. 422
Comonfort, Ignacio 69–70, 96, 114, 166, 167, 193, 194, 195
Comoro Islands 412, 419
Compagnie Danjou, La 426, 427; descendant company 325, 334, *see also* Camerone, Combat at
Compagnie franche montee (Company of Mounted Partisans) 207, 230, 236, 249, 263
Compagnie franche a pied (Company of Partisans) 193, 230, 234
Compagnie Irlandaise 278, 279
Compagnies d'elites 23, 43, 46, 273
Compagnon, Jean 397
Congo Brazzaville, Republic of 419
Conrad, Joseph 25, 25–6
Conrad, Peter 156, 161
Constant, Lt. 110
Constantine, Laurent 93; at Camerone 142, 145, 146; after Camerone 147, 155, 177, 183, 214–15
Contre-guerilla 100–2, 251–2; raids 111, 115–16, 172, 173; escorting convoys 157, 159, 160, 170, 216; responsible for death of Foreign Legion officer 192–3; without Dupin 201, 251; expansion 201–2; HQ at Camaron 216–18; during withdrawal from Mexico 266, 269
Convention of La Soledad 72–3, 77–8
Convention of Miramar 203, 209, 259, 265–6
Cooper, Adolphe Richard 310, 311, 317, 346
Copian, Sgt. 178
Cordaba, Mexico 179
Cortina, Juan N. 240

Index 473

Coste, Froment 30, 31
Cotaxtla, Mexico 185, 216, 243, 247
Cotter, Patrick 278, 279
Coulmiers, France: battle at 277
Coulombon, Ernest 285
Cousin, Capt. 287, 293
Coutant, Capt. 362–3, 364
Couttolenc Espinosa, Antonio 406, 407
Crimean Medal, English 49
Crimean war 43–50, 274

Dael, Constant 155, 171
d'Agen, Boyer 288, 289, 290, 291, 294
Daglincks, Therese-Francois 137, 155, 166, 171, 181, 185
Dally, Frederic 252
Danjou, Jean 39; map-making 40; loses hand 40; during Crimean war 42, 43, 47, 48, 49; back in Algeria 51, 52, 55; on Italian campaign 57, 61, 62; on Mexican Expedition 96, 111, 114, 119; scouting assignment 119–21, 123; at Camerone 124, 125, 125–6, 127, 127–8, 129–31, 156, 161; family request return of his hand 175; hand discovered 245–6; hand taken to Algeria 272; hand on display 287, 293, 299, 329, 409; pictures of 91, 295–6, 331; hand's appearance on Camerone Days 325–6, 334, 402, 412, 416; family donations to museum 330, 333, 335, 414; family home 337–8; hand returns to Mexico 396, 399
Danjou, Jean (nephew) 330, 333
Danjou, Rene 396, 398, 399, 414
Darmuzai, Lt.-Col. 376, 378, 380
Daugan, Gen. 315
d'Aumale, Duc 28, 29
D'Aure, Henri Cartier 260, 263
d'Aurelle de Paladines, Gen. 277
de Barres, Charles 222, 242
de Beauvoir, Roger 295
de Bombelles, Charles 212, 259
de Borelli, Vicomte 286, 287, 385
de Brayer, Col. 55, 92
de Brian, Paul-Amiable 35, 37; on Mexican Expedition 79, 83, 205, 205–6, 215, 216; and Southern Campaign 222, 232, 234, 236; and Northern Campaign 240, 241, 244, 252–3; death at Santa Isabel 253–4, 256
de Briche, Francis 186, 195, 196, 215, 221
de Bru, Sous-Lt. 263
de Caprez, Col. 27, 28, 42, 46–7
de Castellane, Comte Paul 33
de Castries, Christian 360, 361, 363, 364, 366
de Chabriere, Col. 45, 47, 50, 52, 54, 55, 57
de Chauglonne, Gabriel Menard de 207, 260

de Choulot, Jacques 395, 404
de Choulot, Paul 45–6, 404
de Cognord, Courby 31, 32
de Cordoue, Martenot 45, 46
de Corta, Battalion Commander 309, 351
de Courcy, Boussel 246, 252
de Curten, Gen. 278
de Forges, Blanchard 289, 291, 292
de Freycinet, Minister of War 289, 291
de Galard, Genevieve 362, 363, 394–5
de Gaulle, Charles 342, 344, 371, 375, 376, 379, 394
de Granet Lacroix de Chabriere, Louis 29
de Heckeren, George 252, 267, 268
de Keratry, Emile 101, 216, 251, 273–4, 274
de la Graviere, Jurien 70, 71, 72, 73, 76, 77, 78, 100, 203
de La Hayrie, Alexis 95, 241, 246, 250, 257, 289–90
de la Motterrouge, Gen. 276, 277
de Lasselle, Gabriel Collinet 207
de Leuchey, Guyot 205, 215, 232, 234, 241
de Lorencez, Gen. 76, 77, 78
de Mallaret, Joseph 262, 263, 281
de Massol, Louis 45, 46
de Maussion, Ernest 82; on Mexican Expedition 97, 98, 104, 168, 177–8, 193; inspection of Regiment Etranger 189, 393–4
de Montessuit, Paul 226
de Montholon, Marquis de 221, 230
de Montpensier, Duc 29
de Pindray, Count Charles 69
de Recuerdo, Jean Baptiste Munos 90
de Ribens, Abbe 76
de Saint-Arnaud, Leroy 26, 27, 37, 38, 41, 43
de Saint-Maurice, Faucher see Saint-Maurice, Faucher de
de Saligny, Dubois 71, 77, 169, 176, 177
de Stoecklin (of Contra-guerilla) 100, 101, 103–4, 201–2
de Thun, France 229, 240, 244, 245, 268
de Tscharner, Albert 309
de Tuce, Lt.-Col. 258
de Villebois-Mareuil, George 293–4, 296
De Vries, Hartog 93, 126, 155, 156, 173, 184
Debas, Col. 333
Debay, Remi 102, 105
Debay, Yves 418, 419–20
decorations: wearing of 90, see also medals
Degorges, Fus. 254
Degueldre, Roger 372, 376, 379, 381, 383, 384
Delcaretto, Adolfi 93, 137, 155, 168

Delebecque, Capt. 33, 46, 52, 57, 59, 64
Delettre, Jules 90
Deligny, Gen. 52, 64, 66, 68, 80, 81, 87, 91–2
Della Rosa, Adj.-Chef 397, 398, 399
Delpech, Jean 415
Delpech (soldier) 32
Deplanque, Col. 272–3, 277, 278
Des Loiseau, Claude J. 224–5, 274
des Meloizes, Lt.-Col. 280
des Vallieres, Jean 330
Desbordes, Sgt. 254, 255
desertions: during Mexican Expedition 222, 227; problem in early 1920's 309
d'Esparbes, Georges 301–2
D'Esperey, Louis Franchet 322, 324, 326, 334
Detaille, Edouard 285
Deuxieme Soldats (Second Class Soldiers) 273
d'Hurbal, Charles Courtois Roussel 225, 227–8, 229, 230
Diaz, Antonio 111, 116, 117
Diaz, Felix 'Chato' 205, 223, 230, 231
Diaz, Porfirio 169, 205, 223, 230, 235, 236, 244, 266; President of Mexico 282, 292
Dicken, Peter 156, 161, 181
Dien Bien Phu, Battle for 360–6, 415
Diesbach de Torny, Gabriel de 51, 68; on Mexican Expedition 90, 96, 103–4, 111–12, 114, 118, 159, 170, 178, 185, 203; almost in duel 179–80; meets Archduke Maximilian 212; insect hunting 215
discipline 214–15
d'Istria, Philippe Galloni 90, 112, 163
Djemmaa-Ghazouet (Nemours), Algeria 30, 32
Djibouti, Republic of 413
Djintcheradze, Alexander 334, 397
DLECC (Detachment de Legion Etrangere de Comoros) 412
DLEMC (Detachment de Legion Etrangere de Mayotte) 412, 419
Doazan, Jules 219
Doblado, Manuel 71–2, 76, 77, 193, 194, 197, 202
Docir, Louis 103, 232–3, 234, 236
Doldier, Henri 296
Domaine Capitaine Danjou, La (Foreign Legion home), Puyloubier 384, 385, 405, 422–3
Domenech, Emmanuel 274
Dominguez, Honorato 103, 216, 217
Dominguez, Jose 121, 125, 139, 156
Dorian, Jean-Pierre 333
d'Ornano, Emile Colonna 229, 231, 232, 235, 237, 243, 249, 252, 262; death 271

Index

Doty, Bennett J. 317
Douay, Felix 78, 96, 113, 196, 199, 251, 264
Doutrelaine, Louis 213, 229
Dovecar, 'Bobby' 372, 380, 381, 383
Doze, Sgt-Mjr. 26, 297, 298
Druzes 313–14
du Vallon, Capt. 202
Dubois, Charles 156, 161
Dubosq, Jules 56, 60, 90, 105, 116, 178, 179, 267
Dufour, Henri 371, 372, 375, 376
Dufrense, Achille 234
Dugenne, Sous-Lt. 193, 234
Dumas, Alexandre 32–3
Dunant, Henry 61
Dupin, Charles 28, 100, 100–1; commander of *Contre-guerilla* 101–2, 111, 115; escoring convoys 157, 159, 160, 170; wanting to avenge Camerone 166; raids 172, 173; responsible for death of Foreign Legion officer 192–3; sick 201; changes of command 216; sent back to France 239–40; return to Mexico 251; during withdrawal from Mexico 269, 270; death 273
Durer, Max 314–15
Duriez, Lt.-Col. 304
Duronsoy, Jean-Pierre 350
Duroux, Elie 209

earthquakes, in Mexico 223
Edwards, John N. 248
Egel, Adj.-Chef 397, 398, 399
Egyptian Battalion 213, 231, 238, 249, 266, 270–1
Ehrhart, Joseph 299
11th *Regiment Etranger d'Infanterie* (11th REI) 339, 340, 341–2, 342–3, 346, 349
Elite Companies (*Compagnies d'elite*) 23, 43, 46, 273
Elton, J.F. 274
Escobar, Maximo 127
Escobedo, Mariano 169, 240, 246, 250, 257, 258
Esperou, Sgt.-Chef 397
Espinasse, Louis 27, 29, 56, 58
Etienne, Eugene 298
Eugenie (ballad) 94
Evans, Frank E. 328–9

Faidherbe, Col. 68, 79–80, 87
Faucan, Capt. 352
Favas, Aime 93, 132, 156, 161
Favrel, Charles 335, 340
Fenton, Leg. 369
Ferdinand VII, King of Spain 24, 68
Fernandez, Francisco 170
Fez, Morocco 312
Fiala, Sgt. 254, 256
5th Mixed Pacific Regiment (5th RMP) 403, 417
5th *Regiment Etrangere d'Infanterie* (5th REI): in Indo-China 343, 350, 350–1, 351; in Algeria 369, 384, 386; depoyed to French Polynesia 403
Figuerero, Col. 105, 116
1st *Bataillon Etranger de Parachutistes* (1st BEP) 355, 356, 360, 361, 362, 365, 370
I Legion Etranger 45
1st (Regiment) Etranger (1841–1856): created 27; in Algeria 28, 32, 33, 34, 37, 38, 40; during Crimean War 41, 42, 44, 46–7; end of 67
1st (Regiment) Etranger (1856–1862): created 50, 51; in Algeria 54–5, 55; in Italy 56, 57, 58, 59, 59–60, 63–4; return to Algeria 64, 65–6; beomes Regiment Etranger 67–8
1st (Regiment) Etranger (1885 onwards): created 285; in China 286–7; Colonels of 292, 293–4; Regimental Standard and Legion of Honour 297–9; first Camerone Day 300; during World War I 302–4, 305–7; after World War I 308; becomes 1st REI 309; 1st REI becomes 1st Etranger again 357; in North Africa in 1950's & 1960's 368, 369, 381, 384; at Magrin-Vernerey's funeral 405; modern action 415, 418, *see also* 1st Regiment Etranger d'Infanterie
1st *Regiment Etranger de Cavalerie* (1st REC) 309; during World War II 343, 348, 349; in North Africa post-war 369, 384, 385, 386; new base 411–12; modern action 414, 415, 418, 419
1st *Regiment Etranger d'Infanterie* (1st REI) 309; Regimental Standard 321; building work 319, 330, 333; commanders 311, 331, 333; during World War II 343, 346, 348; name changed 357, *see also* 1st (Regiment) Etranger (1885 onwards)
1st *Regiment Etranger d'Infanterie de Marche* (1st REIM) 348, 349
1st *Regiment Etranger de Parachutistes* (1st REP) 370, 371, 372, 375, 376, 379–80, 382
flags: from siege of Puebla 392, 403–4, *see also* Regimental Standards
FLN (National Liberation Front), Algeria 369, 370, 371, 382, 384
Foch, Ferdinand 426
Foreign Legion: origin of 22–3; first action in Algeria 23–4, 24–5; ceded to Spain 24, 25–6; 'new legion' in Algeria 26–9, 32, 33; and new French regime 34; further action in Algeria 35–7, 38, 39–40; life in 40–1; Crimean war 41–9; return to Algeria and reorganisation 49–50, 51–5; Italian Campaign 56–62; back to Algeria 63–6, 67; reorganization 67–8; Regiment Etranger *see* Regiment Etranger; Legion Etrangere *see* Legion Etrangere; divided into two regiments 285; in China 286–7, 300; and Morroco 296, 297, 301, 311–12, 315, 330; during World War I 302–4, 305–7; post-war reorganization 308, 309; in Lebanon 314; Centenary Celebrations (1931) 312–13, 315, 318, 322–7; new regiments 339; World War II 341–3, 344–7, 348–50; in Indo-China 350–1, 352, 355, 356–7, 360–7; GALE created 357; and war of independence in Algeria 369–73, 375–6, 382–4; 'General's Putsch' 376–8, 379–82, 383–4; most leaving Algeria 384–6; official visits to Mexico 396–400, 406–7; Camerone Centenary celebrations 393, 400–2; at time of Camerone Centenary 402–3; new beginnings and modern action 410–11, 411–14, 415, 415–16, 417, 418, 419, 420; 150th anniversary 414; today 418–20; writings on 285–6, 295, 301–2, 317–18, 321–2, 328, 330, 331, 333, 335, 388–9, 400, 416, 418, 419–20, 420–9
Forey, Eli-Frederic: sent to Mexico 78, 82; and Foreign Legion 97, 332; and *Contre-guerilla* 100; and siege of Puebla 96, 113, 166, 167, 168, 169; commending the 3rd Company 167; in Mexico City 172, 176; receives report on Camerone 183–4; recalled to France 177, 190, 193, 218; death 282
Forey, Pierre 313, 320, 326, 333, 343, 352
Forsdyke, Jim 334
4th *Demi-Brigade* 343, 348
4th Regiment Etranger 418, 415
4th *Regiment Etranger d'Infanterie* (4th REI) 308, 313, 343, 369, 384, 386, 405; badges 325, 334
France: and origins of Foreign Legion 22–3; conquest of Algeria 24, 24–5; 1848 Revolution 34; declares war on Russia 41; at war in Italy 55–61; and Mexico 66–7, 70, *see also* Mexican Expedition and Seven Weeks war 259; Franco-Prussian War 275, 275–80; and Morocco 301, 315; World War II 342, 344, 349; and Korea 357; and Indo-China 360, 361, 366; and North Africa 368, 369; war of independence in Algeria 371, 382, 384; student protests 412
Francois, Marie Jules Victor Leon

Index

296–7, 300, 311, 313, 343–4
Frankfurt, Treaty of 280
Franzini, Capt. 45, 46
Free French Foreign Legion 342, 345, 348, 349
French Polynesia 403, 417
French Somaliland 384, 413
Friedrich, Friedrich 156, 161
Friquet, Lt. 249
Fritz, Friedrich 40, 93; during Crimean War 49, 56; at Camerone 126, 129, 131, 135, 136, 137, 140, 141, 142, 143, 145, 146; after Camerone 147–8, 155, 156, 166, 171, 175, 183, 205; visit to Camarone 187–9
Frohlich, Leg. 363
Fuller, Fus. 116
Fursbaz, Georg 156, 161
fusil (weapon) 89

Gaertner, Fusilier 139, 156, 185
GALE (*Groupement Autonome de la Legion Etrangere*) 357
Galleret, Admiral 391, 406
Gallopoli, Turkey 42
Galvin, Barry 420
Gambetta, Leon 276
Gans, Adolphe 53, 88, 90, 93, 119, 178, 205, 270
Garcia, Antonio 231
Gardy, Paul 314, 365, 372, 390; and 'Generals' Putsch' 376, 378, 381, 412; on the run 379, 384
Garfias Magana, Luis 427
Gatling guns 258
Gaucher, Jules 351, 361
Gaulot, Paul 301
Gaultier, Louis 352, 355, 396, 400, 429
Gautrin, Maj. 27
Gazeaux, Sgt.-Maj. 314
'Generals' Putsch' 376–8, 379, 383–4, 411
Gereaux, Capt. 31, 32
Germeys, Jean 45, 56, 58, 93, 142, 155, 168
Giap, Gen. 351, 356, 361, 362
Gibbons, John 325, 328
Giovaninelli, Ange 234, 271
Giraud, Henri 348–9, 349
Giraud, Jean-Baptiste 64, 90; on Mexican Expedition 104, 114, 117, 157, 161, 167, 215
Glass, Corp. 319
Glassier, Francois 267
Godard, Jules 60
Godot, Daniel 375, 379
Gonzalez, Isadore 243, 260
Gonzalez y Montesinos, Manuel 388, 390–1, 397, 398, 403, 406
Gorski, Leon 85; at Camerone 129, 142, 143–4; after Camerone 156, 175, 183, 196, 223; death 228; *Salle D'Honneur* and 333
Goumiers 24
Graff, Henri 207
GRD 97(97th *Groupe Reconnaissance Divissionnaire*)

341, 342, 343
Grenadiers 23, 43, 52, 53, 54, 273; on Mexican Expedition 88–9, 185, 234
Grimaldi, Jean-Luc 207
Grincourt, Sous-Lt. 179
Grisot, Paul 281, 285
Groupement Autonome de la Legion Etrangere (GALE) 357
Groux, Louis 156, 161
Gruber, Karl 237, 245
guerillas, Mexican 98, 201; attacks on convoys 100, 216, 217; *Contra-guerilla* attacks on 115–16; at Camerone 129; attacks on railway 192–3, 243, 249, 260; attacks during French withdrawal 266–8
Guerrero, Vincente 68
Guibert-Lasselle, Battalion Commander 413
Guido, Vicente 136
Guidon, Father 364
Guilhem, Pierre 252, 262, 263, 264, 272, 276
Guiraud, Maurice 375, 376, 377, 380

Hablutzel, Leg. 287
Hacienda de la Trinidad, Mexico 107–8, 122, 216, 284, see also Camerone, Combat at
Hacienda de Santa Isabel 253, 254–5, 266
Haiti 420
Haliburton, Richard 325, 327
Hall, Bert 317
Hallard, Louis 388, 390, 397, 399, 406, 407
Harvey, John 317, 318
Hasey, John F. 344–5, 345
Hauer, Sgt. 36
Herbillon, Emile 36, 37
Herrera, Jesus Gonzalez 255
Hijazi, Salih 247
Hipp, Emile 137, 156, 161
Ho Chi Minh 351, 356
Holler, Fus. 121, 139, 156, 185
Huart, Abel 81–2, 165, 256, 301
Huatusco, Mexico 177–8, 178
Hunter-Choat, Anthony 426
Husband, Edward 286–7

Indo-China 286–7; World War II 343, 350–1; fighting the Viet Minh 351, 352, 355, 356–7, 360–7
Inkermann, battle of 44
Isabella II, Queen of Spain 24
Ischeriden, Algeria 52–3
Isly, Battle of 29
Italy: war in 1859 55–62; World War II 349
Iturbide, Emperor and descendants 68, 244
Ivory Coast 420

Jacquot, Charles 396, 400, 429
Jalapa Road, Mexico 97, 98

Jamapa, Mexico 111, 116
Jameson, Simon 424–5
Japan 343, 350–1
Jaudon, Philippe 59, 61, 90, 178, 185–6
Jeannin, Fusilier 139, 156, 185
Jeanningros, Pierre 25, 75–6; preparing for Mexican Expedition 79, 90, 91; first assignment in Mexico 97, 102–3, 104–5, 106–7, 114, 117, 118; and aftermath of Camerone 150, 151, 152–3, 157, 160, 161, 162, 174; report on Camerone 163–5, 333–4, 335; and convoy to Puebla 160, 161, 162; commanding officer of Veracruz 172; requests commemoration of Camerone 191–2, 194, 333; based at Puebla 203, 205–6; writing home 209–10; on reconnaissance 215, 216; in command at Puebla 223, 225, 227, 236; and Southern Campaign 230, 234, 236; and Northern Campaign 240, 241, 242, 246, 247, 248, 252, 263; promotion to General 246; leaving Mexico 269–70; during Franco-Prussian war 278; death 297
Jeanpierre, Pierre 356, 370, 371, 376
Jennings, Christian 420–1
Jimenez, Anastasio 124
Jimenez, Joaquim 124
John, Colin 354–5, 357–8, 359, 360, 361, 364, 365
Jouhaud, Gen. 375, 376, 379, 381, 384
Joxe, Louis 379
Juarez, Benito 66, 69–70, 70–1, 172, 193, 282
Juin, Alphonse 343, 349, 390

Kabyles (Algerian people) 28, 29, 38, 40, 52, 65–6
Kamienski, Miccilas 58–9
Karageorgevitch, Peter 276, 277
Karayinis, Nick 303, 305
Kaspe, Vladimir 392
Kauffmann, Henri–Guido 51, 64, 68, 90, 112, 280
Kelbel, Jules 281
Kemencei, Janos 356, 356–7, 365, 381, 384
Kepi blanc (magazine) 389, 426
King, David Wooster 303, 317, 347
Kirwan, Martin Waters 278, 279
Koch, Christophe 45, 239, 261
Koenig, Pierre: during World War I 342, 345, 346, 347; and Camerone Monument 390, 391, 392, 394; and Camerone Centenary 401; leads delegation to Mexico 406, 407; and Foreign Legion Museum 409
Kollonitz, Countess Paolo 210, 211, 274

476 Index

Konkewitz, Fus. 116
Konrad, Ulrich 121, 127, 156, 182, 185
Korean War 357, 360
Kubiak, Sgt. 364, 366
Kuhn, Andre 390, 392
Kunassec, Hippolyte: at Camerone 129, 142, 143–4; after Camerone 156, 175, 179, 183, 205, 275; during Franco-Prussian war 276; serving with 2nd Etranger 293, 295; retirement 296, 297
Kurz, Hans 123, 125, 139, 155, 156, 184
Kuwasseg, Hippolyte 67

La Soledad, Convention of 72–3, 77–8
La Soledad, Mexico 97, 104, 106, 117, 266
La Tejeria, Mexico 102, 104, 105
Labastida, Archbishop 176, 194, 195, 198, 243
LaBella, Sgt.-Chef 428
Labrousse, Col. 172
Lafont, Antoine 201, 209
Lafont, Jean Jacques Jules 105–6, 109, 251
Lafontaine, Paul 269, 271
Lai, Casimir 93, 333; new recruit 56, 58; at Camerone 138, 139, 144; after Camerone 151–2, 164, 165, 263; possible death 270
Laimay, Col. 397
Laine, Ramon 129, 162, 171, 178–9
Lalande, Andre 347, 363–4, 365, 366
Lambert, Battalion Commander 276
Lamping, Clemens 27
Lande, Lucien-Louis 284
Landriau, Capt. 313, 314
Langlais, Pierre 363, 366
Langmeier, Felix 137, 156, 161
language of the Foreign Legion 41
Lanusse, Jean Ephrem 59, 61; and Mexican Expedition 76, 78, 186, 256; visits to Camaron 108–9, 186–8, 196–7; after Mexico 272, 273; during Franco-Prussian war 275, 276, 277, 279, 280, 282; at Saint-Cyr writing of Camerone 288–9, 290–1, 294; death 300–1
Laos 360
Latrille, Charles Ferdinand 73
Laurent, Joseph 262, 263
Lavayssiere, Corp. 32
Lavolle, Paulin 215
Le Boudin (Legion anthem) 277
Le Cacher de Bonneville, Battalion Commander 261
Lebanon 415
Lebre, Jean 51, 61, 103, 103–4, 172, 174
Lefort, Gen. 386, 396–7, 398, 399, 411
Legion Etrangere (1875–1885): first proposed as new name 201,
203–4, 207; Regiment Etranger renamed as 283; Regimental Standard 284; divided into 1st and 2nd Etranger 285
Legion Etrangere, La (magazine) 301, 318, 331, 335, 338, 344, 347, 351
Legion of Honour 297–9
Legionnaires Monument, Camerone 390–3, 394, 395, 398–9, 403–4, 406
Legout, Auguste 185, 216
Lelievre, Capt. 26, 27
Lemeunier, Maurice 361, 363
Lemmer, Fus. 126, 155, 185
Lemonnier, Emile 350
Leonard, Jean-Baptiste 93; at Camerone 142, 145, 146; after Camerone 155, 177, 181–2, 183
Leopold, Prince 274
Lernoud, Louis 132, 156, 161
L'Estafette (newspaper) 222
Lesur, Andre 390, 392
L'Heriller, Edmond 218, 230
L'Hopitallier, Lt. 378, 381
Liddell-Hart, Adrian 357, 359
Ligier, Jean-Jules 186, 192
Lissignolo, Capt. 276
Livre d'Or, Le: 1st edition 312–13, 318; 2nd edition 389; 3rd edition 412–13; 4th edition 414–15
Loizillon, Henri 212
Lopez Arias, Fernando 394, 403, 404, 406, 408
Lopez Uraga, Jose 71, 193, 194, 196, 197, 202, 218
Loubet, President Emile 298
Loubet, Sgt. 249
Louis Napoleon, Prince see Napoleon III, Emperor
Louis-Philippe, King of France 22–3, 24, 34
Lozada, Manuel 202
Lyautey, Hubert 296, 301, 303, 315, 332
Lyons, Every 192, 193, 213

Macdonald, Peter 418
MacMahon, Patrice 27; in Algeria 28, 29, 32, 32–3, 38, 52; during Crimean War 48; in Italy 56, 58, 59, 60; during Franco-Prussian war 275, 276, 279; and Bazaine 282
Macta, Algeria 25
Madeira 95
Magenta, Battle of 56–9, 297
Magnin, Karl 93; at Camerone 129, 142, 143; after Camerone 156, 177, 183, 267–8
Magrin-Vernerey ('Monclar'), Raoul 339, 342, 345, 390; Inspector General 351, 353, 357; funeral 405
Maine, Philippe 47, 85–6, 87, 93, 120; at Camerone 129, 131, 135, 139, 142, 143, 144, 145, 146, 147; after Camerone 148, 156, 162, 171, 174–5, 175, 183, 185;
after return to Algeria 272, 275, 276, 279–80; retirement and death 283–4, 292; photograph of 331
Maire, Fernand 305, 309, 319, 325, 331, 332–3, 339, 351
Malakoff, Crimea 47, 47–8
M'Alevey, Frank 67; on Mexican Expedition 92, 95, 103, 104, 120; and Camerone aftermath 150–1, 161; on Southern Campaign 234, 236; and Compagnie Irlandaise 278, 278–9
Mamelon, Crimea 47
Mangin, Louis 36, 52, 103, 229, 232, 236, 240
Manue, Georges-R. 315, 341, 396, 401–2; and Livre d'Or 389, 396, 412, 415
Marechal, J.M. 213, 214, 219, 231, 238–9
Marest, Madame 335
Margot, Leg. 367
Marin, Efren 406, 407
Marion, Jean-Baptiste 186
Mariotti, Capt. 52, 53, 59
Marquez, Leonardo 96, 194, 196, 265, 269
Marrero de Gomez, Juana 165, 167, 179
Marrero, Francisco 134, 162, 178
Marrero, Manuel 134, 178, 250
Marsol, Capt. 334
Martinez, Antonio 26, 33, 38, 52; in Italy 58, 59, 60; back in Algeria 63, 64, 66; end of Foreign Legion career 67–8
Martinique 96, 206
Marty, Capt. 44, 45
Martyn, Frederic 198, 287–8, 292
Masselot, Georges 376, 377
Massu, Jacques 371, 412
Matamoras, Mexico 240, 244, 258
Matehuala, Mexico 252, 257, 261
Maudet, Clement 34–5, 37, 39, 40; during Crimean war 42, 43, 46, 47, 47–8, 49, 50; in Italy 60; back in Algeria 64; on Mexican Expedition 88, 90, 91, 114, 120; at Camerone 125, 126, 137, 140, 141, 142, 145, 146; after Camerone 148, 155, 162, 165; death 166, 167; depicted in Beauce's painting 273; grave 167, 389–90
Maximilian, Archduke of Austria 70, 73; travels to Mexico 203, 209, 210–12; Emperor of Mexico 224, 225, 238, 244; Zede meets 243; Jeannigros on 248; sends wife to France 259; considers abdication 265; death 272
Mazagran, Fort, Algeria 26–7
McGorman, Evan 424, 425
Mechounech, Algeria 29
medals: English Crimean 49; awarded after Camerone 183–4; Expedition du Mexique 191–2, 194, 207, 226–7, 333; wearing of

Index 477

90
Medellin, Mexico 104
Mefredy, Madame 346
Mejia, Tomas 194, 196, 202, 241, 244, 257, 258, 265
Mendoza, Gen. 168
Mercer, Charles 403
Merlet, Fus. 126, 156, 185
Merolli, Aristide 302
Messmer, Pierre 419; in 13th *Demi-Brigade* 344, 347; Minister of Defence 375, 380-1, 391, 401, 405, 407, 409, 410-11
Mexican Expedition 66; arrival in Mexico 70-3; increasing hostilities 76-8; further forces sent 78-9, 82; Regiment Etranger sent to 87-90, 91-6, 97; *Contre-guerilla* 100-2, 111, 115-16; Regiment Etranger assigned to *Terres Chaudes* 97-8, 100, 101, 103-4, 104-5, 105-8, 109-10; siege of Puebla 96, 103, 113-14, 165-6, 166-7; Mexican Army strategy 114, 114-15; Combat at Camerone *see* Camerone, Combat at; convoys 115, 116, 117-18, 157, 158, 160, 166, 170, 172-3; surrender of Puebla 168, 169, 170-1; *Contre-guerilla* raids 172, 173; occupation of Mexico City 172, 176, 185, 193-4, 195-6, 198, 199, 202; French action outside Mexico City 185, 196, 198, 202, 205-6, 213-14, 215-16, 222; Convention of Miramar 203, 209; Southern Campaign 222, 229-36; expedition to Tlalixocyan 238-9; Northern Campaign 240-2, 246, 247-8, 249, 250, 252-3, 256-7, 257-8; continuing action in the South 243, 244-5, 247; increasing unpopularity in France 251; repartriation considered 252; telegraph links 252; Santa Isabel Disaster 252-6; French withdrawal 265-71; losses on expedition 271; later accounts of 251, 273-4, 282, 290-1, 301, 388-9, 393, 414; mementoes exhibited 410
Mexico 66, 68-70; National Guardsmen 133-4; Archduke Maximilian and 203, 209, 210-13; Scientific Commission 213, 226; railways 102, 213, 216, 225, 240, 249, 282-3; 'affair of the flags' 392, 403-4; Foreign Legion Official Visits 396-400, 406-7; modern recognition of Camerone 427, *see also* Mexican Expedition
Mexico City: French occupation 172, 176, 185, 193-4, 195-6, 198, 199, 202; Saint-Maurice in 221-2; after French withdrawal 269

Meyer, Col. 27, 29, 33, 37, 45, 50, 51, 55
Mier, Mexico 258
Milan, Francisco de Paula: commander of Veracruz 113, 114, 115; and Camerone 128, 134, 141, 142-3, 144; report on Camerone 153-4; after action at Camaron 147, 148, 149, 157-8, 162-3, 166, 178-9, 216; grave 388; statue to 408
Miliana, Algeria 27
Milson von Bolt, Ernst 64, 68, 90, 105, 116-17, 230, 277
Minnaert, Corp. 286, 292, 294
Miquel, Gen. 390, 406
Miramar, Convention of 203, 209, 259, 265-6
Miron, Diaz 83
Molina Enriquez, Rafael 398, 399
Monclar *see* Magrin-Vernerey, Raoul
Montagnac, Col. 30-1
Monterrey, Mexico 247, 249, 250, 252
Monument aux Morts 315, 319-21, 326, 385, 402
Moore, Thomas 33
Mordacq, Jules 308
Morel, Gen. 346, 392
Morelia, Mexico 196
Morelos, Jose Maria 68
Morhain, Louis 261, 268
Mori (Mori-Ubaldini), Charles 53, 62, 82, 263
Morocco 296, 297, 301, 308, 309, 311-12, 315, 330, 369
Morris, Louis 28
Morziki, Marie 67, 93, 120; at Camerone 127, 129, 134, 134-5, 142, 145, 156, 161
mosquitoes 112
motto of the Foreign Legion 308-9
Moulay Ishmael, Algeria 25
Moulinier, Capt. 253, 254
Moutier, Sous-Lt. 253, 254, 255, 266
Muhammad, Bilan 192
Munier, Gustave 90; on Mexican Expedition 104, 105, 116, 172, 178, 186; death 272
Murray, Simon 373, 380, 383, 401, 405
Musee de la Legione Etrangere 409-10, 414, 420, 421, 421-2, *see also Salle d'Honneur*
Musee de Souvenir 333, 334

Nagy, E. 322
Nalda, Leg. 382
Napoleon III, Emperor: rise to power 34, 35, 37-8, 40; formation of Swiss regiments 45, 50; visit to Algiers 64; and Mexican Expedition 70, 73, 77-8, 81, 176-7, 185, 249, 252, 259; and European events 202-3; and new Emperor of Mexico 203; and

Regiment Etranger expansion 206-7; Empress Carlota of Mexico visits 259, 262; and Prussia 262-3, 274-5, 275-6
Napoleon, Prince 339-40, 340, 342, 391
National Liberation Front (FLN), Algeria 369, 370, 371, 382, 384
Nayral, Maj. 41, 43, 45, 46
Nazare-Aga, Prince Karaman Khan 303, 306
Negrete, Miguel 169, 193-4, 196, 240, 241, 242
Neigre, Charles 196, 198, 199
Nemours (Djemmaa-Ghazouet), Algeria 30, 32
Ney, Michel, Duke of Elchingen 239
Nicolai, Leon 396
Nicolas, Col. 305-6, 309, 321, 325, 330, 331; death 332
97th *Groupe Reconnaissance Divissionnaire* (GRD 97) 341, 342, 343
Nougues, Lt.-Col. 397, 403

OAS (*Organisation Armee Secrete*) 376, 380, 382, 383
Oaxaca, Mexico: campaign against 222, 229-36, 237
Ochoa, Pablo 132, 136
Ochsenbein, Baron 45
Olaguibel, Juan 404, 408
Old Comrades Associations 426
Olie, Jean 349, 357, 358, 379; and Camerone Association 390, 391; visits to Mexico 396, 398, 399, 400, 406; and Camerone Centenary 401; Camerone Day 1951 427-8
Olivera, Corp. 46
Organisation Armee Secrete (OAS) 376, 380, 382, 383
Orizaba Road, Mexico 97-8, 100, 104, 105-8; attacks on 100, 102, 216, 243
Ortega, Jesus Gonzalez 96, 112-13, 166, 167, 168, 169, 176, 203
Ortiz Garcia, Faustino 392, 393
Osterreichische Freicorps 224, 229, 236-7, 238-9, 240, 244-5, 257, 261, 268

Palmaert, Alfred 93, 156, 177, 182, 183
Palo Verde, Mexico 107, 196-7
Paris, Count of 339-40, 342, 391
Parras, Mexico 252-3, 255
Parris, Bill 421-4
Paso del Macho, Mexico 104, 110, 240, 257, 261
Pataky, Laszlo 397
Pechkoff, Zinovi 303, 310, 339, 351, 390, 410
Pelisser, Jean-Jacques 34, 41-2, 46, 49, 67, 79
Penette, Marcel J.: visits to Camaron 353, 387-8; research

into Regiment Etranger 388–9, 389, 393; and Camerone Association 390, 392, 395, 403; and Foreign Legion visits 397, 398, 399, 400, 406
Pepin-Lehalleur, Francois 391, 397, 400
Perrot-White, Alfred 336, 342, 347
Pertusati, Charles 90, 182
Petain, Philippe 305, 307, 315, 342, 344
Petri, Herbert 381, 383
Petrovski, Leg. 288, 292
Philippeville, Algeria 51, 64
Pied Noir community, Algeria 369, 371, 372, 375, 376, 382
Pierret, Charles 262
Pierron, Capt. 243
Pinzinger, Heindrich 40, 49, 58, 93; at Camerone 142, 143, 155, 177, 183
Poser, Sgt. 293
postage stamp, Camerone 415
Pouilly, Gen. 377, 379
Pouliot, Henri 316
Pourquet, Charles 320
Premier Soldats (First Class Soldiers) 273
Prim, Gen. 71, 73, 77
Prussia 202–3, 259, 262–3, 274–5; Franco-Prussian War 275, 275–80
Puchingo, Mexico 224
Puebla, Mexico 77, 97; convoys to 113, 115, 116, 117–18, 157, 158, 160–1; siege of 96, 103, 113–14, 165–6, 166–7; surrender of 168, 169; Regiment Etranger based at 203, 204, 206; war memorial at 289, 292; 'affair of the flags' 392, 403–4
punishment 214–15
Pyle, Ernie 347–8

Raberin, Col. 357
Racle, Sgt. 254
railway, Mexican 102, 213, 216, 225, 240, 282–3; attacks on 192–3, 243, 249, 260
Rajaud, Louis 193, 196, 267
Randon, Jacques: in Algeria 28, 37, 52, 53; Minister of War 67; and Mexican Expedition 79, 80, 81, 194, 207, 265–6; death 282
ranks in the Foreign Legion 40–1
Raschaya, Lebanon 314
Rausset–Boulbon, Count Gaston 69
Ravix, Lt. 253, 254
razzias 28
Rebers, Joseph 138, 155, 175, 183, 192, 205
recruits and recruitment: 1848 34; 1850's 40–1; prior to Mexican Expedition 84–5; during Mexican Expedition 185, 189–90, 195, 227, 247; post-World War I 309; 1963 402
Redondo, Rafael 136

Reeves, Peter 374, 380, 383
Regiment de Marche de la Legion Etrangere see RMLE
Regiment Etranger: creation of 67–8; eager to go to Mexico 68, 73–4, 79–81, 82–3; ordered to Mexico 87–90; those remaining in Algeria 90–1; on way to Mexico 91–6, 97; assigned to *Terres Chaudes* 97–8, 101, 103–4, 104–5, 105–8, 109–10; based at Chiquihuite 110, 111–12; early duties and action 114, 116–18, 158, 160; Camerone *see* Camerone, Combat at; changes in officers 172; continuing duties 172–3, 174, 175–6, 178, 193, 196; move to Cordoba 179; *vomito negro* and 182–3, 193; recruitment 185, 189–90, 195; mission to Cotaxtla 185–6; officer changes 186; inspection by de Maussion 189, 393–4; Dupin responsible for death of an officer 192–3; *Compagnie franch a pied* formed 193; 3rd Battalion ordered to Mexico 197–8, 200–1, 203, 206, 207; a mass in Mexico 198–9; proposals for expansion and renaming 200–1, 203–4, 206–7, 207; continuing duties in Mexico 201; based at Puebla 203, 204, 205–6, 206, 215; guard Peubla-Orizaba road 209, 211, 212; punishment 214–15; reorganization 215; reconnaissance 215–16; Brincourt inspection 222–3; and Southern Campaign 222, 223–4, 229, 231–6; recreation time 226–7; recruitment and deserters 227; creation of 5th Battalion 239; and Northern Campaign 240–2, 244, 246, 247, 249, 250, 256–7; creation of 6th Battalion 244, 246, 257; at beginning of 1866 252; erecting telegraph line 252; disaster at Santa Isabel 253–6; as 1st Brigade of Legion 257; looting 258; mid-1866 259, 260, 261–2, 263–4, 264–5; withdrawal from Mexico 266–8, 269–71; losses in Mexico 271; return to Algeria 272–3; and Franco-Prussian war 275, 276–9; in Algeria 280; Regimental Standard 78, 91, 194–5, 273, 278, 281; becomes Legion Etranger 283; books on 388–9, 393
Regiment Suisse see 1st (Regiment) Etranger (1856–1862)
Regimental Standards 409; first 24; new for 2nd Etranger 54; Regiment Etranger 78, 91, 194–5, 273, 278, 281; ordered destroyed during Third Republic

281; Legion Etranger 283, 284; 1st Etranger 297–9; World War I 307, 401; change of motto on 308–9; 3rd REI 310, 348, 349; limits on Battle Honours on 321; 1st REI 321; 13th DBLE 340, 345, 346, 350; 11th REI's destroyed 341, 346; RMLE 350; after fall of Dien Bien Phu 360, 365
Regnault, Eloi 90; on Mexican Expedition 104, 111, 112; and convoy to Puebla 157, 160, 162; responsible for 1st Battalion 172, 178, 179; report on Camerone 177, 181–2, 183, 283; orders troops to Cotaxtla 185, 186; return to France 186, 215; death 239
Rehmann, Joseph 90, 182, 185
Rembert, Louis 55, 57, 215, 222
Reus, Johan 85, 156, 161
Reybaz, G.-Jean 318, 328
Richert, Col. 325
Riley, Lou 'Paddy' 373
Rio Jampa, Mexico 107
Ritt, Sgt. 233
RMLE (*Regiment de Marche de la Legion Etrangere*): during World War I 304, 305–7; after World War I 308; reconstituted 309; World War II regiment 349, 349–50, 350
Robert, Capt. 35, 45, 46
Robert, Jean-Baptiste 339
Rockwell, Paul Ayers 303, 306, 317–18
Rohlfs, Gerhardt 53
Rohr, Ludwig 155, 171
Roland (a *Clarion*) 32
Rolland, Elie 90, 197–8, 200, 204, 236
Rollet, Paul 304–5; commanding 3rd REI 306, 308, 309; and Camerone Day 310; takes command of 1st REI 311, 312; and Centenary Celebrations 312–13, 315, 318, 319, 326, 327; General 321, 338; and *La Legion Etrangere* magazine 335; highlighting Camerone 337; death and grave 344, 384–5
Rollin, Paul 318, 321
Romany, Augustin 216
Romero, Jose Maria 221
Romet, Col. 396, 398
Rose, Aunt 226
Rosen, Erwin 299
Rousseau (a Sutler) 100, 105
Rousseau, Sous-Lt. 36, 37, 40, 45
Rouvere, Honore 264
Royaux, Sous-Lt 253, 254
Russia 41
Rustegho, Dr. Alexandre 94, 111, 254
Rwanda 419

sabres 89
Saint-Hillier, Bernard 350

Saint-Louis (troopship) 92, 94, 95
Saint-Marc, Denoix de 376, 377, 379–80, 381
Saint-Maurice, Faucher de 219, 285; arrival in Mexico 219–22, 225–7, 227, 228; on Southern Campaign 228, 229–30, 230–1, 235, 236; illness 240; on Northern Campaign 240, 241–2; in Mexico City 242; leaves Mexico 244; memoirs 282, 285
Salan, Raoul 374–5, 376, 379, 381, 384
Salas, Mariano 172, 176, 195, 198
Salle d'Honneur (Hall of Honour): creation of 286, 287; Zeni and 292–3; visits to 299, 329, 347–8, 368, 369; refurbished 335–7; donations 330, 333, 335, 344; acquires Beauce's picture 360; contents moved to Puyloubier 384, *see also Musee de la Legion Etrangere*
Saltillo, Mexico 240, 241, 242, 252
San Luis Potosi, Mexico 252, 257, 261
Santa Anna, Antonio Lopez de 68, 68–9, 202
Santa Isabel, Hacienda de, action at 253, 254–5, 266
Saurel, Julien 297–8
Saussier, Capt. 45, 52; on Mexican Expedition 90, 122, 178, 182, 185–6, 205, 215, 216; and Southern Campaign 228, 230, 232, 233–4, 234, 236; and Northern Campaign 250; commanding 2nd Battalion 255, 258, 261; leaves Regiment Etranger 272; during Franco-Prussian war 278; Lanusse's book dedicated to 290–1
Schacht, Adj.-Chef 398
Schaefer, Christophe 56
Schaffner, Karl 51, 58, 93, 156, 177, 183, 247
Schal, Adj. 293
Scherer, Lt. 192, 193
Schifer, Fus. 139, 156, 185
Schmidt, Lt. 253, 254
Schneidarek, Leg. 318
Schoenberger, Sgt.-Chef 356
Schreiblich, Josef 132, 156, 175, 183, 196
Schuvetz, Gustave 412
Scientific Commission, Mexico 213, 226
Sebastopol, Crimea, siege of 43–5, 48
2nd *Bataillon Etranger de Parachutistes* (2nd BEP) 355, 362, 370
II Legion Etrangere 45, 50
2nd (Regiment) Etranger (1841–1856): formed 27–8; in Algeria 29, 33, 35, 36; during Crimean War 41, 42, 43, 44, 46–7
2nd (Regiment) Etranger

(1856–1862): formed 50, 51–2; in Algeria 52–3, 55; new Regimental Standard 54; in Italy 56, 56–7, 58, 59, 60, 61; return to Algeria 63, 64, 66, 67
2nd (Regiment) Etranger (1885 onwards): created 285; during World War I 302–4, 305–7; after World War I 308
2nd *Regiment Etranger de Cavalerie* (2nd REC) 339, 343, 384
2nd *Regiment Etranger d'Infanterie* (2nd REI) 343, 351, 360; in North Africa 369, 384, 386; dissolved temporarily 411; re-raised regiment 412, 413, 414, 415, 418, 419
2nd *Regiment Etranger de Parachutistes* (2nd REP) 376, 411; in Algeria 370, 378, 381, 382; based at Bou Sfer 384, 386, 401; in Corsica 405; in Chad 412, 415; in Zaire 413–14; in Lebanon 415; recent action 418, 419; book on 420
Seffrin, Fus. 126, 156, 185
Segers, Fus. 139, 156, 185
Seiler, Daniel 157, 161
Sempe, Edouard 289, 395, 400
Sempe Montalvo, Raul 395, 400
Senihle, Col. 29
Sergent, Pierre 371, 372, 375, 376, 377, 379, 383, 384, 414
Serrano, Manuel 78
Sevestre, Eugene 216
Shelby, Joseph O. 247–8
Sidi Brahim, Algeria 30, 31–3
Sidi-bel-Abbes, Algeria: founded by Foreign Legion 28; City Council and Legion of Honour 298–9; Centenary Celebrations at 323–7; demolition of gateways 330; Foreign Legion leave 384, 385
Signorino, Col. 60, 63
Simon, Jean 344, 347, 377
Simpson, Howard R. 411
6th *Regiment Etranger de Genie* (6th REG) 415–16, 417, 418
6th *Regiment d'Infanterie* (6th REI) 339, 344, 345, 345–6, 416
61st Mixed Engineers Battalion-Legion (61st BMGL) 412, 415–16
Slistan, Francois 397
Sobieski, Leg. 59
Sol la Lande, Louis 348, 388, 389, 390
Sol la Lande, Xavier 348, 388, 391
Solferino, Italy 60–1
Solomirsky, Vladimir 385
Somalia 413, 419
Soos, Sgt.-Chef 364
Sotomayer (Mexican guerilla) 249
Soubic, Paul 395
Sousa, Daniel 388, 389, 390
Sousa, Manuel 115, 388
Spain 24; and Mexico 68, 70, 71,

72–3, 77; Foreign Legion ceded to 24, 25–6; Prussia and 274–5
spies, in Mexico 98
Spinner, Henri 200, 206, 215, 235
Stefanovsky, Ivan 314–15
Stoffel, Christophe 24
Streibler, Thiebald 286
Struszyna, Adj. 352
Swain, Jon 402–3
Swiss Legionnnaires 45
Syrian Campaign, World War II 345, 346
Szecsko, Tibor 415

Talavera, Carlos 398, 399, 406
Talavera, Francisco Dr. 138, 139, 148, 165, 394
Tampico, Mexico 218, 244
telegraph in Mexico 252
Tenne, Claude 372, 380, 381, 383
Tepeji, Mexico 205
Teran, Ismael 132, 166
Terres Chaudes, Mexico 72, 76, 168, 243; Regiment Etranger assigned to 97–8, 101, 103–4, 104–5, 105–8, 109–10; accounts of life in 251
Thevenon, Col. 397
Thiers, President Adolphe 280, 282
3rd *Regiment Etranger d'Infanterie* (3rd REI): created 309; and Camerone Day 310; Regimental Standard 310; change of commander 311; during World War II 348, 349, 350; in Indo-China 356; in Laos 360, 362; in Algeria 369, 384–5; sent to Somaliland 384; recent missions abroad 412, 420
13th *Demi-Brigade de la Legion Etrangere* (13th DBLE) 339; during World War II 340, 341, 342, 344–5, 346–7, 348, 349–50; in Indo-China 351, 352, 360, 361, 362, 364; in Algeria 369; in Somaliland 384, 413; recent action 419
Thoumas, Charles 63
Timmermans, Jean 85, 155, 168
Tirailleurs Algeriens 24, 36, 65; on Mexican Expedition 79, 82, 95, 249; during Franco-Prussian War 275; in China 286; Regimental Standard of 2nd 297; in action in Laos 361
Tissot, Pierre 364
Tlacotalpan, Mexico 213, 214
Tlalixcoyan, Mexico 102, 174, 216, 238
Tonel, Henri 92–3, 95, 119; at Camerone 120, 129, 130, 132, 156, 161
Tonkin, China 286, 343, 350–1, 351, 360; Battle for Dien Bien Phu 360–7
Torne-Sistero, Adj.-Chef 398
Townsend, John 368–9
Treaty of Frankfurt 280
Trevino, Geronimo 252, 253, 254

Trezel, Camille 25
Troupes de Marine 83
Tunisia 368, 369
Turkey 41
Turnbull, Patrick 334, 425–6
Tuyen Quang, China 319; battle at 286–7, 293, 367
12th *Regiment Etranger d'Infanterie* (12th REI) 339, 341, 342, 342–3, 349
21st *Regiment de Marche de Volontaires Etrangers* (21st RMVE) 340, 341, 342
22nd *Regiment de Marche de Volontaires Etrangers* (22nd RMVE) 340, 341, 342
23rd *Regiment de Marche de Volontaires Etrangers* (23rd RMVE) 340, 341, 342

Ulrich, Gen. 65–6
uniforms: Mexican Army 133; Regiment Etranger 88–9
Urtizberea, Gomez 406, 412

Vadot, Michel 361, 363, 405, 406, 409, 410
Vallez, Sous-Lt. 202
Valliant, Col. 378, 381, 382, 386, 396, 398
Valliez, Sgt-Maj. 48
Van den Bulcke, Pharaon Clovis 85, 139, 156, 184
Van der Meersche, Fus. 126, 139, 148, 155, 156, 181
van der Smissen, Alfredo 224, 230, 239, 261
Van-Leyden, Corp. 53
Van Opstal, Luitpold 40; during Crimean War 49, 56; at Camerone 125, 126; after Camerone 155, 156, 177, 184; death 203
Vanderbendt, Leg. 249
Vandesavel, Henri 157, 161
Veracruz, Mexico 71, 98, 113, 172, 271
Verjus, Jean-Baptiste 54, 56, 93, 125, 139, 156, 184

Vert et Rouge (magazine) 351, 359, 366, 389
Victor Emmanual II, King of Sardinia 55, 59
Vienot, Raphael 44, 46, 50
Viet Minh 351, 356, 357, 360, 367; Battle for Dien Bien Phu 360–6
Vilain, Jean 42, 93; during Crimean War 44, 47, 47–8, 48; back in Algeria 51, 55; in Italy 58, 60; back in Algeria 64, 65; on Mexican expedition 88, 90, 118–19, 120; at Camerone 124, 125, 126, 129, 131, 135, 137, 156, 161; pictures of 296, 331
Villebois-Mareuil, Georges de 293–4, 296
Vilmette, Battalion Commander 258, 261, 264, 266
vinogle (wine concentrate) 362, 363, 364
Vinoy, Gen. 28, 43, 44, 56
Voisin, Capt. 260, 261
Voltigeurs 23, 43, 52, 53, 54, 273; on Mexican Expedition 88–9, 116, 117, 185, 223, 234; at Santa Isabel 253, 254, 255
vomito negro 71, 72, 76, 77, 82, 98–9, 208
von Alvensleben, Max 258, 266, 268, 274
von der Tann, Gen. 277
von Hulsen, Col. 26, 27
von Smolinsky, Lt. 193

Wagner, Leg. 362
Wagram (troopship) 92, 94
Waldejo, Louis 213, 214, 238
Walker, William 69
Walton, Emile 225, 274
Ward Price, G. 330
Wattringue, Col. 285, 286, 287, 292
weapons: Foreign Legion 89, 89–90, 133; Mexican 133, 133–4, 258
Wensel, Gottfried 40, 93; during Crimean War 48, 49, 56; at Camerone 142, 145, 146; after Camaron 147, 155, 156, 175,
183
Weygand, Jacques 314, 322–3, 327
Weygand, Maxime 334, 344, 390
Wildermann, Leg. 61
Wilhelm, Monsieur 91, 277
William I of Prussia 202, 274–5, 279
Williamson, Alice 328
Wittgens, Karl 137, 157, 161
Worden, James William 373, 381, 384, 405, 426, 428–9
World War I 302–3
World War II 340–3, 344–7, 348–50
Wren, P.C. 317
Wyke, Sir Charles 71, 73

Yanhuitlan, Mexico 222
yellow fever *see vomito negro*
Yemen 419
Young, John Robert 416
Yowell, John 336–7, 340, 426

Zaatcha, Algeria 35–6, 36–7
Zaire 413–14
Zaragoza, Ignacio 72, 77, 397
Zede, Charles 54, 78, 88; in Italy 58, 61; not going to Mexico 91; on way to Mexico 198, 200, 204–5, 206; arrival in Mexico 207–8, 210; in command at Texmelucan 221; on Southern Campaign 233, 234, 235; in Oaxaca 237, 240; reassigned 243; transfer out of Regiment Etranger 272; death 301; memoirs 301, 330–1, 331, 332
Zeller, Andre 375, 376, 377, 379, 381
Zeni, Col. 281, 292, 292–3
Zey, Fus. 139, 156, 185
Zimmerman, Henri 384, 385
Zouaves, Regiment of 24, 37; during Crimean War 43, 47, 48; in Italy 58, 59, 60, 297–8; on Mexican Expedition 73, 78, 94, 165–6, 229–30, 232; during Franco-Prussian 275